INTERMEDIATE

Mastering Mathematics for WJEC GCSE

Series Editors:
Linda Mason and Roger Porkess

Keith Pledger
Gareth Cole, Heather Davis, Sophie Goldie,
Linda Liggett, Robin Liggett, Andrew Manning,
Richard Perring, Rob Summerson

This material has been endorsed by WJEC and offers high quality support for the delivery of WJEC qualifications. While this material has been through a WJEC quality assurance process, all responsibility for the content remains with the publisher.

Acknowlegements

Photo credits:

p.3 © Ulrich Müller – Fotolia.com; **p.5** © Kate Crossland-Page (t); © Sue Hough (b); **p.10** © HugoCCampos – Fotolia.com; **p.14** © m-gucci – iStockphoto via Thinkstock; **p.16** © Caitlin Seymour; **p.18** © Jürgen Fälchle – Fotolia.com; **p.21** © Coprid – Fotolia.com (b); © Food photo – Fotolia.com (t); **p.24** © Kate Crossland-Page; **p.25** © Sandy Officer; **p.27** © Alexandr Mitiuc – Fotolia.com; **p.32** © pumpuija – Fotolia.com; **p.35** © whitewizzard – iStockphoto via Thinkstock; **p.37** © Steve Mann – Fotolia; **p.42** © Mark Bond; **p.44** © Imagestate Media (John Foxx) / Vol 18 Golddisc I (t); © Sue Hough (b); **p.50** © Pavel Losevsky – Fotolia.com; **p.58** © cherries – Fotolia.com; **p.65** © Marek Kosmal – Fotolia.com; **p.67** © scanrail – iStockphoto via Thinkstock; **p.70** © Kurhan – Fotolia.com; **p.77** © Florin Capilnean – Fotolia.com; **p.78** © Kate Crossland-Page; **p.82 and p.viii** © Dave Gale; **p.92** © Simon Smith/iStockphoto.com; **p.96** © Sasa Komlen – Fotolia.com; **p.97** © Rawpixel – Fotolia.com; **p.103** © ttatty – iStock via Thinkstock; **p.115** © olgataranik – Fotolia.com; **p.122** © Warren Goldswain – Fotolia.com; **p.123** © Sue Hough; **p.128** © klikk – Fotolia.com; **p.136** © picsfive – Fotolia.com; **p.140** (t) © Sue Hough, (b) © Kate Crossland-Page; **p.142** © Corbis/ Education – image100 RFCD697; **p.146** © Kate Crossland-Page; **p.148** © RTimages – Fotolia.com; **p.154** © Claudio Divizia – Fotolia.com; **p.167** © Sandy Officer; **p.168** © GaryBartlett – Thinkstock; **p.175** © Britain On View/VisitBritain / Britain 100 CD001RF; **p.179** (t) © Popartic – iStockphoto via Thinkstock (b) © JaysonPhotography – iStockphoto via Thinkstock; **p.182** © University of Kentucky (http://www.ms.uky.edu/~cyuen/261/index.html); **p.189** © Ingram Publishing Company / Ultimate Business 06; **p.197** © Kautz15 – Fotolia.com; **p.207** © GoodMood Photo – Fotolia.com; **p.216** © Arkady – iStock via Thinkstock; **p.223** © blobbotronic – Fotolia.com; **p.233** The Photos – Fotolia.com; **p.237** © Ingram Publishing Limited / Ingram Image Library 500-Food; **p.242** © Kate Crossland-Page; **p.244** © bloomua – Fotolia.com; **p.247** © Kate Crossland-Page; **p.248** © Sue Hough; **p.250** © alanstenson – Fotolia.com; **p.257** © MADDRAT – Fotolia.com; **p.274** © Sandy Officer; **p.283** © Oleg Prikhodko / iStockphoto; **p.287** © Kate Crossland-Page; **p.290** © absolut – Fotolia.com (t); © GoldPix – Fotolia.com (b); **p.297** © Photodisc/Getty Images/ Business & Industry 1; **p.302** tsuneomp – Fotolia.com; **p.307** © Jupiterimages – Pixland via Thinkstock; **p.316** © Popova Olga – Fotolia.com; **p.324** © Marc Tielemans / Alamy; **p.325** © Sandy Officer (l); © Kate Crossland-Page (r); **p.326** © Kate Crossland-Page; **p.330** © Eric Farrelly / Alamy; **p.338** © Stockbyte/ Photolibrary Group Ltd/ Big Business SD101; **p.345** © arturas kerdokas – Fotolia.com; **p.356** © Tupungato – iStock via Thinkstock; **p.362** © spaxiax – iStock via Getty Images/Thinkstock; **p.375** © Heather Davis; **p.382** © Heather Davis; **p.391** (t) © Minerva Studio – Fotolia.com (b) © Imagestate Media (John Foxx) / Education SS121; **p.403** © oriontrail – Fotolia.com; **p.413** © Ingram Publishing Limited/Ingram Image Library 500-Sport; **p.420** © Igor – Fotolia.com; **p.434** © traffico – Fotolia.com; **p.448** © George.M – Fotolia.com; **p.455** © whitewizzard – iStockphoto via Thinkstock;; **p.466** © Nitiruj – iStockphoto via Thinkstock; **p.469** © yasar simit -Fotolia.com; **p.480** © Heather Davis; **p.490** © Doug Houghton / Alamy; **p.498** © Elaine Lambert; **p.507**, **p.513** © Pumba – Fotolia.com; **p.515** © highwaystarz – Fotolia.om; **p.524** © Andres Rodriguez – Fotolia.com; **p.547** © auryndrikson – Fotolia.com; **p.556** (t) © blvdone – Fotolia.com, (bl) © Kate Crossland-Page, (br) © Caitlin Seymour; **p.565** (t) © AKS – Fotolia.com (b) © Kate Crossland-Page; **p.573** © rusty Elliott – Fotolia.com; **p.574** © Kate Crossland-Page; **p.581** © bennyartist– Fotolia.com; **p.589** © Sean Gladwell – Fotolia.com; **p.596** © Dawn Hudson – Fotolia.com; **p.606** © cherezoff – Fotolia.com; **p.617** (t) © kreizihorse – Fotolia.com (bl) © VRD – Fotolia.com (br) © magann – Fotolia.com; **p.627** ©HelenaT – iStockphoto via Thinkstock.

Although every effort has been made to ensure that website addresses are correct at time of going to press, Hodder Education cannot be held responsible for the content of any website mentioned in this book. It is sometimes possible to find a relocated web page by typing in the address of the home page for a website in the URL window of your browser.

Hachette UK's policy is to use papers that are natural, renewable and recyclable products and made from wood grown in sustainable forests. The logging and manufacturing processes are expected to conform to the environmental regulations of the country of origin.

Orders: please contact Bookpoint Ltd, 130 Milton Park, Abingdon, Oxon OX14 4SB. Telephone: +44 (0)1235 827720. Fax: +44 (0)1235 400454. Lines are open 9.00a.m.–5.00p.m., Monday to Saturday, with a 24-hour message answering service. Visit our website at www.hoddereducation.co.uk

© Gareth Cole, Heather Davis, Sophie Goldie, Linda Liggett, Robin Liggett, Andrew Manning, Richard Perring, Keith Pledger, Rob Summerson 2015

First published in 2015 by

Hodder Education,

An Hachette UK Company

Carmelite House, 50 Victoria Embankment

London EC4Y 0DZ

Impression number	5	4	3	2
Year		2019	2018	2017 2016

All rights reserved. Apart from any use permitted under UK copyright law, no part of this publication may be reproduced or transmitted in any form or by any means, electronic or mechanical, including photocopying and recording, or held within any information storage and retrieval system, without permission in writing from the publisher or under licence from the Copyright Licensing Agency Limited. Further details of such licences (for reprographic reproduction) may be obtained from the Copyright Licensing Agency Limited, Saffron House, 6–10 Kirby Street, London EC1N 8TS.

Cover photo © ShpilbergStudios

Illustrations by Integra

Typeset in ITC Avant Garde Gothic Std Book 10/12 by Integra Software Services Pvt. Ltd., Pondicherry, India

Printed in Italy

A catalogue record for this title is available from the British Library

ISBN 9781471856518

Contents

■ Units with this symbol are required for the Mathematics GCSE only.

How to get the most from this book　　vii

NUMBER

Strand 1 Calculating　　1
Units 1–9 Foundation

Strand 2 Using our number system　　2
Units 1–4 Foundation
Unit 5 Using the number system effectively　　3
Unit 6 Understanding standard form　　10
Unit 7 Calculating with standard form　　14

Strand 3 Accuracy　　20
Units 1–4 Foundation
Unit 5 Approximating　　21
Unit 6 Significance　　27
Unit 7 Limits of accuracy　　32
Unit 8 Upper and lower bounds　　37

Strand 4 Fractions　　43
Units 1–5 Foundation
Unit 6 Dividing fractions　　44

Strand 5 Percentages　　49
Units 1–3 Foundation
Unit 4 Applying percentage increases and decreases to amounts　　50
Unit 5 Finding the percentage change from one amount to another　　58
Unit 6 Reverse percentages　　65
Unit 7 Repeated percentage increase/decrease　　70

Strand 6 Ratio and proportion　　76
Unit 1 Foundation
Unit 2 Sharing in a given ratio　　77
Unit 3 Working with proportional quantities　　82

Contents

Strand 7 Number properties   91

Units 1–3 Foundation
Unit 4 Index notation   92
Unit 5 Prime factorisation   97
Unit 6 Rules of indices   103
Unit 7 Fractional indices   108

ALGEBRA

Strand 1 Starting algebra   114

Units 1–3 Foundation
Unit 4 Working with formulae   115
Unit 5 Setting up and solving simple equations   122
Unit 6 Using brackets   128
Unit 7 Working with more complex equations   136
Unit 8 Solving equations with brackets   142
■ Unit 9 Simplifying harder expressions   148
Unit 10 Using complex formulae   154

Strand 2 Sequences   161

Units 1–2 Foundation
■ Unit 3 Linear sequences   162
■ Unit 4 Special sequences   168
■ Unit 5 Quadratic sequences   175
■ Unit 6 nth term of a quadratic sequence   182

Strand 3 Functions and graphs   188

Unit 1 Foundation
Unit 2 Plotting graphs of linear functions   189
■ Unit 3 The equation of a straight line   197
■ Unit 4 Plotting quadratic and cubic graphs   207
■ Unit 5 Finding equations of straight lines   216
■ Unit 6 Perpendicular lines   223

Strand 4 Algebraic methods   232

Unit 1 Trial and improvement   233
Unit 2 Linear inequalities   237
■ Unit 3 Solving pairs of equations by substitution   244
■ Unit 4 Solving simultaneous equations by elimination   250
■ Unit 5 Using graphs to solve simultaneous equations   257

Contents

Strand 5 Working with quadratics   264

- Unit 1 Factorising quadratics   265
- Unit 2 Solving equations by factorising   271

GEOMETRY AND MEASURES

Strand 1 Units and scales   276

Units 1–6 Foundation
Unit 7 Converting approximately between metric and imperial units   277
Unit 8 Bearings   283
Unit 9 Scale drawing   290
Unit 10 Compound units   297
Unit 11 Dimensions of formulae   302
Unit 12 Working with compound units   307

Strand 2 Properties of shapes   315

Units 1–4 Foundation
- Unit 5 Angles in triangles and quadrilaterals   316
Unit 6 Types of quadrilateral   324
Unit 7 Angles and parallel lines   330
- Unit 8 Angles in a polygon   338
- Unit 9 Congruent triangles and proof   345
- Unit 10 Proof using similar and congruent triangles   356
- Unit 11 Circle theorems   362

Strand 3 Measuring shapes   374

Units 1–3 Foundation
Unit 4 Area of circles   375
Unit 5 Pythagoras' theorem   382

Strand 4 Construction   390

Units 1–2 Foundation
Unit 3 Constructions with a pair of compasses   391
Unit 4 Loci   403

Strand 5 Transformations   412

Units 1–2 Foundation
- Unit 3 Translation   413
- Unit 4 Reflection   420

Contents

■ Unit 5 Rotation — 434
■ Unit 6 Enlargement — 448
Unit 7 Similarity — 458
Unit 8 Trigonometry — 469

Strand 6 Three-dimensional shapes — 479

Units 1–2 Foundation
Unit 3 Volume and surface area of cuboids — 480
Unit 4 2D representations of 3D shapes — 490
Unit 5 Prisms — 498
Unit 6 Enlargement in two and three dimensions — 507
Unit 7 Constructing plans and elevations — 515

STATISTICS AND PROBABILITY

Strand 1 Statistical measures — 523

Units 1–3 Foundation
Unit 4 Using grouped frequency tables — 524
Unit 5 Inter-quartile range — 533

Strand 2 Statistical diagrams — 546

Units 1–2 Foundation
Unit 3 Pie charts — 547
Unit 4 Displaying grouped data — 556
Unit 5 Scatter diagrams — 565
Unit 6 Using lines of best fit — 573

Strand 3 Collecting data — 580

Unit 1 Foundation
Unit 2 Designing questionnaires — 581

Strand 4 Probability — 588

Unit 1 Foundation
■ Unit 2 Single event probability — 589
■ Unit 3 Combined events — 596
■ Unit 4 Estimating probability — 606
■ Unit 5 The multiplication rule — 617
■ Unit 6 The addition rule and Venn diagram notation — 627

How to get the most from this book

This book covers the content for the Intermediate WJEC GCSEs in Mathematics and Mathematics – Numeracy

Sometimes sections are included for completeness as extension material. This is clearly flagged with **Higher Tier only**

The material is split into 22 '**strands of learning**':

Number strands	Algebra strands	Geometry Strands	Statistics Strands
Calculating	Starting algebra	Units and scales	Statistical measures
Using our number system	Sequences	Properties of shapes	Statistical diagrams
Accuracy	Functions and graphs	Measuring shapes	Collecting data
Fractions	Algebraic methods	Construction	Probability
Percentages	Working with quadratics	Transformations	
Ratio and proportion		Three-dimensional shapes	
Number properties			

Each strand is presented as a series of units that get more difficult as you progress (from Band b to Band i). This book mainly deals with units in Bands f to h. In total there are 80 units in this book.

Getting started

At the beginning of each strand, you will find a '**Progression strand flowchart**'. It shows what skills you will develop in each unit in the strand. You can see:

- what you need to know before starting each unit
- what you will need to learn next to progress

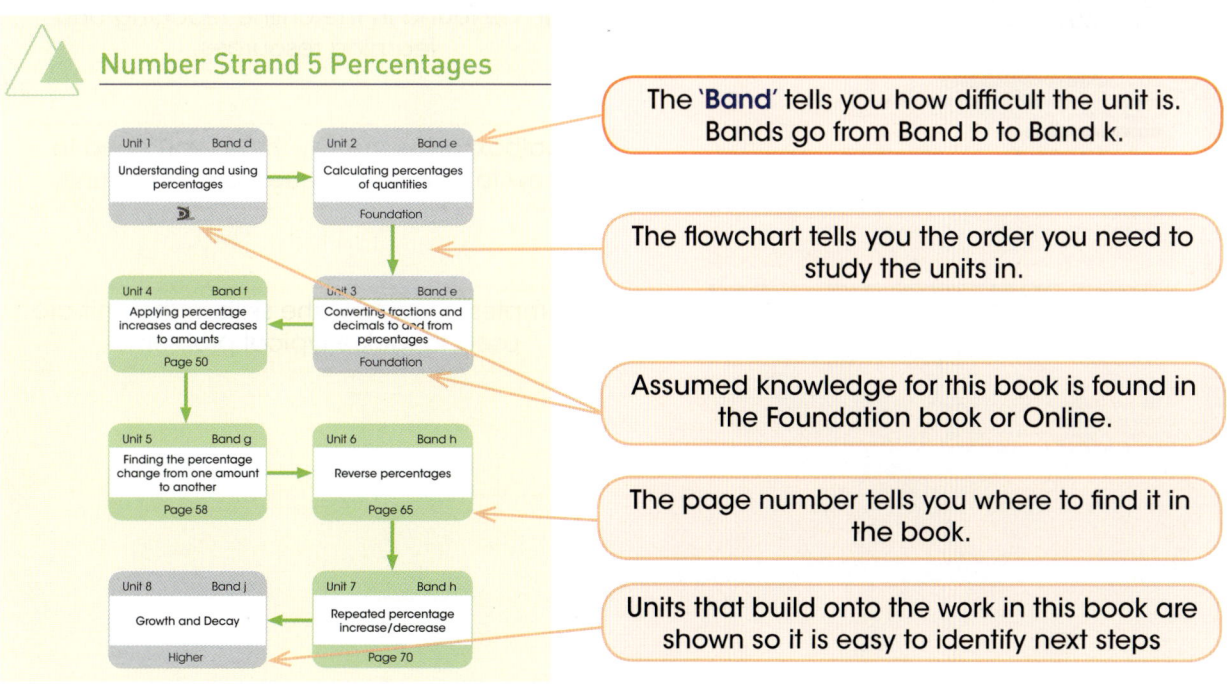

vii

How to get the most from this book

When you start to use this book, you will need to identify where to join each Strand. Then you will not spend time revisiting skills you have already mastered.

If you can answer all the questions in the '**Reviewing skills**' section of a unit then you will not have to study that unit.

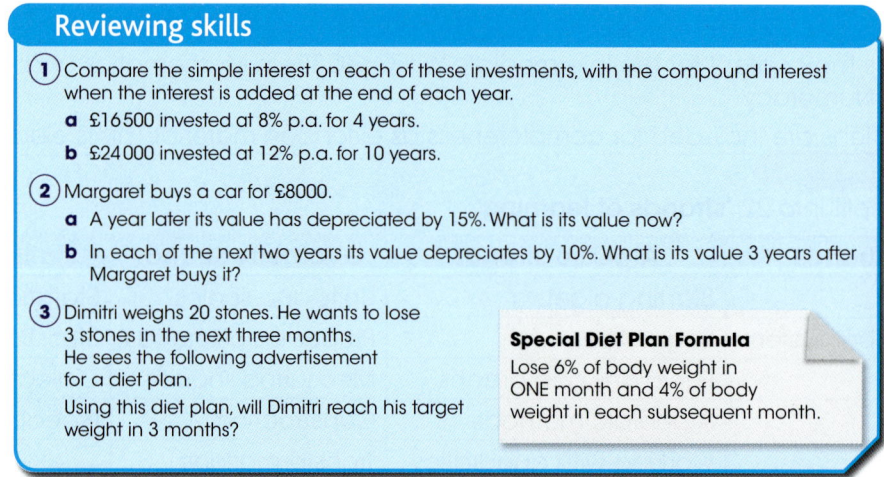

When you know which unit to start with in each strand you will be ready to start work on your first unit.

Starting a unit

Every unit begins with some information:

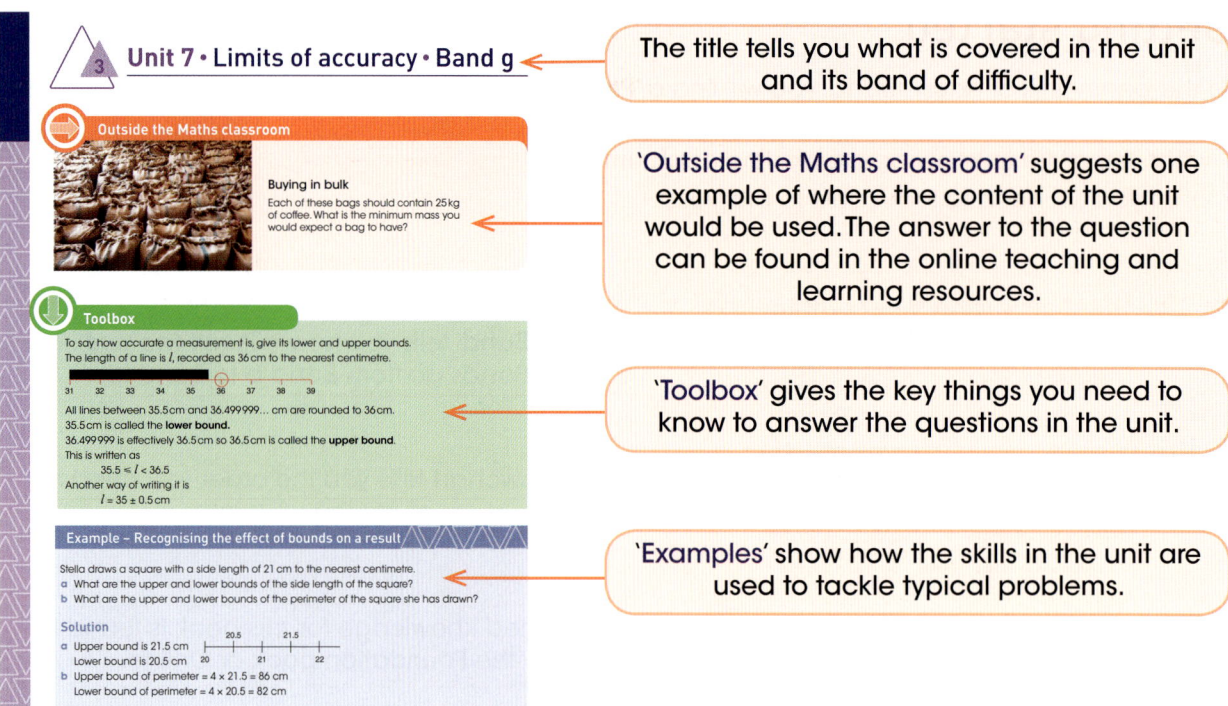

The title tells you what is covered in the unit and its band of difficulty.

'Outside the Maths classroom' suggests one example of where the content of the unit would be used. The answer to the question can be found in the online teaching and learning resources.

'Toolbox' gives the key things you need to know to answer the questions in the unit.

'Examples' show how the skills in the unit are used to tackle typical problems.

How to get the most from this book

Now you have all the information you need, you can use the questions to develop your understanding.

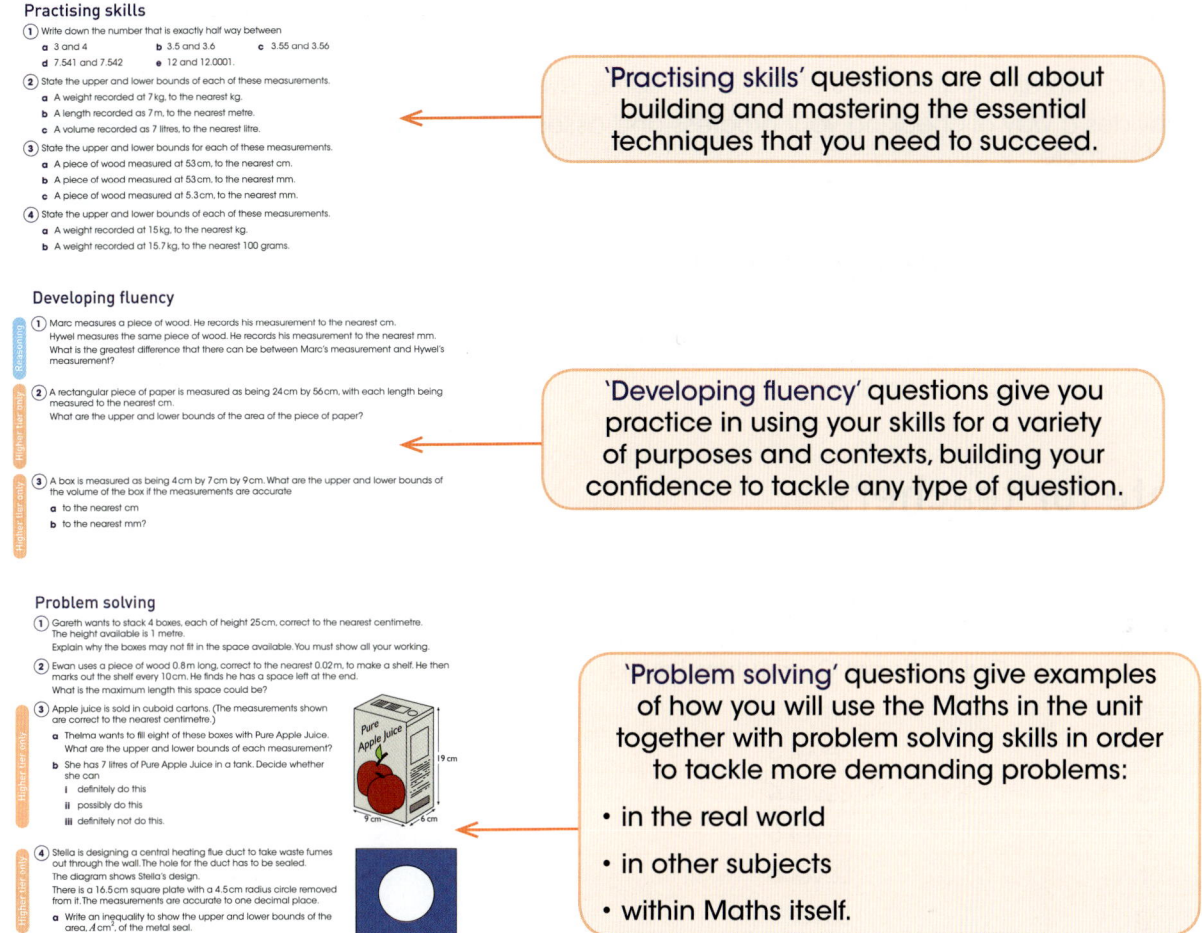

'Practising skills' questions are all about building and mastering the essential techniques that you need to succeed.

'Developing fluency' questions give you practice in using your skills for a variety of purposes and contexts, building your confidence to tackle any type of question.

'Problem solving' questions give examples of how you will use the Maths in the unit together with problem solving skills in order to tackle more demanding problems:

- in the real world
- in other subjects
- within Maths itself.

When you feel confident, use the '**Reviewing skills**' section to check that you have mastered the techniques covered in the unit.

You will see many questions labelled with Reasoning

 Reasoning skills are key skills you need to develop in order to solve problems.

They will help you think through problems and to apply your skills in unfamiliar situations. Use these questions to make sure that you develop these important skills.

How to get the most from this book

About 'Bands'

Every unit has been allocated to a Band. These bands show you the level of difficulty of the Maths that you are working on.

Each Band contains Maths that's of about the same level of difficulty.

This provides a way of checking your progress and assessing your weaker areas, where you need to practise more.

Moving on to another unit

Once you have completed a unit, you should move on to the next unit in one of the strands. You can choose which strand to work on next but try and complete all the units in a particular Band before moving on to the next Band.

A note for teachers

Lower Bands have been assigned to units roughly in line with the previous National Curriculum levels. Here they are, just to help in giving you a reference point.

Band	Approximate Equivalent in terms of Old National Curriculum Levels
b	Level 2
c	Level 3
d	Level 4
e	Level 5
f	Level 6
g	Level 7
h	Level 8
i	No equivalent

Answers and Write-on sheets

Write-on sheets to aid completion of answers are denoted by . These and answers to all the questions in this book are available via **Mastering Mathematics 11-16 Teaching and Learning Resources for WJEC GCSE** or by visiting

www.hoddereducation.co.uk/MasteringmathsforWJECGCSE

Number Strand 1 Calculating

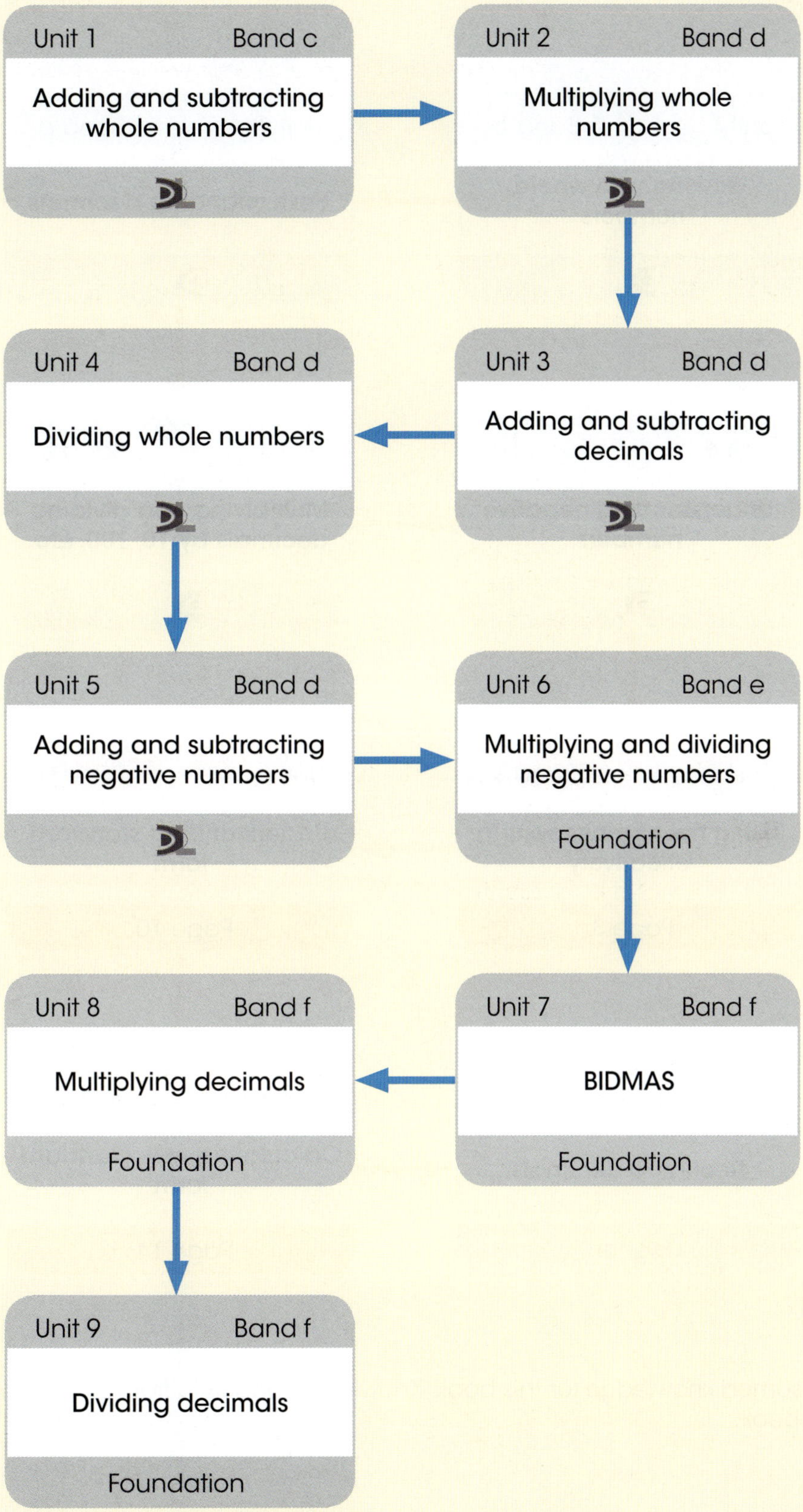

Unit 1 — Band c: Adding and subtracting whole numbers

Unit 2 — Band d: Multiplying whole numbers

Unit 3 — Band d: Adding and subtracting decimals

Unit 4 — Band d: Dividing whole numbers

Unit 5 — Band d: Adding and subtracting negative numbers

Unit 6 — Band e: Multiplying and dividing negative numbers (Foundation)

Unit 7 — Band f: BIDMAS (Foundation)

Unit 8 — Band f: Multiplying decimals (Foundation)

Unit 9 — Band f: Dividing decimals (Foundation)

This strand is assumed knowledge for this book. Knowledge and skills from these units are used throughout the book.

Number Strand 2 Using our number system

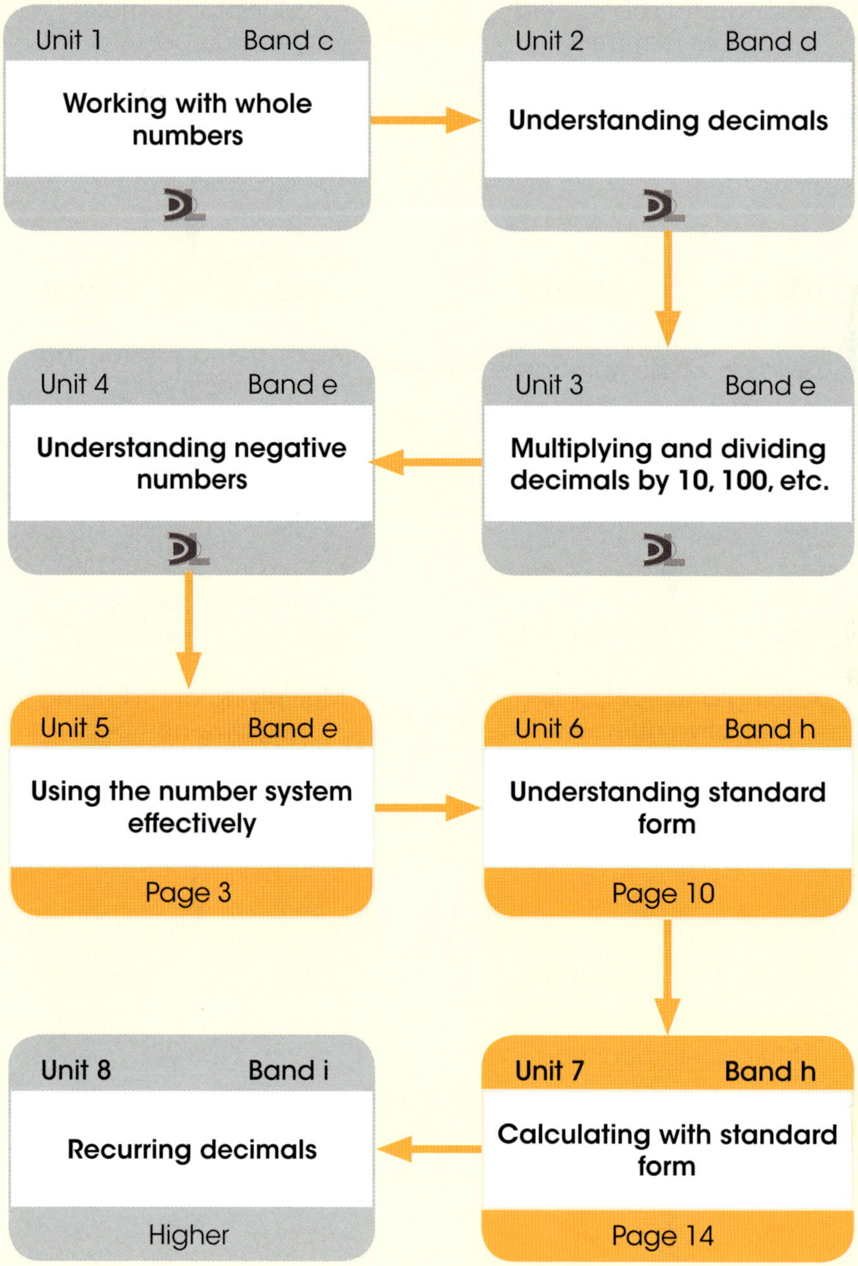

Unit 1	Band c
Working with whole numbers	

Unit 2	Band d
Understanding decimals	

Unit 4	Band e
Understanding negative numbers	

Unit 3	Band e
Multiplying and dividing decimals by 10, 100, etc.	

Unit 5	Band e
Using the number system effectively	
Page 3	

Unit 6	Band h
Understanding standard form	
Page 10	

Unit 8	Band i
Recurring decimals	
Higher	

Unit 7	Band h
Calculating with standard form	
Page 14	

Units 1–4 are assumed knowledge for this book. Knowledge and skills from these units are used throughout the book.

Unit 5 • Using the number system effectively • Band e

Outside the Maths classroom

Building swimming pools

How many tiles are needed to tile an Olympic swimming pool?

Toolbox

Thinking of dividing as 'how many are there in…?'
How many 2s are there in 8?

$$2 + 2 + 2 + 2 = 8$$

There are four 2s in 8 so $8 ÷ 2 = 4$.

How many 0.1s are there in 1.3?

$$0.1 + 0.1 + 0.1 + 0.1 + 0.1 + 0.1 + 0.1 + 0.1 + 0.1 + 0.1 + 0.1 + 0.1 + 0.1 = 1.3$$

There are thirteen 0.1s in 1.3 so $1.3 ÷ 0.1 = 13$.

This is the same as multiplying 1.3 by 10.

This place-value table shows 4.67 divided by 0.01

H	T	U	.	$\frac{1}{10}$	$\frac{1}{100}$
		4	.	6	7
4	6	7	.		

The place-value table shows that dividing by 0.01 has exactly the same effect as multiplying by 100.

In the same way,

- multiplying by 0.1 is the same as dividing by 10
- multiplying by 0.01 is the same as dividing by 100
- multiplying by 0.001 is the same as dividing by 1000 and so on.

Number Strand 2 Using our number system

Example – Multiplying and dividing by 0.1 and 0.01

Work out the answers to these calculations.
a 32×0.1
b 320×0.01
c $32 \div 0.1$
d $32 \div 0.01$

Solution

a Using a place-value table to multiply by 0.1, think of 30 lots of 0.1 which makes 3, and 2 lots of 0.1 which makes 0.2.

H	T	U	.	$\frac{1}{10}$	$\frac{1}{100}$	$\frac{1}{1000}$
	3	2	.			
		3	.	2		

Using a place-value table can help to keep track of the digits when multiplying or dividing by powers of 10.

So 32 lots of 0.1 = 3.2

Using the same idea for the other calculations:
b $320 \times 0.01 = 3.2$
c $32 \div 0.1 = 320$
d $32 \div 0.01 = 3200$

Example – Division using known facts

Use this known fact to work out the calculations below.

$720 \div 0.1 = 7200$

a $7200 \div 0.1$
b $7200 \div 0.01$
c $72 \div 0.1$
d $720 \div 0.01$
e $7200 \div 10$
f $7200 \div 1000$

Solution

a $7200 \div 0.1 = 72\,000$
b $7200 \div 0.01 = 720\,000$
c $72 \div 0.1 = 720$
d $720 \div 0.01 = 72\,000$
e $7200 \div 10 = 720$
f $7200 \div 1000 = 7.2$

Unit 5 Using the number system effectively Band e

Example – Multiplication using known facts

Use this known fact to work out the calculations below.

$720 \times 0.1 = 72$

a 7200×0.1
b 7200×0.01
c 72×0.1
d 720×0.01
e 7200×10
f 7200×1000

Solution

a $7200 \times 0.1 = 720$
b $7200 \times 0.01 = 72$
c $72 \times 0.1 = 7.2$
d $720 \times 0.01 = 7.2$
e $7200 \times 10 = 72\,000$
f $7200 \times 1000 = 7\,200\,000$

Example – Mental calculation using known facts

Work out $5.6 \div 0.07$ in your head.

Salman

Solution

$56 \div 7 = 8$
so $5.6 \div 7 = 0.8$
so $5.6 \div 0.7 = 8$
and so $5.6 \div 0.07 = 80$

Amy

Number Strand 2 Using our number system

Practising skills

1 Work these out.

a
  i 7000 × 1000
  ii 7000 × 100
  iii 7000 × 10
  iv 7000 × 1
  v 7000 × 0.1
  vi 7000 × 0.01
  vii 7000 × 0.001

b
  i 2468 × 1000
  ii 2468 × 100
  iii 2468 × 10
  iv 2468 × 1
  v 2468 × 0.1
  vi 2468 × 0.01
  vii 2468 × 0.001

c Use the word 'less' or 'more' to complete these sentences.
7000 × 10 gives an answer which is _____ than 7000.
7000 × 0.1 gives an answer which is _____ than 7000.

2 Work these out.

a
  i 8000 ÷ 1000
  ii 8000 ÷ 100
  iii 8000 ÷ 10
  iv 8000 ÷ 1
  v 8000 ÷ 0.1
  vi 8000 ÷ 0.01
  vii 8000 ÷ 0.001

b
  i 6500 ÷ 1000
  ii 6500 ÷ 100
  iii 6500 ÷ 10
  iv 6500 ÷ 1
  v 6500 ÷ 0.1
  vi 6500 ÷ 0.01
  vii 6500 ÷ 0.001

c Use the word 'less' or 'more' to complete these sentences.
8000 ÷ 10 gives an answer which is _____ than 8000.
8000 ÷ 0.1 gives an answer which is _____ than 8000.

3 Work these out.
a 40 × 0.1
b 600 × 0.1
c 9 × 0.1
d 8.4 × 0.1
e 125 ÷ 0.1
f 993 ÷ 0.1
g 6.2 ÷ 0.1
h 5.17 ÷ 0.1

4 Work these out.
a 0.6 × 0.01
b 500 × 0.01
c 8000 × 0.01
d 145 × 0.01
e 246.9 ÷ 0.01
f 61.3 ÷ 0.01
g 32 ÷ 0.01
h 2000 ÷ 0.01

5 Work these out.
a 225.9 × 0.001
b 638 × 0.001
c 8 × 0.001
d 0.4 × 0.001
e 5.84 ÷ 0.01
f 0.7 ÷ 0.001
g 24.9 ÷ 0.001
h 0.0815 ÷ 0.001

6 Work these out.
a 6 ÷ 0.1
b 13 × 0.1
c 4.7 ÷ 0.001
d 52.9 ÷ 0.01
e 0.8 × 0.1
f 7.65 ÷ 0.001
g 5 ÷ 0.01
h 46 × 0.01

7 Work these out.

a 180 ÷ 0.01
b 2.3 × 0.01
c 6.91 ÷ 0.01
d 0.7 ÷ 0.01
e 50 × 0.01
f 3.2 ÷ 0.001
g 1.64 × 0.001
h 5.899 ÷ 0.0001

8 Work these out.

a 0.6 ÷ 0.001
b 12.2 × 0.01
c 0.07 ÷ 0.01
d 0.18 ÷ 0.1
e 0.009 ÷ 0.001
f 0.746 × 0.1
g 45.228 ÷ 0.01
h 3.6078 × 0.001

Developing fluency

1 Beef costs £8.60 per kilo.

Copy and complete each sentence.

a 1 kg of beef costs 8.60 × 1 = £☐
b 10 kg of beef costs 8.60 × ☐ = £☐
c 0.1 kg of beef costs 8.60 × ☐ = £☐

2 a Siân has a bag of 10p coins. It is worth £3. How many 10p coins are in the bag?

b Using pence this is written 300 ÷ 10 = 30.
Complete this equivalent statement using pounds. 3 ÷ ☐ = ☐

3 Write the answers to these calculations in order of size, smallest first.

a 17 × 0.1
b 26.5 × 0.01
c 790 × 0.01
d 125.1 × 0.001
e 0.7 ÷ 0.1
f 0.65 ÷ 0.01
g 1.124 ÷ 0.001
h 7 ÷ 0.001

4 Here is Owain's homework.
Mark the homework and correct any answers that are wrong.

> 1 86 × 0.1 = 8.6
> 2 20 × 0.1 = 200
> 3 2.5 ÷ 0.1 = 0.25
> 4 3 ÷ 0.1 = 30
> 5 18 × 0.01 = 0.18
> 6 1121 ÷ 0.01 = 11210
> 7 60 × 0.001 = 0.6
> 8 2.04 ÷ 0.1 = 2.004

5 Find the missing numbers.

a 180 × ☐ = 1800
b 65 × ☐ = 6.5
c 900 × ☐ = 9
d 2.1 × ☐ = 210
e 6.7 × ☐ = 0.67
f 0.9 × ☐ = 0.009

6 Find the missing numbers.

a 4500 ÷ ☐ = 45
b 2 ÷ ☐ = 20
c 7.8 ÷ ☐ = 7800
d 68 ÷ ☐ = 680
e 40 ÷ ☐ = 0.4
f 0.06 ÷ ☐ = 0.6

Number Strand 2 Using our number system

Problem solving

1 Look at this diagram. There are 4 operations in the boxes.

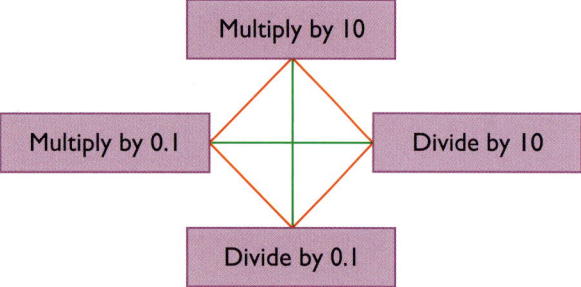

Two pairs of the operations are equivalent; they are joined by green lines.
The other pairs are opposite (or inverse) operations and they are joined by red lines.
Copy and complete the following diagrams.

a

b

c

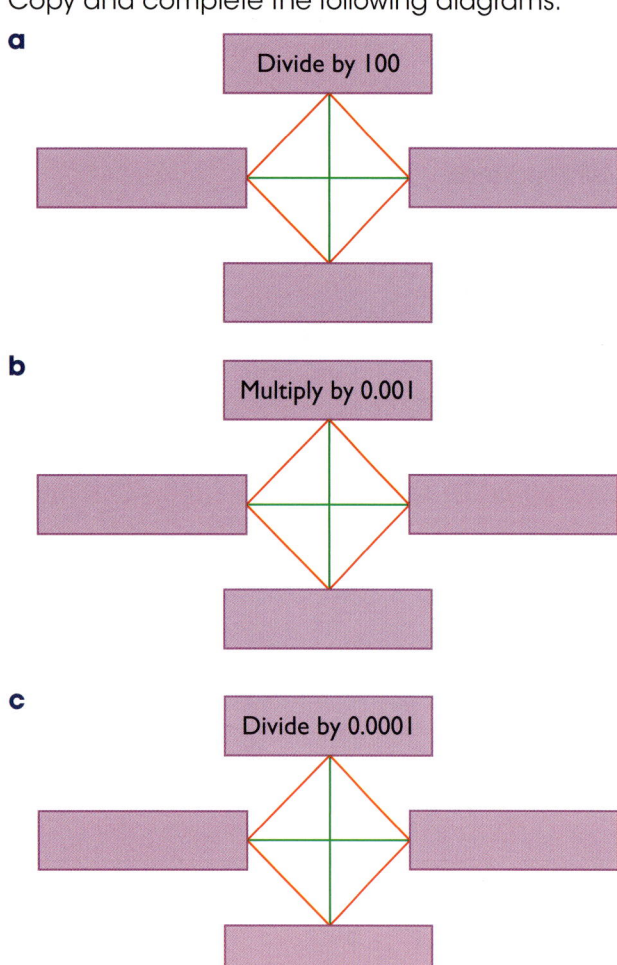

2 Start with 81 × 16 = 1296.

When you go diagonally down to the left, multiply the first number by 2 and divide the second number by 2.

When you go diagonally down to the right, divide the first number by 3 and multiply the second number by 3.

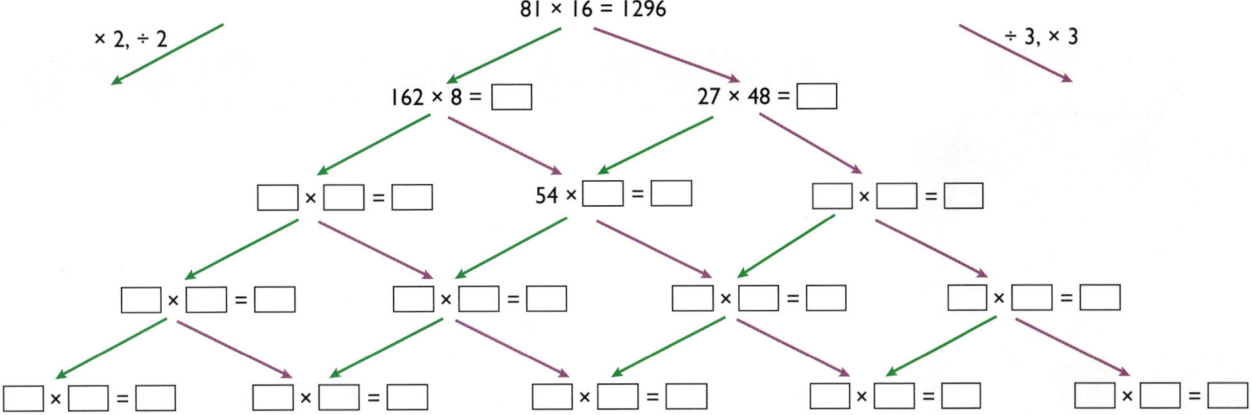

a Complete the diagram.
b What happens if you try to complete another layer?
c What is special about the starting numbers that have been chosen?

Reviewing skills

1 Work these out.
  a 8.2 × 0.1
  b 130 × 0.1
  c 4 × 0.01
  d 8 × 0.001
  e 63 × 0.001
  f 0.9 × 0.01
  g 2.01 × 0.1
  h 0.7 × 0.001

2 Work these out.
  a 2.8 ÷ 0.1
  b 30 ÷ 0.01
  c 0.08 ÷ 0.001
  d 0.2 ÷ 0.001
  e 600 ÷ 0.1
  f 0.004 ÷ 0.01
  g 100 ÷ 0.0001
  h 0.001 ÷ 0.0001

3 How many 1p coins make £100?

Unit 6 • Understanding standard form • Band h

Outside the Maths classroom

Describing the Universe

The speed of light is written in standard form as 3×10^8 m/s. Why do scientists use numbers written in standard form?

Toolbox

Standard form is used to write large numbers and small numbers.

For example, the speed of light is 2.998×10^8 metres per second and the mass of an electron is 9.110×10^{-31} kg.

A number in standard form is
(a number between 1 and 10) × (a power of 10).

So 3.9×10^{-4} is standard form but 39×10^{-5} isn't.

When thinking about numbers in standard form it can be helpful to have a place-value table in mind. The table below shows four million six hundred and seventy thousand (4 670 000), which is sometimes said as 4.67 million.

	M	HTh	TTh	Th	H	T	U	.	$\frac{1}{10}$	$\frac{1}{100}$
							4	.	6	7
4.67 × 10⁶	4	6	7	0	0	0	0	.		

4.67 million is $4.67 \times 1\,000\,000$ or 4.67×10^6. The table shows you that, the $\times 10^6$ moves all of the digits in 4.67 six places to the left; any blanks are filled with zeros.

In 6.8×10^{-3} all of the digits of 6.8 are moved three places to the right and the gaps are filled with zeros.

	H	T	U	.	$\frac{1}{10}$	$\frac{1}{100}$	$\frac{1}{1000}$	$\frac{1}{10000}$
			6	.	8			
6.8 × 10⁻³				.	0	0	6	8

Unit 6 Understanding standard form Band h

Example – Converting small numbers to standard form

A flea weighs around 0.000087 kg. Write this number in standard form.

Solution

For it to be in standard form, it must start 8.7
0.000087 = 0.00087 × 0.1
0.000087 = 0.0087 × 0.01
0.000087 = 0.087 × 0.001
0.000087 = 0.87 × 0.0001
0.000087 = 8.7 × 0.00001
So
0.000087 = 8.7 × 0.00001 = 8.7×10^{-5}

Example – Converting large numbers from standard form

Convert the standard form number 6.387×10^6 to a normal number.

Solution

M	HTh	TTh	Th	H	T	U	.	$\frac{1}{10}$	$\frac{1}{100}$	$\frac{1}{1000}$
						6	.	3	8	7
6	3	8	7	0	0	0	.			

Using a place-value table the digits will move up 6 columns when multiplied by 10^6
So $6.387 \times 10^6 = 6\,387\,000$

The questions in this unit should be answered *without* the use of a calculator.

Practising skills

1 a Write these numbers in standard form.
    i 5120   **ii** 512   **iii** 51.2
    iv 0.512   **v** 0.00512   **vi** 0.000512

  b How would you write 5.12 in standard form?

2 These numbers are expressed in standard form. Write them as ordinary numbers.
  a 5×10^2 **b** 8×10^4 **c** 2.6×10^3 **d** 1.9×10^5
  e 8.17×10^3 **f** 9.05×10^4 **g** 7.4×10^7 **h** 1.004×10^4

3 Write these numbers in standard form.
  a 600   **b** 70 000   **c** 8900   **d** 816
  e 133 000   **f** 4 million   **g** 95 million   **h** 4 billion

Number Strand 2 Using our number system

4 These numbers are written in standard form. Write them as ordinary numbers.
- a 6.8×10^{-2}
- b 5×10^{-3}
- c 2.99×10^{-2}
- d 7×10^{-4}
- e 1.04×10^{-1}
- f 8.6×10^{-5}
- g 5×10^{-6}
- h 3.227×10^{-2}

5 Write these numbers in standard form.
- a 0.69
- b 0.052
- c 0.0114
- d 0.0007
- e 0.0038
- f 0.000006
- g 0.955
- h 0.00009

Developing fluency

1 Which of these are not written in standard form?

5×10^4 1600 0.8×10^3 6.2×10^5 9×100^3 7.1×10^{-4}

2 Write these quantities in standard form.
- a The total length of veins in the human body is 60 000 miles
- b On average a person's heart beats 108 000 times a day
- c The distance between the Sun and the Moon is about 150 000 000 km
- d A single coffee bean weighs about 0.003 kg
- e The mass of a grain of rice is 0.000 002 6 kg

3 These numbers are in standard form. Write them as ordinary numbers and in words.
- a 9×10^3
- b 2.1×10^3
- c 6.8×10^2
- d 9.22×10^2
- e 1.08×10^4
- f 7×10^1
- g 7×10^{-1}
- h 3×10^{-2}

4 Write these numbers in standard form.
- a Six thousand
- b Seventy four
- c Eight hundred and ten
- d Two thousand and fifteen
- e Four tenths
- f Three hundredths
- g 0.000 000 2 24
- h 5 108 000
- i 67 800 000
- j 23 million
- k 4 billion
- l 0.000 000 007 001

5 Write these numbers in order, starting with the smallest.

7100 6.8×10^4 9×10^4 7.95×10^2 7.09×10^3

6 Write these numbers in order, starting with the biggest.

3.82×10^{-2} 0.04 2×10^{-3} 3.9×10^{-2} 2.2×10^{-3}

7 In each of these, fill the box with one of <, > or =
- a 7×10^2 ☐ 750
- b 6.2×10^{-3} ☐ 8×10^{-2}
- c 5×10^3 ☐ 5000
- d 0.009 ☐ 9×10^4
- e 1.65×10^8 ☐ 2.4×10^7
- f 8×10^7 ☐ 9 million

Unit 6 Understanding standard form Band h

Problem solving

1) The table shows the closest distances of the Sun and seven planets from Earth.

Planet	Distance from Earth (in kilometres)
Jupiter	6.244×10^8
Mars	7.83×10^7
Mercury	9.17×10^7
Neptune	4.35×10^9
Saturn	1.25×10^9
Sun	1.496×10^8
Uranus	2.72×10^9
Venus	4.1×10^7

In a school project, Finlay has to list these in order of distance from Earth.
He has to start with the planet that is nearest to Earth.
Finlay writes them in the correct order. Write down Finlay's list.

2) In a test, Rhodri had to write down the value of the first digit of 10 numbers written in standard form.
The table shows Rhodri's answers.

Question	Number	Value of first digit	Question	Number	Value of first digit
1	6.1×10^4	6000	6	2×10^{-2}	2 hundredths
2	3.62×10^4	3 units	7	1.46×10^{-2}	1 unit
3	2.9×10^7	20 million	8	3×10^{-4}	$\frac{3}{10\,000}$
4	4.5×10^9	4 billion	9	6.2×10^{-4}	$\frac{6}{100\,000}$
5	1.236×10^9	1 trillion	10	3.12×10^{-6}	3 millionths

How many correct answers did Rhodri get?

Reviewing skills

1) These numbers are expressed in standard form. Write them as ordinary numbers.
  a 2.008×10^5 b 2.45×10^6 c 7.803×10^9 d 6.45×10^8
  e 9×10^{-1} f 2.07×10^{-7} g 6.145×10^{-3} h 1.007×10^{-1}

2) Write these numbers in standard form.
  a 20 250   b 23 million   c 654.7   d 25 624.87
  e 3 tenths   f 7 hundredths   g 0.00204   h 0.099

3) Write these quantities in standard form.
  a The population of the world is approximately 7 billion.
  b The diameter of a red blood cell is 0.008 mm.

4) Indicate the correct answer a, b, c or d.
3.2 million in standard form.
  a 3.2×10^5 b 3.2×10^6 c 3.2×10^7 d $3.0^2 \times 10^6$

13

Unit 7 • Calculating with standard form • Band h

Outside the Maths classroom

Measuring space

How many stars are there in our galaxy?

Toolbox

Adding or subtracting numbers in standard form is straightforward if the power of ten is the same.

Five million added to three million is eight million, which can be written as
$5 \times 10^6 + 3 \times 10^6 = 8 \times 10^6$.

If the powers of ten are not equal rewrite them so they are.

Then the same strategy can be used.

$6 \times 10^9 + 5 \times 10^8 = 60 \times 10^8 + 5 \times 10^8$ ← Making the powers of 10 the same.

$\qquad = 65 \times 10^8$ ← Adding.

$\qquad = 6.5 \times 10^9$. ← Rewrite the number in standard form.

When multiplying (or dividing) two numbers in standard form, work with each part of the number separately.

$5 \times 10^7 \times 3 \times 10^4 = 5 \times 3 \times 10^7 \times 10^3$ ← $5 \times 3 = 15, 10^7 \times 10^3 = 10^{10}$

$\qquad = 15 \times 10^{10}$ ← Note: This is not standard form.

$\qquad = 1.5 \times 10^{11}$

← The *number* must be between 1 and 10.

Unit 7 Calculating with standard form Band h

Example – Multiplying large and small numbers

The mass of a grain of sand is about 3.5×10^{-10} kg.
It is thought that there are about 7.5×10^{18} grains of sand on the Earth.
Use the figures above to calculate the mass of all of the sand on Earth. Give your answer in standard form.

Solution

$3.5 \times 10^{-10} \times 7.5 \times 10^{18} = 26.25 \times 10^{8}$ ← $3.5 \times 7.5 = 36.25, 10^{-10} \times 10^{18} = 10^{8}$

$\qquad\qquad\qquad\qquad\quad = 2.625 \times 10^{9}$ kg ← Make the *number* between 1 and 10.

Example – Subtraction and division of small numbers

A loaf of bread contains 5×10^{-3} kg of yeast and 1×10^{-2} kg of salt.
a How much do the salt and yeast weigh in total?
b How much greater is the mass of the salt than the mass of the yeast in kg?
c How many times is the mass of the salt greater than the mass of the yeast?

Solution

a $1 \times 10^{-2} + 5 \times 10^{-3} = 10 \times 10^{-3} + 5 \times 10^{-3}$ ← Converting to the same power of ten.
$\qquad\qquad\qquad\qquad\; = 15 \times 10^{-3}$ kg
$\qquad\qquad\qquad\qquad\; = 1.5 \times 10^{-2}$ kg ← In standard form.

b $1 \times 10^{-2} - 5 \times 10^{-3} = 10 \times 10^{-3} - 5 \times 10^{-3}$
$\qquad\qquad\qquad\qquad\; = 5 \times 10^{-3}$ kg
The salt weighs 5×10^{-3} kg more than the yeast.

c $\dfrac{\text{mass of salt}}{\text{mass of yeast}} = \dfrac{1 \times 10^{-2}}{5 \times 10^{-3}}$

$\qquad\qquad\quad = 0.2 \times 10^{-2-(-3)}$
$\qquad\qquad\quad = 0.2 \times 10^{1}$
$\qquad\qquad\quad = 2 (\times 10^{0})$
There is twice as much salt as yeast.

Do the questions in this unit without a calculator first. Use your calculator to check your answers.

Practising skills

1 Work out the values of the following, giving your answers in standard form.
   a $\;3.2 \times 10^{5} + 4.6 \times 10^{5}$
   b $\;6.8 \times 10^{-2} - 5.1 \times 10^{-2}$
   c $\;8000 + 700$
   d $\;6.4 \times 10^{3} + 2000$
   e $\;1.8 \times 10^{-3} + 2.2 \times 10^{-3}$
   f $\;6.4 \times 10^{-2} - 0.033$

2 Work out the following, giving your answers in standard form.
   a $\;7.2 \times 10^{5} + 4.6 \times 10^{5}$
   b $\;7.2 \times 10^{5} + 4.6 \times 10^{4}$
   c $\;7.2 \times 10^{5} + 4.6 \times 10^{6}$
   d $\;7.2 \times 10^{5} - 4.6 \times 10^{5}$
   e $\;7.2 \times 10^{6} - 4.6 \times 10^{5}$
   f $\;7.2 \times 10^{5} - 4.6 \times 10^{6}$

Number Strand 2 Using our number system

3 Without using a calculator work out the value of the following. Give your answers in standard form.
  a $3 \times 10^5 \times 2 \times 10^7$
  b $2 \times 10^3 \times 4 \times 10^5$
  c $2 \times 10^5 \times 5 \times 10^2$
  d $3 \times 10^{-5} \times 3 \times 10^7$
  e $5 \times 10^{-7} \times 2 \times 10^5$
  f $9 \times 10^{-6} \times 7 \times 10^{-4}$

4 Without using a calculator work out the value of these calculations.
  a $6 \times 10^5 \div 2 \times 10^3$
  b $8 \times 10^9 \div 4 \times 10^8$
  c $6 \times 10^7 \div 2 \times 10^3$
  d $3 \times 10^7 \div 2 \times 10^3$
  e $2 \times 10^5 \div 4 \times 10^3$
  f $2 \times 10^6 \div 8 \times 10^8$

5 Using standard form, write down a number that is between:
  a 6×10^5 and 6×10^4
  b 6×10^{-3} and 6×10^{-2}
  c 7.1×10^2 and 7.1×10^3
  d 7.1×10^{-6} and 7.1×10^{-7}

6 Ceri says:

> When you're multiplying numbers in standard form you have to multiply the two numbers at the front together and write down what that comes to, then write '×10' and finally add the two powers together and write that down.

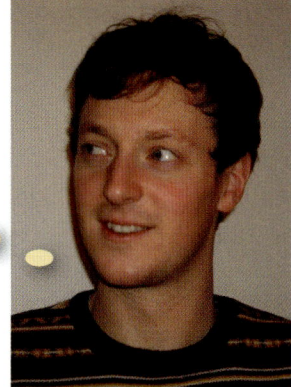

Explain why Ceri's method won't always give the correct answer in standard form.

Developing fluency

1 Work out the following, giving your answers in standard form.
  a $3.204 \times 10^2 + 4 \times 10^{-1}$
  b $3.204 \times 10^2 - 4 \times 10^{-1}$
  c $3.204 \times 10^2 \times 4 \times 10^{-1}$
  d $3.204 \times 10^2 \div 4 \times 10^{-1}$

2 The speed of light is 3×10^8 metres per second and there are roughly 3×10^7 seconds in a year.
A light year is the distance travelled by light in one year.
Approximately how many metres is a light year?
Give your answer in standard form.

3 The masses of some of the planets in our Solar System are:
Jupiter 1.9×10^{27} kg   Mercury 3.3×10^{23} kg
Saturn 5.7×10^{26} kg   Earth 6×10^{24} kg.
  a Place the planets in order of mass.
  b How many times greater than the mass of the Earth is the mass of Jupiter?
  c How many times greater than the mass of Mercury is the mass of Jupiter?
  d How many time greater than the mass of Mercury is the mass of the Earth?

Unit 7 Calculating with standard form Band h

4 Some approximate masses are:
caffeine molecule 3.2×10^{-25} kg
average human cell 1×10^{-12} kg
eyebrow hair 7×10^{-8} kg
water molecule 3×10^{-26} kg.

  a How many water molecules weigh the same as an eyebrow hair?
  b How many water molecules weigh the same as one caffeine molecule?
  c How many times greater than the mass of a water molecule is the mass of an eyebrow hair?

5 A human body contains roughly 1×10^{12} bacteria and there are about 7×10^9 people on the planet.
How many bacteria are there in total within all of the people?

Problem solving

1 The mass of a spacecraft is 7.8×10^4 kg.
The spacecraft is carrying equipment with a total mass of 2.4×10^3 kg.
The spacecraft docks with a space station.
The mass of the space station is 4.62×10^5 kg.
The commander of the space station does not want the total mass on docking to be greater than 5.43×10^5 kg.
Is the total mass within this limit?

2 Rowena is making a scale model of the Solar System.
She wants the distance from Earth to Saturn to be 20 cm on her scale model.
The real distance from the Earth to Saturn is 1.25×10^9 kilometres.
  a Find the scale of the model in the form $1:n$ where n is written in standard form.
Rowena wants to put the position of a spacecraft on the scale model.
The real distance of the spacecraft from Earth is 8.5×10^8 kilometres, correct to 2 significant figures.
  b Work out the distance of the spacecraft from Earth on the scale model.

3 Carwyn is trying to find out the thickness of a piece of paper.
He has a box of paper which contains 3000 sheets of paper positioned on top of each other.
The height of the paper is 0.3 m.
  a Work out the thickness of each sheet of paper.
     Give your answer in metres, in standard form.
Carwyn also wants to know the weight of each sheet of paper.
He weighs the box containing the paper, then he weighs the box when it is empty.
The mass of the box and paper is 54 kg.
The mass of the empty box is 500 g.
  b Work out the mass of each piece of paper.
     Give your answer in kilograms, in standard form.

Number Strand 2 Using our number system

4 Gwenda is estimating how far away a thunderstorm is from her home.

The speed of sound is estimated at 3.3×10^2 metres per second.

The speed of light is estimated at 3.0×10^8 metres per second.

a The thunderstorm is 6 km away and Elaine sees a flash of lightning.

She hears the clap of thunder x seconds later.

Work out the value of x.

Give your answer to the nearest whole number.

b The length of time between seeing the next flash of lightning and hearing the clap of thunder is 3 seconds.

How far away is the thunderstorm now?

State any assumptions that you have made.

5 Lynn is carrying out a survey on the living space per person in six different countries.

The table shows the information that she has collected.

Country	Area (in km^2)	Population	Area (in km^2) per person
Australia	3.0×10^6	2.2×10^7	
Brazil	8.5×10^6	2.0×10^8	
China	9.6×10^6	1.4×10^9	
Germany	3.6×10^5	8.3×10^7	
UK	2.4×10^5	6.4×10^7	
USA	9.8×10^6	3.2×10^8	

She wants to find out which country has the greatest land area per person.

Copy and complete the table and compare the six countries.

6 Rhodri is a keen physicist interested in the wavelengths of sound waves.

Rhodri wants to find the difference between the wavelength of his favourite radio station and the wavelength of his dad's favourite radio station.

Rhodri listens to FM Capital Radio which has a frequency of 102 MHz.

Rhodri's dad listens to AM Radio 5 Live which has a frequency of 909 kHz.

1 MHz = 10^6 waves per second. 1 kHz = 10^3 waves per second.

To find the wavelength (in m), Rhodri uses the formula:

wavelength = $3 \times 10^8 \div$ frequency (in waves per second)

Work out the difference between the wavelength of Rhodri's favourite radio station and the wavelength of his dad's favourite radio station.

Reviewing skills

1 Work out

  a $8.48 \times 10^4 + 8.4 \times 10^3 - 3 \times 10^2$
  Give your answer in standard form.

  b Write the following as ordinary numbers.

  i 8.48×10^4 **ii** 8.4×10^3 **iii** 3×10^2

  c Use your answers to part **b** to check your answer to part **a**.

2 Work out the following, giving your answers in standard form.

  a $6000 \times 1.5 \times 10^9$ **b** $1.6 \times 10^{-4} \times 2 \times 10^{-3}$ **c** $2.3 \times 10^6 + 3$ million

  d $0.0052 - 3.2 \times 10^{-3}$ **e** $7.6 \times 10^2 \times 2 \times 10^{-1}$ **f** $7.6 \times 10^2 \div 2 \times 10^{-1}$

3 Indicate the correct answer **a**, **b**, **c** or **d**.
A hydrogen atom has a mass of 1.67×10^{-27} kg. An oxygen atom has a mass of 2.67×10^{-26} kg. A molecule of water consists of two hydrogen atoms and an oxygen atom. Which of these options is the correct mass for a molecule of water?

  a 6.01×10^{-27} kg **b** 6.01×10^{-26} kg **c** 3.004×10^{-26} kg **d** 3.004×10^{-27} kg

Number Strand 3 Accuracy

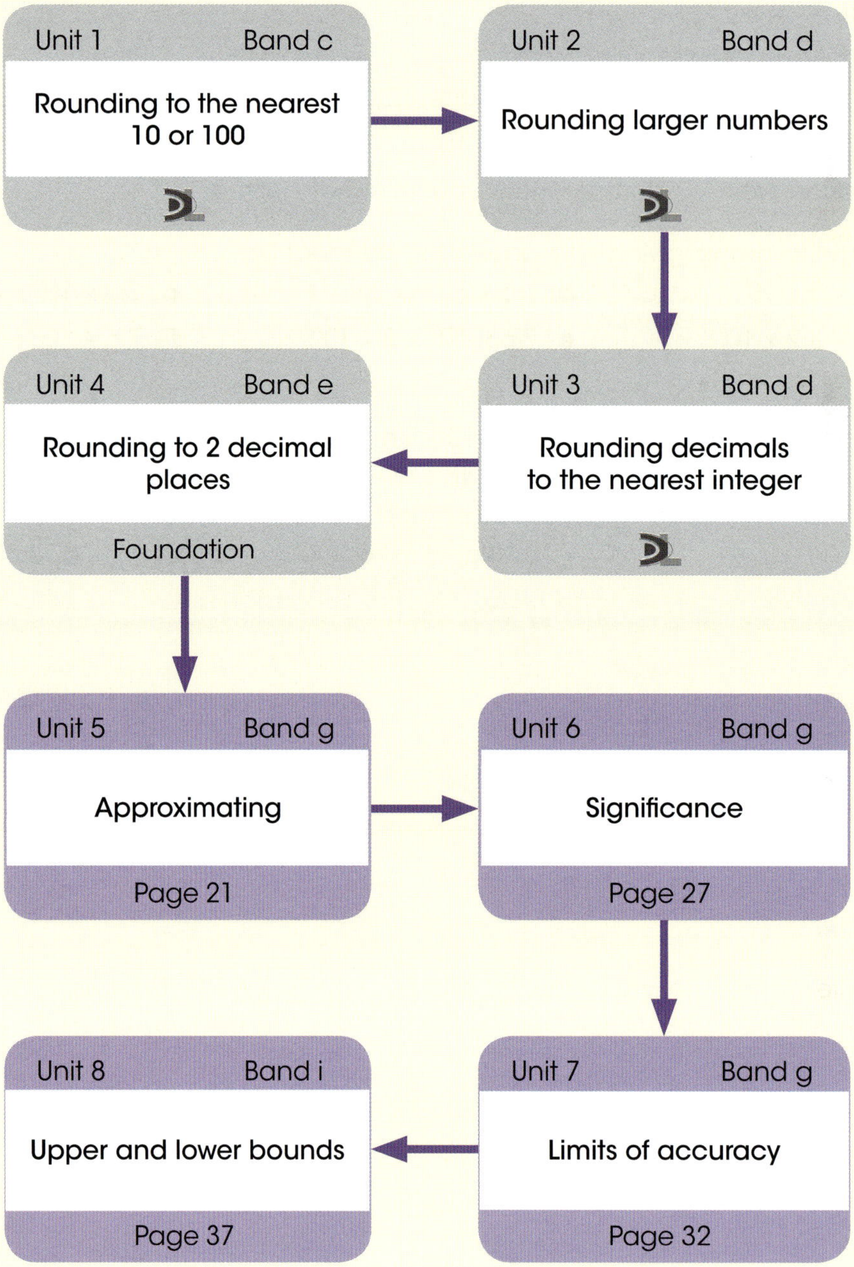

Unit 1 — Band c
Rounding to the nearest 10 or 100

Unit 2 — Band d
Rounding larger numbers

Unit 3 — Band d
Rounding decimals to the nearest integer

Unit 4 — Band e
Rounding to 2 decimal places
Foundation

Unit 5 — Band g
Approximating
Page 21

Unit 6 — Band g
Significance
Page 27

Unit 7 — Band g
Limits of accuracy
Page 32

Unit 8 — Band i
Upper and lower bounds
Page 37

Units 1–4 are assumed knowledge for this book. Knowledge and skills from these units are used throughout the book.

Unit 5 • Approximating • Band g

Outside the Maths classroom

Costing jobs
What factors should a caterer consider when providing a quote for producing a buffet?

Toolbox

Approximating is about:
- rounding numbers for a calculation so that you can do it in your head
- making a rough calculation to anticipate what sort of answer to expect
- recognising when an error has been made
- giving a number to the level of detail that suits the context.

Example – Rounding numbers to make a calculation easier

Mo and Sahar are buying a new radiator for their bedroom.
To choose the right radiator they first need to know the volume of the room.
Mo measures the room in metres. It is 3.8 m long, 3.2 m wide and 2.7 m high.
Use rounded numbers to find the approximate volume of the room.

Solution

- Volume = 3.2 × 2.7 × 3.8
- Approximate values 3 × 3 × 4

The approximate volume is 36 m^3.

Example – Rounding to recognise when an error has been made

Pete's dog is 7 years 10 months old.
Pete says that this is equivalent to a human aged 70 because 1 dog year is like 7 human years.
Is he correct?

Solution

7 years 10 months is nearly 8 years.
7 × 8 = 56 so Pete's dog would be less than 56, not 70.
You could also use an inverse argument to say that, to get a result of 70 when multiplying by 7, you would need to start with 10 (Pete's dog is not yet 10 years old).

The questions in this unit should be answered *without* the use of a calculator.
(However, you may wish to use a calculator to check some of your answers.)

Practising skills

1. Decide if these are good approximations.

    a 82.7 is about 80
    b 9.63 is about 9
    c 312 is about 30
    d 793 is about 800
    e 449 is about 400
    f 6711 is about 6000

2. Estimate the answers to these calculations.

    a 68.79 + 21.96
    b 858.74 − 111.79
    c 30.8 × 45.3
    d 28.4 ÷ 1.99
    e 29.7^2
    f 6371 + 4912

3. For each of these calculations, there is a choice of answers. Use approximation to help you select the correct answer.

    a 6.4 × 8.8
       i 15.2
       ii 28.66
       iii 56.32

    b 7.23^2
       i 5227.29
       ii 52.2729
       iii 14.46

    c 836 ÷ 19
       i 15884
       ii 855
       iii 44

4. Quick checks by rounding the numbers will tell you that three of these answers are wrong. Which three are wrong?

    a 168 × 94 = 1592
    b 18.6 × 4.5 = 83.7
    c $\frac{56}{3.8}$ = 19.74
    d 1200 ÷ 48 = 25
    e 8.9^2 = 79.21
    f 2.8^3 = 31.92

5. A t-shirt costs £7.99 and a pair of shorts costs £11.49.
   Amber wants to buy 2 pairs of shorts and 5 t-shirts.
   She has £60.
   Use a rough estimate to decide if Amber has enough money.

6 Micah has done several calculations.
He then does rough estimates to check his answers.
Here are his results. Which calculations should he look at again?

a Calculation 12.64; rough estimate 80
b Calculation 611; rough estimate 600
c Calculation 0.072; rough estimate 0.08
d Calculation 19.32; rough estimate 6.5
e Calculation 341.8; rough estimate 360
f Calculation 0.0156; rough estimate 0.002

Developing fluency

1 Estimate the answers to these calculations.

a $649 + 382$
b 7.15×13.06
c 62.4^2
d $\dfrac{815 \times 6.4}{2.85}$
e $\dfrac{97 \times 94}{8.96}$
f $(2.1 + 9.4)^2$

2 For each of these calculations, use approximation to help you select the correct answer from the four possible answers given. Explain your choice.

a 514^2
  i 664 196
  ii 26 416
  iii 264 196
  iv 246 196

b 71.4×6.8
  i 4015.52
  ii 465.52
  iii 595.52
  iv 485.52

c $4.2^2 + 2.9^3$
  i 42.029
  ii 430.221 96
  iii 73.08
  iv 0.723

3 Alana saves £18.25 every week for a year.
Approximately how much does she save in a year?

4 Walt's mobile phone bill is £27.49 per month.
Approximately how much does he pay for his mobile phone in a year?

5 A journey of 104 miles, 528 yards took 2 hours and 3 minutes.
Estimate the average speed in mph.

6 Amir's weekly wage is usually between £350 and £400.
4.8% of his wage is deducted for his pension.
Estimate how much is deducted over 2 years.

7 A typical adult sleeps about $7\tfrac{1}{2}$ hours every night.
Estimate how many months an adult sleeps in a year.

Number Strand 3 Accuracy

8. Here are some calculations.
   Estimate the answers.
   Then decide if the answer given is definitely wrong.

   a $\dfrac{6149 \div 28}{3.8 \times 4.7}$ Answer 22.26

   b $\dfrac{8.4^2 \times 9.75}{0.68 - 0.4}$ Answer 2457

   c $\dfrac{5.4^2 - 5.8^2}{61.5 \div 2.2}$ Answer 14.4

9. The diameter of the Sun is about 1 392 000 km.
   The diameter of the Earth is about 12 700 km and the diameter of the Moon is about 3500 km.

   a Estimate roughly how many times bigger the diameter of the Sun is than the diameter of the Earth.

   b Estimate how many times bigger the diameter of the Earth is than the diameter of the Moon.

   c Now estimate how many times bigger the diameter of the Sun is than the diameter of the Moon.

Problem solving

1. The table shows how long Aimee worked at different rates of pay last week.

	Hours worked	Rate of pay
Normal pay	25 hours 45 mins	£7.90 per hour
Overtime	5 hours 20 mins	£9.95 per hour
Sunday	2 hours 40 mins	£12.75 per hour

   Aimee

   This week, Aimee earned £305.

   a Using approximations, show whether Aimee earned more or less last week than she earned this week.

   Aimee is hoping to get a mortgage to buy a house.
   She needs to earn more than £13 000 a year to get a mortgage for the house she wants.
   In a year, Aimee works for 41 weeks and she earns a similar amount each week.
   In the remaining weeks of the year, she is paid holiday pay at a rate of £152 per week.

   b Estimate whether Aimee earns enough each year to be able to get a mortgage.

2. Country Farm yogurt is sold in pots.
   A machine fills the pots in batches of ten at the same time.
   The machine can fill 9040 pots in one hour.

   a Estimate the number of seconds it takes the machine to fill a batch of pots.

   In one week, the machine fills pots for a total of 31 hours.
   The pots of yogurt are then packed in cartons, each holding 96 pots.

   b Estimate how many cartons are filled that week.

3 Andy is treating himself and five friends to a chip shop supper.
Andy orders the food that everyone wants.

Fryin - 2 - Nite

Chips .... 89p per portion
Peas .... 25p per tub
Fish .... £1.95 each
Pies .... £1.49 each
Sausages .... £1.10 per portion
Drinks .... 90p per can

Three portions of fish and chips, two pie and chips and a sausage and chips please.

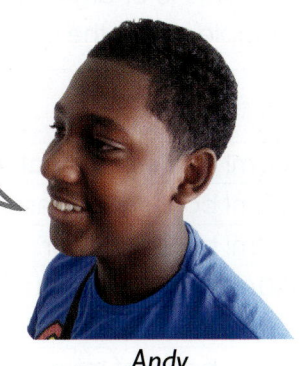

Andy

He then realises that he only has a £20 note.
Andy quickly estimates if he will have enough money.

a Does Andy have enough money?

His friends say that they each would like a drink. Andy does not want one himself.

b Will Andy have to borrow any money from his friends?

4 This is part of a timetable for trains from London to Stoke-on-Trent.

London Euston	07:20	08:00	08:20	09:00	09:20	10:00
Milton Keynes Central	07:50		08:50		09:50	
Stoke-on-Trent	08:48	09:25	09:48	10:25	10:48	11:15

This is part of a timetable for trains from Stoke-on-Trent to London.

Stoke-on-Trent	16:50	17:12	17:50	18:12	18:50	19:12
Milton Keynes Central	17:46		18:46		19:46	
London Euston	18:24	18:43	19:24	19:43	20:24	20:42

Lucy lives in London.
She has a meeting in Stoke-on-Trent at 11 a.m.
It takes Lucy about 15 minutes to walk from her home to London Euston train station.
The journey from the train station in Stoke-on-Trent to her meeting takes about 35 minutes.
The meeting is due to finish at 5.15 p.m.
Show and explain why Lucy is likely to be away from home for about 12 hours.

Number Strand 3 Accuracy

5 Leah runs a beauty salon.
In order to attract new customers, Leah is offering a mini facial.
She wants to charge enough just to cover her costs.
The table shows the facial products that Leah will need.

Product	Amount needed for mini facial	Cost of product
500 ml bottle of exfoliator	50 ml	£27.99 per bottle
200 ml bottle of cleanser	20 ml	£11.99 per bottle
300 ml bottle of toner	15 ml	£29.99 per bottle
450 ml bottle of moisturiser	15 ml	£58.99 per bottle
150 ml jar of eye tonic	10 ml	£74.49 per jar
200 ml bottle of mixed oils	10 ml	£20.99 per bottle
1 face pack (inc. towels etc.)	1 pack	£1.99 per pack

Estimate what Leah should charge for this mini facial.

6 The diagram shows the lines on a netball court.

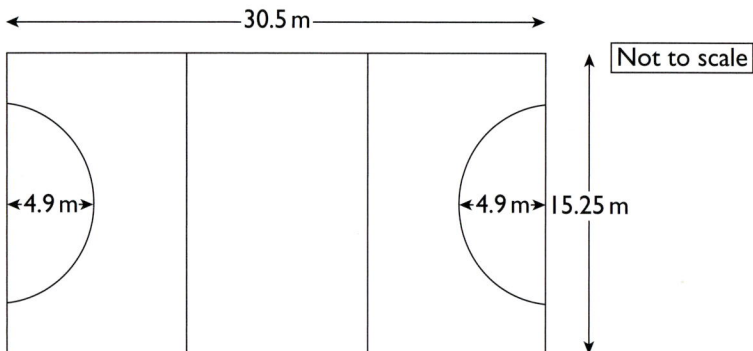

Stuart is painting the lines for 4 netball courts on the floor of a sports hall.
One tin of paint is enough to paint 110 metres of lines.
Estimate the number of tins of paint Stuart needs.

Reviewing skills

1 Estimate the answers to these calculations.
   a 9728 − 9061
   b 814 ÷ 36.9
   c 7.84 × 194.3

2 For each of these calculations, there is a choice of answers. Use approximation to help you select the correct answer.
   a $\dfrac{126 \times 68}{48}$
      i 178.5   **ii** 17.85   **iii** 1785
   b 9398.4 ÷ 26.4
      i 0.002 809   **ii** 9372   **iii** 35.6   **iv** 356

3 Estimate the answers to these calculations.
   a $\dfrac{1684 - 324}{4.93}$
   b $\dfrac{6.93 \times 55.4}{0.132}$
   c $\dfrac{917 + 458}{0.41 - 0.23}$

4 Jake uses about 8.5 litres of petrol every day that he works.
Petrol costs 132.9 p per litre.
Approximately how much does Jake pay for petrol for a 4-day working week?

Unit 6 • Significance • Band g

Outside the Maths classroom

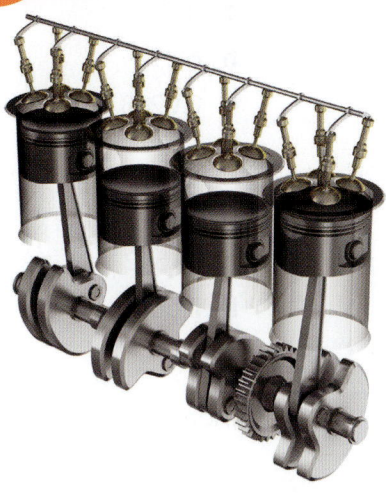

Precision engineering
How do engineers make sure all the pieces fit together?

Toolbox

The length of one year is 365.2422 days. This is 365 when rounded to the nearest whole number. This is the same as saying it has been rounded to 3 **significant figures** (s.f.).

365.2422 is also
400 to 1 significant figure
370 to 2 significant figures
365.2 to 4 significant figures
365.24 to 5 significant figures

The first non-zero digit is always the first significant figure.
After the first significant figure, all digits are significant.

Example – Rounding very small numbers

The answer 0.000 253 745 was given on a calculator. Write the number to 2 significant figures.

Solution

These 3 zeros are place holders.

0.000 253 745

2 is the first significant digit.

3 is smaller than 5 so the number rounds down.

The answer is 0.000 25 (to 2 significant figures).

Number Strand 3 Accuracy

Practising skills

1 Here are some measurements. How many significant figures are in each number?

a 36 cm   b 1297 km   c 0.9 kg   d 0.053 m
e 208 mm   f 0.0251 m   g 30.97 kg   h 700.49 m

2 Round these numbers to 1 significant figure.

a 29   b 45   c 361   d 852
e 7422   f 21 652   g 18.4   h 62.9
i 0.943   j 0.652   k 0.0194   l 0.0248

3 Round these numbers to 2 significant figures.

a 873   b 924   c 615   d 708
e 704   f 3261   g 5119   h 18 642
i 73 281   j 8042   k 0.635   l 0.6041

4 Write the number 384 027 correct to

a 1 significant figure   b 2 significant figures   c 3 significant figures
d 4 significant figures   e 5 significant figures.

5 Write the number 7.999 999 9 correct to

a 1 significant figure   b 2 significant figures   c 3 significant figures
d 4 significant figures   e 5 significant figures.

6 Write the number 0.008 106 049 9 correct to

a 1 significant figure   b 2 significant figures   c 3 significant figures
d 4 significant figures   e 5 significant figures.

7 Write these numbers correct to the number of significant figures (s.f.) shown in brackets.

a 17.65 (1 s.f.)   b 0.597 (2 s.f.)   c 71 046 (3 s.f.)
d 3.74 (1 s.f.)   e 6.5092 (3 s.f.)   f 26.9999 (4 s.f.)

Developing fluency

1) Copy and complete this table.

	Number	Round to 1 significant figure	Round to 2 significant figures
a	742		
b	628		
c	199		
d	4521		
e	3419		
f	8926		
g	8974		
h	36 294		
i	0.2583		
j	0.07961		
k	0.000 397 2		
l	0.001 023		

2) Use a calculator to work these out. Give each answer to the degree of accuracy shown in brackets.

a $861 \div 45$ (1 s.f.)
b 2.3^3 (1 s.f.)
c 7.89×6.45 (2 s.f.)
d $11.6 \div 240$ (2 s.f.)
e 64.8^4 (3 s.f.)
f 0.89×156.11 (1 s.f.)
g $\sqrt{89956}$ (2 s.f.)
h $\sqrt[3]{1.0256}$ (3 s.f.)
i $\dfrac{4.3^2 \times 72}{\sqrt{3.864}}$ (3 s.f.)

3) Calculate the difference between

a 63.8421 (to 2 s.f.) and 63.8421 (to 3 s.f.)
b 81.478 (to 2 s.f.) and 81.478 (to 2 d.p.)

4) Decide if each of these is true or false.

a 91.684 (to 2 s.f.) > 91.684 (to 1 s.f.)
b 0.3079 (to 3 s.f.) = 0.3079 (to 3 d.p.)
c 16.9949 (to 2 s.f.) = 16.9949 (to 2 d.p.)
d 0.002 713 (to 2 s.f.) > 0.002 713 (to 1 s.f.)

5) Five friends round numbers in this way.
Ada rounds to 1 significant figure.
Ben rounds to 2 significant figures.
Cain rounds to the nearest integer.
Dewi rounds to 1 decimal place.
Ella rounds to 2 decimal places.

a They each round the number 9.463. Whose answers are the same?
b They each round the number 59.698. Whose answers are the same?
c They each round the number 109.655. Whose answers are the same?

Number Strand 3 Accuracy

Problem solving

1. At an international football match at Wembley, the attendance was announced to be 80 641.

   Four people who were at the match were asked to round this figure to 2 significant figures.

   Ifor said 80 000.

   Milly said 80 600.

   Ami said 81 000.

   Iwan said, 'You are all wrong, 80 641 correct to 2 significant figures is 81.'

   Who is right?

   Explain your answer, indicating the mistakes that some of the people made.

2. The formula to find the circumference C, of a circle of diameter d, is $C = \pi d$.

   The value of π is 3.141592654... .

   Keith wants to compare the circumference of a circle, diameter 8 cm for different values of π.

   He works out C using π correct to

   a 1 significant figure

   b 2 significant figures

   c 3 significant figures

   d 4 significant figures.

   Work out Keith's results.

3. Hâf has shares in two companies.

   She has 250 shares in company A and 1800 shares in company B.

   Each share in company A is valued at 198.45 pence.

   Each share in company B is valued at 5.075 pence.

   Hâf needs to do a quick estimate of the total value of all of her shares.

   a She rounds the value of each share of each company to 1 significant figure.
      Calculate Hâf's estimate.

   b Work out another estimate. This time round the value of each share to 2 significant figures.

   c Which estimate, **a** or **b**, is the more accurate? Which is the easier to work out?

4. Alwyn wants to find out the thickness of each page in his Maths text book.

   He uses a ruler to measure its thickness. It is between 1.2 and 1.3 cm, not including the cover.

   The pages in the book are numbered i to viii and then 1 to 297.

   At the end there are 7 blank sides.

   a Work out the thickness of each page.
      Give your answer to a suitable number of significant figures.

   b Suggest how Alwyn can get a more accurate answer.

Reviewing skills

1 Round these numbers to 1 significant figure.
  a 0.994
  b 0.00974
  c 993
  d 999 943

2 Round these numbers to 2 significant figures.
  a 6.382
  b 19.84
  c 0.00519
  d 0.00997

3 Use a calculator to work these out. Give each answer to the degree of accuracy shown in brackets.
  a $\dfrac{2.35}{7.66}$ (4 s.f.)
  b $452 \times 60 \times 19$ (4 s.f.)
  c $\dfrac{2.3 \times 4.7}{9.22 - 3.7}$ (2 s.f.)

4 Indicate the correct answer **a**, **b**, **c** or **d**.
34 990 correct to 1 significant figure.
  a 30 000
  b 34 000
  c 34 900
  d 35 000

Unit 7 • Limits of accuracy • Band g

Outside the Maths classroom

Buying in bulk
Each of these bags should contain 25 kg of coffee. What is the minimum mass you would expect a bag to have?

Toolbox

To say how accurate a measurement is, give its lower and upper bounds.
The length of a line is l, recorded as 36 cm to the nearest centimetre.

All lines between 35.5 cm and 36.499 999... cm are rounded to 36 cm.
35.5 cm is called the **lower bound**.
36.499 999 is effectively 36.5 cm so 36.5 cm is called the **upper bound**.
This is written as
$$35.5 \leq l < 36.5$$
Another way of writing it is
$$l = 35 \pm 0.5 \text{ cm}$$

Example – Recognising the effect of bounds on a result

Stella draws a square with a side length of 21 cm to the nearest centimetre.
a What are the upper and lower bounds of the side length of the square?
b What are the upper and lower bounds of the perimeter of the square she has drawn?

Solution
a Upper bound is 21.5 cm
   Lower bound is 20.5 cm
b Upper bound of perimeter = 4 × 21.5 = 86 cm
   Lower bound of perimeter = 4 × 20.5 = 82 cm

Unit 7 Limits of accuracy Band g

Practising skills

1) Write down the lower and upper bounds for each of these measurements.
   a 80 cm (to the nearest cm)
   b 80 cm (to the nearest 10 cm)
   c 300 g (to the nearest g)
   d 300 g (to the nearest 100 g)

2) Write down the lower and upper bounds for each of these measurements.
   a 5000 m (to the nearest m)
   b 5000 m (to the nearest 10 m)
   c 5000 m (to the nearest 100 m)
   d 5000 m (to the nearest 1000 m)

3) Write down the lower and upper bounds for each of these measurements.
   a 600 m (to the nearest 10 m)
   b 600 m (to the nearest 5 m)
   c 600 m (to the nearest 100 m)
   d 600 m (to the nearest 50 m)

4) The mass of a bag of potatoes is m kg. To the nearest kg the mass is 6 kg.
   Copy and complete this statement.
   $\square \leq m < \square$

5) The length of a pencil is l cm. To the nearest cm the length is 9 cm.
   Copy and complete this statement.
   $\square \leq l < \square$

6) Each of these measurements is rounded to 1 significant figure. Write down the lower and upper bound for each measurement.
   a 3 m   b 60 m   c 0.4 mg   d 0.07 km

7) Each of these measurements is rounded to 2 significant figures. Write down the lower and upper bound for each measurement.
   a 24 ml   b 360 g   c 0.83 kg   d 0.019 m

8) Copy and complete this table.

	Number	Lower bound	Upper bound
a	4 (to nearest whole number)		
b	70 (to nearest 10)		
c	600 (to nearest 10)		
d	0.3 (to 1 decimal place)		
e	0.06 (to 2 decimal places)		
f	80 km (to 1 significant figure)		
g	68 mg (to 2 significant figures)		
h	0.032 (to 2 significant figures)		

Number Strand 3 Accuracy

Developing fluency

1) The capacity of a pot of paint is 300 ml, to the nearest 10 ml.
Thabo buys 5 pots. The total volume of paint is V ml.
Copy and complete this statement.

$\square \leqslant V < \square$

2) Mel runs 8 km, to the nearest km, every day.
What is the least possible distance she runs in a week?

3) Ann draws a square with a side length of 14 cm, to the nearest cm.
The area of the square is A cm².
Copy and complete this statement.

$\square \leqslant A < \square$

4) A bag of flour weighs 250 g, to the nearest 10 g. Val needs 740 g of flour for a recipe.
Will three bags of flour definitely be enough?
Explain your answer.

5) A rectangle has length 80 m, to the nearest 10 m, and width 40 m, to the nearest 5 m.
Its perimeter is p m and its area is A m².
Copy and complete these statements.

a $\square \leqslant p < \square$

b $\square \leqslant A < \square$

6) Which is the odd one out among these statements about a length l m?

i $l = 50$ to the nearest 5.

ii $47.5 \leqslant l < 52.5$

iii $l = 50 \pm 5$

iv The upper and lower bounds of l are 52.5 and 47.5.

7) The number n is 680, correct to 2 significant figures.
Copy and complete these statements about n.

a $n = 680 \pm \square$

b $\square \leqslant n < \square$

c The upper and lower bounds of n are $\square$ and $\square$ respectively.

d n is 680 to the nearest $\square$

Problem solving

1. The directors of a golf club issue the following statement about membership.
   'The membership of the club to the nearest 5 members will be 650.'
   At present there are 648 members of the golf club.
   10 people have applied to become members of the golf club.
   How many of these 10 people will definitely not be successful?

2. The measurements of this photograph are accurate to the nearest centimetre.
   Jo has 100 photographs of this size to stick in her photograph album. The measurements of each page of the album are exactly 38 cm by 18.5 cm. There are 9 empty pages in Jo's album.
   Is there definitely enough space in Jo's photograph album for these 100 photographs without overlapping?

3. The following people want to travel in a lift.

   Dafydd 65 kg   Brian 92 kg
   Bronwen 74 kg   Pat 54 kg
   Peter 86 kg   Bruce 95 kg
   Ahmed 89 kg   Marc 93 kg

   **Lift
   Maximum safe load
   8 persons or
   650 kg**

   a Explain why it might not be safe for these people to travel together in the lift.

   b Eight different people get in the lift. They all have the same mass to the nearest kilogram. What is the largest that their mass can safely be?

4. A particular paperback book is 2.6 cm thick, measured to the nearest tenth of a centimetre. Tomos has 50 of these paperback books. His bookshelf is 1.30 m in length to the nearest centimetre.
   What is the greatest possible number of these books Tomos can definitely put on his bookshelf?

Number Strand 3 Accuracy

Reviewing skills

1) Write down the lower and upper bounds for each of these measurements.
   a 40 ml (to the nearest ml)
   b 40 ml (to the nearest 10 ml)
   c 700 kg (to the nearest 100 kg)
   d 700 kg (to the nearest 10 kg)

2) Indicate the correct answer **a, b, c** or **d**.
   The lower and upper bounds when a measurement of 650 m has been given to the nearest 50 m.
   a 625 m and 674.9 m
   b 624.9 m and 674.9 m
   c 625 m and 675 m
   d 625 m and 674.49 m

3) The mass of a fish is m g. To the nearest 10 g, the mass is 320 g.
   Copy and complete this statement.
   $\Box \leq m < \Box$

4) Each of these measurements is rounded to 1 significant figure. Write down the lower and upper bounds for each measurement.
   a 900 cm   b 2000 km   c 0.2 g   d 0.005 m

5) Each of these measurements is rounded to 2 significant figures. Write down the lower and upper bounds for each measurement.
   a 7100 m   b 49 cm   c 520 mm   d 0.0028 km

6) Eve has made a square cake with sides of length 20 cm, to the nearest cm. She wants to put a ribbon round the sides. Her piece of ribbon is 80 cm to the nearest cm. Does she definitely have enough ribbon for the cake? Explain your answer.

Unit 8 • Upper and lower bounds • Band i

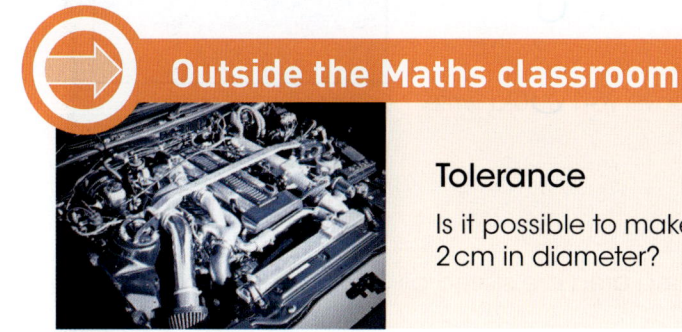

Outside the Maths classroom

Tolerance

Is it possible to make a piston that is exactly 2 cm in diameter?

Toolbox

Any measurement is only as accurate as the instrument used to measure.

If a ruler is marked in centimetres only then a length can be measured to the nearest centimetre, as on Ruler A.

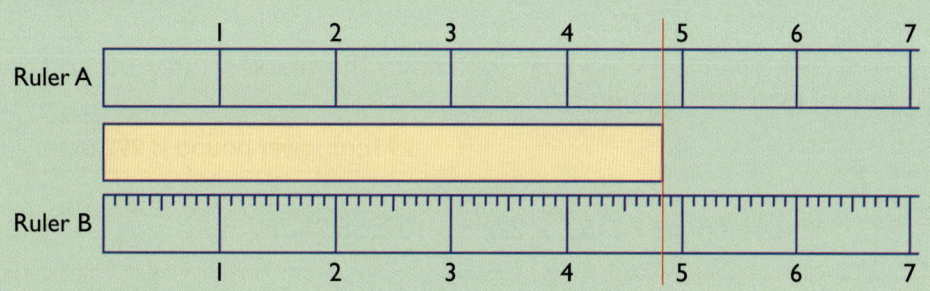

But using Ruler B the same line can be measured to the nearest millimetre.

Ruler B is more accurate but it is still not absolutely precise.

The limits of the accuracy of a measurement, an estimate or a calculation, are called **the upper and lower bounds**.

The bar above is measured as 5 cm to the nearest cm. This means that it must be between 4.5 cm and 5.5 cm.

> The lower bound is 4.5 cm and the upper bound is 5.5 cm.

The same bar is 48 mm to the nearest mm. This means it must be between 47.5 mm and 48.5 mm.

> In this case the lower bound is 47.5 mm and the upper bound is 48.5 mm.

To find the bounds of a calculation you must use the bound values of all the measurements, to give the worst-case scenario.

Number Strand 3 Accuracy

This rectangle has been measured at 3 cm by 4 cm to the nearest cm.
Using the smallest possible lengths
 perimeter = 2.5 + 2.5 + 3.5 + 3.5 = 12 cm
Using the largest possible lengths
 perimeter = 3.5 + 3.5 + 4.5 + 4.5 = 16 cm

Rounding up and down
By convention 5 rounds up, so in the rectangle above you would write
 $2.5\,\text{cm} \leqslant \text{width} < 3.5\,\text{cm}$
 $3.5\,\text{cm} \leqslant \text{length} < 4.5\,\text{cm}$
 $12\,\text{cm} \leqslant \text{perimeter} \leqslant 16\,\text{cm}$
However the upper bounds for the length, width and area are stated as 3.5, 4.5 and 16 cm.

Example – Measures of area and volume

The dimensions of a rectangular room are measured as 346 cm by 293 cm to the nearest cm.
a What is the smallest area that the room could have?
b What is the largest area that the room could have?

Solution

a Measurements are given to the nearest centimetre. The smallest area is found using the lower bounds of the measurements.

293 cm: lower bound is 292.5 cm.

Smallest area = 345.5 × 292.5 = 101 058.75 cm²

346 cm: lower bound is 345.5 cm.

This is the lower bound.

The smallest area that the room could have is 101 058.75 cm².

b The largest area is found using the upper bounds of the measures.

293 cm: upper bound is 293.5 cm.

Largest area = 346.5 × 293.5 = 101 697.75 cm²

346 cm: upper bound is 346.5 cm.

This is the upper bound.

The largest area that the room could have is 101 697.75 cm².

Unit 8 Upper and lower bounds Band i

Example – Density

A cube has length of side of 25 cm, measured to the nearest cm, and weighs 50 grams, measured to the nearest gram.

a Calculate the greatest density that the cube could have.
b Calculate the least density that the cube could have.

Solution

The density of an object is given by $\frac{\text{mass}}{\text{volume}}$.

a The greatest density is found using the greatest mass and dividing it by the smallest volume

$\frac{50.5}{24.5^3} = 0.00343$ grams per cm³ (3 s.f.) ← *The greatest possible mass is 50.5 g. The least possible side length is 24.5 cm.*

The greatest density that the cube could have is 0.00343 grams per cm³.

b The least density is found using the lowest mass and dividing it by the greatest volume

$\frac{49.5}{25.5^3} = 0.00299$ grams per cm³ (3 s.f.) ← *The least possible mass is 49.5 g. The greatest possible side length is 25.5 cm.*

The least density that the cube could have is 0.00299 grams per cm³.

Practising skills

1 Write down the number that is exactly half way between

  a 3 and 4   *3.5*
  b 3.5 and 3.6   *3.55*
  c 3.55 and 3.56   *3.5585*
  d 7.541 and 7.542   *7.5411*
  e 12 and 12.0001.

2 State the upper and lower bounds of each of these measurements.

  a A weight recorded at 7 kg, to the nearest kg.
  b A length recorded as 7 m, to the nearest metre.
  c A volume recorded as 7 litres, to the nearest litre.

3 State the upper and lower bounds for each of these measurements.

  a A piece of wood measured at 53 cm, to the nearest cm.
  b A piece of wood measured at 53 cm, to the nearest mm.
  c A piece of wood measured at 5.3 cm, to the nearest mm.

4 State the upper and lower bounds of each of these measurements.

  a A weight recorded at 15 kg, to the nearest kg.
  b A weight recorded at 15.7 kg, to the nearest 100 grams.
  c A weight recorded at 15.36 kg, to the nearest 10 grams.

5 The weight of a metal block is measured as 6 kg, correct to the nearest gram. A machine includes 25 of these metal blocks. They are all identical.

What are the upper and lower bounds of the total weight of the blocks?

Number Strand 3 Accuracy

Developing fluency

(1) Marc measures a piece of wood. He records his measurement to the nearest cm.
Hywel measures the same piece of wood. He records his measurement to the nearest mm.
What is the greatest difference that there can be between Marc's measurement and Hywel's measurement?

(2) A rectangular piece of paper is measured as being 24 cm by 56 cm, with each length being measured to the nearest cm.
What are the upper and lower bounds of the area of the piece of paper?

(3) A box is measured as being 4 cm by 7 cm by 9 cm. What are the upper and lower bounds of the volume of the box if the measurements are accurate

   a to the nearest cm

   b to the nearest mm?

(4) Elen measures the length of a sports pitch. She records her measurement as 98 metres to the nearest metre.
Marged measures the width of the pitch. She records her measurement as 51.2 metres to the nearest 0.1 metre.
They calculate the area of the pitch.

   a What are the largest and smallest areas that they will find?

   b They say 'This area is 5000 square metres.'
      To how many significant figures is that statement correct?

(5) Ginny measures the radius of a circle to be 30.9 cm.
She claims this is accurate to the nearest mm.
Find upper and lower bounds for the perimeter of the circle, based on Ginny's claim.

(6) The radius of the Earth at the equator is 6380 km correct to the nearest 10 km.

   a Find the upper and lower bounds of the radius of the Earth.

   b Find the greatest and least value for the circumference of the Earth at the equator.

(7) Gareth says 'it says here that, if a length is 6 cm to the nearest cm, the upper bound is 6.5 cm. But 6.5 cm will round to 7 cm! This is a printing error!'
Explain why Gareth is wrong.

Problem solving

1. Gareth wants to stack 4 boxes, each of height 25 cm, correct to the nearest centimetre. The height available is 1 metre.
   Explain why the boxes may not fit in the space available. You must show all your working.

2. Ewan uses a piece of wood 0.8 m long, correct to the nearest 0.02 m, to make a shelf. He then marks out the shelf every 10 cm. He finds he has a space left at the end.
   What is the maximum length this space could be?

3. Apple juice is sold in cuboid cartons. (The measurements shown are correct to the nearest centimetre.)
   a Thelma wants to fill eight of these boxes with Pure Apple Juice. What are the upper and lower bounds of each measurement?
   b She has 7 litres of Pure Apple Juice in a tank. Decide whether she can
      i   definitely do this
      ii possibly do this
      iii definitely not do this.

4. Stella is designing a central heating flue duct to take waste fumes out through the wall. The hole for the duct has to be sealed.
   The diagram shows Stella's design.
   There is a 16.5 cm square plate with a 4.5 cm radius circle removed from it. The measurements are accurate to one decimal place.
   a Write an inequality to show the upper and lower bounds of the area, A cm^2, of the metal seal.

5. Two speed cameras are set up on a section of motorway 0.5 mile apart.
   The police use these cameras to enable them to work out the average speed of a vehicle over this distance.
   The cameras give the time taken to travel 0.5 mile.
   The time is measured correct to the nearest 0.5 of a second. The distance of 0.5 mile has been measured to the nearest hundredth of a mile.
   Viv is driving on this section of the motorway. The time she takes between the two cameras is timed at 25.5 seconds.
   The speed limit is 70 mph. The police caution Viv. They say she was travelling at 71 mph. Viv disagrees with this and says that she was driving under the speed limit.
   Show
   a how the police get their figure
   b how Viv could be right.

6. Irfan runs a 200-metre race in a local athletics event.
   His time for the race was given as 23.4 seconds.
   Irfan realises that these measurements were not accurate. The 200 metres was measured to the nearest metre. His time was measured to the nearest tenth of a second.
   Irfan is interested to know his average speed. Write an inequality to show the upper and lower bounds of Irfan's average speed.

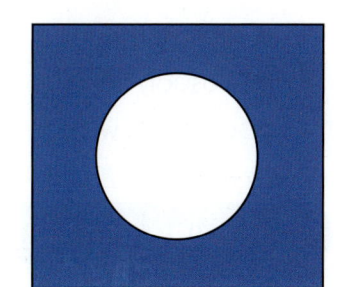

Number Strand 3 Accuracy

7 Hywel wants to find the height of this telegraph pole.

He measures the horizontal distance from the foot of the pole to be 70 m, to the nearest metre.
He measures the angle of elevation of the top of the pole to be 36°, to the nearest 2 degrees.

a Find upper and lower bounds for the height of the pole.

b State the height of the pole to an appropriate degree of accuracy.

8 The diagram shows a can of Fiz Pop in the shape of a cylinder.
Malcolm measures the height and the diameter of the can. He says the height is 10 cm, to the nearest mm, and the diameter is 6.5 cm, also to the nearest mm.
Malcolm says 'The can is not big enough to hold 330 ml of Fiz Pop.'
Decide whether Malcolm is:

a definitely right

b possibly right, or

c definitely wrong.

Reviewing skills

1 The maximum safe load of a lift is 500 kg, to the nearest 50 kg.
6 people enter the lift. Their masses, to the nearest kg, are:

82 kg   64 kg   84 kg   59 kg   87 kg   73 kg

Can the lift safely carry all 6 people? Explain your answer.

2 A CD case has a thickness of 0.7 cm to the nearest mm.

What is the minimum number of CDs that can fit on a shelf of length 125 cm to the nearest cm?

3 A rectangle has a length of 26 cm and a width of 18 cm, both measurements are correct to the nearest cm.
Calculate the upper and lower bounds of the area of the rectangle.

Number Strand 4 Fractions

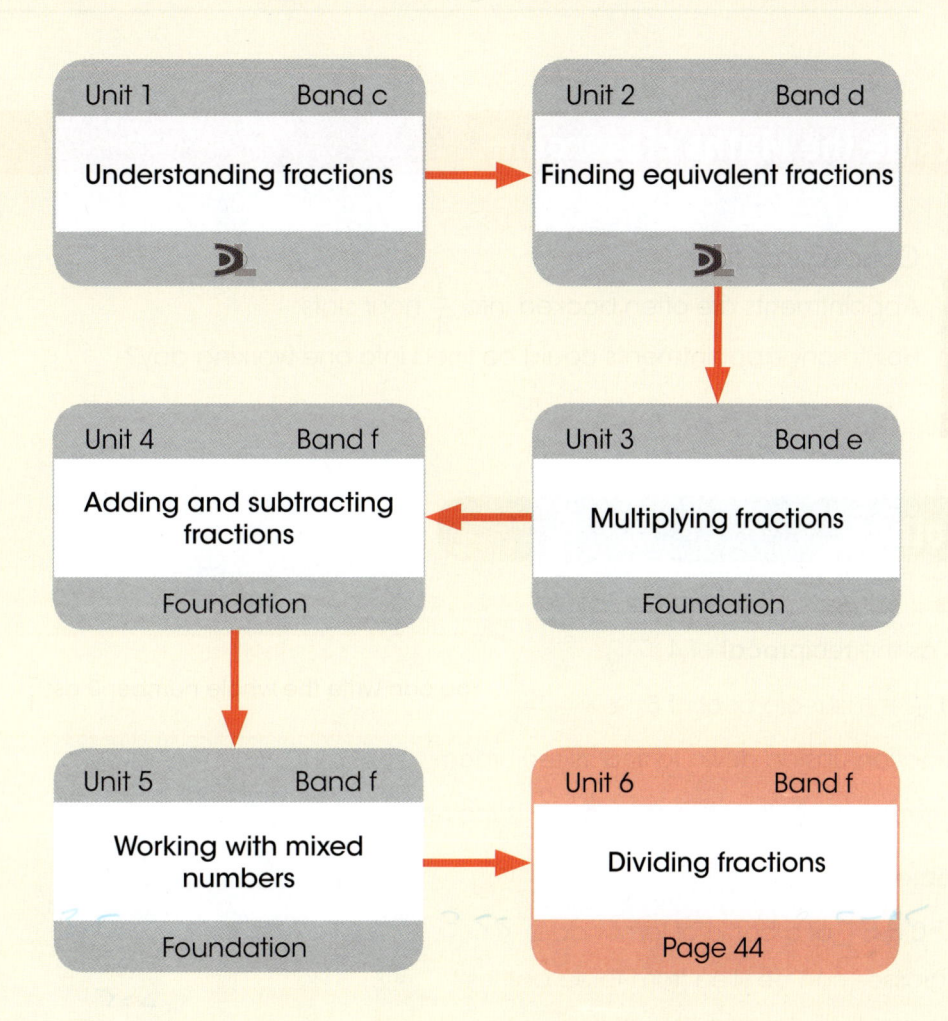

Unit 1	Band c
Understanding fractions	

→

Unit 2	Band d
Finding equivalent fractions	

↓

Unit 3	Band e
Multiplying fractions	
Foundation	

←

Unit 4	Band f
Adding and subtracting fractions	
Foundation	

↓

Unit 5	Band f
Working with mixed numbers	
Foundation	

→

Unit 6	Band f
Dividing fractions	
Page 44	

Units 1–5 are assumed knowledge for this book.
Knowledge and skills from these units are used throughout the book.

Unit 6 • Dividing fractions • Band f

Outside the Maths classroom

Organising time
Appointments are often booked into $\frac{1}{4}$ hour slots.
How many appointments could be fitted into one working day?

Toolbox

Reciprocals
$\frac{1}{4}$ is known as the **reciprocal** of 4.
The fraction $\frac{1}{3}$ is the reciprocal of 3.

You can write the whole number 3 as $\frac{3}{1}$.

You turn a fraction upside down to find its reciprocal.
$\frac{5}{2}$ is the reciprocal of $\frac{2}{5}$. In the same way $\frac{2}{5}$ is the reciprocal of $\frac{5}{2}$.

Division problems
Each glass holds $\frac{1}{4}$ of a bottle of lemonade.
How many glasses can be filled from three bottles?
The problem can be solved by finding how many quarters in 3.

$$3 \div \frac{1}{4} = 12$$

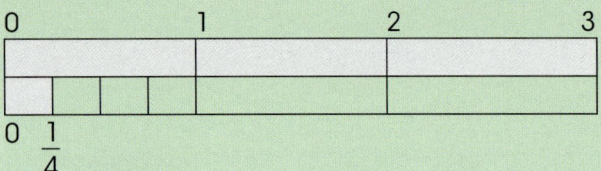

It can also be solved as a multiplication.

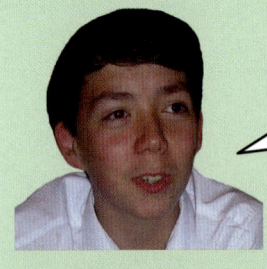

One bottle can fill 4 glasses. How many glasses can three bottles fill?

So dividing by a fraction is the same as multiplying by its reciprocal.
$3 \times 4 = 12$
You should change mixed numbers into improper fractions before dividing.

Unit 6 Dividing fractions Band f

Example – Dividing a fraction by a fraction

Work out $\frac{5}{4} \div \frac{2}{3}$.

Solution

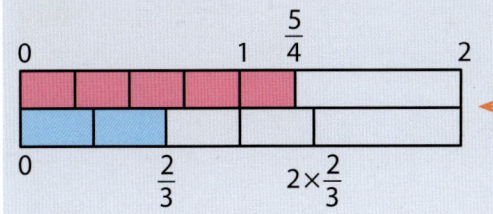

The bar diagram shows the answer will be just less than 2.

You find the answer by multiplying by the reciprocal.

The reciprocal of $\frac{2}{3}$ is $\frac{3}{2}$.

$$\frac{5}{4} \div \frac{2}{3} = \frac{5}{4} \times \frac{3}{2}$$
$$= \frac{15}{8}$$

The questions in this unit should be answered *without* the use of a calculator. (However, you may wish to use a calculator to check some of your answers.)

Practising skills

1 Write down the reciprocal of each of these.

a $\frac{1}{7}$ b $\frac{5}{7}$ c 20 d $1\frac{1}{2}$

e $2\frac{5}{8}$ f $4\frac{5}{6}$ g $3\frac{7}{8}$ h $6\frac{2}{9}$

2 Change each of these into a multiplication and then work out the answer.

a $\frac{1}{5} \div 2$ b $\frac{1}{3} \div 4$ c $\frac{3}{4} \div 5$ d $\frac{3}{5} \div 3$

e $\frac{7}{9} \div 6$ f $\frac{9}{10} \div 4$ g $\frac{1}{20} \div 2$ h $\frac{1}{20} \div 5$

3 Change each of these into a multiplication and then work out the answer.

a $3 \div \frac{1}{2}$ b $2 \div \frac{1}{4}$ c $3 \div \frac{1}{5}$ d $2 \div \frac{2}{3}$

e $5 \div \frac{3}{5}$ f $6 \div \frac{3}{4}$ g $6 \div \frac{1}{12}$ h $12 \div \frac{1}{6}$

4 Change each of these into a multiplication and then work out the answer.

a $\frac{1}{3} \div \frac{3}{4}$ b $\frac{1}{6} \div \frac{2}{5}$ c $\frac{2}{9} \div \frac{1}{2}$ d $\frac{2}{7} \div \frac{3}{4}$

e $\frac{3}{5} \div \frac{9}{10}$ f $\frac{5}{8} \div \frac{2}{3}$ g $\frac{1}{6} \div \frac{2}{3}$ h $\frac{2}{3} \div \frac{1}{6}$

5 Change each of these into a multiplication and then work out the answer.

a $1\frac{1}{4} \div 3$ b $2\frac{1}{3} \div \frac{1}{2}$ c $3 \div 2\frac{3}{4}$ d $2\frac{4}{5} \div 1\frac{1}{2}$

e $2\frac{2}{7} \div 3\frac{1}{5}$ f $3\frac{1}{8} \div 1\frac{5}{8}$ g $4\frac{1}{3} \div 1\frac{1}{8}$ h $1\frac{1}{8} \div 4\frac{1}{5}$

Number Strand 4 Fractions

6 Work out these.

a $\dfrac{1}{7} \div \dfrac{3}{5}$ b $\dfrac{1}{9} \div \dfrac{3}{4}$ c $\dfrac{7}{10} \div \dfrac{1}{3}$ d $\dfrac{3}{7} \div \dfrac{3}{5}$

e $\dfrac{5}{8} \div 6$ f $\dfrac{9}{10} \div 4$ g $5 \div \dfrac{2}{3}$ h $1\dfrac{1}{2} \div 7$

i $8 \div 3\dfrac{1}{2}$ j $1\dfrac{1}{3} \div 2\dfrac{3}{4}$ k $1\dfrac{7}{8} \div 5\dfrac{1}{4}$ l $3\dfrac{2}{5} \div 1\dfrac{3}{5}$

Developing fluency

1 $\dfrac{7}{8}$ of a litre of cola is shared between 3 friends.

What fraction of a litre of cola does each receive?

2 Daryl eats $\dfrac{2}{3}$ of a pizza.

The rest is divided between his two little sisters.
What fraction of the pizza does each sister eat?

3 Decide if these are true or false.

a $\dfrac{1}{3} \div 4 = 4 \div \dfrac{1}{3}$ b $6 \div \dfrac{1}{2} = 3 \div \dfrac{1}{4}$ c $\dfrac{2}{5} \div 3 = \dfrac{3}{5} \div 2$

4 Copy and complete this multiplication grid.

×		$\dfrac{2}{3}$
$\dfrac{1}{5}$	$\dfrac{1}{20}$	
		$\dfrac{5}{9}$

5 A room has area $30\,m^2$ and length $6\dfrac{1}{4}$ m.
Work out these:

a the width of the room

b the perimeter of the room

6 Work out these.

a $\dfrac{1}{2} \div \dfrac{5}{8} + \dfrac{1}{6}$ b $\dfrac{7}{8} - \dfrac{5}{8} \div \dfrac{5}{6}$ c $\dfrac{9}{10} + \dfrac{3}{5} \div \dfrac{2}{7}$ d $\dfrac{4}{5} \div \dfrac{3}{4} + \dfrac{1}{3}$

7 It takes Jenny $\dfrac{3}{4}$ of an hour to drive the $26\dfrac{1}{4}$ miles to her friend Glain's house.
What is her average speed? [Use the formula speed = distance ÷ time]

Unit 6 Dividing fractions Band f

Problem solving

1 This was part of an article in a local newspaper.

> **Local Millionaire Leaves Fortune**
>
> Martin Miller, local millionaire, left $\frac{1}{2}$ of his fortune of £$17\frac{1}{2}$ million to his wife of 32 years.
>
> His children are to share the rest of the money, each receiving £$1\frac{3}{4}$ million.

When Liz read this article, she asked 'How many children did Martin Miller have?'
Work out the answer to Liz's question.

2 Alwyn is an engineer.
He makes parts for car engines.
The diagram shows a part that Alwyn has to cut from a piece of metal of length 1 metre.

$\longleftarrow 3\frac{1}{8}$ cm $\longrightarrow$

Alwyn needs to make 100 of these parts.
He has three 1 metre lengths of metal.
Can Alwyn make these 100 parts from the metal he has available?

3 Mrs Coch is organising a birthday party for her daughter Jessica.
Including Jessica, there are 35 children at the party.

Mrs Coch has $5\frac{1}{2}$ litres of juice.

Each glass holds $\frac{1}{6}$ litre when full.

a Will there be enough juice for one glassful for each child at the party?

Mrs Coch has five $3\frac{1}{2}$ kg bars of chocolate.

She shares them equally between the 35 children at the party.

b What fraction of a bar of chocolate does she give each child?

At the end of the party, $\frac{4}{5}$ of the children are collected by their parents.

Jessica and her best friend Sophie stay at Jessica's house.
The rest of the children walk home.

c What fraction of the number of children at the party walk home?

Number Strand 4 Fractions

4 Carwyn provides the wood for workers to make toy cars.

All the toy cars are the same. It takes 5 hours and 45 minutes to make one toy car. Carwyn decides to pay each person the same amount. He thinks that a payment of £34.65 per toy car is fair.

Calculate the rate of pay per hour for the people making the toy cars, correct to the nearest penny.

Reviewing skills

1 Write down the reciprocal of each of these.
   a 8   **b** $\frac{3}{4}$ **c** $2\frac{1}{3}$ **d** $1\frac{4}{5}$

2 Change each of these into a multiplication and then work out the answer.
   a $\frac{7}{8} \div 2$ **b** $\frac{5}{6} \div 10$ **c** $4 \div \frac{1}{6}$ **d** $7 \div \frac{3}{8}$

3 Change each of these into a multiplication and then work out the answer.
   a $\frac{3}{10} \div \frac{1}{3}$ **b** $\frac{2}{9} \div \frac{5}{6}$ **c** $\frac{5}{9} \div 1\frac{2}{3}$ **d** $6\frac{1}{4} \div 2\frac{2}{3}$

4 Meena has a pendant.

She wants to know what it is made of and so she tries to measure its density.

She finds its weight is $34\frac{1}{5}$ grammes and its volume is $1\frac{4}{5}$ cubic centimetres.

Find the density of the pendant.
Use the formula density = $\frac{mass}{volume}$

5 Indicate the correct answer **a**, **b**, **c** or **d**.
The reciprocal of $8\frac{2}{5}$.
   a $\frac{5}{42}$ **b** $\frac{42}{5}$ **c** $10\frac{1}{2}$ **d** $2\frac{5}{8}$

Number Strand 5 Percentages

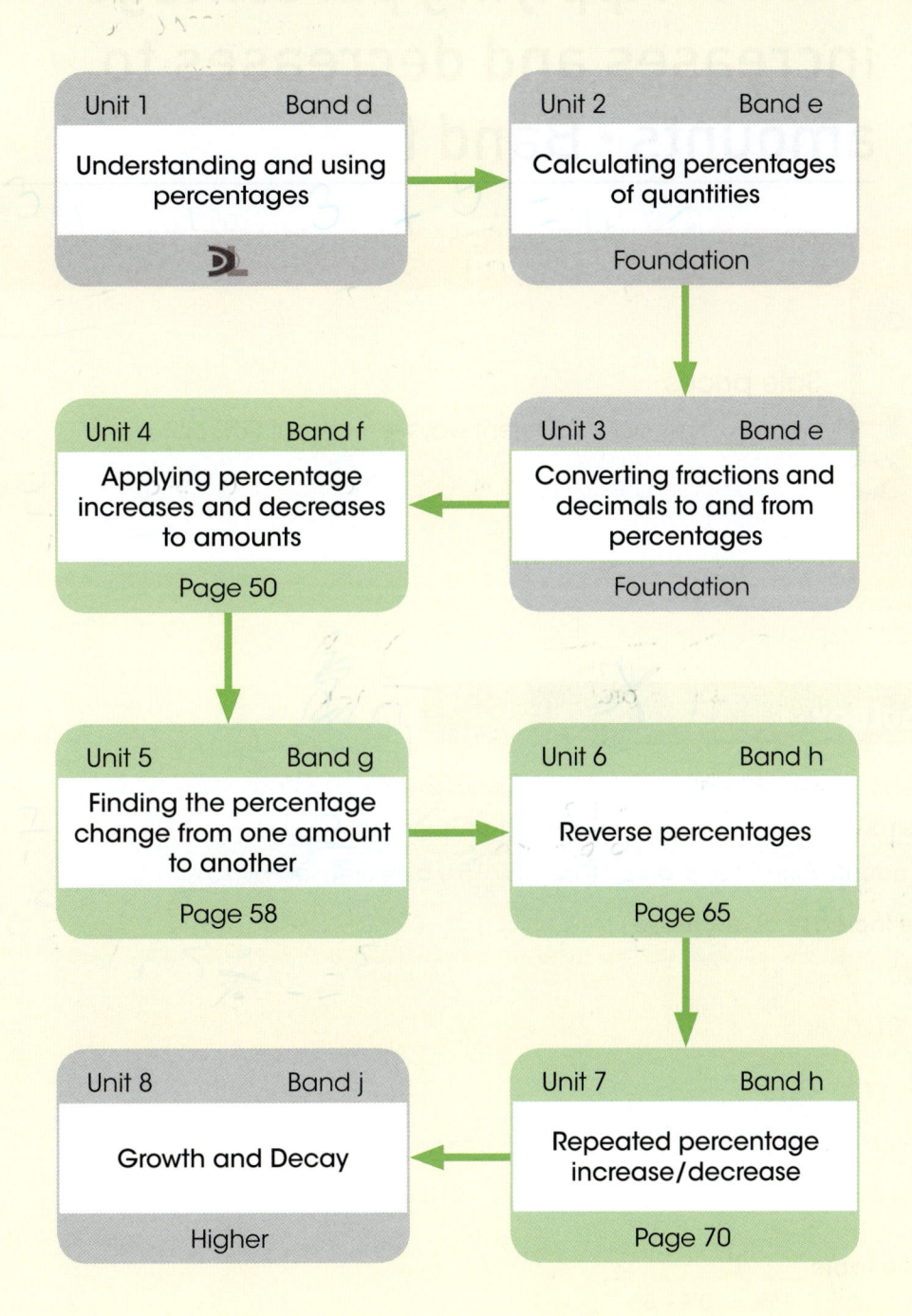

Unit 1 — Band d
Understanding and using percentages

Unit 2 — Band e
Calculating percentages of quantities
Foundation

Unit 3 — Band e
Converting fractions and decimals to and from percentages
Foundation

Unit 4 — Band f
Applying percentage increases and decreases to amounts
Page 50

Unit 5 — Band g
Finding the percentage change from one amount to another
Page 58

Unit 6 — Band h
Reverse percentages
Page 65

Unit 7 — Band h
Repeated percentage increase/decrease
Page 70

Unit 8 — Band j
Growth and Decay
Higher

Units 1–3 are assumed knowledge for this book.
Knowledge and skills from these units are used throughout the book.

5 Unit 4 • Applying percentage increases and decreases to amounts • Band f

Outside the Maths classroom

Sale prices

Can you think of two different ways to work out 20% off?

Toolbox

There are several ways to work out percentage increases and decreases.

These are shown here using, as an example, the question:

Find the amount when £120 is **a** increased by 15% **b** decreased by 15%

Finding the increase or decrease

100% is £120

1% is $\frac{1}{100} \times £120$

15% is $\frac{15}{100} \times £120 = £18$

a An increase of 15% gives

　　£120 + £18 = £138

b A decrease of 15% gives

　　£120 − £18 = £102

Using a ratio table

15% = 10% + 5%

%	100	10	5	15	115	85
Amount	120	12	6	18	138	102

£120 − £18 = £102

b A decrease of 15% gives £102

£120 + £18 = £138

a An increase of 15% gives £138

This is the amount of the increase or decrease. In this case it is £18

Unit 4 Applying percentage increases and decreases to amounts Band f

Using a percentage bar chart

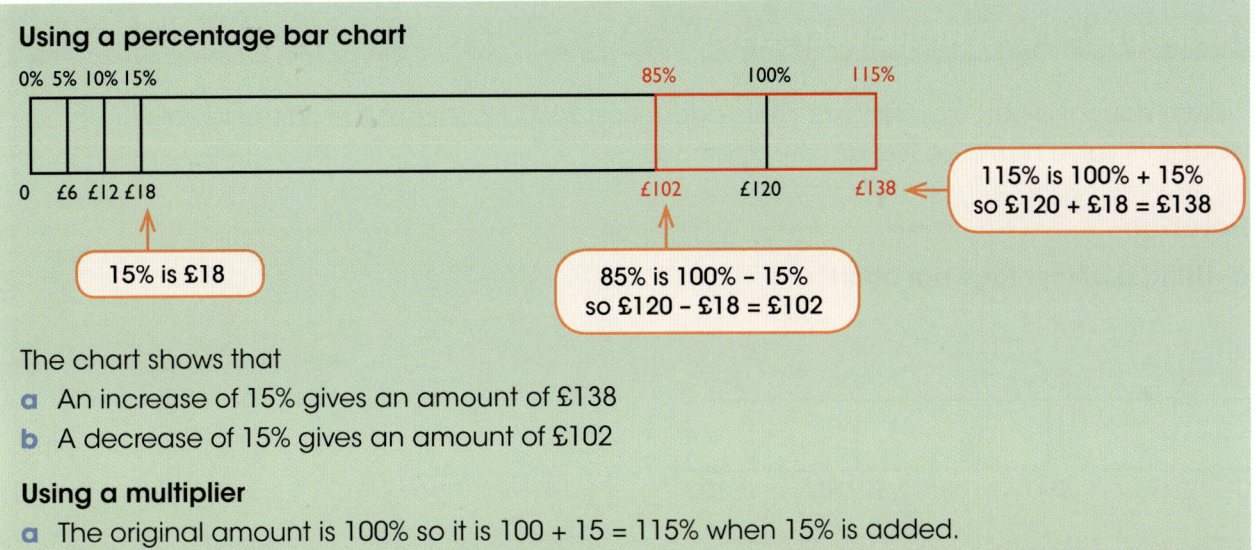

- 15% is £18
- 85% is 100% − 15% so £120 − £18 = £102
- 115% is 100% + 15% so £120 + £18 = £138

The chart shows that
a An increase of 15% gives an amount of £138
b A decrease of 15% gives an amount of £102

Using a multiplier

a The original amount is 100% so it is 100 + 15 = 115% when 15% is added.

So the new amount is 115% of £120 = $\frac{115}{100} \times £120$
= £138

You can also write this as 1.15 × £120

b In the same way, the amount is 100 − 15 = 85% when 15% is subtracted.

$\frac{85}{100} \times £120 = 0.85 \times £120$
= £102

Example – Percentage increase

Anneka earns £21 000 per year. She is given a 3% increase.
Calculate how much she now earns in a year. Use two different methods.

Solution

Using a ratio table

100%	1%	3%	103%
£21 000	£210	£630	£21 630

103% of £21 000 = £21 630

Finding the increase or decrease

100% is £21 000

1% is $\frac{1}{100} \times £21\,000 = £210$

3% is $\frac{3}{100} \times £21\,000 = £630$

An increase of 3% gives
£21 000 + £630 = £21 630

Number Strand 5 Percentages

Example – Percentage decrease

William bought a new bicycle three years ago. It cost £300. Now it has lost 30% of its value. What is its value now? Use two different methods.

Solution

a **Using a percentage bar chart**

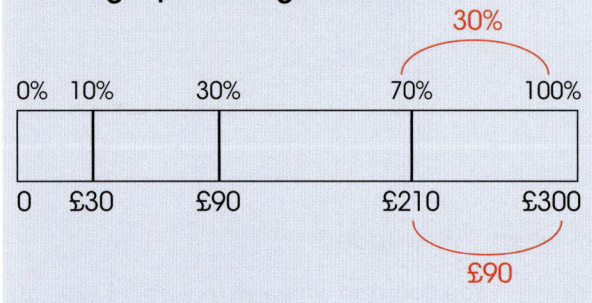

```
        30%
0%  10%   30%    70%   100%
|----|-----|------|-----|
0   £30   £90   £210   £300
                  £90
```

70% of £300 = £210

b **Using a multiplier**

The new amount is 100% − 30% = 70%

This is $\frac{70}{100} \times £300 = 0.7 \times £300 = £210$

Example – Percentage increase using a multiplier

Increase £78 by 24%.

Solution

As £78 represents 100% of the amount and we need to add on 24%, what we really need is 124% of £78.

$\frac{124}{100} \times 78$ ← This can more easily be thought of by converting the fraction $\frac{124}{100}$ to a decimal.

= 1.24 × 78 ← 1.24 is known as **the multiplier**.
= 96.72

So, £78 increased by 24% is £96.72.

Unit 4 Applying percentage increases and decreases to amounts Band f

Example – Percentage decrease using a multiplier

Decrease 460 metres by 16%.

Solution

100% − 16% = 84%   ← 460 metres represents 100% and we wish to subtract 16%.

$84\% = \frac{84}{100} = 0.84$ ← 0.84 is known as **the multiplier**

So, 84% of 460 metres = 0.84 × 460
= 386.4 metres

Practising skills

1. Work out these.
   a. 10% of £70 *7*
   b. Increase £70 by 10% *77*
   c. Decrease £70 by 10% *63*

2. Work out these.
   a. 50% of 18 kg *9 kg*
   b. Increase 18 kg by 50% *27 kg*
   c. Decrease 18 kg by 50% *9 kg*

3. In a sale there is 10% off.
   Find the sale price of each item.
   a. jeans £20 *18 pound*
   b. shirt £18 *£16.20*
   c. tie £6.50 *5.85p*

4. The price of each of these items goes up by 30%.
   What are the new prices?
   a. coat £40 *52*
   b. jumper £32 *41.60*
   c. socks £9.20 *£12.50*

5. In a sale there is a reduction of 25%.
   For each item find the reduction in price and the new price.
   a. chair £68 *13 oth £52*
   b. table £244 *183*
   c. lamp £19 *14.25*

6. Work out these.
   a. Increase 30 by 10% *33*
   b. Decrease 35 by 20% *28*
   c. Decrease 32 by 25% *24*
   d. Increase 80 by 50% *120*
   e. Decrease 60 by 30% *42*
   f. Decrease 170 by 40% *102*
   g. Increase 15 by 100% *30*
   h. Increase 10 by 200% *30*
   i. Increase 200 by 10% *220*

Number Strand 5 Percentages

Answer questions 1 to 7 without using your calculator.

Developing fluency

1. Match each card to its pair with the same answer.

   | A: 124 raised by 25% | B: 220 decreased by 30% | C: 750 reduced by 80% | D: 110 increased by 40% |

   | E: 130 increased by 20% | F: 620 decreased by 75% | G: 390 reduced by 60% | H: 75 increased by 100% |

2. In a sale all prices are reduced by 30%.
   Glenys buys shoes priced at £28, a coat priced at £43 and a shirt priced at £17.50.
   What is her total bill when she buys them during the sale?

3. Boxes of confectionary are labelled '25% extra free'.
   Work out the new number of contents when the original amount was

   a 48 bars

   b 60 lollipops

   c 160 chews

4. Steffan buys a car for £7200.
   He sells it and makes 15% profit.
   What price does he sell the car for?

5. Sid buys a house at £185 000.
   After one year its value has risen by 3%.
   What is the value of the house after one year?

6. Mair earns £9.50 per hour.
   She gets a pay rise of 6% starting in June.
   She works 32 hours in the first week of June.
   What is her pay for that week?

7. A carton of cream normally contains 230 ml.
   The label says 20% extra free.
   Ffion buys five cartons.
   How many litres of cream does she buy?

8. Put these amounts in order of size, starting with the smallest.

   150 g reduced by 4%   140 g increased by 6%   115 g increased by 26%,
   245 g reduced by 41%   141 g increased by 2.5%   224 g reduced by 35.5%

9 Osian is at a DIY store.

He buys a drill, a wheelbarrow and a hammer.

£38.00 plus VAT   £40.00 plus VAT   £18.00 plus VAT

What is Osian's final bill when the VAT is included? (VAT is 20%.)

10 Top Rates Bank offers simple interest at a rate of 1.6% per annum.
Work out the total value when each amount is invested for these times.

  a £700 for 2 years   **b** £1340 for 3 years   **c** £190 for 6 months   **d** £825 for 9 months

11 Elen invests £410 for 3 years at 2.1% per annum simple interest.

Emyr invests £520 for $2\frac{1}{2}$ years at 1.9% per annum simple interest.

Who gains more interest and by how much?

Problem solving

Reasoning

1 Natasha joins a small company. Her starting salary is £16 000 a year.

  a In her first year the company does very well. Everyone is given a 25% pay rise for the next year.
  What is Natasha's new salary?

  b The next year the company does not do at all well. Everyone's salary is reduced by 25% for the following year.
  What is Natasha's salary now?

  c Natasha says, 'That's not fair! + 25 − 25 should be zero'.
  Comment on this statement.

Reasoning

2 Marcus owns a house and an apartment.
He bought his house for £160 000.
He bought his apartment for £90 000.
Marcus decides to sell both properties.
He makes a 20% loss in selling the house and a 40% profit in selling the apartment.
Show that overall Marcus makes a profit.
Is his profit greater than 2%?

Number Strand 5 Percentages

3 Ali bought his car for £20 000.
The car depreciated by 20% in the first year.
During the second year, the car depreciated by 10% of its value at the start of the year.
During the third year, the value of Ali's car depreciated by 25%.
What was the value of the car after the three years?

4 Cars depreciate in value as they get older.
Mansoor is buying a car.
He finds three cars that he likes. He wants to buy a car that has depreciated by the least amount of money after one year.

	Original cost	Rate of depreciation after one year
Car A	£17 500	9%
Car B	£23 000	7%
Car C	£15 650	10%

a Which car should Mansoor buy?

b What is the value of this car after one year?

5 Heddwen wants to go on holiday.
She is going to take out a loan of £1500 to help pay for the holiday.
Heddwen will have to pay back the £1500 plus 20% interest over 12 months.
She will pay back the same amount of money each month.
How much money will she need to pay back each month?

6 In a European country the tax rules are as follows:
Earn 3000€ per annum tax free.
Pay 15% tax on the next 10 000€ of annual income.
Pay 50% tax on all additional income.

a How much, per annum, is it possible to earn before having to pay 50% tax?

b Liam earns 12 500€ per annum. How much will he pay in tax?

c Idris earns 45 850€ per annum. How much will he pay in tax?

7 Dimitri bought a car in Moscow for 250 550 Russian Rubles. Each year, the value of Dimitri's car depreciates by 14% of its value at the start of the year.

a At the end of two years, by how much has the value of Dimitri's car depreciated?

Dimitri had agreed to pay for his car in instalments. After a 100 000 Ruble deposit, he agreed to make 23 payments of 7000 Rubles.

b Compared with the value of the car in 2 years' time, what is the loss for Dimitri?

8 Petrol in Austria costs the equivalent of 17% per litre less than it does at home in Wales. Carys usually pays 119p per litre for her petrol at home.
How much per litre will Carys pay for petrol in Austria, in Euros?

9 In 2012 the cost of heating Mr Evans' house was £792.49. At the start of 2013, Mr Evans spent £160 on improving the insulation of his house. He spent a further £155 on insulation at the start of 2014. Mr Evans found that his heating bill in 2013 was 20% less than in 2012, and that his heating bill for 2014 was 20% less than in 2013.

   a Find the cost of Mr Evans' heating bill for 2014.

   b Was it worth Mr Evans spending money on improving the insulation in his house? You must give a reason for your answer.

Reviewing skills

1 Work out these.

   a 20% of £80   **b** Increase £80 by 20%   **c** Decrease £80 by 20%

2 In a sale there is a reduction of 20%.
   For each item find the reduction in price and the new price.

   a shirt £30   **b** coat £99   **c** rugby shirt £55.50

3 Work out these.

   a Increase 120 by 5%   **b** Increase 160 by 35%   **c** Decrease 150 by 3%

4 Sonya's car cost £9600.
   After one year its value has depreciated by 12%.
   By how much has the value of her car fallen?

Unit 5 • Finding the percentage change from one amount to another • Band g

Outside the Maths classroom

Inflation rates

This basket of shopping costs more to buy this year than it did last year. Will the increase be the same as the inflation rate?

Toolbox

To calculate a percentage change, follow the method illustrated in this example.
The population of an island increases from 500 to 650 people. What is the percentage increase?
The increase is 650 − 500 = 150 people

As a fraction this is $\frac{150}{500}$ ← the increase / the original population

Either
Find the equivalent fraction with 100 on the bottom line

$$\frac{150}{500} = \frac{30}{100} = 30\%$$

Or
Write the fraction as a decimal
$$\frac{150}{500} = 0.3$$
Then multiply by $\frac{100}{100}$ to make it a percentage

$$0.3 \times \frac{100}{100} = \frac{30}{100} = 30\%$$

You may find it helpful to use a percentage bar or a ratio table to illustrate this.

Example – Percentage increase

Maya deals in musical instruments. She buys a guitar for £75 and restores it. She sells it for £120. Find her percentage profit.

Solution

Profit = £120 − £75   ← Profit = sale price − cost price
     = £45

As a fraction this is $\frac{45}{75}$ ← Remember to always put the original value on the bottom line.

$$\frac{45}{75} = \frac{90}{150} = \frac{30}{50} = \frac{60}{100}$$

So Maya's profit is 60%.

Unit 5 Finding the percentage change from one amount to another Band g

Example – Percentage decrease

Zorro was an overweight dog. He was 14.0 kg.
His owner put him on a programme of long daily walks. After six months his weight is 9.8 kg.
What percentage weight has Zorro lost?

Solution

Weight lost = 14.0 − 9.8 = 4.2 kg

As a fraction $\frac{4.2}{14.0}$

Percentage decrease = $\frac{4.2}{14.0} \times \frac{100}{100}$ ← Find an equivalent fraction with 100 on the bottom line.

$= \frac{420}{1400} = \frac{60}{200} = \frac{30}{100}$ ← This is the equivalent fraction.

The fraction lost is $\frac{30}{100}$

So Zorro has lost 30% of his weight.

Practising skills

1 Write these percentages.

a 3 as a percentage of 10
b 11 as a percentage of 20
c 6 as a percentage of 24
d 32 as a percentage of 80
e 64 as a percentage of 200
f 42 as a percentage of 150
g 80 as a percentage of 160
h 160 as a percentage of 180

2 Write the first quantity as a percentage of the second quantity.

a £7, £100
b €9, €10
c 5 cm, 25 cm
d 12 g, 300 g
e 30p, £2
f 14 cm, 1 m
g 90 cm, 3 m
h 85p, £5
i 800 m, 5 km

3 Work out the profit and percentage profit for each of these items in a DIY store.
The first one has been done for you.

	Item	Cost price	Selling price	Profit	Percentage profit
	Drill	£30	£33	£3	10%
a	Saw	£12	£21		
b	Hammer	£10	£17		
c	Plane	£20	£32		
d	Spanner set	£35	£56		

Number Strand 5 Percentages

4) Work out the loss and percentage loss for each of these items at a car boot sale.

	Item	Cost price	Selling price	Loss	Percentage loss
a	Book	£10	£2		
b	Saucepan	£25	£22		
c	Dinner set	£200	£184		
d	Armchair	£70	£63		
e	Bicycle	£120	£84		
f	Cushion	£2	96p		

5) A carton of juice used to contain 750 ml.
It now contains 810 ml.
   a What is the increase in ml?
   b What is the percentage increase?

6) A packet of biscuits used to contain 30 biscuits.
It now contains 24 biscuits.
   a What is the decrease in the number of biscuits?
   b What is the percentage decrease?

Developing fluency

1) Write £12 as a percentage of £60.

2) Write 60p as a percentage of £2.50.

3) A chair cost £60 and is sold for £75.
Work out the percentage profit.

4) A TV cost £250 and is sold for £240.
Work out the percentage loss.

5) Gareth's rent last year was £400 per month.
This year it is £460 per month.
Work out the percentage increase in his rent.

6) Ned's weight fell from 90 kg to 81 kg.
Work out the percentage decrease in his weight.

7) A tree grew in height from 75 cm to 1.2 m.
Work out the percentage increase in height.

Unit 5 Finding the percentage change from one amount to another Band g

8 Using a calculator find the percentage change from the first quantity to the second quantity.
Give your answers correct to 1 decimal place.
State whether it is an increase or a decrease.

	First quantity	Second quantity	% increase/decrease
a	30	37	
b	65	40	
c	148	200	
d	£1.14	81p	
e	£12.60	£13.60	
f	64 cm	1.1 m	
g	2.15 kg	900 g	
h	3 mm	1.1 cm	
i	1.02 km	999 m	

9 Garth's prize calf's weight increased from 40 kg to 43 kg.
Marged's prize calf's weight increased from 46 kg to 49 kg.
Which calf had the greater percentage increase in weight?

10 The value of Glenda's house fell from £160 000 to £147 000.
The value of Griff's house fell from £185 000 to £172 000.
Whose house had the greater percentage fall in value?

11 Mr Tell bought 10 DVDs for £6 each.
He sold 8 of them for £10 each and 2 of them for £5 each.
Work out his percentage profit.

Problem solving

1 Last year, Gwyn and Henry were looking at ways to reduce their heating bills.
Gwyn had wall insulation installed in his house.
Henry had loft insulation installed in his house.
For this year, Gwyn's heating bill is reduced from £640.50 to £544.43.
Henry's heating bill is reduced from £650 to £520.
Compare the percentage saving of wall insulation and loft insulation.

Number Strand 5 Percentages

2) Sheila is writing an article in a magazine about the changes in transport and travel between 1961 and 2011.

She uses this information taken from government statistics.

Transport and travel	1961	1971	1981	1991	2001	2011
Road vehicles (millions)						
Licensed road vehicles	9.0	14.0	19.3	24.5	28.9	34.5
Motor vehicles registered for the first time	1.3	1.7	2.0	1.9	2.9	2.4
Length of network (thousand km)						
All public roads	314.0	325.0	342.0	360.0	392.0	393.0
Motorways	0.2	1.3	2.6	3.1	3.5	3.6

    a Calculate the percentage increase in licensed road vehicles between 1961 and 2011.

    b Compare the percentage increase in the length of motorways with the percentage increase in the length of all public roads over each 10-year period.

3) Nigel's rent increased from £200 to £220 per week.

At the same time, Nigel's wages increased from £450 to £490 per week.

Work out the percentage increase in the amount of money Nigel has left to spend each week.

4) This headline was taken from a newspaper from 1977.

Cost of food increases by nearly 200% in the last 5 years

The table shows some information about the prices of some foods in 1972 and in 1977.

Food	1972 price	1977 price
1 lb sausages	21p	44p
4 oz coffee	29p	72p
1 lb potatoes	2p	12p
12 eggs	20p	48p
2 lb sugar	10p	21p
1 pt milk	6p	10p
1 lb carrots	3p	14p

Mrs Evans wants to see if this headline is true.
Here is a typical shopping list from 1977.
By considering this shopping list, comment on the headline.

1 lb sausages
8 oz coffee
5 lb potatoes
6 eggs
3 pts milk
1 lb carrots

5) The table shows some information about the number of students in a college.

Year	2009	2010	2011	2012
Number	581	620	641	672

    a In which year was the percentage increase in the number of students the greatest?

In 2013, the number of students was 48 more than in 2012.

    b Work out the percentage increase in the number of students from 2009 to 2013.

Unit 5 Finding the percentage change from one amount to another Band g

6 Each year, Grace goes to France for her summer holiday.
She rents a villa which costs €850 per week.
The exchange rate last year was £1 = €1.12
The cost in euros of renting the villa was the same this year but she actually paid £680.
Work out the percentage change in the exchange rate.

7 The table gives information about the length of a lap at two motor racing tracks.

Motor racing track	Lap length
Brands Hatch	2.3 miles
Silverstone	3.67 miles

At Brands Hatch, there are 85 laps in a race.
At Silverstone, there are 60 laps in a race.
The organisers want to make both races the same length.

  a Find the percentage change required in the length of the race at Brands Hatch to make this happen.

  b Find the percentage change that would be required at Silverstone.

8 Raffi takes out a mortgage for £150 000. He pays a deposit of £30 000, then £1000 per month for 25 years.
Calculate the overall percentage interest payable over the term of the mortgage on the amount borrowed, excluding the deposit.

9 Marged wants to take out a mortgage for £180 000. Reef bank offers her a mortgage for 20 years with a 20% deposit and fixed monthly payments of £855. Rhudd building society offers her a mortgage for 20 years with a 15% deposit and fixed monthly payments of £925.

  a Which would be the better option for Marged, provided she is able to pay the deposit required?

  b Over the period of the mortgage, what would be the overall percentage interest rate on the actual amount borrowed, excluding the deposit?

10 Rita is offered a payday loan. She wishes to borrow £50 for 10 weeks. She has to pay back £8.50 per week for the 10 weeks.

  a How much in total will Rita have to pay back?

  b What is the percentage interest Rita pays by taking out this loan?

Number Strand 5 Percentages

Reviewing skills

1) Work out these percentages.
   a 9 as a percentage of 90
   b 54 as a percentage of 72
   c 75 as a percentage of 125
   d 20.8 as a percentage of 26

2) Write the first quantity as a percentage of the second quantity.
   a 8 mm, 3.2 cm
   b 240 m, 1 km
   c 8.4, 20
   d 84 ml, 0.75 litres

3) Work out the profit and percentage profit for each item.

	Item	Cost price	Selling price	Profit	Percentage profit
a	Dress	£80	£84		
b	Pencil	80p	£1.08		
c	Dressing gown	£120	£84		
d	Notebook	£2	96p		

4) Iolo bought 3 cars.
   Car A cost £5000, car B cost £6100 and car C cost £6300.
   He sold the 3 cars for £5100, £5800 and £6000, respectively.
   a Work out his total percentage loss to the nearest whole number.
   b On which car did he make the greatest percentage loss?

Unit 6 • Reverse percentages • Band h

Outside the Maths classroom

Reclaiming VAT

Resources cost £600 including VAT at 20%.

Beth says the VAT is 20% of £600. Why is Beth wrong?

Toolbox

Sometimes you know the value of something and the percentage change but not the original value. Finding the original value involves reverse percentages, as in this example.

A coat costs £45 in a sale. It has been reduced by 10%. What was its original cost?

This percentage bar shows what you know and what you need to find out.

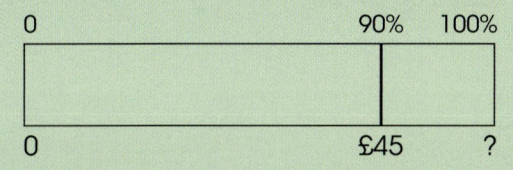

The original cost was £50.

Alternatively,

90% is £45

1% is $\frac{45}{90} = 0.5$

100% is 0.5×100
 = £50

Example – When an amount is reduced

The sale price of a pair of designer sunglasses is £96.

a The reduction in the sale is 20%. What percentage of the original price is the sale price?
b Find the original price.

Solution

a The sale price is 80% of the original price.
b 80% is £96   [100% − 20% = 80%]
  1% is $\frac{96}{80}$ = £1.20
  100% is 1.2×100
       = £120
  So the original price was £120.

Number Strand 5 Percentages

Example – When an amount is increased

A shop sells boots for £56 a pair. The shop makes a profit of 40%.
What price did the shop pay for the boots?

Solution

Cost price = 100%; profit = 40% so the selling price = 140%.
140% is £56

1% is $\frac{56}{140}$ = £0.40

100% is 0.4 × 100
= £40

so the shop paid £40 for the boots.

Practising skills

1. A shirt costs £48 which includes VAT at 20%. This means 120% = £48.
   Work out the cost of the shirt without VAT.

2. A tie costs £12 following a reduction of 20%. This means 80% = £12.
   Work out the cost of the tie before the reduction.

3. A lamp costs £27 following a reduction of 10%.
   Work out the cost of the lamp before the reduction.

4. A table costs £138 which includes VAT at 20%.
   a Work out the cost of the table without VAT.
   b How much VAT was paid?

5. Work out the original length for each of these.
   a ☐ cm was increased by 30% to give 91 cm.
   b ☐ m was reduced by 25% to give 96 m.
   c ☐ km was reduced by 14% to give 387 km.
   d ☐ m was increased by 4% to give 5.2 m.
   e ☐ km was reduced by 38% to give 527 km.

6. a Increase £200 by 15%.
   b An amount was increased by 15% to give £200. What was the original amount?
   c Increase your answer to part **b** by 30%. Is your answer the same as in part **a**? Explain your answer.

Developing fluency

1. The table shows the sale price and the percentage discount for some items.
   Work out the original price of each item.

	Item	Sale price	Discount	Original price
a	Necklace	£63	10%	
b	Watch	£102	15%	
c	Bracelet	£57	5%	
d	Earrings	£12	40%	

2) The table shows the cost of some household bills. Each bill includes VAT at 20%.
Work out the cost without VAT.

	Bill	Cost with VAT	Cost without VAT
a	Telephone	£96	
b	Satellite TV	£21.60	
c	Insurance	£210	
d	Carpet	£1500	

3) The contents of a carton of juice have been reduced by 12%.
The contents are now 792 ml. What was the original content?

4) A nurse worked 52 hours this week. This was an increase of 30% compared to last week.
How many hours did the nurse work last week?

5) Dylan got a reduction of 15% on the cost of his new car. He paid £7990.
What was the original cost?

6) House prices have risen by 3% this year compared to last year.
A house is valued at £185 400 this year. What was its value last year?

7) A jeweller buys a watch and makes 55% profit when he sells it for £124. How much profit did he make?

8) A photocopier printed 1131 pages this month. This was a reduction of 22% compared to the previous month. How many fewer pages were printed this month compared to last month?

9) Ned travelled 60% more miles in September than he did in August. He travelled 2240 miles in September. What was his total mileage for August and September?

10) Naomi bought a computer for £432, a TV for £270 and a mobile phone for £138. All three items included VAT at 20%. How much VAT did she pay in total?

Number Strand 5 Percentages

Problem solving

1. Ken shops at CashLimited wholesale warehouse where all items are priced without VAT. Ken buys a box of printing paper, 4 ink cartridges and a pack of folders.

   A box of printing paper is priced at £11.00; a pack of folders is priced at £9.00 and there is no price on the ink cartridges.

   Including VAT, at 20%, Ken pays £84.

   Work out the price of an ink cartridge.

2. Morgan and Rowan buy identical cars. Morgan buys his car from Car Market Sales and Rowan buys his car from Jeff's Autos.

   Car Market Sales offers Morgan a 12% reduction on the showroom price for the car. Morgan accepts the offer and buys the car.
   At Jeff's Autos, Rowan buys the identical car for £6250.
   Morgan pays £86 more than Rowan.
   What was the showroom price of the car at Car Market Sales?

3. In a sale there is 20% off all items.
   Siobhan buys these three items of clothing. The diagram shows the sale prices of two of them.
   Siobhan pays €137 for these three items. What was the original price of the shoes?

   A   B   C
                €65   €32

4. Guto buys and sells antique furniture. At an auction, Guto buys a grandfather clock.
   As well as the price he bids, he pays an additional 15% commission to the auction house.
   He later sells the grandfather clock for £1288 making a 40% profit on what he paid at the auction house.
   How much did Guto bid for the clock?

5. As a result of an economic crisis in 2010, Tony and his wife Elen have to take a cut in salary.
   Tony's salary is reduced by 10%.
   Elen's salary is reduced by 5%.
   After the cuts, Tony's salary is £28 800 per annum and Elen's salary is £42 750 per annum.
   Tony needs to know the total percentage cut in the sum of their salaries. Elen says the total percentage cut is 7.5%, their average reduction.
   Show that Elen is wrong.

6 Ace Parking owns two car parks, one at Franton and one at Cefn.
Ace Parking wants to increase the capacity of their car parks.
Franton is to increase by 20%.
Cefn is to increase by 25%.
The capacity of the car park in Cefn will be twice that of the car park in Franton.
In total there will be 1800 places to park vehicles.
How many more spaces are there now at Cefn than there are at Franton?

7 Gordon wants to reduce his annual energy bill. Wall insulation reduces annual heating costs by 15%. The cost to install wall insulation for his house is £1620.
After he insulated the walls of his home, Gordon's annual heating cost was £765.
How many years will it take for Gordon to save enough money to cover the cost of installing wall insulation?

8 This article appeared in the local newspaper in the Algarve, Portugal in August 2014.
It went on to say that the rainfall in July 2014 was an increase of 460% on the July average.

> **The wettest July since records began**
>
> With a total rainfall of 5.6 cm, it has been the wettest July since records began. In 2012, just 0.9 cm of rain fell in the month of July.

Compare the rainfall in July 2012 to the average rainfall for the month of July.

Reviewing skills

1 Indicate the correct answer **a, b, c** or **d**.
An electricity bill was £126 which included VAT at 5%. How much VAT was paid?
   a £6   **b** £6.30   **c** £120   **d** £119.70

2 Thabo's parents measure his height every birthday. On his 14th birthday his height is 147 cm. His father says 'You grew 5% last year.'
   a How tall was Thabo on his 13th birthday?
   b How much did he grow when he was 13 years old?

3 This year there are 204 registered players in a cricket league. This is a reduction of 15% compared to last year.
   a How many registered players were there last year?
   b What is the reduction in the number of registered players?

4 There is 10% off coats and 25% off shirts in T.C. Clothing. Neil paid £54 for a coat and £48 for a shirt when the offers were on. How much in total did he save?

Unit 7 • Repeated percentage increase/decrease • Band h

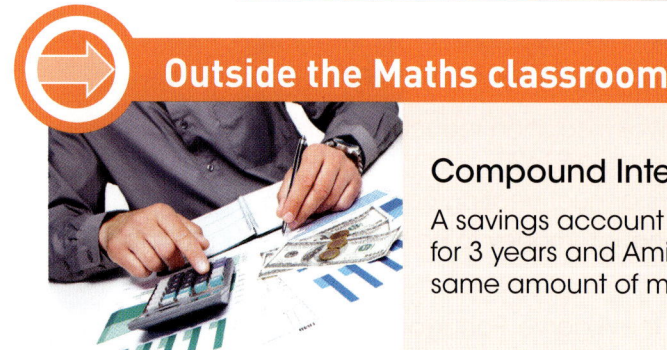

Outside the Maths classroom

Compound Interest

A savings account pays interest at a rate of 2%. John invests £500 for 3 years and Amid invests £1500 for 1 year. Do they have the same amount of money at the end of each of these periods?

Toolbox

A common use of repeated percentage increase is for savings where interest is added to an account and the next year's interest is calculated on the new balance. **This is called compound interest.**

A common use of percentage decrease is for depreciation. Assets such as cars reduce in value each year by a percentage of their value at the start of the year.

It is important to recognise when to use these techniques.

Example – Repeated percentage increase

£2000 is invested at 3.5% interest. Calculate the amount at the end of four years when
a The interest is not added to the investment
b The interest is added to the investment.

Solution

a 3.5% of £2000 = $\frac{3.5}{100} \times 2000$
  = £70

This is the interest earned each year.

At the end of four years, the total amount received is the original amount plus four years of interest:

£2000 + 4 × 70 = £2280

b Each year the investment increases by 3.5% i.e. 103.5% of the investment at the start of that year.

Year 1   103.5% of 2000 = $\frac{103.5}{100} \times 2000$
                           = £2070

Year 2   103.5% of 2070 = $\frac{103.5}{100} \times 2070$
                           = 2142.45

Unit 7 Repeated percentage increase/decrease Band h

Year 3 103.5% of $2142.45 = \dfrac{103.5}{100} \times 2142.45$

$= 2217.44$

Year 4 103.5% of $2217.44 = \dfrac{103.5}{100} \times 2217.44$

$= £2295.05$

This can be done in one calculation:
$2000 \times \left(\dfrac{103.5}{100}\right)^4 = £2295.05$

Practising skills

1 The number A is 6000.
   a A is increased by 10% to give B. What is number B?
   b B is increased by 10% to give C. What is the number C?
   c C is increased by 10% to give D. What is the number D?
   d What is the percentage increase from A to D?

2 Asaph buys a field for £6000. For each of the next 3 years it increases in value by 10%.
   a What is its value at the end of 3 years?
   b What is the percentage increase in its value since Asaph bought it?
   c Explain why the increase is greater than 30%.

3 The number P is 5000.
   a P is decreased by 20% to give Q. What is the number Q?
   b Q is decreased by 20% to give R. What is the number R?
   c R is decreased by 20% to give S. What is the number S?
   d What is the percentage change from P to S?

4 Pepe buys a car for £5000. For each of the next 3 years the car decreases in value by 20%.
   a What is the value of Pepe's car at the end of 3 years?
   b What is the percentage decrease in its value since Pepe bought it?
   c After how many more years is Pepe's car worth less than £2000?
      (It continues to depreciate at 20% per year.)

5 Match these percentage changes with the decimal multiplier.

% change	Decimal multiplier
20% increase	× 1.5
60% decrease	× 0.88
12% increase	× 1.2
12% decrease	× 0.4
150% increase	× 1.12

Number Strand 5 Percentages

Reasoning

6 Start with the number 200.

    a Increase it by 50%.
       Then decrease the answer by 40%.
       Then decrease that answer by 10%.

    b Find the percentage change from 200 to the final answer in part **a**.

    c Work out $200 \times 1.5 \times 0.6 \times 0.9$

    d What do you notice about the answers to parts **a** and **c**? Explain the connection.

Developing fluency

1 Elis invests £500 at 6% per annum.

    a How much interest does Elis receive at the end of the first year?

    b He reinvests the £500 but not the interest. What is his total investment at the end of the first year?

    c His reinvestment earns interest for another year at 6%. How much interest does he receive at the end of the second year?

2 Interest is paid on the following investments but not reinvested.

    a How much interest is received in total on

       i £1000 at 5% p.a. for 2 years

       ii £2000 at 10% p.a. for 5 years

       iii £500 at 3.5% p.a. for 3 years?

    b Now find the interest paid on these investments when the interest is reinvested each year.

3 A riverbank has been colonised by mink. They are an alien species that attacks local wildlife. The river authority traps the mink and removes them. Each year it reduces the number of mink by 60%.
What percentage of mink remain after

    a 1 year   **b** 2 years   **c** 3 years   **d** 4 years   **e** 5 years?

4 Hannah buys her first car for £3000.

    a After she has owned it for a year, she is told that its value has depreciated by 20%.

       i How much is the car worth after 1 year?

       ii How much value has the car lost in the first year?

    b The rate of depreciation continues at 20% per year from the start of the second year.

       i Show that after two years the car is worth £1920.

       ii How long will it be before Hannah's car is worth less than £500?

5 One Monday, 100 people have a highly infectious disease.
The number of people with the disease increases by 20% each day.
How many have the disease the following Monday?

Unit 7 Repeated percentage increase/decrease Band h

6 In 2002, Iwan bought a house for £87 000. The house appreciated in value by 6% per year from the start of the year.

 a How much was the house worth in 2003?

 b How much was the house worth in 2004?

 c In which year did the value of the house become greater than £100 000?

7 'The world is now losing its tropical forest at the rate of 7% per year.'

 a If this trend continues, what percentage of the existing tropical forest will be left in 5 years' time?

 b Show that 10 years from now, just under half of the tropical forest will have disappeared.

 c How much tropical forest will remain after 50 years?

 d How much tropical forest will remain after 100 years?
 You may find a spreadsheet useful.

8 Look at this information about compound interest rates.

Allied Afon savings accounts compound interest rates	
Standard saver	6% p.a.
Junior saver	7.5% p.a.
Super saver	11% p.a.

Find the amount and the compound interest paid on each of the following.

 a £580 invested for 3 years in a standard savings account.

 b £1650 invested for 4 years in a junior savings account.

 c £24 000 invested for 10 years in a super savings account.

9 Nathan increases the number of kilometres he runs each day by 25%. He went running on Monday, Tuesday and Wednesday. On Wednesday he ran 18.75 km. How far did he run on the previous two days?

Problem solving

1 Keith and Mari organised a closing-down sale in their clothes shop. They reduced the prices of all the items in the shop by 30%. Two weeks before the end of the sale, Keith reduced the prices by a further 20%.

Mari said that all the prices had then been reduced by 50%. Keith said that all the prices had been reduced by over 50%.

Who was right?

2 In 2012, the population of a country is 36 million. If the population decreases at an annual rate of 2.5%.

 a What was the population in 2010?

 b What will the population be in 2015?
   Write your answers to the nearest thousand.

Number Strand 5 Percentages

3) In 2010, the total number of crimes recorded in the town of Afonwen was 1250. 40% of these crimes were robberies.

In 2011, the number of robberies recorded decreased by 8%. In 2012, the number of robberies recorded increased by a further 10% on the numbers in 2011. In 2013, there were 30 more robberies recorded in Afonwen than in 2011.

The Chief of Police in Afonwen has to give details about the robberies committed in 2013. What will she be able to say about the percentage change in the number of robberies committed in 2013 in Afonwen, compared with the previous year?

4) In 2013, a young footballer playing in the Premier League was earning £30 000 per week. At the end of 2013, he signed a new 2-year contract, giving him an increase of 25% in the first year and a further increase of 30% in the second year.

He tells his mum that by the end of 2015, he will have earned over £4 million in these two years. Is he correct?

5) Dan wants to invest £5000 for 3 years in the same bank.

At the end of 3 years, Dan wants to have as much money as possible.

Which bank should Dan invest his £5000 in?

The International Bank
Compound interest
4.5% for the first year
1% for each extra year

The Friendly Bank
Compound interest
5.8% for the first year
0.5% for each extra year

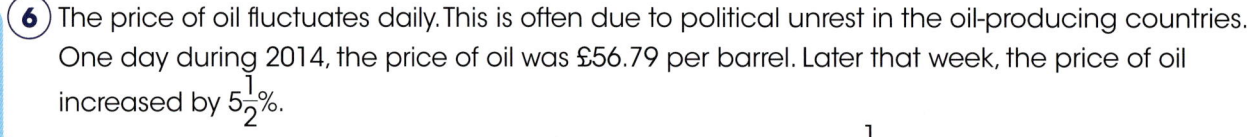

6) The price of oil fluctuates daily. This is often due to political unrest in the oil-producing countries.

One day during 2014, the price of oil was £56.79 per barrel. Later that week, the price of oil increased by $5\frac{1}{2}$%.

During the following week, after the price of oil had decreased by $5\frac{1}{2}$%, a newspaper headline read 'The price of oil is back to what it was last week.'

Explain why this headline is incorrect.

7) Miguel owns a Spanish villa with a swimming pool. On Monday, the depth of the swimming pool was 1.5 m. As a result of the hot weather, the depth decreased each day for 4 days, by 1.5% of the depth on the previous day.

On Friday, Miguel had to refill the pool to a depth of 1.5 m. The surface area of the water in the pool is 200 m^2.

Work out the amount of water that Miguel had to use to fill the pool.

8) Tina invests £1500 in a bank account for 4 years. The bank pays compound interest at an annual rate of 2.5% for the first year and 1.5% for the next 3 years.

Andy also invests £1500 in a bank account for 4 years. Andy's is a variable rate compound interest account. The interest is 2% for the first year, 1.8% for the second year and 1.7% for the third and fourth years.

Who has made the better investment?

Unit 7 Repeated percentage increase/decrease Band h

9 Jodie buys a painting for £800. The painting increases in value by 12% in the first year and then by a further 10% in the second year.
Jodie says that after two years, the value of the painting has increased by 22%.
Is she right?

10 Leonie invests £800 at compound interest at 8% p.a. The interest is added to the balance each year.

a Copy and complete this table.

Year	Principal	Interest	Amount at end of year
1	£800	£64	£864
2	£864		
3			

Use this amount as the next principal.
Amount from year before.

b The amount, £A, can also be calculated by using the formula
$$A = P\left(1 + \frac{R}{100}\right)^T$$
Use the formula with $P = 800$, $R = 8$ and $T = 1, 2$ and 3 to check your answers to part **a**.

c Explain why the formula works.

d Use the formula to find the final amount in these cases.
   i £900 invested for 5 years at 7.5% p.a. compound interest.
   ii £650 invested for 4 years at 3.9% p.a. compound interest.
   iii £110 invested for 18 months at 5.4% p.a. compound interest.

11 Henri thinks that if interest is paid quarterly then the AER % rate is always higher than the Gross annual % rate.
Explain why Henri is correct.

Reviewing skills

1 Compare the simple interest on each of these investments, with the compound interest when the interest is added at the end of each year.
   a £16 500 invested at 8% p.a. for 4 years.
   b £24 000 invested at 12% p.a. for 10 years.

2 Margaret buys a car for £8000.
   a A year later its value has depreciated by 15%. What is its value now?
   b In each of the next two years its value depreciates by 10%. What is its value 3 years after Margaret buys it?

3 Dimitri weighs 20 stones. He wants to lose 3 stones in the next three months.
He sees the following advertisement for a diet plan.
Using this diet plan, will Dimitri reach his target weight in 3 months?

Special Diet Plan Formula
Lose 6% of body weight in ONE month and 4% of body weight in each subsequent month.

Number Strand 6 Ratio and proportion

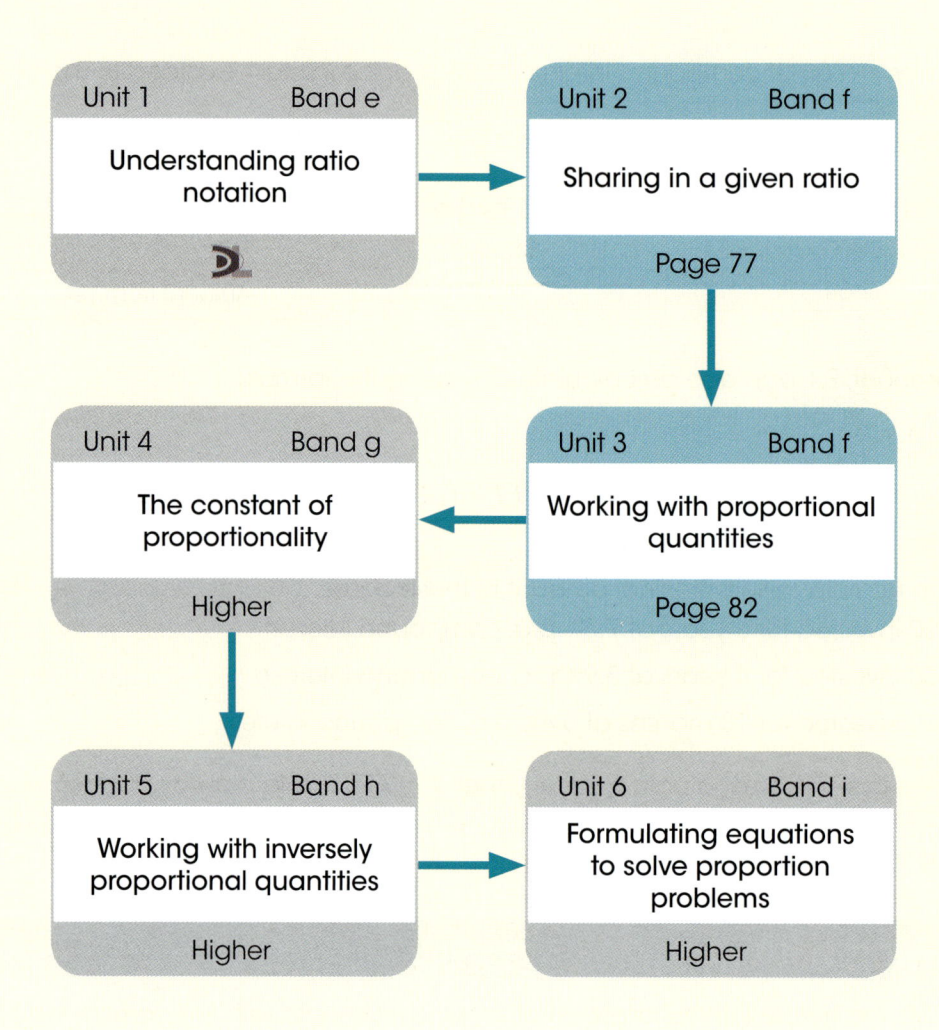

Unit 1 — Band e
Understanding ratio notation

Unit 2 — Band f
Sharing in a given ratio
Page 77

Unit 3 — Band f
Working with proportional quantities
Page 82

Unit 4 — Band g
The constant of proportionality
Higher

Unit 5 — Band h
Working with inversely proportional quantities
Higher

Unit 6 — Band i
Formulating equations to solve proportion problems
Higher

Unit 1 is assumed knowledge for this book. Knowledge and skills from this unit is used throughout the book.

Unit 2 • Sharing in a given ratio • Band f

Outside the Maths classroom

Mixing concrete
How do builders make sure they end up with the right mix?

Toolbox

In sharing problems, start by finding the total number of 'parts'. Then decide how the parts are allocated.

You can use a rectangular bar as in this example.

Kate and Pam share the cost of their £8.40 pizza in the ratio 3 : 4. How much does each pay?

The ratio is 3 : 4

3 + 4 = 7 so there are 7 parts.

Draw a bar with 7 equal parts.

K	K	K	P	P	P	P
£1.20	£1.20	£1.20	£1.20	£1.20	£1.20	£1.20

Kate has 3 shares and Pam has 4.

Divide £8.40 into 7 shares £8.40 ÷ 7 = £1.20

So Kate's share is 3 × £1.20 = £3.60
   Pam's share is 4 × £1.20 = £4.80

Alternatively, you can use proportions.

Kate pays $\frac{3}{7}$ of £8.40 = £3.60

Pam pays $\frac{4}{7}$ of £8.40 = £4.80

These fractions are called proportional

$\frac{1}{7}$ of £8.40 is £1.20

Number Strand 6 Ratio and proportion

Example – Sharing in a given ratio

Matthew and Harry go to a car boot sale.
They have a lucky find and buy a box of old Star Wars figures for £10.
Matthew pays £4 and Harry pays £6.
There are 40 figures in the box.

a Do you agree with Harry? Why?
b The ratio of their money is 2 : 3.
   They share the figures in this ratio.
   Find how many each of them gets using
   i proportions ii a rectangular bar.

Matthew: That's 20 each.

Harry: No, that's not fair.

Solution

a Yes. Harry paid more than Matthew so it seems right that Harry should get more of the figures than Matthew.

b The ratio is 2 : 3
   2 + 3 = 5 so there are 5 parts

   i Matthew gets $\frac{2}{5}$ of 40 = 16 figures $\frac{1}{5}$ of 40 is 8

      Harry gets $\frac{3}{5}$ of 40 = 24 figures

   ii

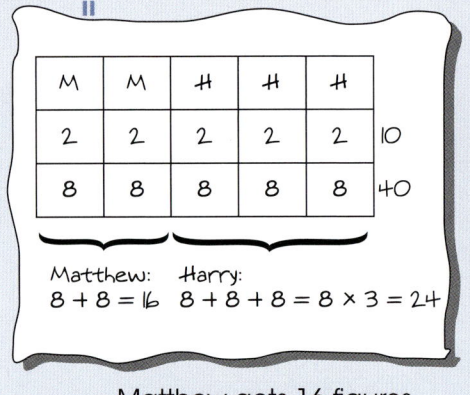

M	M	H	H	H	
2	2	2	2	2	10
8	8	8	8	8	40

   Matthew: Harry:
   8 + 8 = 16   8 + 8 + 8 = 8 × 3 = 24

   ← There are two parts for Matthew and three parts for Harry so there are five parts altogether.

   ← This row shows how the £10 they paid in total was shared between them. Matthew paid £4 and Harry paid £6.

   ← There are 40 figures to share. 10 × 4 = 40 so multiply each number in the row above by 4.

   Matthew gets 16 figures.
   Harry gets 24 figures.

Practising skills

1 £36 is shared between Islwyn and Mari in the ratio 1 : 2.

   a How many equal parts are there?
   b How much is each equal part?
   c How much does Islwyn get?
   d How much does Mari get?
   e What is the total of Islwyn and Mari's amounts?

2 Jared and Raheem share a packet of 45 stickers in the ratio 2:7.
  a How many equal parts are there?
  b How many stickers are in each equal part?
  c How many does Jared get?
  d How many does Raheem get?
  e What is the total of Jared and Raheem's amounts?

3 Jalel mixes blue and yellow paint in the ratio 1:5.
He ends up with 480 ml of green paint.
  a How many equal parts are there?
  b How much is each equal part?
  c How much blue paint did he use?
  d How much yellow paint did he use?
  e How much more yellow than blue did he use?

4 Work these out.
  a Share £60 in the ratio 2:3.
  b Share £96 in the ratio 5:1.
  c Share 160 in the ratio 3:5.
  d Share 126 ml in the ratio 7:2.

5 The ratio of red apples to green apples on a market stall is 3:7.
  a What fraction of the apples are red?
  b What fraction of the apples are green?
  c How much bigger is the fraction of green apples than red apples?

6 Work these out.
  a Share £90 in the ratio 3:2.
  b Share £120 in the ratio 1:7.
  c Share 225 in the ratio 5:4.
  d Share 480 m in the ratio 7:3:2.

Developing fluency

1 £336 is shared between Alex and Abbie in the ratio 5:7.
How much more does Abbie get than Alex?

2 A café sold 168 meals one day.
The ratio of beef meals to chicken to fish was 4:2:1.
How many more beef than fish meals were sold on that day?

Number Strand 6 Ratio and proportion

3 Jeff is 12 years old and Joseph is 20 years old.
Plan A is to share £5280 in the ratio of their ages now.
Plan B is to wait until Jeff is 18 years old and to share £5280 in the ratio of their ages then.
How much will Jeff gain by waiting until he is 18 years old?

4 In a rectangle the ratio of the length to width is 9 : 5.
The perimeter of the rectangle is 196 cm.
What are the length and width of this rectangle?

5 A canteen serves glasses of milk or water at lunchtime.
On Monday they serve 128 glasses.
The ratio of glasses of milk to glasses of water is 5 : 3.
On Tuesday the ratio is 4 : 3.
The number of glasses of milk is 12 more than on Monday.
How many more glasses of water are served on Tuesday than on Monday?

Problem solving

1 Llew says he could share this bar of chocolate in the ratio 1 : 3.
Berwyn says he could share it in the ratio 5 : 7.
How many different ratios could the bar be shared into?

2 Ninety girls are asked what their favourite sport is from hockey, tennis and netball.
The ratio of the results of hockey to tennis to netball is 1 : 3 : 5.

  a How many girls chose tennis as their favourite sport?

The pie chart shows these results.

  b Work out the angle of each sector of the pie chart.

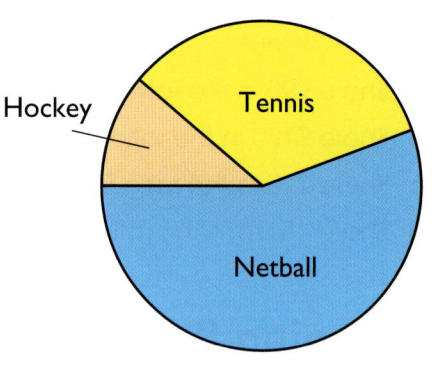

3 Glenys and Jenny are sisters.
At Christmas 2004, Glenys was 3 years old and Jenny was 12 years old.
Their father gave them a present of £300 shared in the ratio of their ages.

  a How much money did Glenys receive?

Each Christmas, their father carried on giving them a sum of money shared in the ratio of their ages.

  b In which year did Jenny receive twice as much money as Glenys?

4 Lesley takes the penalties for her football team.
During her career, she has taken 56 penalties.
There are three possible outcomes from a penalty:
- a goal is scored
- it is saved by the goalkeeper
- it misses the target

For Lesley's penalties, the ratio of these outcomes is $5:2:1$ respectively.
Lesley's brother Lionel also takes penalties for his football team.
Lionel has scored 30 goals from penalties.

a Who has scored more goals from penalties?

Of the penalties that Lionel has taken, 6 were saved by the goalkeeper and 4 missed the target.

b Compare Lionel's record of taking penalties with Lesley's record of taking penalties.

5 Arfan and Benny each have a box of chocolates.
In each box, there are milk chocolates, dark chocolates and white chocolates.
Arfan's box contains 27 chocolates.
The ratio of milk to dark to white chocolates in Arfan's box is $4:3:2$.
Benny's box contains 28 chocolates.
The ratio of milk to dark to white chocolates in Benny's box is $3:3:1$.
Arfan says, 'I have more milk chocolates than Benny has.'
Is Arfan right?

Reviewing skills

1 The ratio of oranges to lemons in a recipe for marmalade is $1:4$.
  a How many equal parts of fruit are there?
  b What fraction of the fruit are oranges?
  c What fraction of the fruit are lemons?

2 a Share 105 g in the ratio $4:3$.
  b Share 330 in the ratio $7:8$.
  c Share 286 g in the ratio $1:2:10$.
  d Share 245 in the ratio $1:2:4$.

3 Ceri goes to the gym on Mondays and Fridays.
He always divides his time between using the treadmill and doing weights in the ratio $3:2$.

On Monday he was there for $1\frac{1}{2}$ hours.

On Friday he spends the same time on weights as he had spent on the treadmill on Monday.
How long is he at the gym on Friday?

Unit 3 • Working with proportional quantities • Band f

Outside the Maths classroom

Supermarket prices

Why do supermarkets often give the price per 100g?

Toolbox

It is important to choose the most suitable method to solve a problem involving ratio and proportion.
- A ratio table can be very helpful for understanding a situation.
- The unitary method is good when the numbers are not quite straightforward and can be helpful for comparing quantities using unit costs.

Example – Comparing unit costs

Orange juice can be bought in different-sized cartons.
Holly needs 6 litres of orange juice for a party.
Which size carton should Holly buy?

Solution

Smaller carton
1.5 litres cost £2.40
1 litre costs $\frac{1}{1.5} \times £2.40 = £1.60$
Unit cost = £1.60

Larger carton
2 litres cost £3.00
1 litre costs $\frac{1}{2} \times £3.00 = £1.50$
Unit cost = £1.50

The larger carton has a lower unit cost.
Holly should buy the larger carton.

Example – Using the unitary method

These ingredients for apple crumble make enough to serve two people.

Apple Crumble (serves 2)
1 large cooking apple
25 g white sugar
$\frac{1}{4}$ teaspoon cinnamon
90 g wholemeal flour
40 g butter
75 g brown sugar

Inga needs to make an apple crumble for five people.
How much of each ingredient should she use?

In the unitary method you find for 1.

Solution

Then you scale up by multiplying.

Ingredients	For 2	For 1 (÷2)	For 5 (×5)
Cooking apple	1	$\frac{1}{2}$	$2\frac{1}{2}$
White sugar	25 g	12.5 g	62.5 g
Cinnamon	$\frac{1}{4}$ tsp	$\frac{1}{8}$ tsp	$\frac{5}{8}$ tsp
Wholemeal flour	90 g	45 g	225 g
Butter	40 g	20 g	100 g
Brown sugar	75 g	37.5 g	187.5 g

This column gives all the answers.

Example – Solving problems with a ratio table

40 blank CDs cost £20.
a Find the cost of 50 blank CDs.
b Find the cost of 24 blank CDs.

Solution

a

Number of CDs	40	20	10	50
Cost (£)	20	10	5	25

← 40 + 10 = 50
← 20 + 5 = 25

50 CDs cost £25.

b

Number of CDs	40	20	4	24
Cost (£)	20	10	2	12

← 20 + 4 = 24
← 10 + 2 = 12

24 CDs cost £12.

Number Strand 6 Ratio and proportion

Practising skills

1) 4 apples cost 96p.

   a How much does 1 apple cost?   b How much do 3 apples cost?

2) 6 carrots cost 90p.

   a How much does 1 carrot cost?   b How much do 8 carrots cost?

3) 100 litres of heating oil cost £60.

   a How much do 10 litres of oil cost?   b How much do 230 litres cost?

4) Look at the prices on these two market stalls.

Bev's Bargains
6 oranges £1.86
8 cans of cola £2.80
8 bananas £2.60

Dan's Discounts
4 oranges £1.28
6 cans of cola £1.80
12 bananas £2.88

   a i   How much does 1 can of cola cost in Bev's Bargains?
      ii How much does 1 can of cola cost in Dan's Discounts?
      iii Which market stall is better value for cans of cola?

   b i   How much do 4 bananas cost in Bev's Bargains?
      ii How much do 4 bananas cost in Dan's Discounts?
      iii Which is better value for bananas?

   c i   How much do 12 oranges cost in Bev's Bargains?
      ii How much do 12 oranges cost in Dan's Discounts?
      iii Which is better value for oranges?

5) Vincent has a recipe for shepherd's pie which serves 5 people.
   Copy and complete this table to help him find the quantities needed for 8 people.

Ingredient	Quantity for 5 people	Quantity for 1 person	Quantity for 8 people
Minced beef	900 g		
Stock	480 ml		
Onion	2		
Tin of tomatoes	1		
Potatoes	700 g		
Worcestershire sauce	40 ml		

Developing fluency

1. Three concert tickets cost £42.
   How much do eight of these tickets cost?

2. Nine cups of coffee cost £15.30.
   How much do four cups of coffee cost?

3. Last Saturday Mrs Boston paid £4.30 for five lemonades and £14.40 for six burgers at a café.
   She plans to go back this Saturday and order four lemonades and four burgers.
   How much less will it cost this Saturday?

4. For each of these work out which is better value. Explain your answer.

   a 6 kg for £14.70 or 7 kg for £17.50

   b 100 ml for £18 or 150 ml for £24

   c 80 g for £16.40 or 60 g for £12.06

5. A window cleaner charges a fixed rate of £5 plus an amount for each window he cleans.
   He cleaned a house with 6 windows and charged £9.80.
   Tom's house has 12 windows.
   He thinks the window cleaner will charge him £19.60.
   Is Tom right?
   Explain your answer.

6. Roland lives in France and is going on holiday to Iceland. The bank offers him an exchange rate of 1 Euro to buy 153.24 Icelandic Krona. Roland wants to exchange 400 Euros, but no more than this, into Icelandic Krona. The bank only has 10 Krona notes.
   Calculate the maximum number of Krona that Roland can buy and also how much this is going to cost him.

7. Elinor's favourite perfume comes in 3 sizes.

   £16.20 — Perfume 40 ml
   £18.50 — Perfume 50 ml
   £30 — Perfume 100 ml

   She sees these two offers online.
   Which is the best offer? Explain fully.

   OFFER 1
   Buy two 40 ml bottles and get one 40 ml bottle free
   USE CODE TWO40 AT CHECKOUT

   OFFER 2
   Buy one 50 ml bottle and get one 50 ml bottle half price
   USE CODE ONE50 AT CHECKOUT

8 Megan went on holiday to Poland. Before going, she went into her local travel money exchange shop to buy some Polish Zloty. Megan only had £150 to spend on buying Zloty. She wanted to buy as many Zloty as possible. Unfortunately, the travel money exchange shop only had 20 Zloty notes. The exchange rate to buy Zloty was £1 = 4.42 Zloty.

   a i How many Zloty did Megan buy?

     ii How much did she pay for the Zloty?

Whilst in Poland, Megan spent 84.40 Zloty. On returning from her holiday Megan changed her Zloty back to pounds. Unfortunately, the money exchange shop would only buy back a whole number of Zloty. The exchange rate used for changing Zloty back to pounds was £1 = 4.51 Zloty.

   b Calculate how much Megan received back from the money exchange shop. Give your answer to the nearest penny.

9 Dafydd is paid the same rate from Monday to Friday.

On Saturday he is paid time and a half.

Last week he worked 7 hours on Tuesday and 8 hours on Wednesday.

His pay was £123.

This week he is due to work 6 hours on Monday, 5 hours on Thursday and 8 hours on Saturday.

How much more will his pay be this week?

10 A car production line uses robot-operated machinery. A machine fits 5 identical windscreen wipers in 42 minutes.

How long would it take this machine to fit 15 of these windscreen wipers? Give your answer in hours and minutes.

11 At a water station, it takes 2 hours for 19 pumps to deliver 20 thousand litres of water.

How long would it take for 5 of these pumps to deliver 50 thousand litres of water?

The rate of delivery is equal and constant for each pump.

12 At an oil refinery, it takes 5 hours for 22 pumps to pump 25 thousand litres of oil.

How long would it take for 9 of these pumps to deliver 45 thousand litres of oil?

The rate of delivery is equal and constant for each pump.

Problem solving

1) Farah works in the retail industry.
The table shows some information about the hours she worked and her pay for the last three weeks.

Day	Hours worked		
	Week 1	Week 2	Week 3
Monday	8	9	8
Tuesday	6	4	8
Wednesday	10	10	
Thursday	4	8	10
Friday	10	12	4
Total pay	£475		£450

a Work out Farah's pay for Week 2.

b How many hours did Farah work on Wednesday of Week 3?

2) The ingredients for apple crumble make enough to serve two people.
Inga is going to make some apple crumble using this recipe.
In her kitchen, Inga has the following quantities of each ingredient:

24 large cooking apples
200 g of white sugar
6 teaspoons of cinnamon
1.2 kg of wholemeal flour
300 g of butter
500 g of brown sugar.

Apple Crumble (serves 2)
1 large cooking apple
25 g white sugar
$\frac{1}{4}$ teaspoon cinnamon
90 g wholemeal flour
40 g butter
75 g brown sugar

Work out the maximum number of servings of apple crumble that Inga can make.

3) Here are three boxes of the same type of chocolates.

Average contents 12 chocolates — 89p
Average contents 30 chocolates — £2.04
Average contents 50 chocolates — £3.45

Melanie and her friend go shopping for chocolates.
Melanie says, 'You always get the best value for money by buying the largest box'.
Is Melanie right?

Number Strand 6 Ratio and proportion

4) Albert and Harvey are salesmen. They work for different companies.
They are both allowed to claim for the use of their car for work.
During one month, Albert claimed £108 for driving 240 miles.
During the same month, Harvey claimed £135 for driving 270 miles.
In the next month, Albert's company increased the rate of car allowance by 10%.
Whose company now has the higher rate of car allowance?

5) There are 28 children in Mrs Davies' class.
She is going to buy a pen, a pencil and an eraser for each of the children in her class.
In a stationery catalogue, she sees the following information.

Pens: 30p each or a pack of 5 for £1.20

Pencils: 20p each or a pack of 3 for 50p

Eraser: 12p each or a pack of 10 for £1

Mrs Davies has just £15 to spend.
Has she got enough money to buy a pen, a pencil and an eraser for each of the children in her class?

6) Sara lives in the UK. Her friend Anton lives in France. They are both going on holiday to America. Anton is offered an exchange rate of 1 Euro to 1.32 US Dollars. Sara is offered an exchange rate of £1 to 1.68 US Dollars.
Sara states:

Using these exchange rates, £1 is worth .... Euros.

Copy and complete Sara's sentence.

7) Malcolm is working overseas.
He posts 120 letters.
Some of the letters are 1st class.
Some of the letters are 2nd class.
The number of 1st class letters is 5 times the number of 2nd class letters.
Malcolm knows that it costs 32 cents to post a 2nd class letter.
The total cost of posting all 120 letters is $47.40. There are 100 cents in 1 dollar.
Work out the cost of posting one 1st class letter.

8 Here is a list of ingredients for making a cheese soufflé.
Frances is going to make 12 cheese soufflés.
She has 150 grams of flour and 2 litres of milk.
Does she have enough flour and milk?

1 oz = 28 grams and 1 pint = 568 millilitres.

Cheese soufflé
3 eggs
1 oz of butter
$\frac{1}{2}$ oz of flour
$\frac{1}{4}$ pint of milk
3 oz of grated cheese

9 Ten 5p coins weigh 33.5 grams.
Five 2p coins weigh 35.6 grams.
Brynmor works in a bank.
A customer gives him a bag of 2p coins weighing 3.026 kg.
The customer also gives him 7 bags of 5p coins.
Each bag of 5p coins weighs 402 g.
Brynmor gives the customer a receipt for the total amount of money.
The receipt is for £50.50.
Show that the amount shown on this receipt is correct.

10 In the summer of 2014, £1 was worth 1.12 Euros. In the summer of 2015, £1 was worth 1.32 Euros.

The Davies family went to Italy for 10 nights during both of these summers. They stayed for the 10 nights in both 2014 and in 2015 at the Hotel Luca. The room rate for the family was 135 Euros per night in 2014. In 2015 the room rate had increased by 11%.

a Giving your answer in pounds, how much more did it cost to stay for the 10 nights in 2015 than in 2014?

b If the exchange in 2016 was midway between that of 2014 and 2015, and the cost per night had increased only by 2% from 2015, how much should the Davies family have budgeted for staying at the Hotel Luca for 10 nights in 2016?

11 In a factory, it takes 2 hours for 11 conveyor belts to deliver 6000 sandwiches to packing boxes.
How long would it take for 8 of these conveyor belts to deliver 4000 sandwiches to the packing boxes?
The rate of delivery is equal and constant for each conveyor belt.
Give your answer in hours and minutes.

Number Strand 6 Ratio and proportion

Reviewing skills

1) 5 adult bus tickets cost £11.70.
   a How much does 1 adult bus ticket cost?
   b How much do 9 adult bus tickets cost?

2) For each of these work out which is better value. Explain your answer.
   a 2m for £8.10 or 60cm for £2.49
   b 600g for £5.40 or 750g for £7.20
   c 2 litres for £22.12 or 800ml for £8.92

3) A particular brand of shampoo comes in 3 sizes.

   300 ml — £2.16
   400 ml — £2.72
   500 ml — £3.45

   a Work out the cost of 100ml for each size of bottle.
   b Which size is the best value?

Number Strand 7 Number properties

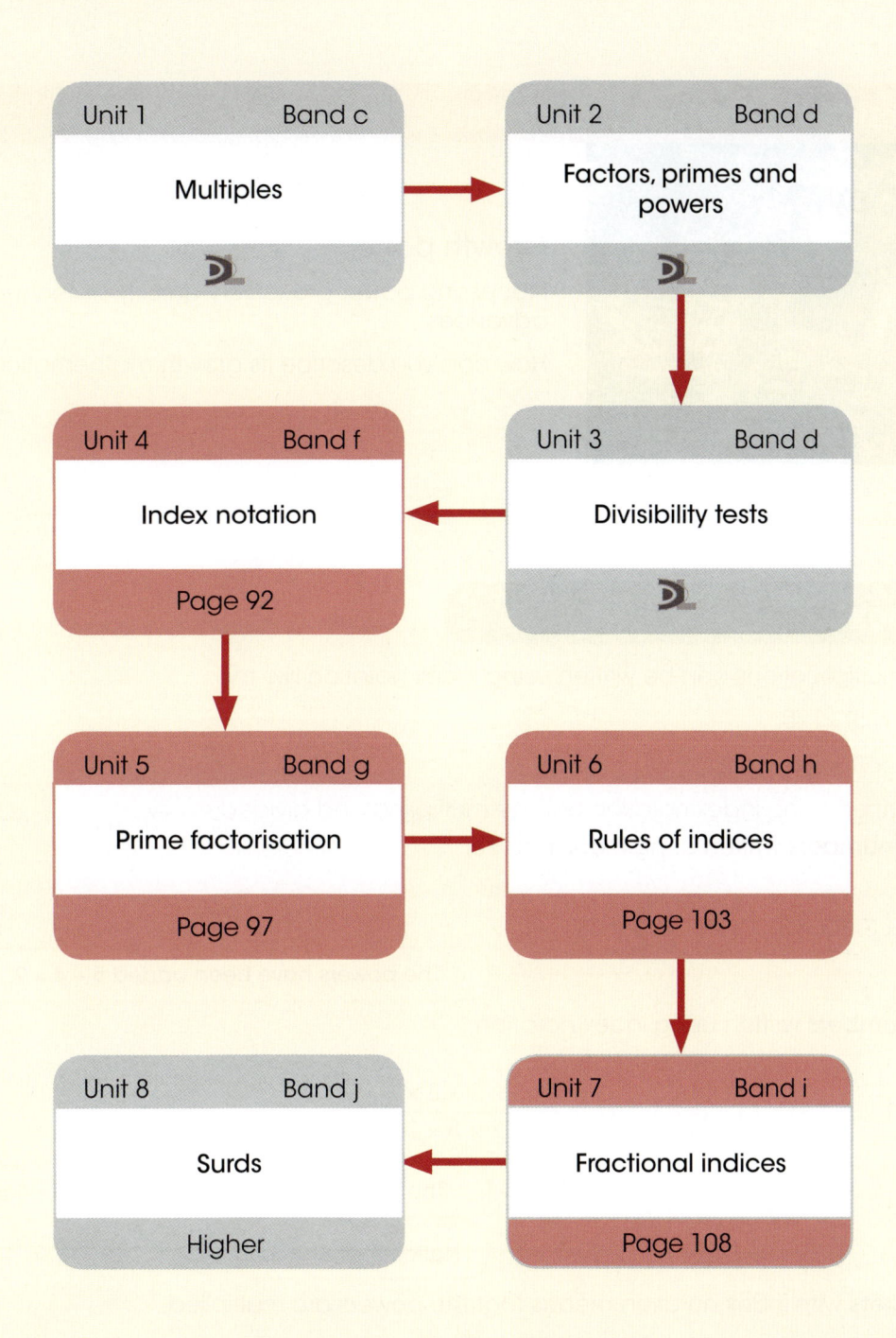

Unit 1	Band c
Multiples	

Unit 2	Band d
Factors, primes and powers	

Unit 3	Band d
Divisibility tests	

Unit 4	Band f
Index notation	
Page 92	

Unit 5	Band g
Prime factorisation	
Page 97	

Unit 6	Band h
Rules of indices	
Page 103	

Unit 7	Band i
Fractional indices	
Page 108	

Unit 8	Band j
Surds	
Higher	

Units 1–3 are assumed knowledge for this book.
Knowledge and skills from these units are used throughout the book.

7 Unit 4 • Index notation • Band f

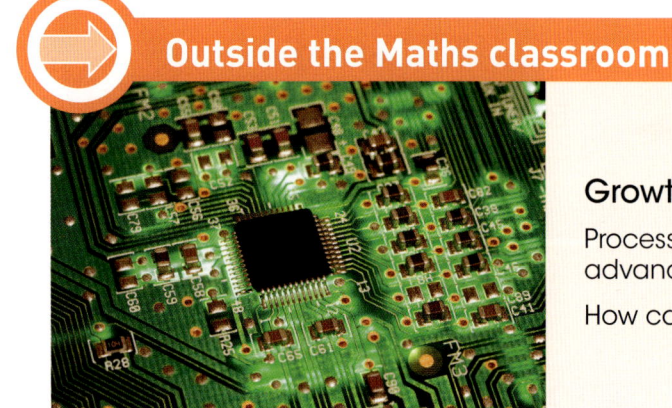

Outside the Maths classroom

Growth patterns
Processing power grows very quickly as technology advances.

How can you describe its growth mathematically?

Toolbox

Repeated multiplications can be written using index notation like this:
- $5 \times 5 \times 5 = 5^3 = 125$.
- $3 \times 3 \times 3 \times 3 \times 3 = 3^5 = 243$.

Numbers written using index notation can be multiplied and divided easily.

To **multiply numbers** written using index notation,

$3^5 \times 3^4$
$= (3 \times 3 \times 3 \times 3 \times 3) \times (3 \times 3 \times 3 \times 3)$
$= 3^9$ ← The powers have been added $5 + 4 = 9$.

To **divide numbers** written using index notation,

$3^5 \div 3^4$

$(3 \times 3 \times 3 \times 3 \times 3) \div (3 \times 3 \times 3 \times 3) = \dfrac{3 \times \cancel{3} \times \cancel{3} \times \cancel{3} \times \cancel{3}}{\cancel{3} \times \cancel{3} \times \cancel{3} \times \cancel{3}}$

$= 3^1$ ← The powers have been subtracted $5 - 4 = 1$.

$= 3$ ← Notice that $3^1 = 3$.

Using brackets with index notation means that the powers are multiplied.

$(3^5)^4 = 3^5 \times 3^5 \times 3^5 \times 3^5$
$= (3 \times 3 \times 3 \times 3 \times 3) \times (3 \times 3 \times 3 \times 3 \times 3) \times (3 \times 3 \times 3 \times 3 \times 3) \times (3 \times 3 \times 3 \times 3 \times 3)$
$= 3^{20}$ ← 4 lots of 5 is 20

Example – Equivalent amounts

Match these cards into pairs of the same value.

4×4^3	$4^9 \div 4^2$
$4^9 \div 4^3$	$4^5 \times 4^2$
$(4^2)^3$	$(4^2)^2$

Solution

Simplify each amount.

$4 \times 4^3 = 4 \times 4 \times 4 \times 4$
$ = 4^4$

$4^9 \div 4^3 = \dfrac{\cancel{4} \times \cancel{4} \times \cancel{4} \times 4 \times 4 \times 4 \times 4 \times 4 \times 4}{\cancel{4} \times \cancel{4} \times \cancel{4}}$
$ = 4^6$

$(4^2)^3 = (4 \times 4) \times (4 \times 4) \times (4 \times 4)$
$ = 4^6$

$4^9 \div 4^2 = \dfrac{\cancel{4} \times \cancel{4} \times 4 \times 4 \times 4 \times 4 \times 4 \times 4 \times 4}{\cancel{4} \times \cancel{4}}$
$ = 4^7$

$4^5 \times 4^2 = (4 \times 4 \times 4 \times 4 \times 4) \times (4 \times 4)$
$ = 4^7$

$(4^2)^2 = (4 \times 4) \times (4 \times 4)$
$ = 4^4$

So $4 \times 4^3 = (4^2)^2$
$ 4^9 \div 4^3 = (4^2)^3$
$ 4^9 \div 4^2 = 4^5 \times 4^2$

Practising skills

1 Write each of these as a power of 3.

    a 3×3 **b** $3 \times 3 \times 3 \times 3 \times 3$

    c $3 \times 3 \times 3 \times 3$ **d** $3 \times 3 \times 3 \times 3 \times 3 \times 3 \times 3$

2 Write each of these in index form.

    a $5 \times 5 \times 5$ **b** $2 \times 2 \times 2 \times 2 \times 2 \times 2$ **c** $2 \times 5 \times 2 \times 5$

    d $7 \times 7 \times 7 \times 7 \times 7$ **e** $11 \times 11 \times 11 \times 17 \times 17$ **f** $3 \times 3 \times 3 \times 3 \times 3 \times 3 \times 3 \times 3$

    g $2 \times 2 \times 2 \times 2 \times 2 \times 19$ **h** $5 \times 5 \times 7 \times 5 \times 7 \times 7$

3 Use a calculator to work out the value of these.

    a 5^3 **b** 2^{10} **c** 7^4 **d** 1^{30}

    e 3^6 **f** 6^5 **g** 4.5^2 **h** 8^7

    i 29^1 **j** 15^4 **k** 2^{16} **l** $(-6)^4$

Number Strand 7 Number properties

4 Write each of these as a single power of 2.
- a $2^2 \times 2^2$
- b 16
- c 2×8
- d 64
- e $2^3 \times 2^4 \times 2$
- f $2 \times 2 \times 2 \div 2$
- g $2^3 \div 2$
- h $2 \times 8 \times 16$

5 Write each of these as a single power of 3.
- a $3^{10} \div 3^2$
- b $3^7 \div 3^4$
- c $3^6 \div 3$
- d $3^9 \div 3^3$
- e $3^8 \div 3^2$
- f $3^{11} \div 3^5$
- g $3^{10} \div 3$
- h $\dfrac{3^6}{3^2}$
- i $\dfrac{3^9}{3^4}$

6 Write each of these as a single power of 5.
- a $(5^3)^2$
- b $(5^2)^4$
- c $(5^6)^2$
- d $(5^4)^3$
- e $(5^6)^6$
- f $(5^7)^3$
- g $(5^5)^4$
- h $(5^2)^9$
- i $(5^8)^4$

Developing fluency

1 Write down the equal pairs in this list.
2^{10} 8^3 9^3 2^9 4^5 3^6

2
- a How much greater is 2^6 than 6^2?
- b How much smaller is 5^3 than 5^4?
- c What is the sum of 2^8 and 3^4?
- d What is the product of 6^3 and 1^{10}?

3 Write these in order of size, starting with the smallest.
4^4 7^3 2^9 43×6 3^5

4 Work out the value of these. Give your answers as ordinary numbers.
- a $3^2 + 3$
- b $5^3 - 5$
- c 4×4^2
- d $10^3 - 10$
- e $7^2 \div 7$
- f $2^3 + 3^2$
- g $2^3 \times 3^2$
- h $2^3 - 3^2$

5 Write each of these in index form.
- a $2 \times 2 \times 7 \times 7 \times 7$
- b $6 \times 5 \times 6 \times 6$
- c $3 \times 5 \times 3 \times 5 \times 5 \times 5$
- d $2 \times 3 \times 3 \times 2 \times 3 \times 2 \times 2$
- e $7 \times 6 \times 6 \times 2 \times 7 \times 6$
- f $5 \times 3 \times 7 \times 3 \times 5 \times 7 \times 5$

6 Write each of these as a single power of 2.
- a $2^3 \times 2^4$
- b $2^8 \div 2^4$
- c $(2^4)^2$
- d $(2^5)^3$
- e 2×2^9
- f $2^{12} \div 2^3$
- g $\dfrac{2^{10}}{2^2}$
- h $2^3 \times 2 \times 2^4$

7 Write each of these as a single power of 2.
- a $\dfrac{2^4 \times 2^5}{2^2}$
- b $\dfrac{(2^4)^3}{2^3}$
- c $\dfrac{2^{11} \div 2^3}{2^4}$
- d $\dfrac{2^{15}}{2^3 \times 2^4}$
- e $\dfrac{2^6 \times 2^8}{(2^2)^2}$
- f $\dfrac{2^9 \times 2^6}{2^5 \div 2^3}$
- g $\dfrac{2^{10} \div 2^2}{2^7 \div 2^4}$
- h $\dfrac{2 \times 2^4}{2^2 \times 2^2}$

8 Find the missing numbers.

a $3^4 \times 3^{\square} = 3^{10}$
b $7^6 \div 7^{\square} = 7^3$
c $(5^{\square})^2 = 5^{12}$
d $2^6 = 2^{\square} \div 2$

9 In the men's singles at Wimbledon, the champion has to win 7 matches. How many men play in the first round?

Problem solving

1 The thickness of an A4 sheet of paper is 0.1 mm.

Bill cuts an A4 sheet of paper in half and places the two halves on top of each other. He then cuts the two halves in half and places these two halves on top of each other. He repeats this a further 4 times.

a Work out the height of the pile of paper formed.

b Explain why it would be very difficult for Bill to do this a further 10 times.

2 Dyfed is a free-range pig farmer. The diagram shows his field. Its shape is a trapezium.

Dyfed gives each pig an area of 2×5^3 m² of land. Work out the greatest number of pigs that Dyfed can put in this field.

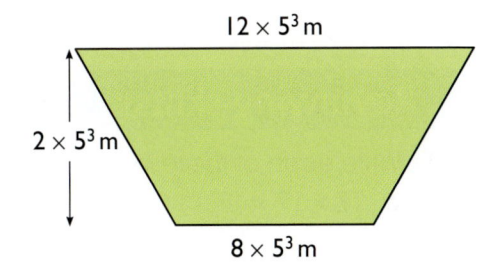

12×5^3 m

2×5^3 m

8×5^3 m

3 In a game of 'Double Your Money', contestants are asked a number of questions.

Contestants who answer the first question correctly win £1. If they answer the second question correctly, their winnings are doubled to £2, and so on.

Monica is a contestant on 'Double Your Money'. She answers 10 questions correctly.

a How much money had she won after answering the 10 questions? Give your answer using index notation.

b Work out the minimum number of questions she would have to answer correctly to win over £1 million.

4 You are given that
$x = 2^5 \times 8^4$
$y = 16^2 \div 4^6$
and that
$xy = 2^n$
Show that $n = 13$.

Number Strand 7 Number properties

5 Archie organises a *Ludo* knockout competition. Four people take part in each game and one (the winner) goes through to the next round. There are five rounds in this competition.

   a Work out the number of competitors in this competition. Give your answer using index notation and as an ordinary number.

   b Only 820 people turn up for the competition. Archie gives 68 of them a bye into the second round, so they don't have to play in the first round. Explain how this allows the competition to work out.

6 You are given that
   $a = 3 \times 10^5$
   $b = 5 \times 10^3$
   $c = 2 \times 10^3$
   Show that $a(b + c) = ab + ac$.

Reviewing skills

1 Write each of these in index form.
   a $17 \times 17 \times 17$
   b $2 \times 2 \times 5 \times 5 \times 5$
   c $3 \times 5 \times 3 \times 3 \times 3 \times 5$
   d $2 \times 3 \times 3 \times 11 \times 3 \times 11$

2 Indicate the correct answer **a**, **b**, **c** or **d**.
   The number 32 written as a single power of 2.
   a 2^3 **b** 2^4 **c** 2^5 **d** 2^6

3 Work out the value of these. Give your answers as ordinary numbers.
   a $4^3 + 4^3$
   b $6^3 - 6^2$
   c $2^3 \times 2^2$
   d $19^2 \div 19^2$

4 Work out the missing numbers.
   a $7^8 \times 7^2 = 7^\square \div 7^2$
   b $3^\square \times 3^2 = (3^2)^4$
   c $5^9 \div 5^2 = 5^\square \times 5$
   d $(2^6)^3 = 2^\square \div 2^2$

Unit 5 • Prime factorisation • Band g

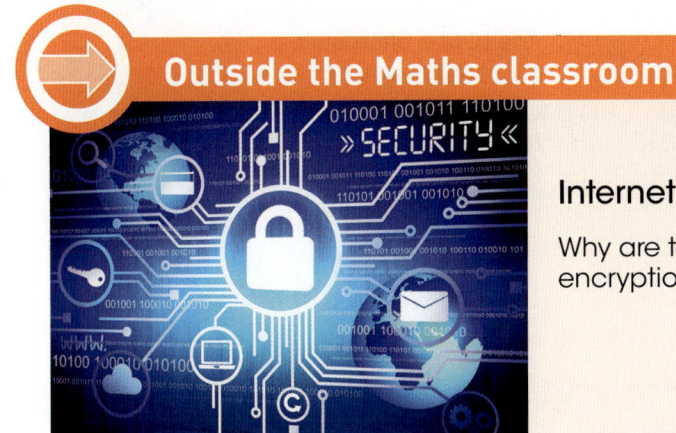

Outside the Maths classroom

Internet security

Why are telephone numbers used in code encryption?

Toolbox

The factors of a number divide into it exactly.
The factors of 12 are 1, 2, 3, 4, 6 and 12.
Prime factors are the factors of a number that are also prime numbers.
The prime factors of 12 are 2 and 3.
Every number can be written in terms of its prime factors.

Remember 1 is not a prime number.

$12 = 2 \times 2 \times 3 = 2^2 \times 3$

A factor tree is often used to write a number as a **product of its prime factors**.

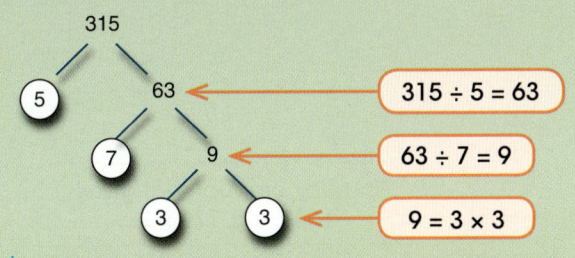

Factor tree for 315:
- 315 → 5, 63 ($315 \div 5 = 63$)
- 63 → 7, 9 ($63 \div 7 = 9$)
- 9 → 3, 3 ($9 = 3 \times 3$)

From this diagram, you can see that $315 = 5 \times 7 \times 3 \times 3 = 3^2 \times 5 \times 7$.

Any number's set of prime factors is unique. A different set of prime factors will give a different number.

The **highest common factor (HCF)** of two numbers is the largest factor that they share.
You can find the HCF of two numbers by listing their factors, as in this example for 20 and 30.

Factors of 20   1   2   4   5   ⑩   20
Factors of 30   1   2   3   5   6   ⑩   15   30

The highest number in both lists is 10 and this is the HCF. *The HCF is often quite a small number.*

Number Strand 7 Number properties

The **lowest common multiple (LCM)** of two numbers is the lowest multiple that they share.
You can find the LCM of two numbers by listing their multiples, as in this example, again using 20 and 30.

Multiples of 20   20   40   60   80   100
Multiples of 30   30   60   90   120   150

The lowest number in both lists is 60 and this is the LCM.

The LCM is often quite a large number.

Another way of finding the HCF and LCM of two numbers is to place their prime factors in a Venn diagram. In the following example this is done for 315 and 270.

$315 = 3 \times 3 \times 5 \times 7$ $\qquad\qquad 270 = 2 \times 3 \times 3 \times 3 \times 5$

Placing these factors in a Venn diagram gives

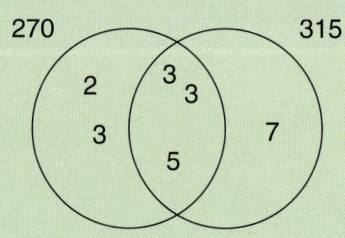

The HCF is found by multiplying the numbers in the intersection:

$\qquad 3 \times 3 \times 5 = 45$

The LCM is found by multiplying all of the numbers in the diagram:

$\qquad 2 \times 3 \times 3 \times 3 \times 5 \times 7 = 1890$

Example – Finding prime factors using a factor tree

Write 1540 as a product of its prime factors.

Solution

Using a factor tree:

Find any product that gives 1540, e.g. 770 × 2.

Find any product that gives 770, e.g. 77 × 10.

Stop when all the factors are prime numbers.

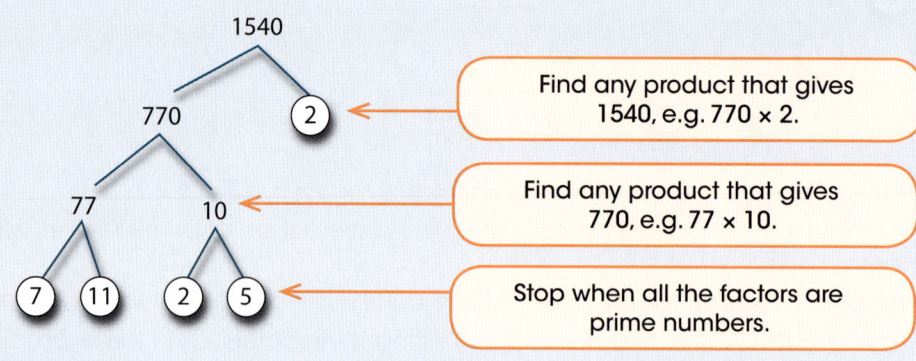

So $1540 = 7 \times 11 \times 2 \times 5 \times 2$
$\qquad\quad = 2^2 \times 5 \times 7 \times 11$

Unit 5 Prime factorisation Band g

Example – Prime factors

a Find the prime factors of 24 and 90 and display this information on a Venn diagram.
b List the multiples and factors of 24 and 90.
c Use your answers to **a** and **b** to identify the HCF and LCM.

Solution

a The prime factors of 24 are $2 \times 2 \times 2 \times 3 = 2^3 \times 3$.
The prime factors of 90 are $2 \times 3 \times 3 \times 5 = 2 \times 3^2 \times 5$.
On a Venn diagram these are placed like this.

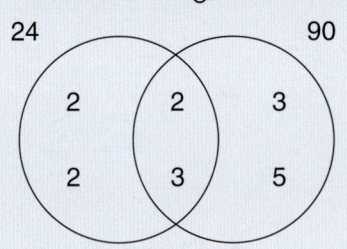

24　　　　　　90

(Venn diagram: left only: 2, 2; intersection: 2, 3; right only: 3, 5)

HCF = 2 × 3 = 6　← The numbers in the intersection give the HCF.

LCM = 2 × 2 × 2 × 3 × 3 × 5 = 360　← All the numbers are needed for the LCM.

b Factors of 24　　　1　2　3　4　6　8　12　24
   Factors of 90　　　1　2　3　5　6　9　10　15　18　30　45　90
   Multiples of 24　　24　48　72　96　120　144　168　192　216　240　264　288
   　　　　　　　　　312　334　360　384
   Multiples of 90　　90　180　270　360　450 …

c The HCF is 6.　← The highest number which is in both lists is 6.

This is found from the intersection of the Venn diagram.
2 × 3 = 6

The LCM is 360.　← 360 is the first number which is in both lists.

This is found by multiplying the numbers in the Venn diagram.
2 × 2 × 2 × 3 × 3 × 5 = 360

Practising skills

1 Find these numbers. They have been written as the products of their prime factors.

a □ = 2 × 3 × 5
b □ = 2 × 5 × 11
c □ = $2^2 \times 3$
d □ = 2×3^2
e □ = 3×5^2
f □ = 2×5^3
g □ = $3 \times 5 \times 7^2$
h □ = $3^3 \times 5^2 \times 7$

2 Write each of these numbers as a product of its prime factors, in index form.

a 60
b 126
c 100
d 54
e 225
f 154
g 105
h 495
i 300
j 405
k 500
l 624

Number Strand 7 Number properties

3 a Write down all the factors of 12.
  b Write down all the factors of 20.
  c Which numbers are common factors of 12 and 20?
  d What is the highest common factor (HCF) of 12 and 20?

4 Find the HCF of each pair.
  a 6 and 10   **b** 15 and 20   **c** 24 and 30   **d** 9 and 18
  e 16 and 24   **f** 26 and 52   **g** 40 and 75   **h** 36 and 54
  i 48 and 60   **j** 29 and 37   **k** 66 and 154   **l** 51 and 85

5 a Write down the first ten multiples of 6.
  b Write down the first ten multiples of 8.
  c Which numbers are common multiples of 6 and 8?
  d What is the lowest common multiple (LCM) of 6 and 8?

6 Find the LCM of each pair.
  a 6 and 9   **b** 5 and 8   **c** 7 and 10   **d** 12 and 20
  e 6 and 14   **f** 15 and 30   **g** 16 and 10   **h** 5 and 13
  i 24 and 40   **j** 50 and 60   **k** 18 and 27   **l** 30 and 36

Developing fluency

1 Work out the missing numbers in these.
  a $2 \times 3^{\square} \times 7^2 = 882$
  b $2^{\square} \times 3 \times 5^2 = 1200$
  c $3 \times \square^3 \times 11 = 4125$
  d $\square^{\square} \times 7 \times \square = 5824$

2 a Write 60 as a product of its prime factors.
  b Write 126 as a product of its prime factors.
  c Place the prime factors in a Venn diagram.
  d Find the HCF of 60 and 126.
  e Find the LCM of 60 and 126.

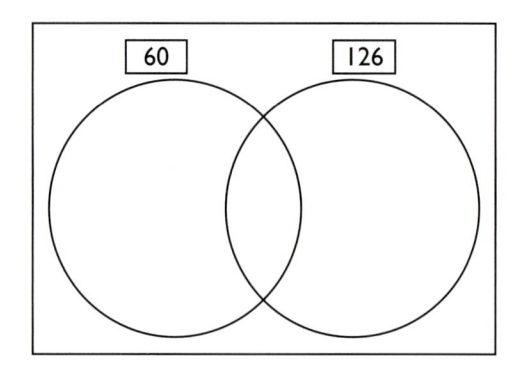

3 a Write 180 as a product of its prime factors.
  b Write 63 as a product of its prime factors.
  c Place the prime factors in a Venn diagram.
  d Find the HCF of 180 and 63.
  e Find the LCM of 180 and 63.

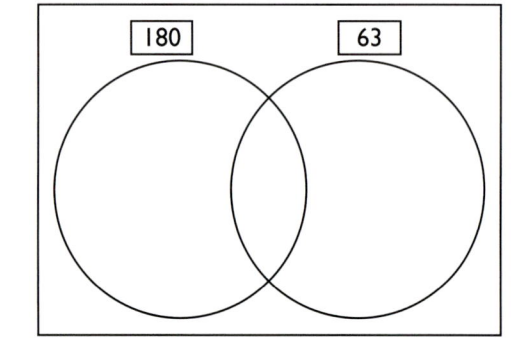

4) Find the HCF and LCM of each set of numbers.
   a 12, 20 and 28
   b 45, 60 and 90
   c 168, 700 and 1470
   d 210, 490 and 875

5) Amy is in hospital. Her medication consists of:
   paracetamol, 2 tablets to be taken every 4 hours
   antibiotics, 1 tablet every 3 hours
   steroids, 1 injection every 6 hours.
   At 8.30 a.m. this morning, Amy had all three of her medications. When will Amy next have all three medications at the same time?

6) a Work out these numbers.
   i 3×37
   ii 11×101
   iii $7 \times 11 \times 13$
   iv 41×271

   b Write 111 111 as the product of its prime factors.

Problem solving

1) Nadir is planning a party. She wants to buy some samosas, some sausage rolls and some cakes. The table shows the quantities and costs of each item.

	Samosas	Sausage rolls	Cakes
Number in a box	24	16	18
Cost per box	£5.80	£2.50	£7.10

Nadir wants to buy exactly the same number of samosas, sausage rolls and cakes so that each of the people at the party will have one of each. She has £120 to spend on this food.
Does she have enough money to buy the food she needs?

2) Linda has her car serviced every 6000 miles. Here are some of the checks they carry out.

Check	Required every
Brake fluid	6000 miles
Change oil filter	12 000 miles
Tyres	6000 miles
Wiper blades	18 000 miles
Change timing belt	24 000 miles

How many miles does the car travel before it has a service that includes all five checks?

3) Bradley and Mark cycle around a cycle track. Each lap Bradley cycles takes him 50 seconds. Each lap Mark cycles takes him 80 seconds.
Mark and Bradley start cycling at the same time at the start line. How many laps behind Bradley will Mark be when they are next at the start line together?

Number Strand 7 Number properties

4 The map shows the route of a charity walk.

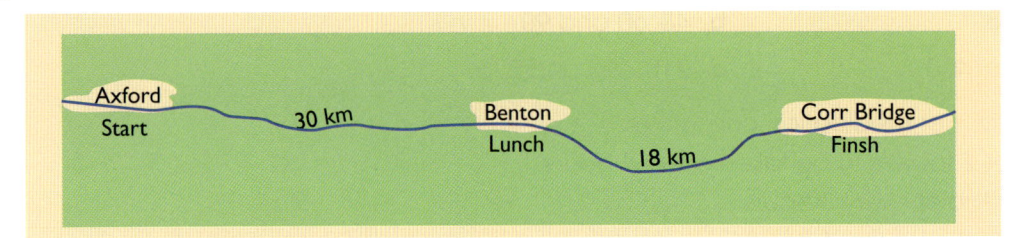

Axford Start — 30 km — Benton Lunch — 18 km — Corr Bridge Finish

Marshals stand at equally spaced intervals along the route, including the lunch stop, the start and the finish. The distance between marshals is always a whole number of kilometres.

What is the smallest possible number of marshals?

5 Buses to Ashinton leave a bus station every 28 minutes. Buses to Cardsbury leave the same bus station every 35 minutes.

A bus to Ashinton and a bus to Cardsbury both leave the bus station at 08:15. These are the first buses of the day to leave the bus station. The last bus of the day to leave this bus station leaves at 22:45.

How many times during the day will a bus to Ashinton and a bus to Cardsbury leave the bus station at the same time?

6 Nomsa is reading a book about numbers. It says, 'Every number has just one set of prime factors.'

Nomsa says, 'That's not true. I can factorise the number 24 871 in two completely different ways. It can be 209 × 119 or it can be 187 × 133.'

Explain the mistake in Nomsa's reasoning.

Reviewing skills

1 Work out these numbers. They have been written as the products of their prime factors.
   a $2^2 \times 5$
   b $2^4 \times 5^2$
   c $2 \times 3 \times 5 \times 7 \times 11$
   d $2^2 \times 3 \times 5^2 \times 7 \times 11$
   e $2^4 \times 3 \times 5^4 \times 7 \times 11$

2 Write each number as a product of its prime factors, using index form.
   a 90
   b 165
   c 770
   d 819
   e 1400
   f 1750
   g 1584
   h 2912

3 a Write down all the prime factors of 54 and 60, using index form.
   b Find the highest common factor (HCF) of 54 and 60.
   c Find the lowest common multiple (LCM) of 54 and 60.

Unit 6 • Rules of indices • Band h

Outside the Maths classroom

Estate agents
How big is a house that has a floor area of 151 square metres?

Toolbox

The rules of indices can be used provided the base number is the same in all numbers used.

$$a^m \times a^n = a^{m+n}$$
$$a^m \div a^n = a^{m-n}$$
$$(a^m)^n = a^{mn}$$

Powers are repeated multiplication.
Looking at the pattern helps you to understand what happens if the power is negative.

$4^3 = 4 \times 4 \times 4 = 64$
$4^2 = 4 \times 4 = 16$
$4^1 = 4$
$4^0 = 1$
$4^{-1} = \left(\dfrac{1}{4}\right)^1 = \dfrac{1}{4}$
$4^{-2} = \left(\dfrac{1}{4}\right)^2 = \dfrac{1}{16}$
$4^{-3} = \left(\dfrac{1}{4}\right)^3 = \dfrac{1}{64}$

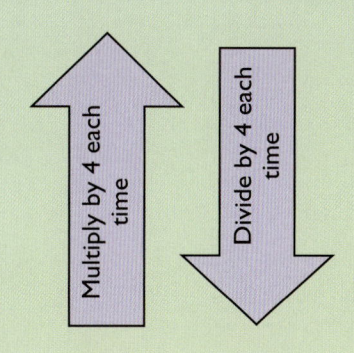

Multiply by 4 each time ↑

Divide by 4 each time ↓

It is helpful to know common square and cube numbers.

$1^2 = 1$	$11^2 = 121$	$1^3 = 1$
$2^2 = 4$	$12^2 = 144$	$2^3 = 8$
$3^2 = 9$	$13^2 = 169$	$3^3 = 27$
$4^2 = 16$	$14^2 = 196$	$4^3 = 64$
$5^2 = 25$	$15^2 = 225$	$5^3 = 125$
$6^2 = 36$		$6^3 = 216$
$7^2 = 49$		$7^3 = 343$
$8^2 = 64$		$8^3 = 512$
$9^2 = 81$		$9^3 = 729$
$10^2 = 100$		$10^3 = 1000$

Example – Using the rules of indices

Calculate the following.
Give your answers using indices.

a $6^4 \times 6^9$
b $6^9 \div 6^4$
c $6^4 \div 6^9$
d $(6^4)^9$
e How many times bigger is your answer to **b** than your answer to **c**?

Solution

a $6^4 \times 6^9 = 6^{(4+9)}$
   $= 6^{13}$
b $6^9 \div 6^4 = 6^{(9-4)}$
   $= 6^5$
c $6^4 \div 6^9 = 6^{-5}$
d $(6^4)^9 = 6^{(4 \times 9)}$
   $= 6^{36}$
e $6^5 \div 6^{-5} = 6^{(5-(-5))}$
   $= 6^{10}$
f 6^5 is 6^{10} times bigger than 6^{-5}.

Practising skills

1 a Copy and complete this table.

Index form	In full	Ordinary number
2^5	$2 \times 2 \times 2 \times 2 \times 2$	32
2^4	$2 \times 2 \times 2 \times 2$	16
2^3		
2^2		
2^1		
2^0		1
2^{-1}	$\dfrac{1}{2}$	$\dfrac{1}{2}$
2^{-2}	$\dfrac{1}{2 \times 2}$	
2^{-3}	$\dfrac{1}{2 \times 2 \times 2}$	

b Write down the value of
  i 2^7
  ii 2^{-4}.

2 a Copy and complete this table.

Index form	In full	Ordinary number	In words
10^3	$10 \times 10 \times 10$	1000	One thousand
10^2			
10^1			
10^0		1	
10^{-1}	$\dfrac{1}{10}$	$\dfrac{1}{10}$	
10^{-2}	$\dfrac{1}{10 \times 10}$		
10^{-3}			One thousandth

b Write 10^6 as a number and in words.

c Write 10^{-6} as a decimal and in words.

3 Jasmine is working out $2^2 \times 2^4$.
This is what she writes.

a Use Jasmine's style to write out the answers to these calculations.
  i $3^2 \times 3^3$
  ii $5^4 \times 5^2$
  iii $10^3 \times 10^4$

b Copy and complete the rule for multiplying numbers in index form, $a^m \times a^n = \square$

$$2^2 \times 2^4$$
$$2 \times 2 \times 2 \times 2 \times 2 \times 2$$
$$2^6 \quad \text{Answer}$$
Check
$$4 \times 16$$
$$64$$
and $2^6 = 64$ ✓

Number Strand 7 Number properties

4) Multiply the following. Give your answers both in index form and as ordinary numbers.
  a $2^3 \times 2^3$
  b $3^4 \times 3^2$
  c 5×5^2
  d $5^5 \times 5^{-2}$

5) Niamh is working out $3^5 \div 3^2$.
This is what she writes.

  a Use Niamh's style to write out the answers to these calculations.
  i $3^6 \div 3^4$
  ii $5^4 \div 5^3$
  iii $10^5 \times 10^2$

  b Copy and complete the rule for dividing numbers in index form, $a^m \div a^n = \square$

$3^5 \div 3^2$

$\dfrac{3 \times 3 \times \cancel{3} \times \cancel{3} \times \cancel{3}}{\cancel{3} \times \cancel{3}}$

3^3 Answer

Check
$243 \div 9 = 27$
$3^3 = 27$ ✓

6) Carry out these divisions. Give your answers both in index form and as ordinary numbers.
  a $2^6 \div 2^3$
  b $3^4 \div 3^3$
  c $10^6 \div 10^3$
  d $5 \div 5^{-2}$

7) Sanjay is working out $(7^2)^3$.
This is what he writes.

  a Use Sanjay's style to work these out.
  i $(2^4)^3$
  ii $(3^2)^5$
  iii $(10^3)^2$

  b State a rule for simplifying numbers in the form $(a^m)^n$.

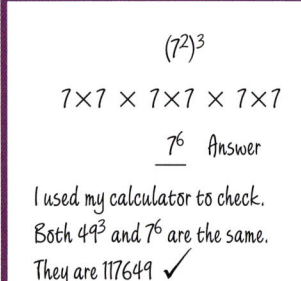

$(7^2)^3$

$7 \times 7 \times 7 \times 7 \times 7 \times 7$

7^6 Answer

I used my calculator to check.
Both 49^3 and 7^6 are the same.
They are 117649 ✓

8) Simplify the following. Give your answers both in index form and as ordinary numbers.
  a $(2^2)^5$
  b $(2^5)^2$
  c $(10^3)^4$
  d $(10^2)^6$

Developing fluency

1) Without using a calculator, decide which numbers in each pair is larger, or whether they are equal in value.
  a 2^1 or 1^2
  b 2^3 or 3^2
  c 2^4 or 4^2
  d 2^5 or 5^2
  e 2^6 or 6^2
  f 2^{-1} or 1^{-2}
  g 2^{-3} or 3^{-2}
  h 2^{-4} or 4^{-2}

2) You are given that $5^a \times 5^b = 5^{10}$.
How many different pairs of values can you find for a and b if they
  a are both positive whole numbers
  b can be any whole numbers, positive or negative?

3) Work out the following. Give your answers in index form.
  a $3^2 \times 3^4 \times 3^7$
  b $2^3 \times 2^4 \times 2^5$
  c $10 \times 10^2 \times 10^3$
  d $5^4 \times 5 \times 5$

4) Work out the following. Give your answers in index form.
  a $6^7 \times 6^4 \div 6^2$
  b $6^7 \times 6^4 \times 6^{-2}$
  c $(6^7 \times 6^4)^2$
  d $(6^{-7} \times 6^{-4} \div 6^{-2})^{-1}$

5 Work out the following. Give your answers in index form.

a $\dfrac{3^6 \times 3^7}{3^8}$
b $3^6 \times 3^7 \div 3^{-8}$
c $\dfrac{3^3 \times 3^{10}}{3^4 \times 3^4}$
d $\dfrac{3^3 \times (3^2)^5}{(3^2)^4}$

6 Work out the following. Give your answers in index form.

a $2^3 \times (2^5 - 2^5)$
b $2^3 \times (2^5 + 2^5)$
c $2^8 \div (2^5 \div 2^3)$
d $\dfrac{3^4}{(3^3 + 3^3 + 3^3)}$

7 Place these numbers in order of size, largest first. If two or more are the same size, put them together.

a 2^5
b 5^2
c 19^0
d $\dfrac{3^2 \times 3^5}{3^7}$

e $\dfrac{2^4}{2^7}$
f $10^3 \div 10^4$
g $\left(\dfrac{3^7}{3^6}\right)^3$
h $\left(\dfrac{3^6}{3^7}\right)^{-3}$

i $\dfrac{2^4 + 2^5}{2^0}$
j $\dfrac{10^2 \times 10^3}{10^4 \times 10^4}$

8 Marged says, 'I know that 2^{10} is just over a thousand. So 2^{20} must be just over a million and 2^{40} must be just over a billion.'

How much of Marged's statement is correct? Use the rules of indices to explain your answer.

Problem solving

1 Here are some powers of x.

x^{-2} x^4 x^{-1}

a Select two of them (you can have the same one twice if you want) and either multiply them or divide them.

b How many different answers can you make?

c Can you choose another set of three indices that will give you a greater number of different answers?

Reviewing skills

1 Work out the following. Give your answers in index form.

a $5^2 \times 5^3 \div 5^4$
b $\dfrac{5^2 \times 5^3}{5^4}$
c $5^2 \times 5^3 \times 5^{-4}$

2 Work out the following. Give your answers in index form.

a $\dfrac{10^3 \times 10^3}{10^8}$
b $10^2 \times 10^2 \times 10^3 \times 10^{-8}$
c $\dfrac{(10^2)^3}{(10^2)^4}$

3 Work out the following. Give your answers in index form.

a $(2^3)^4 \div 2^{10}$
b $(7^3)^5 \times (7^{-2})^7$
c $\dfrac{(10^{-6})^2}{(10^{-3})^4}$

4 Use the rules of indices to show that $23^0 = 1$.

Unit 7 • Fractional indices • Band i

Outside the Maths classroom

	A	B	C	D	E
1	Period of investment in years	Interest rate needed for investment to grow by:			
2		25%	50%	75%	100%
3	1	25%	50%	75%	100%
4	2	12%	22%	32%	41%
5	3	8%	14%	21%	26%
6	4	6%	11%	15%	19%
7	5	5%	8%	12%	15%
8	6	4%	7%	10%	12%
9	7	3%	6%	8%	10%
10	8	3%	5%	7%	9%
11	9	3%	5%	6%	8%
12	10	2%	4%	6%	7%

Investment

What formula tells you the interest rate required for your investment to double in 5 years?

Toolbox

You know that when you multiply numbers in index form, you add the powers

So $a^{\frac{1}{3}} \times a^{\frac{1}{3}} \times a^{\frac{1}{3}} = a^{\frac{1}{3}+\frac{1}{3}+\frac{1}{3}} = a^1 = a$

So $a^{\frac{1}{3}}$ means the cube root of a.

Example: $27^{\frac{1}{3}} = 3$, since $3^3 = 27$.

In the same way $a^{\frac{1}{7}}$ is the 7th root of a.

Example: $128^{\frac{1}{7}} = 2$, since $2^7 = 128$.

In general $a^{\frac{1}{n}}$ **is the nth root of a.**

Now look at $a^{\frac{2}{3}}$

This can be written $(a^{\frac{1}{3}})^2$ or $(a^2)^{\frac{1}{3}}$.

Example: $8^{\frac{2}{3}}$ can be written $(8^{\frac{1}{3}})^2$ or $(8^2)^{\frac{1}{3}}$

2^2 or $64^{\frac{1}{3}}$

4 or 4 ← $4^3 = 64$

In general $a^{\frac{m}{n}}$ is

either $(a^{\frac{1}{n}})^m$, the nth root of a, raised to the power m.

or $(a^m)^{\frac{1}{n}}$, the nth root of a^m.

Unit 7 Fractional indices Band i

Example – Unit fractions as indices

Without using a calculator simplify:

a $32^{\frac{1}{5}}$

b $(1000\,000)^{\frac{1}{6}} - (1000)^{\frac{1}{3}}$

Solution

a $32 = 2 \times 2 \times 2 \times 2 \times 2 = 2^5$

So $(32)^{\frac{1}{5}} = (2^5)^{\frac{1}{5}} = 2^1 = 2$

b $(1000\,000)^{\frac{1}{6}} = (10 \times 10 \times 10 \times 10 \times 10 \times 10)^{\frac{1}{6}}$

$(10^6)^{\frac{1}{6}} = 10^1 = 10$

$(1000)^{\frac{1}{3}} = (10 \times 10 \times 10)^{\frac{1}{3}} = 10^1 = 10$

So $(1000\,000)^{\frac{1}{6}} - (1000)^{\frac{1}{3}} = 10 - 10 = 0$

Example – Simplifying fractional indices

Find the value of:

a $16^{\frac{3}{2}}$

b $27^{\frac{4}{3}}$

Solution

a $16^{\frac{3}{2}} = (16^{\frac{1}{2}})^3$

$= (\sqrt{16})^3$

$= 4^3$

$= 64$

You get the same answer when you cube 16 first and then square root, but the arithmetic is harder!

b $27^{\frac{4}{3}} = (27^{\frac{1}{3}})^4$

$= (\sqrt[3]{27})^4$

$= 3^4$

$= 81$ ← $3^4 = 3^2 \times 3^2$

Number Strand 7 Number properties

Unless otherwise stated do not use a calculator.

Practising skills

1) Match the following.

$3^{\frac{1}{2}}$	$\sqrt[7]{3}$
$3^{\frac{1}{7}}$	$\sqrt[3]{2}$
$7^{\frac{1}{2}}$	$\sqrt[7]{2}$
$2^{\frac{1}{3}}$	$\sqrt{3}$
☐	$\sqrt[3]{7}$
$2^{\frac{1}{7}}$	$\sqrt[2]{7}$

Fill in the missing number.

2) Write the following as roots.

a $8^{\frac{1}{2}}$ b $11^{\frac{1}{2}}$ c $107^{\frac{1}{2}}$ d $3^{\frac{1}{9}}$ e $113^{\frac{1}{12}}$ f $18^{\frac{1}{18}}$

3) Write the following using indices.

a $\sqrt[2]{19}$ b $\sqrt{29}$ c $\sqrt[3]{15}$ d $\sqrt[3]{3}$ e $\sqrt[8]{3}$ f $\sqrt[13]{7}$

4) Copy and complete these number statements with the correct digits.

a $\square^{\frac{1}{3}} = \sqrt[\square]{8} = \square$

b $196^{\frac{1}{\square}} = \sqrt[\square]{\square\square\square} = 14$

c $\square\square^{\frac{1}{4}} = \sqrt[\square]{\square\square} = 2$

5) State the value of each of these.

a $64^{\frac{1}{2}}$ b $4^{\frac{1}{2}}$ c $100^{\frac{1}{2}}$ d $125^{\frac{1}{3}}$ e $1331^{\frac{1}{3}}$ f $225^{\frac{1}{2}}$

Unit 7 Fractional indices Band i

Developing fluency

1 Match the following.

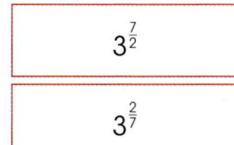

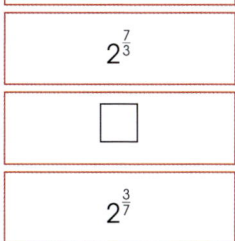

$3^{\frac{7}{2}}$	$\sqrt[7]{2^3}$
$3^{\frac{2}{7}}$	$\sqrt[3]{2^7}$
$7^{\frac{3}{2}}$	$\sqrt{3^7}$
$2^{\frac{7}{3}}$	$\sqrt[3]{7^2}$
$\square$	$\sqrt[2]{7^3}$
$2^{\frac{3}{7}}$	$\sqrt[7]{3^2}$

Fill in the missing number.

2 Write the following as roots of integers. Where possible go on to write them as integers.

a $4^{\frac{3}{2}}$ b $8^{\frac{2}{3}}$ c $625^{\frac{1}{4}}$

d $36^{\frac{3}{2}}$ e $1^{\frac{7}{9}}$ f $32^{\frac{2}{5}}$

3 Write the following using indices

a $\sqrt[2]{75}$ b $\sqrt{11^3}$ c $\sqrt[3]{15^4}$

d $\sqrt[3]{3^8}$ e $\sqrt[8]{3^3}$ f $\sqrt[13]{7^{14}}$

4 Complete these number statements with the correct digits.

a $\square^{\frac{2}{3}} = \sqrt[\square]{8^{\square}} = \square$

b $196^{\frac{3}{\square}} = \sqrt[\square]{\square\,\square\,\square^{\square}} = 14$

c $\square\square^{\frac{3}{\square}} = \sqrt[\square]{\square\,\square^{\square}} = 2^{\square} = 8$

5 Arrange the digits 3, 4 and 5 into the frame so that the result is:

a as large as possible

b as small as possible.

$\square^{\frac{\square}{\square}}$

6 Place three different digits in the frame so that the result is:

a 2
b 3
c 4.

$\square^{\frac{\square}{\square}}$

Number Strand 7 Number properties

Problem solving

1) Write these numbers in order of size, smallest to largest.

   a $8^{\frac{2}{3}}$ **b** $9^{\frac{3}{2}}$ **c** $81^{\frac{1}{4}}$ **d** $3025^{\frac{2}{5}}$ **e** $128^{\frac{4}{7}}$

2) **a** Show that $a = b^{\frac{a}{b}}$ if $a = b$.

   b Find values of a and b that are not equal for which $a = b^{\frac{a}{b}}$.

3) A cube has volume V cm³ and surface area A cm².

   a Prove that $A = 6V^{\frac{2}{3}}$.   **b** Make V the subject of this equation.

4) In this question give your answers to three significant figures.

   The time T years that it takes a planet at a mean distance R million kilometres from the Sun to complete one orbit of the Sun is given closely by $T = 0.000544 \times R^{\frac{3}{2}}$

   a The Earth is 150 million kilometres from the Sun.
   Use the formula to find how many years it takes the Earth to complete the orbit.

   b Jupiter is 779 million kilometres from the Sun. How long does it take Jupiter to complete one orbit?

   c It takes Venus 224.7 days to complete one orbit. How far is it from the Sun?

5) Here is a product pyramid. To work out the number in a box you multiply the numbers in the two boxes below it.

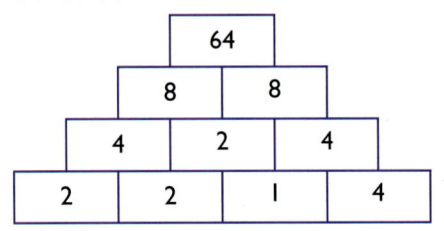

   ```
              64
           8     8
         4    2    4
       2   2    1    4
   ```

   All of the pyramids below are equivalent to the one above.

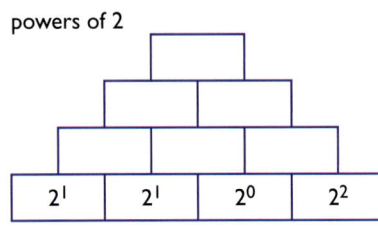

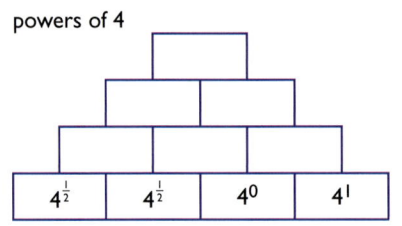

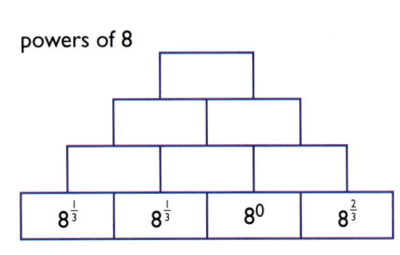

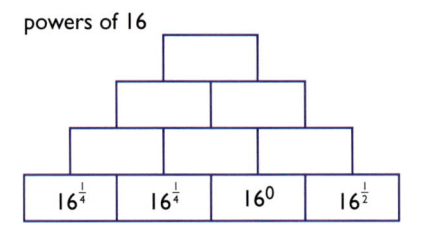

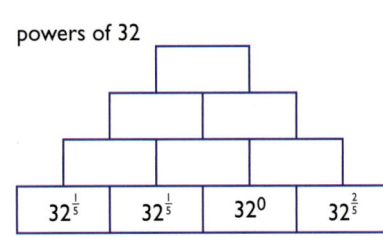

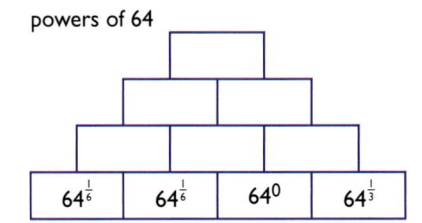

   powers of 2: 2^1, 2^1, 2^0, 2^2

   powers of 4: $4^{\frac{1}{2}}$, $4^{\frac{1}{2}}$, 4^0, 4^1

   powers of 8: $8^{\frac{1}{3}}$, $8^{\frac{1}{3}}$, 8^0, $8^{\frac{2}{3}}$

   powers of 16: $16^{\frac{1}{4}}$, $16^{\frac{1}{4}}$, 16^0, $16^{\frac{1}{2}}$

   powers of 32: $32^{\frac{1}{5}}$, $32^{\frac{1}{5}}$, 32^0, $32^{\frac{2}{5}}$

   powers of 64: $64^{\frac{1}{6}}$, $64^{\frac{1}{6}}$, 64^0, $64^{\frac{1}{3}}$

Complete them, giving each one as a power of the same number.
Check that all of the top numbers are equivalent to 64.

Reviewing skills

1 Match the terms on the top row with the equivalent term on the bottom row.

$5^{\frac{1}{2}}$	$3^{\frac{5}{2}}$	$5^{\frac{2}{3}}$	$3^{\frac{2}{5}}$	$3^{\frac{1}{2}}$	$2^{\frac{2}{3}}$	$2^{\frac{5}{3}}$	$5^{\frac{3}{2}}$	$2^{\frac{1}{2}}$
$\sqrt[5]{3^2}$	$\sqrt[3]{5^2}$	$\sqrt{3}$	$\sqrt{2}$	$\sqrt[3]{2^5}$	$\sqrt{5}$	$\sqrt{5^3}$	$\sqrt[3]{2^2}$	$\sqrt{3^5}$

2 Find the value of
   a $16^{\frac{1}{2}}$
   b $9^{\frac{3}{2}}$
   c $8^{\frac{2}{3}}$

3 Complete these statements.
   a $\square^{\frac{1}{3}} = 2$
   b $25^{\frac{3}{\square}} = (\sqrt{})= \square$
   c $32^{\frac{\square}{5}} = 8$

Algebra Strand 1 Starting algebra

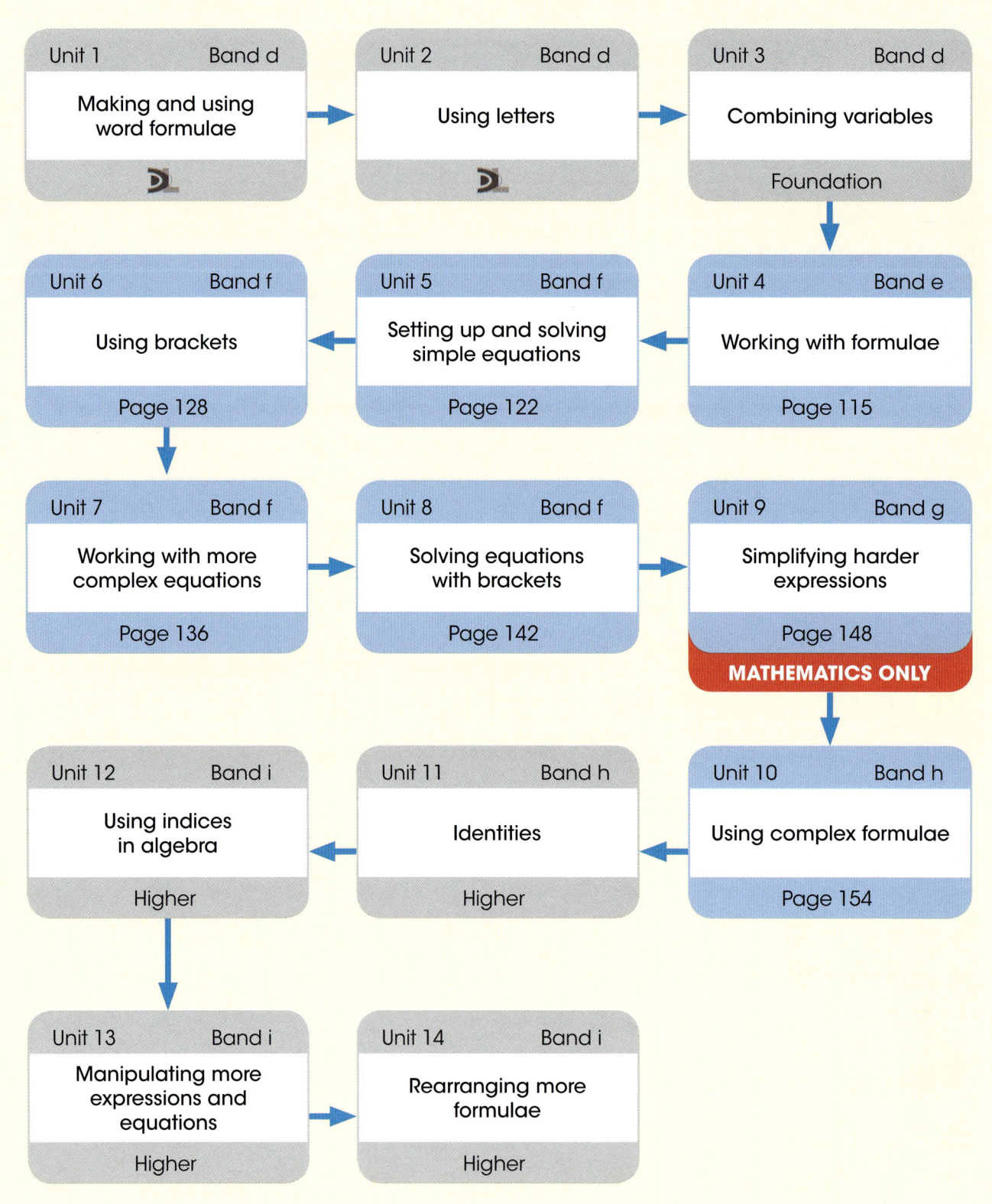

Unit 1 — Band d	Unit 2 — Band d	Unit 3 — Band d
Making and using word formulae	Using letters	Combining variables
		Foundation

Unit 6 — Band f	Unit 5 — Band f	Unit 4 — Band e
Using brackets	Setting up and solving simple equations	Working with formulae
Page 128	Page 122	Page 115

Unit 7 — Band f	Unit 8 — Band f	Unit 9 — Band g
Working with more complex equations	Solving equations with brackets	Simplifying harder expressions
Page 136	Page 142	Page 148 — MATHEMATICS ONLY

Unit 12 — Band i	Unit 11 — Band h	Unit 10 — Band h
Using indices in algebra	Identities	Using complex formulae
Higher	Higher	Page 154

Unit 13 — Band i	Unit 14 — Band i
Manipulating more expressions and equations	Rearranging more formulae
Higher	Higher

Units 1–3 are assumed knowledge for this book. Knowledge and skills from these units are used throughout the book.

Unit 4 • Working with formulae • Band e

Outside the Maths classroom

Building regulations
What are the regulations about the size of steps?

Toolbox

Number machines can help you work with formulae.

The cost, C pence, of a bus ticket for a journey of m miles is given by the formula

$$C = 20m + 50$$

You can write this using a number machine.

$m \longrightarrow \boxed{\times 20} \xrightarrow{20m} \boxed{+ 50} \longrightarrow 20m + 50 = C$

For a journey of 7 miles, $m = 7$.

$7 \longrightarrow \boxed{\times 20} \xrightarrow{140} \boxed{+ 50} \longrightarrow 190$

The cost is 190 pence or £1.90.

You can use a number machine in reverse.

This will tell you the number of miles you can travel for a certain amount of money.

Work from right to left with the **inverse operations**.

So, for a fare of £1.30, the number machine looks like this.

$4 \longleftarrow \boxed{\div 20} \xleftarrow{80} \boxed{- 50} \longleftarrow 130$

You can travel 4 miles.

Algebra Strand 1 Starting algebra

Example – Changing a formula

The Williams family are going on holiday to Florida.
a The exchange rate is 1.6 dollars to the pound.
  Write a formula to represent this information.
b They wish to take $1200 with them.
  How many pounds should they change into dollars?

Solution

a Number of dollars = number of pounds × 1.6
  If D is the number of dollars and P is the number of pounds then $D = 1.6P$
b The formula is used in reverse to find the number of pounds.
Number of pounds = number of dollars ÷ 1.6
$$= 1200 ÷ 1.6$$
$$= 750$$
They need to change £750 into dollars.

> To find the number of dollars you multiplied by 1.6, so to find the number of pounds you must divide by 1.6.

Example – Substituting values into a formula

This formula gives p in terms of e and g.
$$p = \frac{3e - g}{4}$$
Find the values of p when
a $e = 4$ and $g = 0$
b $e = 5$ and $g = 7$
c $e = 8$ and $g = 20$
d $e = 4$ and $g = 12$
e $e = 100$ and $g = 296$

Solution

a $\frac{3e - g}{4} = \frac{3 \times 4 - 0}{4}$ ← Substitute the values given for the variables.

$= \frac{12 - 0}{4} = \frac{12}{4} = 4$ ← Calculate the numerator first.

b $\frac{3e - g}{4} = \frac{3 \times 5 - 7}{4}$

$= \frac{15 - 7}{4} = \frac{8}{4} = 2$

c $\frac{3e - g}{4} = \frac{3 \times 8 - 20}{4}$

$= \frac{24 - 20}{4} = \frac{4}{4} = 1$

d $\frac{3e - g}{4} = \frac{3 \times 4 - 12}{4}$

$= \frac{12 - 12}{4} = \frac{0}{4} = 0$

e $\frac{3e - g}{4} = \frac{3 \times 100 - 296}{4}$

$= \frac{300 - 296}{4} = \frac{4}{4} = 1$

Unit 4 Working with formulae Band e

Example – Using number machines

A train company uses a formula to work out the time, t minutes, for a rail journey from London to Plymouth.
The number of stops along the way is s.

$$t = 5s + 165$$

a Use a number machine to find the time for a journey with seven stops.
b A train takes 3 hours and 10 minutes to travel from Plymouth to London. How many stops did it make?

Solution

a Here is the number machine for this formula.

$$s \xrightarrow{} \boxed{\times 5} \xrightarrow{5s} \boxed{+165} \xrightarrow{} 5s + 165 = t$$

When there are seven stops,

$$7 \xrightarrow{} \boxed{\times 5} \xrightarrow{35} \boxed{+165} \xrightarrow{} 200$$

It takes 200 minutes or 3 hours and 20 minutes.

b For a journey of 190 minutes, reverse the number machine.

> Convert 3 hours and 10 minutes into minutes.

$$5 \xleftarrow{} \boxed{\div 5} \xleftarrow{25} \boxed{-165} \xleftarrow{} 190$$

The train made five stops.

Practising skills

1 Find the output for each of these number machines.

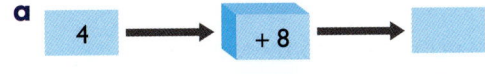

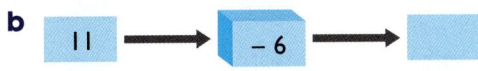

a $4 \rightarrow \boxed{+8} \rightarrow \square$

b $11 \rightarrow \boxed{-6} \rightarrow \square$

c $4 \rightarrow \boxed{\times 7} \rightarrow \square$

d $21 \rightarrow \boxed{\div 3} \rightarrow \square$

2 Work out the addition or subtraction rules for these number machines.

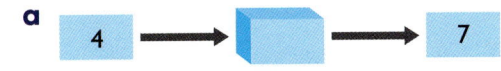

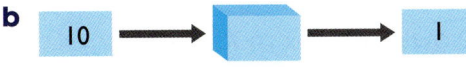

a $4 \rightarrow \boxed{} \rightarrow 7$

b $10 \rightarrow \boxed{} \rightarrow 1$

c $6 \rightarrow \boxed{} \rightarrow 5$

d $17 \rightarrow \boxed{} \rightarrow 31$

3 Write down the opposite of these.

   a turn left
   b sit down
   c turn 68° anti-clockwise
   d walk 6 steps forward

4 Write down the inverse of each of these operations.

   a $+7$
   b -4
   c $+129$
   d $\times 5$
   e $\times 3.9$
   f $\div 8$
   g $\div 0.5$

Algebra Strand 1 Starting algebra

5 The number machines in question 2 can be written the other way.
Work out the new addition or subtraction rules for these number machines.

a 4 ← ☐ ← 7
b 10 ← ☐ ← 1
c 6 ← ☐ ← 5
d 17 ← ☐ ← 31

6 Dyfan pays £1.40 for each litre of petrol.
   a How much does he pay for 37 litres?
   b Copy and complete this number machine to work out how much he pays for his petrol.

   Number of litres → ☐ → Cost of fuel

   c Dyfan pays £78.40 for petrol. Reverse your number machine to find out how many litres he buys.
   d i Emyr pays £62.16 for diesel costing £1.48 per litre. Draw a number machine to help you work out how many litres he buys.
     ii Mai pays £42.18 for diesel. How much does she buy?

Developing fluency

1 a Work out the value of y in each of the four cases below when $x = 9$.

   i $x \rightarrow \times 3 \rightarrow + 5 \rightarrow y$
   ii $x \rightarrow \times 5 \rightarrow + 3 \rightarrow y$
   iii $x \rightarrow + 5 \rightarrow \times 3 \rightarrow y$
   iv $x \rightarrow \div 3 \rightarrow + 5 \rightarrow y$

   b Match the four number machines in part **a** with the equivalent formulae below.

A	B	C	D
$y = (x + 5) \times 3$	$y = 3x + 5$	$y = \frac{1}{3}x + 5$	$y = 5x + 3$

2 a Draw a number machine for $y = 4x - 3$.
   b Draw the reverse number machine for your answer to part **a**.
   c Use your answer to part **b** to find the value of x which gives $y = 65$.

3 a Copy and complete the number machine below.

   14 → ×2 → ☐ → 37

   b Use the number machine to find the output when the input is 7.
   c Draw the reverse number machine. Use it to find the input when the output is 55.

4 Here is a number machine. Use it to complete the tables in parts **a** and **b**.

input → ×4 → −7 → output

a

Input	Output
3	
10	
7	
1	

b

Input	Output
	41
	17
	73
	−7

5 In a city the cost of a taxi journey in euros is worked out using these steps.
Multiply the number of kilometres by 2.
Add 3.

   a Find the cost of these journeys.
      i 10 km   **ii** 20 km

   b Find the length of a journey costing €27.

   c Write down a formula connecting the cost €c and the length of the journey, d km.

6 The exchange rate for pounds and euros is £1 = €1.15.

   a Work out how many euros you will get for these amounts in pounds.
      i £100   **ii** £25   **iii** £40   **iv** £2000

   b Work out how many pounds you will get for these amounts in euros.
      i €23   **ii** €460   **iii** €1840   **iv** €9200

7 This formula gives the cost, $C(£)$, of buying n tickets for a football match.
$C = 18n$

   a Work out the cost of buying these numbers of tickets.
      i 30   **ii** 45   **iii** 124   **iv** 356

   b Work out how many tickets can be bought for these amounts.
      i £1548   **ii** £414   **iii** £2556   **iv** £634

8 Here is a formula to work out the time, T minutes, to cook a piece of meat of weight, w kg.
$T = 15w + 12$

   a For how long should a 4 kg piece of meat be cooked?

   b What weight of meat takes 102 minutes to cook?

Problem solving

1 Euler developed a relationship that connects the number of faces, vertices and edges of a solid shape. He worked out that

      faces + vertices = edges + 2

   a Show that this works for a cube.

   b A shape has five faces and six vertices.
      How many edges does it have?
      Draw this shape.

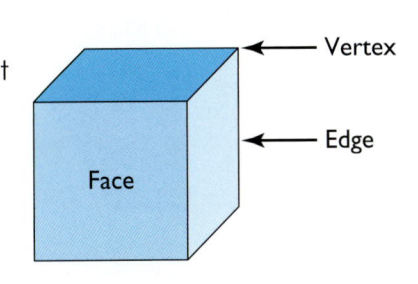

Algebra Strand 1 Starting algebra

2 Gethin uses this formula to find the perimeter of a rectangle.
$P = 2l + 2w$

   a Find the value of P when $l = 10$ and $w = 6$
   b Find the value of l when P is 20 and $w = 4$
   c A square has a perimeter of 36 cm
   Find the length of one of the sides.

3 a Ben hires a cement mixer from Mixers R Us.
   He hires the cement mixer for 10 days.
   Work out the cost.

   b The cost of hiring a mixer from Hire Shop for n days is £C. Write down a formula for C.

   c Show that the costs for 4 days are the same.

Mixers R Us — £15 a day
Hire Shop — £20 deposit then £10 a day

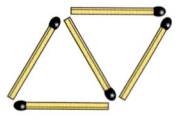

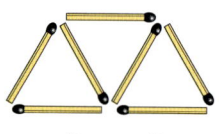

4 Here are three patterns made from sticks.

Pattern 1   Pattern 2   Pattern 3

   a Write down the number of sticks in pattern 3.
   b Write down the number of sticks in pattern 4.
   c Write down the number of sticks in pattern n.
   d Write down the number of sticks in pattern 20.

5 Here is a table that gives information about how long it takes to cook a turkey.

Weight of turkey (w), in kg	3	4	5	6
Time (t), in minutes	140	180	220	260

Siân is cooking a turkey that weighs 7.6 kg.
She wants the turkey to have finished cooking at 7 p.m.
At what time should she put the turkey into the oven?

6 In the grid at the top of the facing page you are told which quantity to work out, having been given the values of the other letters.
Start in the bottom left corner.
If an answer is a prime number then move → to the next square.
If an answer is a multiple of 10 then move ← to the next square.
If an answer is a square number then move ↑ to the next square.
If an answer is a factor of 31 then move ↓ to the next square.

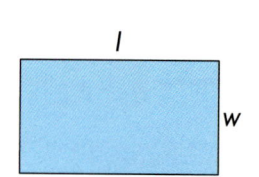

	work out $W = FD$ when $F = 14$ and $D = 17$	work out $t = \dfrac{d}{s}$ when $d = 14$ and $s = 4$	work out $t = \dfrac{s}{d}$ when $s = 15$ and $d = 6$	**FINISH**
	work out $V = IR$ when $I = 0.3$ and $R = 31$	work out $A = \dfrac{1}{2}bh$ when $b = 11$ and $h = 2$	work out $F = \dfrac{W}{D}$ when $W = 68$ and $D = 4$	work out $v = at + u$ when $a = 8$ and $t = 5$ and $u = 9$
	work out $b = \dfrac{A}{h}$ when $h = 2$ and $A = 17$	work out $d = st$ when $s = 27$ and $t = 3$	work out $P = VI$ when $I = 2.5$ and $V = 8$	work out $A = b \times h \div 2$ when $b = 5$ and $h = 7$
START here →	work out $y = 2x + 3$ when $x = 2$	work out $P = \dfrac{F}{A}$ when $F = 39$ and $A = 3$	work out $A = b \times h$ when $b = 4$ and $h = 9$	work out $s = \dfrac{d}{t}$ when $t = 15$ and $d = 45$

a Which of the formulae are equivalent to each other?

b Describe your path from the start to the finish.

Reviewing skills

1 a Draw a number machine for $C = 60d + 30$

  b Find the value of C when
    i $d = 4$ **ii** $d = 10$

  c Draw the reverse number machine.

  d Find the value of d when
    i $C = 390$ **ii** $C = 570$

2 To convert a temperature in Fahrenheit into Celsius (centigrade), you take these steps.
Subtract 32.
Multiply by 5.
Divide by 9.

  a Convert these Fahrenheit temperatures into Celsius.
    i 212° **ii** 32° **iii** 95°

  b Convert these Celsius temperatures into Fahrenheit.
    i 10° **ii** 30° **iii** 205°

3 The cost, £C, of a meal for n people at a fixed price restaurant is given by
$C = 15n + 5$

  a Work out the costs of meals for
    i 4 people **ii** 10 people

  b A meal costs £125. How many people are there?

  c Explain the numbers 5 and 15 in the formula.

Unit 5 • Setting up and solving simple equations • Band f

Outside the Maths classroom

Fencing enclosures
What factors affect the shape of a play park?

Toolbox

An **equation** says that one expression is equal to another.
For example:

$$4x - 3 = 17$$

Solving an equation means finding the value of x that makes the equation true.

You can solve an equation using the balance method.
You must keep the equation balanced, like a pair of weighing scales, by doing the *same* operation to *both* sides.

$$\begin{aligned} 4x - 3 &= 17 \\ 4x &= 20 \\ x &= 5 \end{aligned}$$

+3 / +3: The inverse of subtract 3 is add 3. Make sure you add 3 to *both* sides.

÷4 / ÷4: The inverse of multiply by 4 is divide by 4.

$x = 5$ is the solution.

Unit 5 Setting up and solving simple equations Band f

Example – Solving 'think of a number' problems

Amy thinks of a number. What is her number?

Amy: When I multiply my number by 9 and subtract 11, the answer is 52.

Solution

You can write an equation and solve it to find Amy's number.

Let n represent her number.

$$n \times 9 - 11 = 52$$
$$9n - 11 = 52$$

Using the balance method rewrite this using correct algebraic notation.

$9n - 11 = 52$ ← The inverse of subtract 11 is add 11.
$+11$ $+11$ ← Add 11 to both sides.
$9n = 63$
$\div 9$ $\div 9$ ← The inverse of multiply by 9 is divide by 9.
$n = 7$

Check: $9 \times 7 - 11 = 63 - 11 = 52$ ✓ ← Always check your work.

Example – Solving word problems

Three friends run a relay race.
Altogether their time is 65 seconds.
Harry takes 4 seconds longer than Dan.
Millie takes 5 seconds less than Dan.
How many seconds does each person take?

Solution

First write the expressions for the time each person takes.
Let s stand for the number of seconds that Dan takes.

Dan: s seconds
Harry: $s + 4$ seconds
Millie: $s - 5$ seconds
Total: 65 seconds

So,

$s + s + 4 + s - 5 = 65$ ← The total of the three expressions is 65.
$3s - 1 = 65$ ← Collect like terms.
$3s = 66$ ← Add 1 to both sides.
$s = 22$ ← Divide both sides by 3.

So Dan takes 22 seconds.
Harry takes 26 seconds. ← Harry's time is $s + 4 = 22 + 4 = 26$ seconds.
Millie takes 17 seconds. ← Millie's time is $s - 5 = 22 - 5 = 17$ seconds.
Check: $22 + 26 + 17 = 65$ ✓

Algebra Strand 1 Starting algebra

Practising skills

1 Work out the weights of the boxes.

a [balance: boxes vs 20 kg]
b [balance: boxes + 4 kg vs 25 kg]
c [balance: boxes + 2 kg vs 20 kg]
d [balance: boxes + 3 kg vs 48 kg]

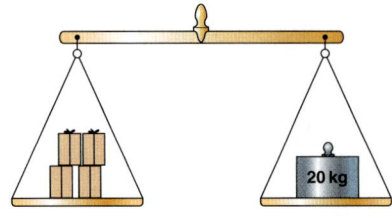

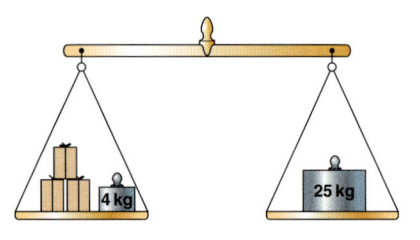

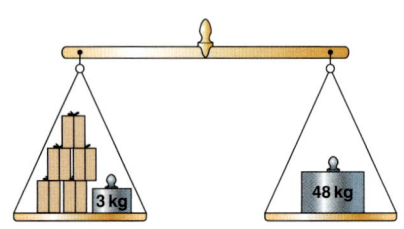

2 Solve these equations by subtracting the same number from both sides.

   a $d + 4 = 9$ **b** $f + 6 = 17$ **c** $3 + x = 7$ **d** $m + 2 = 5$

3 Solve these equations by adding the same number to both sides.

   a $x - 3 = 8$ **b** $n - 6 = 2$ **c** $p - 7 = 7$ **d** $e - 10 = 9$

4 Solve these equations.

   a $f - 6 = 1$ **b** $g + 3 = 11$ **c** $d + 1 = 6$ **d** $b - 7 = 4$

5 Solve these equations by dividing both sides by the same number.

   a $2b = 18$ **b** $5f = 30$ **c** $3x = 12$ **d** $6g = 72$

6 Solve these equations by multiplying both sides by the same number.

   a $\frac{t}{2} = 5$ **b** $\frac{y}{5} = 3$ **c** $\frac{h}{4} = 6$ **d** $\frac{d}{9} = 2$

7 Solve these equations.

   a $6s = 42$ **b** $d - 7 = 3$ **c** $a + 2 = 8$ **d** $5h = 40$
   e $\frac{x}{7} = 8$ **f** $u - 3 = 14$

8 Cynthia and Hardip both try to solve the equation $4x - 2 = 32$.

This is what they write.

Whose answer is correct? Explain what is wrong with the incorrect solution.

Cynthia
$4x - 2 = 32$
$4x - 2 + 2 = 32 + 2$
$4x = 34$
$\frac{4x}{4} = \frac{34}{4}$
$x = 8.5$

Hardip
$4x - 2 = 32$
$x - 2 = 8$
$x - 2 + 2 = 8 + 2$
$x = 10$

9 Solve these equations.

   a $3g + 4 = 25$ **b** $5h - 3 = 17$ **c** $10y - 2 = 58$ **d** $4d - 4 = 4$
   e $6s + 7 = 25$ **f** $2k + 5 = 23$ **g** $8r - 5 = 11$ **h** $7u + 9 = 37$

Developing fluency

1 Andrea is a years old and Benny is b years old.

Explain what these mean in words.

a $a + b = 21$ **b** $a = 2b$ **c** $b - a = 7$

2 Write an equation for this situation and solve it to find the number.

> I think of a number, multiply it by 5 and add 12 and the answer is 47.

3 Solve these equations.

a $-5x = -10$ **b** $-5x = 10$ **c** $10 = 5x$
d $10 + 5x = 0$ **e** $-5x - 10 = 0$ **f** $0 = 10 - 5x$

4 Match each equation with its solution.

i $2x - 9 = 15$ **ii** $8x + 3 = 19$ **iii** $5x - 1 = 54$
iv $4x + 16 = 4$ **v** $3x - 1 = -16$ **vi** $6x - 24 = 0$

| $x = 2$ | $x = 4$ | $x = 11$ | $x = -3$ | $x = 12$ | $x = -5$ |

5 Solve these equations.

a $\frac{s}{5} = 12$ **b** $\frac{f}{2} = 8$ **c** $\frac{g}{3} = -3$ **d** $\frac{x}{6} + 3 = 6$
e $\frac{t}{4} - 1 = -2$ **f** $\frac{u}{10} + 6 = 18$ **g** $\frac{v}{12} + 4 = 4$ **h** $\frac{y}{12} + 4 = -4$

6 Grace buys eight text books and a teachers' guide costing £24. The total cost is £138. Write an equation for this situation and solve it to find the price of a text book.

7 Alys bought a £28 railcard and two adult train tickets and the total came to £204. Write an equation for this situation and solve it to find the price of an adult ticket.

8 Glyn buys two oranges at 32p each and four apples. The total comes to £1.72. Write an equation for this situation and solve it to find the price of an apple.

9 Solve these equations.

a $s + 6.8 = 14.2$ **b** $5f = 7.8$ **c** $g - 0.48 = 7.3$
d $3d = 56.4$ **e** $32 - 3x = 17$ **f** $10 - 3b = 16$

10 Amy is a years old. Her sister Ffion is 8 years older.

a Write down an expression for Ffion's age.

Their brother Darren is 10 years old. The total of their ages is 30 years.

b Use their information to write an equation for part **a**.
Solve your equation.
How old are Amy and Ffion?

Algebra Strand 1 Starting algebra

Problem solving

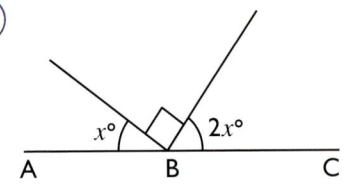

1)

ABC is a straight line.
Find the value of x.

2) ABCD is a quadrilateral.

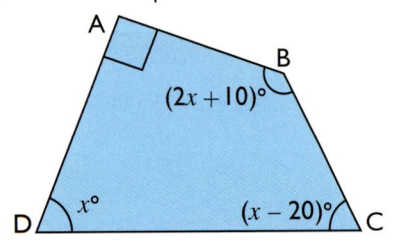

Find the value of the largest interior angle of the quadrilateral.

3) Ami is x years old.
Ben is twice as old as Ami.
Ceri is four years younger than Ami.
The total of their three ages is 36.
Write this information as an equation.
Solve the equation to find x.
How old are Ami, Ben and Ceri?

4) Sam has a field. It is rectangular, with a length l m.
The perimeter of the field is 400 m.
The width of the field is 50 m less than the length.
Write this information as an equation.
Solve the equation to find l.
Find the area of the field.

5) Explain why it is not possible for the angles of an equilateral triangle to have values
$2x + 40°$, $6x°$ and $7x - 24°$.

6) A small bottle of water contains l litres.
A large bottle of water contains five times as much water as the small bottle.
The difference in the amount of water they contain is 2 litres.
Write this information as an equation.
Solve the equation.
How much water does each bottle contain?

Unit 5 Setting up and solving simple equations Band f

7 Lily hires a car from Auto Hire.

   a Write a formula for the cost, £C, of hiring a car for n days.

   b Lily pays £280. How many days does she hire the car for?

Auto Hire
£40 plus £30 a day

8 The equal angles of an isosceles triangle are 30° greater than the third angle, $a°$.

   a Write an equation for a.

   b Solve the equation.

   c Find all three angles of the triangle.

9 Abi is desperate to get full marks for her algebra homework. One of the questions on the sheet is smudged and she cannot read the last number.

> Solve: $3x + 2 =$ ▇

Abi realises that the final number could be anything at all.

For example, if it is $3x + 2 = 4$ then she can solve it to get $x = \frac{2}{3}$.

If it is $3x + 2 = 101$ then she can solve it to get $x = 33$,

but she is fairly sure that the teacher will have written a question where

the value of x is an integer.

   a How many different possibilities for the right-hand side of the equation are there? Is there anything special about those numbers?

   b Could the right-hand side number be 100? Explain your answer.

   c The next question is also difficult to read. Abi knows it starts with $4x + 3$ and thinks that x will be an integer and that the right-hand side might be 10. Can all of her guesses be accurate? What types of number should Abi look at this time?

Reviewing skills

1 Solve these equations.

   a $3c - 6 = 15$ **b** $4f + 7 = 19$ **c** $2x + 3 = -11$ **d** $6 + 4y = 50$

   e $6t + 9 = 3$ **f** $9u + 14 = -40$ **g** $5y + 2 = 17$ **h** $3p + 18 = 12$

2 Solve these equations.

   a $4u + 94 = 15.6$ **b** $8.1 - 2k = 10.5$ **c** $\frac{h}{6} - 12.5 = 2.9$ **d** $24 - \frac{m}{4} = 8$

3 So-shan needs 1 kg of chickpeas for a soup recipe.
She buys 3 packets and 2 large tins to give her the correct amount.
Each packet contains 230 g.
Write an equation for the total amount of chickpeas and solve it to find the size of a large tin.

4 Indicate the correct answer **a**, **b**, **c** or **d**.

The solution to $1.6 + \frac{f}{2} = 9.8$

   a 4.1   **b** 11.4   **c** 16.4   **d** 22.8

Unit 6 • Using brackets • Band f

Outside the Maths classroom

Sales forecasting
Why do companies need to predict sales?

Toolbox

When you **expand** an expression you multiply out the brackets.
When you rewrite an expression using brackets you are **factorising.**

$$5a + 10 = 5(a + 2)$$

- $5a + 10$ is the expanded expression.
- $5(a + 2)$ is the factorised expression.

When you expand (or multiply out) brackets you must multiply every term inside the bracket by the term outside the bracket.

$$b \times (a + 3b - 2) = b \times a + b \times 3b + b \times -2$$
$$= ab + 3b^2 - 2b$$

There are three terms inside the bracket so there will be three terms in your answer.

When you factorise an expression, look at the numbers first and then the letters.

$$2fg + 6f^2 = 2 \times fg + 2 \times 3f^2$$
$$= 2f \times g + 2f \times 3f$$
$$= 2f(g + 3f)$$

2 goes into 2 and 6.

f goes into fg and f^2

so $2f$ goes outside the bracket.

$2f$ is the highest common factor (HCF) of both terms.

Example – Expanding brackets

Expand the brackets in these expressions.
a $3(4a - 7)$
b $t(s - u)$

Solution

a $3(4a - 7) = 3 \times 4a - 3 \times 7$
            $= 12a - 21$

> Multiply every term inside the brackets by the term outside the brackets.

b $t(s - u) = t \times s - t \times u$
            $= st - tu$

> Remember to use correct algebraic notation. You don't write the × sign and you arrange the letters alphabetically.

Example – Factorising expressions

Factorise these expressions.
a $12x - 18$
b $6y^2 + 2y$

Solution

a $12x - 18 = 6 \times 2x - 6 \times 3$
            $= 6 \times (2x - 3)$
            $= 6(2x - 3)$

> 6 goes into $12x$ and 18.

> Write the 6 outside the brackets. Be careful to keep the minus sign.

> Remember to use correct algebraic notation. You don't write the × sign.

b $6y^2 + 2y = 2y \times 3y + 2y \times 1$
              $= 2y \times (3y + 1)$
              $= 2y(3y + 1)$

> 2 and y go into $6y^2$ and $2y$.

> Don't forget to write the 1 in the brackets.

Check: $2y(3y + 1) = 2y \times 3y + 2y \times 1$
                  $= 6y^2 + 2y$ ✓

It is always a good idea to check your factorising by expanding the expression again.

Algebra Strand 1 Starting algebra

Practising skills

1 Lexmi and Kabil need to work out 8 × (30 + 4). Here is some of what they wrote.

Lexmi
8 × (30 + 4)
= 8 × 30 + 8 × 4
= ___ + ___
= ___

Kabil
8 × (30 + 4)
= 8 × ___
= ___

a Copy and complete their answers.
b Are they both right?
c Whose method is better?

2 Work out each of these
  i by expanding the brackets first
  ii by working out inside the brackets first.

a 6 × (20 − 1)   b 3 × (40 + 2)   c 4 × (30 − 3)
d 8 × (6 + 4 − 3)   e 2 × (9 − 5 + 2)   f 5 × (10 + 3 − 6)

3 Work these out by first expanding the brackets.

a 6 × 29 = 6 × (30 − 1)   b 4 × 52 = 4 × (50 + 2)
c 5 × 37 = 5 × (40 − 3)   d 8 × 93 = 8 × (90 + 3)

4 Factorise these expressions and work out their values.

a 6 × 3 + 6 × 7   b 4 × 8 − 4 × 7
c 3 × 3 + 3 × 8   d 45 × 3 + 45 × 9 + 45 × 8

5 a Find the areas of these rectangles.

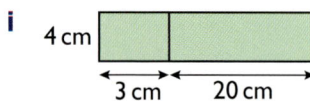

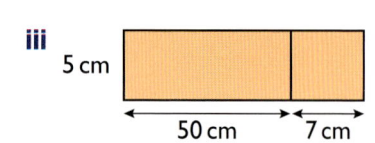

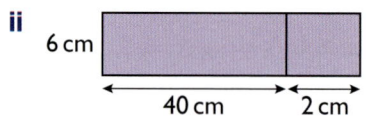

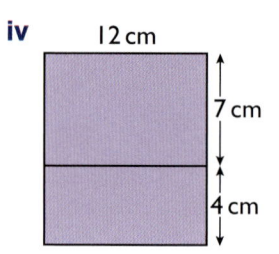

i 4 cm; 3 cm, 20 cm
ii 6 cm; 40 cm, 2 cm
iii 5 cm; 50 cm, 7 cm
iv 12 cm; 7 cm, 4 cm

b Use your answers to write down the value of:
  i 5 × 57   ii 4 × 23   iii 12 × 11   iv 6 × 42

6 For each of these rectangles
  i write down an expression for the area using brackets
  ii find the area when $x = 7$.

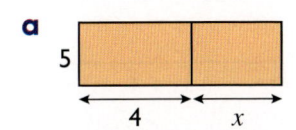

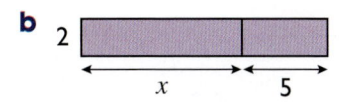

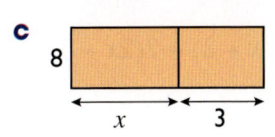

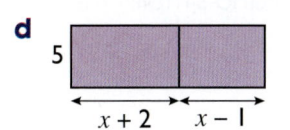

a rectangle with height 5, width split into 4 and x

b rectangle with height 2, width split into x and 5

c rectangle with height 8, width split into x and 3

d rectangle with height 5, width split into $x + 2$ and $x - 1$

7 Expand these brackets.

  a $3(2a + 7)$
  b $6(7 - 4b)$
  c $2(8c - 11)$
  d $5(1 - 8d)$
  e $4(2x + 3y)$
  f $3(5e + 2f + 6)$
  g $7(2p + 4q)$
  h $5(8g - 3h + 2)$

Developing fluency

1 Match each expression with its equivalent.

$5(x - 3)$	$15x + 5$	$3(5x + 2)$	$8(x + 2)$	$12x + 18$
$8 - 2x$	$2(4x - 1)$	$12 - 2x$	$4(2x - 1)$	$3(2x + 5)$
$6(2x + 3)$	$2(4 - x)$	$5x - 15$	$6x + 15$	$8x - 2$
$8x - 4$	$8x + 16$	$5(3x + 1)$	$15x + 6$	$2(6 - x)$

2 Factorise these expressions fully.

  a $4x + 8$
  b $3y - 12$
  c $16 - 8f$
  d $12g + 18$
  e $15m - 10$
  f $7a + 21b$

3 Simplify these expressions and factorise your answers.

  a $5x + 4y - 3x + 8y$
  b $6a + 2b + 4a + 3b$
  c $4x + 9y - 4 + 7 - x - y + 2x - 3y + 2$

4 Find the value of $5(3x - 2y)$ when

  a $x = 4$ and $y = -3$
  b $x = 2$ and $y = 3$
  c $x = y = 1$
  d $x = 0$ and $y = 4$

5 In each of these pairs choose which expression is larger and give reasons why.

  a $5n - 1$ and $5(n - 1)$
  c $5(3n + 7)$ and $7(2n + 5)$
  b $3(2n + 3)$ and $2(3n + 5)$

Algebra Strand 1 Starting algebra

6 Find the height of each of these rectangles.

a area = $8x + 16$; width $x + 2$; height ?

b area = $10x - 5$; width $2x - 1$; height ?

c area = $12x + 16$; width $3x + 4$; height ?

7 Expand the brackets and simplify the expression.

a $3(2x + 4) + 5(3x + 1)$
b $4(2x + 6) - 2(3x + 1)$
c $6(x + 3) - 2(2x - 3)$

8 Expand these brackets.

a $2(4x + 10)$
b $x(4x + 10)$
c $3x(x - 3)$
d $4x(2x + 5)$
e $3x^2(x - 2)$
f $6x(3x + 2y)$

9 Factorise these expressions fully.

a $4x^2 - 4x$
b $10x^2 + 5$
c $10x^2 + 5x$
d $6x^2 - 12x$
e $12cd - 8c$
f $6x^2 + 4x$
g $4x^2 - 8xy$
h $6c^2d + 18cd^2$

10 Chocolate flakes cost 99p.
During one week a family buy these numbers of flakes:
Monday 6   Tuesday 3   Wednesday 0   Thursday 4   Friday 8   Saturday 7   Sunday 4
Using brackets to help you, work out how much they spend on flakes.

11 Expand the brackets and simplify each of the following:

a $3(4d + 3c) + 5(5b - 6c)$
b $4(3x - 5y) + 3(x - y)$
c $5(2x + 3y) - 2(x + 2y)$
d $4(6a + 7b) - 3(2a - 3b)$

12 Simplify each of the following:

a $4(5t - 6h) + 2(4t - 3h)$
b $3(5g - 6h) - 3(2g - 4h)$
c $3(4d + 3e) - 2(3d - e)$
d $4(5k - m) + 3m - 5(k + m)$

Problem solving

1 Ifor sells vegetable planters for gardens.
The planters are in the shape of a square, of side s metres, and an equilateral triangle.

The length of each side of the equilateral triangle planter is 50 cm longer than each side of the square planter.

a Find the perimeter of the triangular planter.
Give your answer in terms of s.

b The perimeters of both shapes are the same.
Find the lengths of their sides.

2 The tile is used in a child's toy.
It is in the shape of parallelogram.

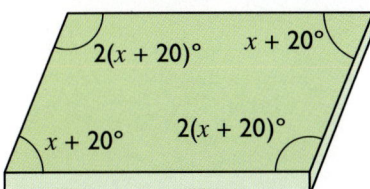

Angles shown: $2(x+20)°$, $x+20°$, $x+20°$, $2(x+20)°$

Find the value of the smallest angles in the parallelogram.

3 ABCD is a rectangle.

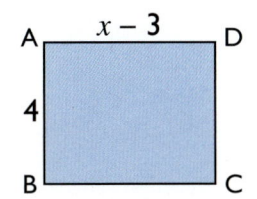

Rectangle with AD = $x - 3$, AB = 4.

All measurements are in centimetres.
The area of the rectangle is $24\,\text{cm}^2$.

a Find the value of x.

b Find the perimeter of the rectangle.

4 Ric is x years old.
Steph is 6 years older than Ric.
Tom is 3 times Steph's age.
The total of their ages is 84.
How old is Tom?

5 Wil hires a car.

Speed Well Cars
£10 a day + 5p a mile

a Write an expression for the cost of hiring the car for one week and driving m miles.

Wil hires a car for 3 weeks and pays a total of £390.

b How many miles does he drive each week (on average)?

6 Here are a square and a right-angled triangle.

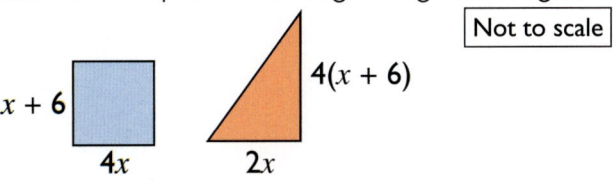

Not to scale

Square: sides $x + 6$ and $4x$. Triangle: legs $2x$ and $4(x+6)$.

Show that the square and the triangle have the same area.

Algebra Strand 1 Starting algebra

7 Here is a rectangle drawn on squared dotted paper. It has a width of 5 and a height of 4.

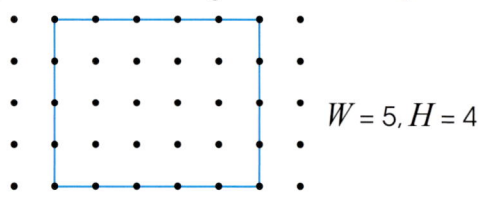

$W = 5, H = 4$

Squares have now been drawn around the inside edge.

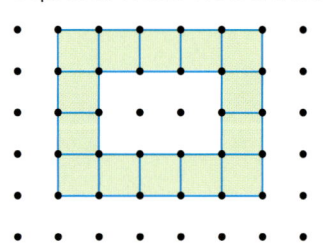

In this picture there are 14 squares.
Here is a general diagram.

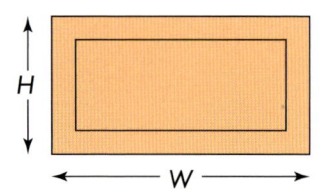

Use it to work out four different expressions for the number of squares around the inside edge.

a Method 1: Add up the number along each side and then subtract the corners (why?).

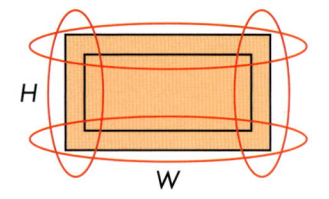

b Method 2: Subtract two from the width and subtract two from the length. Add these together. Add one for the bottom left-hand corner. Double this and add 2 (why?).

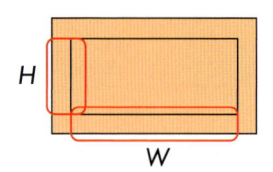

c Method 3: Add the number along the top to the number down the side. Double this and subtract 4 (why?).

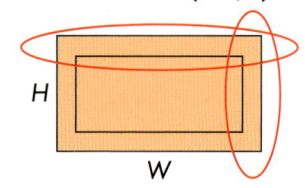

d Method 4: Subtract one from each side and add them all together.

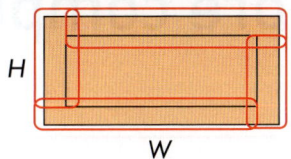

e Show that all of the expressions you get are equivalent.

Reviewing skills

1. Work out each of these
   i by expanding the brackets first
   ii by working out inside the brackets first.

   a $5 \times (100 - 1)$ **b** $6 \times (40 + 5)$ **c** $12 \times (20 + 1)$
   d $15 \times (4 + 3 - 1)$ **e** $7 \times (8 - 5 - 3)$ **f** $11 \times (100 + 1 - 2)$

2. Work these out by first expanding the brackets.
   a $17 \times 999 = 17 \times (1000 - 1)$ **b** $9 \times 82 = 9 \times (80 + 2)$
   c $12 \times 109 = 12 \times (100 + 9)$ **d** $99^2 = 99 \times (100 - 1)$

3. Factorise these expressions and work out their values.
   a $5 \times 8 + 5 \times 12$ **b** $7 \times 3 + 7 \times 2 - 7 \times 5$ **c** $11 \times 13 + 11^2 - 11 \times 4$

4. For each of these rectangles
   i write down an expression for the area using brackets
   ii find the area when $x = 5$.

   a rectangle with height 8, widths x and 11
   b rectangle with height x, widths $2x$ and $x + 1$

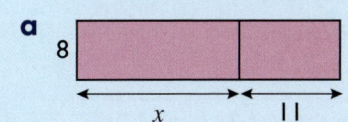

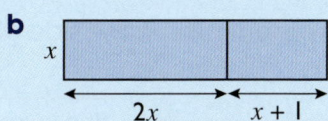

5. Expand these brackets and simplify the expression.
   a $5(2a + 3b) + 2(4a + b)$ **b** $3(5a + 6b) - 3(2a + 4b)$
   c $8(a - b) + 6(3a + 2b)$ **d** $4(3a + 2b) - 5(a - 3b)$

6. Simplify these expressions and factorise your answers.
   a $8f + 3g - 5f + 6g$ **b** $12k - 3m - 4k - 5m$ **c** $7x + 5 + 3x - 4 - 2x + 8$

Unit 7 • Working with more complex equations • Band f

Outside the Maths classroom

Working to deadlines
How can solving equations help someone to manage their workload?

Toolbox

You can use the **balance method** to solve equations with an unknown on both sides.

The first step is to get all the unknowns onto the same side of the equation:

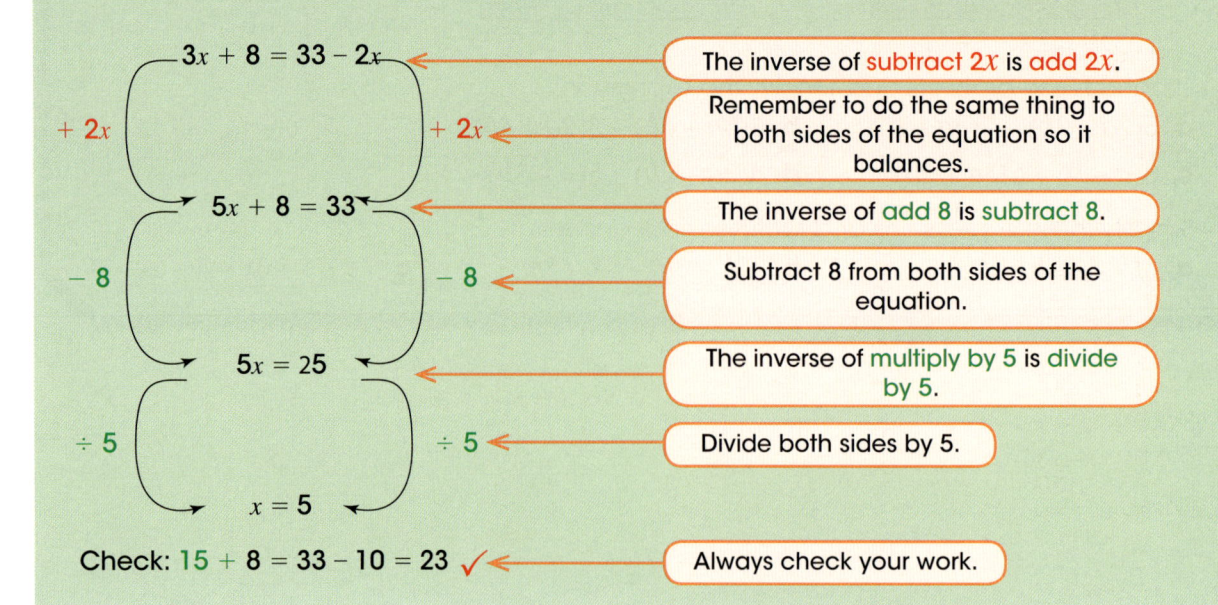

$3x + 8 = 33 - 2x$ — The inverse of subtract $2x$ is add $2x$.

$+2x$ ... $+2x$ — Remember to do the same thing to both sides of the equation so it balances.

$5x + 8 = 33$ — The inverse of add 8 is subtract 8.

-8 ... -8 — Subtract 8 from both sides of the equation.

$5x = 25$ — The inverse of multiply by 5 is divide by 5.

$\div 5$ ... $\div 5$ — Divide both sides by 5.

$x = 5$

Check: $15 + 8 = 33 - 10 = 23$ ✓ — Always check your work.

Example – Solving an equation with an unknown on both sides

Solve $3x - 8 = 20 - x$.

Solution

$3x - 8 = 20 - x$

$4x - 8 = 20$ ← Add x to both sides.

$4x = 28$ ← Add 8 to both sides.

$x = 7$ ← Divide both sides by 4.

Check: $3x - 8 = 20 - x$

$3 \times 7 - 8 = 20 - 7$

$21 - 8 = 13$

$13 = 13$ ✓

Example – Solving word problems

Jamie and Holly both had the same amount of credit on their mobile phones.
Jamie sent 18 texts and has £1.40 credit left.
Holly sent 12 texts and has £2 credit left.
They both pay the same amount for one text.

a Find the cost of one text message.
b How much credit did Jamie and Holly start with?

Solution

a Let t represent the cost of one text message in pence. Change pounds to pence because whole numbers are easier to work with.

Jamie's credit = Holly's credit

$18t + 140 = 12t + 200$ ← Subtract $12t$ from both sides.

$6t + 140 = 200$ ← Subtract 140 from both sides.

$6t = 60$ ← Divide both sides by 6.

$t = 10$

So a text message costs 10p.

b Substitute $t = 10$ into the expression for Jamie's credit.

$18t + 140 = 18 \times 10 + 140$

$= 320$

So Jamie's starting credit was 320p or £3.20
Check that Holly's credit is also 320p:

$12t + 200 = 12 \times 10 + 200$

$= 320$ ✓

Algebra Strand 1 Starting algebra

Practising skills

1 Write an equation for each balancing problem and solve it.

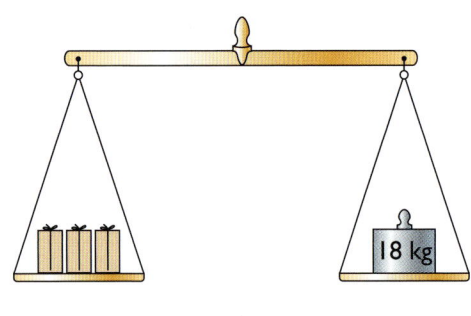

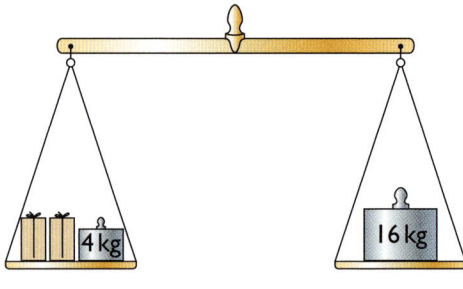

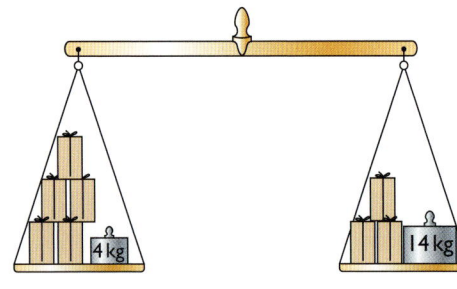

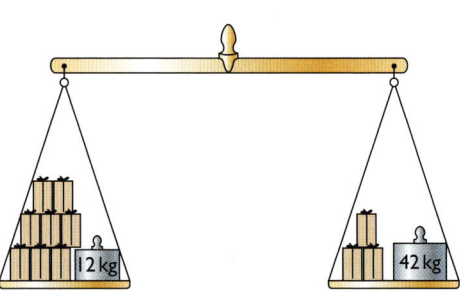

a, b, c, d (balance scales: a — boxes vs 18 kg; b — boxes + 4 kg vs 16 kg; c — boxes + 4 kg vs boxes + 14 kg; d — boxes + 12 kg vs boxes + 42 kg)

2 Solve these equations.
- a $6s = 27$
- b $5x + 14 = 49$
- c $18 - 3h = 3$
- d $\frac{y}{4} - 6 = 9$
- e $12 = 2 - 5m$
- f $14 = 29 + 6g$
- g $8 = 5 + \frac{1}{2}p$
- h $-8 = -5 - \frac{1}{2}p$

3 Solve these equations.
- a $4a + 7 = 3a + 3$
- b $7f + 3 = 2f + 18$
- c $7x - 3 = 6 - 2x$
- d $17 - 2y = 8 - y$

4 Solve these equations.
- a $5a + 8 = 7a + 22$
- b $6b + 15 = -2b - 9$
- c $5c - 3 = c - 1$
- d $11 - 2f = 8 - 8f$

Developing fluency

1 Elena works out that if she buys 6 apples she will have 20p left over but if she buys only 4 apples she will have 64p over.

a Write an equation to represent this situation.

b Solve the equation to find the cost of an apple.

2 Glynis tries to solve this equation.
$11 - 4x = 6x + 5$

a Here is her attempt.

> $11 - 4x = 6x - 4x$
> $11 + 5 = 6x - 4x$
> $16 = 2x$
> $16 \div 2 = x$
> $x = 8$ ✗

Explain what she has done wrong.

b Using the same steps as Glynis, write out a correct answer.

c Check your solution by substituting it in the original equation.

3 Lowri and Tara need to solve this equation.
$4.1x - 3.7 = 3.6x - 2.2$
Here is how they start.

Lowri
$4.1x - 3.7 = 3.6x - 2.2$
$4.1x - 3.6x = -2.2 + 3.7$
$0.5x = 1.5$
$x = \dfrac{\ldots}{\ldots}$
$x = \ldots$

Tara
Multiply both sides by 10.
$41x - 37 = 36x - 22$
$41x - 36x = 37 - 22$
....
....
....

a Complete their answers.

b Whose method do you prefer? Say why.

4 Solve these equations.

a $2.1a + 3.6 = 1.1a + 5.7$

b $4.5b - 2.9 = 3.6b + 4.3$

c $3.7 - 2.2c = 1.8c - 5.4$

d $8.5 - 5.3d = 3.6 - 1.8d$

e $2\frac{1}{2}x - 6 = 3 - \frac{1}{2}x$

f $2\frac{1}{2}x - 6 = 3 + \frac{1}{2}x$

g $4.11x - 2 = 4.1x - 1$

h $0.001x - 0.005 = 0.003 - 0.003x$

Algebra Strand 1 Starting algebra

5) Mali and Zoe are sisters. They are making dresses from the same material. Their parents give them the same amount of money to buy it. The cost of 1 metre of the material is £m.
Mali gets 3.5 metres and has £4.25 left over.
Zoe gets 2 metres and has £11.00 left over.

   a Write this information as an equation for m.

   b Solve the equation.

   c How much money was each girl given?

6) Sam is tiling his bathroom wall. The tiles go part of the way up. Above them the wall is painted.
11 rows of tiles would leave 108 cm of wall to be painted.
14 rows of tiles would leave 72 cm of wall to be painted.

   a Write this information as an equation for the height of a tile, w cm.

   b Solve the equation.

   c How many rows of tiles would cover the whole wall?

7) *I think of a number.*
I multiply it by 5 and take away 8.
My answer is 12 more than if I'd doubled my number and added 10.

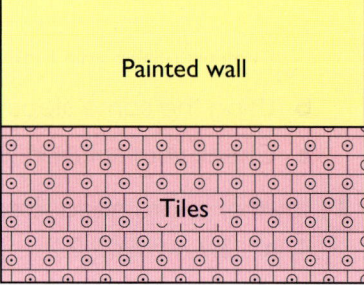

   a Write this information as an equation.

   b What number did Charlie think of?

Problem solving

1) *I think of a number.*
I multiply it by 5 and subtract 3.
My answer is 7 more than if I'd multiplied my number by 3.

   a Write this information as an equation.

   b What number did Ava think of?

2) Here is a rectangle. All the measurements are in centimetres.

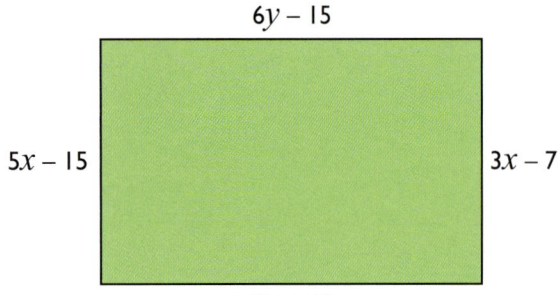

Top: $6y - 15$
Left: $5x - 15$
Right: $3x - 7$
Bottom: $2y + 15$

Find the area of the rectangle.

3) Here is part of a polygon.
  a Angles A and B are equal.
     How many degrees are they?
  b Show that angle C is also equal to A and B.
  c What can you say about the polygon?

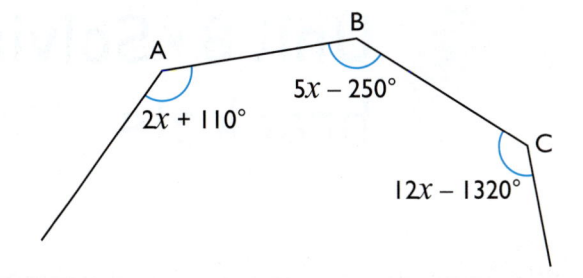

Angles shown: A: $2x + 110°$, B: $5x - 250°$, C: $12x - 1320°$

4) Jack has £400 which he gives to his 3 grandchildren.
He gives Ellie twice as much as Harry.
He gives Tom £40 less than Harry.
Let £h stand for the amount of money that Harry gets.
  a Write down expressions for the amount of money given to
     i Ellie   ii Tom
  b How much money does Jack give to each grandchild?

5) The angles in this triangle are $3a°$, $(5a + 12)°$ and $(96 - 2a)°$.
Show that the triangle is isosceles.

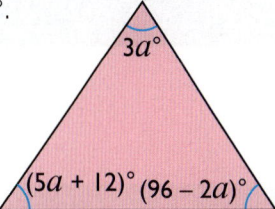

Reviewing skills

1) Solve these equations.
  a $8g - 5 = 5g + 40$
  b $8 + 2d = d + 2$
  c $9t - 4 = t - 8$
  d $24 + 5c = 16 - 3c$

2) Solve these equations.
  a $23 - 4d = 3d + 2$
  b $7e + 4 = 18 - 3e$
  c $17 + g = 6 - g$
  d $5 - 3h = 1 + h$

3) Solve these equations.
  a $1.4x + 2.1 = 0.5x + 5.7$
  b $3.88 - 1.02x = 1.38 + 1.48x$
  c $4\frac{1}{4}x + 1\frac{1}{2} = 16\frac{1}{2} - \frac{3}{4}x$
  d $5 - \frac{3}{4}x = 1\frac{1}{2} - \frac{1}{4}x$

4) Zorro is buying USB pens for his computer. They cost £p each.
Zorro could buy 5 USB pens and have £4.25 change from the money in his pocket.
Instead he buys 2 USB pens and spends £16.50 on a game.
That leaves him with just 20 pence.
  a Form an equation for p.
  b Solve the equation.
  c What is the cost of a USB pen?
  d How much money did Zorro have?

Unit 8 • Solving equations with brackets • Band f

Outside the Maths classroom

Brainteasers
How do equations help solve brainteasers?

Toolbox

When an equation has a bracket it is usually easiest to expand the brackets first.

$5(3x - 6) = 12$

$5 \times 3x - 5 \times 6 = 12$ ← First multiply out the brackets.

$15x - 30 = 12$ ← Add 30 to both sides.

$15x = 42$ ← Divide both sides by 15.

$x = 2.8$

Alternatively you can choose to divide both sides of the equation by the number outside the brackets.

$4(n + 13) = 80$

$n + 13 = 20$ ← Divide both sides by 4.

$n = 7$ ← Subtract 13 from both sides.

Unit 8 Solving equations with brackets Band f

Example – Solving equations with an unknown on one side

Solve these equations.
a $6(5a - 2) = 33$ b $5(4b + 3) = -25$

Solution

a
$6(5a - 2) = 33$
$6 \times 5a - 6 \times 2 = 33$ ← First multiply out the brackets.
$30a - 12 = 33$ ← Simplify.
$30a = 45$ ← Add 12 to both sides.
$a = 1.5$ ← Divide both sides by 30.

b
$5(4b + 3) = -25$
$4b + 3 = -5$ ← It is easiest to divide both sides by 5 first.
$4b = -8$ ← Subtract 3 from both sides.
$b = -2$ ← Divide both sides by 4.

Example – Solving equations with an unknown on both sides

Solve $2(3 - x) = 9 + x$.

Solution

$2(3 - x) = 9 + x$
$2 \times 3 - 2 \times x = 9 + x$ ← First multiply out the brackets.
$6 - 2x = 9 + x$ ← You can subtract x from both sides or add $2x$ to both sides.
$6 = 9 + 3x$ ← Subtracting x from both sides gives a negative x term so it is easier to add $2x$ to both sides.
$-3 = 3x$ ← Subtract 9 from both sides.
$-1 = x$ ← Divide both sides by 3.
$x = -1$ ← Swap the two sides of the equation over. $-1 = x$ means the same as $x = -1$.

Check by substituting $x = -1$ back into the original equation.
$2(3 - x) = 9 + x$
$2 \times (3 - -1) = 9 + -1$
$2 \times 4 = 8$ ✓

143

Algebra Strand 1 Starting algebra

Practising skills

1) Solve these equations by expanding the brackets first.

   a $5(2x + 3) = 75$ **b** $3(x + 2) = 33$ **c** $4(5x - 3) = 18$ **d** $8(5 - x) = 16$

2) Solve these equations by dividing both sides by the number outside the brackets first.

   a $10(3a + 6) = 180$ **b** $2(5b - 3) = 74$ **c** $5(4c + 7) = 195$ **d** $4(2d - 9) = 52$

3) a Copy and complete the table to build an equation to find the number.

Instruction	Algebra
I think of a number, n	n
I multiply it by 5	
I add 6	
I multiply it by 3	
The answer is 123	

   b Solve your equation to find the number.

   c Work through the instructions to check your answer is correct.

4) Solve these equations.

   a $4(x + 6) + 3x = 38$ **b** $2(3x - 5) - 3x + 4 = 6$

   c $5(2x + 1) - x - 3 = 56$ **d** $4x + 9 - 2(x - 4) = 27$

5) Solve these equations.

   a $8(x + 3) = 3x - 11$ **b** $2(4x - 2) = 11 - 2x$

   c $3(5x - 6) = 4x + 15$ **d** $10(3x - 5) = 5x$

6) Solve these equations.

   a $7(3x - 4) = 4(2x + 3) - 1$ **b** $6(2x - 5) = 3(x + 2)$

   c $5(x + 4) = 3(2x - 8)$ **d** $3(4x + 2) = 4(5x + 2)$

Developing fluency

1) Solve these equations. Each answer represents a letter. What word does this spell?

-3	-2	-1	2	3	4	8	24
L	A	T	S	V	E	P	O

   a $2(x + 3) = 10$

   b $3(x - 10) = 2x - 6$

   c $2(6x + 3) = 10(x + 1) - 10$

   d $4(2x + 1) = 2(x + 5) + 12$

   e $5(3x - 2) - 4x = 3(x + 5) + 7$

2 The perimeter of this rectangle is 28 cm.

a Write down an expression for the perimeter of the rectangle.

b Write down and solve an equation for x.

c Find the area of the rectangle.

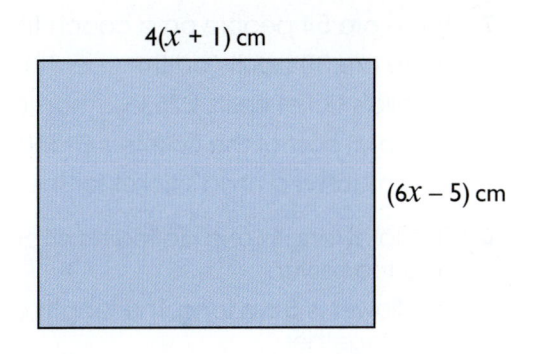

$4(x + 1)$ cm

$(6x - 5)$ cm

3 Isobel thinks of a number, n.

When she subtracts 2 and then multiplies the results by 3 she gets the same answer as when she subtracts her number from 30.

a Write down an expression for 'subtracts 2 and then multiplies the results by 3'.
Use n for Isobel's number.

b Write down an equation for n.

c What number is Isobel thinking of?

d Show how you can check your answer is correct.

4 The sum of the ages of Gethin and his Dad is 42.

a Gethin is p years old now.
Copy and complete this table.

	Age now	Age in 4 years
Gethin	p	
Dad		

In 4 years' time, Gethin's Dad will be four times as old as Gethin.

b Write down an equation for p.

c Solve the equation.

d How old are Gethin and his Dad now?

e Show how you can check you answer is correct.

5 a Expand the brackets.

i $\frac{1}{2}(4x + 2)$ ii $\frac{1}{3}(3x + 6)$

b Solve this equation.

$\frac{1}{2}(4x + 2) = \frac{1}{3}(3x + 6)$

6 a Simplify

i $6 \times \frac{1}{2}(4x + 2)$ ii $6 \times \frac{1}{3}(3x + 6)$

b Multiply both sides of the equation $\frac{1}{2}(4x + 2) = \frac{1}{3}(3x + 6)$ by 6.

c Using your answer to part **b**, solve the equation $\frac{1}{2}(4x + 2) = \frac{1}{3}(3x + 6)$.

Algebra Strand 1 Starting algebra

7 There are 54 people on a coach trip to a theme park.
There are 30 adults on the coach trip.
A child's ticket costs £25 less than an adult's.
The total cost of the tickets is £1560.
How much is a child's ticket for the trip?

8 The total length of a daffodil is 44 cm. This is made up from three parts: the bulb, the stem and the flower.
The flower is 5 cm long. The length of the stem is three times the length of the flower and bulb together.
Find the lengths of each of the parts.

Problem solving

1 I think of a number and call it n.
I add 12 to the number.
I then multiply by 3.
This gives me the same answer as when I subtract n from 60.

   a Write this as an equation for n.

   b What number is Louise thinking of?

2 Jeremy's present age is y years.
Today, Jeremy's sister, Kate, is twice as old as Jeremy.
Two years ago Kate was three times as old as Jeremy was then.

   a Write this information as an equation for y.

   b Solve your equation. How old are Jeremy and Kate today?

3 Mr MacDonald has 120 animals on his farm.
He has hens, cows and sheep. The number of cows is c.
The number of hens is 20 more than the number of cows.
He has twice as many sheep as hens.

   a Write this information as an equation for c.

   b How many cows are there on the farm?

   c How many hens and sheep are there?

4 Here is a quadrilateral.
Show that the quadrilateral is not a square.

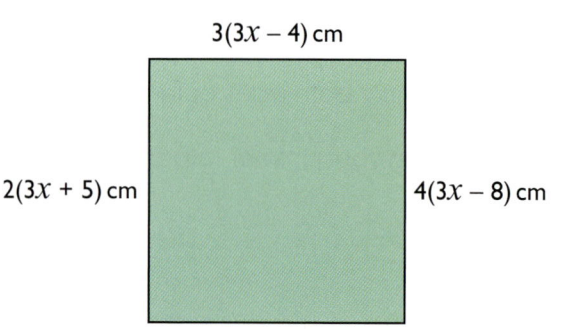

$3(3x - 4)$ cm

$2(3x + 5)$ cm

$4(3x - 8)$ cm

5 Jody and Ben went to the leisure centre together.
Jody spent 40 minutes in the gym then went for a swim. Jody swam for m minutes.
Ben spent all the time swimming. He was swimming for three times longer than Jody.
How long were Jody and Ben in the leisure centre?

6 Here is a quadrilateral.
Use the given angles to decide whether or not this quadrilateral is a parallelogram.

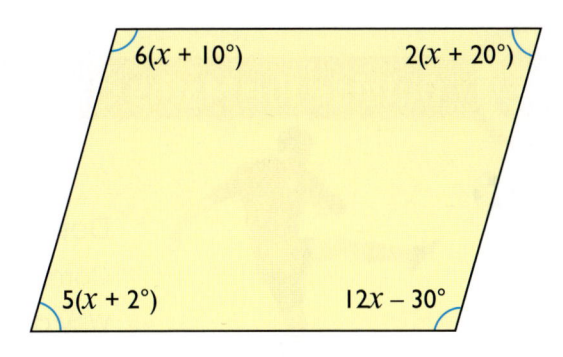

Angles: $6(x + 10°)$, $2(x + 20°)$, $5(x + 2°)$, $12x - 30°$

Reviewing skills

1 Solve these equations.
  a $6(5a - 1) = 114$
  b $3(2b + 4) = 6$
  c $5(4c - 3) = 165$
  d $7(4d - 5) = 0$

2 Solve these equations.
  a $3(2x - 5) = 5x - 14$
  b $2(4x + 1) = 7x + 4$
  c $5(3x - 4) = 2(5 - x) - x$
  d $4(2x - 3) = 5(x - 1) + 2$

3 Here is a rectangle.
The perimeter of the rectangle is 136 cm.
What is the area of the rectangle?

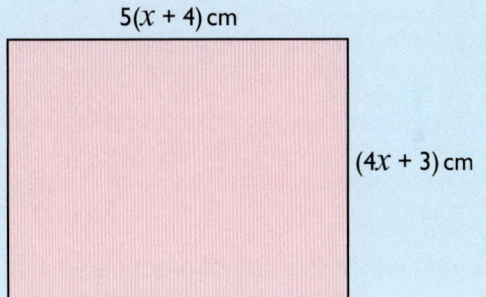

Rectangle dimensions: $5(x + 4)$ cm by $(4x + 3)$ cm

Unit 9 • Simplifying harder expressions • Band g

Outside the Maths classroom

Designing platform games
Computer games model real-life situations.
Why do games designers need to use formulae?

Toolbox

These are the **laws of indices**.

$a^n = \underbrace{a \times a \times a \times \ldots \times a}_{n \text{ factors of } a}$ So $a^5 = \underbrace{a \times a \times a \times a \times a}_{5 \text{ factors of } a}$

$a^1 = a$

$a^0 = 1$

$a^x \times a^y = a^{x+y}$ So $a^5 \times a^7 = a^{5+7} = a^{12}$

$a^x \div a^y = a^{x-y}$ So $a^9 \div a^4 = a^{9-4} = a^5$

$(a^x)^y = a^{x \times y}$ So $(a^5)^3 = a^{5 \times 3} = a^{15}$

When you expand a pair of brackets you multiply every term in the second bracket by every term in the first bracket then simplify your answer.

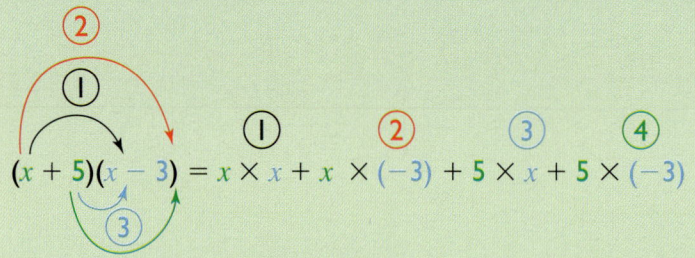

$(x + 5)(x - 3) = x \times x + x \times (-3) + 5 \times x + 5 \times (-3)$

$= x^2 + (-3x) + (+5x) + (-15)$

$= x^2 + 2x - 15$

$= x^2 + 2x - 15$

Alternatively, you can use a table

	x	$+5$
x	x^2	$5x$
-3	$-3x$	-15

$x^2 + 5x - 3x - 15$
$= x^2 + 2x - 15$

Unit 9 Simplifying harder expressions Band g

Example – Simplify harder expressions

Simplify these expressions.

a $2a^3b^7 \times 4ab^5$

b $\dfrac{12a^4b^3}{4ab^2}$

Solution

a Use the rules of indices: $a^x \times a^y = a^{x+y}$.

$2 \times 4 = 8$

$a^3 \times a = a^3 \times a^1 = a^{3+1} = a^4$

$b^7 \times b^5 = b^{7+5} = b^{12}$

So, $2a^3b^7 \times 4ab^5 = 8a^4b^{12}$

b Use the rules of indices: $a^x \div a^y = a^{x-y}$.

$12 \div 4 = 3$

$a^4 \div a = a^4 \div a^1 = a^{4-1} = a^3$

$b^3 \div b^2 = b^{3-2} = b^1 = b$

So, $\dfrac{12a^4b^3}{4ab^2} = 3a^3b$

Example – Expanding a pair of brackets

Expand $(x - 4)(x - 2)$.

Solution

You can use a grid to help you.

	x	-4
x	x^2	$-4x$
-2	$-2x$	8

Put the contents of one bracket along the top and the other down the side then multiply at each cross-section.

$(x - 4)(x - 2) = x^2 - 4x - 2x + 8$

$ = x^2 - 6x - 8$

Then add the results.

Higher tier only

149

Algebra Strand 4 Algebraic methods

Practising skills

1 Write these as single powers.

a $5 \times 5 \times 5$

b $2 \times 2 \times 2 \times 2 \times 2$

c $(9 \times 9 \times 9 \times 9 \times 9 \times 9 \times 9)^2$

d $(7 \times 7)^5$

2 Write these as single powers.

a $f \times f$

b $g \times g \times g \times g$

c $(d \times d \times d)^2$

d $(a \times a \times a \times a \times a \times a \times a \times a)^3$

3 Write each of these in index form and work out their values.

i $x^2 \times x^3$

ii $x^3 \times x^2$

iii $x^3 \div x^2$

iv $x^2 \div x^3$

v $(x^2)^3$

vi $(x^3)^2$

4 Simplify these expressions.

a $5a^3 \times 4a^2$

b $6b^5 \div 3b^4$

c $2c^8 \times 3c^6$

d $10d^7 \times 3d$

e $(2e^2)^3 \div 4e^5$

f $4f^3g^2 \times 2f^2g^6$

g $8m^3p \times 3mp^4$

h $10s^8t^5 \div 5s^5t^5$

5 Simplify these expressions.

a $\dfrac{12a^5}{4a^3}$

b $20c^{12} \div (5 \times c^5 \times c)$

c $\dfrac{15(d^3)^2}{3d}$

d $6(ef^2)^3 \div (2 \times e^2 \times ef)$

6 a i Copy and complete this grid to expand $(x + 2)(x + 4)$.

×	x	4
x	x^2	
2		

ii Now add the four terms together and simplify your answer.

b Copy and complete these grids and add the terms together, simplifying your answers.

i $(x + 3)(x + 5)$

×	x	5
x		
3		

ii $(x + 6)(x - 4)$

×	x	-4
x		
6		

iii $(x - 5)(x - 7)$

×	x	-7
x		
-5		

Unit 9 Simplifying harder expressions Band g

Developing fluency

1 Copy and complete these algebra pyramids.
Each brick is the product of the two beneath it.

a

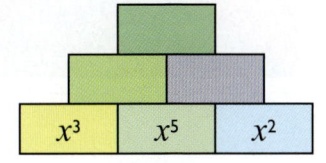

x^3 x^5 x^2

b

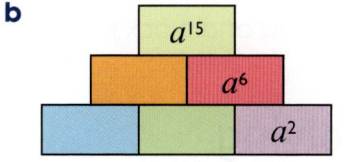

a^{15}
a^6
a^2

2 Match to give six pairs of equivalent expressions.

n^2 $n^4 \times n^2$ n^8 $n^3 \times n^2$

$n^{12} \div n^4$ n^3 $n^3 \div n$ $(n^5)^2$

$n^6 \div n^3$ n^5 n^{10} n^6

3 Expand these expressions and simplify your answers.

   a $(x + 2)(x + 9)$ **b** $(x + 5)(x - 3)$
   c $(x - 4)(x + 1)$ **d** $(x - 2)(x - 5)$

4 Copy and complete these algebra pyramids. Each brick is the product of the two beneath it.

a

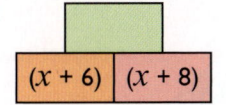

$(x + 6)$ $(x + 8)$

b

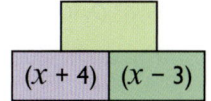

$(x + 4)$ $(x - 3)$

5 a Tim and Harry have expanded the brackets $(x + 5)^2$.
   Tim says the answer is $x^2 + 10x + 25$ and Harry says it is $x^2 + 25$.
   Who is correct? What has the other one done wrong?

   b Expand these brackets and simplify the answers.

   i $(a + 3)^2$

   ii $(b + 6)^2$

   iii $(c - 4)^2$

6 a Multiply $(x + 5)$ by $(x + 10)$.

   b This rectangle has sides $(x + 5)$ and $(x + 10)$.
   It is divided into four parts. One of them is a square of side x.
   Copy the rectangle and mark the areas of the four parts on the rectangle.

   c Explain the connection between your answers to parts **a** and **b**.

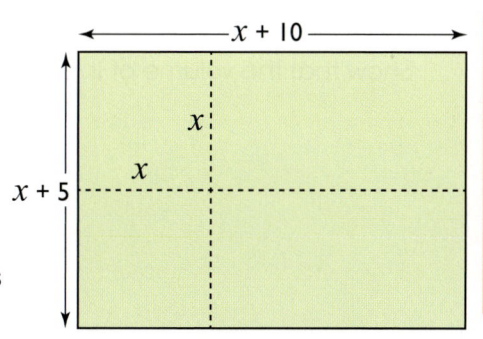

151

Algebra Strand 4 Algebraic methods

7 The sides of this rectangle are $2x + 4$ cm and $2x$ cm.

    a Find, in terms of x,

       i The area of the whole rectangle

       ii The area that is coloured red.

    b Show that the red and black regions have the same area.

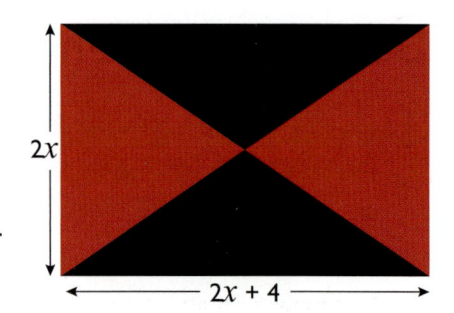

Problem solving

1 A farmer has a field in the shape of a rectangle.
The length of the field is 20 m greater than the width.
Write an expression, in terms of w, for the area of the field.

2 Find an expression, in terms of a, for the area shaded red.

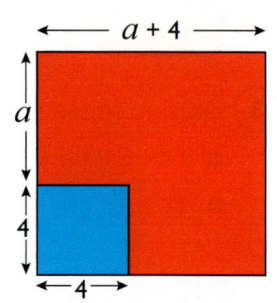

3 Here is a rectangle.
Find an expression, in terms of b, for the area shaded red.

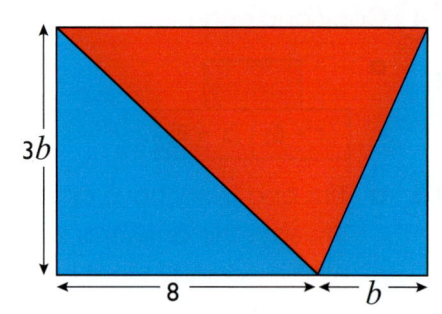

4 A hole in the shape of a square prism is cut through the middle of a cube.
The cube has side $4s$.
The square hole has side s.
Show that the volume of the shape remaining is $60s^3$.

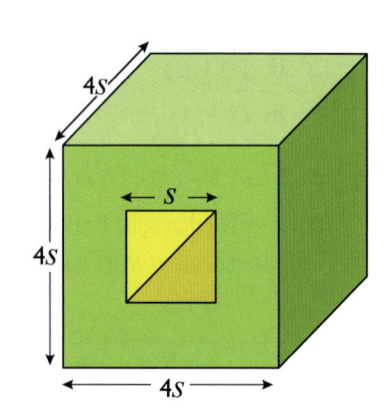

5 Find the value of n to make these statements true.

a $a^4 \times a^n = a^{12}$
b $\dfrac{12p^9}{3p^n} = 4p^3$
c $(y^n)^4 = y^{12}$

6 All measurements are in cm.

a Find an expression, in terms of x, for the blue area on this flag.

b Show that it is the same as the red area.

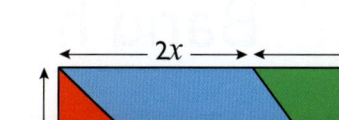

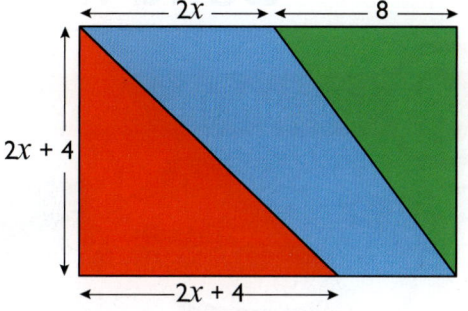

Reviewing skills

1 Write these expressions as single powers.

a $a^6 \times a^8$
b $b^{12} \div b^6$
c $c^{16} \div (c^4 \times c^{12})$
d $(d^9)^2$

2 Simplify these expressions.

a $6a^4 \times 2a^3$
b $\dfrac{8b^{10}}{2b^5}$
c $\dfrac{3a^2b \times 2ab^2}{6(ab)^3}$
d $\dfrac{30g^{12}h^4}{6g^4h^4}$

3 Expand these expressions and simplify your answers.

a $(a+5)(a+6)$
b $(b-3)(b+7)$
c $(c+1)(c-5)$
d $(d-3)(d-5)$

4 a Find the area of the red rectangle in terms of x. The blue square has sides of x cm.

b Find the areas of each of the three regions in terms of x.

c Find the area of the whole figure in terms of x.

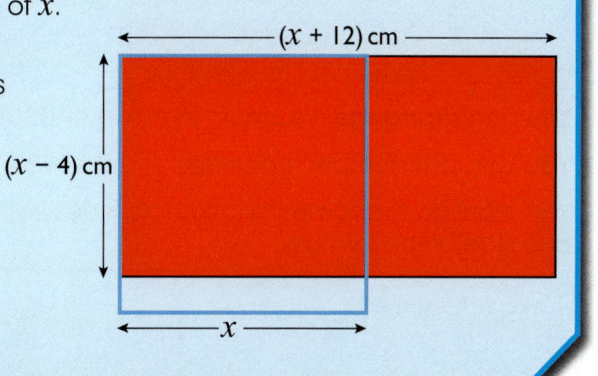

Unit 10 • Using complex formulae • Band h

Outside the Maths classroom

Savings plans
What is the difference between compound interest and simple interest?

Toolbox

You can substitute numbers into formulae, these may include negative numbers and decimals.

v^2 is the **subject** of the formula $v^2 = u^2 + 2as$.

Find v when $u = -3$, $a = 9.8$ and $s = 20$.

$v^2 = u^2 + 2as$
$v^2 = (-3)^2 + 2 \times 9.8 \times 20$ ← Substitute the values given into the formula.
$v^2 = 9 + 392$
$v^2 = 401$ ← Square root both sides of the formula to find v.

$v = +20.02$ or -20.02 to 2 d.p. ← Remember that there are two answers when you square root a number, one positive and one negative.

You can **rearrange** a formula to make another letter the subject.

You can use number machines. A better way is to use a method similar to solving an equation.

You must do the same thing to both sides of the formula to get the variable you want by itself on one side of the formula.

Make s the subject.

$-u^2$: $u^2 + 2as = v^2$: $-u^2$
$\div 2a$: $2as = v^2 - u^2$: $\div 2a$
$s = \dfrac{v^2 - u^2}{2a}$

Make u the subject.

$-2as$: $u^2 + 2as = v^2$: $-2as$
square root : $u^2 = v^2 - 2as$: square root
$u = \pm\sqrt{v^2 - 2as}$

Unit 10 Using complex formulae Band h

Example – Substituting negative numbers into a formula

Work out the value of a when $b = -2$ in this expression

$$a = \frac{3b^2 - 6}{b + 4}$$

Solution

$$a = \frac{3b^2 - 6}{b + 4}$$ ← Substitute $b = -2$ into the expression.

$$= \frac{3 \times (-2)^2 - 6}{(-2) + 4}$$ ← Note that $(-2)^2$ means -2×-2 which is equal to 4.

$$= \frac{3 \times 4 - 6}{2}$$

$$= \frac{6}{2} = 3$$

Example – Working with formulae

The area of this trapezium is $48 \, cm^2$.
Work out the height of the trapezium.

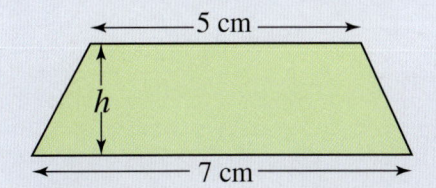

(Trapezium with parallel sides 5 cm (top) and 7 cm (bottom), height h.)

Solution

The formula for the area of a trapezium is

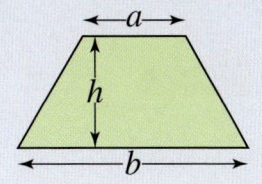

(Trapezium with parallel sides a (top) and b (bottom), height h.)

$$A = \frac{1}{2}h(a + b)$$

So $\quad 48 = \frac{1}{2}h(5 + 7)$ ← Substitute $A = 48$, $a = 5$ and $b = 7$ into the formula.

$\frac{1}{2}h(5 + 7) = 48$ ← It is usual to work with the variable on the LHS of the equation.

$\frac{1}{2}h \times 12 = 48$

$6h = 48$

$h = 8$

So the height of the trapezium is 8 cm.

155

Algebra Strand 1 Starting algebra

Example – Rearranging a formula

The formula for the perimeter of a rectangle is
$P = 2(l + w)$

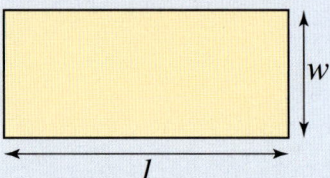

Rearrange the formula to make l the subject.

Solution
Method 1
Look at how Beth and David rearrange the formula:

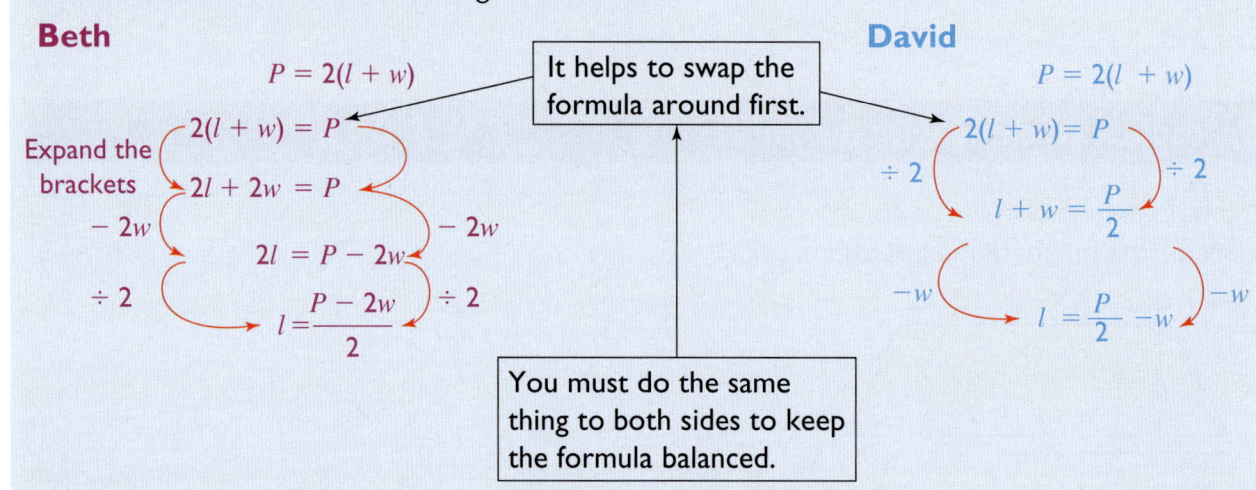

Beth

$P = 2(l + w)$

Expand the brackets: $2(l + w) = P$

$2l + 2w = P$

$-2w$

$2l = P - 2w$

$\div 2$

$l = \dfrac{P - 2w}{2}$

It helps to swap the formula around first.

David

$P = 2(l + w)$

$2(l + w) = P$

$\div 2$

$l + w = \dfrac{P}{2}$

$-w$

$l = \dfrac{P}{2} - w$

You must do the same thing to both sides to keep the formula balanced.

Method 2
You can also use a function machine.

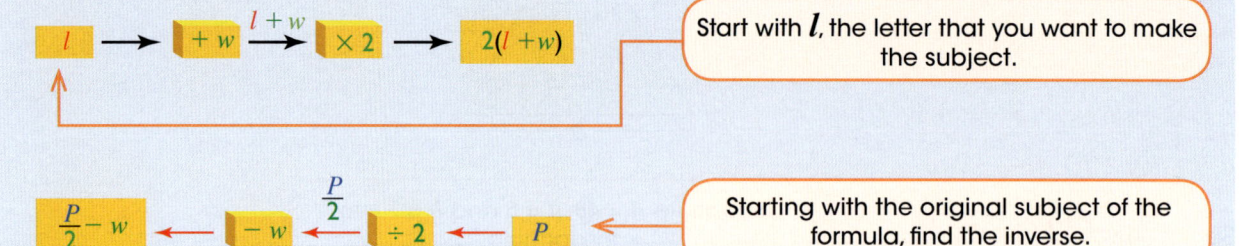

$l \longrightarrow [+w] \xrightarrow{l+w} [\times 2] \longrightarrow 2(l+w)$

Start with l, the letter that you want to make the subject.

$\dfrac{P}{2} - w \longleftarrow [-w] \xleftarrow{\frac{P}{2}} [\div 2] \longleftarrow P$

Starting with the original subject of the formula, find the inverse.

So $l = \dfrac{P}{2} - w$

Practising skills

1 Find the value of $5a - 3b + 2c$ when
  a $a = 4, b = 6, c = 5$
  b $a = 8, b = -3, c = -2$
  c $a = 5, b = -1, c = 6$
  d $a = 0.5, b = 1.5, c = 2.5$

2 Find the value of $6d + 3e - 4f$ when
  a $d = 2, e = 4, f = 1$
  b $d = 7, e = 3, f = -4$
  c $d = 3, e = -9, f = 2$
  d $d = 0.1, e = -0.4, f = 0.3$

3 Find the value of $3x^2 - 6x$ when
  a $x = 4$
  b $x = 5$
  c $x = -2$
  d $x = -1$

4 Find the value of $5x(2y - 4)$ when
  a $x = 3, y = 5$
  b $x = 4, y = 7$
  c $x = 2, y = -3$
  d $x = -5, y = -2$

5 Make x the subject of the formulae.
  a $y = x - 8$
  b $y = 3x$
  c $y = \dfrac{x}{5}$
  d $y = 2x + 1$

6 Make the bold letter the subject of these formulae.
  a $y = \mathbf{x} + 4$
  b $y = 4\mathbf{x} - 3$
  c $a = 6\mathbf{b}$
  d $p = m\mathbf{t}$

7 Work out the value of $4t^2 - 3w$ when
  a $t = 3, w = 4$
  b $t = 5, w = -2$
  c $t = -4, w = 5$
  d $t = -3, w = -6$

8 Given that $a = \dfrac{1}{2}, b = \dfrac{2}{3}$ and $c = 6$, evaluate each of the following.
  Give your answer as a mixed number or a fraction in its simplest form.
  a $\dfrac{8a - 3b}{6}$
  b $7a + 9b$
  c $c - 3a$
  d $2c - 4b$

9 Given that $e = \dfrac{1}{4}, f = \dfrac{1}{5}$ and $h = -3$, evaluate each of the following.
  Give you answer as a mixed number.
  a $6e + h$
  b $15f - h$
  c $5e + 2h$
  d $8e + 6f$

Developing fluency

1 Football teams use the formula $3w + d$ to work out the number of points they have, where w is the number of wins and d is the number of draws.

  a Work out the points these teams have.
    i   8 wins and 3 draws
    ii 10 wins and 2 draws
    iii 7 wins and 5 draws

  b Make w the subject of the formula.

  c A team has 20 points. It has drawn 5 matches. How many matches has it won?

Algebra Strand 1 Starting algebra

2 A taxi driver uses the formula $c = 2p + 1.5m$ to work out the fares, where £c is the fare, p is the number of passengers and m miles is the distance travelled.
  a Work out the fares for these journeys.
    i 2 passengers and 6 miles
    ii 1 passenger and 8 miles
    iii 3 passengers and 10 miles
  b Make m the subject of this formula.
  c Find the length of a journey for 3 passengers costing £10.50.

3 A plumber charges £35 per hour plus £18 call-out charge.
  a Write a formula for the cost of a job, £C, lasting h hours.
  b How much does he charge for a job lasting
    i 2 hours
    ii 6 hours
    iii 10 hours?
  c Rearrange your formula to make h the subject.
  d How long did the job last if it cost
    i £158
    ii £438
    iii £963?

4 The surface area of a sphere is given by the formula $S = 4\pi r^2$ where r is the radius of the sphere. Use the π key on your calculator.
  a Find the surface area of the spheres with radius
    i 6 cm
    ii 12 m
    iii 400 km
  b The radius of the Earth is approximately 6400 km. Find its surface area.
  c Rearrange the formula to make r the subject.
  d Find the radius of a marble with surface area 50.265 cm^2.
    Give your answer to 2 decimal places.

5 The formula to convert temperatures in Fahrenheit, $F°$, to degrees Celsius, $C°$, is $C = \frac{5}{9}(F - 32)$.
  a Convert these Fahrenheit temperatures to degrees Celsius.
    i 32°
    ii 95°
    iii 212°
    iv −40°
  b Make F the subject of this formula.
  c Find the value of F when
    i $C = 0$
    ii $C = 35$
    iii $C = 300$
    iv $C = -40$

6 Here is a formula.
$$P = \frac{4Mt^2}{h}$$
  a Work out the value of P when $M = 200$, $t = 4$ and $h = 25$.
  b Rearrange the formula to make these the subject.
    i M
    ii t
    iii h
  c Use the appropriate formula to work out the values of
    i M when $P = 4000$, $t = 10$ and $h = 5$
    ii h when $P = 640$, $t = 8$ and $M = 50$
    iii t when $P = 98$, $M = 4$ and $h = 8$.

7 Make the bold letter the subject of these formulae.
  a $y = 5\mathbf{x} - 6$
  b $y = 5(\mathbf{x} - 6)$
  c $T = 4m\mathbf{p}$
  d $T = m^2 + 4\mathbf{p}r$

Problem solving

1. Tara uses the formula $C = 30h + 15$ to work out how much she is going to charge a customer, £C, for working on a car for h hours.
   a. How much does she charge for working on a car for 5 hours?
   b. Make h subject of the formula.
   c. Tara charges Tom £52.50 for working on his car.
      For how long does Tara work on Tom's car?

2. The cost, £C, of hiring a cement mixer for d days is given by the formula $C = 12d + 20$.
   Rob hires a cement mixer for 7 days.
   a. How much does it cost?
   b. Make d the subject of the formula.
   c. Celia hires a cement mixer and pays £200.
      How many days did Celia hire the mixer for?

3. Nia's monthly bill, £B, for using a mobile phone when she makes c calls and sends t texts is given by the formula $B = \dfrac{10c + 5t}{100} + 15$.
   Last month Nia made 120 calls and sent 450 texts.
   a. How much was her bill?
   b. Make c the subject of the formula.
   c. This month Nia's bill was £28. She sent 100 texts. How many calls did she make?

4. The density, d, of a solid object is given by the formula $d = \dfrac{m}{V}$, where m is the mass of the object and V is its volume.
   a. Make m the subject of the formula.
   b. A packet of butter in the shape of a cuboid has dimensions 10 cm by 6 cm by 4 cm.
      The density of the butter is 1.05 g/cm³.
      Find the mass of the butter.

5. The volume, V, of tomato soup in a can is given by the formula $V = \pi r^2 h$, where r is the radius of the can and h is the height of the can.
   a. Make h the subject of the formula.
   b. The radius of the can is 3.5 cm and the volume of the soup in the can is 400 cm³. Find the height of the can.
      Give your answer to the nearest 0.1 cm.

Algebra Strand 1 Starting algebra

6 The area of a trapezium is given by the formula
$A = \frac{1}{2}(a + b)h$

  a Find the area of the trapezium when $a = 6$, $b = 10$, and $h = 4$.

  b Make h the subject of the formula.

  c Find the value of h when $A = 30$, $a = 4.75$ and $b = 7.25$.

  d Now make a the subject of the formula.

  e Find the value of a when $A = 32.5$, $h = 7$ and $b = 5.28$.

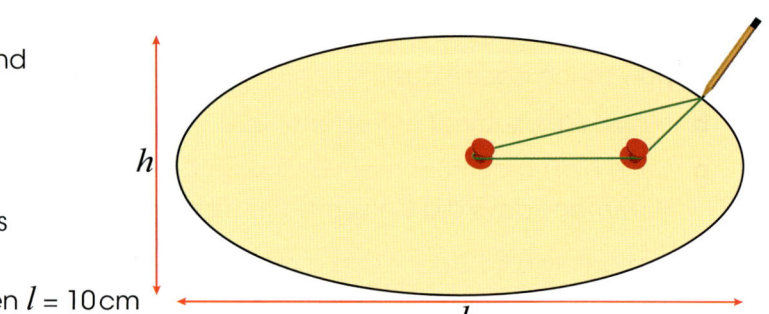

7 Dave draws an ellipse on a piece of paper using a piece of string and two drawing pins.

The area of an ellipse is given by the formula $A = \frac{\pi l h}{4}$ where l is the length of the ellipse and h is its height.

  a Find the area of the ellipse when $l = 10$ cm and $h = 4$ cm. Give your answer in terms of π.

  b Make l the subject of the formula.

  c Dave draws another ellipse. The height of this ellipse is 6 cm, and its area is 15π cm². Find the length of this ellipse.

Reviewing skills

1 Make the bold letter the subject of these formulae.

  a $d = \mathbf{e} + f$
  b $s = a\mathbf{t} + b$
  c $f = \frac{g}{\mathbf{h}}$
  d $v = 4\mathbf{w} - 3$

  e $C = 2\pi \mathbf{r}$
  f $A = \pi \mathbf{r}^2$
  g $P = \frac{Mt\mathbf{r}}{100}$
  h $S = 3\mathbf{t}^2$

2 The final velocity, v, of particles in an experiment is given by the formula $v = u + at$, where a is the acceleration, u is the initial velocity and t is the time of travel.

  a Find the value of v when

   i $u = 4$, $a = 2$, $t = 3$

   ii $u = -10$, $a = 5$, $t = 2$,

   iii $u = 20$, $a = -10$, $t = 4$

   iv $u = 30$, $a = 0$, $t = 7$

  b Make a the subject of the formula.

  c A particle accelerates from 10 m/s to 25 m/s in 5 seconds. Calculate its acceleration.

3 Indicate the correct answer **a**, **b**, **c** or **d**.
The formula $3s^4 = t^2$ is rearranged.

  a $t = 9s^2$
  b $t = 9s^3$
  c $t = \sqrt{3}s^2$
  d $t = s^2\sqrt{3}$

Algebra Strand 2 Sequences

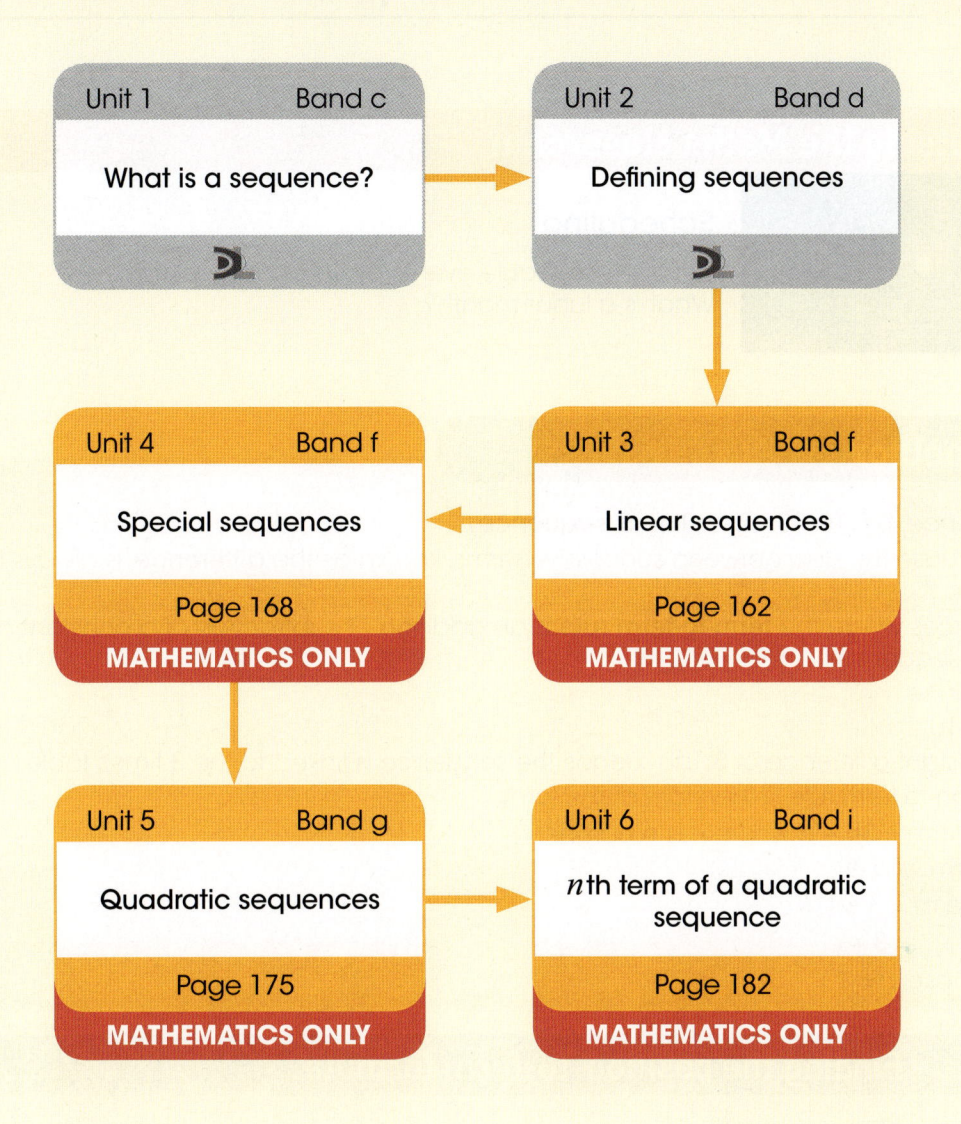

Unit 1	Band c
What is a sequence?	

Unit 2	Band d
Defining sequences	

Unit 3	Band f
Linear sequences	
Page 162	
MATHEMATICS ONLY	

Unit 4	Band f
Special sequences	
Page 168	
MATHEMATICS ONLY	

Unit 5	Band g
Quadratic sequences	
Page 175	
MATHEMATICS ONLY	

Unit 6	Band i
nth term of a quadratic sequence	
Page 182	
MATHEMATICS ONLY	

Units 1–2 are assumed knowledge for this book. Knowledge and skills from these units are used throughout the book.

Unit 3 • Linear sequences • Band f

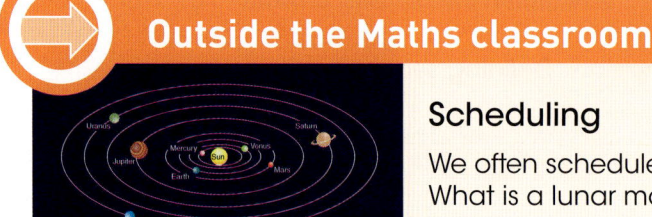

Outside the Maths classroom

Scheduling
We often schedule events by week or by month.
What is a lunar month?

Toolbox

The sequence 4, 7, 10, 13, ... is a **linear sequence**.
This is because the gap between successive terms, known as the **difference**, is always the same, in this case 3.
All sequences where the **term-to-term rule** is an addition or subtraction of a constant amount are linear sequences.
The sequence
$$4, 7, 10, 13, \ldots$$
has a constant difference of 3. This means the sequence is linked to the 3 times table.
The position-to-term rule is therefore of the form
$$n\text{th term} = 3n + c \text{ where } c \text{ is a number.}$$
The first term will be
$$\text{1st term} = 3 \times 1 + c$$
$$= 3 + c$$
So in this case, $c = 1$

Example – Finding the position-to-term formula

For each of the sequences below
  i   find the next three terms
  ii find the position-to-term formula

  a 8, 16, 24, 32, 40, ...   b 27, 25, 23, 21, 19, ...

Solution

a i To get the next term, add 8 each time.
      So the next three terms are 48, 56, 64.
   ii Since the sequence is linear, nth term = $8n$ + a number. ← *The difference is 8 so the sequence is related to the 8 times table.*
      Look at the first term of the sequence.
      It is 8 so there is no need to add a number in this case.
      So nth term = $8n$.
b i To get the next term, subtract 2 each time.
      So the next three terms are 17, 15, 13.
   ii Since the sequence is linear, nth term = $-2n$ + a number. ← *The difference is –2 so the sequence is related to the –2 times table.*
      The first term of the sequence is 27. ← *$n = 1$ for the first term.*
      So nth term = $-2n + 29$.
      Or, more neatly, nth term = $29 - 2n$.

Unit 3 Linear sequences Band f

Example – Generating a sequence using a position-to-term rule

Write down the first five terms of the sequence with this position-to-term rule.

nth term = $14n + 45$

Solution

Method 1 – using nth term formula for all terms:

When $n = 1$, 1st term = $14 \times 1 + 45 = 59$ ← Substitute the term number into the nth term formula.
When $n = 2$, 2nd term = $14 \times 2 + 45 = 73$
When $n = 3$, 3rd term = $14 \times 3 + 45 = 87$
When $n = 4$, 4th term = $14 \times 4 + 45 = 101$
When $n = 5$, 5th term = $14 \times 5 + 45 = 115$

Method 2 – using position-to-term rule for first term only:

When $n = 1$, 1st term = $14 \times 1 + 45 = 59$
From the formula, the common difference is 14.
2nd term = $59 + 14 = 73$ ← Add 14 to previous term.
3rd term = $73 + 14 = 87$
4th term = $87 + 14 = 101$
5th term = $101 + 14 = 115$

Practising skills

1) For each of these describe the sequence by giving the first term and the term-to-term rule.
   a 4, 11, 18, 25, 32, …
   b 6, 11, 16, 21, 26, …
   c 38, 35, 32, 29, 26, …
   d 12, 15, 18, 21, 24, …

2) For each of these position-to-term rules write down the first five terms of the sequence.
   a nth term = 3 × position
   b nth term = 4 × position + 2
   c nth term = 2 × position + 25

3) Look at these linear sequences.
   A 30, ☐, ☐, 54, 62, …
   B 84, ☐, ☐, 75, 72, …

   a Work out the missing terms.
   b The 100th terms are for **A** 822 and for **B** −213.
      Write down the 101st term for each sequence.
   c Complete these position-to-term rules for each sequence.
      i ☐ × position + 22
      ii −3 × position + ☐

4) The first term in a sequence is a and the number added on to each term to get the next term is d.
   In each sequence
      i   find the values of a and d
      ii give the next two terms.
   a 23, 27, 31, 35, …
   b 38, 44, 50, 56, …
   c 46, 43, 40, 37, …
   d −4, −2, 0, 2, …
   e 6, 1, −4, −9, …

Algebra Strand 2 Sequences

5 Here are the position-to-term formulae for three sequences.

   a $3n + 1$ **b** $6n - 2$ **c** $4n + 3$

In each case

   i write down the first 4 terms, and the 100th term

   ii write down the differences between each term, and write down the first term

   iii what is the connection between your answers to part **ii** and the formulae?

6 Write down the position-to-term formulae for these sequences.

   a 5, 8, 11, 14, …   **b** 4, 6, 8, 10, …   **c** 5, 9, 13, 17, …

7 Use these position-to-term formulae to work out the first five terms and the 20th term for these sequences.

   a $3n + 6$ **b** $2n + 5$ **c** $7n - 3$

8 For each of these sequences

   i write down the position-to-term formula

   ii work out the 100th term.

   a 11, 15, 19, 23, …   **b** 2, 12, 22, 32, …   **c** 11, 18, 25, 32, …

Developing fluency

1 Match the sequences to their rules.

3, 6, 9, 12, … $5n + 1$

7, 9, 11, 13, … $3n$

6, 11, 16, 21, … $2n + 5$

2 For each of these number machines, copy and complete the table and then write down the rule as a formula for the output.

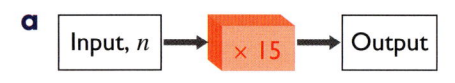

a Input, n → × 15 → Output

Input, n	2		5		12
Output	30	45		150	

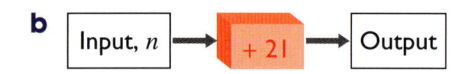

b Input, n → + 21 → Output

Input, n	6			15	
Output		33	35		53

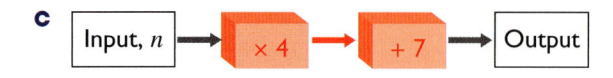

c Input, n → × 4 → + 7 → Output

Input, n	1	2	5		
Output	11			47	87

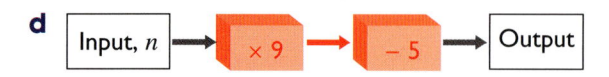

d Input, n → × 9 → − 5 → Output

Input, n	1	6		20	
Output			85		202

Unit 3 Linear sequences Band f

3) Here is a sequence of pentagonal matchstick patterns.

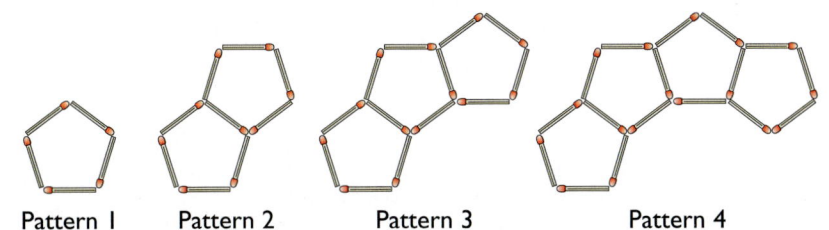

Pattern 1   Pattern 2   Pattern 3   Pattern 4

a Draw the next two patterns.

b Copy and complete this table for the first six patterns.

Number of pentagons	1	2	3	4	5	6
Number of matchsticks	5					

c Predict the number of matchsticks for seven pentagons. Explain how you found your answer.

d Write down the position-to-term formula.

e Predict the number of matchsticks for
   i 10 pentagons   ii 20 pentagons.

f How many pentagons will 101 matchsticks make?

4) Write these position-to-term formulae with the correct notation.

a the nth term is found by $n \times 5$ subtract 2

b the nth term is found by $n \times 3$ add 8

c the nth term is found by multiplying n by 6 and subtracting 5

d the nth term is found by dividing n by 2 and adding 3

5) Here are the first four terms of a sequence.
   6, 10, 14, 18

a i Write down the next term.   ii Explain how you found your answer.

b Write down the position-to-term formula for this sequence.

c Use your formula to work out the 40th term.

d Which position is the term 350?

6) Here are the first four terms of a sequence.
   3, 9, 15, 21

a i Write down the next term.   ii Explain how you found your answer.

b Write down the position-to-term formula for this sequence.

c Use your formula to work out the 40th term.

d Which position is the term 267?

Algebra Strand 2 Sequences

7 Here is a sequence of square matchstick patterns.

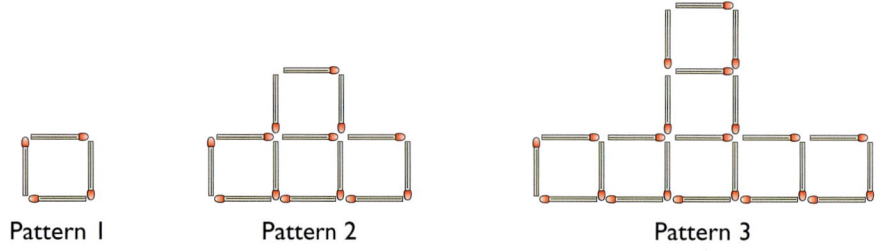

Pattern 1   Pattern 2   Pattern 3

a Draw the next two patterns.

b Copy and complete the table for the first six patterns.

Pattern number	1	2	3	4	5	6
Number of matchsticks	4					

c i Predict the number of matchsticks for pattern number seven.
  ii Explain how you found your answer.

d Write down the position-to-term formula.

e Predict the number of matchsticks for
  i pattern 10   **ii** pattern 20.

f Why is the number of matchsticks for pattern 20 **not** double that for pattern 10?

g How many **squares** will 85 matchsticks make?

8 Owain has written a sequence.
8, 14, 20, 26, 32, 38, 44, …
Owain continues his sequence.
Which of these numbers would be in Owain's sequence? You must give a reason for your answer.

  a 52   **b** 74   **c** 122   **d** 200

9 Lois has written the nth term of a sequence, $5n - 8$.
Which of the following numbers are in Lois's sequence? You must give a reason for your answer.

  a 32   **b** 42   **c** 94   **d** 119

Problem solving

1 A school uses hexagonal tables in its dining hall.
The tables are always laid out according to this pattern.
One chair is placed at each open edge of each table.

  a How many chairs are needed for a pattern with 4 tables?

  b How many chairs are needed to fit around a pattern with n tables?

  c 77 students need to be seated on tables and chairs laid out in this pattern.
  Show that there will be one empty chair if the least number of tables are used.

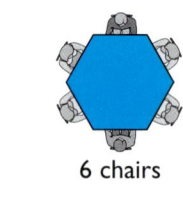

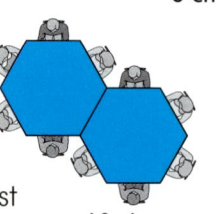

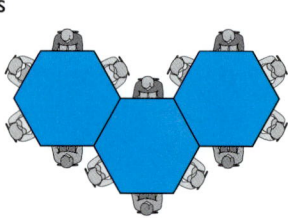

6 chairs

10 chairs

14 chairs

Unit 3 Linear sequences Band f

2 Andy makes a sequence by counting back from 40 in threes.
The sequence starts 40, 37, 34, … .

40, 37, 34,…

  a Write down the next two terms in Andy's sequence.

  b State which one of the following is the formula for the nth term of Andy's sequence.

  i $40 - 3n$ **iii** $43 - 3n$ **ii** $40 + 3n$ **iv** $43 + 3n$

  c Explain whether 2 is a member of this sequence.

Andy

3 The mth term of sequence A is $4m - 3$.
The nth term of sequence B is $63 - 7n$.
How many terms do the sequences have in common?

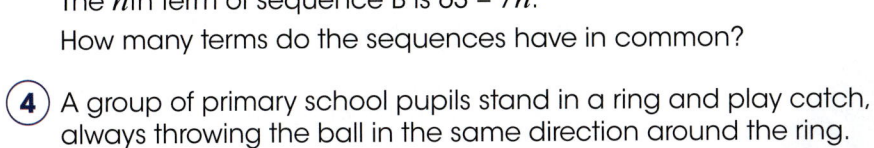

4 A group of primary school pupils stand in a ring and play catch, always throwing the ball in the same direction around the ring.
When they throw the ball they say a number, with the first person (person A) saying '1', the second (person B) saying '2', and so on.
The game stops with the person saying '100' being the winner.
When four people play, Billy works out that he can win if he stands in position D.

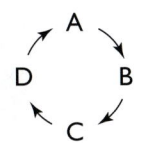

  a Explain how he knows this.

  b Where should Billy stand if there are five people?

  c What about

  i six people   **ii** seven people?

Reviewing skills

1 Here are the first few terms of a sequence.
9, ☐, ☐, ☐, 41, ☐, 57, …

  a Work out the term-to-term rule.

  b Write down the position-to-term formula for this sequence.

  c Find the 50th term.

  d Which position is the term 449?

2 For each of these sequences

  i write down the position-to-term formula   **ii** work out the 100th term.

  a 80, 76, 72, 68, …   **b** 100, 95, 90, 85, …

  c 60, 58, 56, 54, …   **d** 80, 86, 92, 98, …

3 Here are the first three of a sequence of cross-shaped patterns.

  a How many dots are there in patterns 4 and 5?

  b Give a formula for the number of dots, d, in pattern number n.

  c How many dots are there in

  i pattern 90   **ii** pattern 120?

  d What pattern has 645 dots?

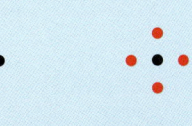

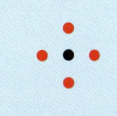

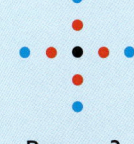

Pattern 1   Pattern 2   Pattern 3

167

Unit 4 • Special sequences • Band f

Outside the Maths classroom

Patterns in nature
What do the spirals on these pine cones have in common with flower petals?

Toolbox

There are some important number sequences that are not linear (i.e. that do not have a constant difference between terms).

- **The triangular numbers:** 1, 3, 6, 10, ... (that is, 1, 1 + 2, 1 + 2 + 3, 1 + 2 + 3 + 4, etc.).

  The difference between successive terms increases by one each time.

  The position-to-term formula for the triangular numbers is nth term = $\frac{n(n+1)}{2}$.

- **The square numbers**: 1, 4, 9, 16, 25, ... (that is 1 × 1, 2 × 2, 3 × 3, 4 × 4, 5 × 5, etc.).

  The difference between successive terms is 1, 3, 5, 7, 9, etc. and the position-to-term formula is nth term = n^2.

- **The Fibonacci numbers**: 1, 1, 2, 3, 5, 8, 13, 21, ... where each term (after the initial two) is the sum of the two previous terms.

  The difference between successive terms is the Fibonacci sequence itself!

Many sequences are variations of these.
For example,

    101, 104, 109, 116, ... is the sequence of square numbers plus 100.
    3, 12, 27, 48, ... is the sequence of square numbers multiplied by 3.

Unit 4 Special sequences Band f

Example – Investigating triangular numbers

Look at this sequence of patterns.

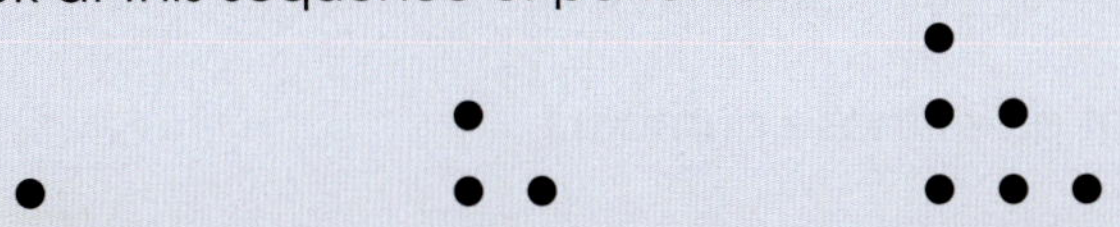

Triangle 1   Triangle 2   Triangle 3

a Draw the next three triangles.
b How many dots are there in each triangle?
c What pattern do you notice in the number sequence?
d The formula for the nth term of the sequence is $\frac{n(n+1)}{2}$.

   Use this formula to check your answer for triangle 5.
e Find the 10th triangular number.

Solution

a

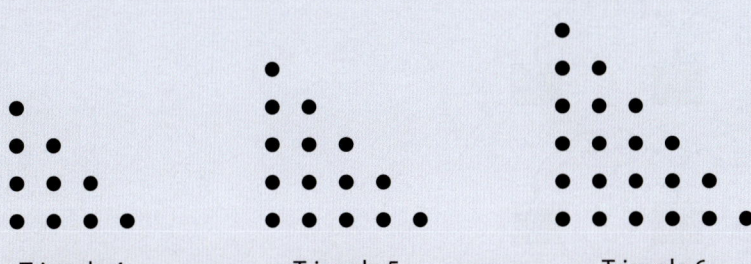

Triangle 4   Triangle 5   Triangle 6

b Triangle 1 has 1 dot.
Triangle 2 has 3 dots – 2 dots are added.
Triangle 3 has 6 dots – 3 dots are added.
Triangle 4 has 10 dots – 4 dots are added.
Triangle 5 has 15 dots – 5 dots are added.
Triangle 6 has 21 dots – 6 dots are added.

c The number of dots added increases by one each time.

d For $n = 5$,
$$\frac{n(n+1)}{2} = \frac{5 \times 6}{2} = 15$$

Substitute $n = 5$ into the formula.

So the answer for triangle 5 is right.

e When $n = 10$,
$$\frac{n(n+1)}{2} = \frac{10 \times 11}{2} = 55$$

So the 10th triangular number is 55.

Algebra Strand 2 Sequences

Practising skills

1) For each of these sequences
  i describe the sequence
  ii draw the first 4 patterns in a sequence that gives these numbers
  iii find its position-to-term formula.

  a 2, 4, 6, 8, 10, 12, ...
  b 1, 4, 9, 16, 25, 36, ...
  c 1, 8, 27, 64, 125, ...

2) Find the missing numbers in each of these sequences.

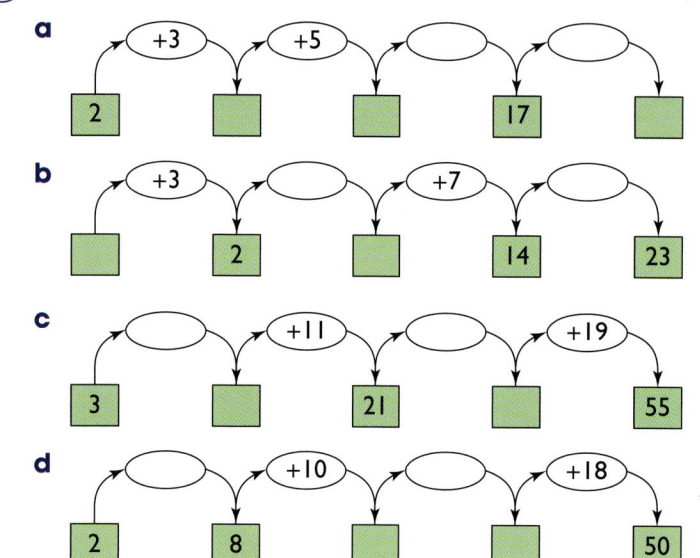

  a 2 → +3 → ☐ → +5 → ☐ → ☐ → 17 → ☐ → ☐

  b ☐ → +3 → 2 → ☐ → ☐ → +7 → 14 → ☐ → 23

  c 3 → ☐ → ☐ → +11 → 21 → ☐ → ☐ → +19 → 55

  d 2 → ☐ → 8 → +10 → ☐ → ☐ → ☐ → +18 → 50

3) Write down the first five terms of these sequences.
  a $n^2 + 10$
  b $n^3 - 1$
  c $\dfrac{(n^2 + n)}{2}$

  What name is given to the numbers in the last sequence?

4) Find the position-to-term formulae for these sequences.
  a 1, 4, 9, 16, 25, ...
  b 2, 5, 10, 17, 26, ...
  c 0, 3, 8, 15, 24, ...
  d 2, 8, 18, 32, 50, ...

5) Find the position-to-term formulae for these sequences.
  a 11, 14, 19, 26, 35, ...
  b 1, 8, 27, 64, 125, ...
  c 6, 13, 32, 69, 130, ...
  d 2, 16, 54, 128, 250, ...

Unit 4 Special sequences Band f

Developing fluency

1 Here are the first three patterns in a sequence made from triangles.

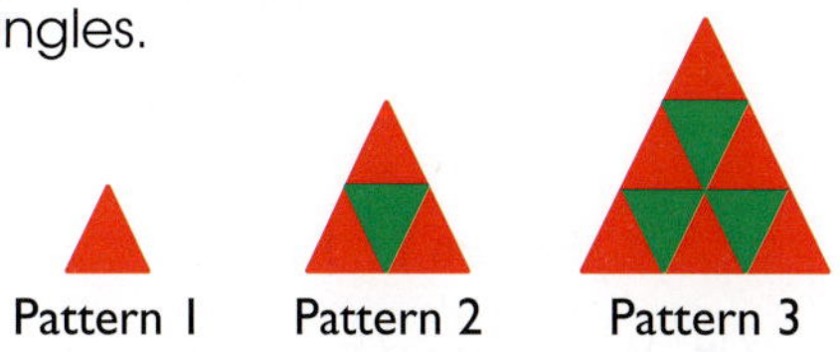

   a Draw pattern number 4.

   b Copy and complete the table.

Pattern number	1	2	3	4	5
Number of red triangles	1	3			
Number of green triangles	0	1			
Total number of triangles, T	1				

Pattern 1   Pattern 2   Pattern 3

   c What are the names of the sequences in the table?

   d Work out the total number of triangles in the 10th pattern.
      In the 10th pattern, how many triangles are
       i red   **ii** green?

   e Find a formula for the total number of triangles, T, in pattern n.

2 Look at these sequences.
     i 2, 4, 8, 16, …   **ii** 1, 2, 4, 7, 11, …

   a What is the rule for finding the next term in each sequence?

   b Write down the first 16 numbers in each sequence.

   c Which numbers are in both sequences?

   d Which square numbers are in sequence **i**?

3 Lucy is making tiling patterns.

   a Draw pattern number 4.

   b Copy and complete the table.

Pattern number	1	2	3	4	5
Number of black tiles	4	4			
Number of blue tiles	1	4			
Total number of tiles, T	5				

Pattern 1   Pattern 2   Pattern 3

   c Work out the total number of tiles in the 10th pattern.

   d Which pattern uses 229 tiles?

   e Find a formula for the total number of tiles, T, in pattern n.

   f Lucy has 400 tiles.
      i Can she use them all to make a single pattern?
         Give a reason for your answer.
      ii Write down the pattern number she can make.
         How many tiles (if any) does she have left over?

Algebra Strand 2 Sequences

4 Here are the first four patterns in a sequence made from coloured counters.

Pattern 1   Pattern 2   Pattern 3   Pattern 4

a Write down how many counters are added to
  i pattern 1 to make pattern 2
  ii pattern 2 to make pattern 3
  iii pattern 3 to make pattern 4.

b How many counters need to be added to make pattern 5?

c How many counters are in pattern 10?

d How many counters are in the nth pattern?

e Which pattern number has $(1 + 3 + 5 + 7 + 9 + 11 + 13)$ counters?

f What is the sum of the first 100 odd numbers?

5 a Write down the first five terms of the sequence with this position-to-term formula.

nth term = $n(n + 1)$

b i Use your answer to part **a** to write down the position-to-term formula for this sequence.
    1, 3, 6, 10, 15, …
  ii Describe the numbers in this sequence.
  iii Draw the first five patterns in a sequence that gives these numbers.
  iv Find the value of the 40th term.

c i Now look at these patterns.

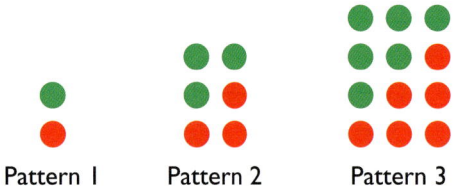

Pattern 1   Pattern 2   Pattern 3

Draw patterns 4 and 5 of this sequence.
  ii The number of circles in **pattern 1** is 1×2.
    In **pattern 2** it is 2×3.
    How many circles are there in pattern n?
  iii In pattern n, how many circles are red?
    How many circles are green?
  iv How is this connected to part **b** of this question?

Unit 4 Special sequences Band f

6 Look at these matchstick patterns.

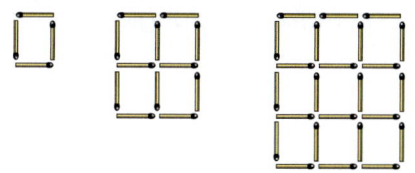

Pattern 1   Pattern 2   Pattern 3

a Draw pattern number 4.

b Copy and complete the table.

Pattern number	1	2	3	4	5
Number of matches, M	4	12			

c Work out the total number of matches in the 8th pattern.

d i Write down the first five triangular numbers.

  ii How is the sequence for the number of matches related to the triangular numbers?

  iii The nth triangular number is $\frac{1}{2}n(n+1)$.

    How many matchsticks are in the 20th pattern?

  iv Write down a formula for the total number of matches, M.

Problem solving

1 Here is a sequence of Fibonacci numbers.
0, 1, 1, 2, 3, 5, 8, 13, …

  a Continue the pattern for all Fibonacci numbers less than 200.

  b List the Fibonacci numbers under 200 that are prime numbers.

  c Find the Fibonacci numbers under 200 that can be factorised using other Fibonacci numbers.

2 Here is an old puzzle.
A cow produces its first female calf at age two years and after that she produces another female calf every year.
The table shows the number of cows after six years.

Year	Original cow	First new cow's calf	Second new cow's calf	Total
1	1			1
2	1			1
3	1 + 1			2
4	1 + 1 + 1			
5	1 + 1 + 1 + 1	1		
6	1 + 1 + 1 + 1 + 1	1 + 1	1	

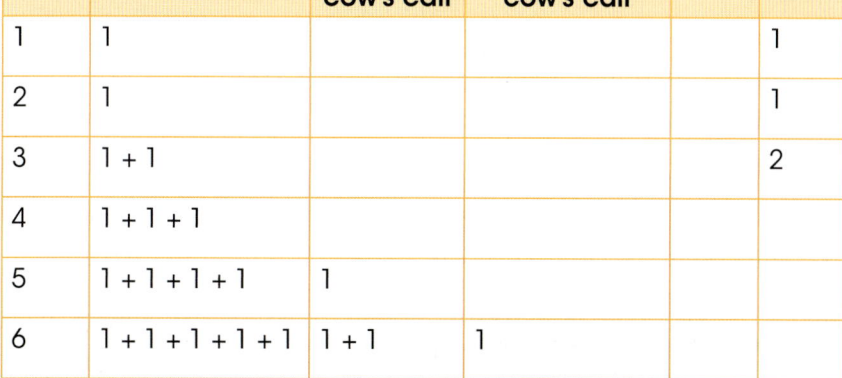

How many female cows are there after 12 years, assuming none die?

173

Algebra Strand 2 Sequences

3 Elen is making rectangles out of dominoes. They are always the height of a domino.
When she has two dominoes there are two ways she can make a rectangle.

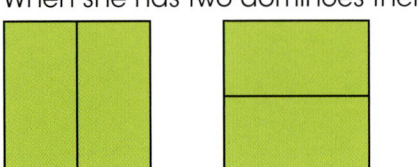

✓

Putting the dominoes end to end doesn't work because the rectangle is not the height of a domino.

✗

a How many different rectangles that are the height of a domino can Elen make if she has
  i 3 dominoes   **ii** 4 dominoes   **iii** 5 dominoes?

b Describe the sequence you have generated.

c How can you explain the pattern?

Reviewing skills

1 Write down the first five terms of these sequences.
  a $n^2 + 5$ **b** $2n^2 - 1$ **c** $n^3 + 3$ **d** $n(n - 1)$

2 Find the position-to-term formulae for these sequences.
  a 3, 6, 11, 18, 27, …   **b** −2, 1, 6, 13, 22, …   **c** 2, 9, 28, 65, 126, …   **d** 3, 12, 27, 48, 75, …

3 Look at these tiling patterns.

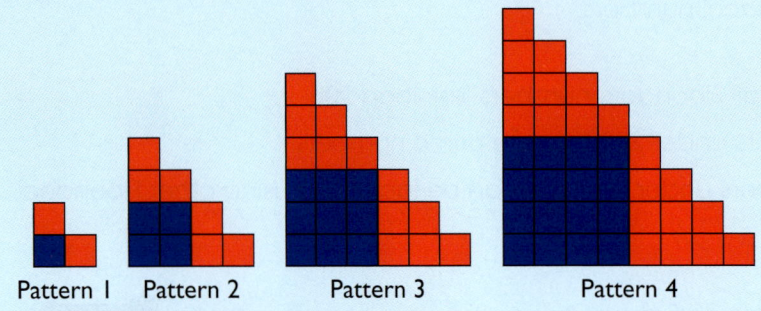

Pattern 1   Pattern 2   Pattern 3   Pattern 4

a Copy and complete the table.

Pattern number	1	2	3	4	5
Number of blue squares					
Number of red squares					
Total number of squares					

b Write down an expression for the number of blue squares in pattern n.
Ben realises that the total number of red squares follows this pattern:

Number of red squares in pattern 1 = 1 × 2 = 2
Number of red squares in pattern 2 = 2 × 3 = 6
Number of red squares in pattern 3 = 3 × 4 = 12

c How many red squares are in pattern 10?

d Write down an expression for the number of red squares in pattern n.

e Ben says that it is impossible for a pattern to have 500 red squares.
Is Ben right? Give a reason for your answer.

f Hence find a rule for the total number of squares. What type of numbers are these?

Unit 5 • Quadratic sequences • Band g

Outside the Maths classroom

Building bridges
What shape is the curve on this bridge?

How does knowing the equation of the curve help the engineers build the bridge?

Toolbox

The sequence of **square numbers** begins 1, 4, 9, 16, 25, ...

The differences between these terms are 3, 5, 7, 9, ... and the difference between these differences is constant. In this case, it is 2.

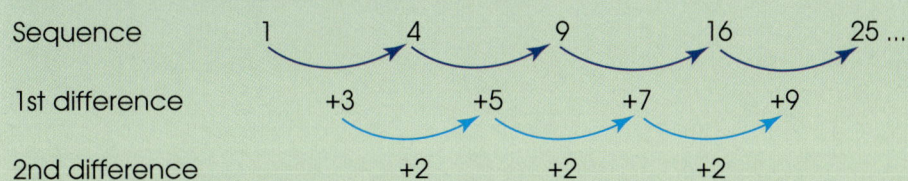

Sequence   1   4   9   16   25 ...

1st difference   +3   +5   +7   +9

2nd difference   +2   +2   +2

Such sequences are known as **quadratic sequences** and the expression for the nth term always contain a term in n^2.

For example, the formula for the nth term of a simple quadratic sequence rule might be $n^2 + 1$, which would give 2, 5, 10, 17, 26, ...

To find the rule for a quadratic sequence, look at the relationship between the square numbers (1, 4, 9, 16, 25) and the sequence itself.

Example – Generating terms of a quadratic sequence

Find the fourth and sixth terms of the sequence whose nth term is given by $3n^2 - 8$.

Solution

When $n = 4$,
$3n^2 - 8 = 3 \times 4^2 - 8$
$= 3 \times 16 - 8$ ← Squaring first.
$= 48 - 8$ ← Then multiplication.
$= 40$

When $n = 6$,
$3n^2 - 8 = 3 \times 6^2 - 8$ ← Substitute 6 into the formula.
$= 3 \times 36 - 8$ ← Squaring first.
$= 108 - 8$ ← Then multiplication.
$= 100$

Algebra Strand 2 Sequences

Example – Finding the nth term of a quadratic sequence

Here is a sequence of patterns.

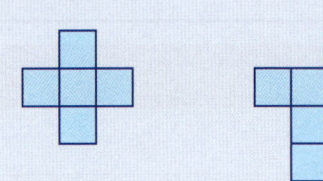

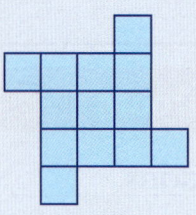

Pattern 1   Pattern 2   Pattern 3

a Draw pattern 4.
b The number of squares in the patterns form a sequence.
  What are the first five terms of the sequence?
c Find the nth term of this sequence.
  Explain how the patterns help you to find the nth term of the sequence.

Solution

a

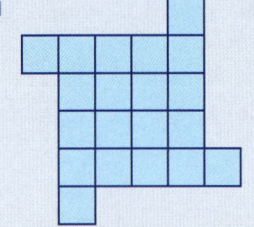

Pattern 4

b From the diagrams, the first four terms are 5, 8, 13, 20.

Sequence   5   8   13   20 ...
1st difference   +3   +5   +7
2nd difference   +2   +2

The next first difference will be 9, so the fifth term is 29.

c The first differences are not the same so the sequence is not linear.
  The second differences are the same so this is a quadratic sequence.

Square numbers   1   4   9   16   25   ← Start with the square numbers.
                +4   +4   +4   +4   +4
This sequence   5   8   13   20   29   ← To get the required sequence, add 4.

The nth term is therefore $n^2 + 4$.
Look at the pattern.
- The first pattern is a 1 × 1 square plus four single squares.
- The second pattern is a 2 × 2 square plus four single squares.
- The third pattern is a 3 × 3 square plus four single squares.

So the nth pattern will be an $n \times n$ square plus four single squares, giving $n^2 + 4$ squares in total.

Unit 5 Quadratic sequences Band g

Practising skills

1 Write down the first five terms for these sequences.
  a nth term $= 5n^2$
  b nth term $= n^2 + 5$
  c nth term $= 2n^2 - 1$
  d nth term $= 3n^2 + 4$
  e nth term $= 10n^2 - 5$

2 Match each sequence with its position-to-term formula.
  a 9, 8, 7, 6, 5, ...   **i** $n^2 + 10$
  b 90, 80, 70, 60, 50, ...   **ii** $10 - n$
  c 10, 40, 90, 160, 250, ...   **iii** $100 - 10n$
  d 11, 14, 19, 26, 35, ...   **iv** $10n^2$

3 Find the missing term in each of these sequences and then write down the position-to-term formula.
  a 1, 4, 9, ☐, 25
  b 2, 5, 10, ☐, 26
  c 2, 8, ☐, 32, 50
  d 5, 11, 21, ☐, 53

4 a Copy and complete this table for the sequence with nth term $n^2 + 3$.
  (You may find compiling a spreadsheet useful for this.)

Term	$n^2 + 3$	1st difference	2nd difference
1	4		
2	7	3	
3	12	5	2
4			
5			

  b Repeat part **a** for
   i $n^2 - 1$ **ii** $n^2 + 2$ **iii** $2n^2 - 3$
   iv $5n^2$ **v** $3n^2 + 5$

  c Do all quadratic sequences have the same second difference?

5 Match each sequence with its position-to-term formula.
   i $2n^2 + 2$ **ii** $n^2 + 2$ **iii** $4n^2 + 6$ **iv** $5n^2 + 5$ **v** $100 - 2n^2$
  a 10, 22, 42, 70, 106, ...
  b 98, 92, 82, 68, 50, ...
  c 4, 10, 20, 34, 52, ...
  d 3, 6, 11, 18, 27, ...
  e 10, 25, 50, 85, 130, ...

Algebra Strand 2 Sequences

6 a Which of these sequences are quadratic?
  i   5, 8, 13, 20, 29, …
  ii 10, 20, 30, 40, 50, …
  iii 3, 12, 27, 48, 75, …
  iv 2, 16, 54, 128, 250, …
  v   5, 11, 21, 35, 53, …

  b For the quadratic sequences, write down the position-to-term formula.

Developing fluency

1 Look at this table of sequences.
  a Write down the next term in each sequence.
  b Write down the rule for the nth term of sequence **A** and **B**.
  c i How is sequence **C** related to sequence **B**?
    ii Write down the nth term of sequence **C**.
  d i How is sequence **D** related to sequences **A** and **B**?
    ii Write down the nth term of sequence **D**.
  e i Which two sequences are used to make sequence **E**?
    ii Write down the nth term of sequence **E**.

	1	2	3	4	5	…
A	2	4	6	8	10	…
B	1	4	9	16	25	…
C	0	3	8	15	24	…
D	3	8	15	24	35	…
E	2	7	14	23	34	…

2 Katrina is making a sequence of patterns from square tiles.
  a Draw the next pattern in the sequence.
  b Copy and complete the table.

Pattern	1	2	3	4	5
Number of tiles					

  c Which pattern uses 100 tiles?
  d How many tiles are there in the nth pattern?

Katrina removes some tiles from each pattern to make the following sequence of patterns.

  e i   How many tiles does Katrina remove from the 50th pattern?
    ii How many tiles are left in the 50th pattern?
    iii How many tiles are left in the nth pattern?

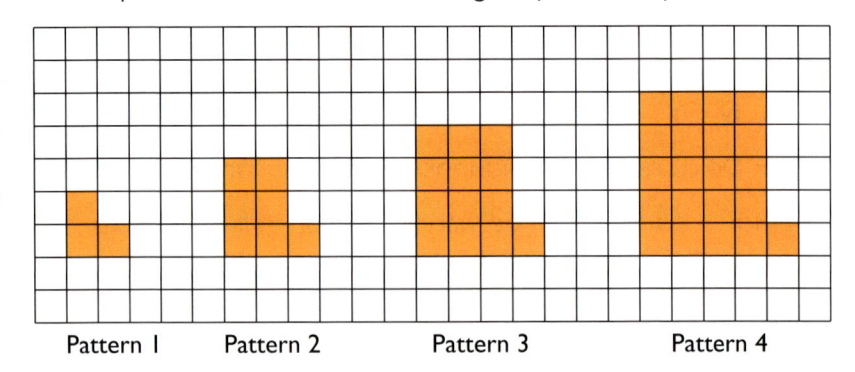

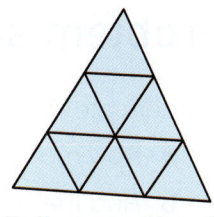

Unit 5 Quadratic sequences Band g

3) Here is a pattern made from triangular tiles.

a How many tiles would be needed for Pattern number 8?

b How many tiles are needed for Pattern number n?

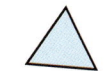

Pattern number 1   Pattern number 2   Pattern number 3

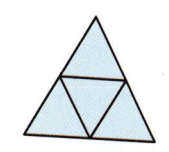

c Which pattern has 100 tiles?

d Explain why the difference between 2 adjacent pattern numbers is always an odd number.

4) Ben is stacking tins of baked beans.

a How many tins are in stack 5?

The 20th stack needs 210 tins.

b How many tins are needed for the 21st stack?

Ben has 120 tins to stack.

c How many tins should he place in the bottom row?

Stack 1   Stack 2   Stack 3

The nth stack has $\frac{1}{2}n(n+1)$ tins.

d How many tins are in the 100th stack?

Comfort has 169 tins to stack.

e i Can she make one stack out of these tins? Explain your answer fully.

ii Comfort uses all of the 169 tins to make 2 stacks. How many tins are in each stack?

5) Look at this Rubik's cube.
It is made up of small cubes around a central mechanism.

a Write down how many cubes have
 i 1 sticker   ii 2 stickers   iii 3 stickers.

b How many cubes have at least one sticker on them?

c You can get different-sized Rubik's cubes. The smallest is a 2 by 2 by 2 cube. You can also get larger cubes like a 5 by 5 by 5 cube.

Copy and complete this table for different-sized cubes.

Cube size	2	3	4	5	10	n
1 sticker						
2 stickers						
3 stickers						
Total number of stickered cubes						

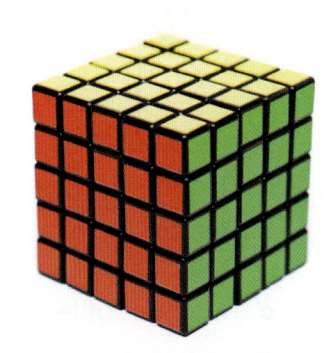

Algebra Strand 2 Sequences

Problem solving

1. Here are the first 3 shapes in a rectangular pattern made from dots.

   a. How many dots are there in pattern number 6?

   b. Find the number of dots in the nth pattern.

   c. Find an expression, in terms of n, for the difference in the number of dots between the nth pattern and the $(n + 1)$ pattern.

   d. Between which two consecutive patterns is the difference in the number of dots 102?

2. Jake draws a circle. He marks points around the circumference of the circle, joining each point to every other point.

Points	Number of lines at each point	Total number of lines
2	1	1
3	2	3
4	3	6
5	4	
6	5	
7	7	
8	8	
n		

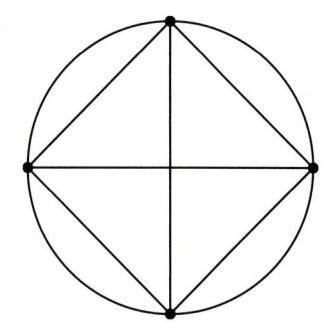

   a. Copy and complete this table for the number of points around the circle.

   b. Mair made a circle pattern by marking points at every 10° from the centre of the circle. How many lines did Mair draw?

3. The nth term of a quadratic sequence is $n^2 + 8$.
   The nth term of a different quadratic sequence is $49 - n^2$.
   Which numbers are in both sequences?

4. The diagrams show the numbers of diagonals in some regular polygons.

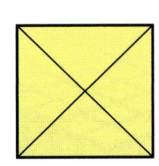

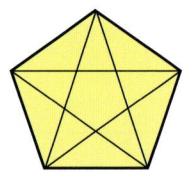

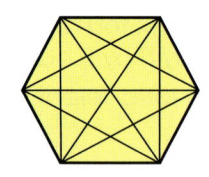

   a. Find the number of diagonals in a regular decagon.

   b. Find an expression, in terms of n, for the number of diagonals at each vertex of an n-sided polygon.

   c. Hence, or otherwise, find the number of diagonals in an n-sided regular polygon.

   d. An n-sided polygon has over 100 diagonals. What is the smallest possible value of n?

Unit 5 Quadratic sequences Band g

Reviewing skills

1. Find the missing term in each of these sequences and then write down the position-to-term formula.

   a 20, 30, 40, 50, 60, ☐, ...

   b 3, 12, 27, ☐, 75, ...

   c 99, 96, 99, ☐, 75, ...

   d 12, 45, 100, ☐, 276, ...

2. Copy and complete this table for the sequence with nth term $n^2 + 5$.

   (You may find compiling a spreadsheet useful for this.)

Term	$n^2 + 5$	1st difference	2nd difference
1	6		
2	9	3	
3	14	5	2
4			
5			

3. Here are some patterns made from square tiles.

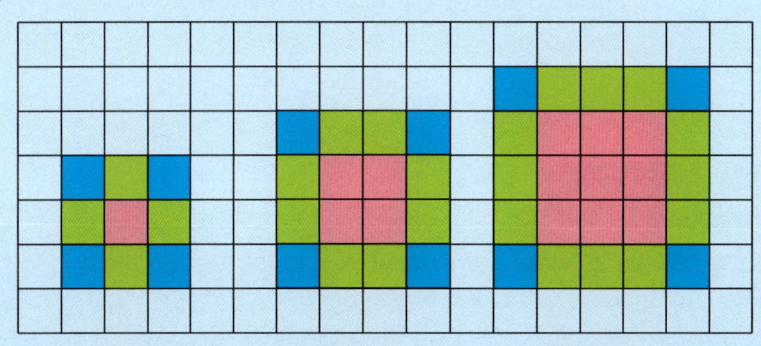

   Pattern 1   Pattern 2   Pattern 3

   a Draw pattern number 4.

   b Copy and complete the table.

Pattern number	1	2	3	4	5
Number of green squares					
Number of blue squares					
Number of red squares					
Total number of squares, S					

   c Write down how many of these are in the 10th pattern.

      i green squares   ii blue squares   iii red squares

      iv Work out the total number of squares in the 10th pattern.

   d Write down how many of these are in the nth pattern.

      i green squares   ii blue squares   iii red squares

   e Write down a formula for the total number of squares, S, in the nth pattern.

   Write your formula in two different ways.

Unit 6 • nth term of a quadratic sequence • Band i

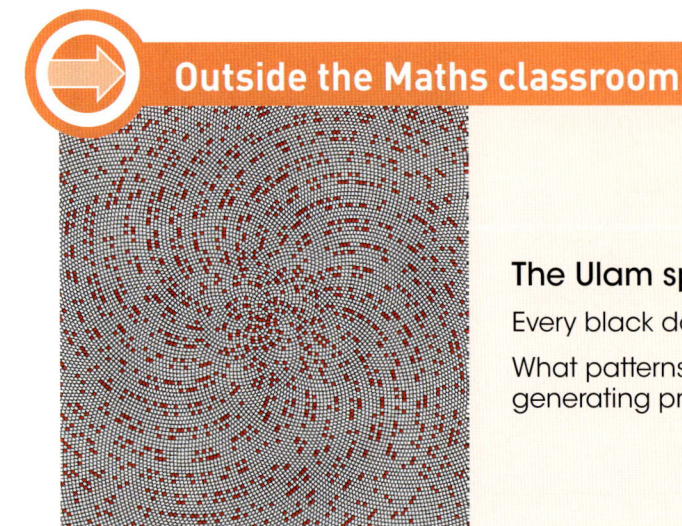

Outside the Maths classroom

The Ulam spiral

Every black dot in this picture represents a prime number.

What patterns can you see in this picture? Is there a rule for generating primes?

Toolbox

A **quadratic sequence** has 2 as the highest power of n in the formula for the nth term.

For example, $u_n = n^2 - 4n + 7$.

A quadratic sequence has second differences that are equal.

The constant in the second row of differences is double the **coefficient** of n^2 in the formula for the nth term.

> The **coefficient** of a term is the number multiplying the variable. For example, the coefficient of n in $n^2 - 4n + 7$ is '**−4**'.

1		10		23		40		61	Sequence
	9		13		17		21		First differences
		4		4		4			Second differences

2 is the coefficient of n^2 as it is half of 4

Example – Finding the rule

Work out the formula for the nth term of this sequence:
$$9, 15, 23, 33, 45, \ldots$$

Solution

9   15   23   33   45   ← Work out the first differences.
    6   8   10   12   ← Work out the second differences.
      2   2   2

The second difference is constant (2).

Half of 2 is 1, so the coefficient of n^2 is 1, which means that it is a quadratic sequence.

There is an 'n^2' in the formula which contributes:

The rest of the formula contributes:

	9	15	23	33	45 …
	1	4	9	16	25 …
	8	11	14	17	20 …

The formula for the rest is $3n + 5$,

so $u_n = n^2 + 3n + 5$.

Check: when $n = 1$, $1^2 + 3 \times 1 + 5 = 1 + 3 + 5 = 9$ ✓

when $n = 2$, $2^2 + 3 \times 2 + 5 = 4 + 6 + 5 = 15$ ✓

when $n = 3$, $3^2 + 3 \times 3 + 5 = 9 + 9 + 5 = 23$ ✓

Example – Using patterns

The diagram shows a sequence of growing shapes. The shapes are made with cubes and there are no 'gaps' in the shapes.

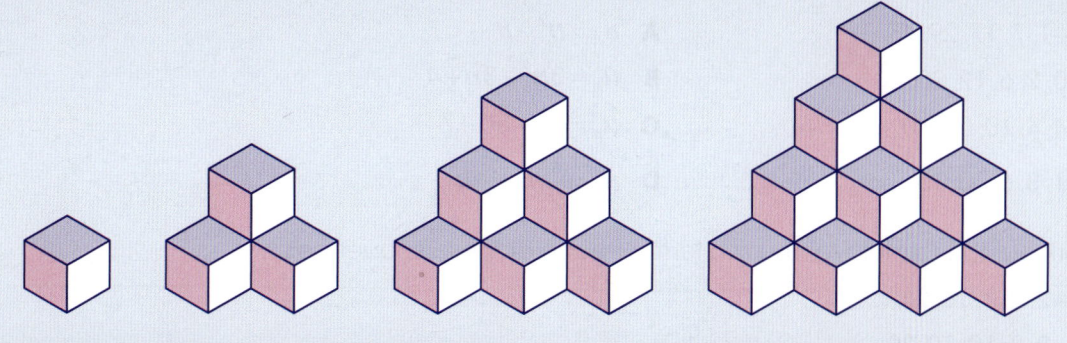

a Write down the first four terms in the sequence for the number of faces in each shape.

b Work out the formula for the nth term of the sequence.

Algebra Strand 2 Sequences

Solution

a 6, 18, 36, 60 ← Don't forget to count the hidden faces.

b 6   18   36   60
    12   18   24 ← Work out the first differences.
       6   6 ← Work out the second differences.

The second difference is constant so it is a quadratic sequence,
$6 \div 2 = 3$, so the sequence is based on $3n^2$.

There is a '$3n^2$' in the formula, which contributes:
The rest of the formula contributes:

    6 18 36 60 ...
    3 12 27 48 ...
    3   6   9 12 ...

The formula for the rest is $3n$.
So the formula for the nth term is $u_n = 3n^2 + 3n$.
Check: when $n = 1$, $3 \times 1^2 + 3 \times 1 = 3 + 3 = 6$ ✓
           when $n = 2$, $3 \times 2^2 + 3 \times 2 = 12 + 6 = 18$ ✓
           when $n = 3$, $3 \times 3^2 + 3 \times 3 = 27 + 9 = 36$ ✓

Practising skills

1 The nth term of the sequence 1, 2, 5, 10, 17, ... is $t_n = n^2 - 2n + 2$.
Use this result to write down the nth term for the sequences:

    a 3, 4, 7, 12, 19, ...

    b 0, 1, 4, 9, 16, ...

    c 6, 7, 10, 15, 22, ...

    d 6, 8, 14, 24, 38, ...

    e 1, 3, 9, 19, 33, ...

2 Match the nth term formula to the sequence:

    a −1, 7, 17, 29, 43, ...   **A** $u_n = n^2 - n$

    b 0, 2, 6, 12, 20, ...   **B** $u_n = 3n^2 - 3n + 4$

    c 4, 4, 10, 22, 40, ...   **C** $u_n = n^2 + 5n - 7$

    d 1, 3, 6, 10, 15, ...   **D** $u_n = \frac{1}{2}n^2 + \frac{1}{2}n$

3 Work out the formula for the nth term of each of these sequences:

    a −2, 2, 8, 16, 26, ...

    b −2, 3, 10, 19, 30, ...

    c 8, 15, 24, 35, 48, ...

    d 1, 3, 7, 13, 21, ...

4 Work out the formula for the nth term of these sequences:
   a 0, 9, 22, 39, 60, …
   b 1.5, 1, 1.5, 3, 5.5, …
   c 0, 4, 14, 30, 52, …
   d 2, −4, −12, −22, −34, …

Developing fluency

1 Many of the terms of the sequence defined by $t_n = n^2 - n + 11$ are prime numbers.
   a Check the first five terms.
   b Are all the terms of this sequence prime numbers? Explain your answer.

2 The nth term of a sequence is given by $u_n = n^2 - an + 3$.
   The first five terms are 2.5, b, 7.5, 13 and 20.5.
   Work out the values of a and b.

3 A sequence has nth term given by $t_n = n^2 + an + b$.
   The first five terms are 5, 11, c, 29 and 41.
   Work out the values of a, b and c.

4 Many of the terms of the sequence $u_n = n^2 - n + 41$ are prime numbers.
   a Check the first five terms.
   b Find a term that is not prime.

5 This sequence of shapes is made using matchsticks.

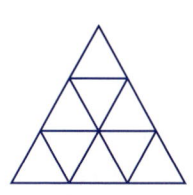

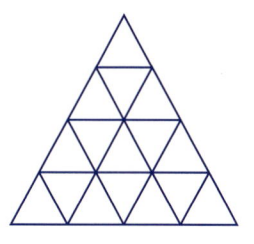

The length of one matchstick is the side length of the first triangle.
The number of matchsticks in each shape forms a sequence.
Work out the nth term of the sequence.

Algebra Strand 2 Sequences

Problem solving

1 Teams of footballers play each other in a league.
Each team plays every other team once.

a How many matches are played when there are 2, 3 and 4 teams in the league?

b How many matches are played when there are 8 teams in the league?

c Find the number of matches when there are n teams in the league.

There are 20 teams in the Premier League. They each play each other twice.

d How many matches are played?

2 Here is a pattern made from sticks.

a How many triangles are there in pattern 4?

b How many triangles are there in pattern n?

c Which pattern has 168 triangles?

Pattern 1   Pattern 2

3 Here are some shapes made from centimetre cubes.

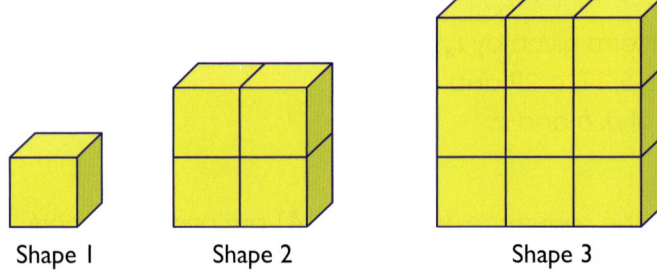

Shape 1   Shape 2   Shape 3

Five faces, each of area 1 cm², are visible in shape 1.

a How many 1 cm² faces are visible in shapes 2 and 3?

b How many 1 cm² faces are visible in shape 5?

c Find an expression, in terms of n, for the number of 1 cm² faces visible in shape n.

Two of each of these shapes are placed side by side to make a new pattern.

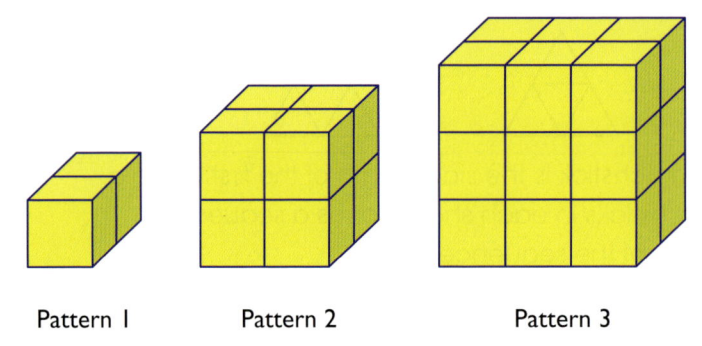

Pattern 1   Pattern 2   Pattern 3

Eight faces, each of area 1 cm² are now visible in pattern 1.

d Find an expression, in terms of n, for the number of 1 cm² faces visible in pattern n.

Unit 6 nth term of a quadratic sequence Band i

4) The nth term of a sequence is $2n^2 + 3n + 12$.
The nth term of a different sequence is $(n+2)(2n+1)$.
One number has the same position in both sequences. Find the number.

Reviewing skills

1) Work out the formula for the nth term of each of these sequences:
   a −4, −3, 0, 5, 12, ...
   b 11, 4, −7, −22, −41, ...

2) A sequence has nth term given by $t_n = an^2 + bn + c$.
The first five terms are 4, d, 20, 37 and e.
Work out the values of a, b, c, d and e.

Algebra Strand 3 Functions and graphs

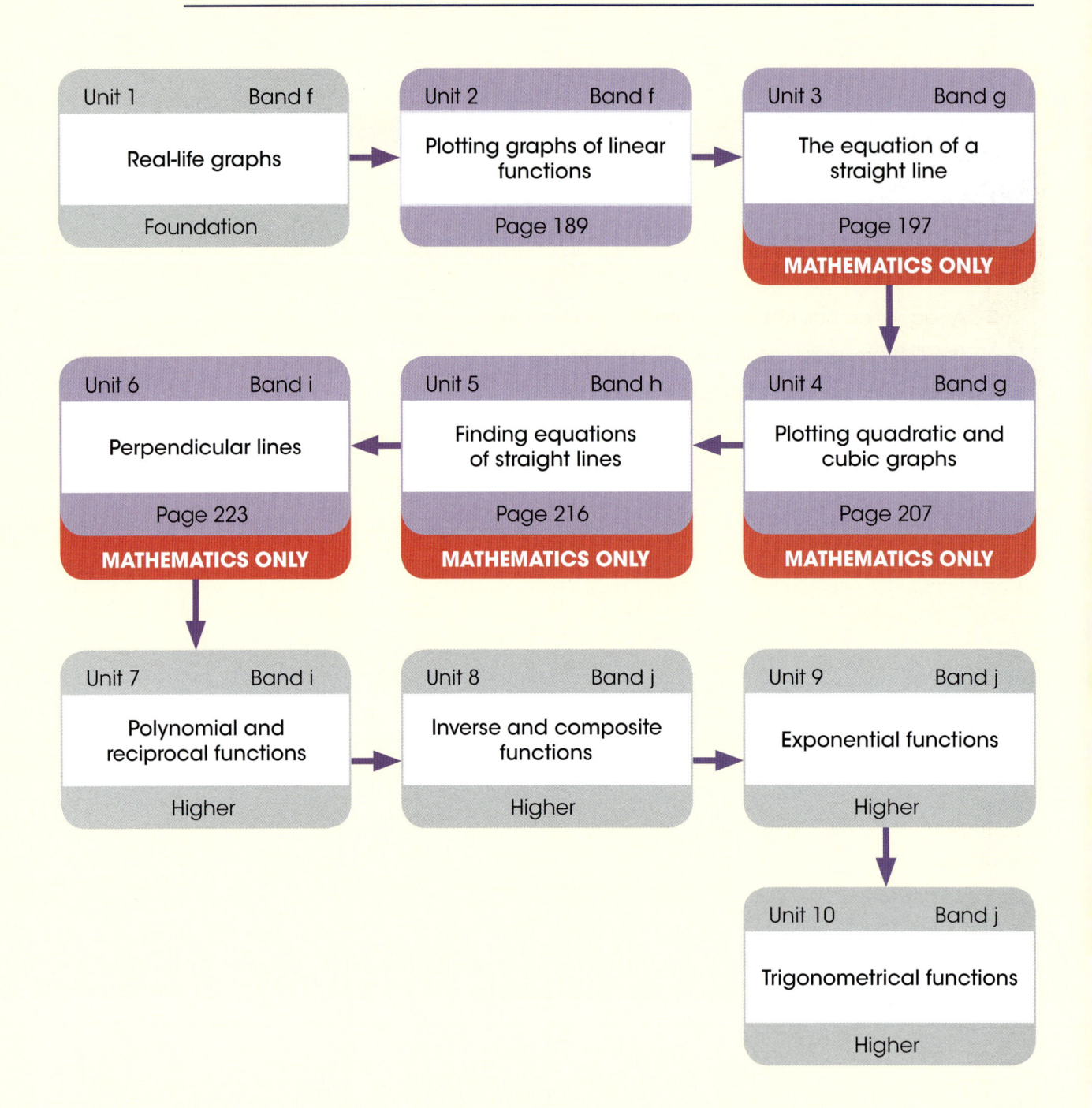

Unit 1 — Band f	Unit 2 — Band f	Unit 3 — Band g
Real-life graphs	Plotting graphs of linear functions	The equation of a straight line
Foundation	Page 189	Page 197 — MATHEMATICS ONLY

Unit 6 — Band i	Unit 5 — Band h	Unit 4 — Band g
Perpendicular lines	Finding equations of straight lines	Plotting quadratic and cubic graphs
Page 223 — MATHEMATICS ONLY	Page 216 — MATHEMATICS ONLY	Page 207 — MATHEMATICS ONLY

Unit 7 — Band i	Unit 8 — Band j	Unit 9 — Band j
Polynomial and reciprocal functions	Inverse and composite functions	Exponential functions
Higher	Higher	Higher

Unit 10 — Band j
Trigonometrical functions
Higher

Unit 1 is assumed knowledge for this book. Knowledge and skills from this unit is used throughout the book.

Unit 2 • Plotting graphs of linear functions • Band f

Outside the Maths classroom

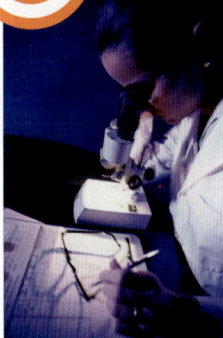

Scientific research
Why do scientists try to work with straight line relationships?

Toolbox

Functions can be represented on a mapping diagram.

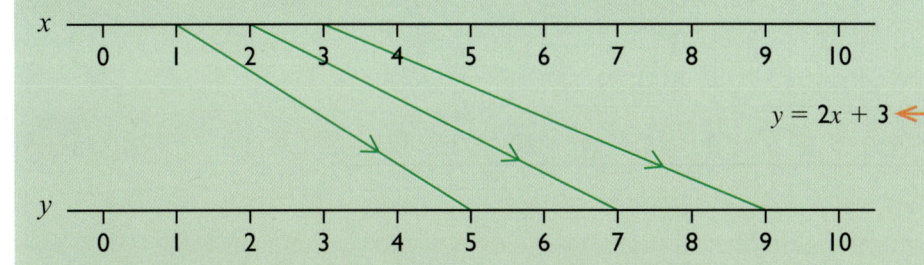

$y = 2x + 3$

This is sometimes written $x \rightarrow 2x + 3$

Every value on the x line maps to a corresponding value on the y line.
Inverse mappings return you to where you started.
Another way to represent a function is to plot its graph.

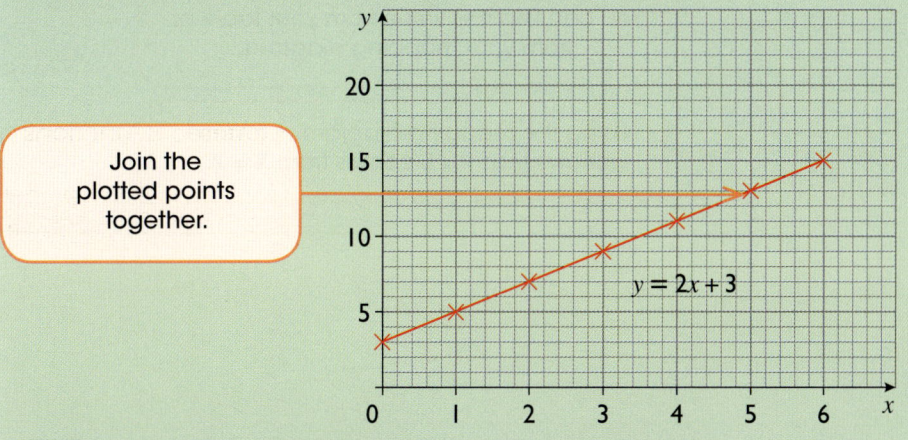

Join the plotted points together.

$y = 2x + 3$

A linear function is represented by a straight line graph.
Conversion graphs are an example of linear functions.

Algebra Strand 3 Functions and graphs

Start by drawing a table of values.
This table is for the function $y = 2x + 3$.

x	1	2	3	4	5	6
$2x$	2	4	6	8	10	12
$+3$	3	3	3	3	3	3
$y = 2x + 3$	5	7	9	11	13	15

Example – Drawing and using a mapping diagram

1 For the function $x \to x + 3$:
 a make a table of values with x from 0 to 6
 b draw a mapping diagram
 c write down the value of y when $x = 4$
 d find the value of x when $y = 5$.

Solution

a

x	0	1	2	3	4	5	6
$+3$	3	3	3	3	3	3	3
$y = x + 3$	3	4	5	6	7	8	9

b

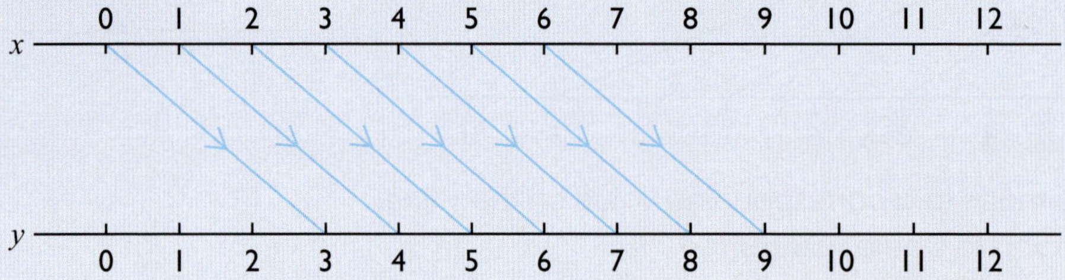

c When $x = 4$, $y = 7$. ← You can find this value from your table or from your mapping diagram.

d When $y = 5$, $x = 2$. ← Using the mapping diagram in reverse shows that $y = 5$ comes from $x = 2$.

Example – Drawing and using a graph of a linear function

In a science experiment, the length of a piece of elastic is recorded when different masses are hung on it.
Here are the results.

Mass (grams), m	0	10	20	30	40
Length of elastic (cm), l	30	40	50	60	70

a Plot the graph.
b Find the mass that stretched the elastic to 56 cm.

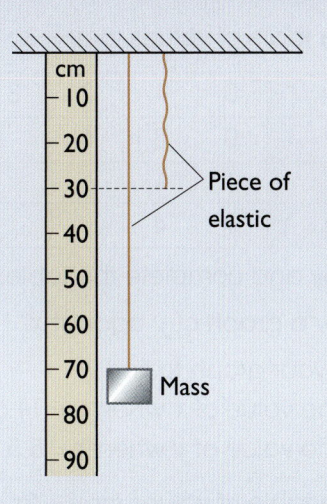

Solution

a

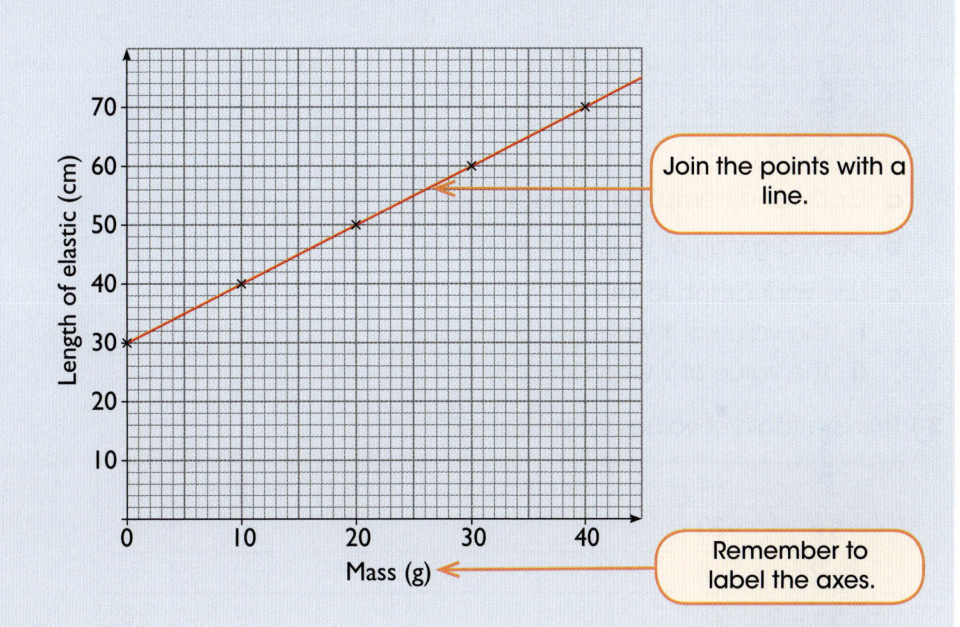

Join the points with a line.

Remember to label the axes.

b The mass would have been 26 g. Draw a horizontal line from 56 cm on the vertical axis. Read off the value on the horizontal axis of the point where this line meets the graph line.

Algebra Strand 3 Functions and graphs

Practising skills

1 This is a table of values for $y = 3x + 1$.

x	0	1	2	3	4	5	6
$3x$	0	3	6				18
$+ 1$	1	1					1
$y = 3x + 1$	1	4					19

a Copy and complete the table.

b Draw a graph of y against x.

c Use your graph to find
  i the value of x when $y = 11.5$
  ii the value of y when $x = 5.5$.

2 This is a table of values for $y = 2x - 3$.

x	0	1	2	3	4	5	6
$2x$	0	2	4				12
$- 3$	-3						
$y = 2x - 3$	-3						9

a Copy and complete the table.

b Draw a graph of y against x.

c Use your graph to find
  i the value of x when $y = 5$
  ii the value of y when $x = 2.5$.

3 This is a table of values for $y = 5x - 2$.

x	-4	-3	-2	-1	0	1	2	3	4
$5x$	-20								
$- 2$	-2								
$y = 5x - 2$	-22								18

a Copy and complete the table.

b Draw a graph of y against x.

c Use your graph to find
  i the value of x when $y = -10$
  ii the value of y when $x = 3.5$.

Unit 2 Plotting graphs of linear functions Band f

4) This is a table of values for $y = 4x - 3$.

x	0	1	2	3	4	5	6
$4x$	0	4	8				
-3	-3						
$y = 4x - 3$	-3						

a Copy and complete the table.

b Draw a graph of y against x.

c Use your graph to find
   i the value of x when $y = 15$
   ii the value of y when $x = 5.5$.

5) This is a table of values for $y = 2x + 5$.

x	0	1	2	3	4	5	6
$2x$	0						
$+5$	5						
$y = 2x + 5$	5						

a Complete the table.

b Draw a graph of y against x.

c Use your graph to find
   i the value of x when $y = 16$
   ii the value of y when $x = 3.5$.

Developing fluency

1) The rule for cooking meat is 40 minutes per kilogram plus 20 minutes.

a Copy and complete the table to show the time to cook some meat.

Weight (kg)	1	2	3	4	5	6	7	8
$40W$	40							
$+20$	20							
Time ($T = 40W + 20$)	60							

b Draw a graph to show the time to cook the meat.
   Put W on the horizontal axis and T on the vertical axis.

c i Where does the line cross the T axis?
   ii What does this number represent?

d Use your graph to find the time to cook meat weighing 6.5 kg.

e Use your graph to find the weight of meat that takes 3 hours 20 minutes to cook.

Algebra Strand 3 Functions and graphs

2 Boats are hired for £3 per hour plus £4 fixed charge.

a Complete the table to show the cost £C of hiring a boat for t hours.

Number of hours, t	1	2	3	4	5	6	7	8
$3t$								
$+4$								
$C = 3t + 4$								

b Draw a graph to show the cost of hiring a boat. Put the cost on the vertical axis.
c Use your graph to find the cost of hiring a boat for 4.5 hours.
d Use your graph to find how many hours a boat can be hired for £11.50.

3 Apples are sold for £6 for 5 kg.

a Complete this table.

Weight of apples (kg)	5	10	15	20
Cost (£)	6	12		

b Draw a graph to show the cost of the apples. Put the cost on the vertical axis.
c Use your graph to find the cost of 8 kg.
d Use your graph to find how many packs can be bought for £21.

4 A shop charges £0.80 per kg for potatoes. As a promotion, they give anyone buying potatoes 1 kg free.

a Complete this table to show the cost of some weights of potatoes.

Weights of potatoes (kg)	1	2	3	4	5	6
Cost (£)	0	0.80			3.20	

b Draw a graph to show the cost of potatoes. Put the cost on the vertical axis.
c Use your graph to find the cost of 4.5 kg.
d Use your graph to find the weight of potatoes you get for £2.00.
e i Where does the line cross the vertical axis?
  ii What does this number represent?

5 a Construct a table of values for $y = 4x - 2$ with x from −2 to 5.
b Use your table of values to draw the graph of $y = 4x - 2$.
c Use your graph to find the value of x when $y = 0$.

6 a Construct a table of values for $y = 8 - x$ with x from −2 to 10.
b Use your table of values to draw the graph of $y = 8 - x$.
c Use your graph to find the value of y when $x = -1$.
d Use your graph to find the value of x when $y = -1$.

7 a Construct a table of values for $y = 12 - 2x$ with x from −2 to 8.
b Use your table of values to draw the graph of $y = 12 - 2x$.
c Use your graph to find the value of x when $y = 15$.

Problem solving

1 The cost, C, in pounds, of n business cards is $20 + 0.05n$.

  a Copy and complete this table of values.

n	0	200	400	600
20		20		
$0.05n$		10		
$C = 20 + 0.05n$		30		

  b Draw a graph of C against n. Plot C on the vertical axis.

  c Sally has £120 to spend on buying business cards.
  How many business cards can she buy?

2 The thickness, T mm, of a hard-cover book is given by the formula
$$T = 5 + \frac{n}{20}$$
where n is the number of pages.

  a Construct a table of values of T for $n = 0, 200, 400$ and 600.

  b Draw a line graph from $n = 0$ to $n = 600$ on the horizontal axis to show this information.

  c Sonia has a hard-cover book that is 40 mm thick.
  How many pages are there in the book?

3 a Construct a table of values for $y = 2x - 1$, taking x from -3 to 3.

  b Draw the graph of $y = 2x - 1$.

  c Find the value of y when $x = 1.7$.

  d Find the value of x when $y = -4.5$.

  e Explain why the point $(-1.5, 2)$ does not lie on the line $y = 2x - 1$.

Algebra Strand 3 Functions and graphs

Reviewing skills

1 a Copy and complete this table of values for $y = 2x - 5$.

x	5	4	3	2	1	0	-1	-2
2x	10					0	-2	
-5	-5	-5					-5	
y	5						-7	

b Draw a graph of $y = 2x - 5$.
c Use your graph to find the value of
  i y when $x = 2.5$
  ii x when $y = -8$.

2 a Construct a table of values for $y = 3x + 5$ with x from -3 to 5.
b Use your table of values to draw the graph of $y = 3x + 5$.
c Use your graph to find the value of x when $y = 4$.

3 A taxi company makes a fixed charge of £4 and then charges a certain amount per minute.
This gives the formula $C = 4 + 0.5m$, when £C is the cost of a journey in minutes.
a What is the cost per minute?
b Construct a table of values of C for journeys of up to half an hour.
c Draw a graph of C against m. Plot C on the vertical axis.
d Use your graph to find
  i the cost of a journey of 18 minutes
  ii the time taken when the cost is £11.

Unit 3 • The equation of a straight line • Band g

Outside the Maths classroom

Making predictions

How can you use current data to predict the future?

Toolbox

Straight lines have an equation of the form $y = mx + c$.
- The value of m represents the gradient or 'steepness' of the line.
- The value of c tells you where the line crosses the y axis.

Special cases are:
- Horizontal lines which have an equation of the form $y = a$ where a is a number.
- Vertical lines which have an equation of the form $x = b$ where b is a number.

Parallel lines have the same gradient.
The y intercept is the value where the line cuts the y axis.
To find the gradient of a straight line
1. choose any two points
2. subtract the y co-ordinates
3. subtract the x co-ordinates
4. the gradient is the change in y divided by the change in x.

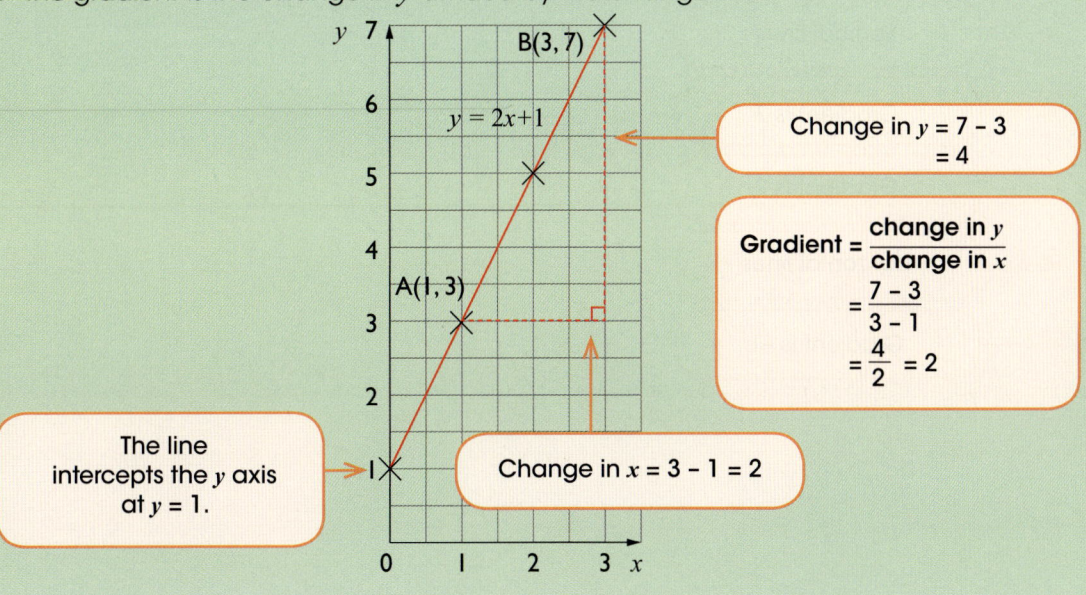

Change in $y = 7 - 3 = 4$

$$\text{Gradient} = \frac{\text{change in } y}{\text{change in } x} = \frac{7-3}{3-1} = \frac{4}{2} = 2$$

The line intercepts the y axis at $y = 1$.

Change in $x = 3 - 1 = 2$

Algebra Strand 3 Functions and graphs

If the line slopes down from left to right the gradient is negative.

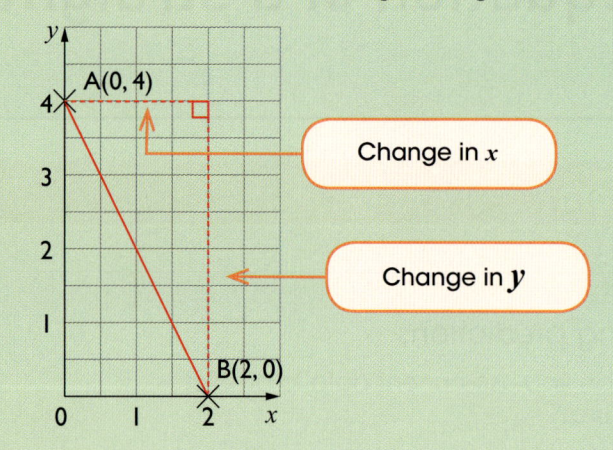

Gradient $= \dfrac{0-4}{2-0}$

$= \dfrac{-4}{2} = -2$

Example – Finding the gradient from the equation of a line

Here are the equations of ten lines.
Write down which ones are parallel.

a $x = 7$
b $y = 3 + 7x$
c $y = 2x + 3$
d $y = -5$
e $y = 2x - 4$
f $x = -2$
g $y = 5 - x$
h $y = -x$
i $y = 7x + 5$
j $y = 4$

Solution

a and f ← Vertical lines

b and i ← Gradient is 7

c and e ← Gradient is 2

d and j ← Horizontal lines

g and h ← Gradient is −1

Unit 3 The equation of a straight line Band g

Example – Finding an equation from a graph

Match the lines in this diagram with the correct equations.

$x = 3$
$x = -3$
$x = 0$
$y = 3$
$y = -3$
$y = 0$
$y = x + 1$
$y = x - 2$
$y = 2x - 1$
$y = 1 - x$

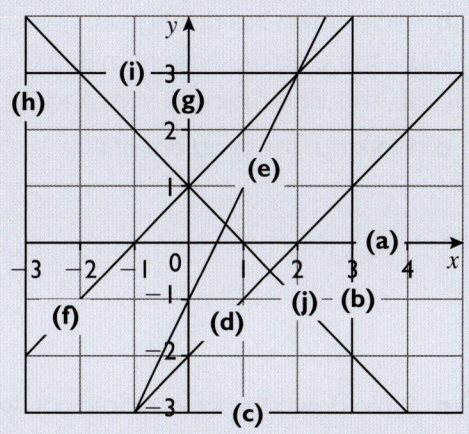

Solution

a is the x axis. Its equation is $y = 0$
b is a vertical line. Every point on the line has an x co-ordinate of 3.
   The equation of the line is $x = 3$
c is a horizontal line. Every point on the line has a y co-ordinate of -3.
   The equation of the line is $y = -3$
d has a gradient of 1 and a y intercept of -2. The equation of the line is $y = x - 2$
e has a gradient of 2 and a y intercept of -1. The equation of the line is $y = 2x - 1$
f has a gradient of 1 and a y intercept of 1. The equation of the line is $y = x + 1$
g is the y axis. Its equation is $x = 0$
h is a vertical line. Every point on the line has an x co-ordinate of -3.
   The equation of the line is $x = -3$
i is a horizontal line. Every point on the line has a y co-ordinate of 3.
   The equation of the line is $y = 3$
j has a gradient of -1 and a y intercept of 1. The equation of the line is $y = -x + 1$ or $y = 1 - x$

Practising skills

1 Look at this graph.

  a Which points lie on these lines?
     i $x = 2$ **ii** $y = 8$
  b Write down the equation of these lines.
     i BD   **ii** CD

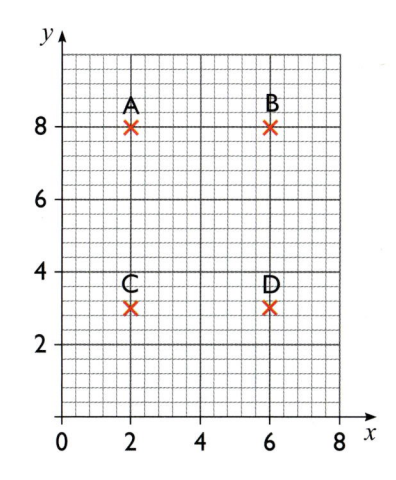

Algebra Strand 3 Functions and graphs

2 Look at this graph.
  a Write down the co-ordinates of
   i A   **ii** B   **iii** C.
  b Write down the change in
   i the y co-ordinate from B to C
   ii the x co-ordinate from A to B.
  c Work out the gradient of AC.

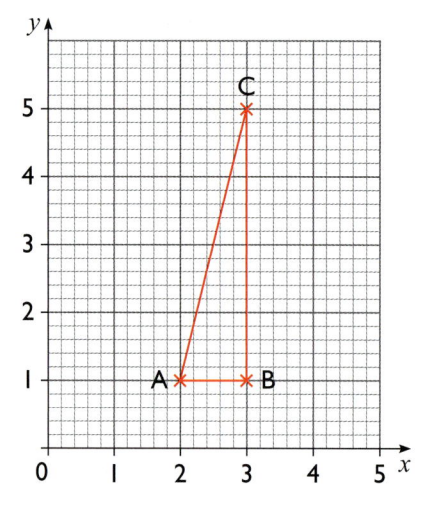

3 a Write down the co-ordinates of two points on each of these lines.

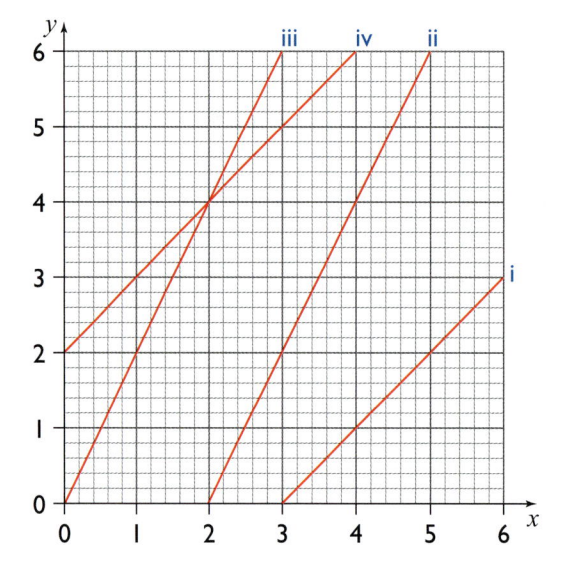

  b Work out the gradient of each line.
  c Which pairs of lines are parallel? What can you say about the gradients of parallel lines?

4 Work out the gradient and the equation for each of the lines going through these points.
  a (1, 2) and (3, 8)   **b** (5, 6) and (6, 7)   **c** (3, 0) and (5, 0)   **d** (−1, −2) and (1, 6)
  e (0, 2) and (2, 0)   **f** (0, 5) and (3, −1)   **g** (0, −3) and (5, −18)   **h** (0, 8) and (2, −2)

Unit 3 The equation of a straight line Band g

5 a Write down the co-ordinates of two points on each of these lines.

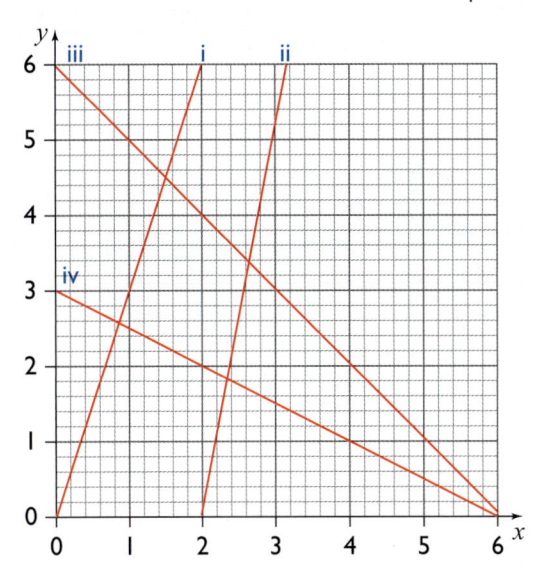

b Work out the gradient of each line.

c What can you say about the gradients of lines that slope down from left to right?

6 a Find the co-ordinates of two points on the line $y = 2x - 3$.

b Draw the graph of $y = 2x - 3$ taking values of x from -1 to 4.

c Find
   i the gradient of the line
   ii the y intercept (the value of y where it crosses the y axis).

d Where can you see the answers to part **c** in the equation of the line?

7 a Copy and complete these tables.

x	-2	-1	0	1	2
$4x$	-8				
-3	-3				
$y = 4x - 3$	-11				

x	-2	-1	0	1	2
$5x$	-10				
$+2$	$+2$				
$y = 5x + 2$	-8				

b Draw these lines on the same graph.

c Work out the gradient of each line.

d Write down the y intercept of each line.

e Explain why you did not need to draw the graphs of the two lines to answer parts **c** and **d**.

f Write down the gradient and the y intercept of the line $y = 8x - 5$.

Algebra Strand 3 Functions and graphs

8 Look at the five lines on this graph.
  a For each line
   i write down two points
   ii work out the gradient
   iii write down the y intercept.
  b Match each line with one of these equations.
   i $y = 2x - 2$
   ii $y = -x + 5$
   iii $y = -2x + 8$
   iv $y = x + 3$
   v $y = 1$ ← This is $y = 0x + 1$

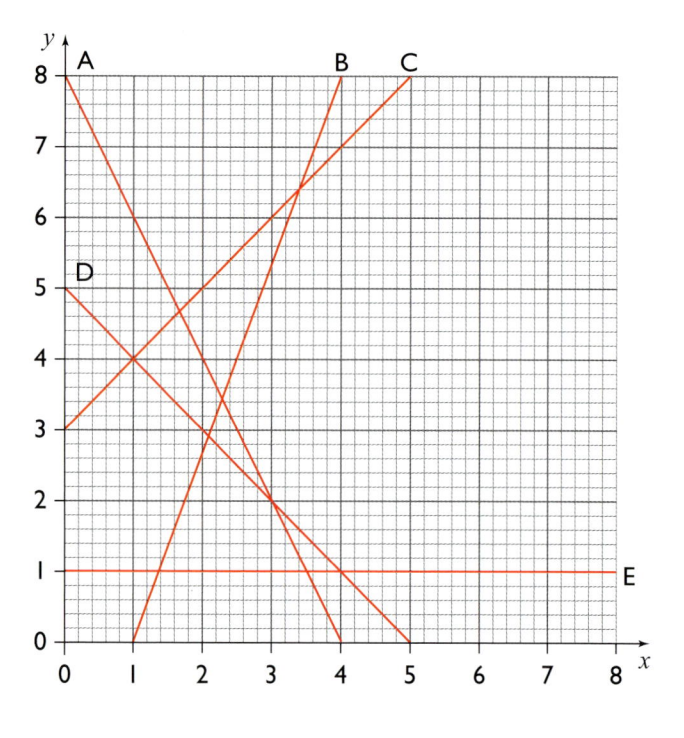

Developing fluency

1 Here are three road signs showing the gradient of three hills.

A: 15%   B: 1:15   C: 1 in 15

Arrange the gradients of these hills in order of size.
Start with the smallest gradient.

2 Here are the equations of some lines.
  A $y = 2x + 7$
  B $y = -2x + 7$
  C $y = 7x$
  D $y = 7x + 2$
  E $y = -7x - 2$
  F $y = 2x - 7$

Which of these line(s) has the property
  i   goes through the origin
  ii parallel to $y = 2x$
  iii has y intercept of $+7$
  iv parallel to $y = -7x + 2$
  v   has y intercept of -2?

3 a Draw the lines with these equations on the same axes.
  A $y = x + 5$
  B $y = 3x - 5$
  C $y = 5x + 3$
  D $y = 3x$
  E $y = x - 5$
  F $y = 5x + 5$

  b Which lines have the same gradient (are parallel)?

  c Which lines have the same y intercept?

4 Find the equations of the lines going through these pairs of points.
  a (0, 0) and (5, 15)   **b** (0, 3) and (4, 11)   **c** (0, 1) and (10, 41)   **d** (0, −2) and (6, 4)

5 a Draw these lines on a sheet of graph paper.
  i $x = 4$ **ii** $y = -3$
  iii $x + y = 6$ **iv** $2x + y = 4$
  v $y = -2x + 5$ **vi** $y = -x + 5$
  vii $y - 3 = 0$ **viii** $x - 2 = 0$

  b Which pairs of lines are parallel?

  c How can you tell which pairs are parallel from their equations?

6 This graph shows the charges (£C) that ABCars make for hiring a car for m miles.

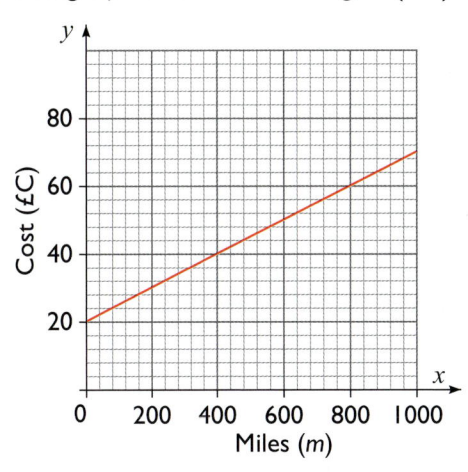

  a Find the formula in the form $C = $ _____ .

  b Work out the cost for 1200 miles.

  c How many miles can you drive a hire car for a cost of £100?

Algebra Strand 3 Functions and graphs

Problem solving

1. Here is the graph that can be used to find the cost C, in pounds, of hiring a hedge-trimmer for d days.

   a Write down the equation of the straight line in terms of C and d.

   b Write in words the cost C of hiring this hedge-trimmer for d days.

   c i Explain what the gradient of the straight line represents

   ii Explain what the intercept with the vertical axis represents.

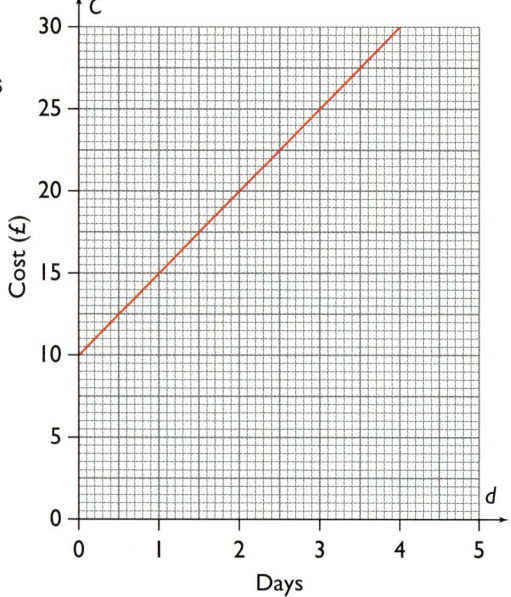

2. Here are the equations of some straight lines.
   A $y = -x + 6$
   B $y = 2x + 3$
   C $y = 3 - 2x$
   D $y = -2x + 6$
   E $y = 2x - 6$

   a Which of these lines are parallel to each other?

   b Which of the lines meet at (0, 3)?

3. Ayesha is comparing the daily cost of van hire. She compares these three firms.
   A £50 plus 10p a mile
   B £25 plus 30p a mile
   C £65 a day with no mileage charge

   a Ayesha writes the cost, £C, for m miles for company A as the formula $C = 50 + 0.1m$
   Write similar formulae for the other two companies.

   b Draw a graph showing the three formulae.
   Put m on the horizontal axis with values from 0 to 200.
   Put C on the vertical axis.

   c Ayesha thinks she will drive the van about 160 miles.
   Which company should she choose?

Unit 3 The equation of a straight line Band g

4 Look at the straight line l on this graph.
  a **i** Find the gradient of l.
      ii Find the y intercept of l.
  b Write down the equation of l.
  c If the line was drawn on a bigger piece of graph paper, would it go through the point (8, 12)?
  d Find the equation of the line parallel to l passing through the point (0, 1).

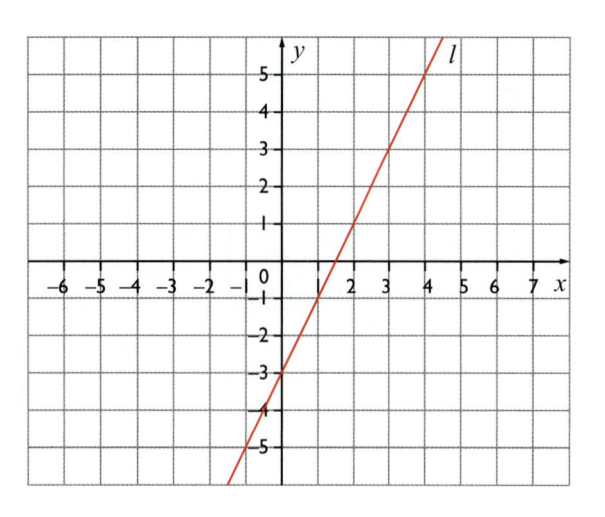

Reviewing skills

1 The table gives information about some lines.

Line	Gradient	y intercept
A	4	3
B	8	2
C	2	−2
D	−5	4
E	−1	−5
F	6	−3

Write down the equation of each line.

2 Write down the equation of each line.
  a 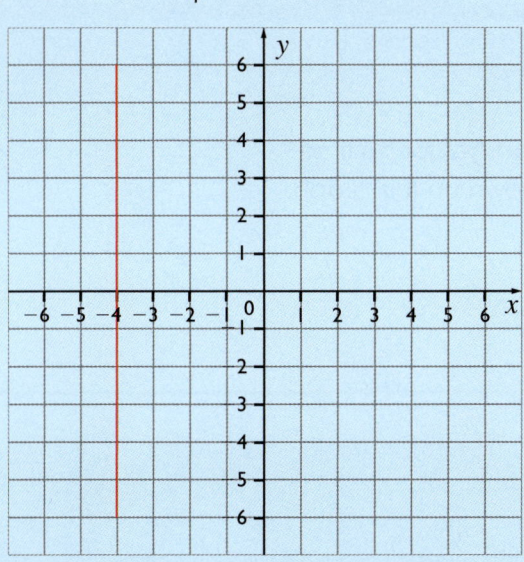
  b

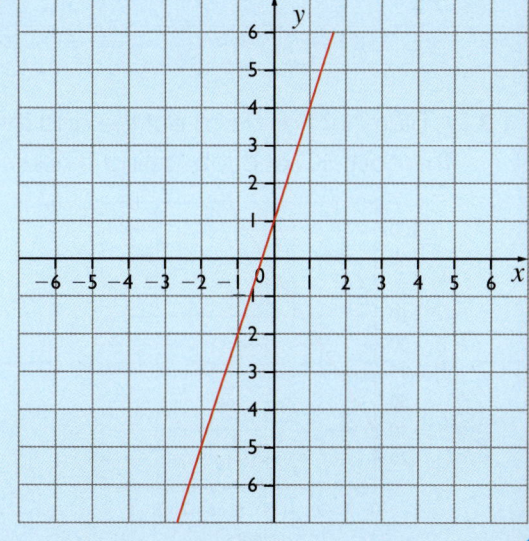

Algebra Strand 3 Functions and graphs

c

d

e

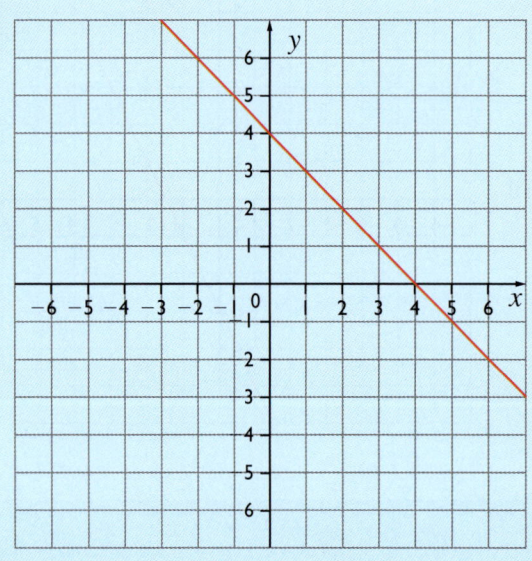

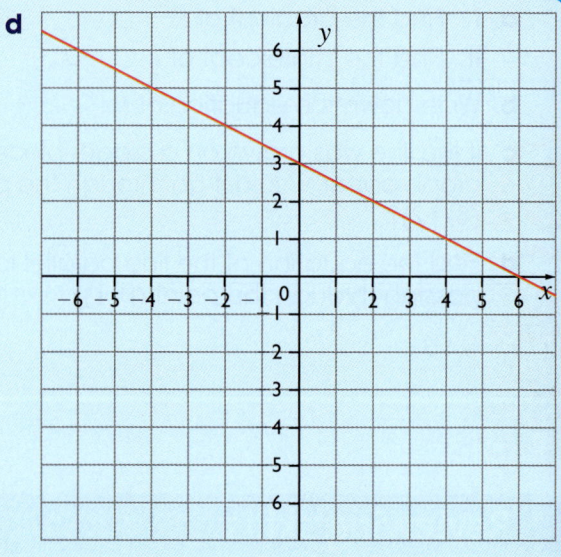

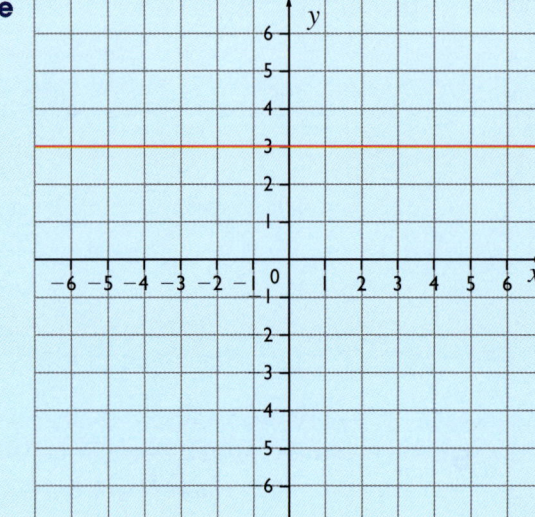

3 A plumber has a call out fee and then charges for his time.
The cost, £C, of a job lasting h hours is shown on this graph.

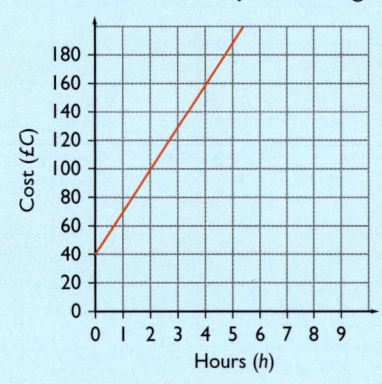

a Find the plumber's formula in the form C = ☐ + ☐ h

b i What is his call out fee?

ii How much does he charge per hour?

c For one job the bill is £250. How many hours did the plumber work?

Unit 4 • Plotting quadratic and cubic graphs • Band g

Outside the Maths classroom

Maximising profit
What would a graph of profit against selling price look like?

Toolbox

Equations which contain powers of x greater than 1 (e.g. x^2, x^3) are not linear functions; instead they produce curved lines.

Equations with x^2 terms but no x^3 terms produce **quadratic** curves.

x	−3	−2	−1	0	1	2	3
$y = x^2$	9	4	1	0	1	4	9

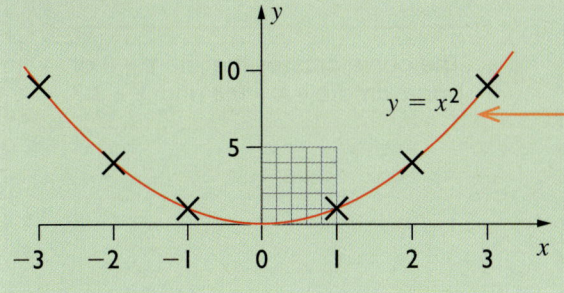

The points are joined by a smooth curve.

Equations with x^3 terms produce **cubic** curves.

x	−3	−2	−1	0	1	2	3
$y = x^3$	−27	−8	−1	0	1	8	27

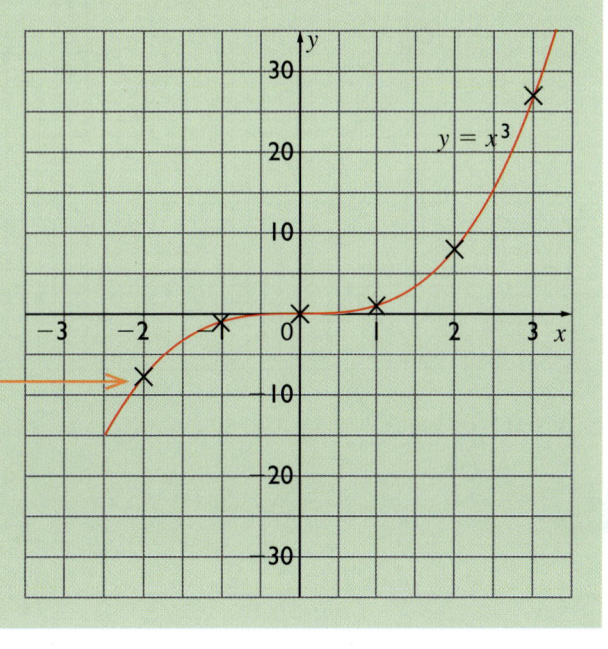

The points are joined by a smooth curve.

Algebra Strand 3 Functions and graphs

Example – Drawing and using quadratic curves

a Make a table of values for $y = x^2 - 4x + 1$, taking values of x from -1 to 5.
b Draw the graph of $y = x^2 - 4x + 1$.
c Use your graph to solve the equation $x^2 - 4x + 1 = 0$.

Solution

a

x	-1	0	1	2	3	4	5
x^2	1	0	1	4	9	16	25
$-4x$	4	0	-4	-8	-12	-16	-20
$+1$	1	1	1	1	1	1	1
$y = x^2 - 4x + 1$	6	1	-2	-3	-2	1	6

b

> All quadratic equations produce a curve in the shape of a parabola. Draw it as smoothly as you can.

> The curve crosses the line $y = 0$ at approximately $x = 0.3$ and $x = 3.7$.

> The solution to the equation $x^2 - 4x + 1 = 0$ is given by the x values at the points where the curve crosses the x axis (the line $y = 0$).
> Values taken from a graph are only approximate.

c $x = 0.3$ or $x = 3.7$

Unit 4 Plotting quadratic and cubic graphs Band g

Example – Drawing and using cubic curves

a Make a table of values for $y = x^3 - 5x$, taking values of x from -3 to 3.
b Draw the graph of $y = x^3 - 5x$.
c Find the values of x where this curve crosses the x axis.
d Write down the solution of the equation $x^3 - 5x = 0$.

Solution

a

x	-3	-2	-1	0	1	2	3
x^3	-27	-8	-1	0	1	8	27
$-5x$	15	10	5	0	-5	-10	-15
$y = x^3 - 5x$	-12	2	4	0	-4	-2	12

b

[Graph of $y = x^3 - 5x$ plotted from $x = -3$ to $x = 3$]

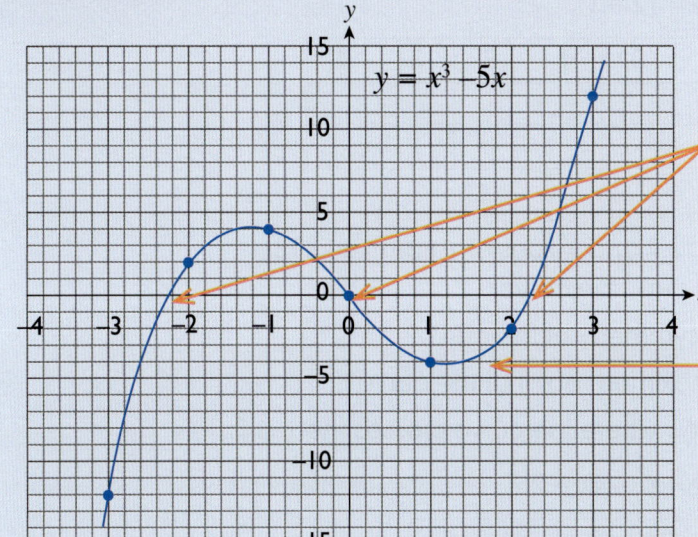

The curve crosses the line $y = 0$ at $x = 0$ and approximately $x = -2.2$ and $x = 2.2$.

All cubic equations produce an S-shaped curve.

Draw it as smoothly as you can.

c $x = 0, x = -2.2$ or $x = 2.2$

The value $x = 0$ is accurate and you could have found it from your table.

The other two values are only approximate.

209

Algebra Strand 3 Functions and graphs

Practising skills

1 a Copy and complete this table for the quadratic curve $y = x^2 + 1$.

x	−3	−2	−1	0	1	2	3
x^2	9						
+1	1						
$y = x^2 + 1$	10						

  b Draw axes with values of x from −3 to 3 and values of y from 0 to 10. Plot the points from your table and join them with a smooth curve.

  c What is the equation of the line of symmetry of the curve?

  d What are the co-ordinates of the minimum point of the curve?

  e Use your graph to find the values of x when $y = 2.5$.

2 a Copy and complete this table for $y = 12 − x^2$.

x	−4	−3	−2	−1	0	1	2	3	4
12	12								
$-x^2$	−16								
$y = 12 - x^2$	−4								

  b Draw axes with values of x from −4 to 4 and values of y from −5 to 15. Plot the points from your table and draw the curve.

  c What is the equation of the line of symmetry of the curve?

  d What are the co-ordinates of the maximum point of the curve?

  e Use your graph to find the values of x where the curve crosses the x axis.

3 a Copy and complete this table for $y = x^2 − 4x + 2$.

x	−1	0	1	2	3	4	5
x^2							
$-4x$							
$+2$							
$y = x^2 - 4x + 2$							

  b Draw axes with values of x from −1 to 5 and values of y from −3 to 7. Draw the curve.

  c What is the equation of the line of symmetry of the curve?

  d What are the co-ordinates of the minimum point of the curve?

  e What are the values of x when $y = −1$?

Unit 4 Plotting quadratic and cubic graphs Band g

4 a Copy and complete this table for $y = (x - 2)^2$.

x	−2	−1	0	1	2	3	4	5	6
$x - 2$	−4								
$y = (x - 2)^2$	16								

b Draw axes with values of x from −2 to 6 and values of y from 0 to 16. Draw the curve.

c What is the equation of the line of symmetry?

d What are the co-ordinates of the minimum point of the curve?

e What are the values of x when $y = 7$?

5 a Copy and complete this table for $y = 2x^2 + 3$.

x	−4	−3	−2	−1	0	1	2	3	4
$2x^2$	32								
$+ 3$	+3								
$y = 2x^2 + 3$	35								

b Draw axes with values of x from −4 to 4 and values of y from 0 to 40. Draw the curve.

c Describe the main features of the curve.

6 a Copy and complete this table for $y = x^3 + 2$.

x	−3	−2	−1	0	1	2	3
x^3	−27						
$+ 2$	+2						
$y = x^3 + 2$	−25						

b Draw axes with values of x from −3 to 3 and values of y from −25 to 30. Draw the curve.

c Use your graph to find the co-ordinates of the points where the curve crosses the x axis and the y axis.

d Describe the symmetry of the graph.

Developing fluency

1 a Draw the graph of $y = x^2 - 4x + 3$, taking values of x from −1 to 5.

b Use your graph to solve the equation $x^2 - 4x + 3 = 0$.

c Use your graph to estimate the values of x when $y = 6$.

d Explain why it is not possible to find a value of x for which $y = -2$.

2 a Draw the graphs of $y = x^3 - 8$ and $y = -x^3 + 8$ on the same sheet of paper, taking values of x from −2 to 3.

b Use your graphs to solve the equation $x^3 - 8 = 0$.

c For what values of x is $x^3 - 8$ greater than $-x^3 + 8$?

d Describe the relationship between the two curves.

Algebra Strand 3 Functions and graphs

3 **a** Copy and complete this table of values for the curve $y = x^3 - 6x^2 + 11x - 6$.

x	0	1	2	3	4
x^3					
$-6x^2$					
$11x$					
-6					
$y = x^3 - 6x^2 + 11x - 6$					

b Draw the curve.

c Use your graph to solve the equation $x^3 - 6x^2 + 11x - 6 = 0$.

d For how many values of x is $y = 1$? Use your graph to find them to 1 decimal place.

e Find the values of x (again to 1 decimal place) when $y = 4$.

4 Mo stands on top of a cliff 60 m high. He throws a stone into the air.
The equation for the height, y metres, of the stone above the beach is
$y = 60 + 20t - 5t^2$ where t is the time in seconds.

a Draw the graph of y against t. Take values of t from 0 to 6 and y from 0 to 100.

b What is the greatest height of the stone above the beach?

c Find how long the stone is in the air.

5 Use a co-ordinate grid with values of x from -3 to $+3$ with 2 cm intervals and values of y from -15 to 15 with 5 units every 2 cm.

a Draw the graphs of $y = (x - 1)^2 - 4$ and $y = 5x - x^3$.

b Find the values of x where the two graphs cross. Give your answers to 1 decimal place.

6 Alex stands at the edge of a 10 m high cliff and throws a pebble into the sea.
The height above sea level of the pebble at time t seconds is modelled by the equation $h = 10 + 8t - 5t^2$.

a Copy and complete this table of values.

t	0	0.5	1	1.5	2	2.5
10						
$+8t$						
$-5t^2$						
$h = 10 + 8t - 5t^2$						

b Draw the graph of h against t.

c What is the maximum height reached by the pebble?

d How long is the pebble above the height of the cliff?

e **i** When does the pebble hit the sea?

   ii Does your graph have any meaning after this time?

Unit 4 Plotting quadratic and cubic graphs Band g

Problem solving

1 Here are the graphs of $y = (x - 4)(x + 1)$ and $y = (x + 4)(1 - x)$:

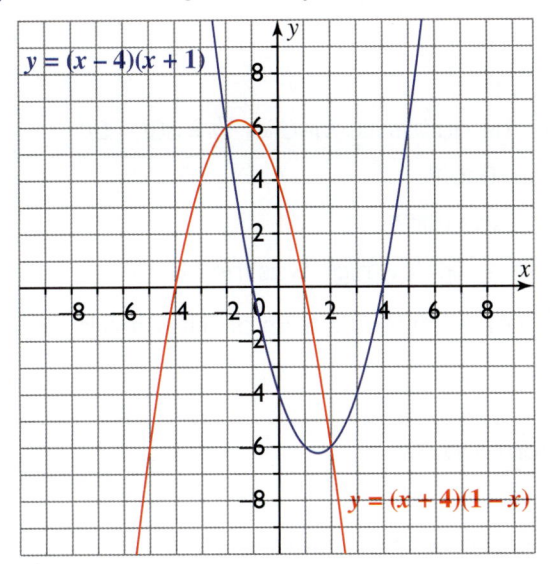

    a For which values of x is $y = (x + 4)(1 - x)$ always positive?
    b For which values of x is $y = (x - 4)(x + 1)$ always negative?
    c Find the values of x when the blue line is below the red line.
    d What is the minimum point of $y = (x - 4)(x + 1)$?
    e What is the maximum point of $y = (x + 4)(1 - x)$?

2 Here are the graphs of $y = x^3 - 4x$ and $y = 4x - x^3$:

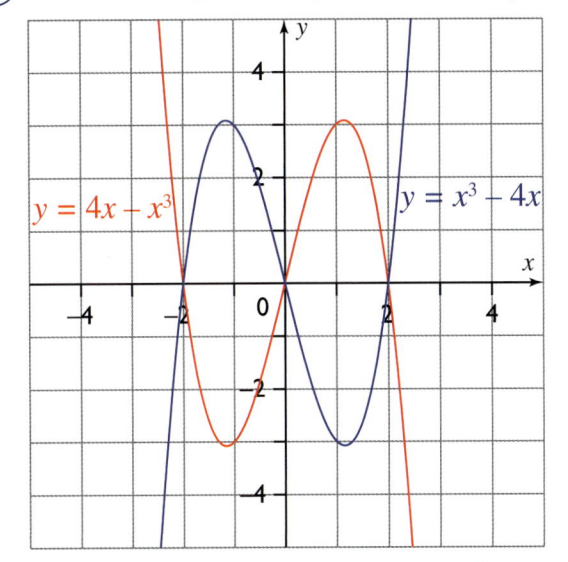

    a For which values of x is $y = 4x - x^3$ positive?
    b For which values of x is $y = x^3 - 4x$ negative?
    c Find the values of x when $4x - x^3$ is greater than $x^3 - 4x$.
    d Describe the relationship between the two curves.
    e Describe the symmetry of $y = x^3 - 4x$.

Algebra Strand 3 Functions and graphs

3) Mair's company manufactures golf balls. Mair and Gwilym tested one of the balls by throwing it into the air from the top of the cliff. Pete made a video.
Back at work, they found the height of the ball at 2 second intervals.

Time (s) t	2	4	6	8
Height (m) h	40	40	0	−80

    a Show that the path of the ball is consistent with the quadratic function $h = 30t - 5t^2$.
    b Draw the graph of h against t, for values of t from 0 to 8.
    c For how long was the ball more than 25 m above the cliff?
    d The ball landed 8 seconds after Mair threw it in the air. How high was the cliff?

4) Narinder makes rectangular table mats. The length of each mat is x cm and its area is A cm^2. Each mat he makes has a perimeter of 80 cm.
    a Show that $A = x(40 - x)$.
    b Draw the graph of A against x for values of x from 0 to 40.
    c Find the length of a table mat with area 375 cm^2.
    d Explain how your graph shows you that the table mat with the greatest area is square-shaped.

5) José makes garden ornaments out of concrete. They stand on a base of radius x cm. The volume of concrete needed, V cm^3, is given by the formula
$V = 2x^2(10 - x)$.
    a Draw a graph of V against x, taking values of x from 0 to 10.
    b A base needs 200 cm^3 of concrete. Use your graph to estimate its radius.
    c One day, José has an order for 5 ornaments of radius 6.2 cm.
       Use your graph to estimate how much concrete he needs.

6) An oil tanker carries a cargo of oil at a speed of v km per hour. The cost, £C, per hour of carrying the oil is given by the formula $C = 20v + \dfrac{6000}{v}$, for values of v between 5 and the maximum speed of 40.
    a Make a table of values.
    b Draw the graph of C against v.
    c Use your graph to estimate the speed at which the value of C is the least.

Reviewing skills

1 a Copy and complete this table for $y = 5x - x^2$.

x	–1	0	1	2	3	4	5	6
$5x$	–5							
$-x^2$	–1							
$y = 5x - x^2$	–6							

  b Draw axes with values of x from –1 to 6 and values of y from –8 to 8.
  Draw the curve.

  c Describe the main features of the curve.

  d Use your graph to solve the equation $5x - x^2 = 0$.

2 Fauzia is a junior rugby player. She is learning to take place kicks. The ball must go over the posts; the bar is 3 m high.
When the ball has travelled x m horizontally its height is y m.
For Fauzia's kicks $y = 0.7x - 0.02x^2$

  a Make a table of values of y, taking x to be 0, 10, 15, 20, 25 and 35.

  b Draw the graph of y against x.

  c How far from the posts can Fauzia make a successful kick?

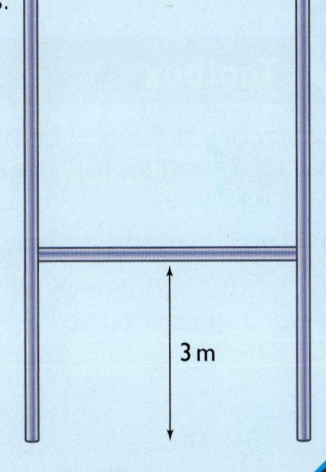

Unit 5 • Finding equations of straight lines • Band h

Outside the Maths classroom

Calculating acceleration
A tourist simultaneously drops a small coin and a cricket ball from the top of the Leaning Tower of Pisa. Which would land first?

Toolbox

How many different straight lines can you draw through two points, say (3, 6) and (5, 10)? The answer, of course, is one. Two points define a straight line.

It is usual in maths that anything described as a **line** is straight.

If a graph produces something that is not straight then this is usually described as a '**curve**'

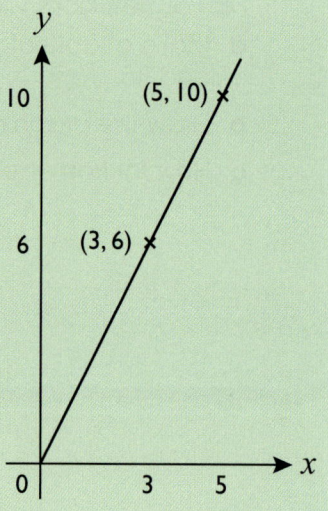

To find the equation of the line, think of the two points as part of a right-angled triangle like this. The line through (3, 6) and (5, 10) goes 2 units across and 4 units up. So the gradient of the line is 2 ÷ 4 or 0.5.

If you know the gradient of a line and a point on that line, then the equation of the line can be found.

$$y = mx + c$$

For example, for a line with gradient of 0.5 that goes through (3, 6) we know that $y = 6$ when $x = 3$.

So, using $y = mx + c$ gives

$6 = 0.5 \times 3 + c$

$6 = 1.5 + c$,

$c = 4.5$.

So the equation of the line with gradient 0.5 that goes through (3, 6) is $y = 0.5x + 4.5$.

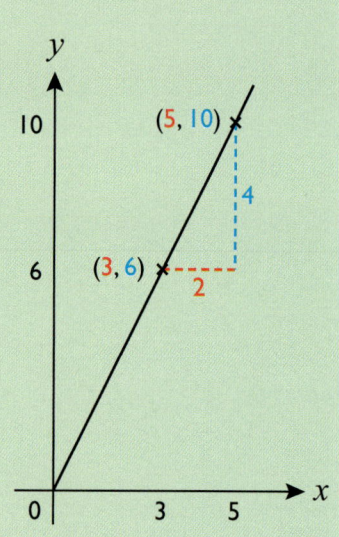

Unit 5 Finding equations of straight lines Band h

Example – Using one point and the gradient

A line has a gradient of 3 and passes through the point (1, 8).
a Calculate the y-intercept of the line.
b Find the equation of the line.

Solution

a Here is a sketch of the line.

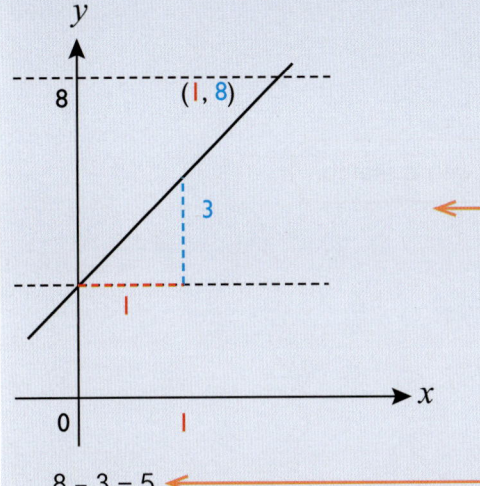

8 – 3 = 5 ← *From $x = 0$ to $x = 1$ the graph goes up 3…*

So the y-intercept is at (0, 5). ← *…so it goes from $y = 5$ to $y = 8$*

The y-intercept is the point where the graph cuts the y axis.

b The equation of a straight line is $y = mx + c$ where m is the gradient and c is the y-intercept.

The gradient is 3, so $m = 3$. ← *From the question.*

The y-intercept is at (0, 5) so $c = 5$. ← *From part a.*
So $y = 3x + 5$.

217

Example – Using two points

A line goes through (2, 9) and (3, 7).
a Find the gradient of the line.
b Find the equation of the line.

Solution

a

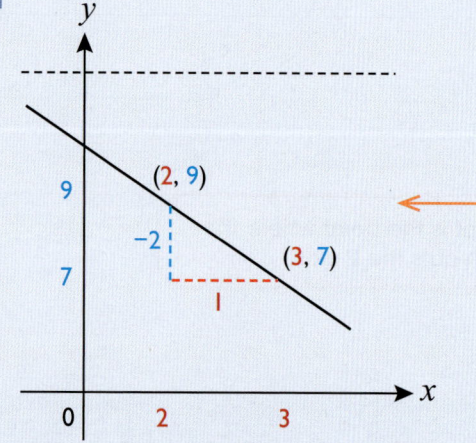

Always start with a sketch.

$$\text{Gradient} = \frac{\text{change in } y}{\text{change in } x}$$

$$= \frac{-2}{1}$$

$$= -2$$

'Downhill lines' have a negative gradient.

b The equation of a straight line is $y = mx + c$.

The gradient is -2 so $m = -2$.
So $y = -2x + c$.
You can find the value of c by substituting the co-ordinates of one point on the line into $y = -2x + c$.
For the point (2, 9):   *You could use (3, 7) instead.*
substituting $x = 2$, $y = 9$ into $y = -2x + c$
gives $9 = -2 \times 2 + c$
$9 = -4 + c$
$13 = c$
So $c = 13$
The equation of the line is $y = -2x + 13$.   *You can write this as $y = 13 - 2x$.*

Practising skills

1. The lines $y = 5x + 2$ and $y = 5x - 2$ are parallel. Match these lines into pairs that are parallel and find the odd one out.

   a $y = 3x + 7$ b $y = 7x + 3$ c $y = -3x + 2$ d $y = 7x - 5$

   e $y = -5x + 9$ f $y = 3x + 9$ g $y = -3x - 10$

   h Write the equation of a line that is parallel to the odd one out.

2. All of the lines in this question have a gradient of 2.

   a Draw the graphs of the lines that go through these points.

       i (1, 5)   ii (1, 12)   iii (1, 1)   iv (5, 7)   v (−2, 1)

   b Find their y-intercepts.

   c Write down their equations.

3. A line has equation $y = 3x + k$.

   a What is the gradient of the line?

   The line passes through the point (2, 11).

   b How does this give you the equation $11 = 6 + k$?

   c Find the value of k and write down the equation of the line.

   d Where does the line cross the y axis?

4. Find the equation of the line that has a gradient of

   a 3 and goes through (1, 1)

   b 7 and goes through (2, 5)

   c 2 and goes through (10, 1)

   d $\frac{1}{2}$ and goes through (2, 2)

   e $-\frac{1}{2}$ and goes through (2, 2).

5. A line goes through the points (2, 1) and (4, 9).

   a Show that the gradient of the line is 4.

   b Find the equation of the line with gradient 4 that passes through (2, 1).

   c Check that (4, 9) lies on your line.

6. For the following pairs of points

   a find the gradient of the line joining them.

   b find the equation of the line through them.

   c check that both points lie on the lines by substituting x- and y-co-ordinates into the equation.

       i (1, 1) to (5, 7)   ii (1, 3) to (5, 7)   iii (3, 4) to (5, 7)

       iv (−2, 3) to (5, 7)   v (2, 9) to (5, 7)

Algebra Strand 3 Functions and graphs

Developing fluency

① These two lines meet at (−1, 2). One has a gradient of 2 and the other has a gradient of 3.

  a Find the equation of each line.

  b Find the co-ordinates of the points where they cross the y axis.

  c State whether these points are on the red line, the blue line or neither.
   i   (1, 6)
   ii (−2, 0)
   iii (2, 8)
   iv $\left(-1\tfrac{1}{2}, 0\right)$
   v $\left(-\tfrac{1}{2}, 3\right)$

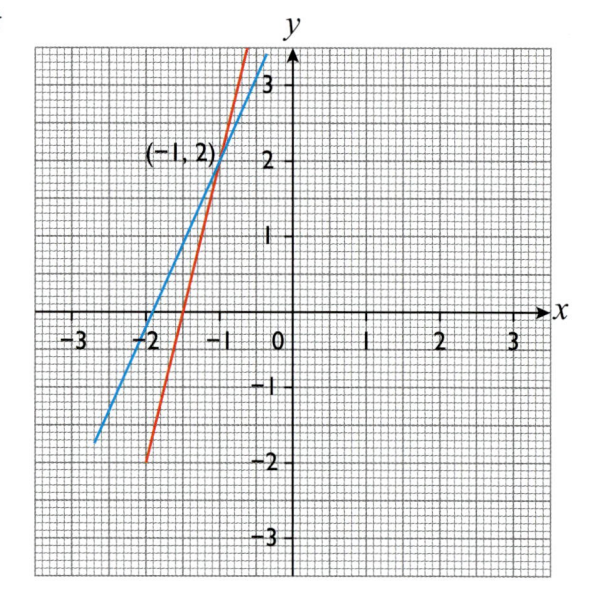

② Write down the equation of a straight-line graph that fits into each section of this two-way table.

	Gradient is 3	Gradient is −7
y-intercept is 6		
y-intercept is −5		

③ The line l goes through the points (4, 0) and (0, 4).
The line m goes through the points (4, 2) and (0, −2).

  a Find the equations of the lines l and m.

  b Draw a graph showing the lines l and m. Use the same scale for both the x axis and the y axis.

  c Find the angle between the two lines.

④ Find the equations of these lines.

  a Through (1, 2) and (3, 4).

  b Through (1, 3) and (5, 7).

  c Through (1, 5) and (9, 13).

  d Through (5, 9) with gradient 1.

  e Gradient 1 and y-intercept 2.

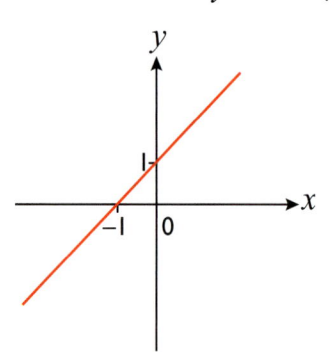

  f

Which lines are the same as each other?

Unit 5 Finding equations of straight lines Band h

5) The co-ordinates of point A are (a, b) and the co-ordinates of point B are (b, a).
Is it always, sometimes or never true that the line through A and B has a negative gradient?
If you think always or never, you must explain how you can be so certain.
If you think sometimes, then you must explain when the statement is and isn't true.

6) A triangle is drawn on a co-ordinate grid. It has vertices at (1, 1), (6, 6) and (1, 11).
   a Find the equations of the three lines used to make the triangle.
   b Draw the triangle on graph paper, using the same scales for the x axis and the y axis.
   c Describe the triangle.
   d Find the area of the triangle.

7) ABCD is a quadrilateral. The equations of its sides are:
   AB $y = -3x + 7$
   BC $y = 2x - 3$
   DC $y = -2x + 13$
   DA $y = 3x - 17$
   a Draw the four lines on a graph.
   b Find the co-ordinates of A, B, C and D.
   c What sort of quadrilateral is ABCD?
   d The diagonals AC and BD meet at E. What are the co-ordinates of E?
   e What are the equations of AC and BD?

Problem solving

1) l and m are two straight lines.
   l has a gradient of 2 and crosses the y axis at (0, −1).
   m has a gradient of −3 and crosses the y axis at (0, 4).
   a Find the equations of l and m.
   b Draw lines l and m on a graph.
   c Find the co-ordinates of their point of intersection.

2) p and q are two straight lines.
   p has a gradient of 3 and passes through the point (3, 2).
   q has a gradient of −2 and passes through the point (1, −4).
   a Draw lines p and q on a graph.
   b Find the equations of p and q.
   c Write down the co-ordinates of R, the point of intersection of p and q.
   d Show that R lies on the line $y = -4x$.

3) A straight line r is parallel to the line $y = x + 3$ and passes through the point (0, 5).
   Another straight line s is parallel to the line $x + y = 5$ and passes through the point (0, 1).
   a Find the equations of the lines r and s.
   b Find, by drawing, the co-ordinates of the point of intersection of the two straight lines.
   c Substitute the x- and y-values you found in part b into the equations of the lines r and s.
      How does this check your answers?

Algebra Strand 3 Functions and graphs

4 A straight line l is parallel to the line $y = 4x - 3$ and passes through the point $(-1, 2)$.
Another straight line m is parallel to the line $4x + 3y = 2$ and passes through the point $(3, -2)$.
   a Draw the lines l and m on a graph.
   b Find the equations of l and m.
   c Find the point of intersection of l and m.
   d Use your answer to part c to check your equation of l and m.

5 a On the same axes, draw the lines
   p: $y = 1$
   q: $x = 3$
   r: $y = 3x + 1$
   b Write down co-ordinates of the point, C, where line p and line q meet.
   c Line m is parallel to r and passes through C.
   Write down the equation of line m.
   d Find the area of the region bounded by the y-axis and the lines q, r and m.

6 Line l passes through the points $(-1, 6)$ and $(1, 2)$.
Line m has equation $y + 2x = 9$.
   a Show that the lines l and m are parallel.
   b Draw lines l and m on the same co-ordinate axes.

Line n has gradient $\frac{1}{2}$ and the same y-intercept as line l.
   c Find the equation of line n.
   d By substituting for x and y, show that the point $(2, 5)$ lies on both lines m and n.
   e Find the area of the triangle bounded by line m, line n and the y axis.

Reviewing skills

1 Find the equations of these lines.
   a Parallel to $y = 2x + 3$ with y-intercept 5.
   b Gradient -1 through the point $(5, 2)$.
   c Through the points $(-1, -4)$ and $(2, 5)$.

2 a Draw a graph showing the lines $y = 2x + 3$ and $y = -x + 6$.
   b Find the co-ordinates of the point of intersection, P.
   c Show algebraically that the line joining $(0, 7)$ to $(3.5, 0)$ passes through P.

3 A is $(0, 0)$, B is $(3, 4)$, C is $(9, 4)$ and D is $(6, 0)$.
   a Show that the quadrilateral ABCD is a parallelogram, but not a rhombus.
   b Find the equations of the lines AC and BD.
   c Use algebra to show that the point E $(4.5, 2)$ lies on both lines AC and BD.
   d Show points A, B, C, D and E on a graph. Show also the parallelogram ABCD and its diagonals.

4 Indicate the correct answer **a**, **b**, **c** or **d**.
A line parallel to $2y = 4x + 5$.
   a $y = 4x + 5$ b $y = 2x - 5$ c $y = -2x + 5$ d $2y = 6x + 5$

Unit 6 • Perpendicular lines • Band i

Outside the Maths classroom

Computer software
Some computer software uses Cartesian grids to construct lines. How could a computer game designer ensure lines are perpendicular?

Toolbox

To calculate the gradient of a line, draw a triangle on the line, like this. Then divide the height of the triangle by its base.

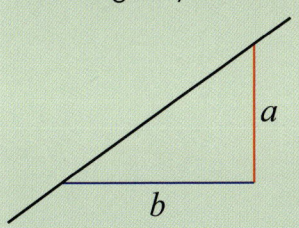

In this diagram the gradient is $a \div b$, so

$$\text{gradient} = \frac{\text{vertical distance}}{\text{horizontal distance}}.$$

Rotating the line by 90° gives a line that is perpendicular to the original. It can be seen that what was originally the horizontal distance is now vertical, and what was vertical is now horizontal.

Rotating 90° gives

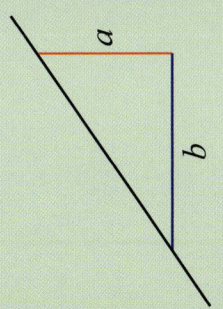

The gradient of this perpendicular line is $\frac{b}{a}$ and, since the line is sloping downwards, it is negative. The gradient is $-\frac{b}{a}$.

So the gradient of the line **perpendicular** to $y = mx + c$ will be $-\frac{1}{m}$.

The two gradients of two perpendicular lines multiply together to give −1 or $mm = -1$.

Algebra Strand 3 Functions and graphs

Example – Calculating the gradient

The diagram shows two lines. They are perpendicular.

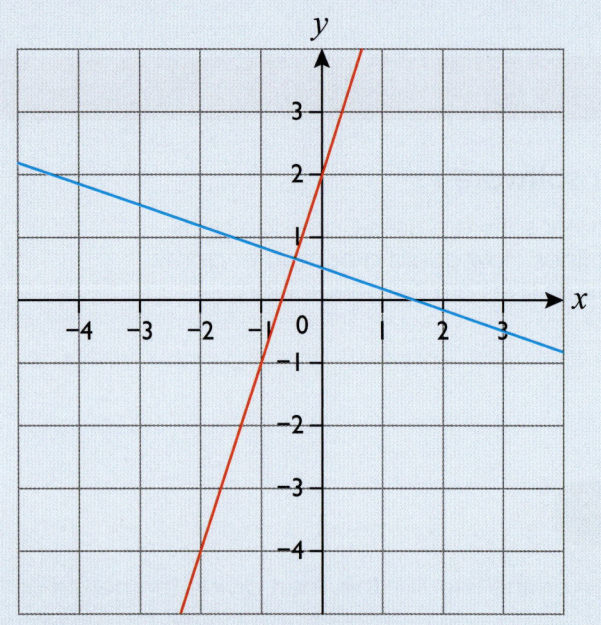

a Find the gradient of the red line.
b Find the equation of the red line.
c Find the gradient of the blue line.
d Find the equation of the blue line.

Solution

a

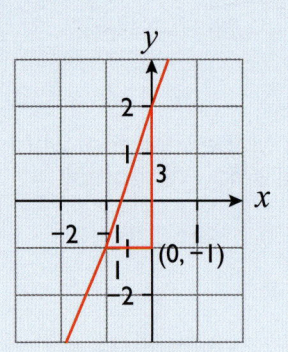

In this triangle,

$$\frac{\text{height}}{\text{base}} = \frac{3}{1} = 3$$

so the gradient is 3.

b The red line has intercept 2 and gradient 3, so its equation is $y = 3x + 2$. ← In $y = mx + c$, $m = 3$ and $c = 2$.

c The red and blue lines are perpendicular, so the gradient of the blue line is $\frac{1}{3}$. ← Using $mm^1 = -1$

d The blue line crosses the y-axis at $\frac{1}{2}$, so the $c = \frac{1}{2}$.

The equation of the blue line is $y = -\frac{1}{3}x + \frac{1}{2}$. ← $m = \frac{-1}{3}$

Unit 6 Perpendicular lines Band i

Example – Solving problems

ABCD is a quadrilateral.
A is (1, −1), B is (5, 2), C is (2, 6) and D is (−2, 3).
a   Show that AB is parallel to DC and that BC is parallel to AD.
b   Show that AD is perpendicular to AB.
c   What can you say now about the quadrilateral?

Solution

a   Gradient = $\dfrac{\text{change in } y}{\text{change in } x} = \dfrac{\text{'rise'}}{\text{'run'}}$.

Gradient of AB = $\dfrac{2-(-1)}{5-1} = \dfrac{3}{4}$. ← A is at (1, −1) and B is at (5, 2).

Gradient of DC = $\dfrac{6-3}{2-(-2)} = \dfrac{3}{4}$. ← D is at (−2, 3) and C is at (2, 6).

The gradients are the same, so AB and DC are parallel.

Gradient of BC = $\dfrac{6-2}{2-5} = -\dfrac{4}{3}$. ← B is at (5, 2) and C is at (2, 6).

Gradient of AD = $\dfrac{3-(-1)}{(-2)-1} = -\dfrac{4}{3}$. ← A is at (1, −1) and D is at (−2, 3).

The gradients are the same, so BC and AD are parallel.

b $m_{AD} \times m_{AB} = -\dfrac{4}{3} \times \dfrac{3}{4} = -1$ ← The 4s and the 3s cancel.

Since the product of the gradients is −1, the lines are perpendicular. ← Or you could say that the gradients are the negative reciprocal of each other.

c   The quadrilateral is a rectangle. ← Two pairs of parallel sides and four right angles.

Practising skills

1   a   Find the gradient of each of these lines.
    b   Which pairs of lines are perpendicular to each other?

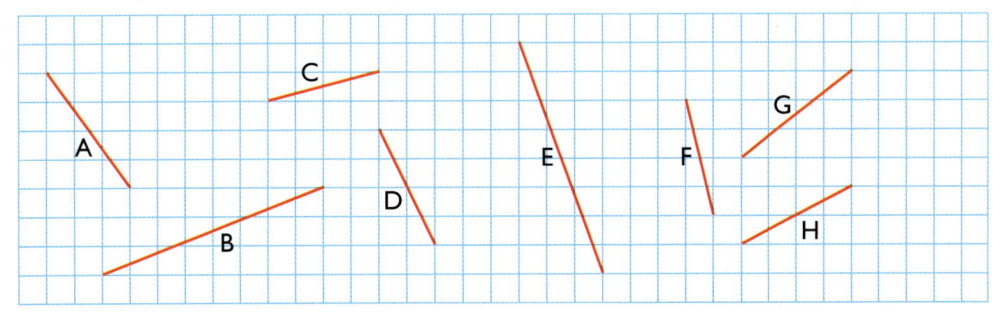

Algebra Strand 3 Functions and graphs

2 a Write down the gradient of each of these lines.
   A $y = 3x + 7$ E $y = x$
   B $y = \frac{-1}{2}x + 7$ F $y = \frac{-1}{3}x + 8$
   C $y = 3x - 4$ G $y = 2x - 2$
   D $y = -5x - 12$ H $y = -x + 3$

   b Which pairs of lines are:
   i parallel to each other
   ii perpendicular to each other?

3 a For each line in **A**, **B**, **C** and **D**, find:
   i the gradient
   ii the y-intercept
   iii the equation of the line.

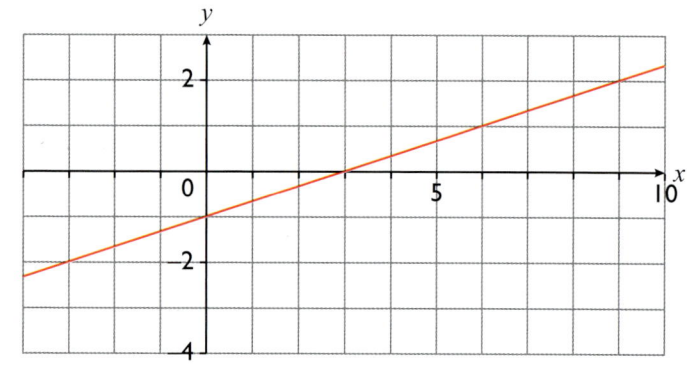

A

B

C

D

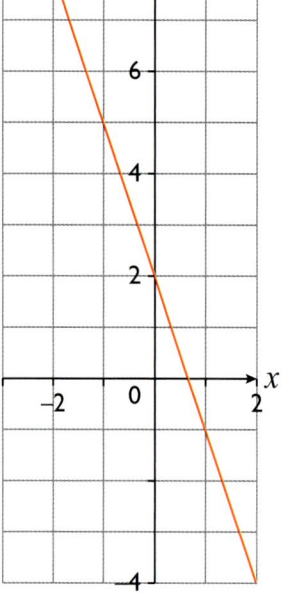

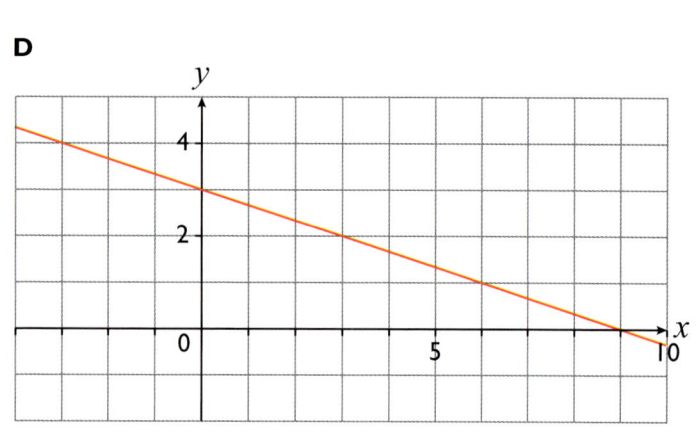

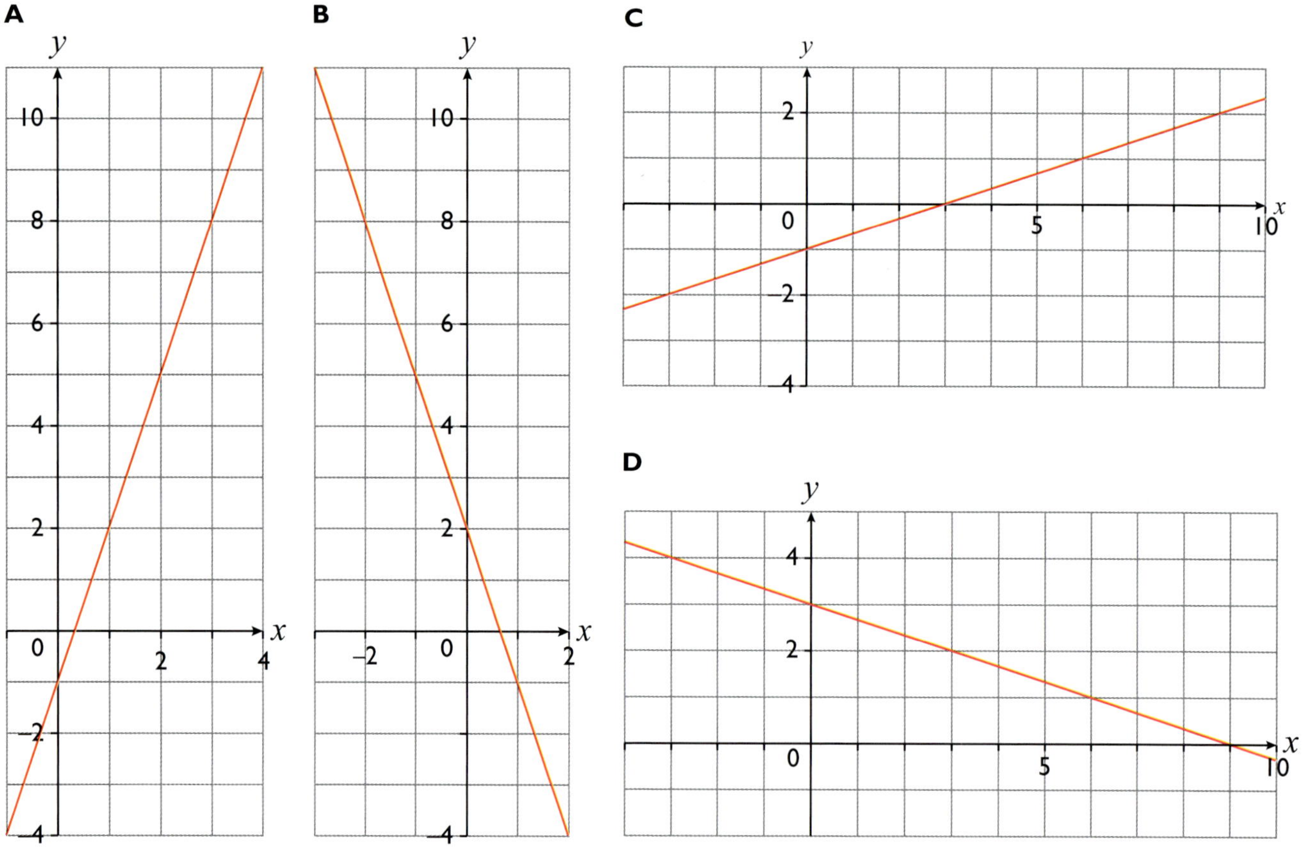

b Which lines are perpendicular to each other?

4.

$2x + 5y + 10 = 0$	$y = \frac{1}{2}x - 3$	$2y = x + 2$
$3y = x + 9$	$y = 2(2x + 1)$	$y - 2x + 4 = 0$
$x + 4y = 1$	$2y + x - 7 = 0$	$y = 3x - 2$

a Match together the pairs of lines which are:
  i parallel
  ii perpendicular
      (Hint: rearrange each equation into the form $y = mx + c$.)
  iii have the same y-intercept.

b Which line is the odd one out?

5. The blue line has equation $y = -2x + 1$.

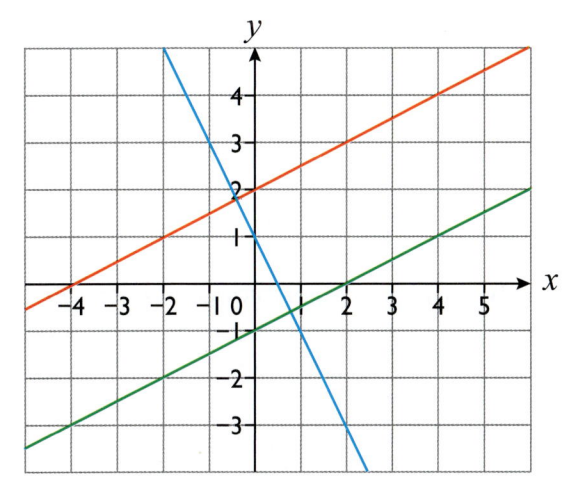

a Show that the red line and the green line are parallel to each other and perpendicular to the blue line.

b Find the equations of the red line and the green line.

6. The line $y = 5x + 3$ has a y-intercept of 3.
Find the equation of the line that is:

a parallel to it and has a y-intercept of 1

b perpendicular to it and has a y-intercept of 1.

Algebra Strand 3 Functions and graphs

Developing fluency

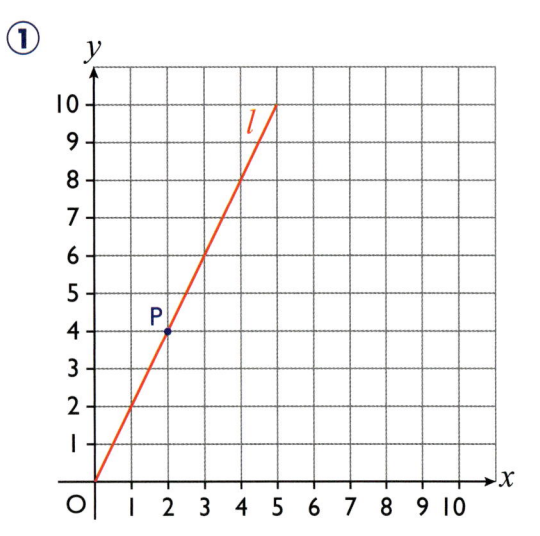

1

a Write down the equation of the line l on this graph.

b Find the equation of the line through point P perpendicular to line l.

This line crosses the x-axis at Q.

c Find the co-ordinates of Q.

d Find the area of the triangle OPQ.

2 a Draw the line $y = 2x + 1$.

b Mark the point P(2, 5) on the line $y = 2x + 1$.

c Find the equation of the line l perpendicular to $y = 2x + 1$ that passes through the point P. Add this line to your diagram.

d Write down the co-ordinates of the y-intercept of the line l.

e Find the equation of the line parallel to $y = 2x + 1$ with the same y-intercept as l. Add this line to your diagram.

The three lines form the three sides of a square.

f Find the equation for the fourth side of the square. (There are two possible answers – find them both.)

Unit 6 Perpendicular lines Band i

3 a Write down the equation of the line w on this graph.

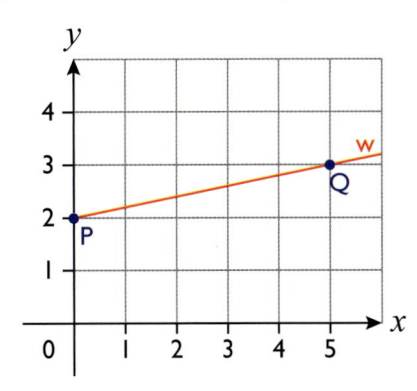

[Graph showing line w passing through P(0, 2) and Q(4, 3)]

b Find the equation of the line through point Q perpendicular to w.
This line crosses the y-axis at S.

c Find the co-ordinates of S.

d Find the area of the triangle SPQ.

4 Two perpendicular lines meet at (1, 1).

a In each of the following cases, draw the pair of lines on graph paper and find their equations.
Where one of the lines has a gradient of:
   i 2   **ii** 3   **iii** 4.

b Write down the equations of the two perpendicular lines when one has a gradient of m.

5 A line goes through the point (2, 3).
It intersects a line that is perpendicular to it at the point (5, 7).
Find the equation of both lines.

6 The line $y = -\frac{1}{2}x - 5$ and a line that is perpendicular to it intersect when $x = 2$.
Find the equation of the perpendicular line.

7 P, Q and R are three straight lines.
P has a gradient of 2 and crosses the y-axis at (0, −1).
Q has a gradient of −3 and crosses the y-axis at (0, 4).
R is perpendicular to P and also crosses the y-axis at (0, −1).

a Draw the lines P, Q and R on graph paper.

b A is the point of intersection of Q and R. Find the co-ordinates of A.

c Find the equations of the lines Q and R.

d Check your answer to part **b** by substituting the co-ordinates of A into the equations of Q and R.

Algebra Strand 3 Functions and graphs

Problem solving

1 The yellow triangle has an area of 4 square units.

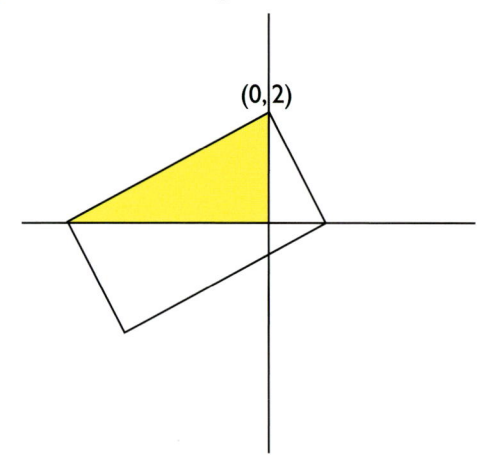

Find:

a the equation of each of the lines making the edges of the rectangle

b the area of the rectangle.

2 Line L is parallel to the line $y = 2x + 3$ and passes through the point $(-2, 5)$.
Line M is perpendicular to the line $y = x - 5$ and passes through the point $(3, -2)$.

a Draw the lines L and M on graph paper.

b Find the co-ordinates of their point of intersection.

c Check your answer to part **b** by substituting it into the equations of the two lines.

3 PQRS is a square, as shown.

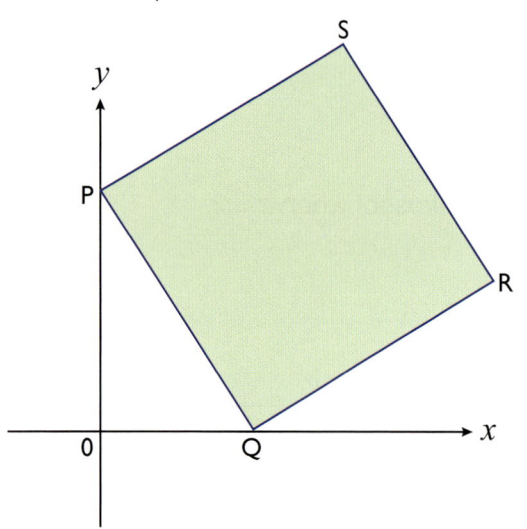

The equation of the line PQ is $4x + 3y = 12$.

a Rearrange the equation of PQ so that y is the subject.

b Write down the co-ordinates of point P and the gradient of PQ.

c Find the co-ordinates of Q and the length of PQ.

d Show that S is the point $(4, 7)$.

④ L, M and N are three straight lines.
L has a gradient of 3 and passes through the point (2, 3).
M has a gradient of −2 and passes through the point (−1, −3).
N is perpendicular to M and passes through the point (4, 1).
Find the point of intersection of L and N.

⑤ Line A is parallel to the line $y = 4x − 3$ and passes through the point (−1, 2).
Line B is perpendicular to the line $4x + 3y = 2$ and passes through the point (2, −4).

   a Draw the lines A and B on graph paper.

   b Find the co-ordinates of their point of intersection.

   c Check your answer to part **b** by substituting it into the equations of the two lines.

⑥ ABCD is a rectangle as shown.

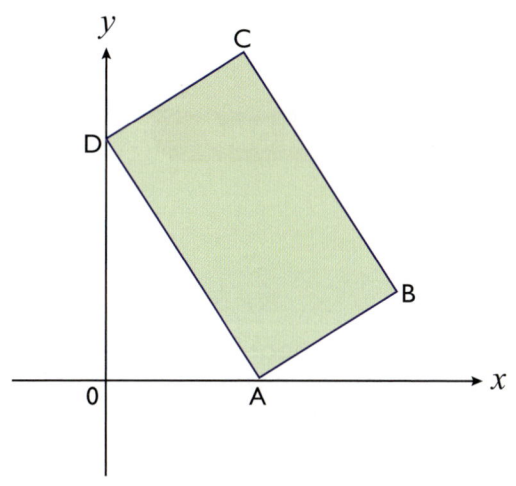

The equation of the line AD is $12x + 5y = 60$. AB has a length of 6.5 units.

   a Draw the rectangle accurately on graph paper.

   b Use your graph to find the co-ordinates of point B.

   c Find the equation of the line BC.

   d Find the equation of the line AB.

   e Find the area of rectangle ABCD.

Reviewing skills

① **a** Draw the line $y = −2x + 1$ on graph paper.

   b Find the equation of the line that is perpendicular to $y = −2x + 1$, which passes through (0, −3).

② Find the equation of the line that is perpendicular to $y = 5x + 1$, which passes through the point (5, 4).

Algebra Strand 4 Algebraic methods

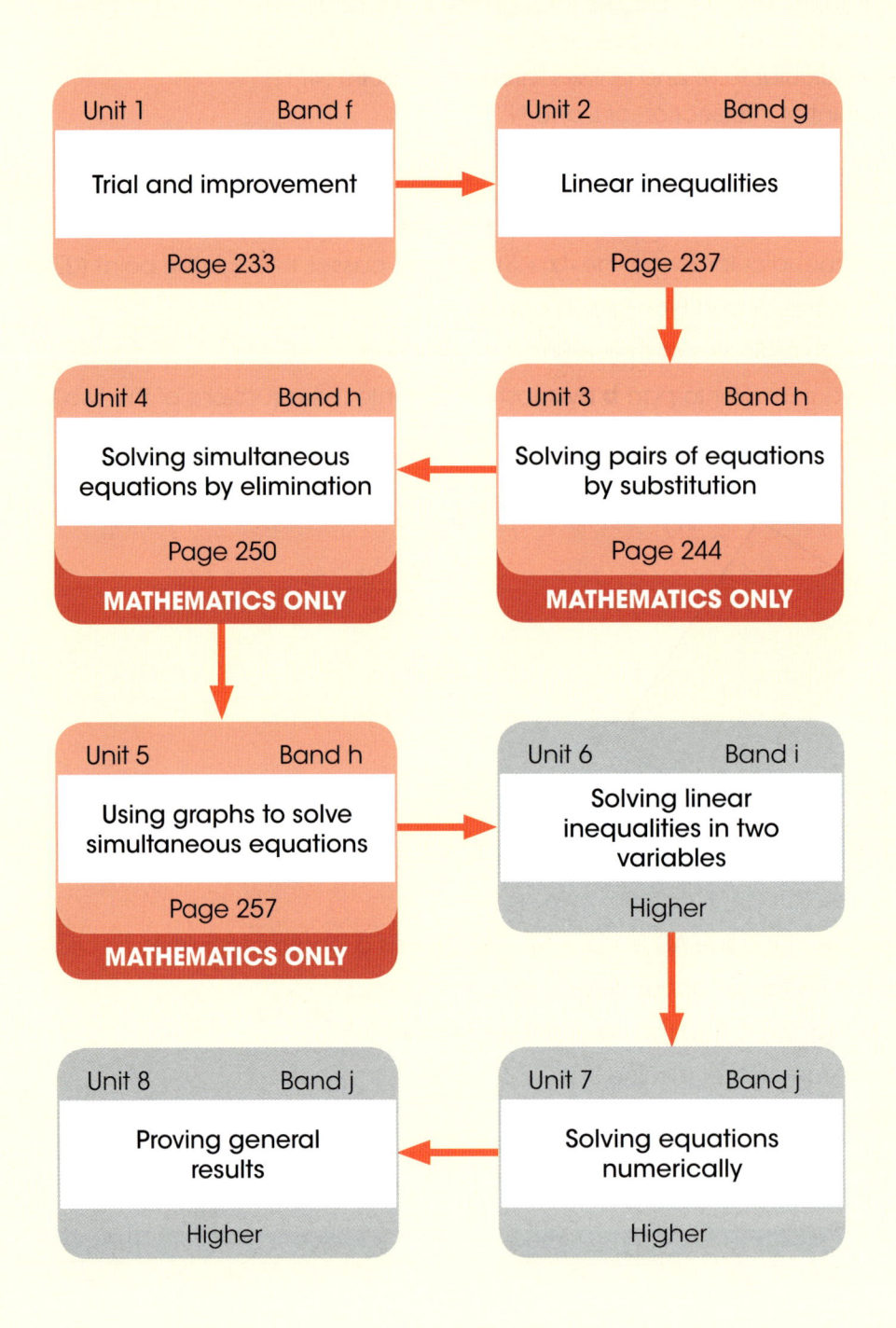

Unit 1 — Band f
Trial and improvement
Page 233

Unit 2 — Band g
Linear inequalities
Page 237

Unit 3 — Band h
Solving pairs of equations by substitution
Page 244
MATHEMATICS ONLY

Unit 4 — Band h
Solving simultaneous equations by elimination
Page 250
MATHEMATICS ONLY

Unit 5 — Band h
Using graphs to solve simultaneous equations
Page 257
MATHEMATICS ONLY

Unit 6 — Band i
Solving linear inequalities in two variables
Higher

Unit 7 — Band j
Solving equations numerically
Higher

Unit 8 — Band j
Proving general results
Higher

Unit 1 • Trial and improvement • Band f

Outside the Maths classroom

Solving complex problems
Is there a relationship between the height of a skyscraper and the depths of its foundations?

Toolbox

When an equation cannot be solved algebraically you can use trial and improvement to solve it.

Trial and improvement means you make a sensible first guess (trial) and then you improve upon it.

Once you have found that the solution lies between two consecutive values, you should check the value halfway between them.

$x = 8$ too small
$x = 9$ too big

Try $x = 8.5$ next.

Keep repeating the process until you have the degree of accuracy you need.

$x = 8.2$ too small
$x = 8.3$ too big
$x = 8.25$ too small

x is between 8.25 and 8.3, so $x = 8.3$ to 1 d.p.

Example – Solving a problem

Zac is designing a tray to hold 75 cm³ of sugar.
The width is 3 times the height.
The length is 4 times the height.
Zac makes a table to find x.
Find x correct to 1 decimal place.

x	$3x$	$4x$	Volume	Too big or too small?
1	3	4	12 cm³	small
2	6	8	96 cm³	
1.5				

Algebra Strand 4 Algebraic methods

Solution

When $x = 1.5$, volume = 40.5 cm³ ← too small
$x = 1.8$, volume = 69.9... cm³ ← too small
$x = 1.9$, volume = 82.3... cm³ ← too big
$x = 1.85$, volume = 75.9... cm³ ← too big

So $x = 1.8$ to 1 d.p. In the end Zac decides to use 1.9 to be on the safe side.

Zac wants to solve

$$a^2 + \frac{1}{x} = 11$$

correct to 2 d.p.

Here is part of Zac's table of results.

Find the value of x correct to 2 d.p.

x	3.27	3.28	3.275
$x^2 + \frac{1}{x} = 11$	10.99...	11.06...	11.03...

Solution

The table shows that x is greater than 3.27 but less than 3.275.
Any number in this range rounds to 3.27 to 2 d.p.
So $x = 3.27$ to 2 d.p.

Practising skills

(1) The equation $x^2 - 3x = 2$ has a solution between 3 and 4.

Robert wants to find this solution, correct to 1 decimal place. Here is his working:

x	$x^2 - 3x$	Comment
3	0	Too small
4	4	Too large
3.5	1.75	Too small
3.6	2.16	Too large
3.55	1.9525	Too small

   a What is the solution correct to 1 decimal place?
   b Explain why Robert calculated the value of $x^2 - 3x + 1$ when $x = 3.55$.

(2) Roy and Jenny are finding the solution to the equation $x^3 + 2x = 110$ that lies between 4 and 5.

Roy's answer is 4.6.

Jenny's answer is 4.7.

Who is correct? Explain how you know.

3) Jerry wants to find the solutions to the equation $x^3 + 2x = 20$.
   a Show that there is a solution between $x = 2$ and $x = 3$.
   b Copy and continue the table below to find that solution to 1 decimal place.

x	$x^3 + 2x$	Comment
2		
3		

4) Rachel is using trial and improvement to find a solution to the equation $x^3 + 6x = 25$. This table shows her first two trials.

x	$x^3 + 6x$	Comment
2	20	Too small
3	45	Too large

   Copy and continue the table to find a solution to the equation. Give your answer to 1 decimal place.

5) The square root key on Paul's calculator has broken. He is trying to find the square root of 70, correct to 1 decimal place.
   a He thinks it lies between 8 and 9.
      Explain why he is correct.
   b He thinks it lies between 8.3 and 8.4.
      Is he correct?
   c Find the answer, correct to 1 decimal place, without using the square root key.

Developing fluency

1) The equation $x^3 + x^2 = 100$ has a solution between 4 and 5.
   Copy and continue the table to calculate this solution, correct to 1 decimal place.

x	x^3	$+x^2$	$x^3 + x^2$	Comment
4	64	−16	80	too small

2) The equation $x^3 - 2x^2 = 40$ has a solution between 4 and 5.
   Find that solution, correct to 1 decimal place.

3) The equation $x(x^2 + 3) = 70$ has a solution between $x = 3$ and $x = 4$.
   Find the solution, to 1 decimal place.

4) x is a number such that $x(x - 1)(x + 2) = 40$.
   Find a value of x between 3 and 4.

Algebra Strand 4 Algebraic methods

5 The equation $x^3 - 3x^3 + x = -1.5$ has a solution between 1 and 2.
  a Find that solution.
  b Show that the equation also has a solution between -1 and 0, and another between 2 and 3.
  c Find the negative solution, correct to 1 decimal place.

Problem solving

1 A cuboid is $x + 2$ cm long, x cm wide and x cm high. The volume of the cuboid is $120\,\text{cm}^3$.

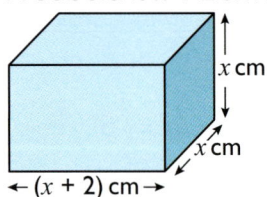

Calculate the length of the cuboid to the nearest mm.

2 Here is the graph of $y = x^3 - 5x^2 + 2x + 10$.

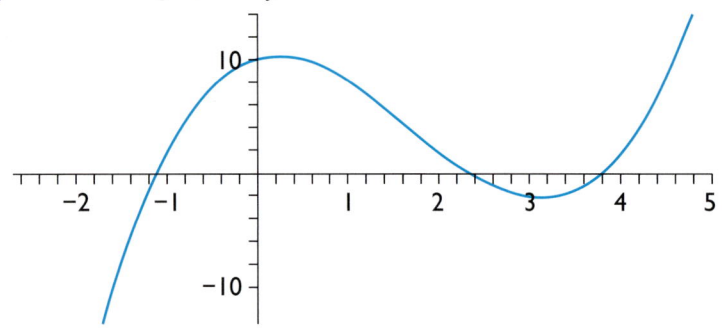

Use trial and improvement to find, correct to 1 decimal place, all three solutions to the equation $x^3 - 5x^2 + 2x + 10 = 5$.

3 Use trial and improvement to find, correct to 1 decimal place, both solutions to the equation $x + \dfrac{1}{x} = 5$.

Reviewing skills

1 Simon wants to find the solutions to the equation $x^3 + x = 9$.
  a Show that there is a solution between $x = 1$ and $x = 2$.
  b Copy and complete table below to find that solution, to 1 decimal place.

x	$x^3 + x$	Comment
1		
2		

2 The equation $x^2(x + 3) = 180$ has a solution between $x = 4$ and $x = 5$. Find the solution, to 1 decimal place.

Unit 2 • Linear inequalities • Band g

Outside the Maths classroom

Manufacturing constraints

What does a baker need to consider when working out how many of each type of cake she should bake?

How can inequalities help?

Toolbox

You can use a **number line** to show an **inequality**.

This number line represents $-2 \leq x < 3$.

```
-4 -3 -2 -1  0  1  2  3  4
 +--+--●--+--+--+--+--○--+
```

The integer (whole number) values of x are $-2, -1, 0, 1$ and 2.

These numbers are said to 'satisfy' the inequality.

You solve linear inequalities in the same way that you solve equations, but remember

- keep the inequality sign pointing the same way

  $x + 6 < 7$ $x + 6 < 7$ $x + 6 < 7$
  $x < 1$ ✓ $x = 1$ ✗ $x > 1$ ✓

- when you multiply or divide by a negative number, turn the inequality sign round.

  $-3x > 12r$ $-4x > 12$ $-\frac{1}{2}x \leq 2$
  $x < -4$ ✓ $x > -3$ ✗ $x \geq -4$ ✓

Example – Solving a word problem with an inequality

An animal shelter has enough kennels to keep 20 dogs.
They never have fewer than 8 dogs.

  a Write an inequality for the number of dogs, d, at the shelter.
  b Show the inequality on a number line.

Solution

  a $8 \leq d \leq 20$ *Use 'less than or equal to' signs to include 8 and 20.*
  b On the number line, draw circles at 8 and 20 and join them with a straight line.
      d can equal 8 and 20, so fill in both of the circles.

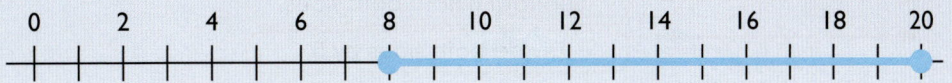

```
 0   2   4   6   8  10  12  14  16  18  20
 +-+-+-+-+-+-+-●--+--+--+--+--+--+--●
```

Algebra Strand 4 Algebraic methods

Example – Using a number line

a Show the inequality $-1 \leqslant x < 4$ on a number line.
b Write down the possible integer (whole number) values of x.

Solution

a

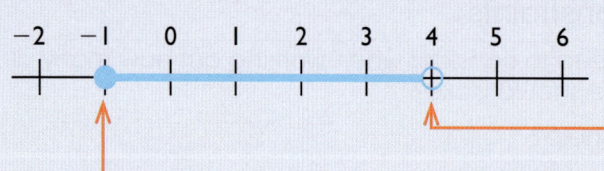

(Number line from −2 to 6 with filled circle at −1 and open circle at 4, shaded between.)

x must be less than 4 so leave this circle open.

x can equal −1, so fill in this circle.

b Include −1, but not 4.
The integer values of x are −1, 0, 1, 2 and 3. ← Remember that 0 is a whole number.

Example – Solving inequalities

Solve these inequalities.
a $5(2x + 3) \geqslant 20$
b $8(x + 1) \leqslant 3x + 18$
c $6 - 3x < 9$

Solution

a $5(2x + 3) \geqslant 20$
$10x + 15 \geqslant 20$ ← Expand the brackets.
$10x \geqslant 5$ ← Subtract 15 from both sides.
$x \geqslant \frac{5}{10}$ ← Divide both sides by 10.
$x \geqslant \frac{1}{2}$

Check: Let $x = 1$. ← Choose any number greater than or equal to $\frac{1}{2}$.
$5(2 \times 1 + 3) \geqslant 20$
$5(2 + 3) \geqslant 20$ ← Calculate the brackets first.
$5 \times 5 \geqslant 20$
$25 \geqslant 20$ ✓

b $8(x + 1) \leqslant 3x + 18$
$8x + 8 \leqslant 3x + 18$ ← Expand the brackets.
$5x + 8 \leqslant 18$ ← Subtract $3x$ from both sides.
$5x \leqslant 10$ ← Subtract 8 from both sides.
$x \leqslant 2$ ← Divide both sides by 5.

Check: Let $x = 2$.
$8(2 + 1) \leq 3 \times 2 + 18$
$8 \times 3 \leq 6 + 18$
$24 \leq 24$ ✓

← Choose any number less than or equal to 2.

← Notice that $\leq$ means less than or equal to so it is true that $24 \leq 24$.

Let $x = 1$.
$8(1 + 1) \leq 3 \times 1 + 18$
$8 \times 2 \leq 3 + 18$
$16 \leq 21$ ✓

← Choose another number less then or equal to 2.

c In this inequality there is a negative x term.
There are two methods you can use to deal with this.

Method 1
$6 - 3x < 9$
$-3x < 3$
$x > \dfrac{3}{-3}$
$x > -1$

← Subtract 6 from both sides.

← Divide both sides by –3 and change the direction of the inequality sign.

Method 2
$6 - 3x < 9$
$6 < 9 + 3x$
$-3 < 3x$
$\dfrac{3}{3} > x$
$-1 < x$
$x > -1$

← Add $3x$ to both sides so the x term becomes positive.

← Subtract 9 from both sides.

← Divide both sides by 3.

← Turn the inequality around.

Check: Let $x = 1$.
$6 - 3 \times 1 < 9$
$6 - 3 < 9$
$3 < 9$ ✓

← Choose a value of x that is greater than –1.

Practising skills

1 Look at the following pairs of numbers.
Put the correct inequality sign, < or > between them.

a 3 ☐ 5 b 7 ☐ 1 c –3 ☐ –5 d –4 ☐ 1
e 1 ☐ –1 f 4.5 ☐ 4.55 g 2.72 ☐ 2.7 h –10 ☐ –8

2 Which of these inequalities matches the following statements?
$x < 5$ $x > 5$ $x \leq 5$ $x \geq 5$ $x > -5$ $x < -5$

a x is bigger than 5
b x is greater than or equal to 5
c x is at most 5
d x is at least 5
e x is lower than –5
f the lowest x can be is –5
g x has a minimum value of 5
h x has a maximum value of 5

Algebra Strand 4 Algebraic methods

3 Write down the inequalities shown on these number lines.

a (closed dot at −2, arrow to the right)

b (arrow to the left, closed dot at 5)

c (open dot at −3, closed dot at 6)

d (closed dot at −6, open dot at 2)

e (open dot at −6, open dot at −1)

f (closed dots at −1 and 0)

4 Show each of these inequalities on a number line.

    a $2 < x < 9$ b $6 \leq x < 8$ c $-4 < x \leq -1$ d $-2 \leq x \leq 5$

5 a Apply the operation '+ 4' to both sides of the inequality $-2 < 10$.
State whether the new inequality is true or false.

   b Now do the same thing using these operations.

      i -7 **ii** $\times 3$ **iii** $\times -3$ **iv** $\div 2$ **v** $\div -2$

   In each case, state whether the new inequality is true or false.

6 Solve these inequalities.

    a $x + 5 < 8$ b $x - 2 > -5$ c $4x < 20$

    d $3x \geq -18$ e $2x + 1 > 9$ f $3x - 5 < 22$

7 For each of these inequalities, list all the possible whole-number values of x.

    a $2 < x < 7$ b $-3 < x < -1$ c $1 \leq x \leq 4$ d $-5 \leq x < 2$

Developing fluency

1 Write each of these statements as an inequality.

    a The hourly pay rate goes from £7 up to £11.

    b To go on this ride you must be at least 18 years old.

    c The seniors' ticket is for anyone over the age of 64 years.

    d There were over 100 but fewer than 150 people at the show.

    e The lift carries a maximum of 16 people.

    f To play in the junior league you must be at least 12 but not over 17 years old.

2 You know that $5 < \sqrt{30} < 6$ because $25 < 30 < 36$.

Write each of these square roots between consecutive positive whole numbers.

    a $\sqrt{38}$ b $\sqrt{90}$ c $\sqrt{199}$ d $\sqrt{5}$

3 Tom is x years old where x is an integer (whole number).
His brother is twice as old as Tom. Tom's sister is 10 years older than Tom.
The total of their ages is less than 40.
  a Write down expressions involving x for the ages of Tom's brother and sister.
  b Complete this inequality for Tom's age.
     $\square < x \;\square\square$
  c What is the oldest that Tom could be?
  d What is the oldest that Tom's siblings could be?
  e Can Tom's brother and sister be twins?

4 The perimeter of this rectangle is at least 18 cm and less than 42 cm.
The length is double the width.

w cm

  a Write down an expression involving w for the perimeter.
  b Complete this inequality for w.
     $\square \leqslant \square w < 42$
  c The width is a whole number of centimetres. Find the minimum and maximum possible area of the rectangle.

5 Solve these inequalities.
  a $5x - 3 \geqslant 2x + 9$
  b $24 + 2x < 30 - 4x$
  c $7(x - 3) < 5(x + 6)$
  d $3(x + 2) + 2(x + 1) \geqslant 4(x + 5)$

6 Solve these inequalities.
  a $4x < 12$
  b $-4x < 12$
  c $4x < -12$
  d $-4x < -12$

7 Trish and Wendy are solving the inequality $-2x < 8$.
Trish says the answer is $x < -4$.
Wendy says the answer is $x > -4$.
Who is correct? Explain why.

8 a i Draw the line $x = 3$ on graph paper.
     ii Shade the region $x < 3$.
  b Draw graphs to show these regions.
     i $x > -3$
     ii $y > 4$
     iii $y > x$

9 Solve these inequalities.
  a $4 - 3x > 19$
  b $2 - x < -5$
  c $6 - 4x \leqslant 12$
  d $5(1 - 2x) \geqslant 15$
  e $2x + 7 < 5x - 5$
  f $4 + \dfrac{x}{2} > 7$

Algebra Strand 4 Algebraic methods

Problem solving

1

I think of a positive whole number.
I double the number and take away 7.
My answer is less than 5.

   a Write this information as an inequality, using n for my number.
   b Which numbers could Salman have thought of?

2

I think of a whole number less than 20.
I take 8 away from the number and double it.
My answer is more than 11.

   a Write this information as an inequality.
   b Which numbers could Aimee have thought of?

3 Sue is x years old. She is over 2.
Ben is twice as old as Sue.
Ceri is 4 years older than Sue.
The total of their 3 ages is less than 28.

   a Write this information as an inequality.
   b What age could Sue be?
   c What are the corresponding ages of Ben and Ceri?

4 Narinder is x years old.
Rashmi is 2 years older than Narinder.
Bhavinda is twice as old as Rashmi.
The total of their ages is less than 42.

   a Write this information as an inequality.
   b Solve the inequality.
   c What is Rashmi's greatest possible age?
   Give your answer as a whole number of years.

5 The perimeter of this rectangle is greater than 21 cm and less than 33 cm. The length is exactly 5 cm more than the width. The width is x cm.

   a Write this information as two inequalities.
   b The width is a whole number of centimetres.
   Find the range of possible values of the rectangle's area.

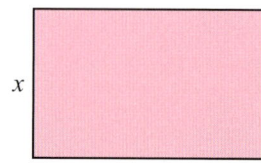

6 Here is the cost of hiring a van from two companies.

Vans 2 go
£80 fixed cost
+
50p a mile

Vans r Us
£1 a mile
No other charges

Dave wants to drive m miles. Vans 2 go will cost him less.

a Write down an inequality for m.

b Solve it to find m.

7 In this diagram, the equation of the green line is $y = x + 1$.

a Write down the equations for the following.
  i the blue line
  ii the red line
  iii the purple line

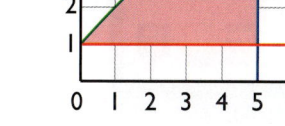

b Write down the inequalities that fully describe the shaded region. The boundary lines are included in the region.

c Sophie draws a straight line within the region. Its length is l units. Complete this inequality.
$\square < l \leq \square$

8 Here are four inequalities.
A $2x + 1 < 15$ B $5 - 4x > 3 - 3x$ C $4x + 5 > x + 2$ D $7 - 4x < 1 - 2x$

a They cannot all be true at the same time. Explain why.

b Find three of them that can all be true. What values can x take?

c How many sets of three of the inequalities work?

Reviewing skills

1 Solve these inequalities.
  a $3x + 2 < 14$ b $2x - 5 > 17$ c $4x - 3 \leq 11 - 3x$ d $2 - 12x \geq 16 - 19x$

2 Solve these inequalities.
  a $2(x + 3) - 5 > 3(2 - x)$ b $x + 5 < 3x + 9$
  c $3(x - 8) < 5x - 28$ d $-12x - 3 > -8x - 23$

3 Abbi is a years old.
Abbi is 5 years older than Cathy.
Bobbi is twice as old as Abbi.
The total of their ages is less than 35.
  a Write this information as an inequality.
  b Solve the inequality.
  c What is Bobbi's greatest possible age?
     Give your answer as a whole number of years.

Unit 3 • Solving pairs of equations by substitution • Band h

Outside the Maths classroom

Best tariffs

What factors should you think about when choosing a new mobile phone?

Toolbox

You can use the **substitution method** to solve this pair of **simultaneous equations**.

$$x + y = 6 \quad \text{①}$$
$$2x + y = 10 \quad \text{②}$$

- Make one of the unknowns the subject of equation ①:
  $$y = 6 - x$$
- Substitute this into equation ②:
  $$2x + 6 - x = 10$$
  $$x + 6 = 10$$
  $$x = 4$$

  Solve to find the value of x.

- Make sure you find the value of both unknowns by substituting the found value into the other equation, in this case equation ①:
  $$4 + y = 6$$
  $$\text{so } y = 2$$
- Substitute the values back into equation ② to check your answer.
  $$2 \times 4 + 2 = 10 \checkmark$$

Example – Solving simultaneous equations using the substitution method

Solve these simultaneous equations using the substitution method.

$$y = 3x - 8$$
$$y = 12 - x$$

Unit 3 Solving pairs of equations by substitution Band h

Solution

$y = 3x - 8$ ①
$y = 12 - x$ ②

$3x - 8 = 12 - x$ ← As both equations equal y, they are equal to each other.
$4x - 8 = 12$ ← Add x to both sides.
$4x = 20$ ← Add 8 to both sides.
$x = 5$ ← Divide both sides by 4.

$y = 3x - 8$ ① ← Substitute the value of x you have just found into either equation to find the value of y.
$y = 3 \times 5 - 8$
$y = 15 - 8$
$y = 7$

Check: $y = 12 - x$ ②
$7 = 12 - 5$ ✓

So the solution is $x = 5, y = 7$. ← You need the values of both x and y for the solution.

Check: $y = 12 - x$ ② ← Check your solution by substituting into the equation you didn't use to find the value of y.
$7 = 12 - 5$
$7 = 7$ ✓

Example – Solving a word problem involving simultaneous equations

At the local shop, birthday cards cost 5 times as much as postcards.
John buys 3 birthday cards and 6 postcards.
The shopkeeper charges him £8.40.
How much does each birthday card and postcard cost?

Solution

Let b stand for the cost of a birthday card in pence.
Let c stand for the cost of a postcard in pence.

$b = 5c$ ① ← Birthday cards cost five times as much as postcards.
$3b + 6c = 840$ ② ← Three birthday cards and six postcards cost 840 pence.

$3b + 6c = 840$ ② ← Substitute this value of b ($5c$) into equation ②.
$3 \times 5c + 6c = 840$
$15c + 6c = 840$ ← Solve the equation to find c.
$21c = 840$
$c = 40$
$b = 5c$ ①
$b = 5 \times 40$ ← Substitute the value you found for c into equation ① to find b.
$= 200$

So a birthday card costs £2 ← Write 200 pence as £2 in your solution.
and a postcard costs 40 pence.

Algebra Strand 4 Algebraic methods

Practising skills

1 Solve these simultaneous equations by substitution.

a $x = 2y$
   $x + 3y = 15$

b $x = 3y$
   $2x + y = 28$

c $x = 2y - 1$
   $2x + 3y = 12$

d $y = 3x + 5$
   $2x + 5y = 8$

2 Solve these simultaneous equations by substitution.

a $y = x - 2$
   $2x - 3y = 8$

b $x = 3y - 2$
   $3x - 2y = 15$

c $x = 5y + 3$
   $2x = 3y - 1$

d $4x - 5y = 3$
   $x = 2y - 3$

3 Solve these simultaneous equations by substitution.

a $5x + 2y = 17$
   $y = 2x - 5$

b $4x - y = -9$
   $y = 2x + 3$

c $x = y - 6$
   $x + y = 14$

d $y = 8x + 1$
   $x + y = 10$

4 Solve these simultaneous equations.

a $y = 6 - x$
   $2x + y = 11$

b $x = 6 - y$
   $2x + y - 11 = 0$

c $y = 11 - 2x$
   $x + y = 6$

d $x = 5\frac{1}{2} - \frac{1}{2}y$
   $x + y - 6 = 0$

5 Solve these simultaneous equations by substitution.

a $x = 3y + 2$
   $4x - 5y = 22$

b $2y = 3x + 14$
   $x = 5y + 4$

c $x = y + 1$
   $2x - 5 = 3y - 6$

d $y = 5x - 6$
   $3x - 2y = -2$

Developing fluency

1 One number, x, is twice another number, y. The 2 numbers add up to give 15.

a Write 2 equations for x and y.

b Solve them to find the two numbers.

2 The sum of two numbers is 6 and the difference is 1.
Write two equations and solve them to find the 2 numbers.

Unit 3 Solving pairs of equations by substitution Band h

3 A hardback book costs £h and a paperback book costs £p.
Hardback books are twice the price of paperback books.
Jo buys 3 hardback books and 4 paperback books, and the total cost is £35.

   a Write this information as 2 equations for h and p.

   b Solve the equations.

   c Find the cost of 1 hardback book and 5 paperback books.

4 At a pet shop a rat costs £r and a mouse costs £m.
A rat costs £2 more than a mouse.
Billy buys 3 rats and 5 mice for £62.

   a Write 2 equations for r and m.

   b Solve the equations to find the costs of a rat and a mouse.

5 In a theatre a seat in the stalls costs £7 more than one in the circle.
Patrick buys 4 tickets for seats in the stalls and 7 tickets for seats in the circle, and the total cost is £523.
Write 2 equations and solve them to find the costs of the 2 types of ticket.

6 Mrs Jones organises a school trip to the theatre for 42 people.
She takes x children and y adults on the trip.
Each adult has paid £40 for their ticket.
Each child has paid £16 for their ticket.
The total cost of the tickets was £1080.

   a Write 2 equations for x and y.

   b How many adults went on the trip and how many children?

7 How can you solve these simultaneous equations by substitution?

   a $3x + y = 29$
   $x - y = 7$

   b $5x - 4y = 17$
   $x - 2y = 7$

8 a Make x the subject of the equation $x + 3y = 17$.

   b Solve these simultaneous equations by substitution.
   $x + 3y = 17$
   $5x - 2y = 0$
   Check your answer by substituting your values for x and y into both equations.

Problem solving

1 Sadie thinks of two numbers, m and n.

   a Write this information as two equations for m and n.

   b Solve the equations. What are the values of m and n?

> When I add my two numbers I get 27. One number is 15 more than the other.

Algebra Strand 4 Algebraic methods

2 Berwyn thinks of a two-digit number, XY.
The sum of the two digits is 12.

  a Write this as an equation for X and Y.

  b Make Y the subject of the equation.

  c The difference between XY and YX is 18.
  Explain why this can be written as the equation
  $(10X + Y) - (10Y + X) = 18$.

  d Solve this equation with the equation you found in part **b**.

  e Show that Berwyn's number is 75.

3 Gerry organises a coach trip to the theatre.
There are a adults and c children.
The number of children is 5 greater than the number of adults.

  a Write this as an equation for a and c.

The cost of an adult ticket is £15 and the cost of a child's ticket is £10.
Gerry spends £550 on tickets.

  b Write another equation for a and c.

  c How many adults went on the trip and how many children?

4 A large tin of beans weighs l g and a small tin weighs s g.
A large tin of beans weighs 100 g more than a small tin of beans.
6 large tins of beans weigh the same as 10 small tins of beans.

  a Write this information as two equations for l and s.

  b Solve the equations.

  c Find the mass of 2 large tins and 5 small ones.

5 Josh is buying dog food.
Dog food is sold in small cans and large cans.
The small can of dog food weighs 140 g less than a large can.
5 large cans together weigh the same as 12 small cans.
A large can costs 90p and a small can costs 40p.
Explain which is the better buy.

Reviewing skills

1) Solve these simultaneous equations by substitution.
   a $x = y + 6$
      $x + y = 12$
   b $y = 3x - 4$
      $2x + 3y = 32$
   c $x = 4y + 3$
      $3x - 5y = -5$
   d $y = 6x + 2$
      $6x - 2y = 14$

2) Solve these simultaneous equations by substitution.
   a $4x - 2y = -12$
      $x = 3y + 2$
   b $y = 2x$
      $3x - 5 = 39 - 4y$
   c $x = 5y + 9$
      $3x + y = 11$
   d $y = x - 2$
      $2y + 3x = 1$

3) A train has f first-class coaches and s standard-class coaches.
   The number of standard class coaches is 3 times the number of first-class coaches.
   A first-class coach seats 40 passengers; a standard-class coach seats 80 passengers.
   The train seats 560 passengers.
   a Use this information to write 2 equations for f and s.
   b Solve the equations.
   c How many coaches does the train have?

Unit 4 • Solving simultaneous equations by elimination • Band h

Outside the Maths classroom

Best tariffs

How can simultaneous equations help you choose between two electricity providers?

Toolbox

A pair of simultaneous equations can be solved by **eliminating** one of the unknowns.
You either **add or subtract the equations** to form a third equation in just one unknown.
- To decide whether to add or subtract look at the signs of the unknown you wish to eliminate.
  If the signs are different, you add.
  If the signs are the same, you subtract.
- Sometimes you need to multiply each term in one (or both) equations by a constant so that one of the unknowns has the same coefficients.

When you have found one unknown, substitute in either equation to find the other.
To check your answer, substitute the values you have found into both equations.

Example – Subtracting simultaneous equations

Solve these simultaneous equations.

$5x + 3y = 18$
$5x - 2y = 13$

Solution

$5x + 3y = 18$ ①   — Both equations have $5x$, so you can eliminate x.
$5x - 2y = 13$ ②   — The signs in front of both $5x$ are the same ($+5x$) so you subtract.
Subtract: $0 + 5y = 5$

$y = 1$ — Divide both sides by 5.

Alternatively,

$5x + 3y = 18$ ①
$-5x + 2y = -13$ ②   — When subtracting one equation from another, you may find it helps to change the signs in the second equation and then add.
Add: $0 + 5y = 5$

① $5x + 3y = 18$
$5x + 3 \times 1 = 18$ ← To find the value of x, substitute $y = 1$ into equation ①.
$5x + 3 = 18$
$5x = 15$ ← Subtract 3 from both sides.
$x = 3$ ← Divide both sides by 5.

So the solution is $x = 3$ and $y = 1$.

Check: $5x + 3y = 18$ ① $5x - 2y = 13$ ②
$5 \times 3 + 3 \times 1 = 18$ $5 \times 3 - 2 \times 1 = 13$
$15 + 3 = 18$ $15 - 2 = 13$
$18 = 18$ ✓ $13 = 13$ ✓

Example – Multiplying simultaneous equations by a constant

Solve these simultaneous equations.
$3s + 2t = 13$
$5s - t = 13$

Solution

$3s + 2t = 13$ ①
$5s - t = 13$ ② ← Multiply equation ② by 2 to eliminate t.

① $\quad 3s + 2t = 13$
② × 2 $\quad 10s - 2t = 26$ ← The signs in front of the $2t$ are different ($+2t$ and $-2t$) so you add.
Add $\quad 13s + 0 = 39$

$s = \dfrac{39}{13}$ ← Divide both sides by 13.

$s = 3$

① $3s + 2t = 13$
$3 \times 3 + 2t = 13$ ← To find the value of t, substitute $s = 3$ into equation ①.
$9 + 2t = 13$
$2t = 4$ ← Subtract 9 from both sides.
$t = 2$ ← Divide both sides by 2.

So the solution is $s = 3$ and $t = 2$.

Check: $3s + 2t = 13$ ① $5s - t = 13$ ②
$3 \times 3 + 2 \times 2 = 13$ $5 \times 3 - 2 = 13$
$9 + 4 = 13$ $15 - 2 = 13$
$13 = 13$ ✓ $13 = 13$ ✓

Algebra Strand 4 Algebraic methods

Example – Solving a word problem using simultaneous equations

Danni has £4.40 in 2p and 5p coins.
She has 100 coins altogether.
Write down 2 equations for this information.
How many of each type of coin does she have?

Solution

Let t = number of 2p coins and
f = number of 5p coins.

$t + f = 100$ ① ⟵ *Choose letters to represent the unknowns.*

$2t + 5f = 440$ ② ⟵ *There are 100 coins altogether.*

Danni has 440 pence altogether. This matches the 2 and 5 which are in pence.

$5 \times$ ① $5t + 5f = 500$ ⟵ *Make the coefficients of one of the unknowns the same in both equations.*

② $\quad 2t + 5f = 440$ ⟵ *The signs on $5f$ are positive in both equations, so subtract.*

Subtract $\quad 3t + 0 = 60$

$t = \dfrac{60}{3}$ ⟵ *Divide both sides by 3.*

$t = 20$

① $t + f = 100$ ⟵ *To find the value of f, substitute $t = 20$ into equation ①.*

$20 + f = 100$

$f = 80$

So Danni has 20 two-pence coins and 80 five-pence coins.

Check: $t + f = 100$ ① $\qquad\qquad 2t + 5f = 440$ ②

$20 + 80 = 100 \qquad\qquad 2 \times 20 + 5 \times 80 = 440$

$100 = 100$ ✓ $\qquad\qquad 40 + 400 = 440$ ✓

Practising skills

1 Simplify these expressions.

   a $5x - 9x$ **b** $3x + (-2x)$ **c** $4x + (-6x)$ **d** $2x - (-3x)$

   e $-4x - (-4x)$ **f** $17 - 23$ **g** $18 - (-27)$ **h** $-15 - (-7)$

2 Solve these simultaneous equations by adding them first.

   a $x + 2y = 0$ **b** $3x + y = 18$ **c** $x - 5y = 2$
       $x - 2y = 4$ $2x - y = 7$ $3x + 5y = -14$

   d $6x + 2y = 6$ **e** $-x + y = 1$ **f** $-2x + 3y = 10$
       $x - 2y = 8$ $x + y = -5$ $2x + y = 6$

Unit 4 Solving simultaneous equations by elimination Band h

3 Solve these simultaneous equations by subtracting them first.

a $2x - 3y = 5$
   $2x + 4y = 12$

b $x + 4y = 1$
   $x + 2y = 3$

c $3x + 4y = 30$
   $x + 4y = 26$

d $2x - 5y = 22$
   $3x - 5y = 23$

e $5x - y = 12$
   $3x - y = 8$

f $x + y = 2$
   $3x + y = 12$

4 Solve these simultaneous equations. Decide for yourself whether to add them or subtract them.

a $3x + y = 7$
   $2x - y = 8$

b $4x - 2y = 14$
   $x - 2y = 11$

c $3x + 4y = 32$
   $3x - 2y = 2$

d $-5x + 3y = 21$
   $5x - 2y = -19$

e $6x - y = 21$
   $3x + y = 15$

f $2x - 4y = 16$
   $3x + 4y = 14$

5 Here are two simultaneous equations.

$3x + 4y = 18$ equation 1

$5x - 2y = 4$ equation 2

a Explain why you cannot eliminate either variable just by adding or subtracting.

b Which equation should be multiplied, and by which value, to ensure you can eliminate a variable?

c Solve the equations.

6 Solve these simultaneous equations by multiplying one equation first.

a $4x - y = 19$
   $2x + 3y = -1$

b $3x + 4y = 7$
   $x + 2y = 1$

c $5x - y = -20$
   $4x + 3y = 3$

d $6x - 3y = 51$
   $3x + 4y = 20$

e $x - 5y = 31$
   $4x - 2y = 16$

f $3x - 2y = -2$
   $2x - 4y = 12$

Developing fluency

1 Here are two simultaneous equations.

$3x + 4y = 23$ equation 1

$2x + 3y = 16$ equation 2

a In this question you need to multiply each equation so that either x or y can be eliminated. Explain 2 ways that this can be done.

b Solve these 2 equations.

2 Solve these simultaneous equations.

a $4a + 3b = 18$
   $3a + 4b = 17$

b $3x + 2y = 20$
   $2x + 5y = 17$

c $3p + 5q = -5$
   $2p - 3q = 22$

d $7x - 4y = 39$
   $3x + 5y = 10$

e $6x - 5y = 38$
   $5x - 3y = 27$

f $-4m + 6n = -4$
   $3m + 2n = 29$

Algebra Strand 4 Algebraic methods

3 In this diagram the perimeter of the triangle is 118 cm and the perimeter of the rectangle is 114 cm.

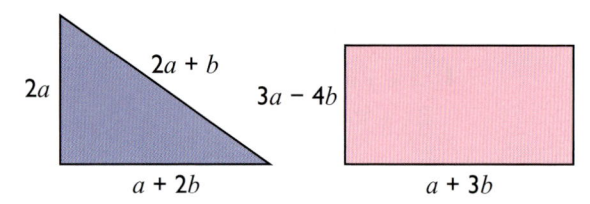

Triangle sides: $2a$, $2a+b$, $a+2b$, with $3a-4b$ labelled.
Rectangle sides: $3a-4b$ and $a+3b$.

 a Write two simultaneous equations for a and b.
 b Solve them to find the values of a and b.
 c Compare the areas of the triangle and the rectangle.

4 In one week, Trefor made 5 journeys to the supermarket and 3 journeys to the park. He travelled a total of 99 kilometres.

During the next week, he made 2 journeys to the supermarket and 4 to the park. He travelled a total of 62 kilometres.

 a Write down 2 simultaneous equations. Use s for the distance to the supermarket and p for the distance to the park.
 b Solve your equations.
 c How far does Trefor travel in a week when he goes 7 times to the park and twice to the supermarket?

5 The price of tickets for a zoo are £a for adults and £c for children.
Rose buys 2 adult tickets and 3 children's tickets for £24.
Amanda buys 3 adult tickets and 5 children's tickets for £38.

 a Write down two simultaneous equations.
 b Solve them to find the price of each ticket.
 c The Singhs have a family outing to the zoo. There are 9 adults and 21 children. How much do they pay?

6 Reya has these 2 equations.
$$5x - 4y = 18$$
$$x - 4y = -6$$
Her next step is to do a subtraction. She says,

   **'My rule is:
   Change the signs on the bottom line and go on as if you were adding.'**

 a Carry out Reya's rule.
 b Explain why Reya's rule works.
 c Solve the equations.

Unit 4 Solving simultaneous equations by elimination Band h

Problem solving

1 A banana costs b pence and an apple costs a pence.
Dewi buys 4 bananas and an apple for 150p.
Marion buys 2 bananas and an apple for 100p.

  a Write this information as 2 simultaneous equations.

  b Solve the equations.

  c Find the cost of 7 bananas and 8 apples.

2 In this diagram, the length and width of the rectangle are l cm and w cm respectively.
The equal sides of the isosceles triangle are also l cm and the base w cm.
The perimeter of the rectangle is 32 cm.
The perimeter of the triangle is 26 cm.

  a Write this information as two simultaneous equations.

  b Find the values of l and w.

3 Bethan leaves her 2 dogs and 3 cats at The Pet Hotel for 7 days and it costs her £315.
Malcolm leaves his dog and 2 cats at The Pet Hotel for 7 days and it costs him £175.
One week The Pet Hotel looks after 15 dogs and 20 cats.
How much money do they collect from their customers in that week?

The Pet Hotel
Leave your pet in our expert care when you go on holiday.

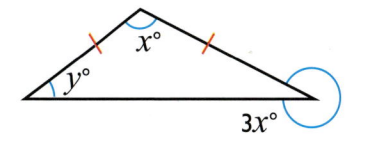

Higher tier only

4 Arwyn makes mountain bikes and sports bikes.
It takes him 4 hours to make a mountain bike and 6 hours to make a sports bike.
Each mountain bike costs him £45 to make and each sports bike costs him £60 to make.
One week Arwyn made m mountain bikes and s Sports bikes in 54 hours.
The cost of making these bikes was £570.

  a Write this information as a pair of simultaneous equations.

  b How many of each type of bike did he make?

5 A mobile phone company charges their pay-as-you-go customers c pence per minute for calls and t pence for each text message.
Ben is charged £7.30 for making 10 minutes of calls and sending 40 texts.
Alicia is charged £7.25 for making 5 minutes of calls and sending 50 texts.

  a Write this information as two simultaneous equations.

  b Solve the equations to find the values of c and t.

  c Ruby has £20 of credit. She makes 15 minutes of calls and sends 100 texts. How much credit does she have left?

6 a Write an equation for the angles in the triangle.

  b Write a second equation connecting the x and y.

  c Solve your equations to find the value of x and y.
Show that, for these values, $x = 3y$.

  d To check your answers replace x by $3y$ in the triangle. Then write an equation for y and solve it.

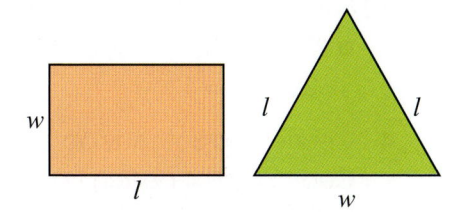

Algebra Strand 4 Algebraic methods

Reviewing skills

1) Solve these simultaneous equations.
   a $3x + 4y = 2$
      $3x - 5y = 11$
   b $2x - 3y = 2$
      $5x - 3y = 14$
   c $x - 4y = 15$
      $2x + 4y = -6$

2) Solve these simultaneous equations.
   a $x - y = 7$
      $5x + 3y = 75$
   b $4x - 6y = 34$
      $3x - 3y = 21$
   c $7x + 4y = 27$
      $3x + 2y = 11$

3) Solve these simultaneous equations.
   a $3x + 2y = 6$
      $2x + 3y = 4$
   b $3x - 5y = 0$
      $4x + 3y = 29$
   c $4x - 5y = 17$
      $3x - 2y = 18$

4) Cedric and Bethany go to a garden centre and buy some trees.
   Cedric buys 4 peach trees and 3 apple trees for £75.
   Bethany buys 3 peach trees and one apple tree for £45.
   a Write this information as a pair of simultaneous equations.
   b Solve the equations.
   c Find the cost of 3 peach trees and 7 apple trees.

Unit 5 • Using graphs to solve simultaneous equations • Band h

Outside the Maths classroom

Best tariffs

Some households have a water meter fitted, so their water bill is worked out according to how much water is used. Other households are charged according to the value of their house.

Which system is fairer?

Toolbox

To solve these equations graphically:
$y = 2x + 1$
$y = 4 - x$

- Plot both equations on the same axes.
- If necessary, extend the lines so that they meet.
- Find the co-ordinates of the point where the two lines meet, in this case (1, 3).
- Make sure you write the solution as $x = \square$ and $y = \square$.
In this case, the solution is $x = 1$ and $y = 3$.

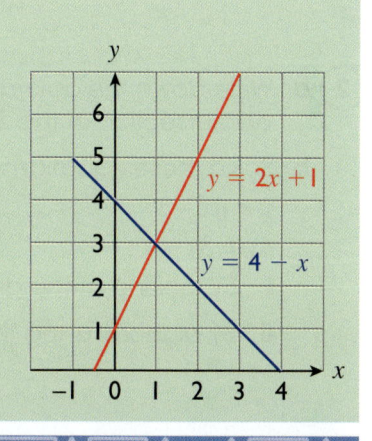

Example – Solving simultaneous equations graphically

Solve these simultaneous equations using a graph.
$y = 2x$
$y = 6 - 2x$

Solution

x	0	1	3
y = 2x	0	2	6

x	0	1	3
6	6	6	6
-2x	0	-2	-6
y = 6 - 2x	6	4	0

Find three points on each line.

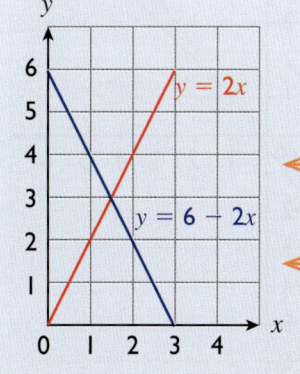

Plot the points for the two lines on the same graph.

The lines cross at the point (1.5, 3).

The solution is $x = 1.5$ and $y = 3$.

257

Algebra Strand 4 Algebraic methods

Practising skills

1 **a** Write down the co-ordinates of the point of intersection of the 2 lines on this graph.

   b Write down the solution of these equations.
   $$x + y = 4$$
   $$y = x - 2$$

   c Check your answer by substituting values for x and y in the 2 equations.

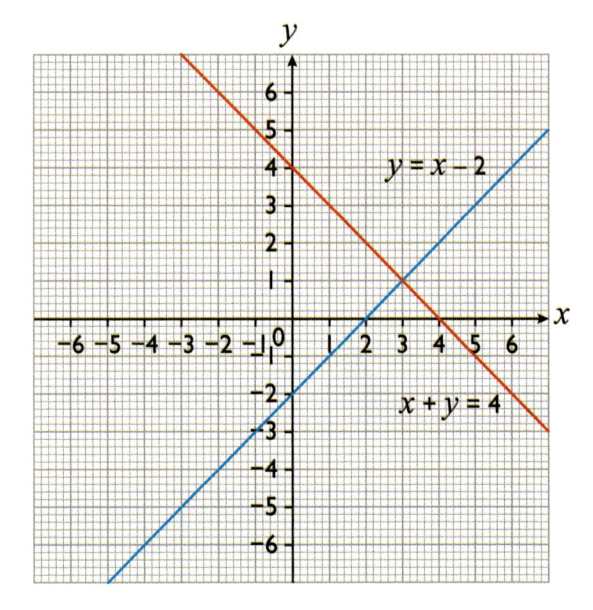

2 **a** Write down the co-ordinates of the point of intersection of the 2 lines on this graph.

   b Solve these equations in 2 ways.
   $$y = 4x - 3$$
   $$4y = 3x + 1$$
   i By looking at the graph.
   ii By algebra, using the substitution method.

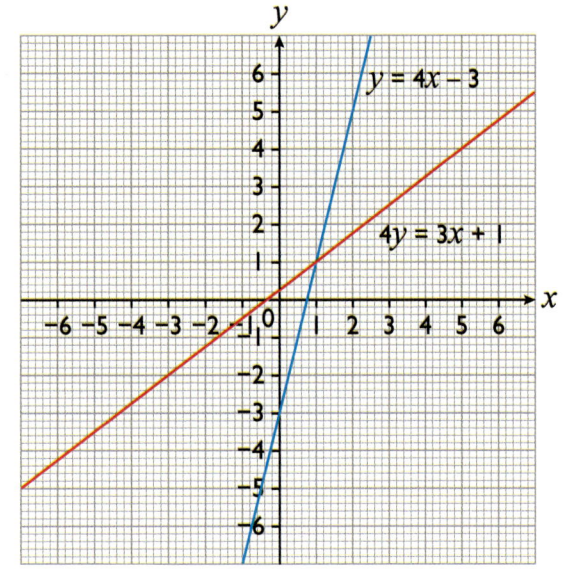

3 **a** One of the lines on this graph is $y = x$ and the other is $3y = 4x - 1$. Which is which?

   b Write down the co-ordinates of the point of intersection of the 2 lines.

   c Solve these simultaneous equations.
   $$y = x$$
   $$3y = 4x - 1$$
   i By looking at the graph.
   ii By algebra, using the substitution method.

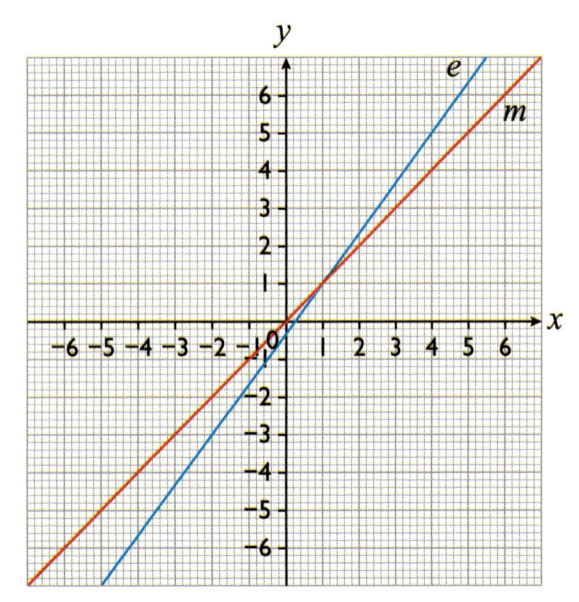

Unit 5 Using graphs to solve simultaneous equations Band h

4 **a** One of the lines on this graph has equation $y = \frac{1}{3}x + 1\frac{2}{3}$.
The other has equation $y = -\frac{1}{2}x + 2\frac{1}{2}$.
Which is which?

b Write down the co-ordinates of the point of intersection of the 2 lines.

c Write down the 2 simultaneous equations for which this point is the solution.

d Check your solution by substituting your x- and y-values in both equations.

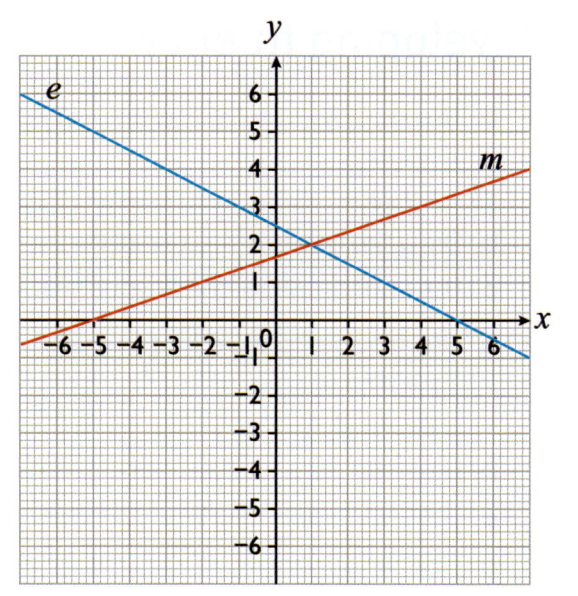

5 **a** Copy and complete this table of values for $y = 3x - 2$.

x	0	1	2	3
$3x$	0			
-2	-2			
$y = 3x - 2$	-2			

b Make a table of values for the line $y = 6 - x$.

c Draw the lines $y = 3x - 2$ and $y = 6 - x$ on the same graph.

d Use your graph to solve the simultaneous equations $y = 3x - 2$ and $y = 6 - x$.

e Use algebra to check your solution.

6 **a** Draw the lines $y = x + 3$ and $y = \frac{1}{4}x + 2\frac{1}{4}$ on the same graph.

b Use your graph to solve the simultaneous equations $y = x + 3$ and $4y = x + 9$.

7 **a** Copy and complete this table of values for $y = 8 - x$.

x	0	1	2	3
$y = 8 - x$	8			

b Make a table of values for the line $y = x + 4$.

c Draw the lines $y = 8 - x$ and $y = x + 4$ on the same graph.

d Use your graph to solve the simultaneous equations $y = 8 - x$ and $y = x + 4$.

e Check your answer using algebra to solve the equations.

8 **a** Draw the lines $y = 3x - 1$ and $y = x - 1$ on the same graph.

b Use your graph to solve the simultaneous equations $y = 3x - 1$ and $y = x - 1$.

c Use algebra to check your answer.

Algebra Strand 4 Algebraic methods

Developing fluency

1. **a** Use algebra to solve these equations.
   $$y = 4x$$
   $$y = 2x^2$$
   b Draw the lines $y = 4 - x$ and $y = 2x - 2$ on the same graph.
   c Use your graph to check your answer to part **a**.

2. **a** Use algebra to solve these equations.
   $$y = 4x - 3$$
   $$y = x + 3$$
   b Draw the lines $y = 4x - 3$ and $y = x + 3$ on the same graph.
   c Use your graph to check your answers to part **a**.
   d Check your answer again, this time by substituting the x- and y-values in both equations.

3. **a** Use a graph to solve the simultaneous equations $y = 2x + 3$ and $x + y = 6$.
   b Check your answer by solving these simultaneous equations by elimination.
   $$-2x + y = 3$$
   $$x + y = 6$$

4. **a** Try to use algebra to solve these simultaneous equations.
   $$y = 2x + 3$$
   $$y = 2x - 1$$
   b What do you notice?
   c Draw these two lines on the same axis.
   d Use your graph to explain the result in part **a**.

5. **a** Draw the lines $2x + 3y = 24$ and $y = x + 3$ on the same graph.
   b Use your graph to solve the simultaneous equations $2x + 3y = 24$ and $y = x + 3$.
   c Check your answer by solving the equations algebraically.
   d Find the area of the region bounded by the lines $2x + 3y = 24$, $y = x + 3$ and the x and y axes.

6. Two electricity companies advertise the following rates.

   Green Power
   Standing charge 30p per day
   Cost of electricity 18p per unit

   Sparkle
   Standing charge 50p per day
   Cost of electricity 16p per unit

   a Write down an equation for the daily cost, C pence, of using u units of electricity for
   　i Green Power　　**ii** Sparkle.
   b On the same graph, draw two lines to illustrate the daily cost of electricity from each company for values of u from 0 to 15.
   c **i** Use your graph to find the number of units for which both companies charge the same amount. How much do they each charge for this number of units?
   　ii Check your answer to **ci** by solving your equations algebraically using the substitution method.
   d The Watts family use an average of 12 units of electricity a day. Which company would you recommend?

Unit 5 Using graphs to solve simultaneous equations Band h

7 A quadrilateral is bounded by these 4 lines

$4y = x + 24$

$y + 4x = 23$

$y + 4x + 11 = 0$

$4y = x - 10$

a Draw the quadrilateral on a graph.

b Use your graph to find the co-ordinates of the vertices of the quadrilateral.

c Show how you can check your answer to **b** by substituting the x and y co-ordinates into the appropriate pair of equations.

d What is the name of the quadrilateral?

Problem solving

1 Pete wants to hire a car. He wants to spend as little as possible.
He can hire it from one of two companies: U hire and Cars 2 go.

U hire	Cars 2 go
50p a mile	£60 plus 20p a mile

a Write down the equations for the cost £C of hiring a car for m miles from each company.

b On the same graph draw lines for your equations.

Use the vertical axis for C with a scale from 0 to 200 and the horizontal axis for m with a scale from 0 to 400.

c Pete expects to drive 250 miles. Which company would you advise him to use?

2 Ros makes an accurate drawing of this diamond shape on graph paper.
The equations of the four lines are

$y = 3x - 3$

$y = 3x - 9$

$y = -3x + 15$

$y = -3x + 9$

a Make tables of values for these lines, taking values of x from 0 to 5.

b Draw a graph showing the parts of the lines that make the shape.

c Write down the co-ordinates of the four vertices, P, Q, R and S.

d Show how Ros could have used algebra to find the co-ordinates of the vertices.
Use this method to check your answers to part **c**.

e What is the mathematical name for this shape?

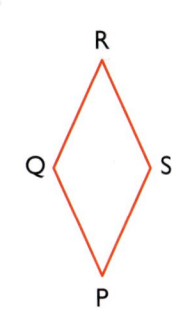

Algebra Strand 4 Algebraic methods

3) Nerys draws a triangle which is bounded by the lines $x + 2y = 12$, $2y = x + 4$ and $y = x - 3$.
   a Draw the three lines on the same graph.
   b i Write the co-ordinates of the vertices of the triangle.
      ii Use your diagram to solve the following pairs of simultaneous equations.
        A $x + 2y = 12$, $2y = x + 4$ **B** $x + 2y = 12$, $y = x - 3$ **C** $2y = x + 4$, $y = x - 3$

   Nerys adds 2 horizontal and 2 vertical lines to her diagram to form a rectangle around her triangle. Each line passes through one of the vertices of the triangle.
   c i Add these lines to your diagram.
      ii State the equations of the lines that Nerys adds.
      iii Find the area of the rectangle bounded by these 4 lines.
   d Find the area of Nerys' triangle.

4) Look at these pay-as-you-go tariffs for 2 mobile phone companies.

   Q-Mobile
   30p per minute for calls
   8p per text

   Pear
   20p per minute for calls
   12p per text

   Let m stand for the number of call minutes and t stand for the number of texts.
   a Write down an equation for m and t for a bill of £5 with
      i Q-Mobile   **ii** Pear.
   b Draw a graph of your equations.

   Chloe uses Q-Mobile and Daisy uses Pear.
   c One week they use the same number of call minutes as each other, and they send the same number of texts. They both use exactly £5 of credit.
   How many call minutes and texts do they each use?
   d Another week both girls make 4 minutes of calls and sent 40 texts.
      i Mark a point on your graph to show this.
      Both girls have £5 credit.
      ii Who has to buy more credit? How much more credit does she need?
      iii Who has credit left over? How much?

5) Here is the graph of the circle $x^2 + y^2 = 4$.
   The line $y = 2x + 1$ cuts the circle at 2 points.
   Find the co-ordinates of these 2 points.

Higher tier only

6 Here is the graph of the ellipse $\frac{x^2}{9} + \frac{y^2}{4} = 1$.

The line $x + y = 1$ cuts the ellipse at two points.
Find the co-ordinates of these two points.

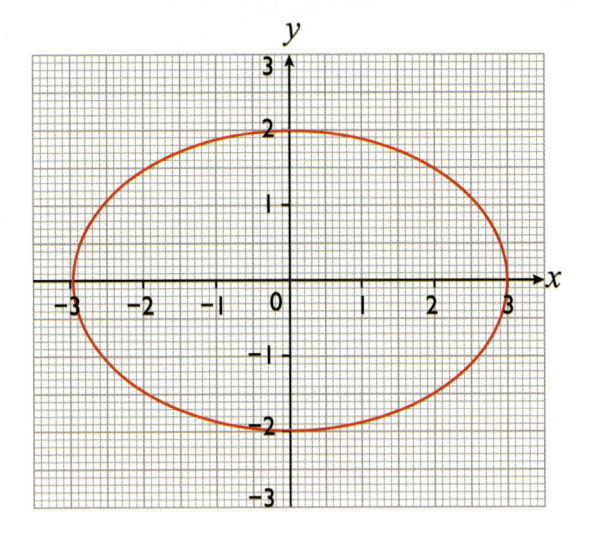

Reviewing skills

1 a Draw the lines $y = 2x - 5$ and $y = 3x - 7$ on the same graph.
   b Use your graph to solve the simultaneous equations $y = 2x - 5$ and $y = 3x - 7$.
   c Check your solution by substituting the x- and y-values in both equations.

2 a Use a graph to solve the simultaneous equations $y = 3x + 4$ and $y = x + 2$.
   b Check your answer algebraically by using the method of substitution.
   c Check your answer again, this time substituting the x and y values in both equations.

3 Afonbedd College compares the cost of two coach companies for a school trip.

Gwilym's Coaches
£150 per day
£2 per mile

Get-Aways!
£100 per day
£4 per mile

a Write down an equation for the cost, £C, of hiring a coach for one day and for m miles for
   i Gwilym's Coaches
   ii Get-Aways!

b On the same graph, draw 2 lines to illustrate the daily cost of hiring a coach from each company for values of m from 0 to 100.

c i Use your graph to find the number of miles for which both firms charge the same amount. How much do they each charge for this number of miles?
   ii Check your answer to **ci** by solving your equations algebraically using the substitution method.

d Afonbedd College are organising a coach for an 80-mile round trip.
   i Which company would you recommend?
   ii How much do Afonbedd College save by choosing this company?

Algebra Strand 5 Working with quadratics

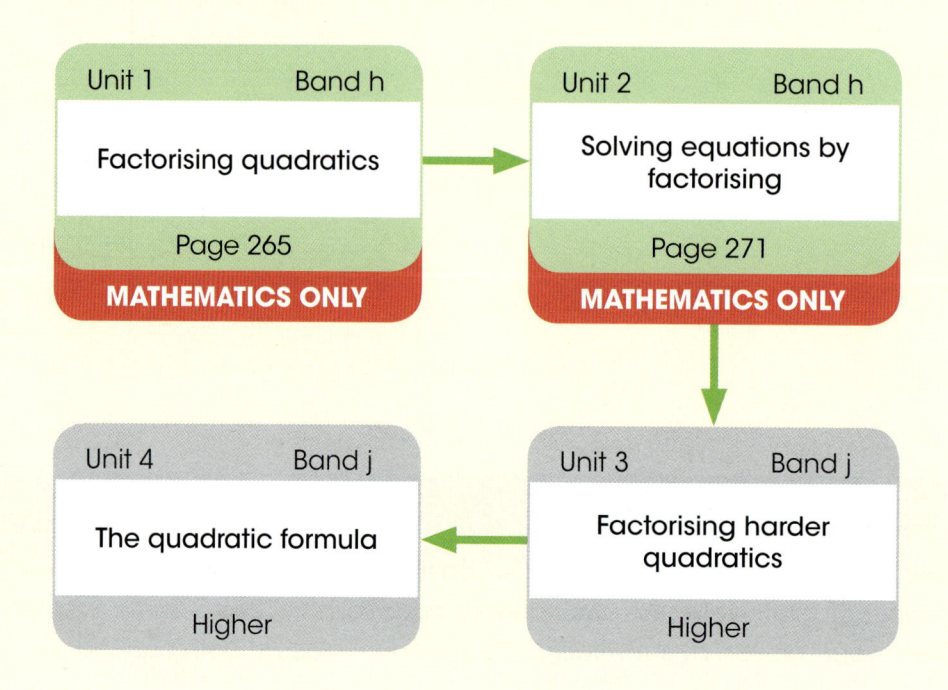

Unit 1	Band h
Factorising quadratics	
Page 265	
MATHEMATICS ONLY	

Unit 2	Band h
Solving equations by factorising	
Page 271	
MATHEMATICS ONLY	

Unit 4	Band j
The quadratic formula	
Higher	

Unit 3	Band j
Factorising harder quadratics	
Higher	

Unit 1 • Factorising quadratics • Band h

Outside the Maths classroom

47,896.49	7130	3565	2139
54,815.62		4896	2448
5,253.16	#DIV/0!	#DIV/0!	#DIV/0!
8,397.00		750	375
101,519.73	15113	7556	4534
97,808.26		8736	4368
10,042.81	2990	1495	897
16,374.15		1463	731

Debugging a spreadsheet
How can altering formulae in a spreadsheet stop errors?

Toolbox

A quadratic expression can sometimes be written as the product of two linear expressions, for example

$$(x + 2)(x - 4)$$

Expanding the brackets

$$(x + 2)(x - 4) = x^2 + 2x - 4x - 8$$
$$= x^2 - 2x - 8$$

Factorising means writing a number or expression as a product of 2 factors. It is the reverse of expanding brackets. So the expression $x^2 - 2x - 8$ factorises to $(x + 2)(x - 4)$.

$x + 2$ and $x - 4$ are **factors** of the original expression.

In general,

$$(x + a)(x + b) = x^2 + ax + bx + ab$$
$$= x^2 + (a + b)x + ab$$

Multiply a and b to give the constant term.

Add to a and b give the coefficient of the x term.

So to factorise $x^2 + 5x + 6$ first find numbers that multiply to give 6.

Possibilities are:

$1 \times 6, 2 \times 3, -1 \times -6$ and -2×-3

Of these, find the two numbers that add up to give 5:

$1 + 6 = 7$ ✗
$2 + 3 = 5$ ✓
$-1 + -6 = -7$ ✗
$-2 + -3 = -5$ ✗

So $x^2 + 5x + 6$ factorises to $(x + 2)(x + 3)$.

Check by expanding the brackets to get back to the original expression.

Algebra Strand 5 Working with quadratics

> **Special case**
> $(x + a)(x - a) = x^2 + ax - ax - a^2$
> $ = x^2 - a^2$
> $x^2 - a^2$ is known as the **difference of two squares**.
> Watch out for this when you need to factorise.
> For example, $x^2 - 100$ is the difference of two squares ($100 = 10^2$).
> So $x^2 - 100 = (x + 10)(x - 10)$.

Example – Factorising quadratics

a Factorise $x^2 - 7x + 10$.
b Factorise $x^2 - x - 12$.

Solution

You need to reverse the process of expanding two brackets.

The first term to consider is the constant term or number 'on its own'.

a $x^2 - 7x + 10 = (x + \square)(x + \square)$
You need two numbers that multiply to give +10.... ⟵ +2 and +5, −2 and −5, +10 and +1, −10 and −1
...and add up to give −7.
$(+2) + (+5) = +7$, right number, wrong sign
$(-2) + (-5) = -7$ ✓ ⟵ So the two numbers are −2 and −5.
Therefore, $x^2 - 7x + 10 = (x - 2)(x - 5)$

	x	-2
x	x^2	$-2x$
-5	$-5x$	$+10$

b $x^2 - x - 12 = (x + \square)(x + \square)$
You need two numbers that multiply to give −12... ⟵ +12 and −1, −12 and +1, +6 and −2, −6 and +2, +4 and −3, −4 and +3

...and add to give −1. ⟵ $(+12) + (-1) = (+11)$ ✗ and $(-12) + 1 = (-11)$ ✗
$(+6) + (-2) = 4$ ✗ and $(-6) + (+2) = (-4)$ ✗

$(+4) + (-3) = 1$, right number, wrong sign
$(-4) + (+3) = -1$ ✓ ⟵ So the two numbers are −4 and +3.
Therefore, $x^2 - x - 12 = (x - 4)(x + 3)$

	x	-4
x	x^2	$-4x$
$+3$	$3x$	-12

Unit 1 Factorising quadratics Band h

Example – Difference of two squares

a Factorise $x^2 - 36$.
b Factorise $x^2 - 1$.

Solution

It is worth checking for the difference of two squares format when a quadratic expression has only 2 terms.

a The first square is x^2 so the brackets have x at the start:
$(x + \square)(x - \square)$
The second square is 36, so 6 fills in the other places.
$x^2 - 36 = (x + 6)(x - 6)$

	x	$+6$
x	x^2	$6x$
-6	$-6x$	-36

b The first square is x^2 so the brackets have x at the start:
$(x + \square)(x - \square)$
The second square is 1, so 1 fills in the other places.
$x^2 - 1 = (x + 1)(x - 1)$

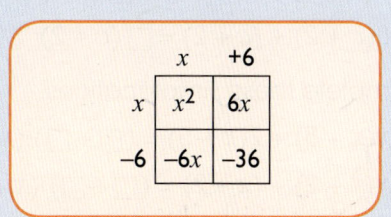

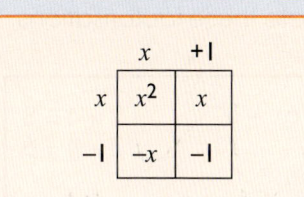

	x	$+1$
x	x^2	x
-1	$-x$	-1

Practising skills

1 Expand and simplify where appropriate:

a $x(x + 3)$
b $x(x - 1)$
c $(x - 5)(x + 5)$
d $(x - 2)(x + 3)$
e $(x + 5)(x - 8)$
f $(x - 4)(x - 1)$
g $(x - 2)(x + 2)$

2 The numbers –3 and 5 can be:
added together to give +2 $-3 + 5 = +2$
multiplied together to give –15 $-3 \times 5 = -15$.
Add up and multiply the following pairs of numbers.

a 3 and 4
b 2 and 6
c 1 and 4
d –1 and 5
e 3 and 3
f 8 and –2
g –3 and –4
h –2 and 2

3 Find pairs of numbers which do the following:

a add up to give 6 and multiply to give 8
b add up to give 2 and multiply to give –8
c add up to give –2 and multiply to give –8
d add up to give –6 and multiply to give 8
e add up to give 9 and multiply to give 8
f add up to give 7 and multiply to give –8
g add up to give –7 and multiply to give –8
h add up to give –9 and multiply to give 8.

Algebra Strand 5 Working with quadratics

4 Find pairs of numbers which do the following:
   a add up to give –5 and multiply to give 6
   b add up to give 5 and multiply to give 6
   c add up to give –1 and multiply to give –6
   d add up to give 1 and multiply to give –6
   e add up to give 7 and multiply to give 6
   f add up to give 5 and multiply to give –6
   g add up to give –7 and multiply to give 6
   h add up to give –5 and multiply to give –6.

5 Complete these simplifications.
   a $2(a + 5) + 7(a + 5) = \Box(a + 5)$
   b $12(b - 6) - 3(b - 6) = \Box(b - 6)$
   c $8(c + 2) + (c + 2) = \Box(c + 2)$
   d $-2(d - 7) + (d - 7) = \Box(d - 7)$

6 Complete these simplifications.
   a $x(x + 5) + 7(x + 5) = (\Box + \Box)(x + 5)$
   b $x(x - 6) - 3(x - 6) = (\Box - \Box)(x - 6)$
   c $x(x + 2) + (x + 2) = (\Box + \Box)(x + 2)$
   d $-x(x - 7) + (x - 7) = (\Box x + \Box)(x - 7)$

7 Complete these factorisations.

a

| $x^2 + 6x + 8$ | $2 \times 4 = 8$ |
| | $2 + 4 = 6$ |

$x^2 + 2x + \Box x + 8$

$x(x + 2) + \Box(x + 2)$

$(x + \Box)(x + 2)$

b

| $x^2 - 8x + 15$ | $-3 \times -5 = 15$ |
| | $-3 + -5 = -8$ |

$x^2 - 3x - \Box x + 15$

$x(x - 3) - \Box(x - \Box)$

$(x - \Box)(x - \Box)$

c

| $x^2 - 2x - 24$ | $4 \times -6 = -24$ |
| | $4 + -6 = -2$ |

$x^2 + 4x - \Box x - 24$

$x(x + \Box) - \Box(x + \Box)$

$(x - \Box)(x + \Box)$

d

| $x^2 + x - 2$ | $2 \times -1 = -2$ |
| | $2 + -1 = 1$ |

$x^2 + \Box x - 1x - 2$

$x(x + \Box) - 1(x + \Box)$

$(x - \Box)(x + \Box)$

8 Factorise:
   a $x^2 + 8x + 15$
   b $x^2 - 9x + 20$
   c $x^2 + 8x + 16$
   d $x^2 + 4x - 21$
   e $x^2 - x - 6$
   f $x^2 + 17x + 16$
   g $x^2 - 15x - 16$
   h $x^2 - 8x - 20$

9 Factorise:
   a $x^2 + 8x$
   b $x^2 - 100$
   c $x^2 - 16x$
   d $x^2 - 16$
   e $x^2 + 7x + 6$
   f $x^2 - 1$
   g $x^2 - 144$
   h $x^2 - 5$

Unit 1 Factorising quadratics Band h

Developing fluency

1. The diagram shows a rectangle PQRS divided up into 4 rectangular regions with dimensions a cm, b cm, c cm and d cm as shown.

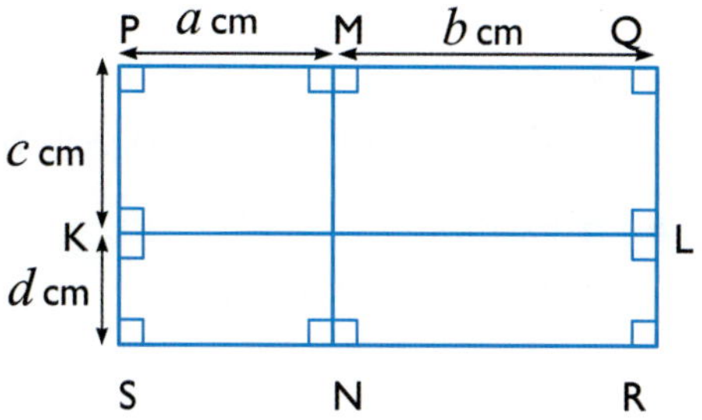

   a Find the areas of the 4 regions.

   b Which regions have areas

      i $a(c + d)$ ii $b(c + d)$

      iii $(a + b)(c + d)$?

   c Factorise $ac + ad + bc + bd$.

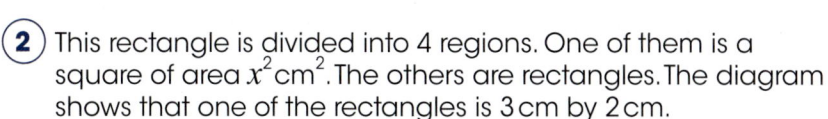

2. This rectangle is divided into 4 regions. One of them is a square of area x^2 cm². The others are rectangles. The diagram shows that one of the rectangles is 3 cm by 2 cm.

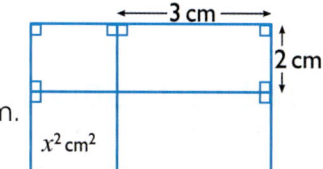

   a Make a copy and mark the areas of the 4 regions on the diagram.

   b Find the length and width of the whole rectangle.

   c Use the diagram to factorise $x^2 + 5x + 6$.

   d Use algebra to check your answer to part c.

3. This rectangle has an area of $x^2 + 6x + 8$ cm².

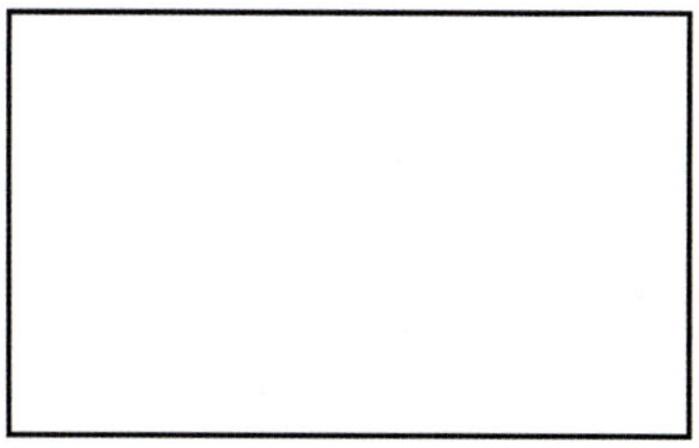

   a Make a copy and divide the rectangle into four regions with areas x cm², $4x$ cm², $2x$ cm² and 8 cm².

   b Show that the perimeter of the rectangle is $4x + 12$ cm and find its area.

   c Use your diagram to factorise $x^2 + 6x + 8$.

   d Use algebra to check your answer to part c.

4. Figure 1 shows a red square of side a cm.

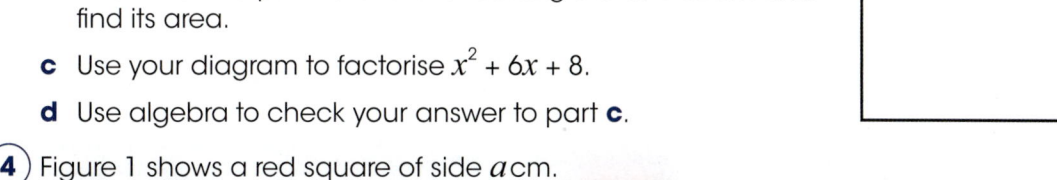

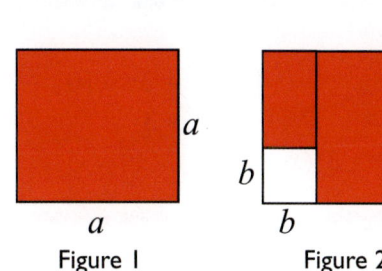

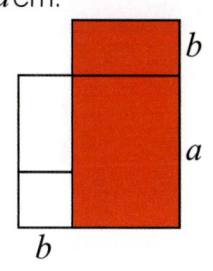

   In Figure 2 a smaller square of side b cm has been removed from the red square. A rectangle has been marked above the small square.

   In Figure 3 the rectangle has been moved and turned so that it lies on the top.

   a Find, in terms of a and b, the area of the red region in each of the 3 Figures.

   b The red region in Figure 3 forms a large rectangle. Write down its dimensions in terms of a and b.

   c Use the diagram to show that $a^2 - b^2 = (a + b)(a - b)$.

   d Use algebra to show the same result.

Algebra Strand 5 Working with quadratics

5 **a** Expand:

i $(x + 10)(x + 1)$

ii $(x + 2)(x + 5)$

b Simplify $(x + 10)(x - 1) - (x + 2)(x + 5)$.

c Check your answer to part **b** by substituting $x = 2$.

6 **a** Expand:

i $(x + 7)(x + 3)$

ii $(x + 7)(x + 2)$

b Simplify $(x + 7)(x + 3) - (x + 7)(x + 2)$.

c How can you work out the answer to part **b** without expanding the brackets?

Problem solving

1 Without using a calculator, work out the area of the region that is shaded red.

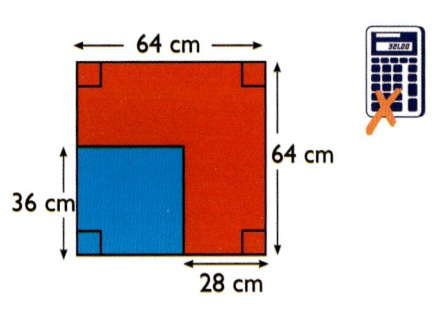

2 Pick an integer that is bigger than 3.

Square it and then subtract 4. Can the answer be a prime number? Explain.

Reviewing skills

1 Factorise these quadratics.

a $x^2 - 6x + 8$
b $x^2 + x - 12$
c $x^2 - x - 12$
d $x^2 + 3x - 10$
e $x^2 - 3x - 10$
f $x^2 - 8x + 16$
g $x^2 - 49$
h $x^2 - 3$

2 Show that $(x + 7)(x + 1) - (x + 2)(x + 6) + (x + 2)(x - 2) = (x + 3)(x - 3)$.

Unit 2 • Solving equations by factorising • Band h

Outside the Maths classroom

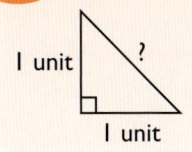

Discovering new numbers

How would you find the exact value of the hypotenuse of this triangle?

Toolbox

Here is a quadratic graph.

The parabola crosses the x axis at $(-2, 0)$ and $(3, 0)$.
-2 and 3 are known as the **roots** of the equation $y = x^2 - x - 6$.

They are also the solution to the equation $x^2 - x - 6 = 0$.

This equation therefore has two solutions or roots, $x = -2$ and $x = 3$.

Quadratic functions can have 0, 1 or 2 roots, depending on where its curve crosses the x axis

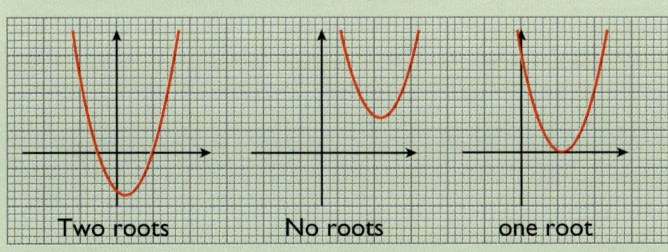

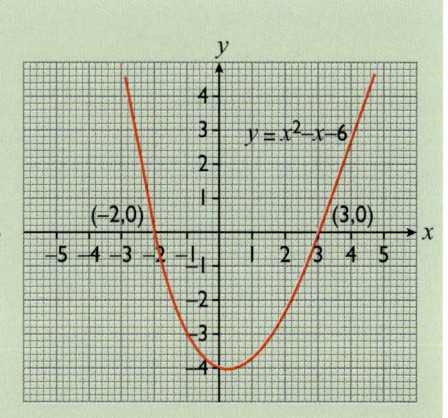

Two roots No roots one root

Some quadratic equations can be factorised and this gives an algebraic method for finding the **roots**.
It uses the fact that if 2 numbers multiply to give zero, then at least one of those numbers must be zero.

$x^2 + (a + b)x + ab = (x + a)(x + b)$ ← Factorising.

$(x + a)(x + b) = 0$ ← Roots are where its curve crosses the x axis, i.e. $y = 0$.

Either $x + a = 0$

$x = -a$ ← Rearranging.

or $x + b = 0$

$x = -b$. ← Rearranging.

For our example, we can find the roots of $y = x^2 - x - 6$ by factorising.

$x^2 - x - 6 = 0$

$(x + 2)(x - 3) = 0$ ← Factorising, $2 - 3 = -1$, $2 \times -3 = -6$.

Either $x + 2 = 0$ so $x = -2$

or $x - 3 = 0$ so $x = 3$.

You can check your answer by substituting back into the equation.

Algebra Strand 5 Working with quadratics

Example – Solving equations

The graph shows the function $y = x^2 + 7x + 12$.
a Solve $x^2 + 7x + 12 = 0$ algebraically.
b Solve $x^2 - 3x = 0$.

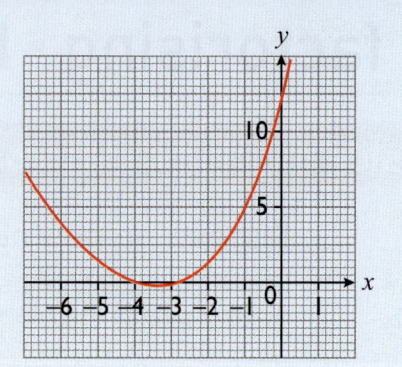

Solution

a $x^2 + 7x + 12 = 0$
Factorise first:
$(x + 3)(x + 4) = 0$ ← Two numbers that multiply to give +12 and add to give +7 are +3 and +4.
Either $x + 3 = 0$
          $x = -3$ ← Check: $(-3)^2 + 7 \times (-3) + 12 = 9 - 21 + 12 = 0$ ✔
or $x + 4 = 0$
          $x = -4$ ← Check: $(-4)^2 + 7 \times (-4) + 12 = 16 - 28 + 12 = 0$ ✔

b $x^2 - 3x = 0$
Factorise first:
$x(x - 3) = 0$ ← There is an 'x' in both terms
Either $x = 0$ ← Check: $0^2 - 3 \times 0 = 0$ ✔
or $x - 3 = 0$
    $x = 3$ ← Check: $3^2 - 3 \times 3 = 9 - 9 = 0$ ✔

Example – Solving geometrical problems

A rectangle has width x metres, and length 1 metre more than its width. The area of the rectangle is $20\,\text{m}^2$.
a Form a quadratic equation for x.
b Solve the equation and find the length and width of the rectangle.

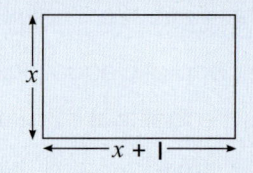

Solution

a Area of rectangle = $x(x + 1)$ ← The area is 20 m².
    So, $x(x + 1) = 20$ ← Expanding.
          $x^2 + x = 20$
          $x^2 + x - 20 = 0$ ← You need to rearrange a quadratic equation into the form $ax^2 + bx + c = 0$ before you can solve it.

b $x^2 + x - 20 = 0$
    $(x + 5)(x - 4) = 0$ ← Two numbers that multiply to give −20 and add to give +1 are +5 and −4.
    Either $x + 5 = 0$,
              $x = -5$ ← Not a valid solution to this problem.
    or, $x - 4 = 0$,
              $x = 4$
The width of the rectangle is 4 metres.
The length of the rectangle is 5 metres. ← The length is 1 metre more than the width.
Check: $4 \times 5 = 20$ ✔

Practising skills

1 Solve these equations.

a $(x+4)(x+1)=0$ b $(x-3)(x+7)=0$ c $(x-1)(x-1)=0$ d $(x+2)(x+1)=0$

2 Solve these equations.

a $x^2-7x+12=0$ b $x^2-x-2=0$ c $x^2+2x-15=0$ d $x^2+6x+5=0$
e $x^2-4=0$ f $x^2-7x=0$ g $x^2+x-12=0$ h $x^2-9=0$

3 Rearrange and solve these equations.

a $x^2+4x=-3$ b $x^2+2x=8$ c $x^2=-x$
d $x^2=3x+4$ e $x^2=49$

4 Solve these equations.

a $x^2-64=0$ b $x^2=9x+36$ c $(x+8)(x-2)=0$
d $x^2+x-2=0$ e $x^2-9x=0$

5 These are the solutions of quadratic equations. Write down each quadratic equation in the form $x^2+bx+c=0$.

a 3 or 5   b −3 or −5   c 6 or −8
d 1 or −1   e 9 or −10   f 0 or −6

Developing fluency

1 A rectangle measures x cm by $(x+4)$ cm.
The area of the rectangle is $45\,\text{cm}^2$.

  a Write the area of the rectangle in terms of x.
  b Form a quadratic equation in x and rearrange it to the form $x^2+bx+c=0$.
  c Solve the quadratic equation.
  d What are the length and width of the rectangle?

2 A rectangle measures x cm by $(x-2)$ cm and has area $48\,\text{cm}^2$.

  a Form a quadratic equation in x and solve it.
  b What are the dimensions of the rectangle?

3 A triangle has height $(x+6)$ cm and base x cm. The area of the triangle is $8\,\text{cm}^2$.
Form and solve a quadratic equation to work out the dimensions of the triangle.

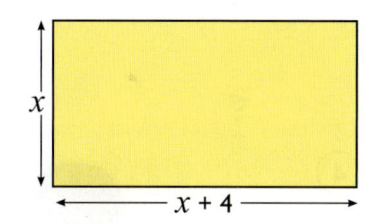

Algebra Strand 5 Working with quadratics

4 The diagram shows the dimensions of a trapezium.
The area of the trapezium is 35 cm².
Form and solve a quadratic equation to work out the dimensions of the trapezium.

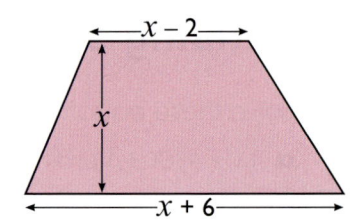

Problem solving

1 The width of this rectangle is $(x - 8)$ cm and its area is $(x^2 - 64)$ cm².

  a Find an expression involving x for its length. The value of x will be different in each of the following parts **b**, **c** and **d**.

  b The area of the rectangle is 36 cm². Find its length and width.

  c Find the value of x for which it is possible to divide the rectangle into two equal squares.

  d The rectangle has the same area as a square of perimeter 60 cm. Find the perimeter of the rectangle.

2 Robin fires an arrow into the air.
The equation for the height, h metres, of the arrow at time, t seconds is $h = 45t - 5t^2$.

  a Find the value of t when the arrow hits the ground.

  b Find the times when the arrow is 100 m above the ground.

3 Here is a rectangle with length $(x + 6)$ cm and width $(x - 5)$ cm.
Find the length and the width of the rectangle.

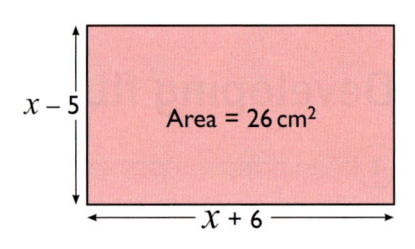

4
I think of a number.
I subtract 5 and square my answer.
My final answer is 4.

What numbers could Arwyl be thinking about?

5 A square of side 5 cm is cut from a square of side $(x + 5)$ cm.
The blue area remaining is 24 cm².

  a Find the length of the original square.

  b Explain why there is only one possible answer.

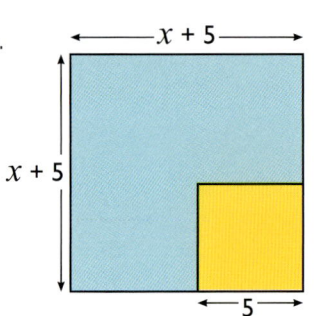

Unit 2 Solving equations by factorising Band h

Reviewing skills

1) Solve these equations.
   a $x^2 + 5x + 6 = 0$
   b $x^2 - 6x + 8 = 0$
   c $x^2 - x - 2 = 0$
   d $x^2 + 3x - 28 = 0$
   e $x^2 + 5x = -4$
   f $x^2 + 6 = 10$
   g $x(x - 2) = 15$
   h $x^2 - 10 = 0$

2) A rectangle has width 3 cm less than its length.
   The area of the rectangle is 54 cm².
   Form and solve a quadratic equation to work out the dimensions of the rectangle.

Geometry and Measures
Strand 1 Units and scales

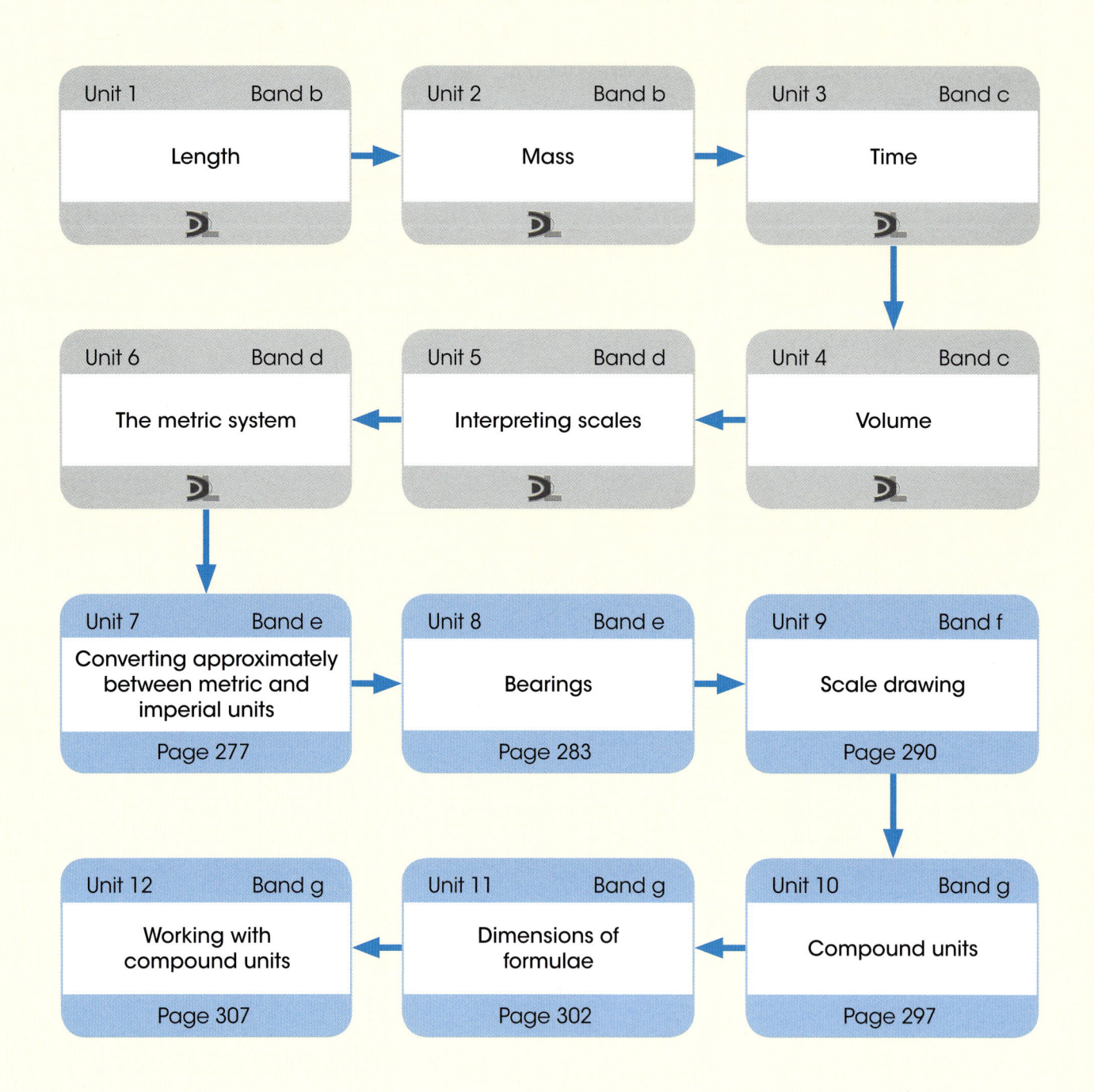

Unit 1	Band b
Length	

Unit 2	Band b
Mass	

Unit 3	Band c
Time	

Unit 6	Band d
The metric system	

Unit 5	Band d
Interpreting scales	

Unit 4	Band c
Volume	

Unit 7	Band e
Converting approximately between metric and imperial units	
Page 277	

Unit 8	Band e
Bearings	
Page 283	

Unit 9	Band f
Scale drawing	
Page 290	

Unit 12	Band g
Working with compound units	
Page 307	

Unit 11	Band g
Dimensions of formulae	
Page 302	

Unit 10	Band g
Compound units	
Page 297	

Units 1–6 are assumed knowledge for this book.
Knowledge and skills from these units are used throughout the book.

Unit 7 • Converting approximately between metric and imperial units • Band e

Example outside the Maths classroom

Following recipes

What would you do if you are following a recipe in pounds and ounces, but using weighing scales in grams and kilograms?

Toolbox

Metric units are units such as metres, grams and litres.
Imperial units include feet, pounds and pints.
You need to be able to convert between the different imperial units.

Mass	Volume (or capacity)	Distance or length
16 ounces = 1 pound	20 fluid ounces = 1 pint	12 inches = 1 foot
14 pounds = 1 stone	8 pints = 1 gallon	3 feet = 1 yard

You can also convert between metric and imperial units.
Here is a table of all the common conversions for mass, volume and length.

Approximate conversions	Mass		Volume (or capacity)		Distance or length			
Metric	1 kg	28 g	1 litre	5 litres	8 km	1 m	30 cm	2.5 cm
Imperial	2.2 pounds	1 ounce	$1\frac{3}{4}$ pints	1 gallon	5 miles	39 inches	1 foot	1 inch

Example – Converting lengths

The world's largest butterfly is the Queen Alexandra Birdwing.
It has a wingspan of 28 cm.
Write the wingspan in inches.

Solution

2.5 cm is about 1 inch.
So the conversion factor is 2.5.
You need to convert cm to inches so you are converting to a larger unit.
This means you need to divide by the conversion factor, 28 ÷ 2.5 = 11.2
The wingspan is about 11.2 inches.

Geometry and Measures Strand 1 Units and scales

Example – Reading a conversion graph

This is a conversion graph between grams and ounces.

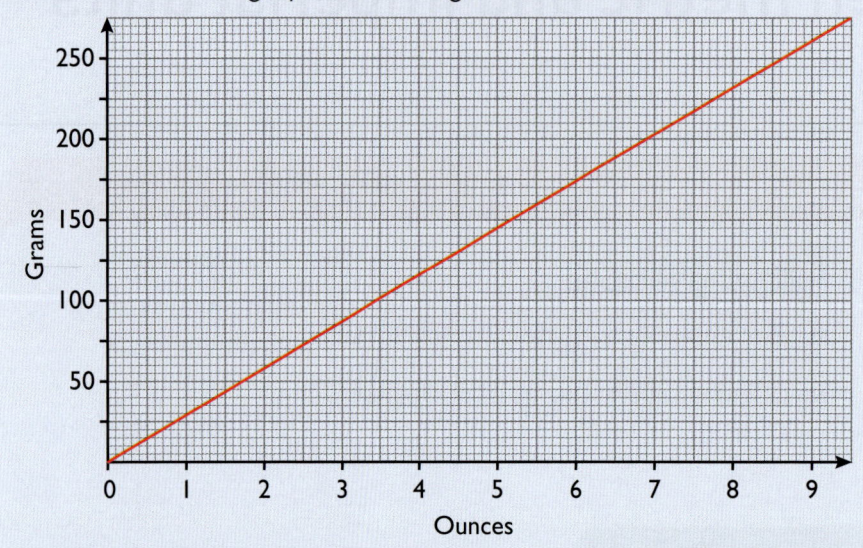

a A packet of butter is labelled 250 g.
   What is this in ounces?
b Paul buys 8 ounces of cheese.
   What is this in grams?

Solution

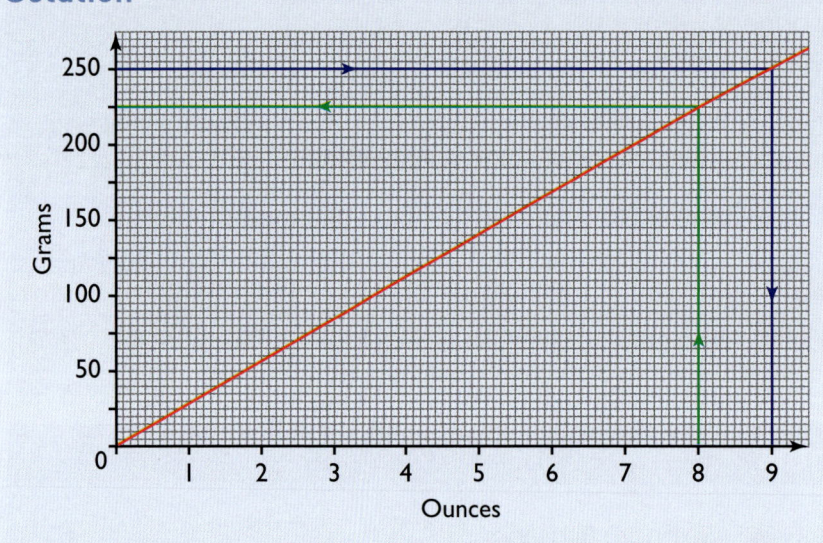

a The blue line on the graph shows 250 g is about 9 ounces.
b The green line on the graph shows that 8 ounces is about 225 grams.

Unit 7 Converting approximately between metric and imperial units Band e

For the following exercises, use the conversion table below.

Approximate conversions	Mass		Volume (or capacity)		Distance or length			
Metric	1 kg	28 g	1 litre	5 litres	8 km	1 m	30 cm	2.5 cm
Imperial	2.2 pounds	1 ounce	$1\frac{3}{4}$ pints	1 gallon	5 miles	39 inches	1 foot	1 inch

Practising skills

1. Convert these volumes to litres.
   - a 3 gallons
   - b 5 gallons
   - c 7 gallons
   - d 15 gallons

2. Convert these lengths to centimetres.
   - a 5 inches
   - b 3 inches
   - c 100 inches
   - d 25 inches

3. Convert these distances to kilometres.
   - a 10 miles
   - b 20 miles
   - c 100 miles
   - d 180 miles

4. Convert these distances to miles.
   - a 64 km
   - b 40 km
   - c 600 km
   - d 2000 km

5. A theme park ride is suitable for people over 130 cm.
   Amy is 4 feet 8 inches tall. Is she tall enough to go on the ride?

Developing fluency

1. Eloise is 5 feet 4 inches tall. Jade is 164 cm.
   Who is taller? By how much?

2. a Which is longer?
   - i 10 metres or 10 yards
   - ii 60 miles or 100 km

   b Which is greater?
   - i 4 pints or 2 litres
   - ii 1 gallon or 4 litres

   c How many gallons are there in 70 pints?

   d How many kilometres are there in 12 miles?

   e How many pounds are there in 40 kg?

   f How many pints are there in 4 litres?

   g How many metres are there in 25 inches?

   h How many litres are there in 10 gallons?

Geometry and Measures Strand 1 Units and scales

3 1 yard is 3 feet.

Football pitches are not all the same size. The actual length of a pitch must be between 100 yards and 130 yards and the width should be between 50 yards and 100 yards.

   a Kay is measuring out a new football pitch on a local field.
      The field measures 85 m by 85 m.
      Is the field large enough to hold a football pitch?

The stadium at Manchester City is 116.5 yards by 78 yards.
The stadium at West Ham United is 110 yards × 70 yards.

   b i Convert the dimensions of Manchester City's stadium to metres.
      ii What is the difference in area between the two stadiums?

4 Look at this recipe for 'Digger biscuits'.
Convert the recipe to metric units.

> 5 oz plain flour
> 8 oz caster sugar
> 4 oz oats
> 3 oz desiccated coconut
> $4\frac{1}{2}$ oz butter
> 1 tbsp golden syrup
> 1 level tsp bicarbonate of soda
> 2 tbsp boiling water

5 Fleur is driving across Spain.
She has enough petrol left for 65 miles.
The next petrol station is 90 km away.

   a Does Fleur have enough petrol to reach the petrol station?
      Explain your answer fully.

Fleur fills her tank with petrol.
The tank takes 14 gallons.

> Petrol
> €1.40 per litre

   b How much does 14 gallons of petrol cost in pounds? (Use the conversion £1 = €1.25.)

Problem solving

1) The BMI of a person is calculated from the rule

$$BMI = \frac{\text{mass in kg}}{(\text{height in m})^2}$$

An ideal BMI lies between 18 and 25.
Bill weighs 154 pounds and has a height of 183 cm.
Does Bill have an ideal BMI? Give a reason for your answer.

2) This conversion graph can be used to exchange between gallons and litres.

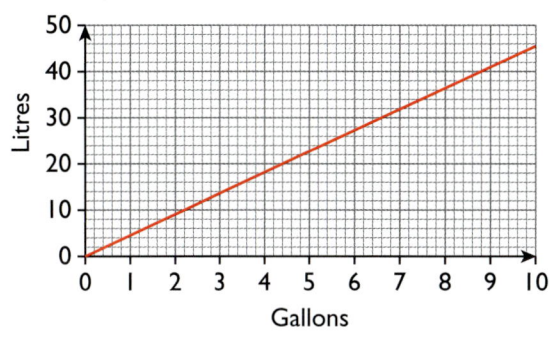

Art has oil-fired central heating. The tank for the oil holds 280 gallons of oil when full.
Art's tank is only $\frac{1}{4}$ full.
Oil costs 50p per litre.
Work out an estimate for the cost of filling the oil tank.

3) Lois is driving from the south of France to Paris.
She sees a road sign.
She knows that it takes one hour to travel 60 miles.
The time now is 10 p.m. Lois wants to get to Paris by 2.30 a.m.
Will she be able to get to Paris by 2.30 a.m.?

Paris
450 km

4) The smallest postage stamp ever was a square, with sides measuring 10 millimetres.

The biggest stamp ever was a rectangle measuring 2 inches by $3\frac{1}{4}$ inches.
How many times bigger is the area of the rectangular stamp than the area of the square stamp?

5 Tyre pressures can be measured in pounds per square inch (psi) or in bars.
The graph can be used to change between pressures in pounds per square inch and bars.

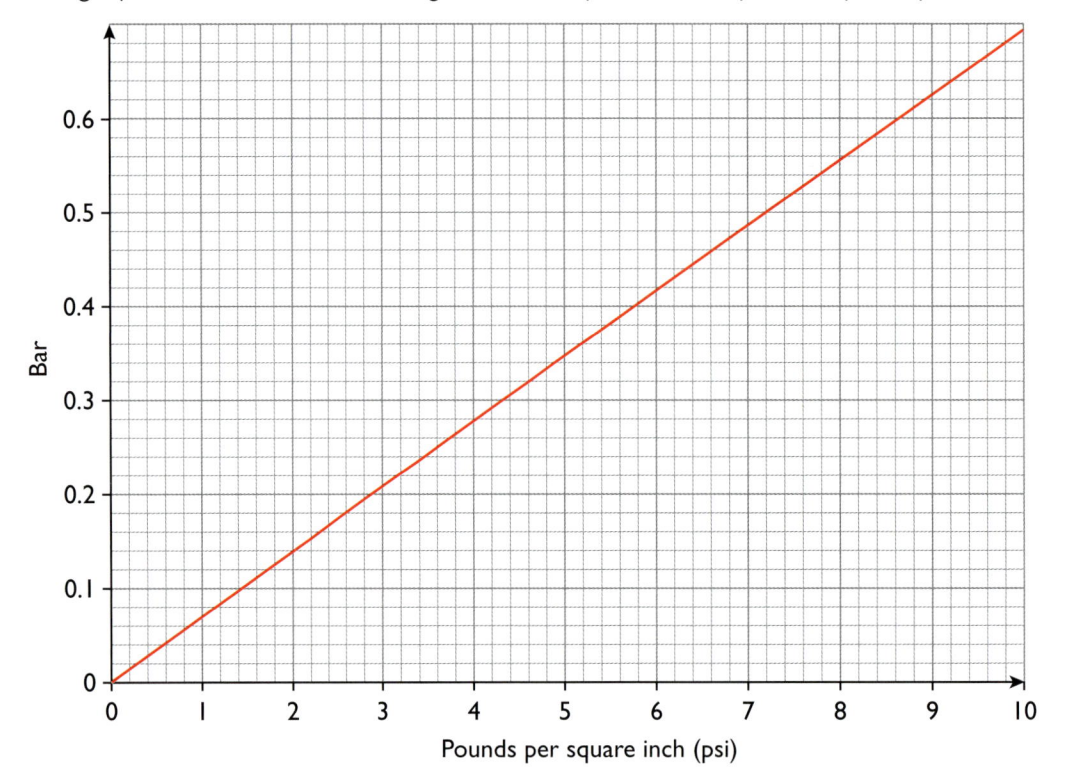

[Graph: Bar (y-axis, 0 to 0.6+) vs Pounds per square inch (psi) (x-axis, 0 to 10), showing a straight line from origin]

a Jensen increases his tyre pressure from 28 psi to 32 psi.
Work out this increase in bars.

Scientists measure pressure in pascals.
100 000 pascals = 15 psi.

b The air pressure at the top of Mount Everest is 0.6 bar. Find this pressure in pascals.

6 Information for this question:
- 1 gallon is approximately 4.55 litres.
- The average cost of diesel last year was £1.29 per litre.

Jac is trying to work out how much it costs per mile to run her car. She spent £1340.28 on diesel for her car last year. On average, Jac's car does 38.9 miles per gallon.
Calculate how many miles Jac travelled in her car last year.

Reviewing skills

1 Convert these masses to pounds.
  a 3 kg   **b** 4 kg   **c** 7 kg   **d** 10 kg

2 Dafydd is 5 feet 3 inches tall. Megan is 163 cm tall.
Who is taller and by how much?

3 Alex buys a 150g bar of chocolate for £1.75 in the UK.
He knows that a $\frac{1}{2}$ pound bar will cost the equivalent of £2.75 in the USA.
Where is it better value, in the UK or in the USA?

1 Unit 8 • Bearings • Band e

Outside the Maths classroom

Navigating
What special problems are there when you navigate at sea?

Toolbox

A **bearing** is given as an **angle** direction.
It is the **angle** measured clockwise from North.
Compass bearings are always given using three figures, so there can be no mistakes.
A **back bearing** is the direction of the return journey.
If a bearing is less than 180°, the back bearing is 180° more than the bearing.
If a bearing is more than 180°, the back bearing is the bearing less 180°.
North is 000°, East is 090°, South is 180° and West is 270°.

Example – Drawing a bearing

B is 3 cm from A on a bearing of 120°.
Draw the bearing of B from A.

Solution

a Draw a North line at A.
b Measure an angle of 120° clockwise from North at A.
c Draw a line at this angle from A.
   Use a ruler to mark point B 3 cm along this line.

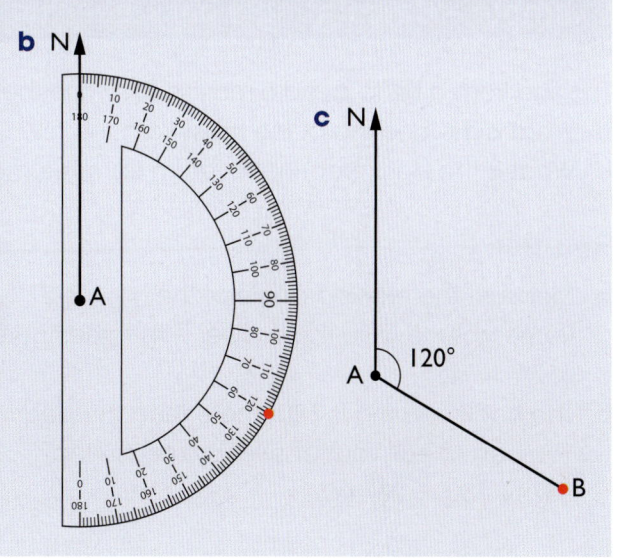

Geometry and Measures Strand 1 Units and scales

Example – Measuring a bearing

Here is a map of Great Britain.
Find the bearing of
a London from Penzance
b Birmingham from London.

Solution

a The bearing is from Penzance so place your protractor on the map with the centre at Penzance and the zero line vertically up.
Use the grid lines to help you.
Measure the angle clockwise from North.
As 70° only has two digits, write your answer with a zero in front.
070°

b The bearing of Birmingham from London is a reflex angle.
Place your protractor on the map with the centre at London and the zero line vertically up.
If you have a 360° protractor you can measure the angle directly.
If you have a 180° protractor, measure the angle anticlockwise from North.
Subtract this angle from 360°.
360° − 53° = 307°

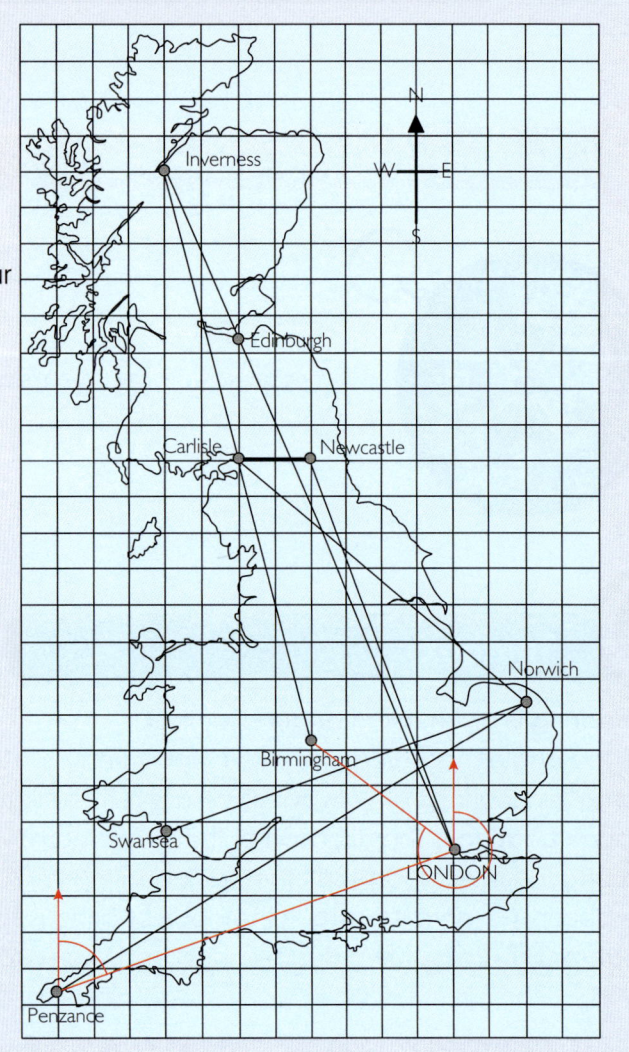

Example – Calculating a back bearing

The line from a hill to a radio mast is shown in the diagram.
a What is the bearing of the mast from the hill?
b What is the back bearing to return from the mast to the hill?

Solution

a Measure the marked angle at the hill. It is 57°.
Remember to write the answer with three figures.
057°

b The back bearing is 180° more than the bearing.
You can check your answer by measuring.
057° + 180° = 237°

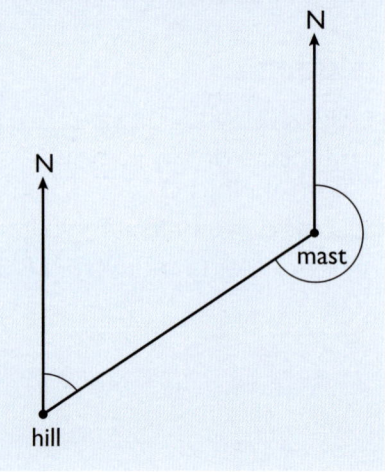

Practising skills

1 Write down the three-figure bearings of A, B, C and D from O.

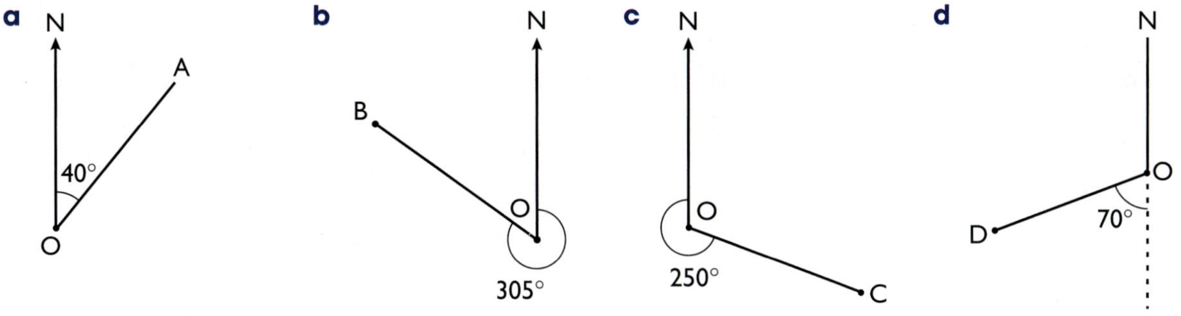
a
N
A
40°
O
b
N
B
O
305°
c
N
O
250°
C
d
N
O
D
70°

2 Measure the bearings of each of the following towns from Avonford.

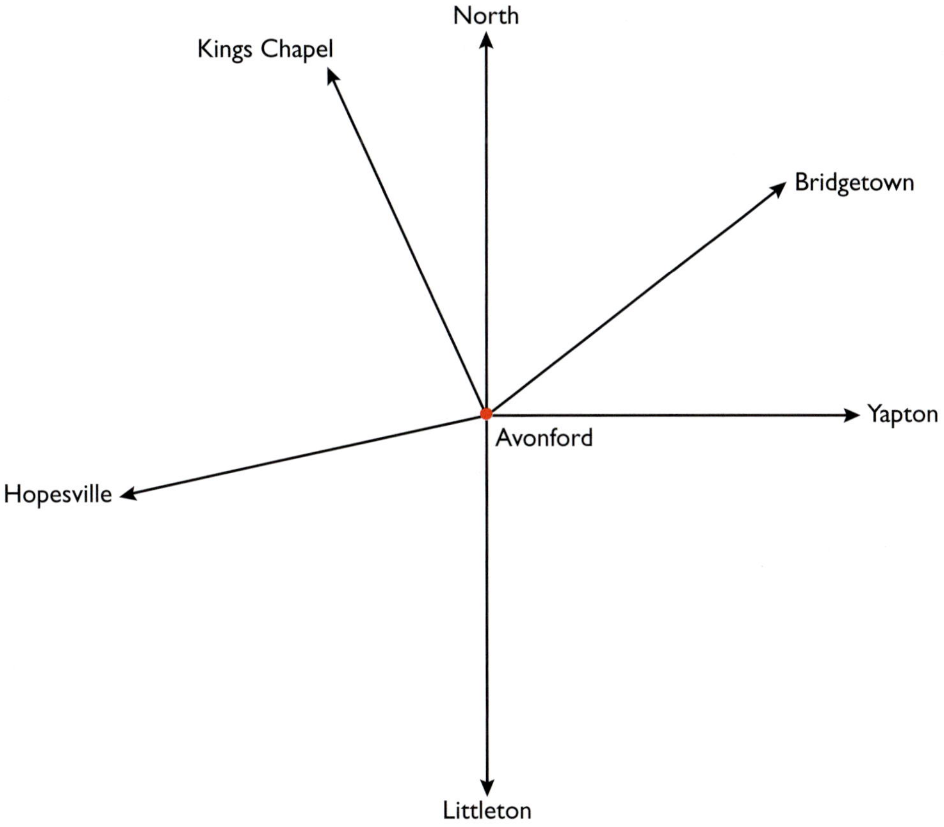
North
Kings Chapel
Bridgetown
Yapton
Avonford
Hopesville
Littleton

3 Write down the bearing for each of these compass directions.

a South **b** East **c** North-East **d** South-West

4 Write down the compass points with these bearings.

a 000° **b** 135° **c** 315° **d** 270°

Geometry and Measures Strand 1 Units and scales

5 For each of these
   i draw an accurate diagram
   ii calculate the angles x and y
   ii give the bearing from A to B
   iv give the back bearing from B to A.

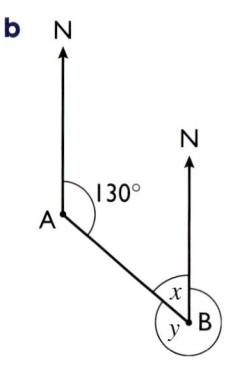

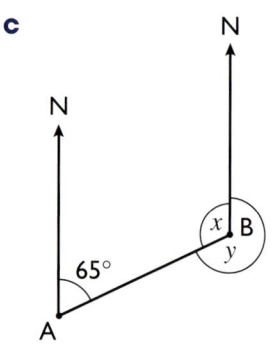

a, b, c [diagrams showing bearings with angles 105°, 130°, and 65° respectively]

6 Draw accurate diagrams to show these bearings.
   a The bearing from A to B is 060°. B is 6 cm from A.
   b The bearing from C to D is 200°. D is 5 cm from C.
   c The bearing from E to F is 330°. F is 4.2 cm from E.
   d The bearing from G to H is 105°. H is 57 mm from G.

7 A helicopter and an aeroplane are flying at the same altitude.
   The bearing of the aeroplane from the helicopter is 070°.
   Jack says the bearing of the helicopter from the aeroplane is 110°.
   Is Jack right?
   Explain your answer fully.

Developing fluency

1 The diagram shows the position of two ships A and B.

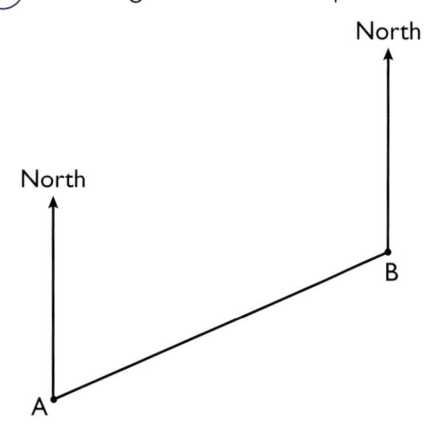

[diagram showing ships A and B with North arrows]

   a Measure the bearing of ship B from ship A.
   b Calculate the back bearing to travel from ship B to ship A.

Unit 8 Bearings Band e

2. Applebury is South-East of Newtown.
   a What is the bearing of Applebury from Newtown?
   b What is the bearing of Newtown from Applebury?

3. a A pilot flies from London to Manchester on a bearing of 312°.
     Calculate the back bearing for the return journey.
   b The flight path from Plymouth to Edinburgh is 017°.
     Calculate the bearing of Plymouth from Edinburgh.

4. The bearing of Sunnyside from Avonford is 133°.
   The bearing of Westbrook from Avonford is also 133°.
   a What can you say about the positions of these three towns?

   Salman: *So the bearing of Westbrook from Sunnyside is also 133°*

   Saidie: *No, it is 313°*

   Aneesa: *We don't have enough information to work it out!*

   b Who is right? Explain your answer fully.

5. Gwen is organising an orienteering competition.
   Checkpoint B is 4 km from checkpoint A on a bearing of 155°.
   Checkpoint C is 7 km from B on a bearing of 220°.
   a Draw an accurate diagram showing the three checkpoints.
   Gwen walks from checkpoint C back to checkpoint A.
   b How far does she walk?
   c What is the bearing of checkpoint A from checkpoint C?
   d What is the bearing of checkpoint C from checkpoint A?

6. The diagram shows the position of two ships P and Q and a nearby lighthouse, L.
   Find the bearing of
   a P from Q   b Q from P
   c Q from L   d L from Q
   e L from P   f P from L.

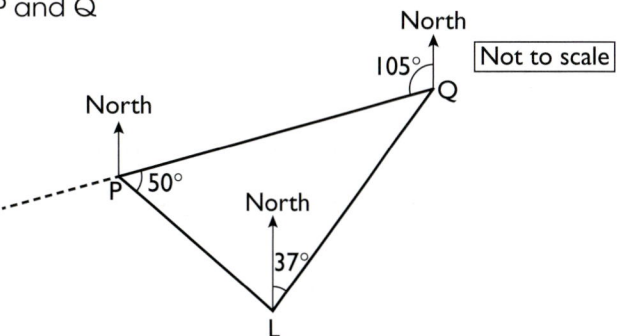

Geometry and Measures Strand 1 Units and scales

7 The distance from Cardiff to Swansea by road is approximately 41 miles.

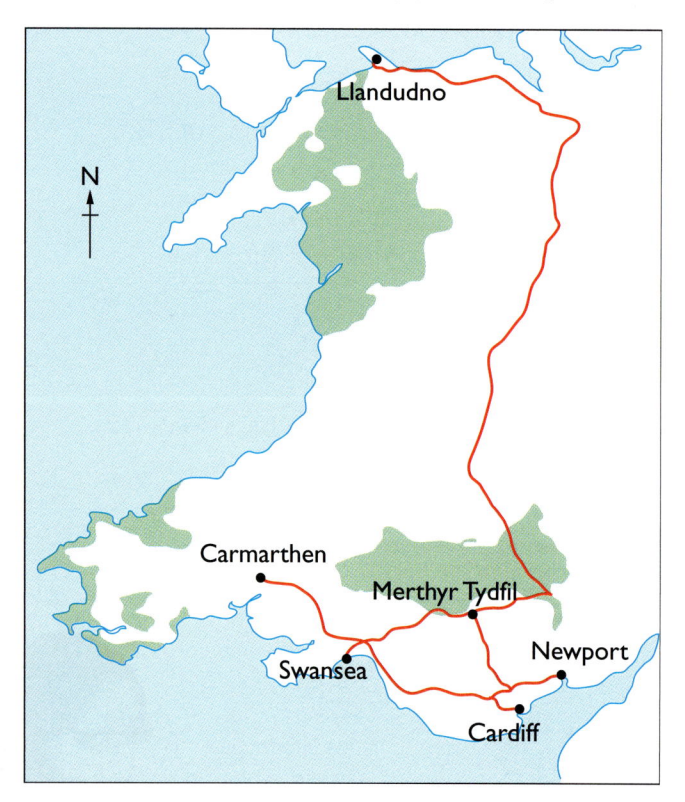

a Approximately how far is Newport from Merthyr Tydfil?
b Approximately how far is Llandudno from Swansea?
c Write down the bearing of:
  i Carmarthen from Cardiff,
  ii Llandudno from Swansea,
  iii Newport from Carmarthen,
  iv Cardiff from Carmarthen.

Problem solving

1 Alton, Broxham and Colton are three villages.
The distance of Alton from Colton is 15 km.
The distance of Broxham from Colton is 15 km.
Alton is due East of Broxham.
The bearing of Alton from Colton is 140°.
  a Draw an accurate diagram showing the three villages.
  b Find the bearing of Colton from Broxham.

2) An aeroplane flies round a triangular route.
It starts from point X and flies 50 km on a bearing of 130° to a point Y.
At Y, it turns and flies to a point Z.
From Z, it turns and flies back to X.
The points X, Y and Z form an equilateral triangle.

   a Draw a diagram showing X, Y and Z.
   b Work out the bearing of Z from Y.
   c Work out the bearing that the aeroplane flies from Z to X.

3) Dalton is a town 4 miles due North of Fflur's home.
Foxham is a village 8 miles from Fflur's home.
The bearing of Foxham from Dalton is 210°.

   a Draw a suitable accurate diagram to find the bearing of Foxham from Fflur's home.
   b State one assumption you made to answer part **a**.

4) A, B and C are 3 markers in the sea.
The bearing of A from B is 040°.
The bearing of C from B is 100°.
The bearing of A from C is 340°.
Prove that A, B and C form the corners of an equilateral triangle.

5) A boat is travelling due East.
It travels a distance of 6 miles every hour.
At 1 p.m. the bearing of an island from the boat is 030°.
At 2.30 p.m. the bearing of the island from the boat is 305°.
Find, by measurement, the closest distance the boat gets to the island between 1 p.m. and 2.30 p.m.

6) In a race, boats sail clockwise around four markers A, B, C and D in the sea.
The markers form a square.
A boat starts from A and sails towards B on a bearing of 110°.
Work out the other three bearings that the boat must travel on to finish the course.

Reviewing skills

1) A boat sails from port A on a bearing of 045°.
The boat sails 5 miles every hour.
B is a point 7 miles due East of A.
A ship leaves B at the same time and sails on a bearing of 030°.
The ship sails 6 miles every hour.
Find, by measurement, the bearing of the boat from the ship after 30 minutes.

1 Unit 9 • Scale drawing • Band f

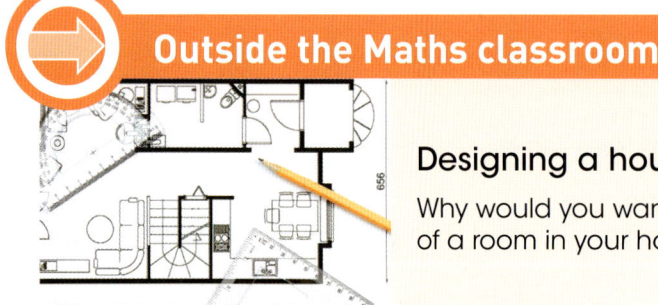

Outside the Maths classroom

Designing a house
Why would you want to make a plan of a room in your home?

Toolbox

A scale drawing is the **same shape** as the original but a **different size**.
All the lengths are in the same **ratio**.
On a scale drawing where 1 cm on the scale drawing represents 2 m on the actual object, the scale can be written as
$\frac{1}{200}$ or
1 cm = 2 m or
1 : 200
$\frac{1}{200}$ is sometimes refered to as the **scale factor**.
Warning: Be careful with areas and volumes.
For example, 1 cm = 10 mm but 1 cm^2 = 10^2 = 100 mm^2 and 1 cm^3 = 10^3 = 1000 mm^3.

Example – Using a scale

Kitty has a toy car on a scale of $\frac{1}{50}$th.
The toy car is 6 cm long.
The real car is 1.7 m wide.
 a How long is the real car?
 b How wide is the toy car?

Solution

The toy car is $\frac{1}{50}$ the size of the real car.
So the real car is 50 times the size of the toy car.
 a Length of real car = 6 × 50 cm ◁ To find the length of the real car, multiply by 50.
              = 300 cm
    The real car is 300 cm or 3 m long.

 b 1.7 m = 170 cm ◁ It is easier to convert to cm first.
    Width of toy car = 170 ÷ 50 cm ◁ To find the width of the toy car, divide by 50.
              = 3.4 cm
    The toy car is 3.4 cm wide.

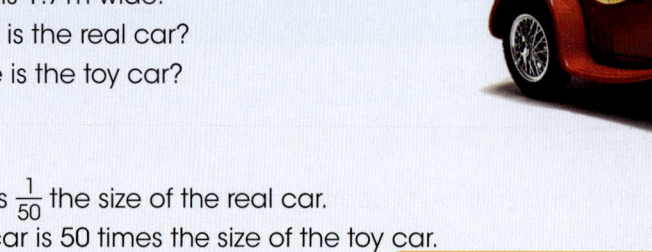

Unit 9 Scale drawing Band f

Example – Reading a map

Adebola is working out distances between places on a map.
The map has a scale of 1 : 50 000.
On the map, the bowling alley is 4.7 cm from the aqueduct.
a How far is the bowling alley from the aqueduct in kilometres?
Adebola's house is 3.8 km from her school.
b How far is her house from her school on the map?

Solution

a 4.7 × 50 000 = 235 000 cm ← To find a distance on the ground, multiply by the scale factor of 50 000.

235 000 ÷ 100 000 = 2.35 km ← There are 100 000 cm in 1 km.

b 3.8 × 100 000 = 380 000 cm ← Convert to centimetres first.

380 000 ÷ 50 000 = 7.6 cm ← To find a distance on the map, divide by the scale factor of 50 000.

Practising skills

1 Look at these rectangles.
Find these scales.

   a The width of red rectangle : the width of green rectangle.
   b The width of red rectangle : the width of blue rectangle.
   c The width of green rectangle : the width of blue rectangle.

2 A map has a scale of 1 : 50 000.
The distance between two villages on the map is 7 cm.

   a What is the actual distance between the villages?

Littleton is 10.4 km from Avonford.

   b How far apart are the two towns on the map?

3 Find the scale of these maps in the form 1 : n.

   a A street map where 3 cm represents 600 m.
   b An ordnance survey map where 20 cm represents 500 m.
   c A road map where 7 cm represents 17.5 km.
   d A map of the world where 8 cm represents 800 km.

4 A model train engine is made to a scale of 1 : 50.
The length of the model is 40 cm.

   a What is the length of the actual train engine?

The height of the actual train engine is 4 m.

   b What is the height of the model?

Geometry and Measures Strand 1 Units and scales

5 A town map is drawn to a scale of 1 : 20 000.
Copy and complete this table showing the distance between various places.

Places	Distance on map (cm)	Distance in real life (km)
Library to Sports centre		1.2
School to park	2.5	
Cinema to supermarket	7.5	
Café to cinema		2
Bowling alley to river		1.8

Developing fluency

1 This is the plan of a flat. It is not drawn to scale.
Using the measurements given on the plan, make an accurate scale drawing.
Use the scale 1 cm = 2 m.

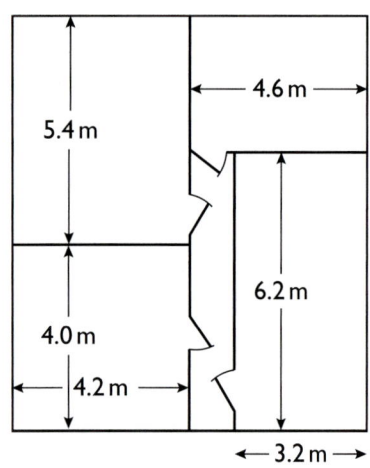

Measurements on the plan: 4.6 m, 5.4 m, 6.2 m, 4.0 m, 4.2 m, 3.2 m

2 Zac is orienteering.
He starts at point A and then walks 6 km East followed by 7 km North-East to reach a lake at point B.

a Make a scale drawing of Zac's journey.

b How far is point B from Zac's starting point?

c What is the bearing from the lake to point A?

d What is the bearing of the lake from point A?

Unit 9 Scale drawing Band f

3) The diagram shows the plan of a garden.
The scale is 1 cm = 2 m.
Copy and complete the table to show the true measurements of the garden.

Item	Plan measurement	True measurement
Length of patio		
Width of patio		
Length of lawn		
Length of vegetable patch		
Width of pond		
Length of pond		
Width of house		
Length of shed		
Width of shed		
Length of path		

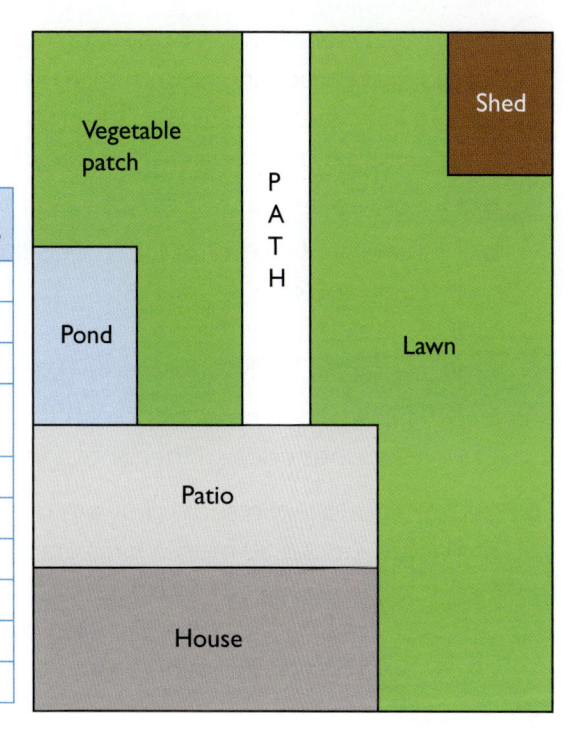

4) A shop sells toy boat sets for 3- to 5-year-olds.
There are different sizes.
The small boat is exactly half the size of the standard boat.
The scale of the small boat : standard boat is 1 : 2.

a The mast in the small set is a cylinder with a height of 20 cm.
   i   What shape is the mast in the standard set?
   ii What is the height of the mast in the standard set?

b This is an accurate drawing of the boat from the small set.

   i   How long is the boat?
   ii   What are the dimensions of the sails?
   iii Make an accurate drawing of the boat from the standard set.

c The shop also sells a super-sized boat.
   It is 20 times bigger than the standard set.
   i   How long is the super-sized boat?
   ii   How tall is it?
   iii Can children climb on it?

Reasoning

293

Geometry and Measures Strand 1 Units and scales

5 Three friends set off on a map-reading activity. They start together at point A and travel for half an hour.
Tom jogs on a bearing of 300° at 10 kilometres per hour.
Molly cycles due West at 20 kilometres per hour.
Evan walks on a bearing of 120° at 6 kilometres per hour.

   a Make a scale drawing to show their travels.

   b At the end of the half hour, what is the distance between
      i Evan and Tom
      ii Tom and Molly
      iii Evan and Molly?

   c The friends then meet at point B. It is 5 km from A on a bearing of 225°.
How far does each of them have to travel?

6 Gemma is making a scale drawing of a swimming pool.
The actual pool is 30 metres long and 15 metres wide.
Gemma has a sheet of A4 paper and needs at least a 1 cm border around her diagram.
Gemma wants to make her drawing as large as possible.
What scale do you think she should use?

7 On a map a forest is shown as a rectangle with an area of 13.6 cm^2. It is 4 cm long.
The scale of the map is 1 : 50 000.

   a i What are the dimensions of the real forest?
      ii What is its area?

   b i What distance on the ground is represented by 1 cm?
      ii What area on the ground is represented by 1 cm^2?

   c Use your answer to check the area you found in part **a ii**.

A lake has a surface area of 0.7 km^2.

   d What is the area of the lake on the map?

Problem solving

1 Here is a sketch of the side view of the roof space of a building.

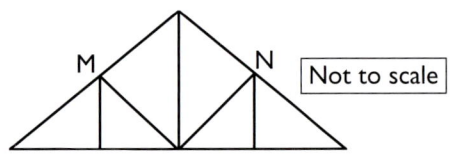

The lines in the sketch show the wooden frame which supports the roof.
The width of the frame is 8 m and the height of the frame is 3 m.
M and N are the midpoints of the sloping sides.
The frame has a single line of symmetry.

   a Make an accurate scale drawing.

   b Find, by measurement, the total length of wood used to make the frame.

2 A hall is 8 m square.
Desks 50 cm square are to be placed in the hall.
The desks are to be at least 1 m apart and at least 1 m from any edge of the hall.
Show how to fit the maximum number of desks in the hall.

3 Hannah wants to make a bird box from wood.
She makes a rough sketch of the front of the bird box.

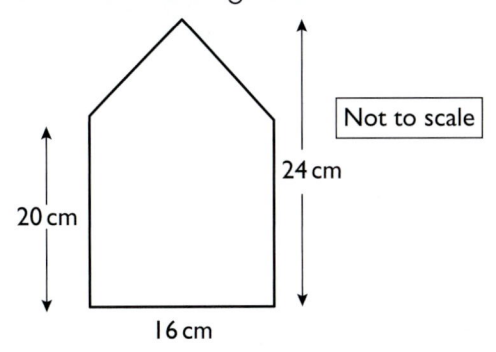

Not to scale
24 cm
20 cm
16 cm

Hannah wants to drill a circular hole of radius 2 cm in the front.
The centre of the hole must be 12 cm from each of the bottom corners.

a Make an accurate scale drawing of the front of the bird box.

b Find, by measurement, the distance of the centre of the circular hole from the top corner.

4 The diagram is a sketch of the gable end of a house.
The end of the house has a vertical line of symmetry.
Building regulations state that the top of the house must be less than 4 m above the level AB.

a Make an accurate scale drawing of the end of the house.

b Find, by measurement, if the top of the house is less than 4 m from the level AB.

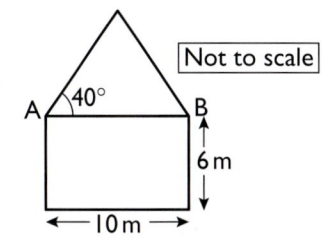

Not to scale
A 40° B
6 m
10 m

5 Rosie sails her boat from port A on a bearing of 070° for 20 miles to a point B.
From B she sails on a bearing of 100° for 15 miles to a point C.

a Make an accurate drawing of Rosie's journey.

b Find, by measurement, the bearing of the course that Rosie must set to get back to port A directly, and how far she has to go.

6 Model trains are made for a 00 gauge track.
The scale is 1:76.
Pete has a model of the Mallard locomotive.
The Mallard is 70 feet long.
Find the length in centimetres of Pete's model.
Use 2.54 cm = 1 inch and 12 inches = 1 foot.

Geometry and Measures Strand 1 Units and scales

Reviewing skills

1 The diagram shows a sketch of a tunnel for a railway. It is a circle of radius 4 m.

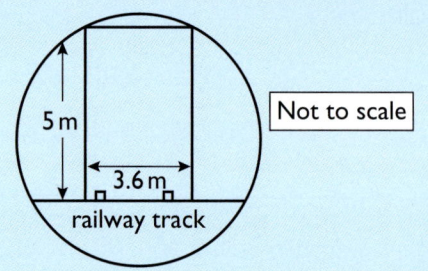

5 m
3.6 m
railway track
Not to scale

The diagram includes a horizontal chord. This shows where the railway track will be laid.
The diagram also includes a rectangle. It shows the space that must be allowed to let trains through.

a Make a scale drawing to show this.

b Find, by measurement, the height of the railway track above the lowest point of the tunnel.

Unit 10 • Compound units • Band g

Outside the Maths classroom

Planning a journey
How do journey planning websites provide an estimated travel time?

Toolbox

A **compound measure** is a measure involving two quantities.
An example is **speed**, which involves distance and time.
$$\text{speed} = \frac{\text{distance}}{\text{time}}$$
The unit of distance might be km and the unit of time might be hours. In this case the compound unit for speed will be kilometres per hour (km/hr or km hr^{-1}).
Other examples are grams per cubic centimetre for density and Newtons per square metre for pressure.

Example – Working with density

A metal block has a volume of 1000 cm^3.
It has a mass of 8.5 kg.
Using the formula
$$\text{density} = \frac{\text{mass}}{\text{volume}}$$
find the density of the block in kilograms per cm^3.

Solution
density = $\frac{\text{mass}}{\text{volume}}$

= 8.5 ÷ 1000

= 0.0085 kilograms per cm^3 ← This unit can also be written as kg cm^{-3} or kg/cm^3.

Geometry and Measures Strand 1 Units and scales

Example – Working with speed

Jason leaves London on a motorbike at 06:00 and travels to his parents' house 432 km away. He arrives at 10:00.

a Find his average speed
   i   in kilometres per hour
   ii in kilometres per minute
   iii in metres per second
b Write the unit 'metres per second' in two other ways.

Solution

a His journey takes from 6 o'clock to 10 o'clock so it lasts 4 hours.

Average speed = $\frac{\text{distance}}{\text{time}}$

i $\frac{\text{distance}}{\text{time}} = \frac{432 \text{ kilometres}}{4 \text{ hours}}$

   = 108 kilometres per hour

ii $\frac{\text{distance}}{\text{time}} = \frac{432 \text{ kilometres}}{240 \text{ minutes}}$ ← 4 hours = 4 × 60 = 240 minutes

   = 1.8 kilometres per minute

iii $\frac{\text{distance}}{\text{time}} = \frac{432\,000 \text{ metres}}{14\,400 \text{ seconds}}$ ← 432 kilometres = 432 × 1000 = 432 000 metres
   ← 4 hours = 4 × 60 × 60 = 14 400 seconds

   = 30 metres per second

b Other ways of writing 'metres per second' include $m\,s^{-1}$ and m/s.

Practising skills

1) Work out the average speed in km/h of each of these.

   a An aeroplane travelling a distance of 900 km in 2 hours.
   b A ferry travelling 8 km in 15 minutes.
   c A car travelling 60 km in $1\frac{1}{2}$ hours.

2) Copy and complete the conversion diagram to convert m/s to km/h.

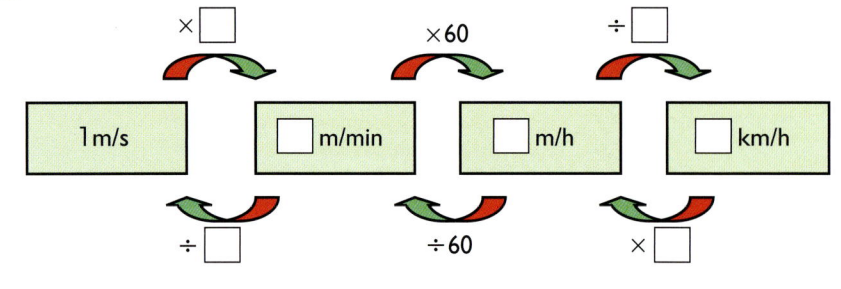

   1 m/s → ×☐ → ☐ m/min → ×60 → ☐ m/h → ÷☐ → ☐ km/h

   (reverse arrows: ÷☐, ÷60, ×☐)

Higher tier only

3 Usain sprints 200 m in 20 seconds.
Work out Usain's average speed in

   a metres per second
   b metres per hour
   c kilometres per hour.

4 a Tom cycles for 3 hours. He travels a distance of 120 km.
Work out his average speed.

   b A tortoise travels for 20 minutes. It travels 40 metres.
   Work out its speed in
      i metres per minute
      ii cm per second.

   c Andrew swims for $1\frac{1}{2}$ hours. He covers 60 lengths, each of 20 metres.
   What is his speed in metres per second?

5 Jamie and Anna have part-time jobs.
In one week, Jamie gets £51 for 6 hours work.
Anna works 9 hours and gets £70.20.
Find their rates of pay.
Who is the better paid?

6 Rhodri records he can cycle 21 km in 1 hour 30 minutes.
Bronwen records she can cycle 16 km in 1 hours 20 minutes.
To calculate the average speeds in km/h this is what Rhodri and Bronwen enter into their calculations.
Rhodri enters 21 ÷ 1.30 into his calculator.
Bronwen enters 16 ÷ 1.20 into her calculator.
They are both incorrect.

   a What is the error Rhodri has made?
   b What calculation should Rhodri be working out?
   c What is the error Bronwen has made?
   d What calculation should Bronwen be working out?

7 Write each of the following in hours. Give your answer using decimals not fractions.

   a 2 hours and 15 minutes
   b 3 hours 45 minutes
   c 5 hours 40 minutes
   d 2 hours 20 minutes

Developing fluency

Remember 5 miles is approximately 8 km.

1 Bob's train departs at 12:38 and arrives at its destination 210 miles away at 14:18.
What is the train's average speed?

2 Jake and Amy go to different garages to fill their cars with petrol.
Jake pays £34.50 for 25 litres.
Amy pays £63.90 for 45 litres.
Who gets the cheaper petrol? Show all of your working.

Geometry and Measures Strand 1 Units and scales

3 Jo's lawn is rectangular.
It is 16 m long and 11.5 m wide.
She wants to feed it with fertiliser.
She buys a 2.5 kg box which covers 500 m².
How many grams should she use?

4 a Harri cycles at 8.5 km/h.
What is his speed in m/s?

b A cheetah can sprint at speeds of up to 30 m/s.
What is this speed in miles per hour?

5 Maya drives her car for 30 minutes at a steady speed of 70 mph.
She then drives for a further 48 miles taking $\frac{3}{4}$ hour.

a Find the total distance she travels.

b Work out Maya's average speed for the whole journey.

6 This conversion graph can be used to change between gallons and litres.

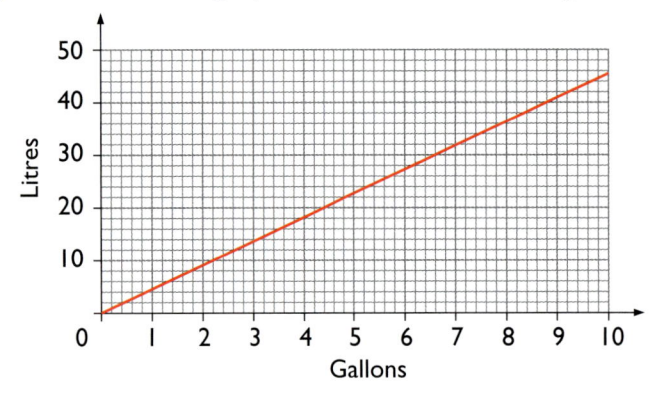

Art has oil-fired central heating.
The tank for the oil holds 280 gallons of oil when full.
Art's tank is only $\frac{1}{4}$ full.
Oil costs 50p per litre.
Work out an estimate for the cost of filling the oil tank.

7 a Find the distance, in km, travelled by a satellite travelling at 8600 metres per second for 1 year.

b What is the speed of the satellite in miles per hour?

8 A company makes metal files for use in engineering and metalwork.
The files have rows of sharp teeth for cleaning surfaces.
A smooth file has 55 teeth per inch. A rough file has 20 teeth per inch.
Both files are 12 cm long.
Work out the difference in the number of teeth on the two files.
You may use 2.5 cm = 1 inch.

Problem solving

1. The speed limit on some main roads in France is 110 kilometres per hour.
   The speed limit on motorways in the UK is 70 miles per hour.
   Which speed limit is higher and by how much?

2. A factory refines precious metal.
   It refines 15 kg of precious metal per hour for 8 hours a day, 5 days a week.
   Work out the amount of precious metal it refines in a year.

3. Hassan drives his car at a constant speed of 60 mph for 1 hour and then for 2 hours at a constant speed of 48 mph.

   a Find the total distance he travels.

   b Work out Hassan's average speed for the whole journey.

Higher tier only

4. Beti has an empty pool.
   She is going to pump water into the pool at the rate of 20 litres per second.
   The pool is in the shape of a cuboid 10 m long by 5 m wide.
   Work out the length of time it will take to fill the pool to a depth of 150 cm.

   $1 m^3 = 1000$ litres

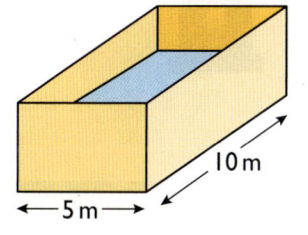

5. A farmer wants to spread fertiliser on a field.
   The field is rectangular and is 600 m long by 90 m wide.

   a Find the area of the field in hectares.   1 hectare = 10000 m^2

   b The farmer puts on the fertiliser at 184 kg per hectare.
      Show that 1000 kg of fertiliser will be enough.

6. A balloon takes off from the ground.
   It ascends at a steady speed of 6.5 metres per second for 10 minutes.
   It then descends at 8.4 metres per second for 6 minutes.
   It then ascends at 6.5 metres per second for a further 3 minutes.
   Work out how far the balloon is now above the ground.

Reviewing skills

1. Wyn drives 130 km in 2 hours.
   Find his average speed in
   a km/h   b m/s.

2. Mel works a 40-hour week and earns £316 per week.
   Toby earns £287 for a 35-hour week.
   Who has the better hourly rate, and by how much?

3. Indicate the correct answer **a**, **b**, **c** or **d**.
   The average speed of a journey of 36.3 miles, which takes 3 hours.
   a 12.1 km/h   b 12.1 mph   c 108.9 mph   d 108.9 km/h

Unit 11 • Dimensions of formulae • Band g

Outside the Maths classroom

Making a clock
How can acceleration and length be useful in the timing of a pendulum?

Toolbox

You can check for errors in formulae by considering the **dimensions** of the variables within it.

Length is a measurement in **one dimension**.

Area is a measurement in **two dimensions**. It is found by measuring two lengths together.

$6\,cm \times 5\,cm = 30\,cm^2$

Volume is a measurement in **three dimensions**. It is found by measuring three lengths together.

$3\,cm \times 5\,cm \times 4\,cm = 60\,cm^3$

In a formula that represents a length, all the terms must represent lengths because when lengths are added or subtracted, the answer is another length.

$8\,cm - 2\,cm = 6\,cm$

These formulae have **dimension 1**.

In a formula that represents an area, all the terms must represent areas because when areas are added or subtracted, the answer is another area.

$8\,cm^2 + 2\,cm^2 = 10\,cm^2$

These formulae have **dimension 2**.

In a formula that represents a volume, all the terms must represent volumes because when volumes are added or subtracted, the answer is another volume.

$8\,cm^3 + 7\,cm^3 = 15\,cm^3$

These formulae have **dimension 3**. If p, q and r are all lengths, the expressions:

$3p + q$, $\frac{1}{2}q$, $\frac{pq}{r}$, $p + q + \frac{\pi r^2}{p}$ and $p + 4$ could all represent lengths

$p^2 + 2pq$, $\frac{4p^2q}{r}$, and $\frac{1}{3}p^2 + \pi rq + 2$ could all represent areas

$p^3 + 2pq^2$, $\frac{3p^2q^2}{r}$ and $\frac{1}{2}p^2q + \pi r^2 + 3$ could all represent volumes.

Unit 11 Dimensions of formulae Band g

Example – Length, area or volume?

p, q and r are lengths. By considering dimensions, say whether each of the following represent a length, an area, a volume, or none of these.

a pq
b pr^2
c $pq + r^2$
d $\dfrac{3r + 5q}{2}$
e $pq + 7r$
f $2\pi r$

Solution

a pq = length × length = AREA (Dimension 2)
b pr^2 = length × length² = VOLUME (Dimension 3)
c $pq + r^2$ = (length × length) + (length × length) = area + area = AREA (Dimension 2)
d $\dfrac{3r + 5q}{2} = \dfrac{3 \times \text{length} + 5 \times \text{length}}{2} = \dfrac{\text{length} + \text{length}}{2} = \dfrac{\text{length}}{2}$ = LENGTH (Dimension 1)
e $pq + 7r$ = (length × length) + (7 × length) = area + length. This expression has mixed dimensions so cannot represent a measurement.
f $2\pi r = 2\pi \times$ length = LENGTH (Dimension 1)

Practising skills

1) p, q and r represent lengths.
For each expression below, state whether it represents a length, an area or a volume.

a $p + q$
b pqr
c $pr + qr$
d $2qr$
e $4\pi p^3$
f $\dfrac{1}{3} p \left(q^2 + \dfrac{r^2}{4} \right)$

2) p, q and r represent lengths. Which of these could represent an area?

a $pq + q^2 + p$
b $pq + 3q^2 + p^2$
c $p(q + p)$
d $\dfrac{p^2 q}{p + q}$

3) a and b are lengths. Which of these have dimension 1?

a ab
b $a + b$
c $\dfrac{3a}{b}$
d $\dfrac{a^2}{b}$

4) a and b are lengths. Which of these could represent a length?

a $3a$
b $3a + b$
c $3a + 4b$
d $3a^2 + 4b$

5) a, b and c are lengths. Which of these have dimension 3?

a $ab + c$
b abc
c $ab^2 + ac^2$
d $ab^2 + 3ab$

6) a, b and c are lengths. Which of these have dimension 2?

a $5b^2 - 4$
b $5b^2 - 4a$
c $5b^2 - 4b$
d $5b^2 - 4a^2$

7) a and b are lengths. Which of these could represent a volume?

a a^3
b $a^3 + 4$
c $a^3 + a$
d $a^2(b + a)$

Geometry and Measures Strand 1 Units and scales

Developing fluency

1. A cylinder of radius r and height h sits on a cuboid with dimensions $h \times 2r \times 2r$.

   Which of these might give:

   a the volume

   b the surface area of the shape?

2. Explain why $2\pi\left(\dfrac{p}{3} + \sqrt{qr}\right)$ is a length.

3. Ismail needs to work out the area of his field so he can work out how many seeds he needs to buy. p, q and r are lengths. Which of these expressions might give Ismail the area of the field?

   a $pq + pr + qr$ b $pq + \pi r$ c $2p + rq$ d pqr

4. p, q and r are lengths. What is the dimension of each of these expressions?

   a $\dfrac{pqr}{\sqrt{pq}}$ b $\dfrac{pqr}{\sqrt{p^2qr}}$ c $\dfrac{r\sqrt{pq}}{\sqrt{qr}}$ d $\sqrt{p^2 + q^2}$

5. Tom is designing some new chess pieces that he is moulding out of clay.

   a This is the shape of a bishop.

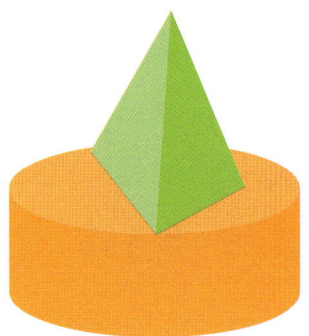

   One of these expressions tells Tom how much clay he will use for each bishop. Which one could it be? Explain how you know.

   i $r^2h\left(\dfrac{1}{10} + \pi\right)$ ii $\dfrac{1}{3}r^2h + \pi r^2$ iii $4r^2 + h^2$ iv $r^2(h + \pi)$

b Here is his castle.

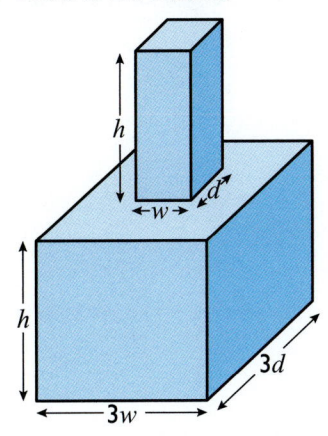

Tom says the volume of clay he will use for this shape is $9wdh + wd + h$.
  i How do you know this is wrong?
  ii What should the expression be?

Problem solving

1 Karen says the surface area of this half cylinder is given by the formula $r(\pi r + 2rh + \pi h)$, where r is the radius and h is the height.
Explain how you know Karen is wrong.

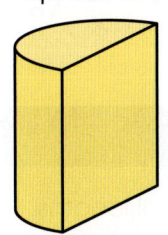

2 This shape is made of a hemisphere and a cone.

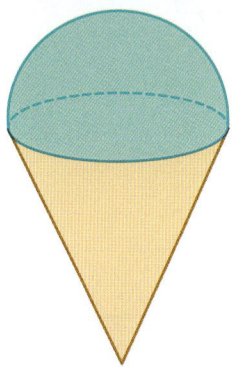

The radius of the hemisphere is r and the overall height is h.

  a Which of these could be an expression for the volume of this shape?

  i $\dfrac{\pi r}{3}(hr + r)$
  ii $\dfrac{\pi r^2}{3}(h^2 + r^2)$
  iii $\dfrac{\pi r^2}{3}(h + r)$

  b Which of these could be an expression for the surface are of this shape?

  i $\pi r\left(2r + \sqrt{h^2 - 2hr + 2r^2}\right)$
  ii $\pi r(2r + h - 2hr)$
  iii $\dfrac{\pi r^2}{3}(h + r)$

Geometry and Measures Strand 1 Units and scales

3 A tube has an outside diameter of R and an inside diameter of r. The height of the tube is h.

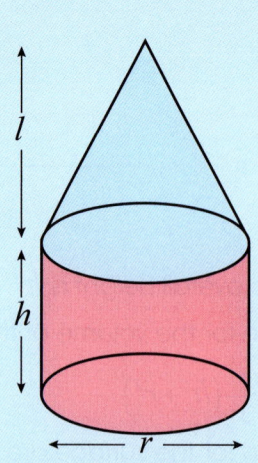

  a Which of these **cannot** be an expression for the surface area of the tube?

  i $2\pi(R+r)(R+h-r)$

  ii $4\pi R - 4\pi r + 2\pi Rh + 2\pi rh$

  iii $2\pi R^2 - 2\pi r^2 + 2\pi Rh + 2\pi rh$

  b Show that the other two expressions are equivalent.

4 g, h and k are lengths.

  a Which of these cannot be an area?

  i $g^2 + h^2 + gk$ 　　 **ii** $\dfrac{g^2h + 3g^3}{k}$ 　　 **iii** $\dfrac{gh + 3gk}{g - k}$ 　　 **iv** $\left(\dfrac{hk}{g}\right)\sqrt{g^2 + hk}$

  b Explain your reasoning.

Reviewing skills

1 State the dimension of each of these expressions, where a, b, c, d and e are all lengths.

  a $abc + cde$ 　　 **b** $\sqrt{ab}$ 　　 **c** $\dfrac{abcd}{e^2}$

  d $ab + c$ 　　 **e** $3a + 2\pi r$ 　　 **f** $3\pi + 2b$

2 Which of these could be an expression for this shape's surface area?

  a $2\pi rh + \dfrac{4}{3}\pi rl + \pi r^2$

  b $\pi r(h + l + r)$

  c $2\pi r(2h + r)$

  d $\pi\left(r^2 + \dfrac{1}{3}h + \dfrac{4}{3}l\right)$

Unit 12 • Working with compound units • Band g

Outside the Maths classroom

Making boats
Why does a stone sink but a piece of wood float?

Toolbox

Common compound measures are:

Measure	Description	Common units
Speed	Distance travelled in 1 unit of time	m/s, km/h
Acceleration	Change in speed over 1 unit of time	m/s^2, km/h^2
Density	Mass of 1 unit of volume	g/cm^3, kg/m^3
Unit price	The price of an item for one unit of weight, area or volume	pence/gram, £/kg, pence/litre, £/gallon, £/m^2
Population density	Number of people in 1 unit of area	people/km^2

The units tell you the calculation to perform to calculate the compound measure.

For example, speed in m/s is calculated as:

$$\text{metres (distance)} \div \text{seconds (time)}.$$

So, to convert from one compound unit to another, e.g. convert $6.7\,g/cm^3$ into kg/m^3:

$6.7\,g = 0.0067\,kg$ ⬅ $1\,kg = 1000\,g$

$1\,cm^3 = 0.000001\,m^3$ ⬅ $1\,cm^3$ is $0.01\,m$ by $0.01\,m$ by $0.01\,m$

$$\text{Density} = \frac{6.7\,g}{1\,cm^3} = \frac{0.0067\,kg}{0.000001\,m^3} = 6700\,kg/m^3$$

Geometry and Measures Strand 1 Units and scales

Speed and acceleration are also known as **rates of change.** They can often be found from the gradient of a graph.

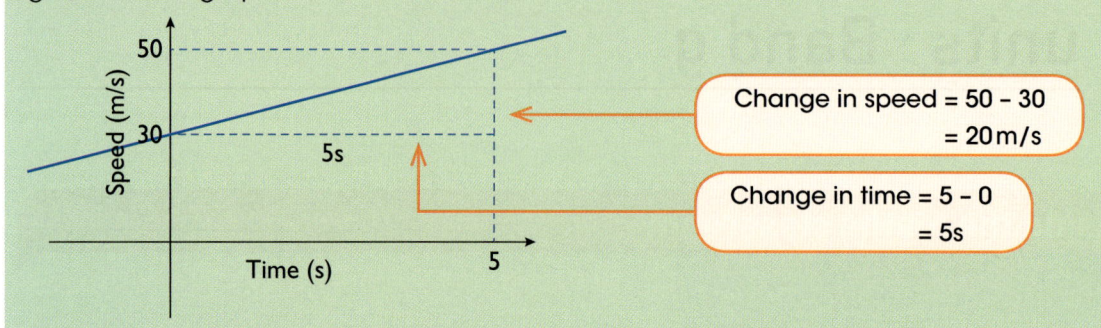

[Graph: Speed (m/s) vs Time (s), line rising from 30 at t=0 to 50 at t=5]

Change in speed = 50 − 30
= 20 m/s

Change in time = 5 − 0
= 5s

Acceleration is the gradient of a graph of speed against time.

Acceleration = $\left(\dfrac{20}{5}\right)$ = 4 m/s^2

Example – Electricity bills

Totals from SuLin's last four electricity bills are given below.
A 1070 kWh   Total cost £145.00
B 850 kWh   Total cost £119.30
C 600 kWh   Total cost £90.09
D 750 kWh   Total cost £107.61

SuLin wants to find out how much she pays per kWh.
Use a graph to find this information.

Solution

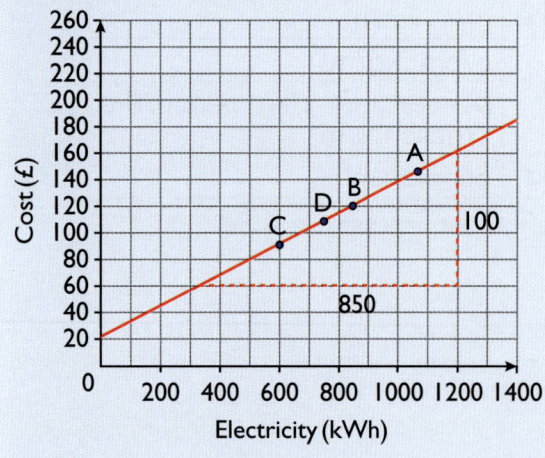

[Graph: Cost (£) vs Electricity (kWh), with points A, B, C, D plotted and a line through them; triangle showing rise 100 over run 850]

Cost per kWh = $\dfrac{100\,(£)}{850\,(\text{kWh})}$

= £0.12 per kWh

= 12p per kWh

Unit 12 Working with compound units Band g

Example – Problems involving density

A brass block has a mass of 187 g and a volume of 22 cm³.
a Calculate the density of brass in g/cm³.
A brass cylinder has a mass of 53 g.
b Calculate the volume of the cylinder.

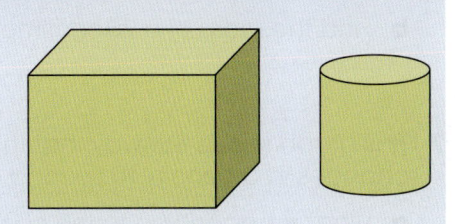

Solution

a Density = mass ÷ volume
= 187 ÷ 22
= 8.5 g/cm³

b Density = $\dfrac{\text{mass}}{\text{volume}}$

$8.5 = \dfrac{53}{v}$

$8.5v = 53$ ← Multiply both sides by v.

$v = \dfrac{53}{8.5} = 6.2$ ← Divide both sides by 8.5.

So the volume is 6.2 cm³.

Practising skills

1) Which is better value?
   a 1.5 litres of lemonade for 65p or 1 litre for 44p?
   b 15 pencils for 99p or 12 for 75p?
   c 3 kg of grass seed for £4.20 or 85 g for 96p?
   d 650 g of dog food for £2.15, 1.5 kg for £4.65 or 5 kg for £18?

2) Lucy swims 500 m in 2 minutes and 20 seconds.
   Calculate her speed in
   a metres per second
   b kilometres per hour.

3) A block of metal has a mass of 475 g and a volume of 225 cm³.
   Calculate the density in
   a g/cm³
   b kg/m³.

4) A cube has sides of 16.4 cm.
   Its mass is 1.2 kg.
   Calculate its density in g/cm³.

5) Dave runs n metres in t seconds. Write his speed in
   a m/s
   b km/h.

Geometry and Measures Strand 1 Units and scales

6 The mass of this block of silver is 1260 g.

   a Calculate the density of silver in g/cm^3.

   b Find the mass of a 20 centimetre cube of silver in kilograms.

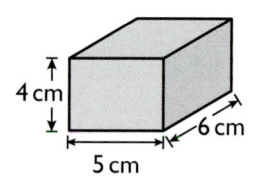

7 This graph shows the way that the speed of one car changes in a certain 10 second period.

   a What is happening to the car between 5 and 7 seconds into its journey?

   b What is the rate of change of speed during the first 5 seconds?

   c What term describes the rate of change of speed?

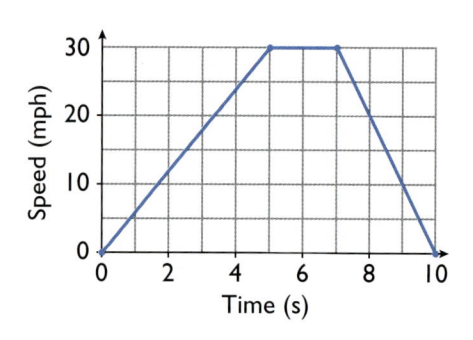

Developing fluency

1 Sioned is driving from the south of France to Paris.
She sees a road sign.
She knows that it takes her 1 hour to travel 60 miles.
The time now is 10 pm.
Sioned wants to get to Paris by 2.30 am.
Will she be able to get to Paris by 2.30 am?

Paris
450 km

2 Alex buys a 150 g bar of chocolate for £1.75 in the UK.
He knows that a $\frac{1}{2}$ pound bar will cost the equivalent of £2.75 in the USA.
Where is it better value, in the UK or in the USA?

3 Salima knows that the fuel tank on her car has a capacity of 9 gallons.
When she was in France she filled up the tank from half full at a cost of €30.
£1 = €1.25
Work out the cost in pounds of a litre of fuel in France.

4 Match the following descriptions with the graphs.

   a An object travels at a constant speed of 15 metres per second for five seconds.

   b An object travels 15 metres in five seconds without accelerating.

   c An object accelerates at a constant rate and reaches a speed of 15 metres per second in five seconds.

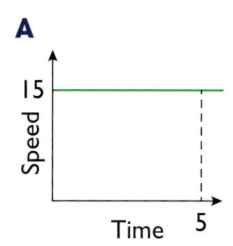

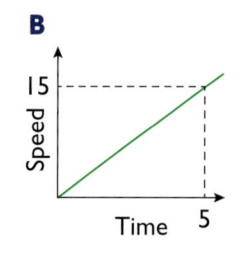

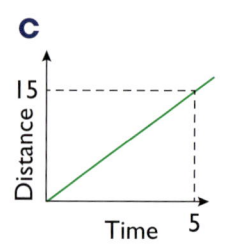

Unit 12 Working with compound units Band g

5 Andy says that these two graphs are for the same car at the same time.
Is Andy correct?
Explain how you know.

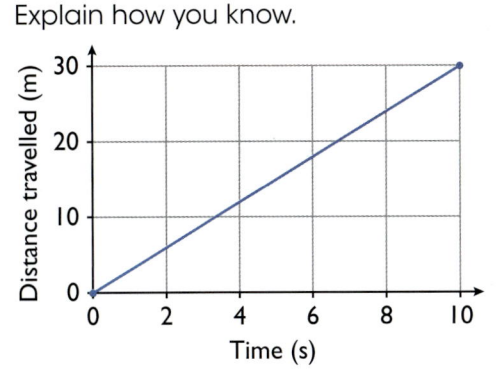

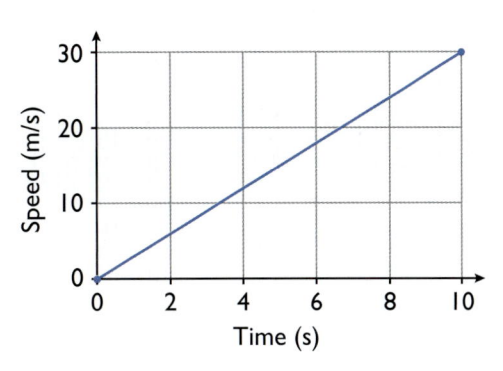

6 A £1 coin has a mass of 9.5 g.
Its diameter is 22.5 mm and its thickness is 3.15 mm.
Calculate the density of a £1 coin in g/cm^3.

7 a A block of metal A weighs 486 g and has a volume of 180 cm^3.
A block of metal B weighs 26 700 kg and has a volume of 3 m^3.
Use the formula density $= \dfrac{\text{mass}}{\text{volume}}$ to calculate the density of each block.

b Ben has a block of metal A and a block of metal B.
Both blocks are identical sizes.
Which block is heavier?

8 The pressure exerted by an elephant's foot is f N/m^2 (newtons per square metre).
Write this in newtons per square centimetre.

9 A concrete block has a volume of v cm^3 and a mass of m g.
Write the density in kg/m^3.

10 Show that V metres per second is about the same speed as $2.25V$ miles per hour.

11 which of these two countries has the greater population density? Show your working.
  i A country with a population of 2 300 000 with a land area of 4500 km².
  ii A country with a population of 48 million and a land area of 92 000 km².

Problem solving

1 A car is travelling at 50 kilometres per hour.
  a Work out how long it will take the car to travel 24 metres.

A bridge is 24 metres long.
  b When you calculate the time a car takes to cross the bridge that is 24 metres long, why could your answer be different from your answer to part **a**?

Geometry and Measures Strand 1 Units and scales

2 Bob is following a fitness programme. He wears a device that monitors his calorie burn.
The graph shows some information about his calorie burn during a period of 15 minutes.

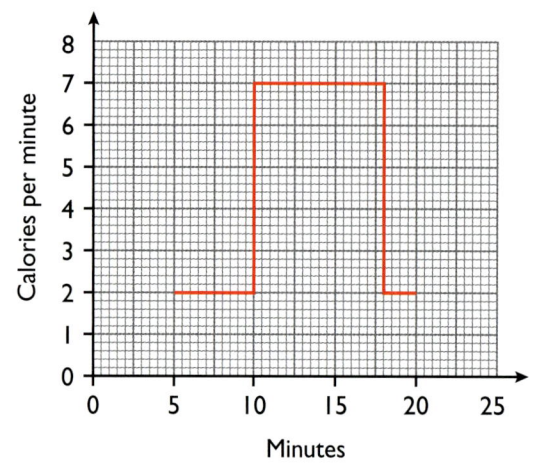

a Work out the number of calories Bob burned over the first 5 minutes of the 15-minute period.

b Work out the average rate at which he burned calories over the 15 minutes.

Bob found that his average rate of calorie burn was 2.5 calories per minute when he was awake and 1.5 calories per minute when he was asleep.

c Work out the total number of calories Bob burned during a 24-hour period when he spent 8 hours asleep.

3 The diagram shows two bottles of the same make of shampoo.

1.8 litres
£4

2.5 litres
£5.80

Which bottle gives the better value for money?
You must show your working to support your choice.

4 The density of wood is 0.9 g/cm.

a Work out the density of the wood in kg/m^3.

x litres of oil have a mass of y grams.

b Work out an expression for the density of the oil in kg/m^3.

5 Luc uses a water meter in his house.
The cost of the water he uses during one year is the sum of the meter charge + the charge for the water used.
The meter charge is £41.
The charge for the water used is £2.10 per 1000 litres.
On average Luc uses 170 litres of water per day.
Work out the cost of the water Luc uses in one year.

Unit 12 Working with compound units Band g

6 The BMI of a person is calculated using the rule
BMI = mass in kg ÷ (height in m)^2
Ideal BMIs lie between 18 and 25.
Wyn weighs 154 pounds and has a height of 183 cm.
Does Wyn have an ideal BMI? Give a reason for your answer.

7 Brass alloy is made by melting together copper and zinc in the ratio 3:2 by mass.
The density of copper is 8.94 g/cm^3.
The density of zinc is 6.57 g/cm^3

  a Find the mass of copper and the mass of zinc in 100 grams of the alloy.

  b Work out the density of brass alloy.

8 A company sells gold bars in the shape of cuboids.
The measurements of a bar are 80 mm by 40 mm by 16 mm.
The density of gold is 19.32 g/cm^3.
Midas thinks that the mass of the block is over 1 kilogram.
Is he correct? Explain your answer.

9 Here is a graph that shows the costs of hiring a cement mixer and a concrete leveller.

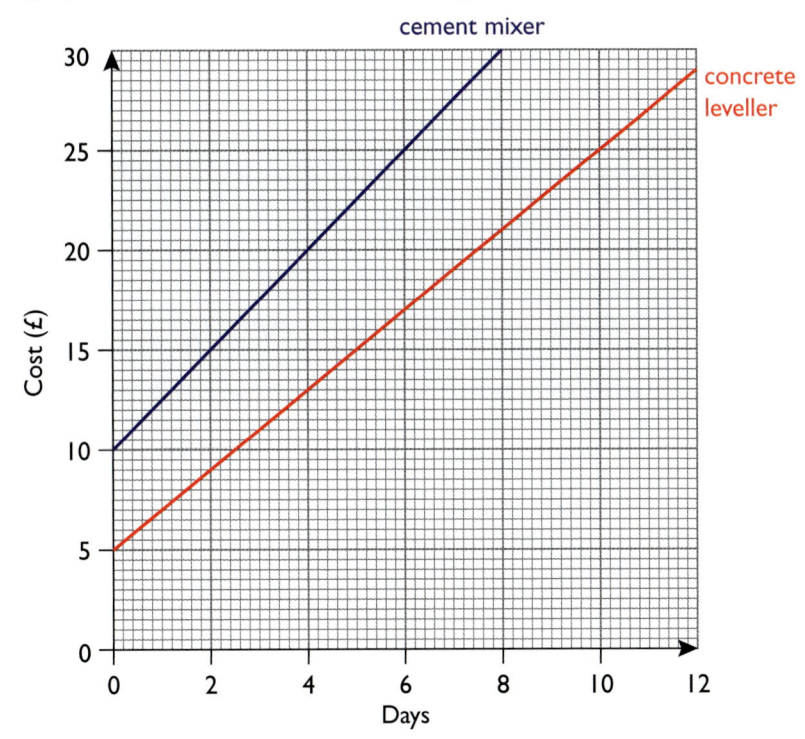

  a Find the difference in the daily rate of hiring each item of equipment.

  b Find the equations of the two graphs.

Geometry and Measures Strand 1 Units and scales

Reviewing skills

1. Morgan is driving in France.
   At 10 a.m. he sees a road sign which says Calais 308 km.
   Morgan knows that he can drive at a maximum speed of 55 miles per hour.
   Work out the earliest time Morgan can get to Calais.

2. A 275 cm^3 block of expanded polystyrene has a mass of 15 g.
   What is the density of expanded polystyrene in kg/m^3?

3. Osian's water is unmetered. His water company provides the graph below so residents can work out how much they will be charged. The chargeable value of Osian's house is £140.

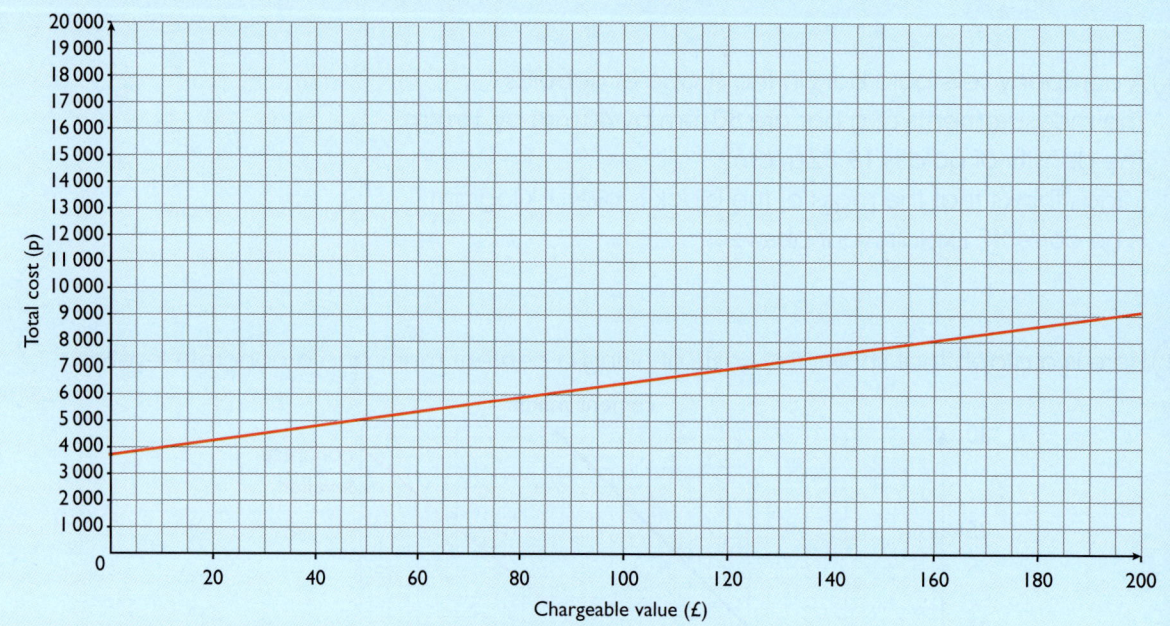

   a How much will Osian be charged? Give your answer in £.
   b How much does the water company charge per £ of chargeable value?

Geometry and Measures
Strand 2 Properties of shapes

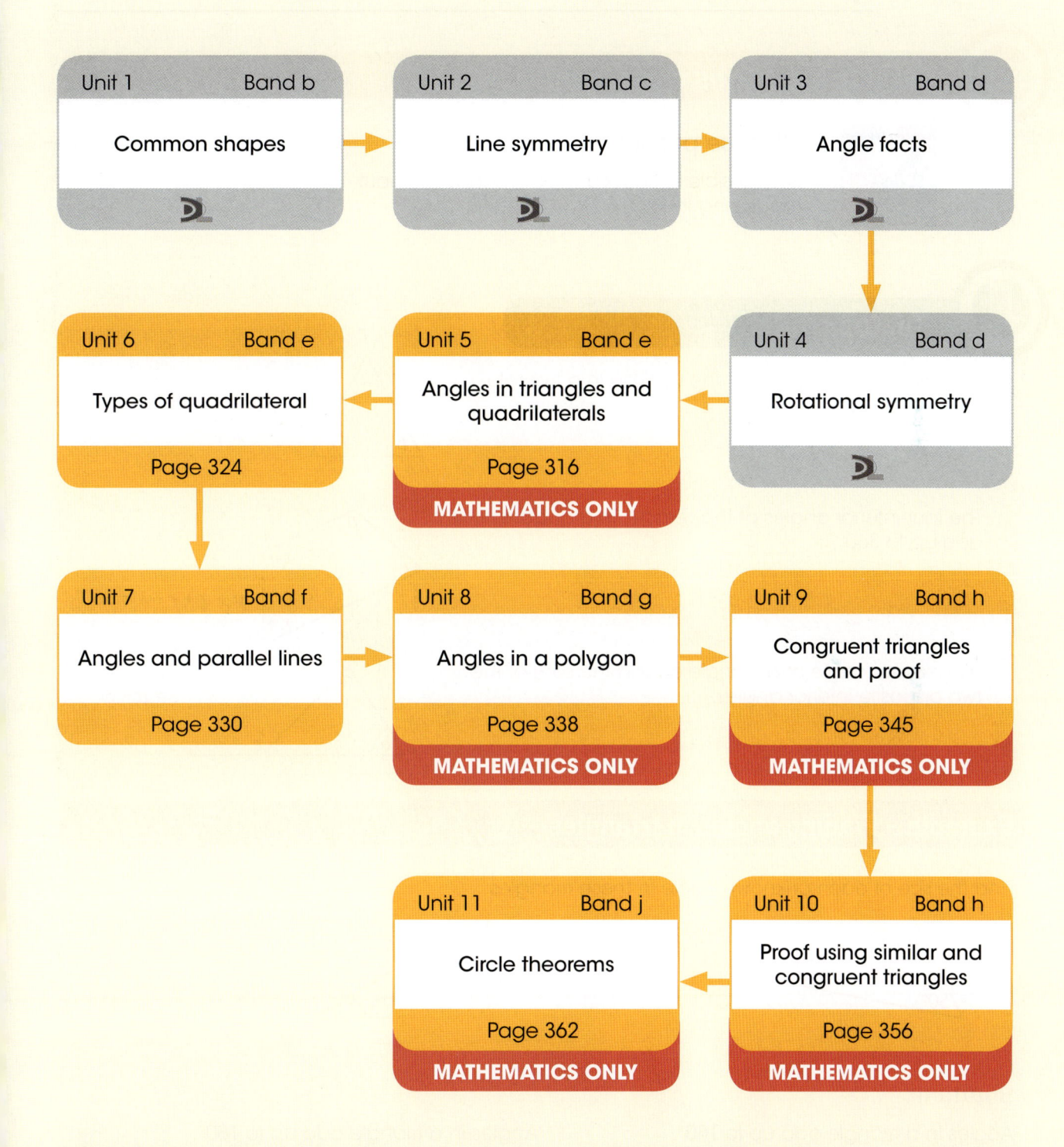

Unit 1 — Band b — Common shapes

Unit 2 — Band c — Line symmetry

Unit 3 — Band d — Angle facts

Unit 4 — Band d — Rotational symmetry

Unit 5 — Band e — Angles in triangles and quadrilaterals — Page 316 — MATHEMATICS ONLY

Unit 6 — Band e — Types of quadrilateral — Page 324

Unit 7 — Band f — Angles and parallel lines — Page 330

Unit 8 — Band g — Angles in a polygon — Page 338 — MATHEMATICS ONLY

Unit 9 — Band h — Congruent triangles and proof — Page 345 — MATHEMATICS ONLY

Unit 10 — Band h — Proof using similar and congruent triangles — Page 356 — MATHEMATICS ONLY

Unit 11 — Band j — Circle theorems — Page 362 — MATHEMATICS ONLY

Units 1–4 are assumed knowledge for this book. Knowledge and skills from these units are used throughout the book.

Unit 5 • Angles in triangles and quadrilaterals • Band e

Outside the Maths classroom

Chinese puzzles
Is it possible to know angles in shapes without measuring them?

Toolbox

- The three interior angles at the vertices in a triangle add up to 180°.

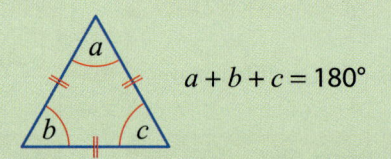

  $a + b + c = 180°$

- The four interior angles at the vertices in a quadrilateral add up to 360°.

  $p + q + r + s = 360°$

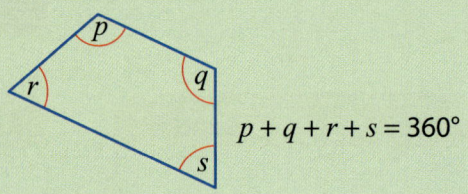

- The exterior angle of a triangle equals the sum of the two opposite interior angles.

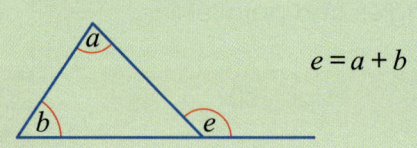

  $e = a + b$

Example – Finding angles in triangles

Find the size of each unknown angle in these triangles.

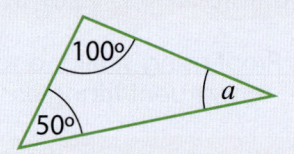

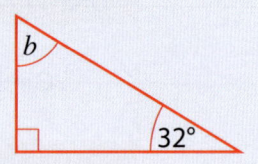

Solution

Angles in a triangle add up to 180°.

$a + 50 + 100 = 180$
$a + 150 = 180$
$a = 180 - 150$
$a = 30°$

Angles in a triangle add up to 180°.

$b + 90 + 32 = 180$
$b + 122 = 180$
$b = 180 - 122$
$b = 58°$

Unit 5 Angles in triangles and quadrilaterals Band e

Example – Finding angles in triangles

Find the size of each unknown angle in these quadrilaterals.

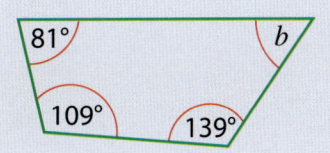

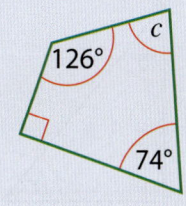

Solution

Angles in a quadrilateral add up to 360°.

$b + 81 + 109 + 139 = 360$
$b + 329 = 360$
$b = 360 - 329$
$b = 31°$

Angles in a quadrilateral add up to 360°.

$c + 74 + 90 + 126 = 360$
$c + 290 = 360$
$c = 360 - 290$
$c = 70°$

Example – Finding unknown angles

Find the size of each unknown angle in these diagrams.

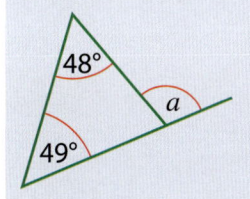

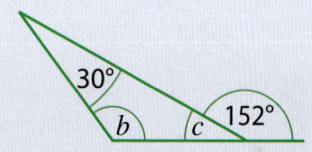

Solution

The exterior angle of a triangle equals the sum of the two opposite interior angles.

$a = 48 + 49$
$a = 97°$

The exterior angle of a triangle equals the sum of the two opposite interior angles.

$b + 30 = 152$
$b = 152 - 30$
$b = 122°$

Angles on a straight line add up to 180°.

$c + 152 = 180$
$c = 180 - 152$
$c = 28°$

Geometry and Measures Strand 2 Properties of shapes

Practising skills

(1) Find the size of each lettered angle in these diagrams.

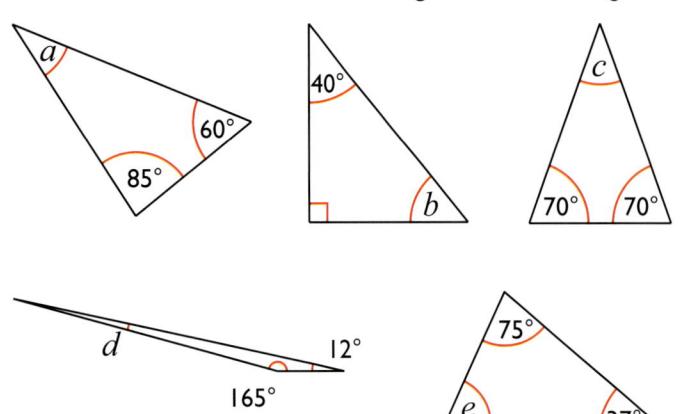

[Triangle with angles a, 60°, 85°]
[Triangle with angles 40°, b, right angle]
[Triangle with angles c, 70°, 70°]
[Thin triangle with angles d, 12°, 165°]
[Triangle with angles 75°, e, 37°]

(2) Find the size of each lettered angle in these diagrams.

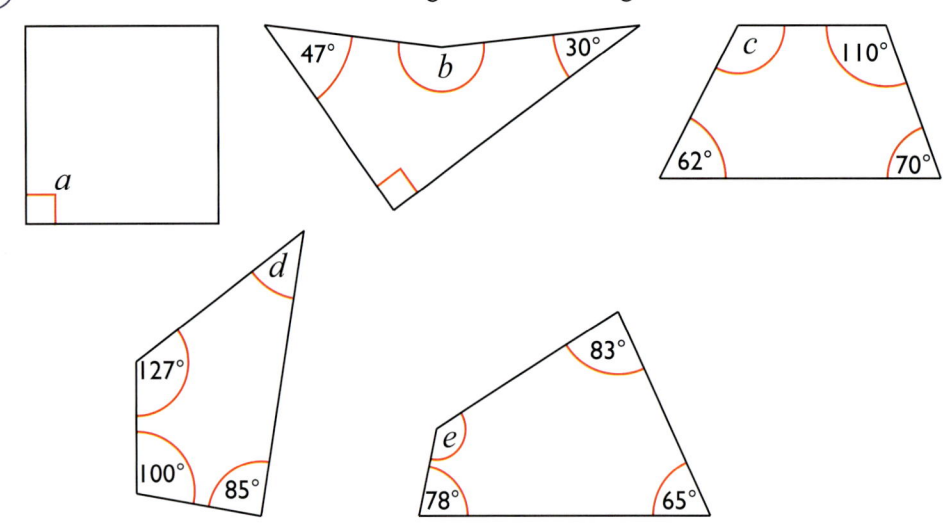

[Square with angle a]
[Quadrilateral with angles 47°, b, 30°, right angle]
[Trapezium with angles c, 110°, 62°, 70°]
[Quadrilateral with angles d, 127°, 100°, 85°]
[Pentagon with angles 83°, e, 78°, 65°]

(3) Find the size of each lettered angle in these diagrams.

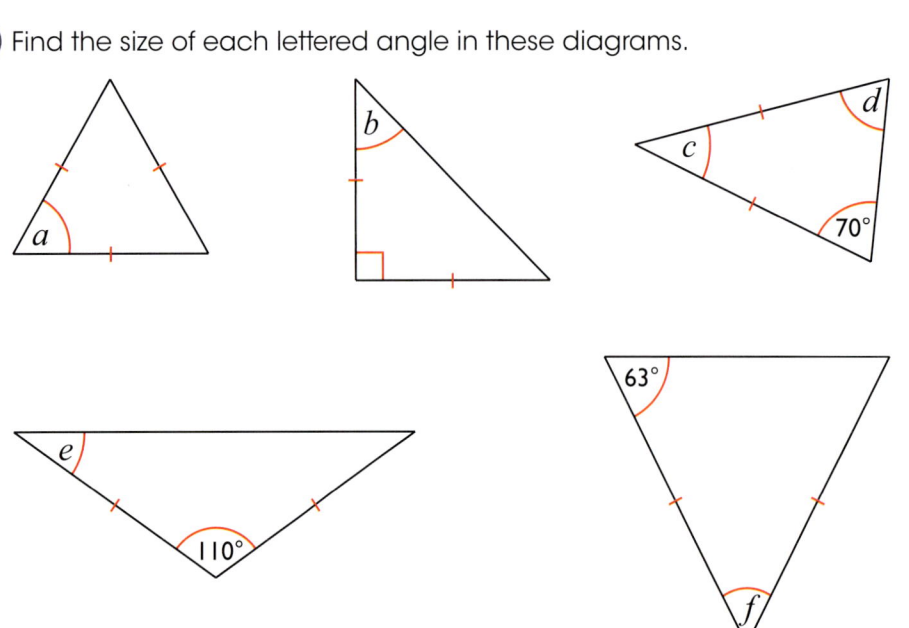

[Equilateral triangle with angle a]
[Right-angled isosceles triangle with angle b]
[Isosceles triangle with angles c, d, 70°]
[Isosceles triangle with angles e, 110°]
[Isosceles triangle with angles 63°, f]

Unit 5 Angles in triangles and quadrilaterals Band e

4 Find the size of each lettered angle in these diagrams.

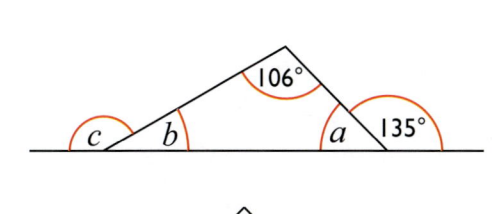

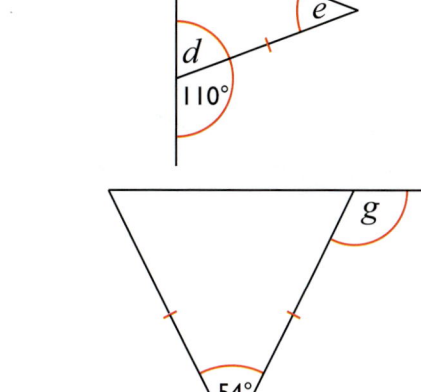

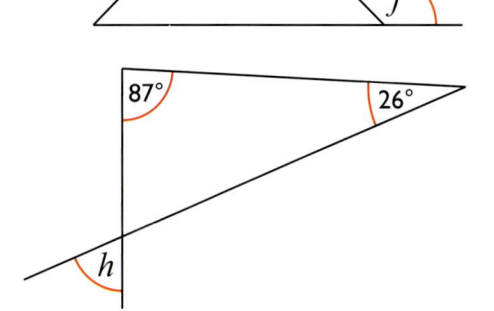

5 Find the size of each lettered angle in these diagrams.

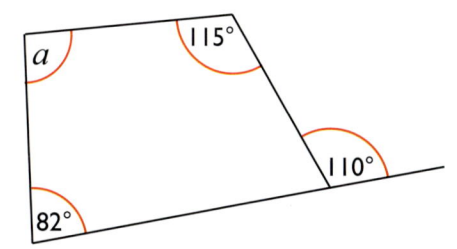

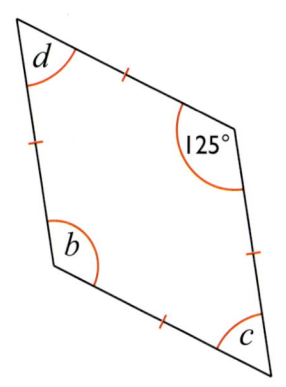

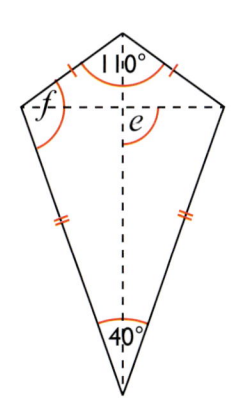

Geometry and Measures Strand 2 Properties of shapes

Developing fluency

1) Find the size of each lettered angle in these diagrams.

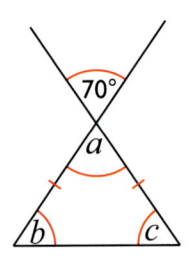

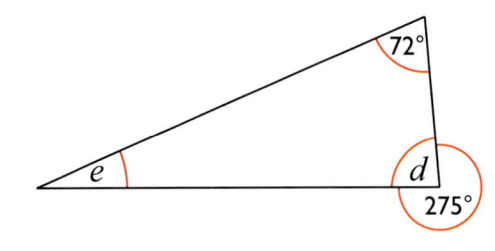

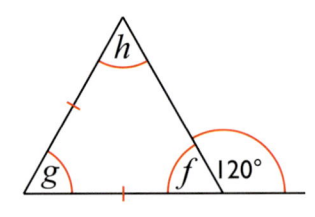

[Diagram 1: Two lines crossing at top with 70° angle, forming isosceles triangle below with angle a at apex, and base angles b and c (tick marks on the two equal sides)]

[Diagram 2: A triangle with exterior angle 72° at top right, angle e at left, angle d at right with reflex 275° marked]

[Diagram 3: Isosceles triangle with apex angle h, base angles g and f, with exterior angle 120° next to f]

2) Calculate the size of the angle at the apex of the tent.

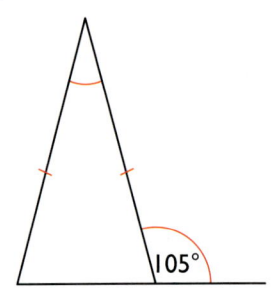

[Diagram: Isosceles triangle (tent) with base angle 105° shown as exterior angle]

3) Look at this diagram.
Angle d is an exterior angle of the triangle.

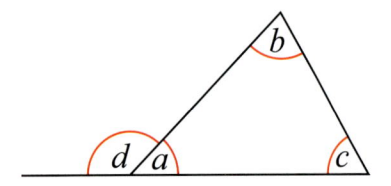

[Diagram: Triangle with interior angles a, b, c and exterior angle d adjacent to a]

Angles b and c are interior angles because they are inside the triangle.
Angles b and c are opposite angle d.
So angles b and c are called interior opposite angles.
Copy and complete these statements.
Angles $a + d =$ _____ because _____
Angles $a + b + c =$ _____ because _____
So angles ___ + ___ = angles ___ + ___ + ___ because _____
So angle $d =$ angles ___ + ___
So the exterior angle of a triangle equals the sum of _____

4) Find the size of each lettered angle in these diagrams.

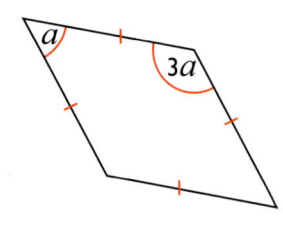

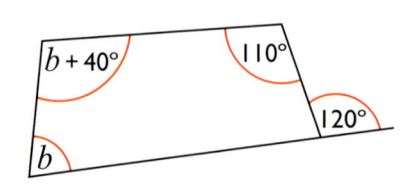

[Diagram 1: Rhombus with angles a and $3a$ shown]

[Diagram 2: Quadrilateral with angles $b + 40°$, $110°$, $120°$, and b]

320

Unit 5 Angles in triangles and quadrilaterals Band e

5 A quadrilateral has interior angles of $x°$, $2x°$, $42°$ and $94°$.
Calculate the size of the angles $x°$ and $2x°$.

6 In a quadrilateral, the smallest angle is acute. Each of the other angles is $20°$ more than the smallest angle.
Find the size of each of the three equal angles.

Problem solving

1 For safety, the angle this ladder makes with the horizontal ground must be between $65°$ and $75°$.
Ben puts up the ladder so that the acute angle between the vertical wall and the ladder is $12°$.

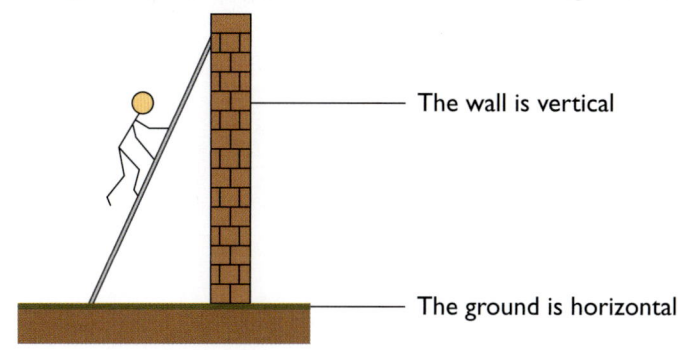

— The wall is vertical

— The ground is horizontal

a Is the ladder safe?

b What is the largest acute angle that the ladder can make with the wall?

2 Look at the angles in this girder bridge.

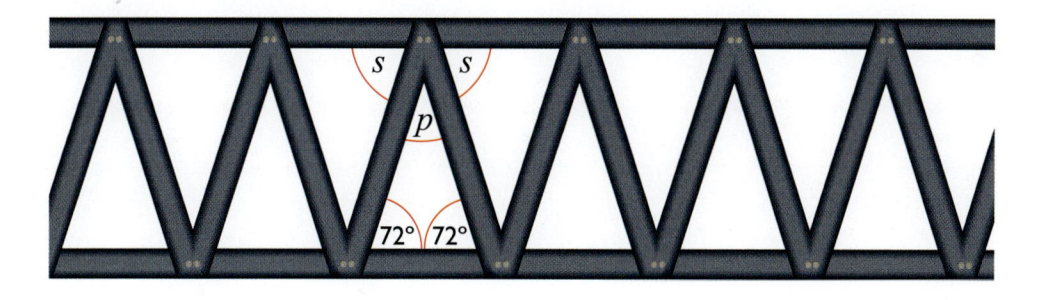

a Calculate the size of angle p.

b Calculate the size of angle s.

3 This quadrilateral is split into two triangles.

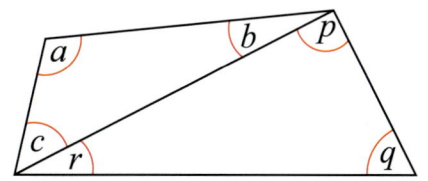

Use the diagram to help you explain why the sum of the interior angles of the quadrilateral is $360°$.

321

Geometry and Measures Strand 2 Properties of shapes

4) For each statement decide whether it is always true, sometimes true or never true.
   a A triangle can have three exterior acute angles.
   b A triangle can have two exterior acute angles.
   c A triangle can have one exterior acute angle.
   d A triangle can have no exterior acute angles.
   Explain your answers.
   If you think *always*, explain how you can be so certain.
   If you think *never*, explain how you can be so certain.
   If you think *sometimes*, explain when it is and when it isn't true.

5) A kite has two interior angles of 135°. Of the other two interior angles, one is double the other. Calculate the size of the other two interior angles.

6) The diagram shows two identical triangles.

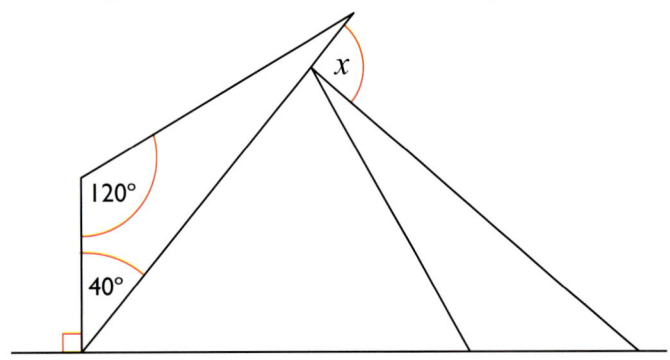

Work out the size of angle x.

Reviewing skills

1 Find the size of each lettered angle in these diagrams.

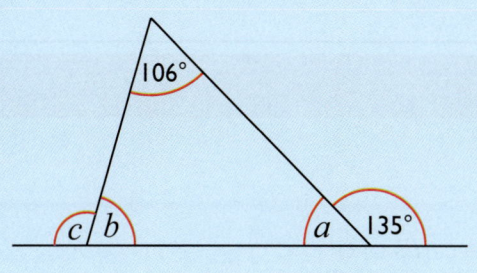

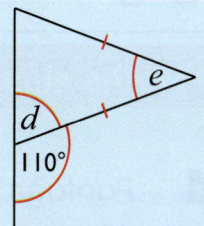

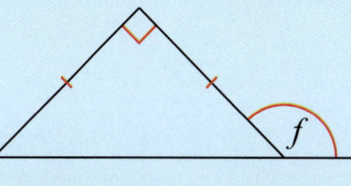

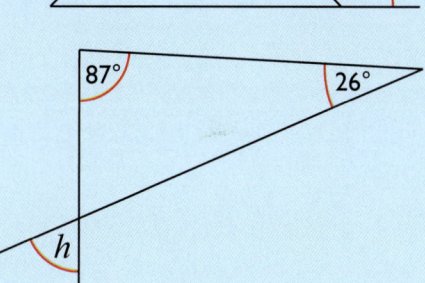

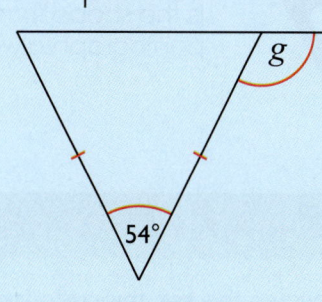

2 a One of the interior angles of a parallelogram is 143°.
  Find the size of all the other interior angles.
  b i Name three quadrilaterals with diagonals that meet each other (intersect) at right angles.
  ii Show the intersecting diagonals in sketches of these three quadrilaterals.
  c An isosceles trapezium has one pair of opposite sides equal.
  One of the interior angles of an isosceles trapezium is 140°.
  Sketch this isosceles trapezium and find the size of all the other interior angles.

3 Here are three identical triangles.

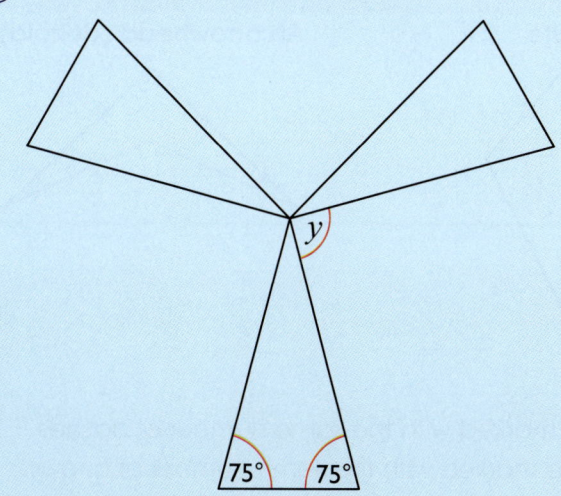

The diagram has rotational symmetry of order 3.

Work out the size of angle y.

Unit 6 • Types of quadrilateral • Band e

Outside the Maths classroom

Pantograph

Is the shape formed by the arms of a pantograph always a parallelogram?

Toolbox

When classifying shapes the key things to look for are
- the number of sides
- the lengths of the sides
- the lines of symmetry
- whether opposite sides are parallel
- the sizes of the angles.

There are seven special types of quadrilateral to remember.

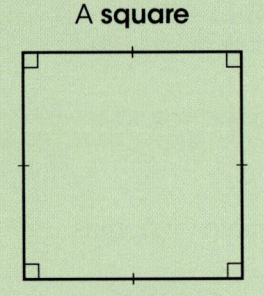

A **square**

A **rectangle**

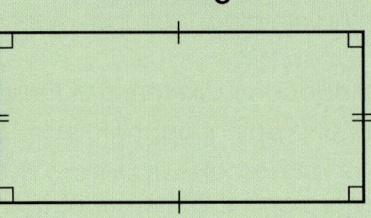

A **parallelogram**

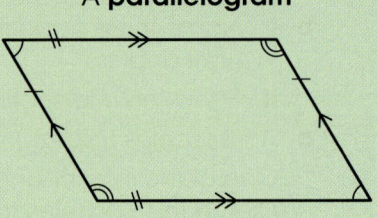

A **rhombus**

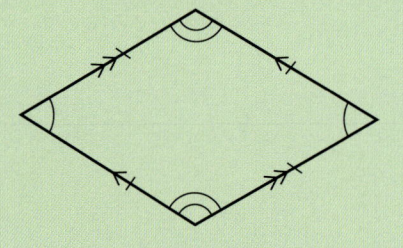

A **kite**

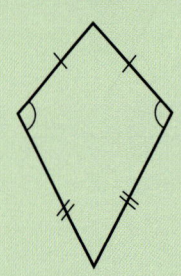

An **arrowhead (deltoid)**

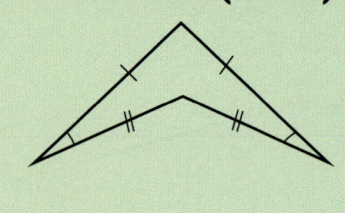

A **trapezium**

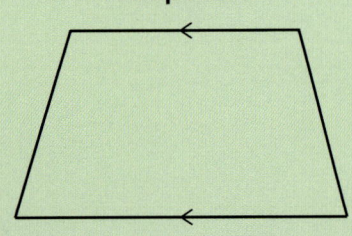

Equal sides are marked with the same number of dashes.
Parallel sides are marked with the same number of arrows.
Equal angles are marked with the same number of arcs.

Example – Classifying quadrilaterals

What type of quadrilateral is Suzanne thinking of?

Andy: Does it have two pairs of parallel sides?

Suzanne: Yes

Andy: Then, in that case, my second question is: are all the angles equal?

Suzanne: Yes

Andy: And now, Suzanne, my final question. Are all its sides equal?

Suzanne: Yes

Solution

Squares, rectangles, parallelograms and rhombuses have two pairs of parallel lines.
Out of these, only squares and rectangles have all angles equal.
Out of these, only a square has equal sides.
Suzanne's quadrilateral must be a square.

Geometry and Measures Strand 2 Properties of shapes

Practising skills

1. Copy and complete this table.

Shape	Name of shape	How many pairs of parallel sides	How many pairs of equal sides	How many lines of symmetry	Order of rotational symmetry	Two pairs of equal angles	Opposite angles are equal
	rectangle	2					
			2				
					0		
				1			

2. What types of quadrilateral must have four equal sides?

3. What types of quadrilateral must have two pairs of parallel sides?

4. Draw all the special quadrilaterals whose diagonals cross at right angles.

5.
   Lucas: I think all rhombuses are squares. So a rhombus is a special type of square.

   Suzanne: No, I think all rhombuses are parallelograms. So a rhombus is a special type of parallelogram.

   Charlie: I think all squares are rhombuses. So a square is a special type of rhombus.

   Who is right?
   Give a reason for your answer.

6. a Draw a kite with one right angle.

   b Draw a kite with two right angles.

   c Is it possible to draw a kite with exactly three right angles?

   d Is it possible for an arrowhead to have a right angle? If so, draw an example.

Unit 6 Types of quadrilateral Band e

Developing fluency

1. Draw x and y axes from 0 to 8.
   Plot the points A(2, 2), B(8, 2) and C(6, 5).
   Plot the point D, and write down its co-ordinates, when ABCD is
   a an isosceles trapezium
   b a parallelogram.

2. Draw x and y axes from 0 to 8.
   Plot the points A(2, 2), B(6, 0) and C(4, 5).
   Plot the point D, and write down its co-ordinates, when ABCD is a kite with a right angle.

3. a Which special quadrilaterals can be formed by joining two congruent triangles?
      Give their names and draw sketches of them.
   b Which special quadrilaterals can be formed by joining two congruent isosceles triangles?

4. a How many different quadrilaterals can you make on a 3 by 3 pinboard?

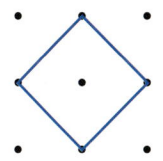

   b How many different quadrilaterals can you make on a 4 by 4 pinboard?

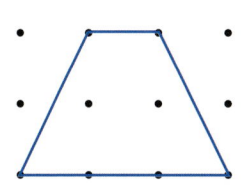

5. The 12 points A to L are equally spaced round a circle.
   a Find which quadrilaterals you can draw by joining some of them.
      Find also which quadrilaterals you cannot draw in this way.
   b Now include the centre O.
      Can you now draw all the quadrilaterals?

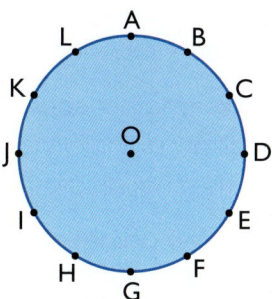

6. Here is the trapezium PQRS. The angles a and b are shown in the diagram.

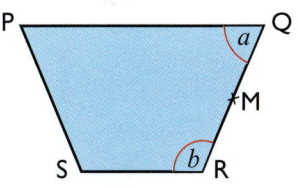

   M is the midpoint of QR.
   a PQRS is rotated through 180° about M to get P'Q'R'S'.
      Draw a diagram showing PQRS and P'Q'R'S' together.
   b Show that $a + b = 180°$.

327

Geometry and Measures Strand 2 Properties of shapes

Problem solving

1. The diagram shows a pattern called a **tangram**.

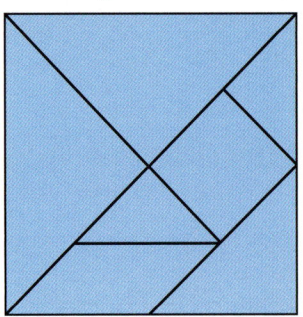

   The diagram has been drawn accurately.
   Show how three of the parts of the tangram can be used to make a rectangle.

2. The diagram shows a square inside a rhombus. One of the angles of the rhombus is 68°.

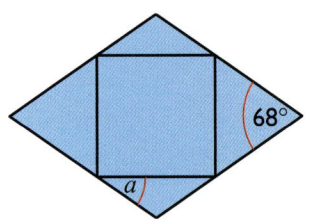

   The corners of the square are the midpoints of the sides of the rhombus.
   Find the size of the angle a.

3. Here is a parallelogram.

   Make a copy of the parallelogram.

   a Draw a single line which divides the parallelogram into two identical trapeziums.
   Each trapezium must have two right angles.

   Make another copy of the parallelogram.

   b Draw a single line which divides the parallelogram into two identical trapeziums.
   The final diagram must have the same order of rotational symmetry as the parallelogram.

4. Here is a parallelogram.

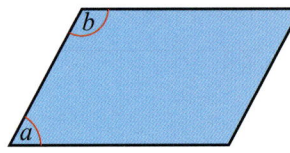

   Use the properties of the angles of a parallelogram to show that $a + b = 180°$.

5 ABCD is a parallelogram. Angle CBF = 68°.
In the diagram, E is a point on the line ABF and angle ADE = angle EDC = x°.
Find the value of x.

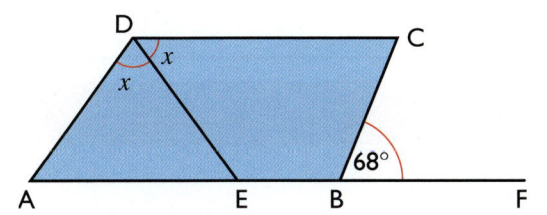

6 The diagram shows a rhombus PQRS. Angle QPR = 42°.

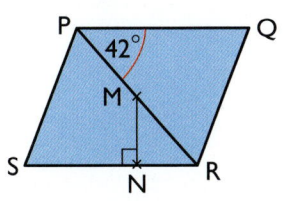

M is the midpoint of PR.
Find the size of the angle RMN.

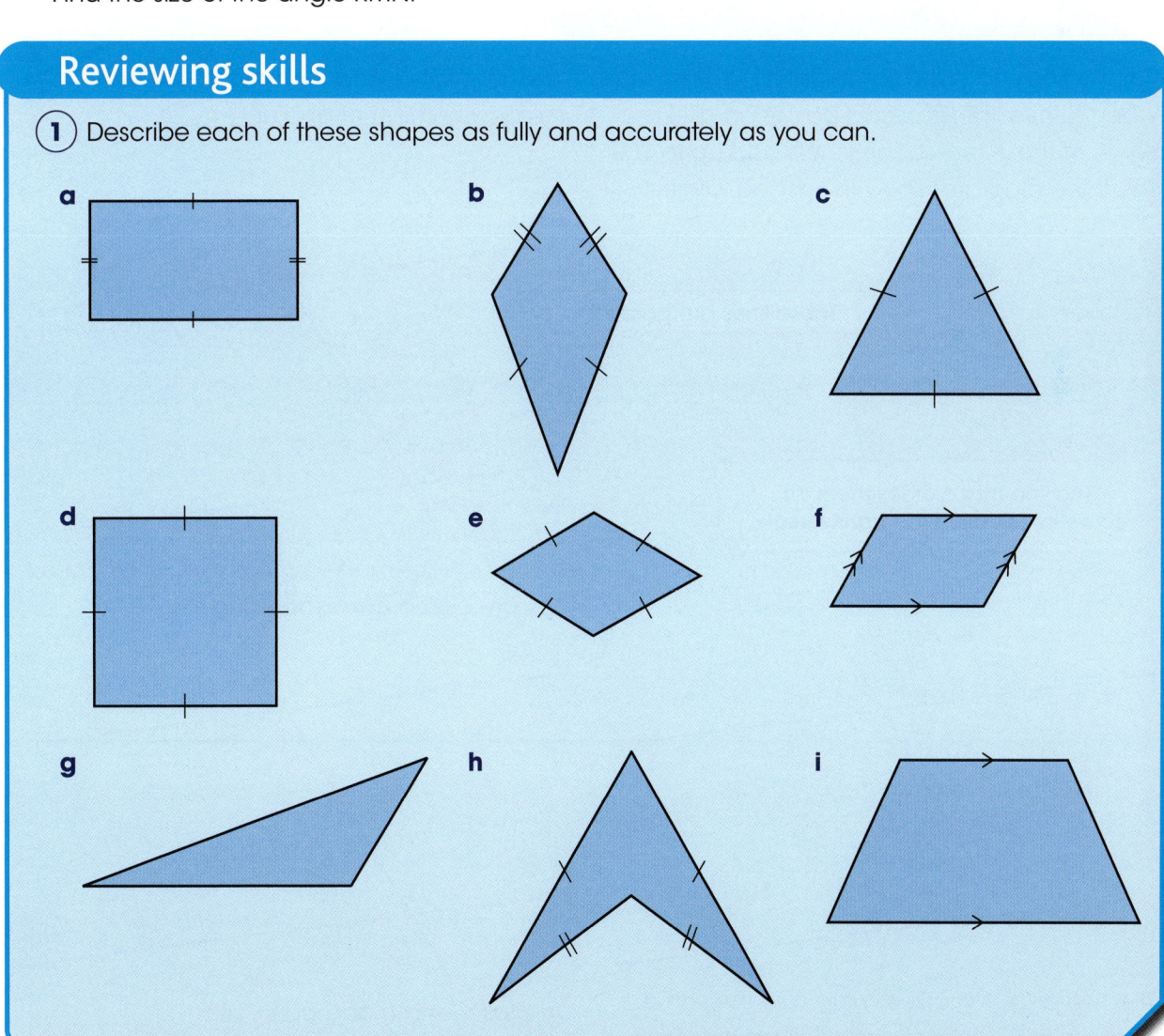

Reviewing skills

1 Describe each of these shapes as fully and accurately as you can.

a b c

d e f

g h i

Unit 7 • Angles and parallel lines • Band f

Outside the Maths classroom

Chart navigation
Why would a navigator need to use a parallel ruler?

Toolbox

Parallel lines go in the same direction. They never meet, no matter how far they are extended.
When a third line crosses a pair of parallel lines it creates a number of angles.
Some of these are equal; others add up to 180°.
The three diagrams show things you will see.

These lines are parallel.

The line that crosses them is sometimes called the **transversal**.

The two angles marked a are exactly the same.
They are called **corresponding** angles.

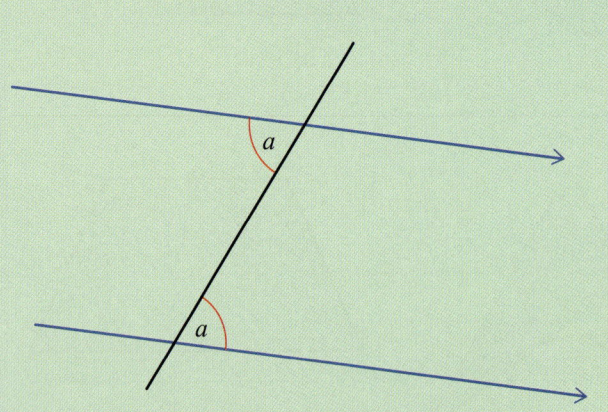

The two angles marked a are also the same.
Angles in this position are called **alternate** angles.

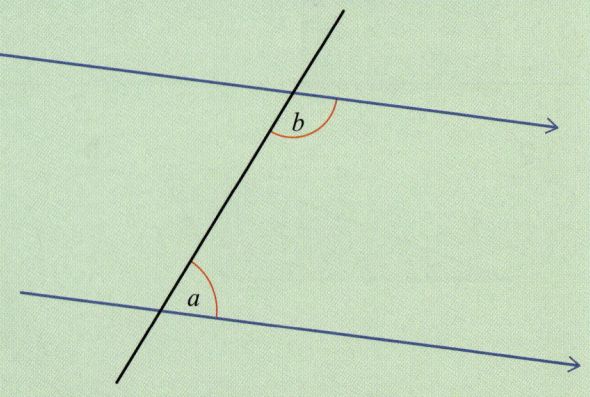

Angles a and b add up to 180°.
They are called **interior** angles.

Unit 7 Angles and parallel lines Band f

Example – Using alternate angles

The diagram shows a pair of parallel lines and an intersecting line.

Work out the size of the lettered angles. Give a reason for each of your answers.

Angle a and the given angle are alternate angles.

Angle b is vertically opposite angle a.

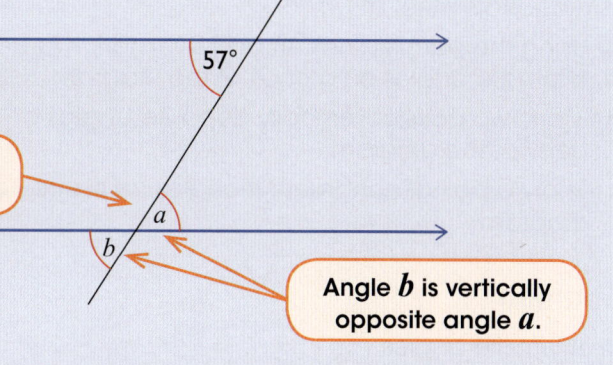

Solution

Alternate angles are equal.
$a = 57°$
Opposite angles are equal.
$b = 57°$

Example – Using interior and corresponding angles

The diagram shows a pair of parallel lines and an intersecting line.

Work out the size of the lettered angles. Give a reason for each of your answers.

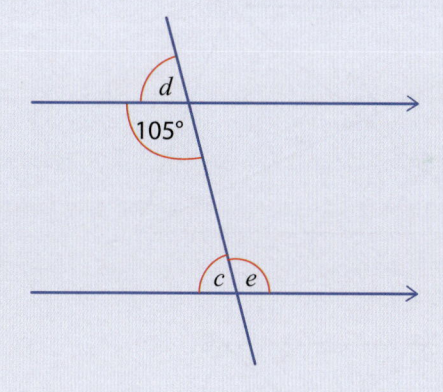

Solution

Interior angles add up to 180°.
$c = 180 - 105 = 75°$
c and d are corresponding angles.
Corresponding angles are equal.
$d = 75°$
Alternate angles are equal.
e is an alternate angle to the given angle.
$e = 105°$

Geometry and Measures Strand 2 Properties of shapes

Example – Finding angles in a parallelogram

ABCD is a parallelogram.

Its diagonals meet at M.

a Using the parallel lines AB and DC, mark two pairs of alternate angles on a copy of the diagram.

b Mark two pairs of vertically opposite angles on a copy of the diagram.

c Show a pair of congruent triangles on a copy of the diagram.

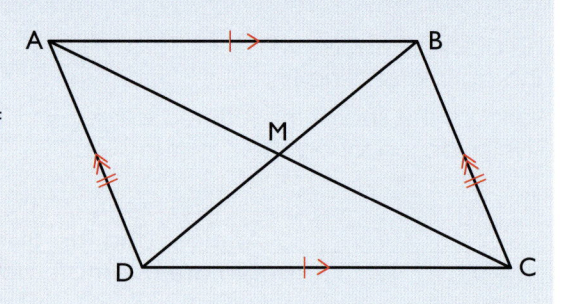

Solution

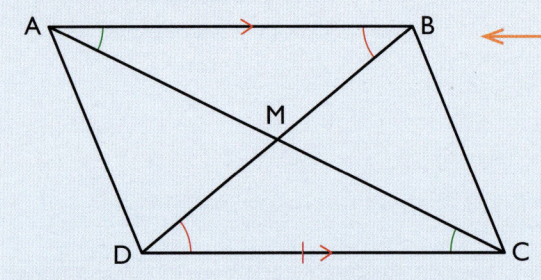

a Alternate angles

The red angles are equal.

The green angles are equal.

b Vertically opposite angles

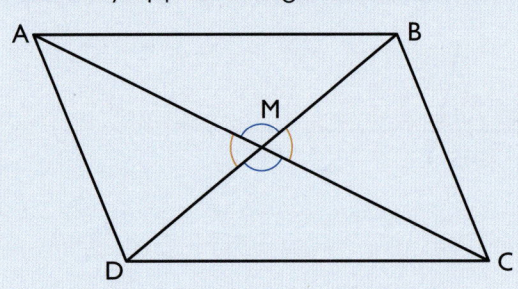

c Congruent triangles

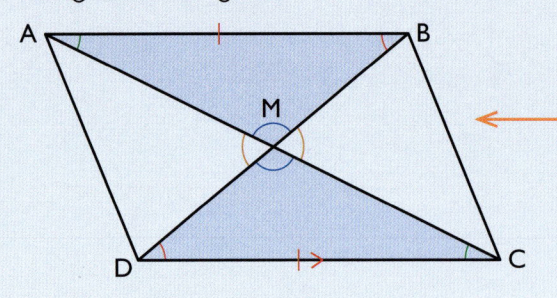

The three angles of these triangles are the same so they are the same shape.
Also AB and CD are the same length so they are the same size.

Unit 7 Angles and parallel lines Band f

Practising skills

1) Find the size of each lettered angle in these diagrams.

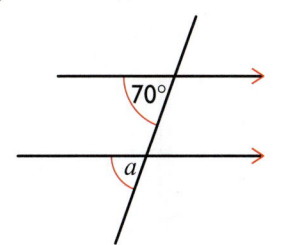

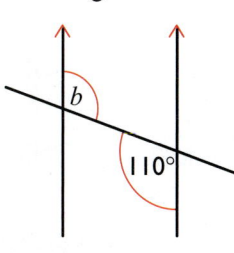

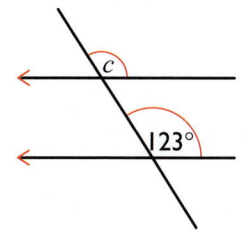

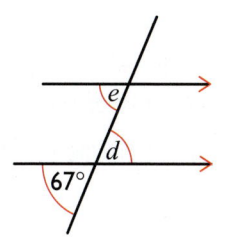

2) Find the size of each lettered angle in these diagrams.

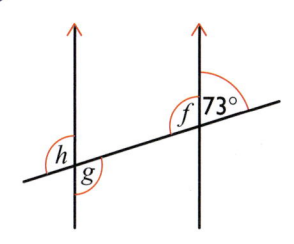

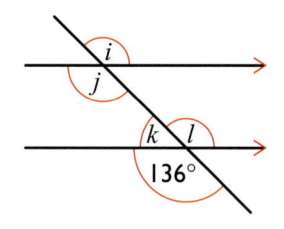

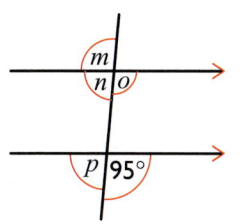

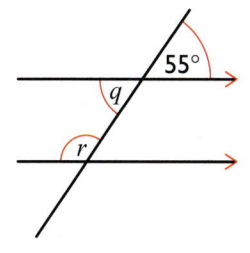

3) Llew says that in this diagram, there are only two different sizes of angle marked.
The angle a is 50°.

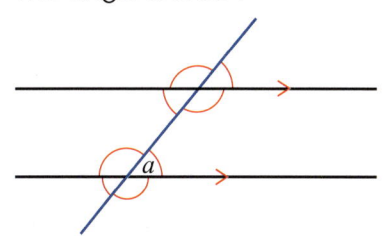

Find the values of the other angles in the diagram.
Is Llew right?

4) Write down the sizes of the lettered angles in this diagram.
For each one give your reason.

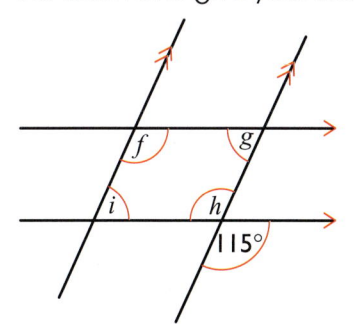

Geometry and Measures Strand 2 Properties of shapes

Developing fluency

1 This fence is going down a hill.
The posts are vertical.
The wires are parallel.

   a What is angle a?

   b What angle do the wires make with the horizontal?

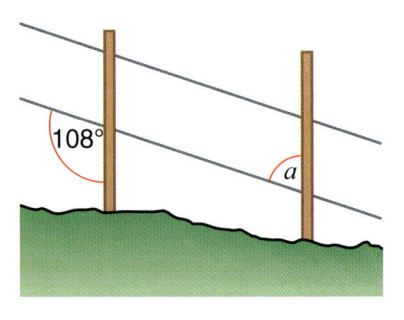

2 The diagram shows part of a fence panel.
Find the angles a, b, c and d.

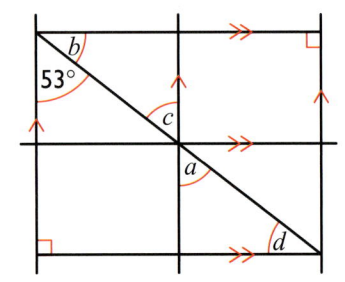

3 Write down the sizes of the lettered angles in these diagrams.
For each one give your reason.

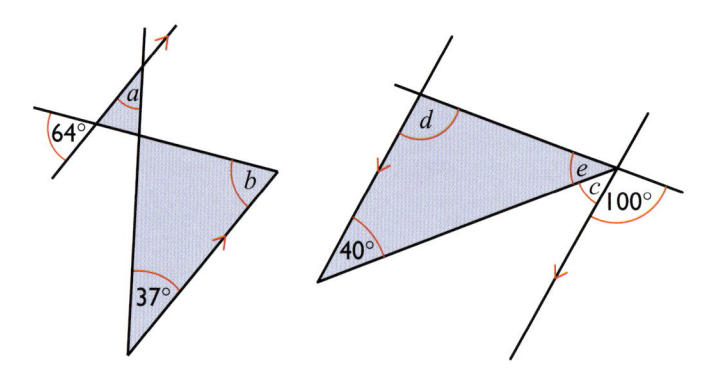

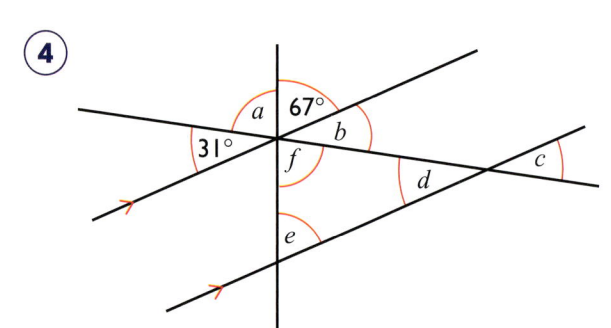

4

   a Write down the size of each lettered angle.
For each one give your reason.

   b What is $f + d + e$?

Unit 7 Angles and parallel lines Band f

5 This diagram represents an electricity pylon.
Find the sizes of the angles marked a, b and c. Give your reasons.

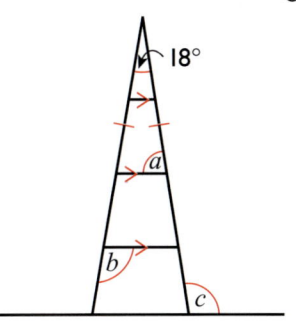

6 In the diagram, the straight lines ABC and DEF are parallel.

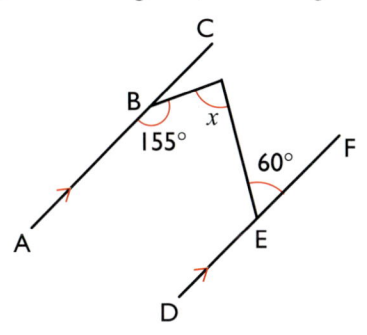

Find the size of angle x. Give your reasons.

Problem solving

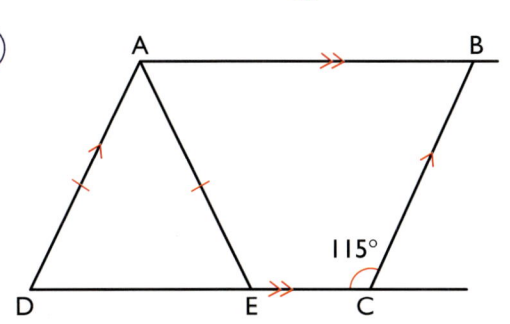

1 AB is parallel to DC. AD is parallel to BC.
E is a point on DC such that ADE is an isosceles triangle.
Find the size of angle DAE. Give your reasons.

2 This diagram has a single line of symmetry and a pair of parallel lines.

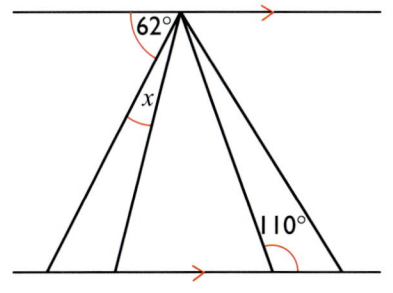

Find the size of angle x. Give your reasons.

335

Geometry and Measures Strand 2 Properties of shapes

3) The diagram shows a square and a pair of parallel lines through two of its vertices.

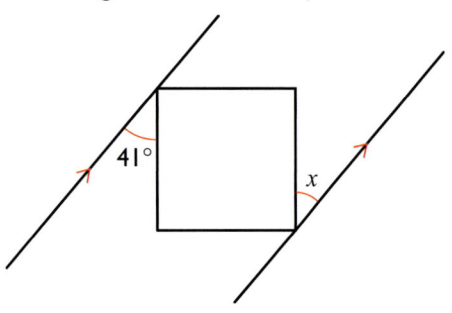

Jim thinks that $x = 41°$.
Is Jim correct?
Give a reason for your answer.

4) The diagram shows an equilateral triangle and a pair of parallel lines, through two of its vertices.
Find the value of x. Give your reasons.

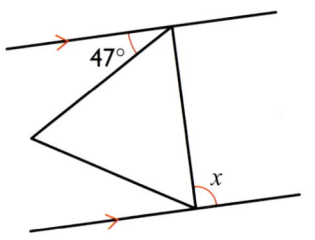

5) ABC and DEF are parallel lines.
Angle ABE is three times angle BED.
Work out the size of angle ABE.

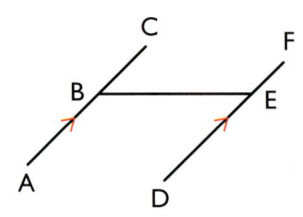

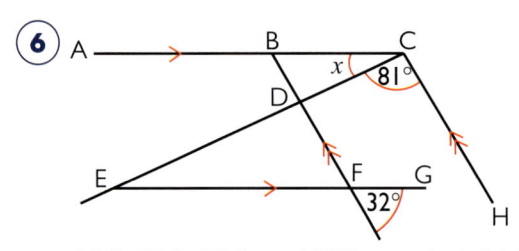

6) ABC, EDC, BDF and EFG are straight lines.
AC is parallel to EG.
BF is parallel to CH.
Find the value of x.

Reviewing skills

1 Find the size of each lettered angle in these diagrams.
For each one write down the angle fact(s) that you use.

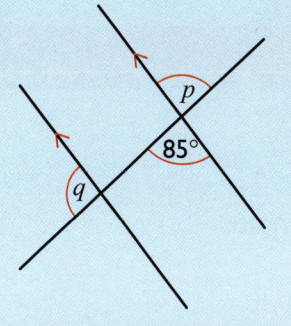

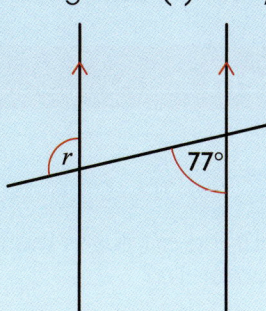

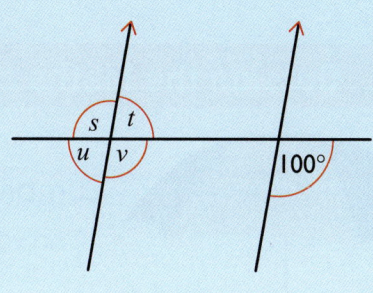

a 85°, p, q

b r, 77°

c s, t, u, v, 100°

2 Jack makes a wire fence.

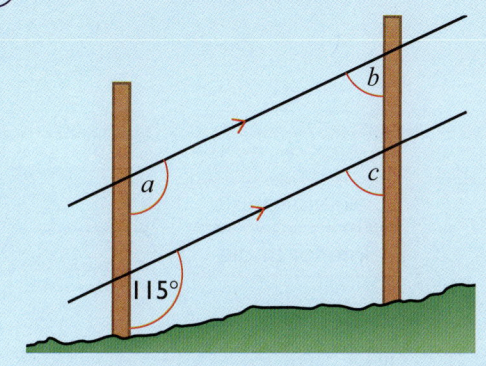

The posts are vertical.
The wires are parallel.
Work out the size of the angles a, b and c.

3 In the diagram, ABCD is a parallelogram.

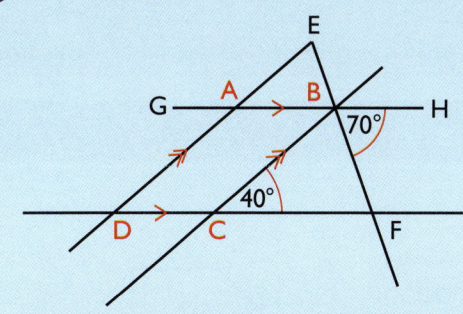

Angle BCF = 40° and angle HBF = 70°.
Show that triangle EDF is an isosceles triangle.

Unit 8 • Angles in a polygon • Band g

Outside the Maths classroom

Umbrellas
Can you work out the angles in the triangles of fabric in this umbrella?

Toolbox

An **interior angle** is the angle inside the corner of a shape.

An **exterior angle** is the angle that has to be turned through to move from one side to the next.

At each vertex,
interior angle + exterior angle = 180°.

In a **regular polygon** all of the interior angles are equal and all of the exterior angles are equal.

The exterior angles of a polygon always make one complete turn and so **add up to 360°**.

The sum of the interior angles of a polygon $=180(n-2)°$ where n is the number of sides.
For example, the sum of the interior angles of a hexagon is
$180 \times (6-2) = 720°$.

Example – Finding angles of regular polygons

The diagram shows a regular octagon.
a Work out the size of an exterior angle of a regular octagon.
b Hence find the size of an interior angle of a regular octagon.

Solution

a The exterior angles of a polygon add up to 360°.
   For a regular octagon,
   each exterior angle = 360° ÷ 8 = 45° ← This is angle a in the diagram.

b Interior angle + exterior angle = 180°
   For a regular octagon,
   each interior angle = 180° − 45° ← This is angle b in the diagram.
   = 135°

Unit 8 Angles in a polygon Band g

Example – Finding the number of sides of a regular polygon

A regular polygon has an interior angle of 162°.
How many sides does the polygon have?

Solution

First find the exterior angle.
Interior angle + exterior angle = 180°
$\qquad$ 162° + exterior angle = 180°
$\qquad\qquad$ exterior angle = 180° − 162° = 18°
The exterior angles add up to 360°.
Number of exterior angles = 360 ÷ 18 = 20
The polygon has 20 sides. ← The number of sides is the same as the number of exterior angles.

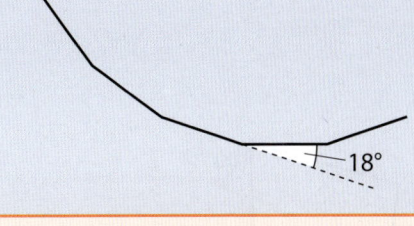

Practising skills

1 a Calculate the exterior angle, a, of a regular hexagon.

  b Calculate the interior angle, b, of a regular hexagon.

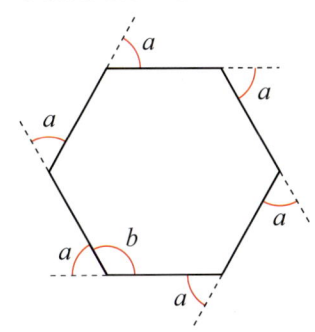

2 a Calculate the exterior angle of a regular octagon.

  b Calculate the interior angle of a regular octagon.

3 Copy and complete the following table:

Regular polygon	Number of sides	Size of each exterior angle	Size of each interior angle	Sum of interior angles
Equilateral triangle				
Square				
Pentagon				
Hexagon				
Octagon				
Decagon				
Dodecagon				
Pendedecagon	15			
Icosagon	20			

339

Geometry and Measures Strand 2 Properties of shapes

4 Calculate the size of each lettered angle.

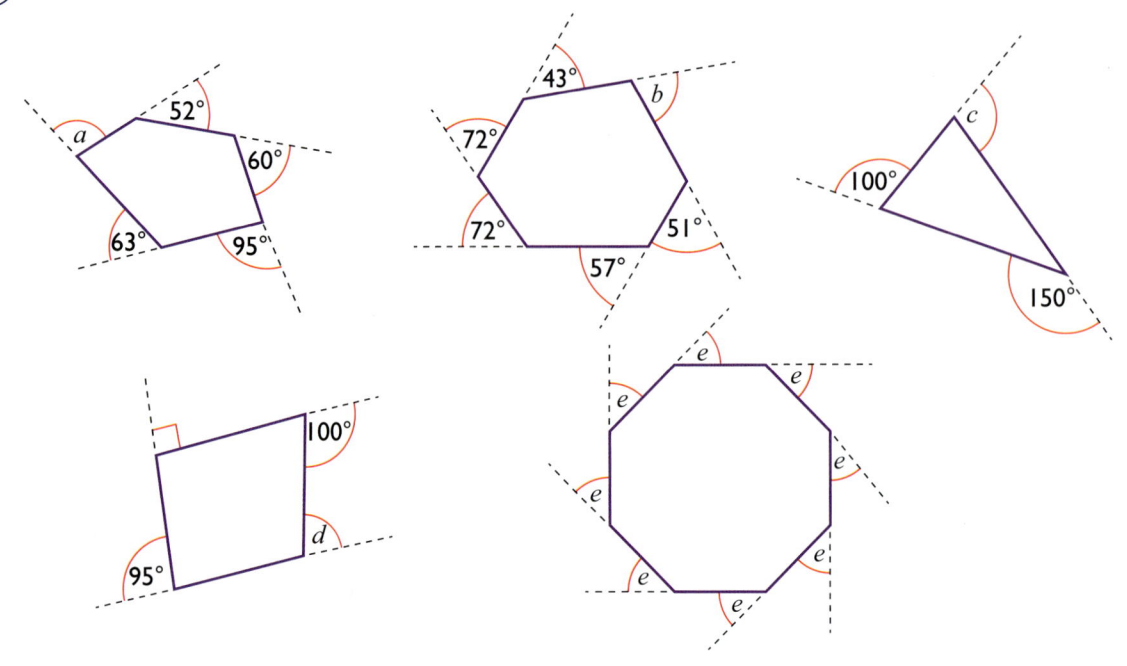

5 The external angle of a regular polygon is 10°.
  a How many sides does the polygon have?
  b What is the size of one interior angle?
  c What is the sum of the interior angles of the polygon?

6 Seb draws a pentagon.

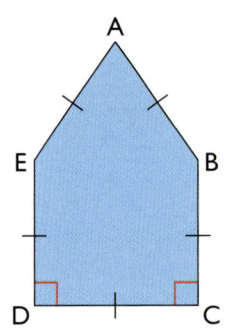

  a Is Seb's pentagon regular?
     Give a reason for your answer.
  b What is the sum of the interior angles of a pentagon?
  c Find each of the interior angles in Seb's pentagon.

Unit 8 Angles in a polygon Band g

Developing fluency

1 The diagram shows a pentagon.

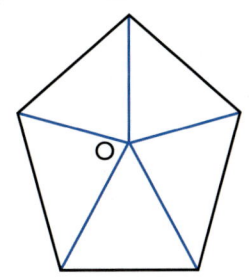

The vertices are all joined to a point O in the middle, making five triangles.
  a Work out the total of all the angles in the five triangles.
  b What is the total of the angles at the point O?
  c Use your answers to parts **a** and **b** to find the total of the interior angles of the pentagon.
  d Find the size of each interior angle if the pentagon is regular.

2 This diagram shows a hexagon.
One of the vertices, D, is joined to all the other vertices.

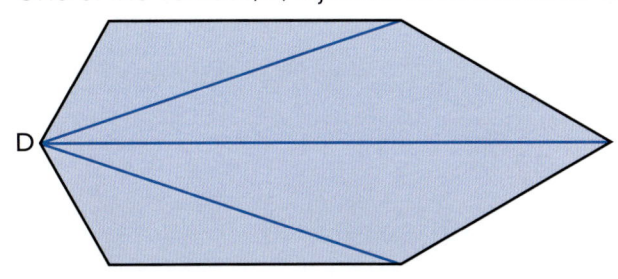

  a The lines from D divide the hexagon into triangles. How many triangles are there?
  b What is the total of all the angles in the triangles?
  c What is the total of all the interior angles of the hexagon?
  d Find the size of each interior angle if the hexagon is regular.

3 The diagram shows a hexagon split into six triangles.

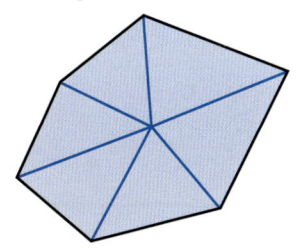

  a What is the sum of
     i   all the angles in all the triangles
     ii the angles at the centre
     iii the interior angles of the hexagon?
  b Use the diagram to explain why the sum of the interior angles of a polygon with n sides is
     $n \times 180° - 360°$
  c Show that the formula in part **b** is the same as $(n - 2) \times 180°$.

341

Geometry and Measures Strand 2 Properties of shapes

4 A regular polygon has exterior angles of 30°.

  a What is the sum of the exterior angles?

  b How many sides does the polygon have?

  c What is the size of each interior angle?

  d What is the sum of the interior angles of the polygon?

5 a A regular polygon has an interior angle of 174°.
How many sides does the polygon have?

  b The sum of the interior angles of a regular polygon is 1980°.
How many sides does the polygon have?

  c A regular polygon has an exterior angle of 10°.
What is the sum of its interior angles?

6 Mark is tiling a floor using polygons for tiles.

  a Mark tiles part of the floor using equilateral triangles. How many tiles meet at each vertex?

  b Can Mark tile the floor using regular hexagons?
Explain your answer fully.

  c Can Mark tile the floor using regular pentagons?
Explain your answer fully.

7

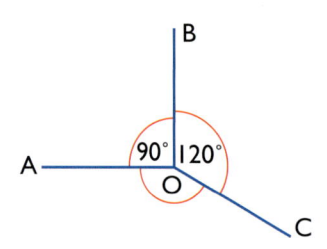

  a In the diagram, the lines AO, BO and CO are all sides of regular polygons.
How many sides does each of the three polygons have?
What are their names?

  b The line CO is rotated by 15° clockwise about O.
How would you answer part **a** when it is in this position?

8

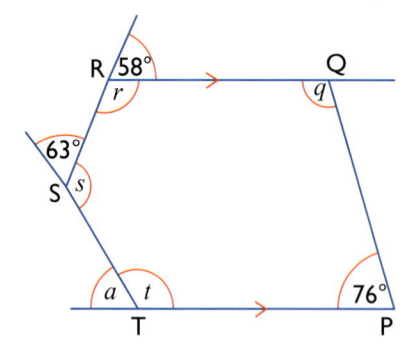

PQRST is a pentagon.
RQ is parallel to TP.

  a Find the size of angle q.

  b Find the sizes of the other interior angles r, s and t of the pentagon.

  c Find the size of angle a.

Unit 8 Angles in a polygon Band g

Problem solving

1) A, B and C are three vertices of a regular 10-sided polygon.
   O is the centre of the polygon.

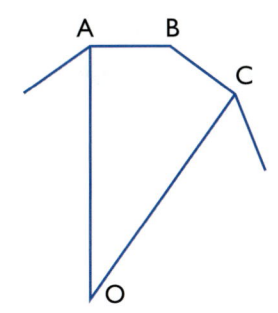

   a Calculate the size of angle AOC.
   b Show that OABC is a kite.

2) The diagram shows a regular hexagon and a square.

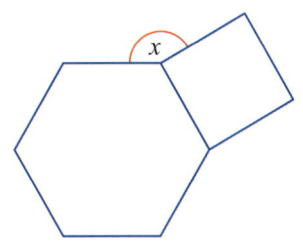

   Work out the size of angle x.

3) The diagram shows a regular pentagon.

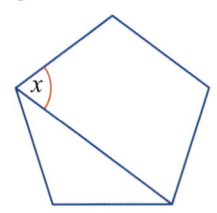

   Find the size of the angle marked x.

4) The diagram shows a regular hexagon and a regular pentagon on the same base.

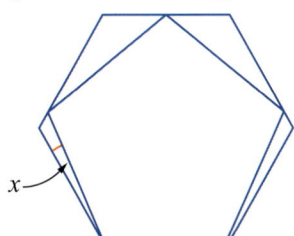

   Work out the size of angle x.

343

Geometry and Measures Strand 2 Properties of shapes

5) The diagram shows two identical pentagons.

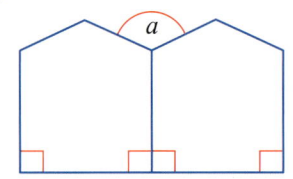

For each pentagon, two of the angles are right angles and the other three angles are the same. Work out the size of angle a.

6) Here is a regular octagon.

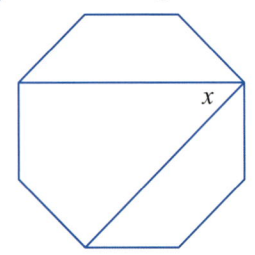

Work out the size of angle x.

Reviewing skills

1) Calculate the size of each lettered angle.

a

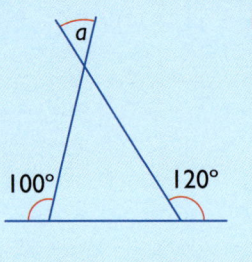

b

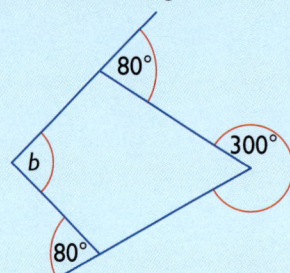

c

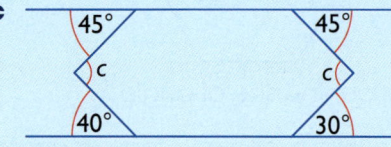

2) a The exterior angle of a regular polygon is 5°.
How many sides does the polygon have?

b Is there a regular polygon with an exterior angle of 7°?
Explain your answer.

3) a Show that the interior angle of a regular dodecagon (12 sides) is 144°.

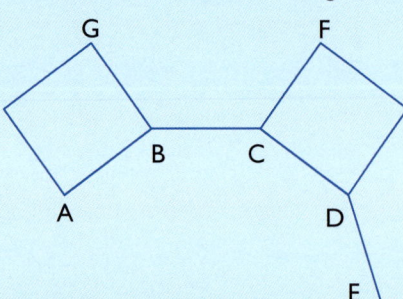

ABCDE is part of a regular dodecagon.
The two quadrilaterals are squares with sides the same length as AB.

b Find the size of the angle GBC.

c Show that angles GBC and FCB are each equal to the interior angle of a regular hexagon.

Unit 9 • Congruent triangles and proof • Band h

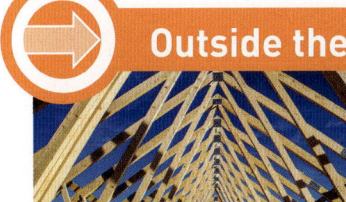

Outside the Maths classroom

Triangular supports
Why do builders use triangular supports?

Toolbox

A **proof** is a water-tight argument that cannot be disputed. A mathematical proof starts from a position that is known to be true. Each step is justified. The explanation is often written in brackets. The proofs in this unit involve angle facts and congruent triangles.

Congruent shapes are exactly the same shape and size.

There are four sets of conditions that prove two triangles are congruent.

1. **SSS.** The three sides of one triangle are equal to the three sides of the other.

2. **SAS.** Two sides of one triangle are equal to two sides of the other, and the angles between those sides are equal.

3. **SAA.** Two angles of one triangle are equal to two angles of the other, and a pair of corresponding sides are equal.

4. **RHS.** Two right-angled triangles have equal hypotenuses and another pair of equal sides.

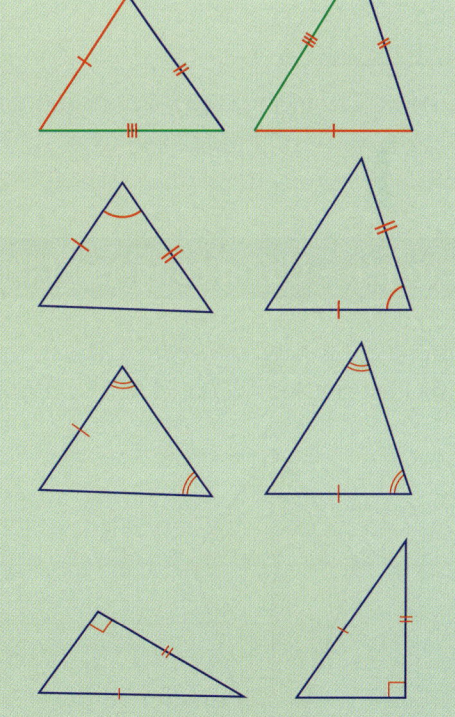

Note that three angles being equal in a pair of triangles (AAA) is not proof of congruence. One triangle may be bigger than the other. It does, however, prove they are similar.

Geometry and Measures Strand 2 Properties of shapes

Example – Recognising congruence

These four triangles have two sides and one angle equal.

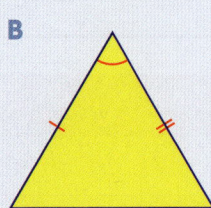

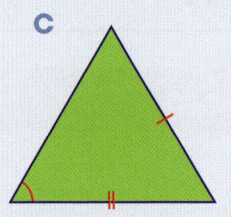

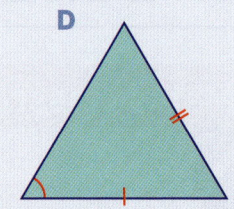

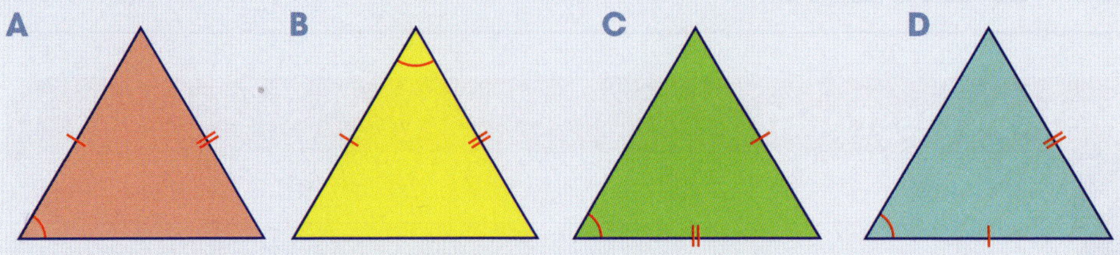

A   B   C   D

a Are any of the triangles congruent?
b Which triangle is congruent to this one?

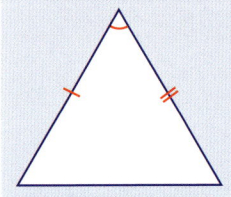

Solution

a **A** and **D** are congruent. If you reflect **D** in the line bisecting the marked angle you get **A** (SAS).

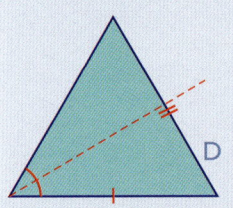

b The yellow triangle (**B**) is congruent to the white one (SAS).

Example – Using congruent triangles

In this kite, AB = AC and BD = CD.
Prove that angles ABD and ACD are equal.

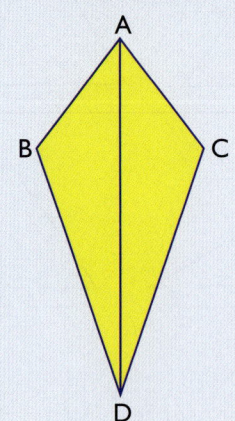

Solution

In triangles ABD and ACD:

AB = AC ← Given

BD = CD ← Given

AD is common.

Therefore triangles ABD and ACD are congruent. ← SSS

So, ∠ABD = ∠ACD ← Corresponding angles of congruent triangles.

Example – Angle proofs

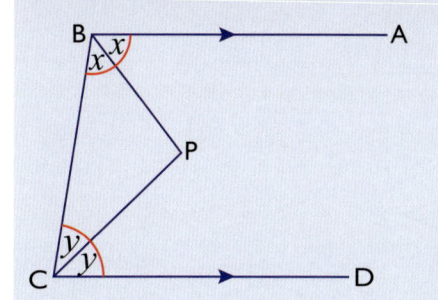

In the diagram, BA and CD are parallel.
The bisectors of ∠ABC and ∠BCD meet at P.
Prove that ∠BPC = 90°.

Solution

Let ∠ABC = $2x$ and ∠BCD = $2y$ as shown in the diagram.

∠ABP = ∠CBP = x ← BP bisects ∠ABC.

∠BCP = ∠DCP = y ← PC bisects ∠BCD.

∠ABC + ∠BCD = 180° ← Interior angles on parallel lines.

$2x + 2y = 180°$

$x + y = 90°$ ← Dividing both sides by 2.

∠CBP + ∠BCP + ∠BPC = 180° ← Angle sum of triangle BPC.

$x + y$ + ∠BPC = 180°

90° + ∠BPC = 180° ← Since $x + y = 90°$.

∠BPC = 90°

Geometry and Measures Strand 2 Properties of shapes

Practising skills

1 Say why the angles in each of the following pairs are equal.
In each case choose a reason from this list.

| Alternate angles | Corresponding angles | Vertically opposite angles |

| Angles in an isosceles triangle | Opposite angles of a parallelogram |

a x, y

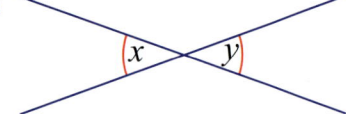

b a, b

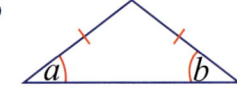

c q, p

d 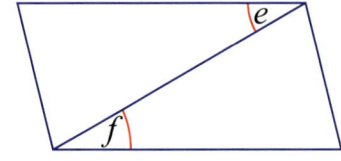 e, 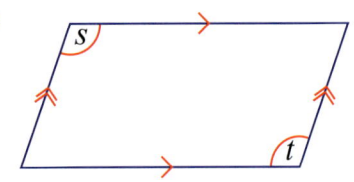 f

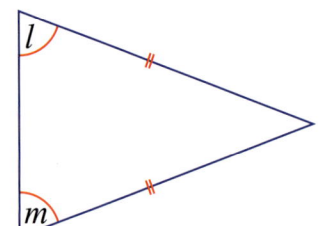

e s, t

f l, m

g u, v

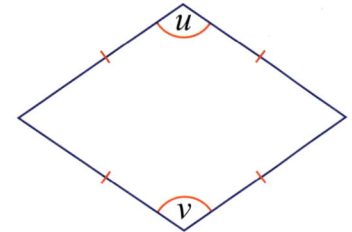

h c, d

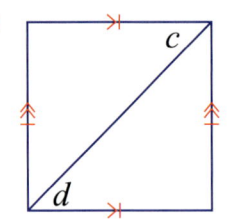

i h, g

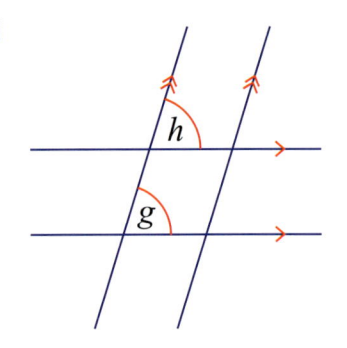

j i, j

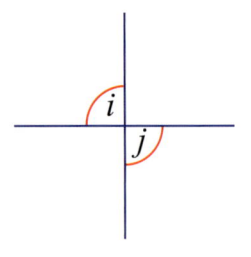

Unit 9 Congruent triangles and proof Band h

2 Say why the lines in each of the following pairs are equal.

a

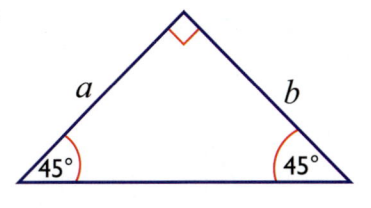

b

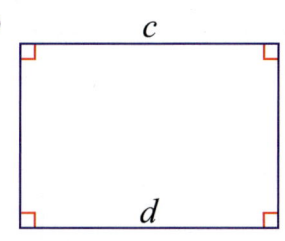

c

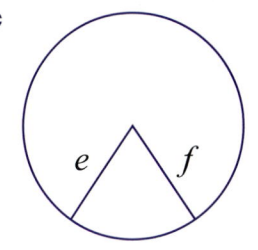

d

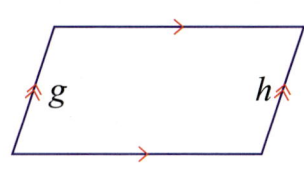

e

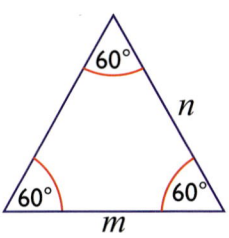

3 a State two pairs of equal angles in this diagram.

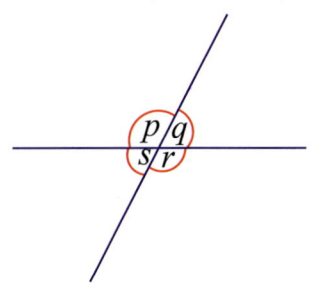

b State four different pairs of angles that add up to 180°.

c Copy and complete this statement.

$p + q + r + s =$ _____ (angles round a ....)

4 a State, giving reasons, three pairs of equal angles in this diagram.

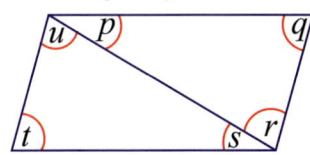

b State, giving reasons, four different sets of three angles that add up to 180°.

5 Say whether the triangles in each pair are congruent. If they are, give a reason (SSS, SAS, ASA, RHS).

a

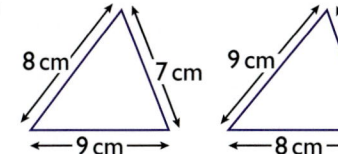

b

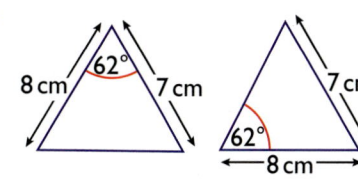

349

Geometry and Measures Strand 2 Properties of shapes

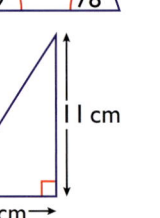

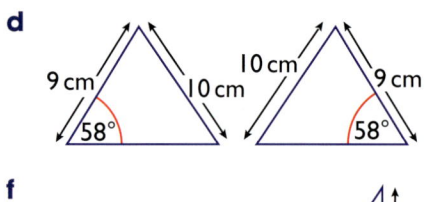

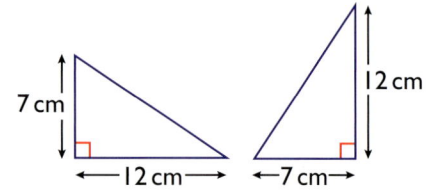

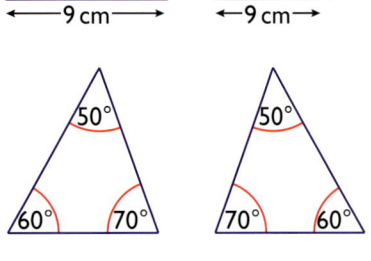

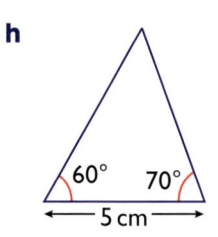

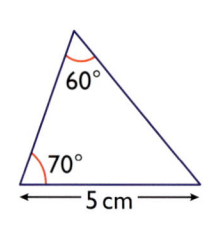

c, **d**, **e**, **f**, **g**, **h** (triangle diagrams)

6 In the diagram, O is the centre of the circle.
The ∠ZOY is 50° as shown.

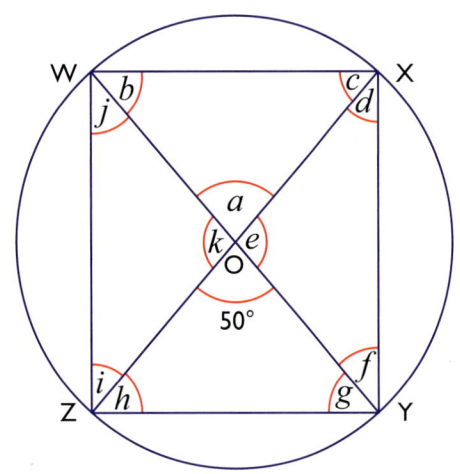

a Find the sizes of the angles marked $a, b, c, d, e, f, g, h, i, j$ and k.
In each case give your reasons.

b Use your answers to prove that WXYZ is a rectangle.

c How many pairs of congruent triangles are there in the diagram?

7 ABC is an isosceles triangle with AB = AC.
AP bisects ∠BAC.
Prove that PB = PC.

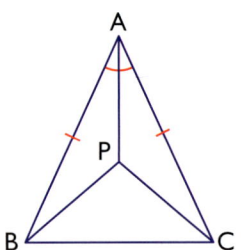

Unit 9 Congruent triangles and proof Band h

Developing fluency

1 In the diagram, AB and DE are parallel.
AC and CE are both 8 cm long.

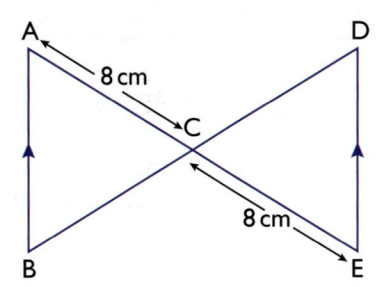

   a Copy and complete this proof that triangles ABC and CDE are congruent.
      In triangles ABC and EDC
      AC = ☐ (both given as 8 cm)
      ∠ACB = ∠ECD (☐)
      ∠BAC = ☐ (alternate angles)
      So triangles ABC and EDC are congruent (☐).

   b What does this tell you about lines AB and DE?

2 The diagram shows a rhombus, ABCD.

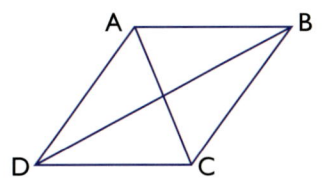

   a Copy and complete this proof that triangles DAB and DCB are congruent.
      In triangles DAB and DCB
      AB = CB (a rhombus has equal sides)
      AD = CD (☐)
      BD is common to both triangles.
      So triangles DAB and DCB are congruent (☐).

   b What does this tell you about ∠ADB and ∠CDB?

3 AB is a chord of a circle, centre O.
ON is perpendicular to AB.

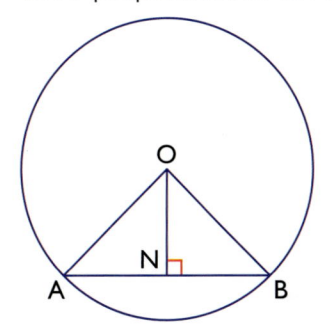

   a Prove that triangles OAN and OBN are congruent.
   b What does this tell you about point N?

Geometry and Measures Strand 2 Properties of shapes

4) Peter has given reasons why the triangles below are congruent.
Explain his errors.

a SAS

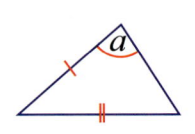

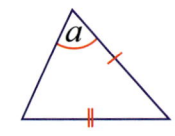

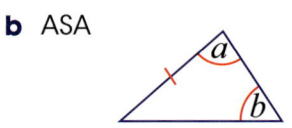

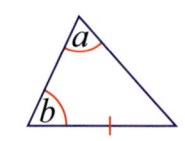

b ASA

c RHS

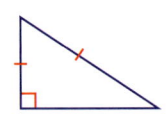

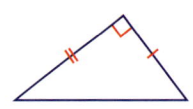

d AAA

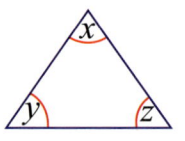

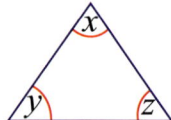

5) In this diagram, angles DAB and CBA are equal and AD = BC.
Prove that BD = AC.

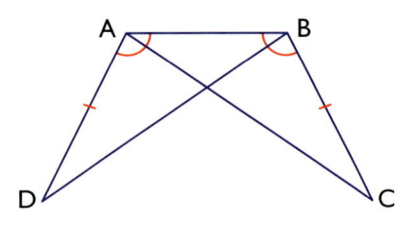

6) In this diagram AQ and BP are perpendicular to AB.
AQ = BP
Prove that AB bisects PQ.

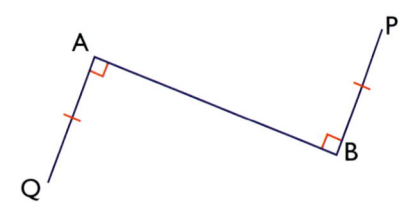

7) In this diagram, D is the mid-point of the line AB.
DM and DN are perpendiculars from D to AC and BC.
DM = DN
Prove that triangle ABC is isosceles.

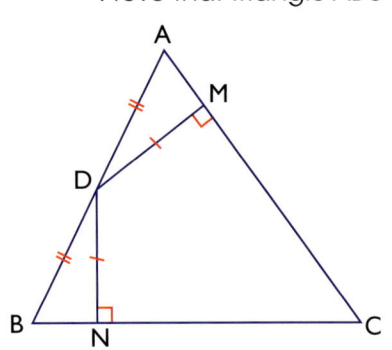

8. ABCD is a quadrilateral. The diagonal AC bisects the angles BAD and BCD.
   Prove that the quadrilateral is a kite.

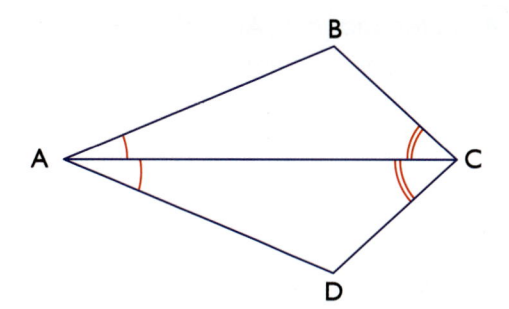

Problem solving

1. ABCDE is a regular pentagon.
   a What does this tell you about its sides?
   b What does this tell you about its interior angles?
   c Use congruent triangles to prove that BE = BD.
   d Which other lines are diagonals of this pentagon?
      Explain how you know that all the diagonals are equal in length.

2. In triangle ABC, AB = AC and D is a point on BC.
   The line AD bisects the angle at A.
   a Prove that the triangles ABD and ACD are congruent.
   b Prove that
      i   D is the mid-point of BC
      ii $\angle ADC = 90°$.

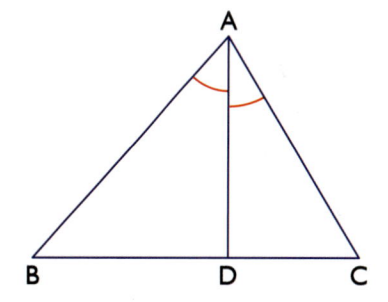

3. In this diagram, $\angle PQS = \angle PRS$.
   PS bisects $\angle QPR$.

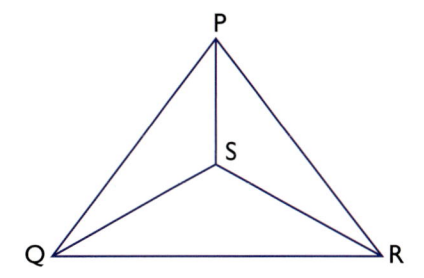

   a Prove that triangle PQR is isosceles.
   b Hence prove that $\angle SQR = \angle SRQ$.

Geometry and Measures Strand 2 Properties of shapes

4 In the diagram, ADB, BCE, AFC and DFE are all straight lines.
∠DBC is a right angle.
AB = BE and AC = DE.
Prove that AD = CE.

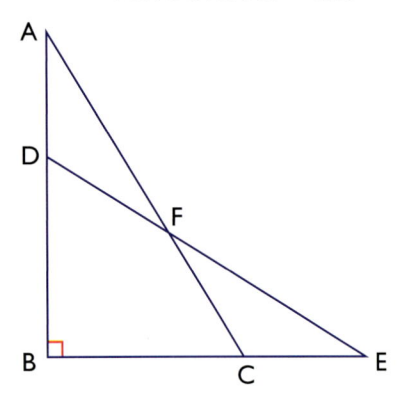

5 PQRS is a parallelogram.
N and M are points on QS such that PM and RN are perpendicular to QS.

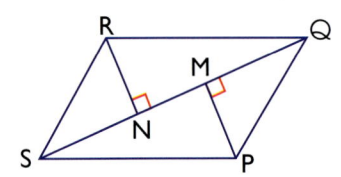

  a Prove that triangles PMQ and RNS are congruent.
  b Prove that SM = QN.

6 All four sides of a rhombus are equal.
  a Taking this as a starting point and using congruent triangles, prove that the opposite sides are parallel.
  b Prove, using congruent triangles, that the diagonals of a rhombus intersect at right angles.

Reviewing skills

1 Say why the following pairs of triangles are similar.
In each case choose a reason from this list.

| Alternate angles | Corresponding angles | Vertically opposite angles |

| Angles in an isosceles triangle | Opposite angles of a parallelogram |

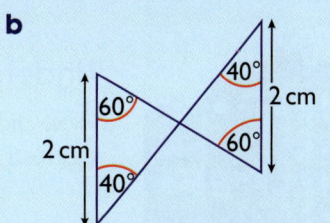

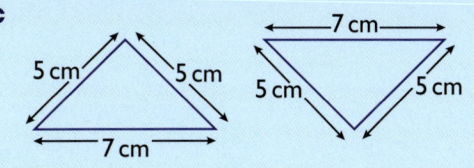

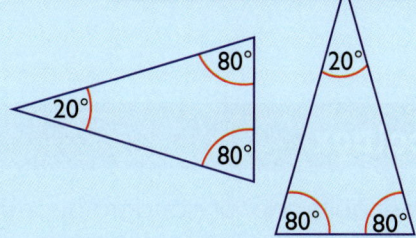

a (Two right-angled triangles: 3 cm, 4 cm and 6 cm, 8 cm)

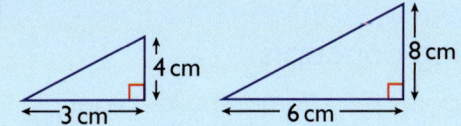

b (Two triangles meeting at a vertex with angles 40°, 60°, 60°, 40° and sides 2 cm)

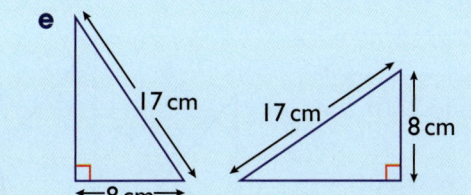

c (Isosceles triangle with sides 5 cm, 5 cm, 7 cm and another with sides 5 cm, 5 cm, 7 cm)

d (Triangle with angles 20°, 80°, 80° and triangle with angles 20°, 80°, 80°)

e (Two right-angled triangles with hypotenuse 17 cm and side 8 cm)

f (Isosceles triangle with 6 cm sides and 72° angle, and another with 6 cm sides and 72° angle)

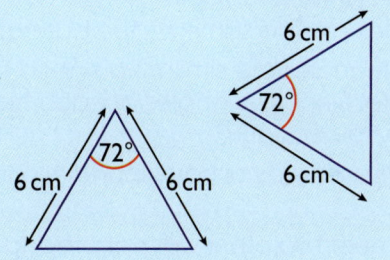

2 CDE is an isosceles triangle with CE = DE.
ABCD is a rectangle, and EF is perpendicular to CD.

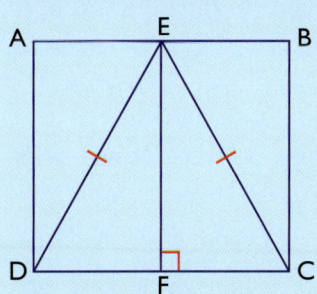

(Diagram showing rectangle ABCD with E on AB, F on DC, and triangle DEC with EF perpendicular to DC)

a Prove that triangles ADE and BCE are congruent.

b What does this tell you about point E?

3 ABCD is a parallelogram. Therefore its opposite sides are equal and parallel.
Prove that the diagonals AC and BD bisect each other.

Unit 10 • Proof using similar and congruent triangles • Band h

Outside the Maths classroom

Understanding concepts
How did Pythagoras help Roman builders get perfect right angles in their buildings?

Toolbox

You have met quite a lot of standard geometry results. These can be proved using angle facts, congruent triangles and similar triangles.

Similar triangles are the same shape but not necessarily the same size.

To prove two triangles are similar, you need to show two pairs of angles are equal (AA). Since the angles of each triangle add up to 180°, the third pair must be equal.

The ratios of the lengths of corresponding sides of similar triangles are equal.

You will also meet two other ways of proving triangles are similar.

a The ratios of all three corresponding sides are the same.

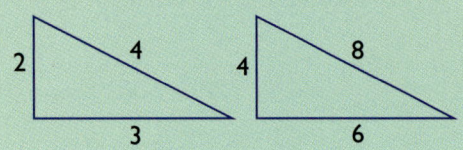

b The ratios of two corresponding sides are the same and the angles between these sides are equal.

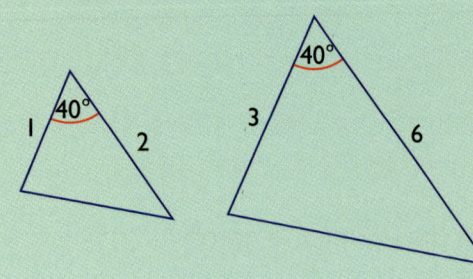

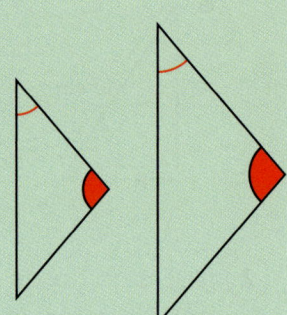

Unit 10 Proof using similar and congruent triangles Band h

Example – Using congruent triangles to prove a standard result

ABC is an isosceles triangle with AB = AC.
Prove that ∠ABC = ∠ACB.

Solution

Mark the mid-point of BC as M.
Join AM.
In the triangles ABM and ACM
AB = AC (Given)
BM = CM (M is mid-point of BC)
AM is common.
Therefore triangles ABM and ACM are congruent (SSS).
So ∠ABM = ∠ACM (Corresponding angles of congruent triangles)
These are the required angles.
∠ABC = ∠ACB

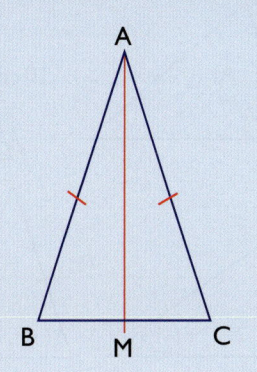

Example – Proof using similar triangles

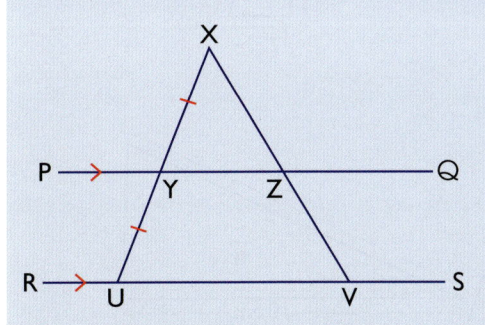

In the diagram, PQ and RS are parallel lines.
XYU and XZV are straight lines.
XY = YU
Prove that UV = 2YZ.

Solution

In the triangles XYZ and XUV
∠XYZ = ∠XUV (Corresponding angles) ← This is because lines PQ and RS are parallel.
∠YXZ is common.
Therefore triangles XYZ and XUV are similar (AA).
So, the sides are in ratio.
$\frac{XU}{XY} = \frac{UV}{YZ} = \frac{VX}{ZX}$
Since XY = YU (given), XU = 2XY and $\frac{XU}{XY} = 2$.
Therefore $\frac{UV}{YZ} = 2$ and UV = 2YZ.

357

Geometry and Measures Strand 2 Properties of shapes

Practising skills

1. Here are 25 triangles. They are 12 pairs and 1 odd one out.
   The pairs are either similar or congruent.
   Identify the pairs (and the odd one out).
   For each pair, justify why you are linking them.

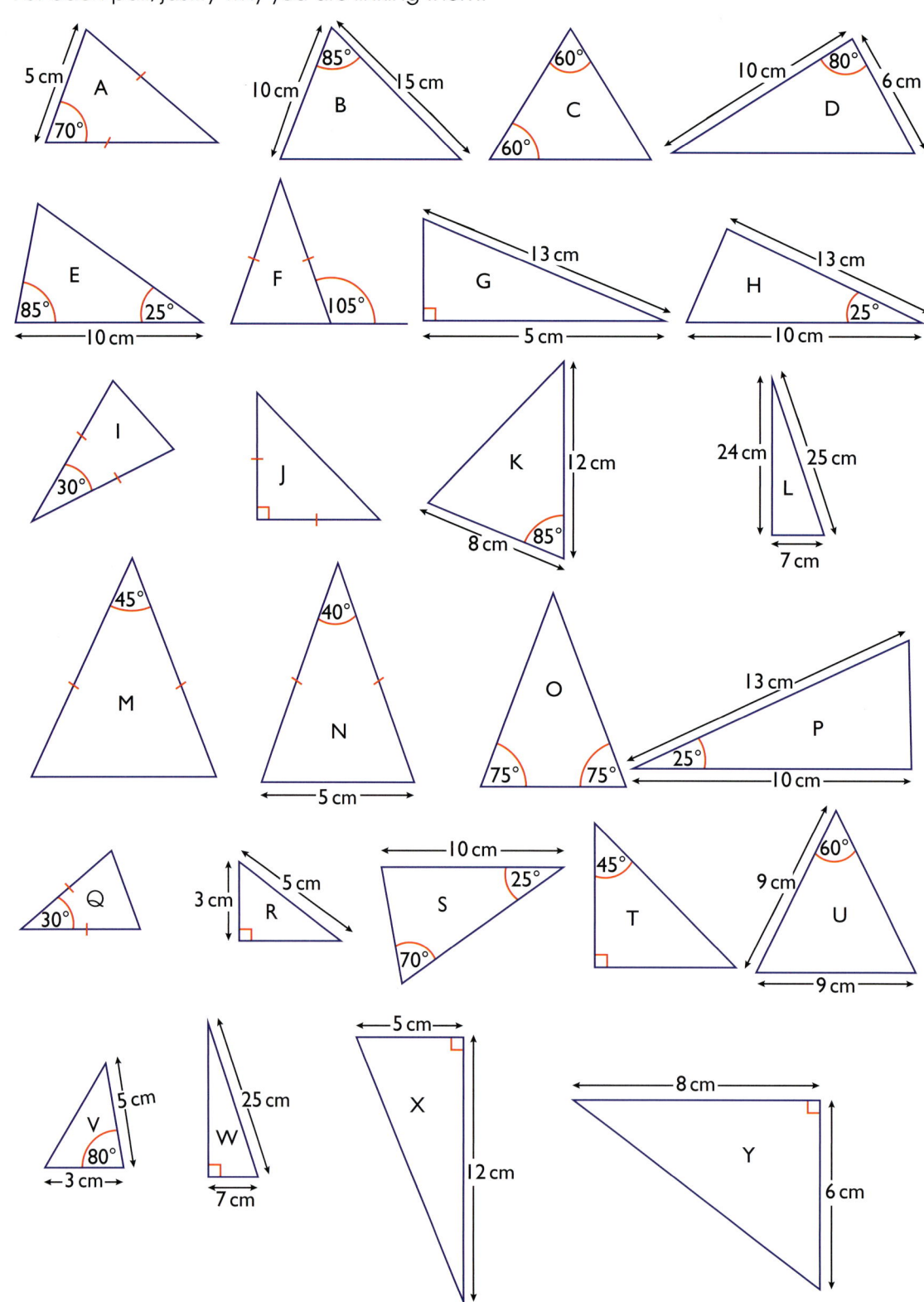

Unit 10 Proof using similar and congruent triangles Band h

Developing fluency

1 ABCDEF is a regular hexagon.
Use congruent triangles to prove that BDF is an equilateral triangle.

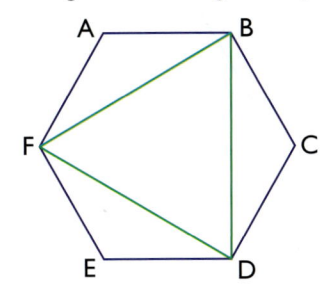

2 ABCD is a quadrilateral.
AB = CD and AD = BC
The angles at A, B, C and D are all 90°.
  a What sort of quadrilateral is ABCD?
  b Prove triangles ADB and BCA are congruent.
  c Hence show that AC = BD.
  d What general result have you proved?

3 ABCD is a kite. The diagonals meet at X.
  a Prove triangles ABC and ADC are congruent.
  b Hence prove triangles ABX and ADX are congruent.
  c Show that X is the mid-point of BD.
  d State this as a general result that is true for all kites.

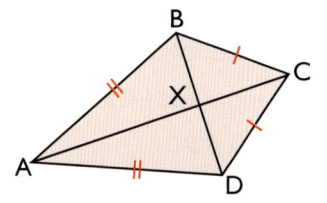

Problem solving

Exam-style questions that require skills developed in this unit are included in later units.

1 The diagram shows the pentagon ADBCE.
ABE is an equilateral triangle.
∠DAB = 90°
∠CEB = 90°
DB = BC.
  a Prove that triangles DAB and CEB are congruent.
  b Prove that ∠DBE = ∠CBA.
  c Explain whether the result in part **a** is still true if triangle ABE is isosceles.

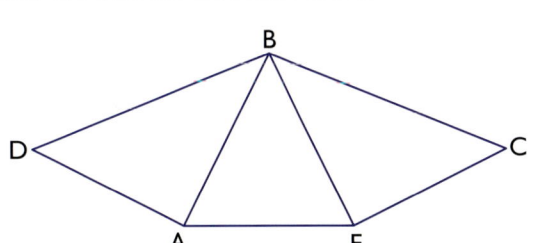

Geometry and Measures Strand 2 Properties of shapes

2 ABCD and CEFG are parallelograms.
BCG and DCE are straight lines.

  a Prove that triangle CFG is similar to triangle CBA.
  Write down reasons at each stage of your working.

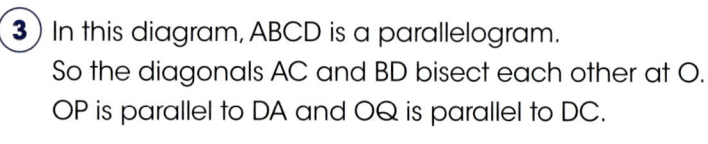

  b Given that DC : CE = 3 : 2, find the value of AF : AC.

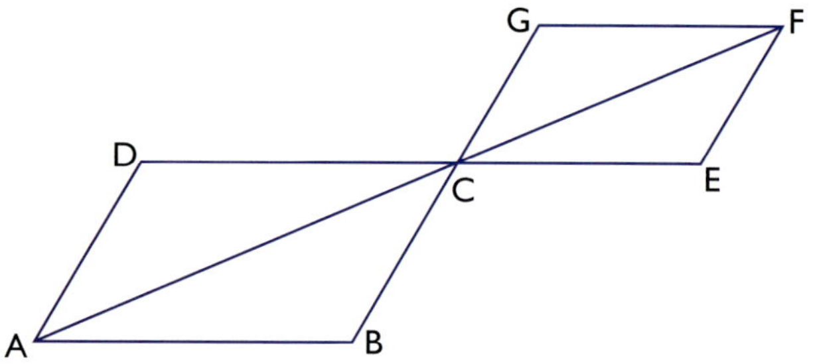

3 In this diagram, ABCD is a parallelogram.
So the diagonals AC and BD bisect each other at O.
OP is parallel to DA and OQ is parallel to DC.

  a Prove that triangles OPB and DAB are similar.

  b Write down another pair of similar triangles.

  c Prove that P is the mid-point of AB.

  d Prove that PQ = $\frac{1}{2}$ AC.

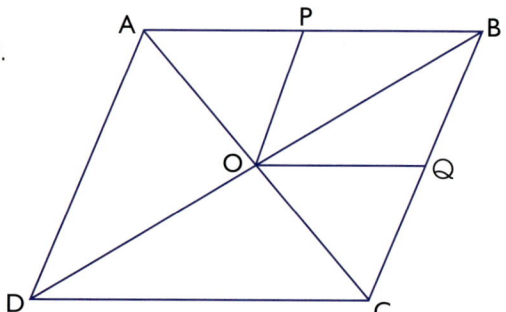

4 PQR is a right-angled triangle. QRS is an isosceles triangle with SQ = SR.
ST is parallel to QP.

  a Prove that triangles SQU and SRU are congruent.

  b Write down the ratio QR : UR.

  c Prove that triangles PQR and TUR are similar.

  d Show that PQ = 2TU.

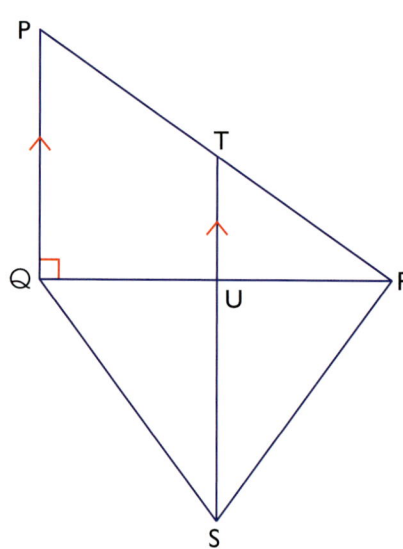

5 In the diagram, ABC is an isosceles triangle with AB = AC.
CF and AB are parallel.
M is the mid-point of BC.
DEMF and DAC are straight lines.

  a Prove that triangles DEA and DFC are similar.

  b Prove that triangles BME and CMF are congruent.

  c Hence show that $\frac{EA}{EB} = \frac{DE}{DF}$.

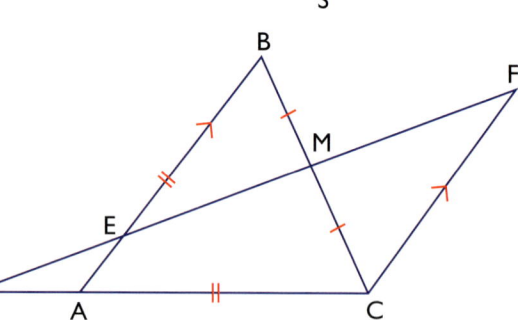

Unit 10 Proof using similar and congruent triangles Band h

6 In this diagram, A and B are the mid-points of PQ and PR.
QBX is a straight line with QB = BX.

  a Prove triangles PAB and PQR are similar.
  What does this tell you about lines AB and QR?

  b Prove triangles QAB and QPX are similar.
  What does this tell you about lines PX and QR?

  c Have you done enough to prove that PXRQ is a parallelogram?
  Explain your answer fully.

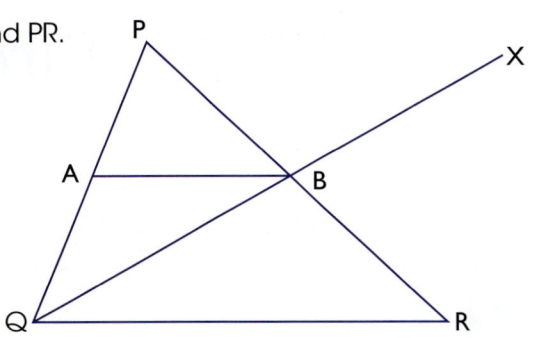

Reviewing skills

1 In the diagram, AC and BD are two straight lines that bisect each other at X.

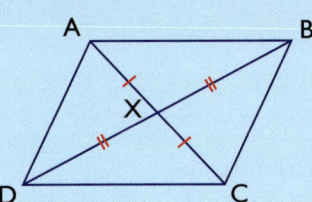

  a Prove that AB = CD and ∠BAX = ∠DCX.

  b What does this tell you about the quadrilateral ABCD? Give reasons for your answer.

Unit 11 • Circle theorems • Band j

Outside the Maths classroom

Jewellery design
A circular pendant has a five-pointed star inside.
The points are equally spaced around the circumference.
What is the size of the angle at each point?

Toolbox

What makes a circle round?
Every radius of a circle has the same length. That's what makes it round.

It means that a triangle like OQP is isosceles because OQ = OP (radii). So the angles OQP and OPQ are equal. They are both marked α.

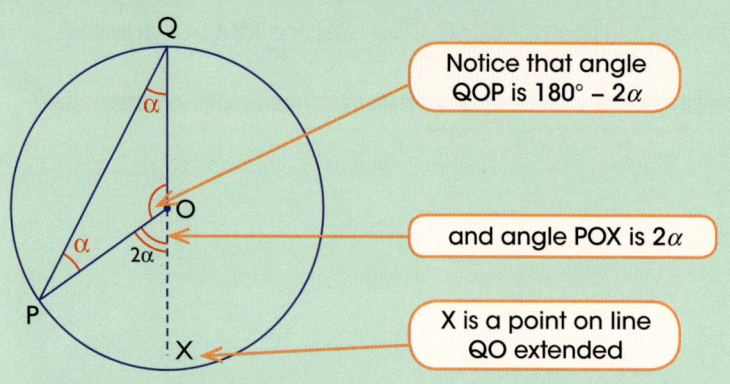

Notice that angle QOP is $180° - 2\alpha$

and angle POX is 2α

X is a point on line QO extended

Circle theorems with angles
The diagram above explains a fundamental circle theorem.

The angle at the centre of a circle is twice the angle at the circumference.

You can see why this is true in the diagram.

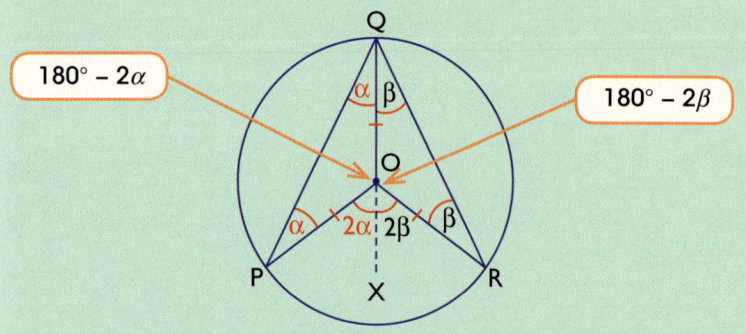

$180° - 2\alpha$

$180° - 2\beta$

The angle PQR is $\alpha + \beta$ and the angle POR is $2\alpha + 2\beta$.
So
$$\angle POR = 2\angle PQR = 2(\alpha + \beta)$$

This theorem gives rise to three more theorems.

The angle in a semicircle is 90°.

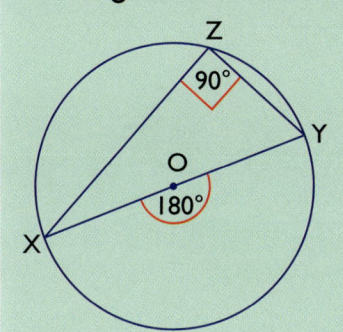

XOY is a diameter and ∠XOY = 180°.
∠XZY is an angle at the circumference. It is $\frac{1}{2}$ of 180° = 90°.
∠XZY is an angle in a semicircle.

Angles in the same segment are equal.

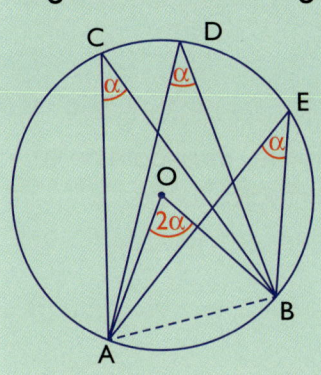

∠AOB = 2∠ACB = 2∠ADB = 2∠AEB = 2α
So ∠ACB = ∠ADB = ∠AEB = α
All the angles stand on the chord AB and are on the same side of it.
They are angles in the same segment.

Opposite angles of a cyclic quadrilateral add up to 180°.

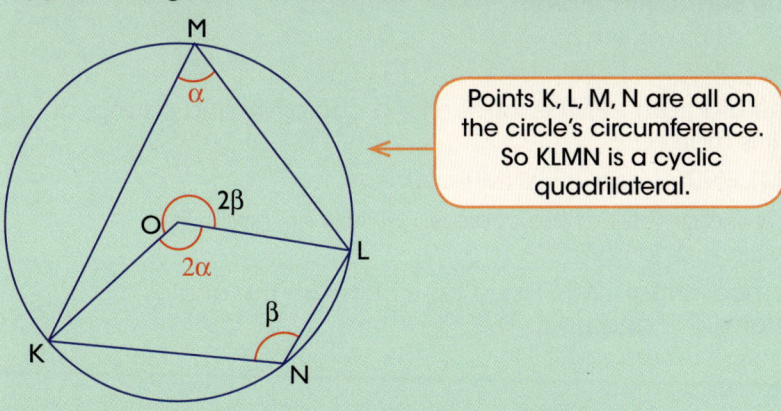

Points K, L, M, N are all on the circle's circumference. So KLMN is a cyclic quadrilateral.

∠KOL = 2∠KML = 2α and ∠KOL (reflex) = 2∠KNL = 2β
At O, 2α + 2β = 360° so α + β = 180°
So ∠KML + ∠KNL = 180°
∠KML and ∠KNL are opposite angles of a cyclic quadrilateral.

Geometry and Measures Strand 2 Properties of shapes

Circle theorems with radii, chords and tangents

Another important theorem is that **the line joining the centre of a circle, O, to the midpoint, M, of a chord, AB is at right angles to it**.

You use congruent triangles to prove this.

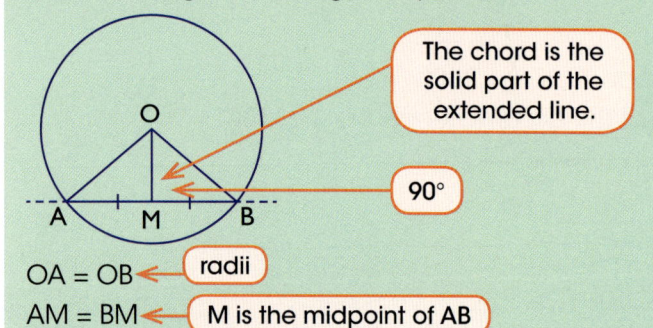

The chord is the solid part of the extended line.

90°

OA = OB ← radii
AM = BM ← M is the midpoint of AB
OM is common
Triangles OAM and OBM are congruent. ← SSS
The sides of OAM are the same lengths as the sides of OBM.
So the angles OMA and OMB are equal and since they make a straight line they must both be 90°.

A special case of this is when the extended line has been translated downwards to the circumference of the circle and becomes a tangent.

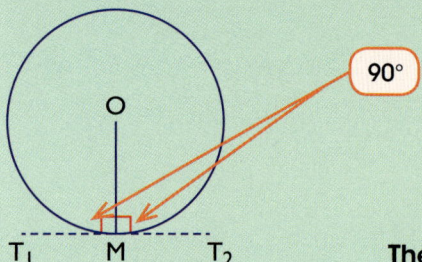

90°

The angle between a radius and a tangent is 90°.

$\angle OMT_1 = \angle OMT_2$

This, in turn, leads on to the '**alternate segment theorem**'

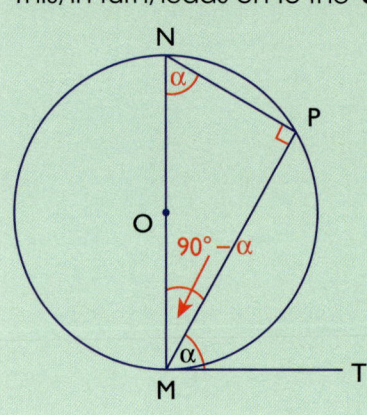

In the diagram $\angle PMT$ is formed by a chord MP and a tangent MT. It is marked α.

$\angle NMT = 90°$ so $\angle NMP = 90° - \alpha$

MN is a diameter of the circle, so MPN is an angle in a semicircle and is 90°.

This means that $\angle MNP$ must be α because the angles of triangle MNP add up to 180°.

Unit 11 Circle theorems Band j

Higher tier only

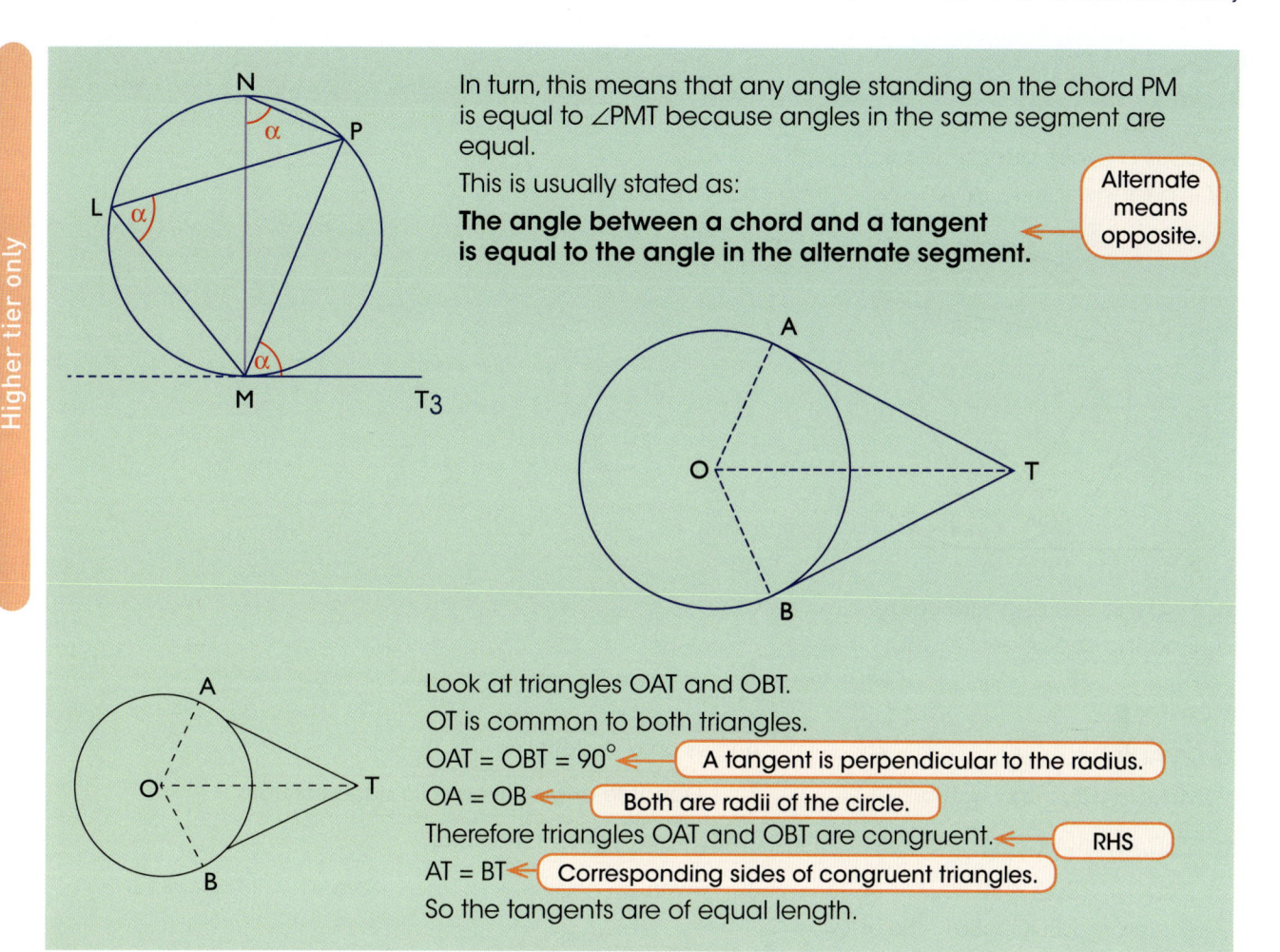

In turn, this means that any angle standing on the chord PM is equal to ∠PMT because angles in the same segment are equal.

This is usually stated as:

The angle between a chord and a tangent is equal to the angle in the alternate segment.

Alternate means opposite.

Look at triangles OAT and OBT.
OT is common to both triangles.
OAT = OBT = 90° ← *A tangent is perpendicular to the radius.*
OA = OB ← *Both are radii of the circle.*
Therefore triangles OAT and OBT are congruent. ← *RHS*
AT = BT ← *Corresponding sides of congruent triangles.*
So the tangents are of equal length.

Example – Using theorems together

A, B, C and D are four points on a circle, centre O.
AD is a diameter. OB is a radius parallel to DC. OB cuts AC at N.
Prove that AN = NC.

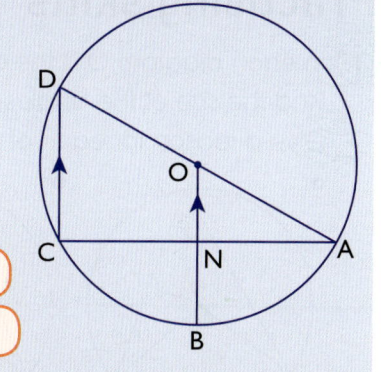

Solution

∠ACD = 90° ← *Angle in a semicircle.*

∠ONA = ∠ACD = 90° ← *Corresponding angles on parallel lines.*

OB bisects AC ← *Angle between radius and chord = 90°.*
So AN = NC

Geometry and Measures Strand 2 Properties of shapes

Example – Using circle theorems

ABCD is a cyclic quadrilateral.
XY is a tangent at A. ∠DAY = 64°, ∠BAX = 56° and ∠CDA = 80°.

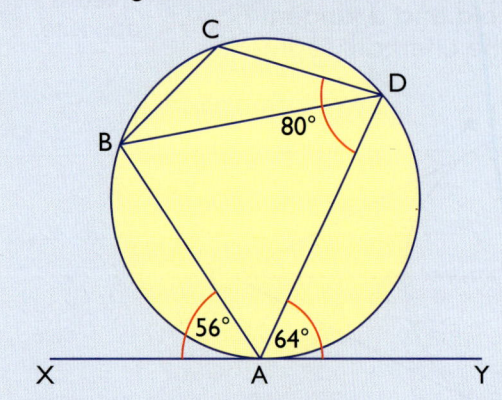

a Find the size of angle BCD.
b Find the size of angle CBD.

Solution

a ∠BAD = 180° − 56° − 64° = 60°   ← Angles on a straight line
   ∠BCD = 180° − 60° = 120°   ← Opposite angles of a cyclic quadrilateral.

b ∠BDA = ∠BAX = 56°   ← Alternate segment theorem.
   ∠BDC + ∠BDA = 80°   ← Given.
   Therefore ∠BDC = 80° − 56° = 24°
   ∠CBD + ∠BCD + ∠BDC = 180°   ← ∠s in a triangle.
   Therefore ∠CBD = 180° − 120° − 24° = 36°

Practising skills

1 In each diagram, O is the centre of the circle.
Find the size of the angles marked with letters.
Give a reason for each of your answers.

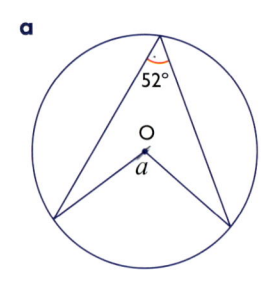

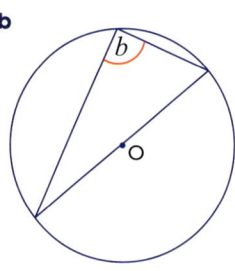

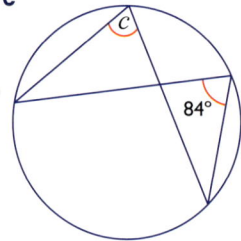

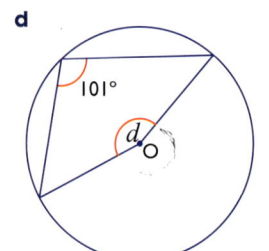

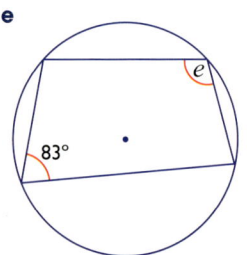

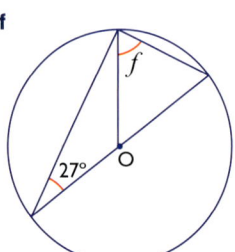

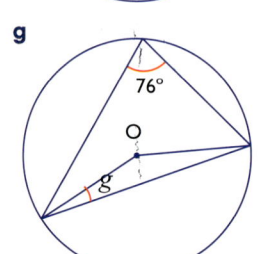

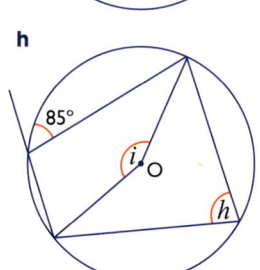

a 52°, a

b b

c c, 84°

d 101°, d

e e, 83°

f f, 27°

g 76°, g

h 85°, i, h

Unit 11 Circle theorems Band j

2) A, B, C and D are points on a circle, centre O.
Angle DCA = 62°. DOB and AOC are straight lines.
Copy and complete the following steps to find the size of angle AOB.
Angle CDO is ☐ because ☐.
Angle COD is ☐ because ☐.
Angle AOB is ☐ because ☐.

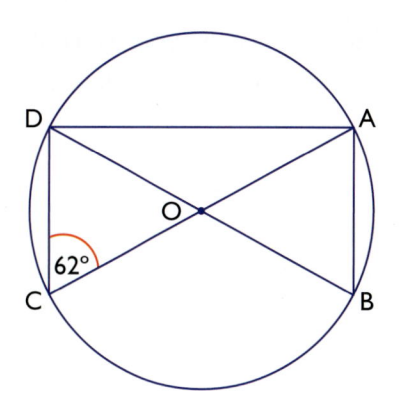

3) A, B, C and D are points on a circle, centre O. Angle BDC = 37°.
AOC is a straight line.
Copy and complete the following steps to find the size of angle ACB, giving reasons.
Angle ADB is ☐ because ☐.
Angle ACB is ☐ because ☐.

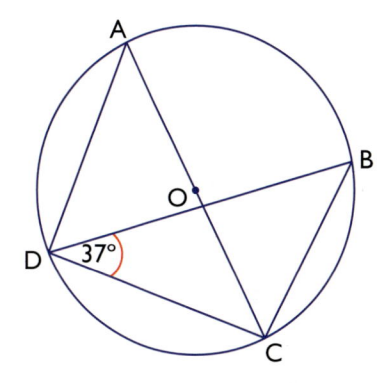

4) A, B, C, D and E are points on a circle. Angle EAD = 43° and DBC = 34°.
Find the size of these angles, giving your reasons:
  a EBD
  b EDC.

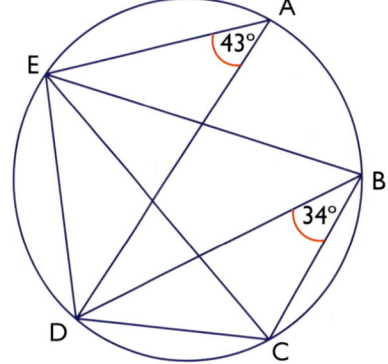

5) ABCD is a cyclic quadrilateral in a circle centre O.
Angle DAB = 78° and angle BDC = 26°.
Find the size of these angles, giving reasons:
  a BOC
  b BCD
  c DCO.

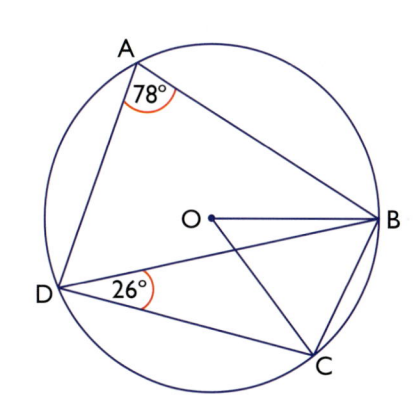

Geometry and Measures Strand 2 Properties of shapes

6 ABCD is a cyclic quadrilateral, centre O.
BD is a diameter. E is a point inside the circle such that CE = DE. Angle DBC = 42°, angle DCE = 30° and angle ADB = 55°.
Find the size of angle ADE.

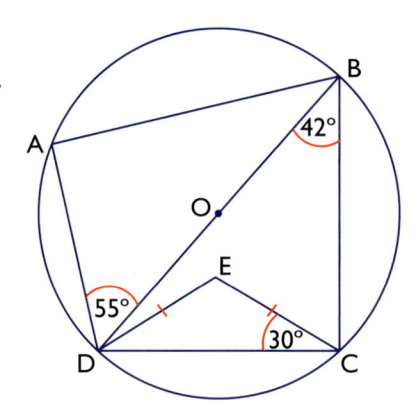

7 A, B and C are points on a circle, centre O. Angle AOB = 136°.
Find the size of angle ACB.

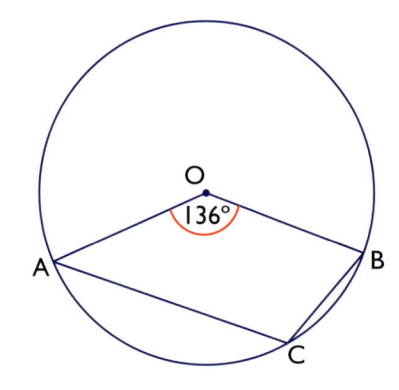

8 A, B, C and D are points on a circle, centre O. DC is a diameter.
Angle DAB = 125°.
Work out the size of angle BDC.

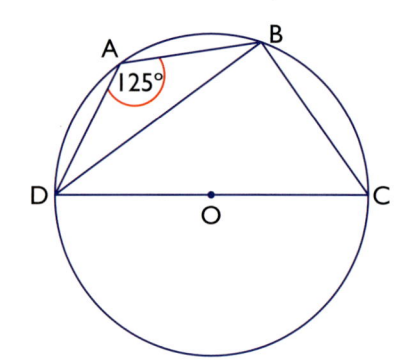

Developing fluency

1 ABC is a triangle with vertices on a circle.
FG is a tangent to the circle at C. Angle BAC = 72° and angle ACF = 54°.
Prove that AC = AB.

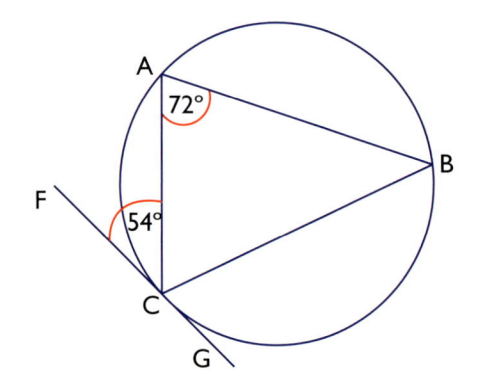

Unit 11 Circle theorems Band j

2) A, B, C, D and E are points on a circle. Angle DBC = 26° and angle AED = 116°.
Prove that AC is a diameter of the circle.

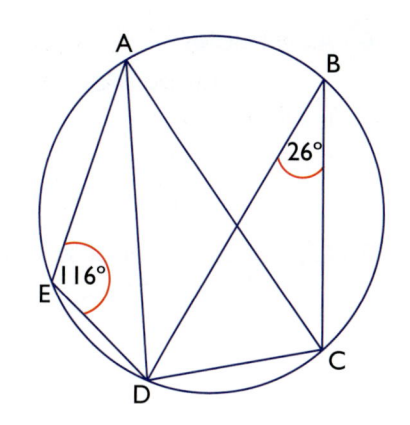

3) A, B, C and D are points on a circle, centre O.
Angle DOC = 100°, angle ABD = 45° and angle ODB = 5°
Prove AB is parallel to DC.

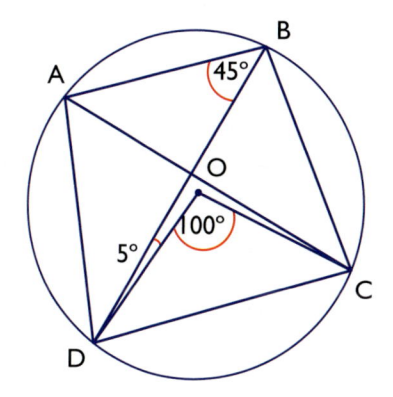

4) A, B, C, D and E are points on a circle.
Angle ADB = x and angle DEC = $2x$.
ED and AC are parallel. DB and EC intersect at P.
Show that angle DPC = $5x$.

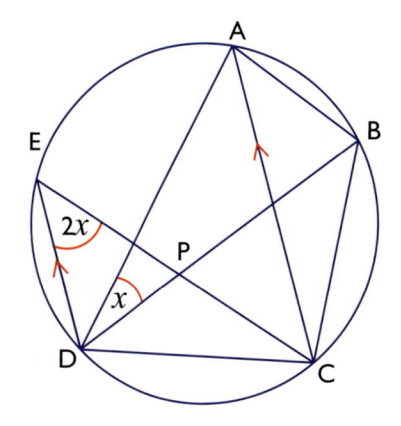

5) ABC is an isosceles triangle with AB = AC.
The vertices lie on a circle, centre O.
MN is a tangent at C. Angle BCN = 60°.
Prove that OC bisects the angle ACB.

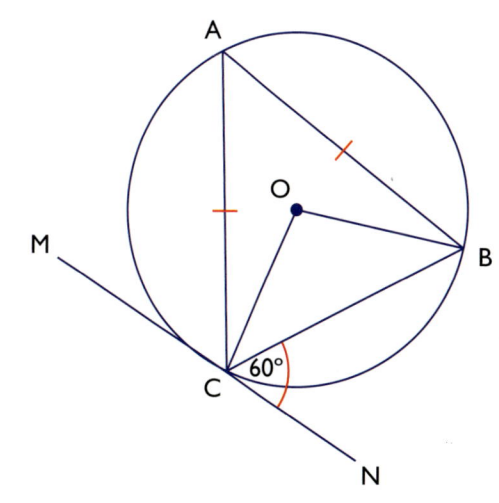

Higher tier only

Geometry and Measures Strand 2 Properties of shapes

6 Albert states:

"The only parallelograms that are cyclic quadrilaterals are those that are also rectangles."

Is Albert correct?

If you answer yes, then give a reason why this should be so.

If you answer no, then give an example to show such a parallelogram.

7 Complete this proof to show that a radius that is perpendicular to a chord bisects it.

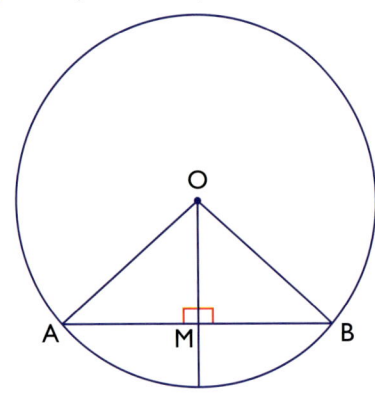

AB is a chord and OM is at right angle to AB.

  i   Prove that triangles OAM and OBM are congruent.

  ii Hence show that OM bisects AB.

8 Complete this proof to show that angle QOR = 2 × angle QPR.

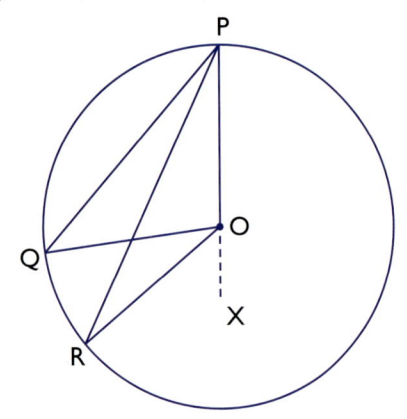

  A Show that angle OPQ = angle OQP.

  Label these two angles a on a copy of the diagram.

  Find the size of angle POQ and mark it on your diagram.

  B Show that angle ORP = angle OQR.

  Label these two angles y.

  Find the size of angle POR and mark it on your diagram.

  C Hence write down expressions for the sizes of angles QPR and QOR, giving your reasons.

  D Hence show that angle QOR = 2 × angle QPR.

Unit 11 Circle theorems Band j

Problem solving

1 Here is a circle, centre O.
PQ and PR are tangents to the circle at Q and R. S is a point on the circumference.
Angle QPR = 50° and angle ORS = 20°.

a Find the size of angle x.

b What can you say about the property of RP and QP?

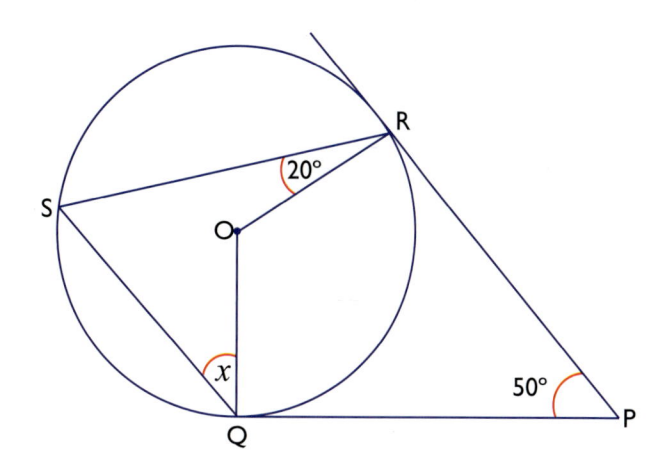

2 ABCD is a tangent at C to a circle, centre O.
E, F and G are points on the circle.
AEOG and FEB are straight lines.
Angle COE = 56°. Angle EBC = 72°.
Calculate the size of angle CGF.
(You must give reasons at each stage of your working.)

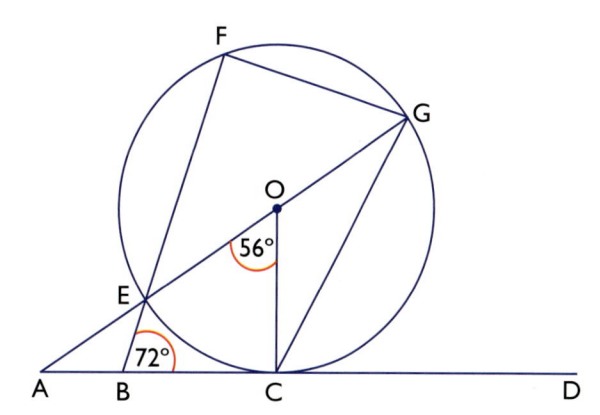

3 AB is a diameter of this circle.
CXD is a straight line perpendicular to AB.

a Prove that triangle AXC is similar to triangle ACB.

b Hence, giving a reason, show that $AC^2 = AX \times AB$.

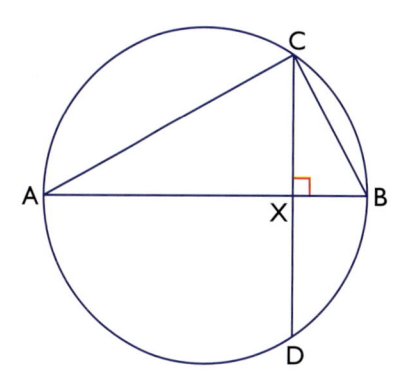

4 P, Q, R and S are points on a circle. PR and SQ meet at X.
PQ is parallel to SR.
Prove that SX = RX.

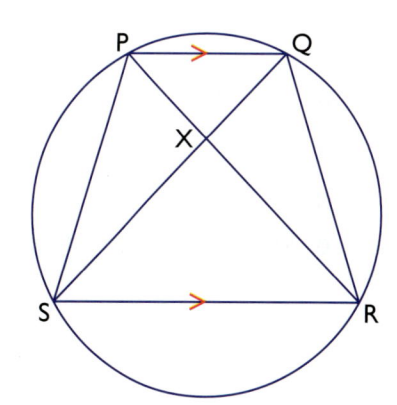

Geometry and Measures Strand 2 Properties of shapes

5 ABCD is a cyclic quadrilateral in a circle, centre O.
AB = AD, angle DBC = 38° and angle BDC = 32°.
Find the size of angle ADO.

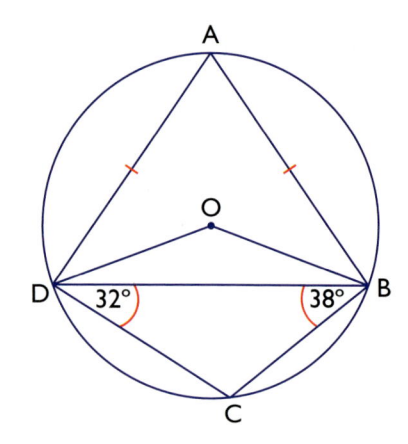

6 ABCD is a cyclic quadrilateral with AB parallel to DC.
Explain why ABCD is an isosceles trapezium.

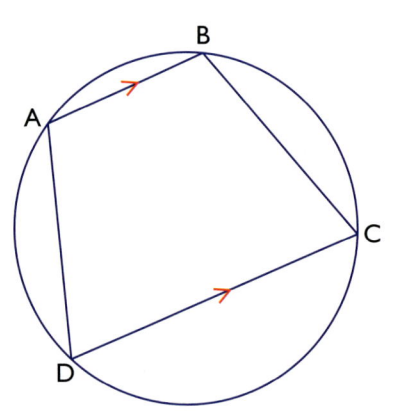

7 In this diagram O is the centre of the circle and A, B, and C are points on the circumference.
∠OAB = ∠OCB = x
∠ABC = $2x$

   a Show that $x°$ can have any value less than 90°.

   b What shape is OABC in the cases:
      i 45° < x < 90°
      ii 0° < x < 45°
      iii x = 45°?

8 Look at the diagram.
You are also given that DT = 6.8 cm.
Find each of the following:

   a length TF

   b ∠TDO

   c ∠DOF

   d ∠ODE

   e length DO (*note trigonometry skills are required)

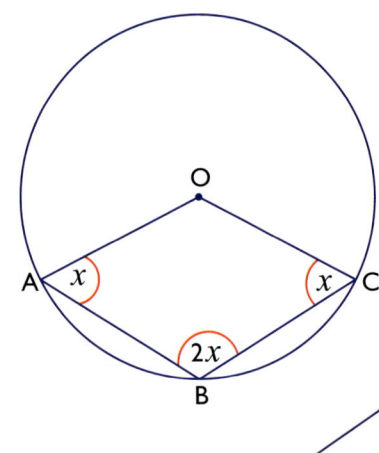

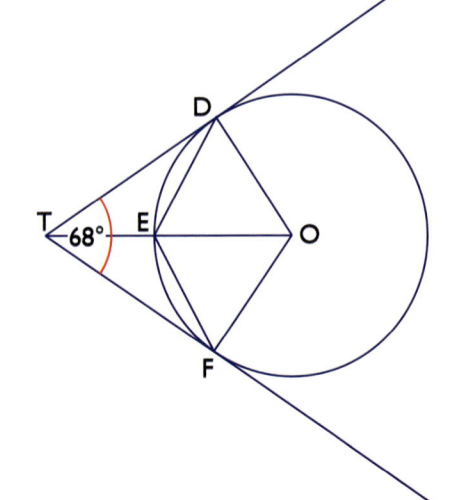

Reviewing skills

1) A, B, C and D are points on a circle.
AT is a tangent to the circle at A. BC is parallel to AT.

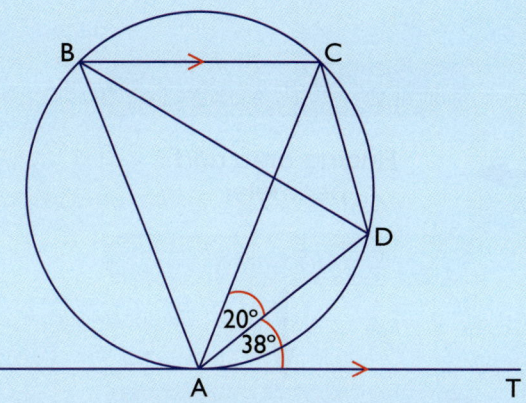

Given that angle DAT = 38° and angle CAD = 20°, find the size of angle BAD.

2) Here is a circle, centre O.
DOB is a diameter. Angle CDB = 58° and angle OAB = 74°.

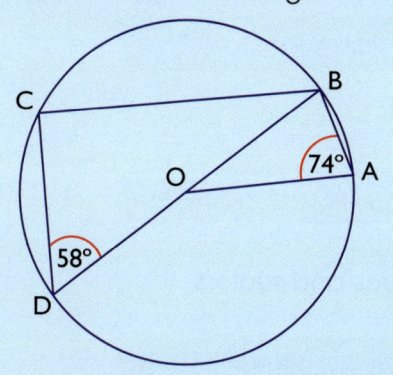

Prove that:

a OA is parallel to BC

b AB is not parallel to DC.

Geometry and Measures
Strand 3 Measuring shapes

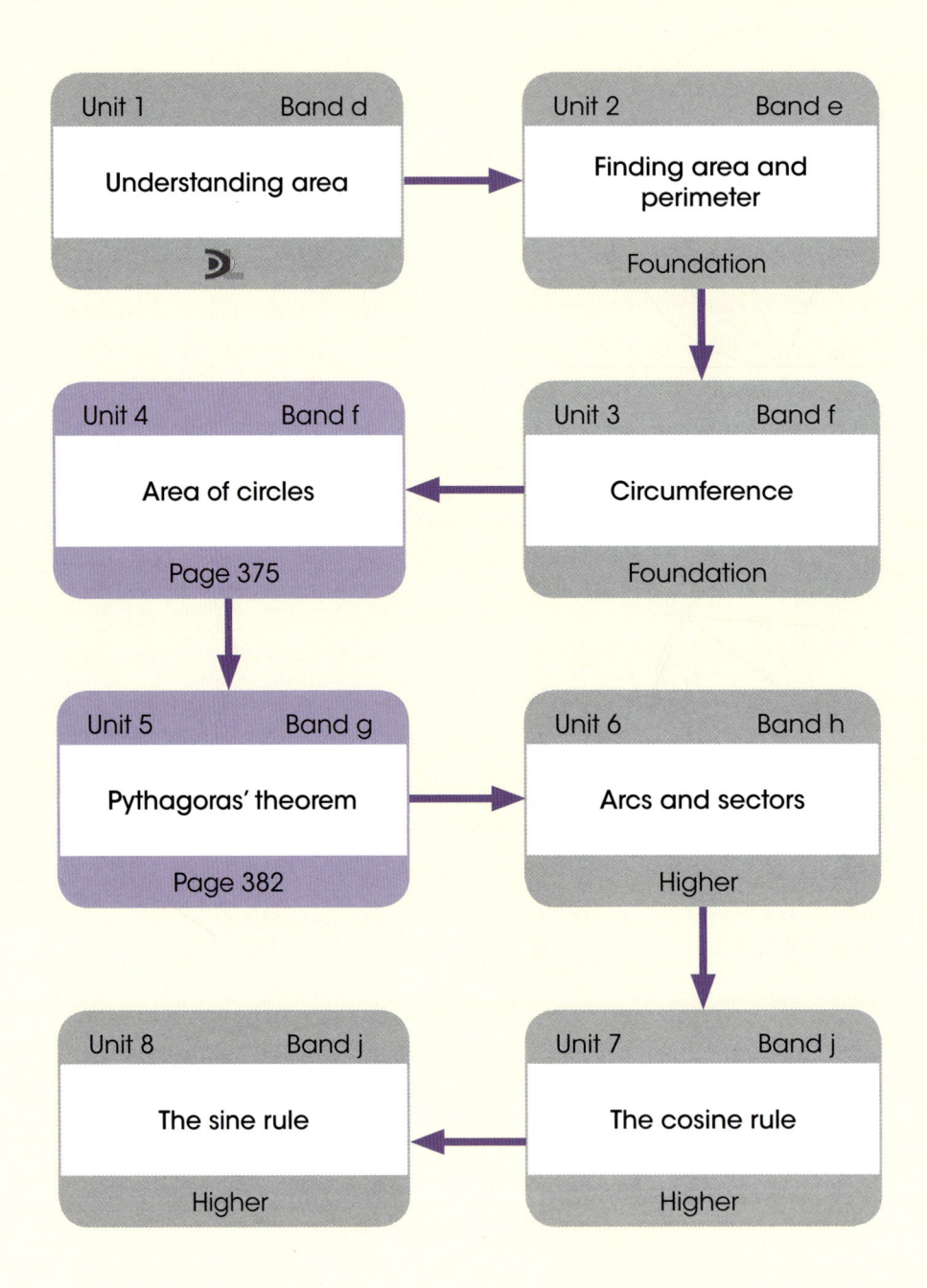

Unit 1	Band d
Understanding area	

→

Unit 2	Band e
Finding area and perimeter	
Foundation	

↓

Unit 3	Band f
Circumference	
Foundation	

←

Unit 4	Band f
Area of circles	
Page 375	

↓

Unit 5	Band g
Pythagoras' theorem	
Page 382	

→

Unit 6	Band h
Arcs and sectors	
Higher	

↓

Unit 7	Band j
The cosine rule	
Higher	

←

Unit 8	Band j
The sine rule	
Higher	

Units 1–3 are assumed knowledge for this book. Knowledge and skills from these units are used throughout the book.

Unit 4 • Area of circles • Band f

Outside the Maths classroom

Amphitheatres
How many seats are there in this amphitheatre?

Toolbox

The area, A, of a circle of radius r is given by $A = \pi r^2$.

A **semicircle** is half a circle.
Its area is $\frac{1}{2}\pi r^2$.

A **quadrant** is a quarter of a circle.
Its area is $\frac{1}{4}\pi r^2$.

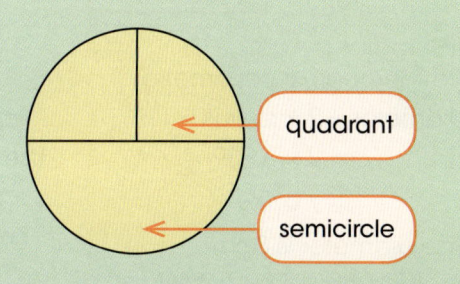

Example – Finding the area of a circle given the diameter

Find the area of this circle.

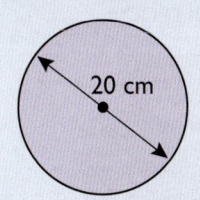

20 cm

Solution

First find the radius.
$r = \frac{d}{2} = \frac{20}{2} = 10\,\text{cm}$

$A = \pi r^2$
$\quad = \pi \times 10^2$
$\quad = \pi \times 100$
$\quad = 314.2\,\text{cm}^2$ (to 1 d.p.)

Geometry and Measures Strand 3 Measuring shapes

Example – Finding the radius and diameter of a circle given the area

The area of this circle is 50 cm².
Calculate
a the radius
b the diameter.
Give your answers to the nearest centimetre.

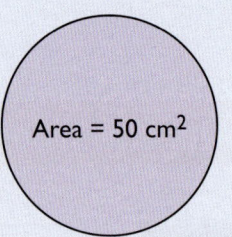

Area = 50 cm²

Solution

a $\quad A = \pi r^2$
$\quad 50 = \pi r^2$
$\quad \dfrac{50}{\pi} = r^2$ ← Divide both sides by π

$\quad \sqrt{\dfrac{50}{\pi}} = r$ ← Take the square root of both sides.

$\quad r = \sqrt{\dfrac{50}{\pi}}$
$\quad r = 3.989...$ ← Your calculator often gives you a long number. Write it like this, using ... for the later digits. That is better than writing them all down.

The radius is 4 cm
(to the nearest centimetre).

b Diameter = 2 × radius
$\quad\quad\quad\quad\ = 2 \times 3.989...$ ← Use the most accurate value.
$\quad\quad\quad\quad\ = 7.979...$

The diameter is 8 cm
(to the nearest centimetre). ← Keep the number on your calculator until you get your final answer.

Practising skills

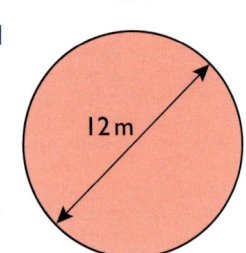

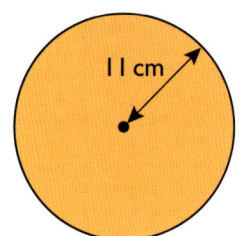

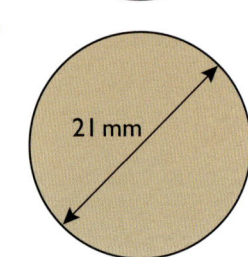

(1) Calculate the area of each of these circles. Give your answers to one decimal place.

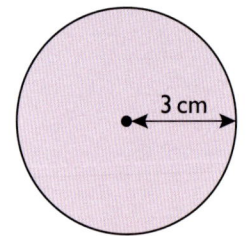

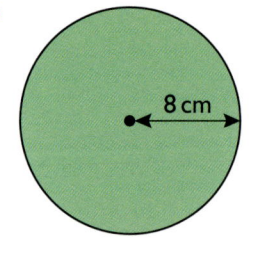

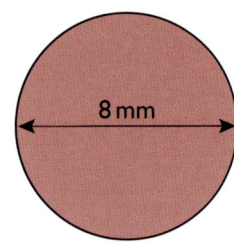

a 3 cm

b 8 cm

c 8 mm

d 12 m

e 11 cm

f 21 mm

Unit 4 Area of circles Band f

2) Calculate the area of each of these circles. Each circle is drawn accurately.

a

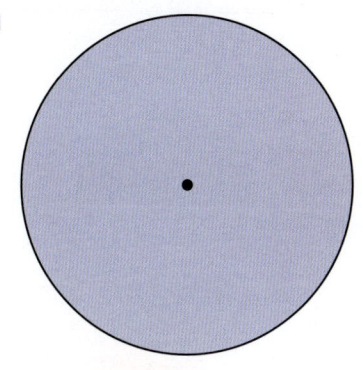

b

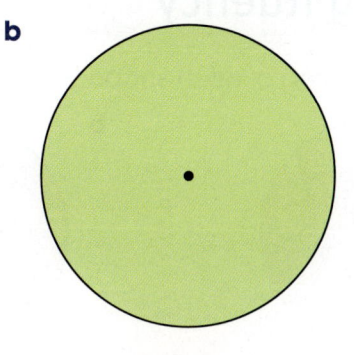

c

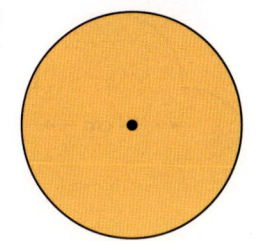

d

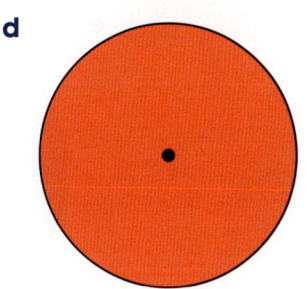

3) A circle has an area of 35 cm².

Use the formula $A = \pi r^2$ to calculate its radius to one decimal place.

4) A circle has an area of 60 cm².

   a Calculate its radius to one decimal place.

   b Write down its diameter.

   c Calculate the circle's circumference.

5) Copy and complete this table which gives some measurements for circles.

	Radius	Diameter	Area	Circumference
a	7 cm			44.0 cm
b		17 cm		
c			80 cm²	
d			250 cm²	56.0 cm

377

Geometry and Measures Strand 3 Measuring shapes

Developing fluency

1. Calculate the area of each shape.

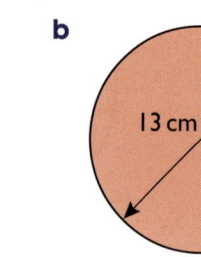

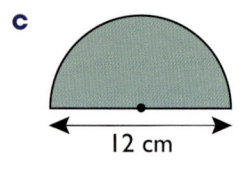

   a 11 cm

   b 13 cm

   c 12 cm

   d 9 cm

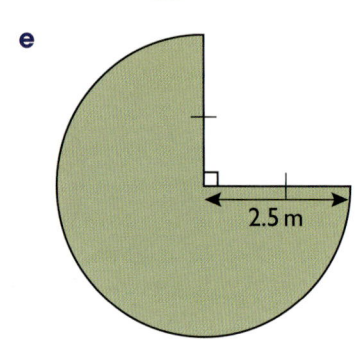

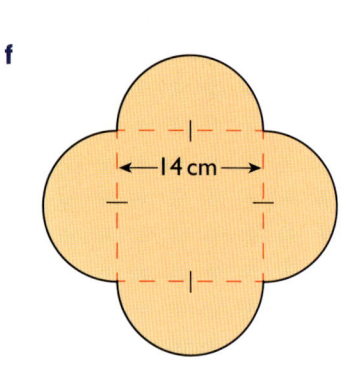

   e 2.5 m

   f 14 cm

2. A circle has area 200 cm². What is its circumference?

3. A circle has circumference 30 cm. What is its area?

4. This semicircle has area 45 cm².

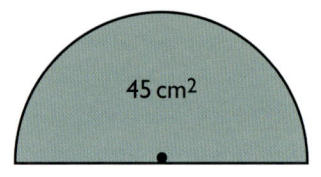

   45 cm²

   Work out the perimeter of the semicircle.

5. Work out the difference between the red area and the blue area of this target board.

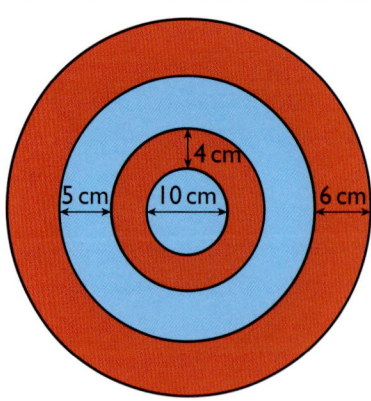

   5 cm, 10 cm, 4 cm, 6 cm

378

Unit 4 Area of circles Band f

6 Candice is making biscuits. She has a rectangular piece of biscuit mixture measuring 32 cm by 16 cm.
She cuts out eight circular biscuits of diameter 8 cm.
She uses the remainder of the mixture to make one last biscuit.
What is its diameter, assuming all the biscuits have the same thickness?

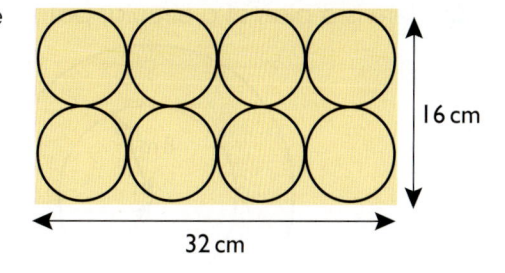

7 Adam ties his goat to the corner of his garden shed.
The shed is 19 m by 8 m. The rope is 12 m long.
Calculate the total area that Adam's goat can graze using this diagram.

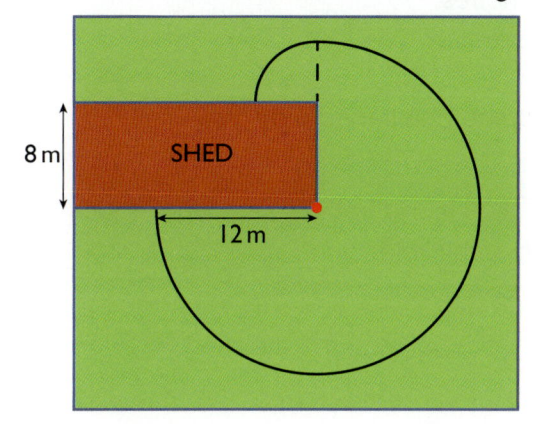

8 Beti is designing a display board for the entrance to her company.
The board is in the shape of a rectangle and two semicircles.
The board has a single line of symmetry.

 a Work out the area of the display board.

 b She uses very expensive paint. It costs her £73 (to the nearest £1).
What is the cost of the paint per square centimetre?

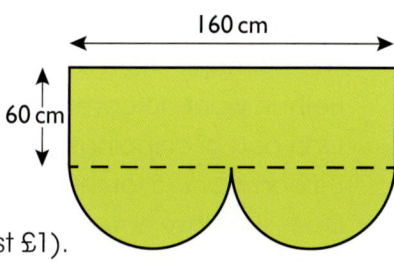

Problem solving

1 Here is a plan of Sophie's garden.

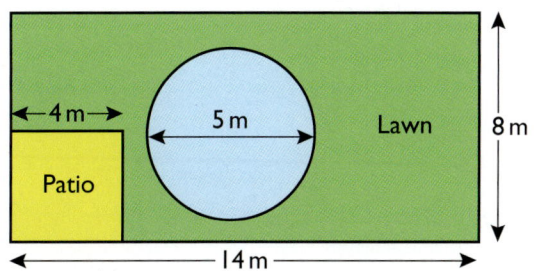

The patio is a square 4 m by 4 m.
The pond is a circle of diameter 5 m.
The rest of the garden is lawn.
Sophie wants to put new turf on the lawn.
Work out the area of the lawn.

379

Geometry and Measures Strand 3 Measuring shapes

2) Here is a plan of a circular path.

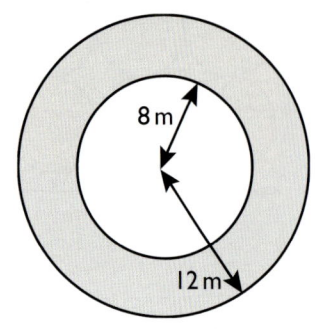

The inner edge of the path is a circle with radius 8 metres.
The outer edge of the path is a circle with radius 12 metres.
Both circles have the same centre.
Helen is going to lay rubber matting on the path, for the children to play on.
The rubber matting costs £30 per square metre.
Work out the total cost of the rubber matting.

3) The diagram shows a garden plot in the shape of a semicircle.

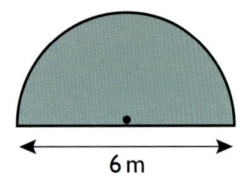

The diameter of the semicircle is 6 m.
Bethan wants to cover the garden plot with wood bark chippings.
One bag of chippings covers an area of $0.6 m^2$ and costs £3.
Bethan has £75 for the chippings.
Does she have enough money?
Show all of your working.

4) Here is a diagram of an athletics field.

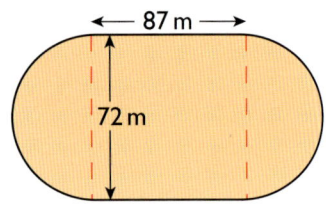

The field has two ends which are semicircles.
Each semicircle has a diameter of 72 m.
The length of each straight part is 87 m.

  a What is the length of the field to the nearest metre?

Fatima is going to spray the field with fertiliser.
One litre of fertiliser is enough for $50 m^2$.

  b How many litres of fertiliser does Fatima need?

Unit 4 Area of circles Band f

5 Here is a diagram of a window made of stained glass.
The window is in the shape of a rectangle and a semicircle.
The width of the window is 60 cm.
The height of the window is 160 cm.
The stained glass in the window needs repairing.
The cost of a repair is £2000 per m^2 of stained glass.
Work out the total cost of the repair.

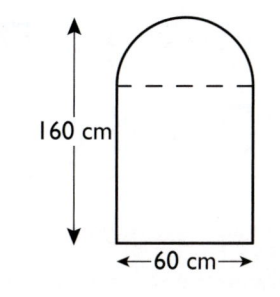

6 A factory makes metal discs by punching out a circle from a piece of metal.
The piece of metal is a square of sides 25 cm.
Any metal left over when the circle is removed is sent for recycling.
The factory makes 800 discs each hour.
Work out the total area of metal sent for recycling each hour.
Give your answer in square metres.

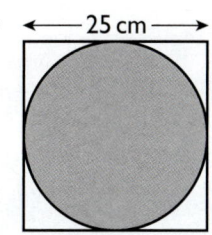

Reviewing skills

1 Calculate the area of each of these circles. Give your answers to one decimal place.

a 5 cm

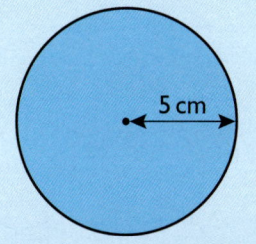

b 7 mm

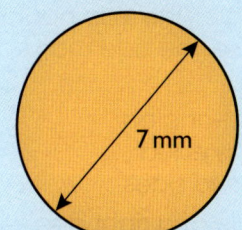

c 2.4 km

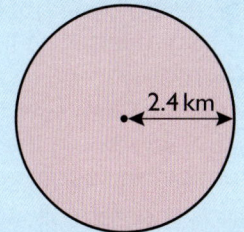

2 A circle has an area of 52 cm^2. Calculate to one decimal place
   a the radius of the circle
   b the diameter of the circle.

3 Calculate the area of each shape.

a 9 cm

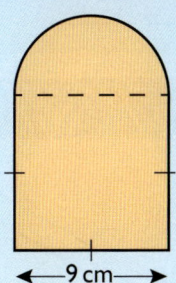

b 8 cm, 15 cm

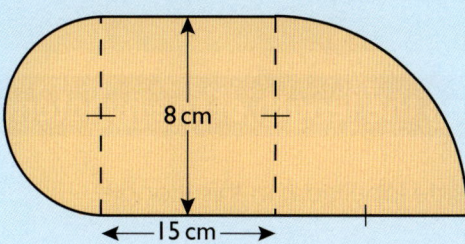

4 The diagram shows part of the cross-section of a building.
The shaded part of the diagram shows a support for the building.
The edges of the support are quarter-circle arcs with the same centre.
The width of the support is 2 metres.
The radius of the inner quarter circle is 3 metres.
Work out the area of the support's cross-section.

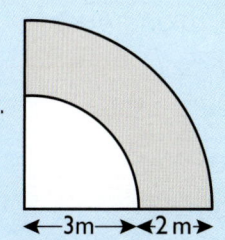

3 m   2 m

381

Unit 5 • Pythagoras' theorem • Band g

Outside the Maths classroom

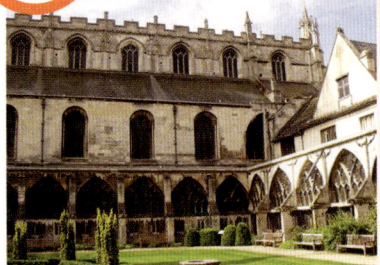

Buildings
Why do most buildings have corners that are right angles?

Toolbox

The longest side of a right-angled triangle (the side opposite the right angle) is called the **hypotenuse**, the side marked h on the diagram.

Pythagoras' theorem says that for a right-angled triangle, the square on the hypotenuse is equal to the sum of the squares on the other two sides.

Pythagoras' theorem allows the third side of a right-angled triangle to be calculated when the other two sides are known.

Pythagoras' theorem:

$a^2 + b^2 = h^2$

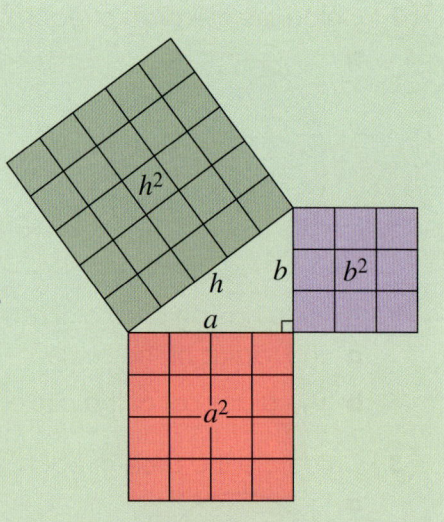

Example – Finding the length of the hypotenuse

Find the length of the side labelled h in this triangle.

Solution

Let $a = 10$ and $b = 6$ ← It could be $a = 6$ and $b = 10$.
$a^2 + b^2 = h^2$ ← Pythagoras' theorem.
$10^2 + 6^2 = h^2$ ← Substitute in the lengths.
$100 + 36 = h^2$
$136 = h^2$
$h = 11.661...$
$h = 11.7$ cm (to 1 d.p.)

Example – Solving a problem involving a right-angled triangle

Gill is a decorator.
She uses a ladder 6m long.
The safety instructions on the ladder say that the foot of the ladder must be at least 1.75m from the base of the wall on horizontal ground.
What is the maximum height her ladder will reach up a vertical wall?

Solution

$1.75^2 + y^2 = 6^2$ ← Pythagoras' theorem rewritten for this problem.

$3.0625 + y^2 = 36$

$y^2 = 36 - 3.0625$

$y^2 = 32.9375$ ← Draw a sketch and label it. y stands for the height reached by the ladder.

$y = \sqrt{32.9375}$ ← Take the square root of both sides.

$y = 5.739...$

Maximum height of ladder = 5.74m (to the nearest centimetre)

Practising skills

1 For each triangle, write down which is the longest side (the hypotenuse).
Then write Pythagoras' theorem in terms of the letters given.

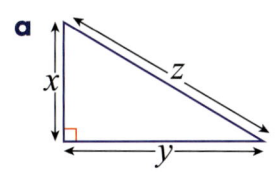

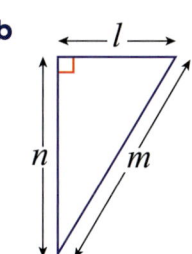

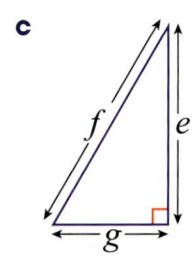

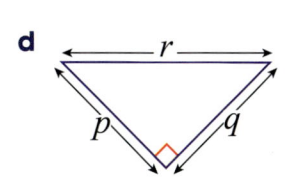

a (triangle with sides x, y, z)

b (triangle with sides l, m, n)

c (triangle with sides e, f, g)

d (triangle with sides p, q, r)

383

Geometry and Measures Strand 3 Measuring shapes

2 Find the length of the hypotenuse of each triangle.
Copy and complete each calculation.

a $x^2 = 5^2 + 12^2$
$x^2 = 25 + \square$
$x^2 = \square$
$x = \sqrt{\square}$
The hypotenuse is $\square$ cm

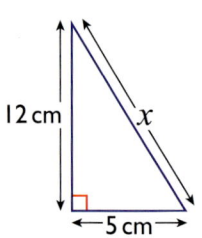

b $y^2 = 6^2 + 8^2$
$y^2 = \square + \square$
$y^2 = \square$
$y = \sqrt{\square}$
The $\square$

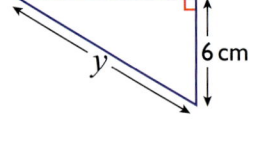

c $z^2 = \square + \square$
$z^2 = \square$
$z^2 = \square$
$z = \sqrt{\square}$
The $\square$

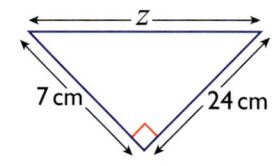

3 Find the length of the unknown side in each triangle. Give each answer correct to 1 decimal place.

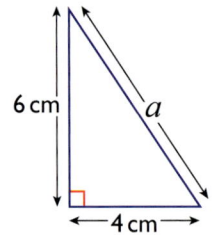

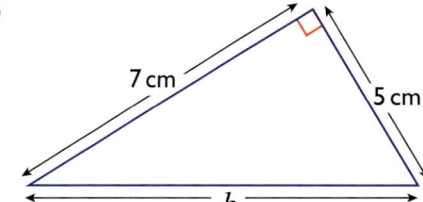

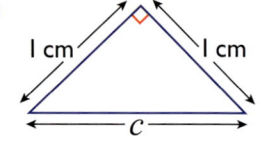

4 Find the length of the hypotenuse in each of these triangles.

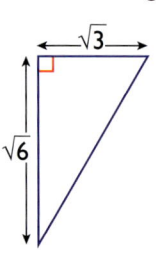

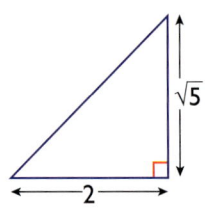

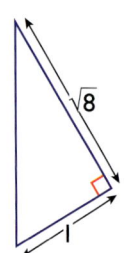

Why did you not need a calculator to answer this question?

5) Find the length of the unknown side of each triangle. Copy and complete each calculation.

a) $x^2 + 4^2 = 5^2$
$x^2 + 16 = 25$
$x^2 = 25 - 16$
$x^2 = \square$
$x = \sqrt{\square}$
The base of the triangle is $\square$ cm

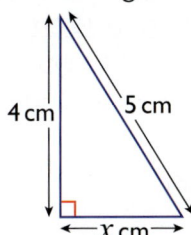

b) $y^2 + 15^2 = \square$
$y^2 + \square = \square$
$y^2 \square = \square$
$\square$
$\square$

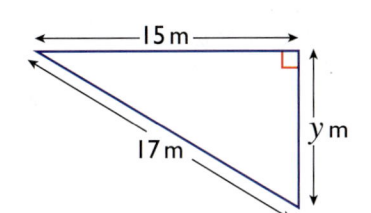

c) $z^2 + \square = \square$
$\square$
$\square$
$\square$
$\square$

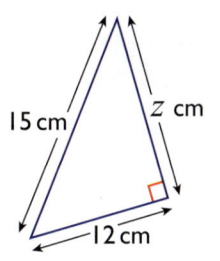

6) Find the length of the unknown side in each triangle. Give the answer correct to 1 decimal place.

a) (triangle with legs 10 cm and 4 cm, hypotenuse a)

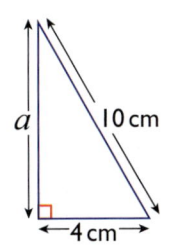

b) (triangle with 9 cm, 6 cm, and b)

c) (triangle with 5 cm, 8 cm, and c)

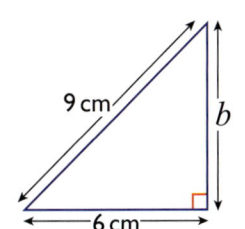

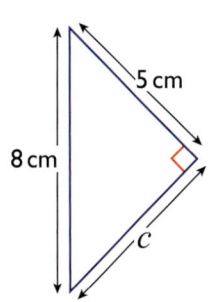

7) Without using a calculator, find the length of the unknown side in each triangle.

a) (triangle with 4 cm, $\sqrt{41}$ cm, and a)

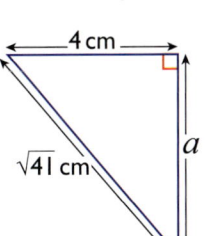

b) (triangle with $\sqrt{19}$ m, $\sqrt{17}$ m, and b)

c) (triangle with 2 miles, $\sqrt{3}$ miles, and c)

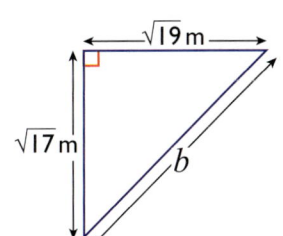

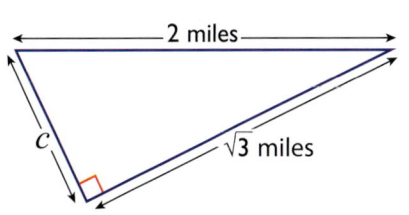

Developing fluency

1) Calculate the perimeter and the area of this triangle.

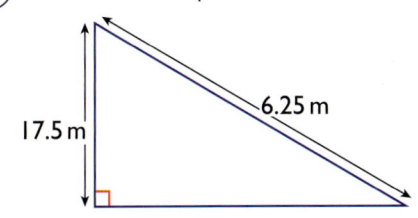

(triangle with 17.5 m, 6.25 m)

Geometry and Measures Strand 3 Measuring shapes

2 The sides of triangle A are 7 cm, 9.4 cm and 12.2 cm.
The sides of triangle B are 7.2 cm, 9.6 cm and 12 cm.
The sides of triangle C are 7.4 cm, 9 cm and 12.4 cm.
Which of the three triangles are right-angled triangles? Explain your answer.

3 A ladder is placed on horizontal ground and leans against a vertical wall.
It reaches a height of 3.2 m up the wall.
The foot of the ladder is 2.4 m from the base of the wall.
Calculate the length of the ladder.

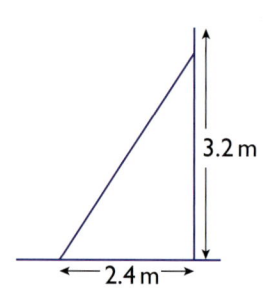

4 Rhys is making a wooden gate with three horizontal lengths, three vertical lengths and one diagonal length as shown.
Work out the total length of timber he needs to make the gate.

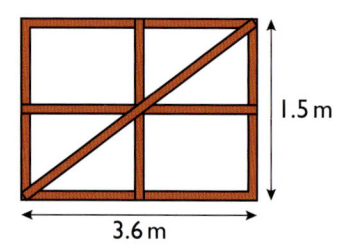

5 A hiker leaves camp and walks south for 8 km, then east for 19.2 km where she stops for a rest.
Then she walks directly back to camp. How much shorter is her return journey?

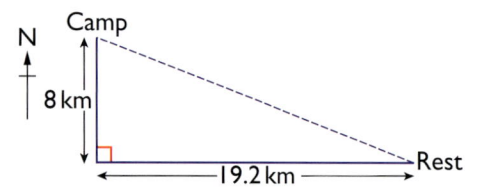

6 In this diagram, find
 a the length CD
 b the perimeter of triangle ABC
 c the area of triangle ABC.

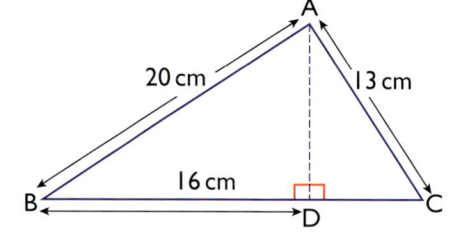

7 Find the perimeter and area of the quadrilateral PQRS.

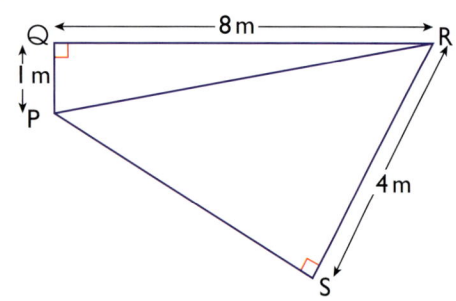

8 KLMN is a rhombus. Its perimeter is 52 cm.
The diagonal LN is 24 cm long.
Find the area of KLMN.

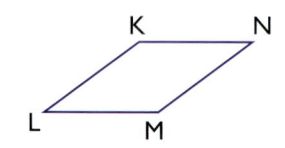

9) A square is drawn with its vertices on the circumference of a circle of radius 5 cm.

   a What is the length of each side of the square?
   b The regions between the square and circle are four segments.
      Find the area of each segment, giving your answer to 3 significant figures.

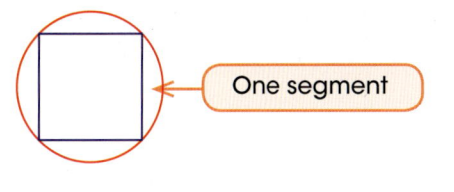

10) Calculate the lengths of x and y.

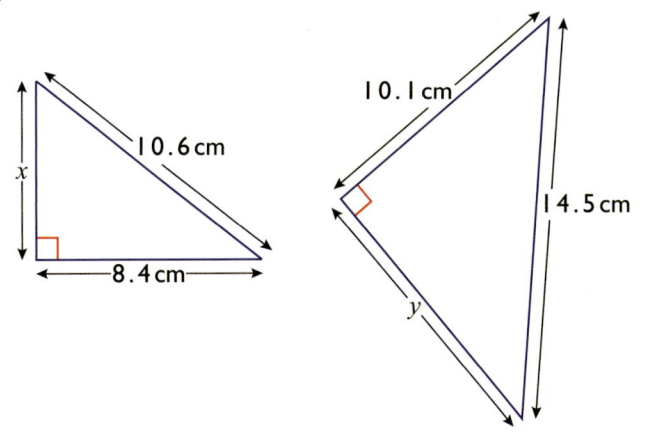

Problem solving

1) This is a field in the shape of a right-angled triangle.
   Fencing is going to be put around the field.
   The fencing costs £17.50 for a 2-metre length.
   Work out the cost to put fencing round the field.
   Give your answer correct to the nearest £10.

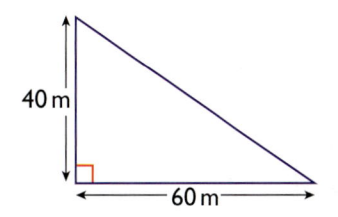

2) The diagram shows a garden in the shape of a trapezium.

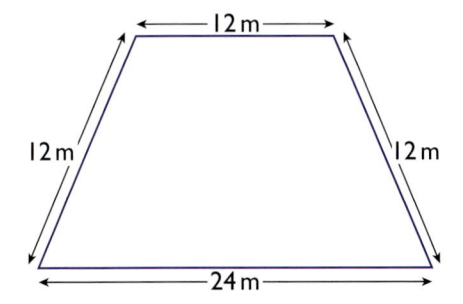

   Turf is going to be put down in the garden.
   Turf costs £2.50 per m^2.
   Work out the total cost of the turf for the garden.

3) Two boats leave a port at the same time.
   The *Sirius* sails due north at 10 km per hour.
   The *Polaris* sails due east at 24 km per hour.
   By how much does the distance between the boats increase each hour?

Geometry and Measures Strand 3 Measuring shapes

4 The diagram shows the end of a modern building.

At a certain wind speed, the wind exerts a force on the building of 128 newtons per square metre.
Norman says that the total force on the end of the building is more than 20 000 newtons.
Rodney says that the total force on the end of the building is less than 20 000 newtons.
Who is correct? You must show all your working.

5 This is a field in the shape of a rectangle ABCD.
The rectangle has a width of 57 m and a length of 76 m.
Ali starts from A and runs once around the field.
He goes from A to B to C to D and back to A.
Beth starts from A and runs along AC and back again.
They both run at the same speed.
They start at the same time.
Show that when Beth gets back to A, Ali is still at D.

6 In the diagram, AD and BC are vertical posts.

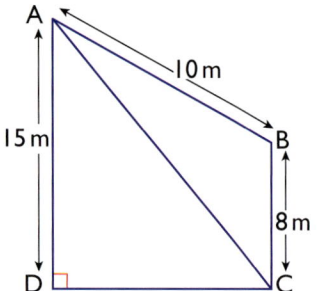

The posts are joined by cables AB and AC.
Mali needs to replace the cables with new ones.
She has 25 m of new cable.

a Explain, without any calculation, how Mali knows she does not have enough new cable.

b How much extra cable does Mali need?

7 The diagram shows the design of an electronic component in the shape of a rectangle.
The rectangle has a total length of 64 mm.
The isosceles triangles are identical and each of the sloping sides has length 20 mm
The parts of the rectangle shown shaded have to be coated.
Calculate the total area of the shaded parts.

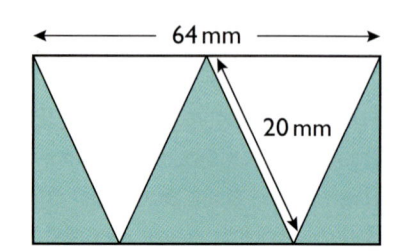

8 Calculate the value of x.

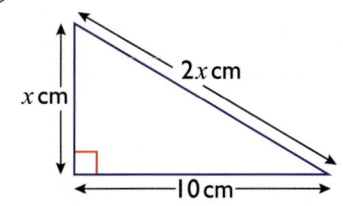

(Triangle with vertical side x cm, hypotenuse $2x$ cm, horizontal side 10 cm, right angle at bottom-left)

Reviewing skills

1 Calculate the length of the unknown side in each triangle.

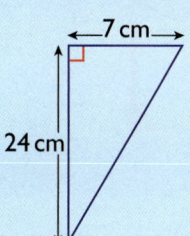

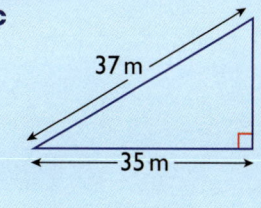

a Right-angled triangle with legs 6 cm and 10 cm.

b Right-angled triangle with legs 7 cm and 24 cm.

c Right-angled triangle with hypotenuse 37 m and one leg 35 m.

2 Calculate the length of the unknown side in each triangle. Give your answer correct to one decimal place.

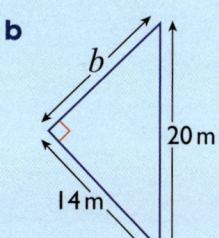

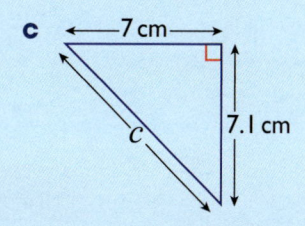

a Triangle with sides 13 cm, 8 cm and unknown a (right angle between 8 and a).

b Triangle with sides 20 m, 14 m and unknown b.

c Right-angled triangle with legs 7 cm and 7.1 cm, hypotenuse c.

3 Calculate the perimeter and area of this field.

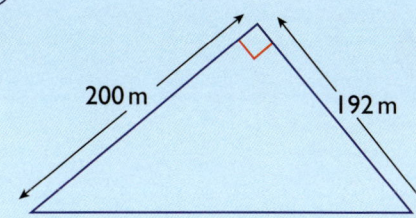

(Right-angled triangle with legs 200 m and 192 m)

4 ABCDEF is a rectangle. Calculate the perimeter of triangle ACE.

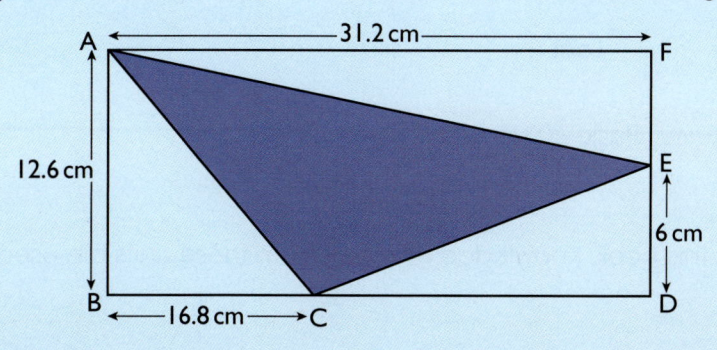

(Rectangle ABCDEF with AF = 31.2 cm, AB = 12.6 cm, BC = 16.8 cm, ED = 6 cm)

Geometry and Measures
Strand 4 Construction

Unit 1	Band d
Angles in degrees	

↓

Unit 2	Band e
Constructions with a ruler and protractor	
Foundation	

↓

Unit 3	Band f
Constructions with a pair of compasses	
Page 391	

↓

Unit 4	Band g
Loci	
Page 403	

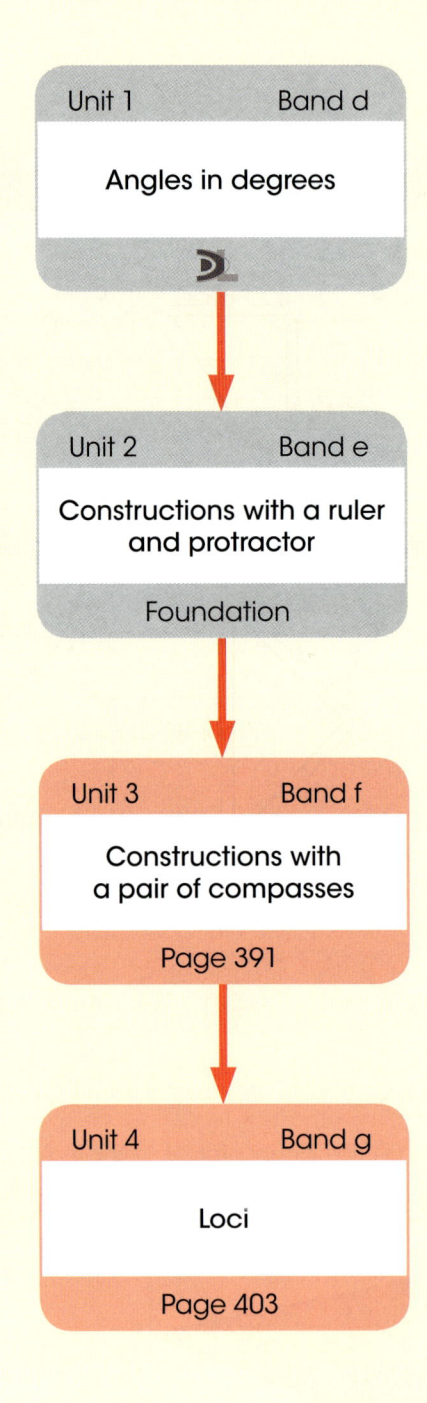

Units 1–2 are assumed knowledge for this book. Knowledge and skills from these units are used throughout the book.

Unit 3 • Constructions with a pair of compasses • Band f

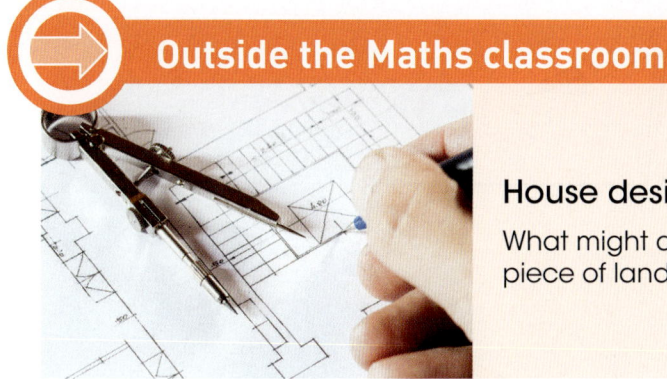

Outside the Maths classroom

House design
What might affect where a house is built on a piece of land?

Toolbox

A circle has a very useful property.
All the points on the circumference are the same distance from the centre.
That distance is the **radius** of the circle.

Part of a circle is called an **arc**.

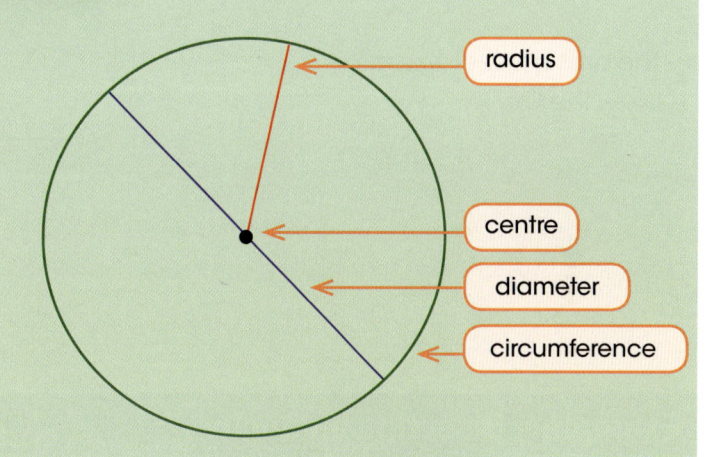

You use a pair of compasses to draw a circle.
You can construct many other things with compasses:
- triangles, given their sides
- line bisectors
- angle bisectors
- perpendicular from a point **to** a line
- perpendicular from a point **on** a line.

Geometry and Measures Strand 4 Construction

Example – Bisecting a line

Bisect the line AB.   A ———— B

Solution

- Open your compasses.
  Put the point on A.
  Draw arcs above and below the line.

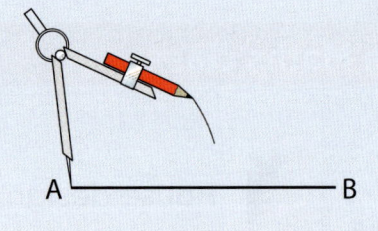

- Do not adjust the compasses.
  Put the point on B.
  Draw two more arcs to cut the first two.

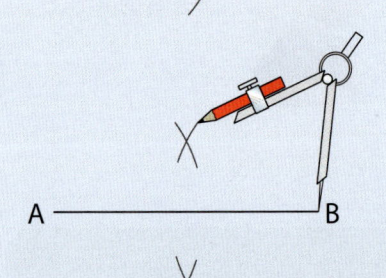

- The arcs meet at X and Y.
  Draw the line XY.

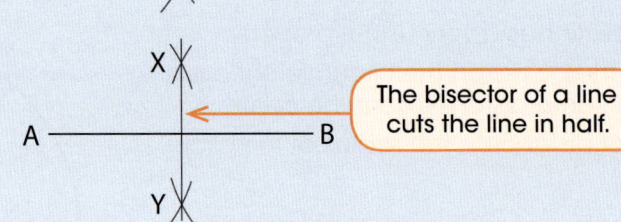

> The bisector of a line cuts the line in half.

Example – Bisecting an angle

Bisect this angle.

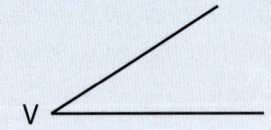

Solution

- Put the point of the compasses on V.
  Draw an arc cutting both lines at points A and B.
- Put the point of the compasses on A.
  Draw an arc.
  Do not adjust the compasses.
  Put the point of the compasses at B.

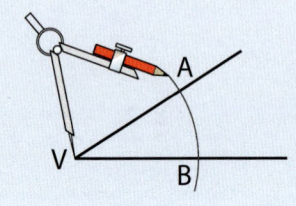

Draw an arc.
These two arcs meet at C.

- Join V to C.

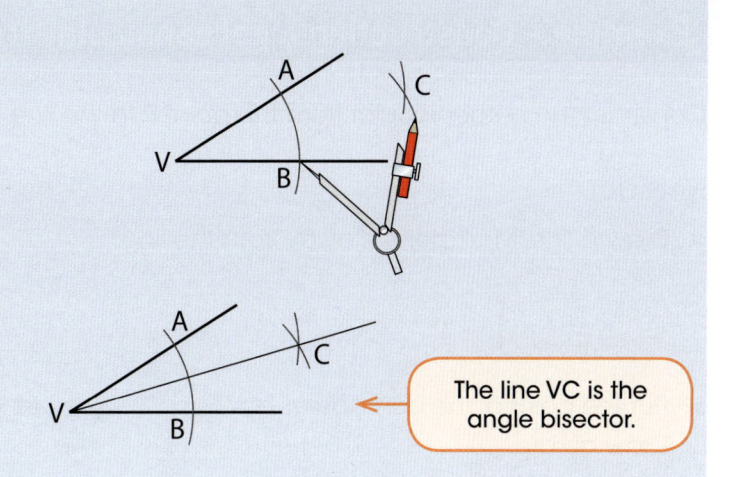

  The line VC is the angle bisector.

Example – Constructing a triangle

Make an accurate drawing of this triangle.

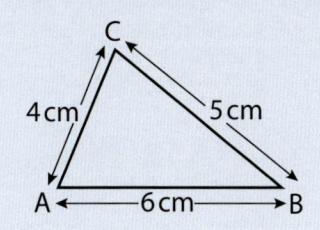

Solution

- Draw a line 6 cm long.

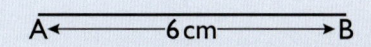

- Draw an arc of radius 4 cm and centre A.
  The point C is on this arc.

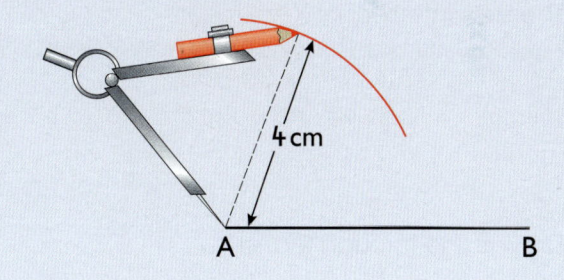

- Now draw an arc of radius 5 cm and centre B.
  C is on this arc too.

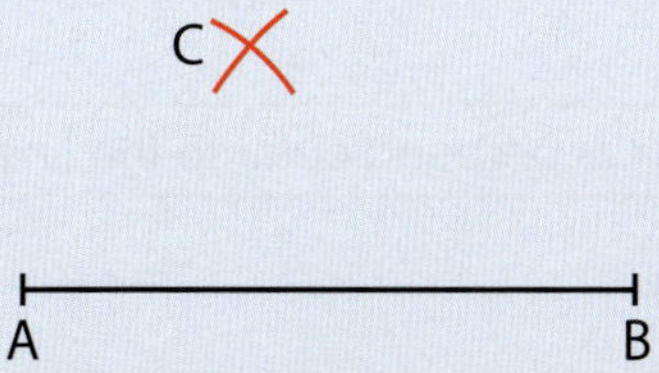

- The two arcs meet at C.
  Join AC and BC to form the triangle.

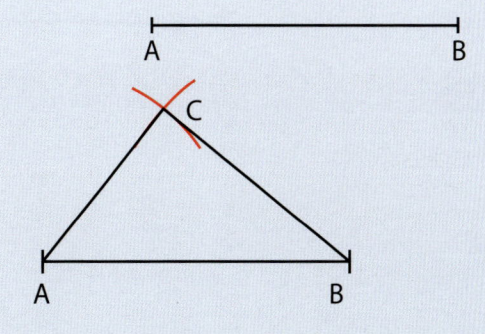

Geometry and Measures Strand 4 Construction

Example – Constructing a perpendicular from a point to a line

Construct the perpendicular from the point R to the line.

Solution

- Draw a line. Mark point R away from the line.

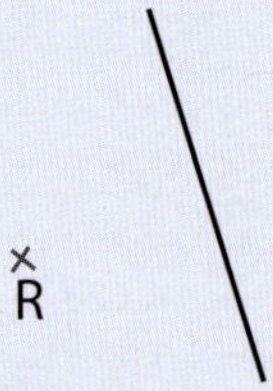

- Put the point of the compasses on R.
  Draw an arc.
  It intersects the line at A and B.

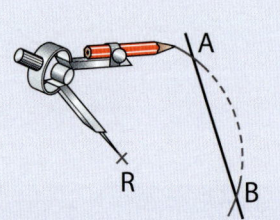

- With the point on A, draw an arc on the opposite side of the line from R.

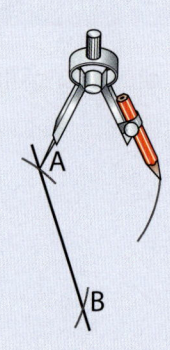

- Do not adjust the compasses.
  With the point on B, draw another arc.
  The arcs intersect at X.

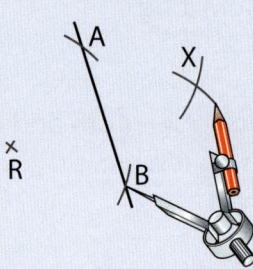

- Draw a line through R and X.

> The line RX is perpendicular to the line AB.

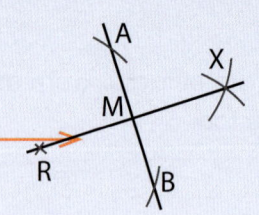

Unit 3 Constructions with a pair of compasses Band f

Example – Constructing a perpendicular from a point on a line

Construct a perpendicular from the point T on this line.

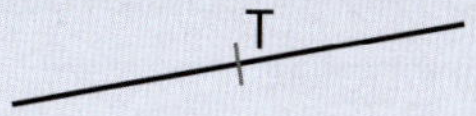

Solution

- Put the point of the compasses on T.
- Mark two points, A and B on the line.
  Each point is the same distance from T.

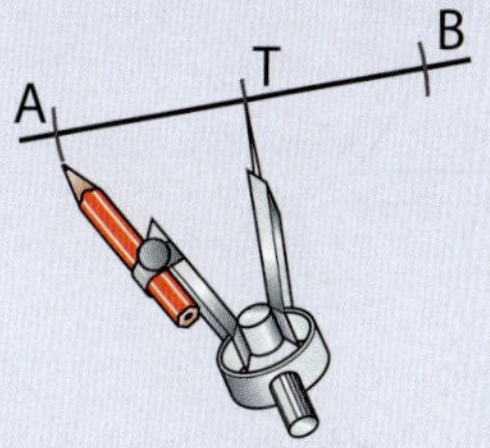

- Open the compasses wider.
  With the point on A draw an arc.

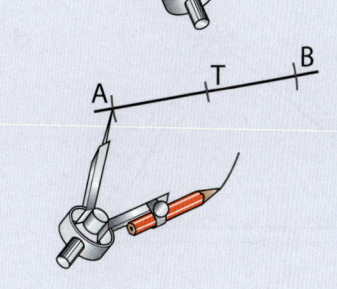

- Do not adjust the compasses.
  With the point on B draw an intersecting arc.

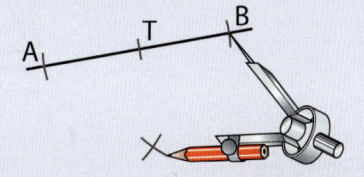

- Draw a line through T and the intersection X.

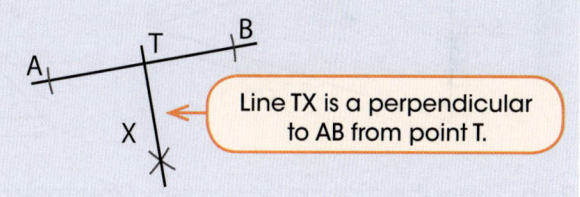

Line TX is a perpendicular to AB from point T.

395

Geometry and Measures Strand 4 Construction

Practising skills

1 Use a ruler and a pair of compasses to construct each triangle accurately. Then measure its angles.

a Triangle with sides 4 cm, 4 cm, 4 cm.

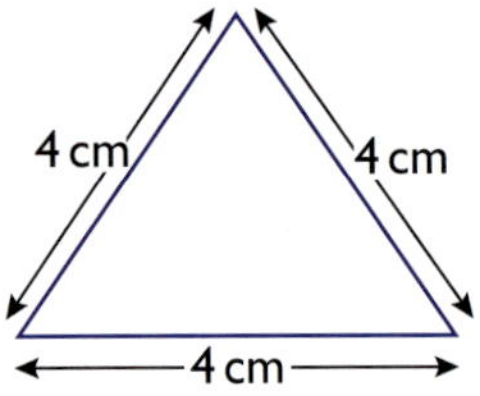

b Triangle with sides 7.5 cm, 7.5 cm, base 5.1 cm.

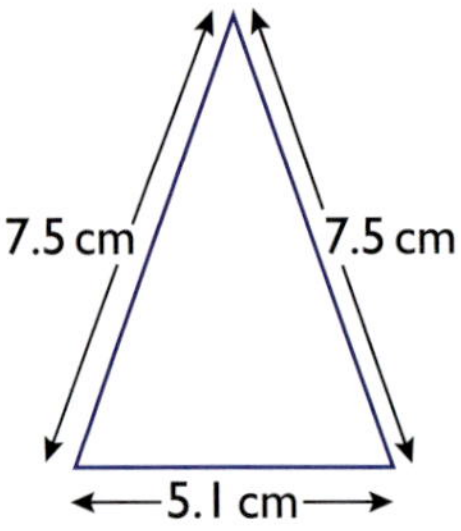

c Triangle with sides 7 cm, 5 cm, base 8 cm.

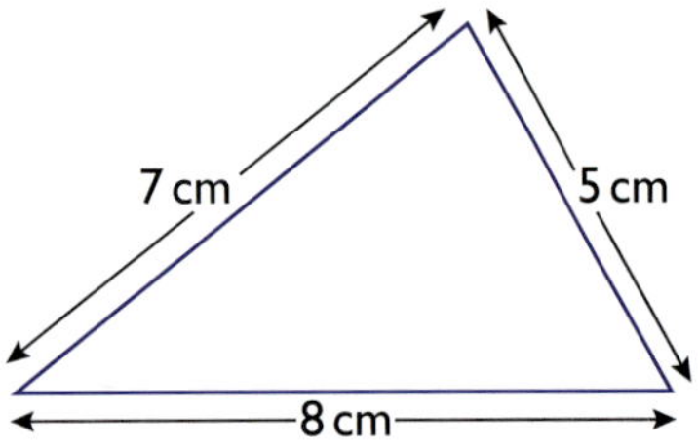

d Triangle with sides 8.5 cm, 7.5 cm, base 4 cm.

e Triangle with sides 5 cm, 10 cm, 8.7 cm.

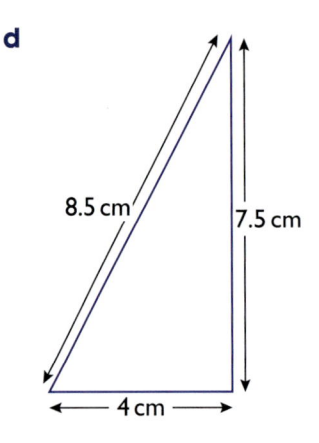

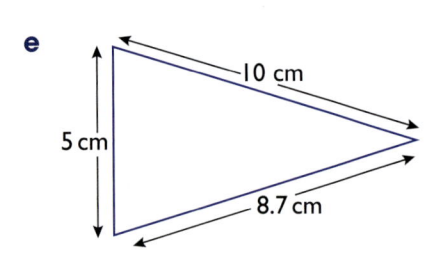

f Triangle with sides 3.9 cm, 5.5 cm, base 7.5 cm.

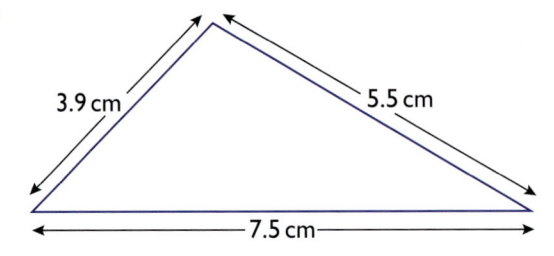

2 a Draw this triangle accurately. (You may use a protractor for the right angle.)

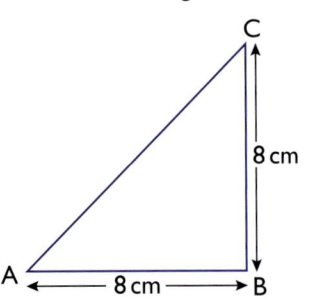

Right-angled triangle with AB = 8 cm, BC = 8 cm, right angle at B.

Using a ruler and a pair of compasses, draw the perpendicular bisectors of AB and BC. What do you notice about the point where they meet?

b Repeat part **a** for the following right-angled triangles.
Do you always notice the same thing?

i

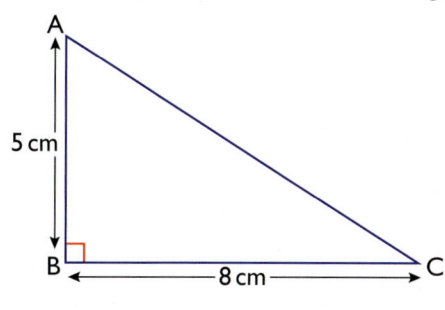

ii

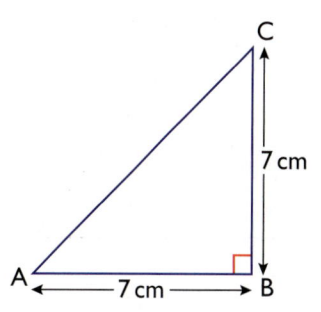

iii

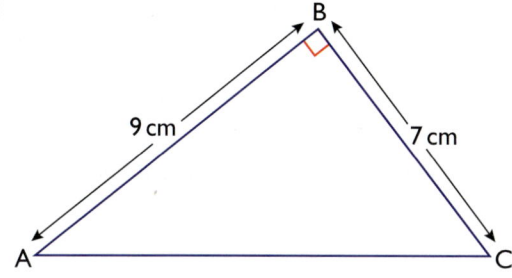

3 a Draw this triangle accurately.

Using a ruler and a pair of compasses, draw the perpendicular bisector of each of the three sides.

You should find that the three lines you have just drawn all go through a point.

Call this point O.

If your lines do not go through a point, start again. You have not done the drawing accurately!

Now draw a circle with centre O and radius OP. What do you notice?

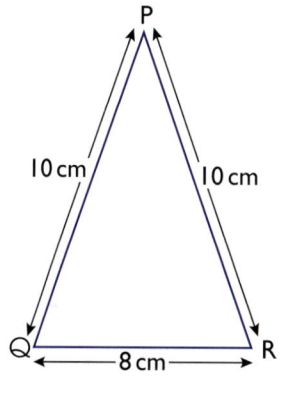

b Repeat part **a** for the following triangles. Do you always notice the same things?

i

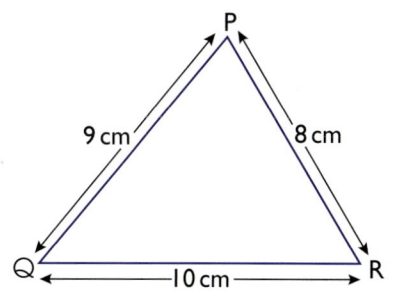

ii

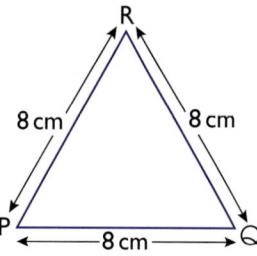

iii

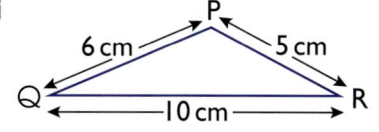

iv

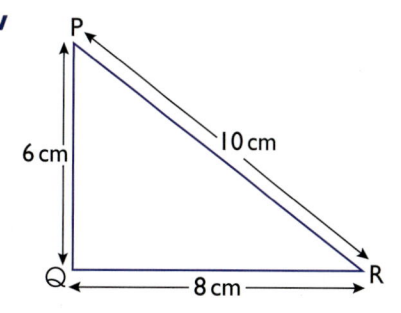

Geometry and Measures Strand 4 Construction

4 a Draw this triangle accurately.

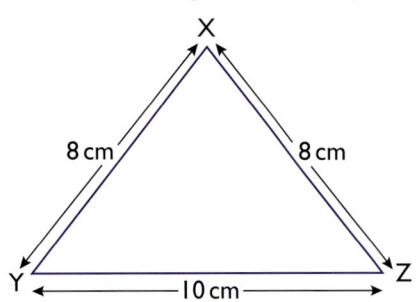

Triangle XYZ with XY = 8 cm, XZ = 8 cm, YZ = 10 cm.

Using a ruler and a pair of compasses (but no protractor), draw the bisectors of the three angles.

You should find that your three lines go through a point. Call it C.

If your lines do not go through a point, start again. You have not done the drawing accurately.

Now draw a circle with centre C. Set your compasses so that the circle just touches the line XY. What do you notice?

b Repeat part **a** for the following triangles. Do you always notice the same things?

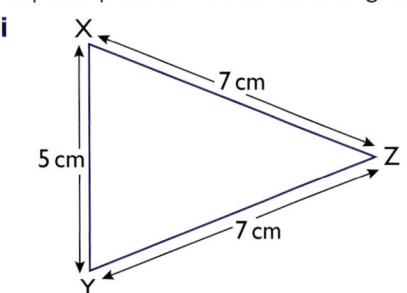

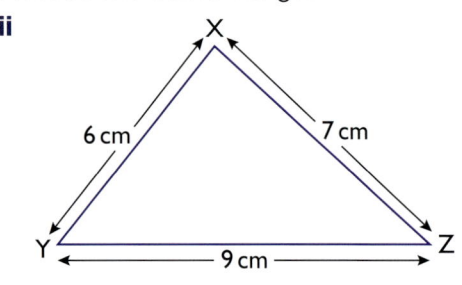

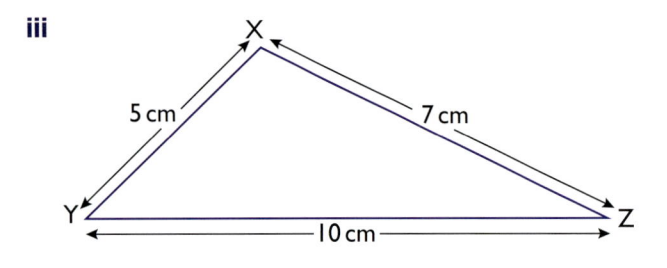

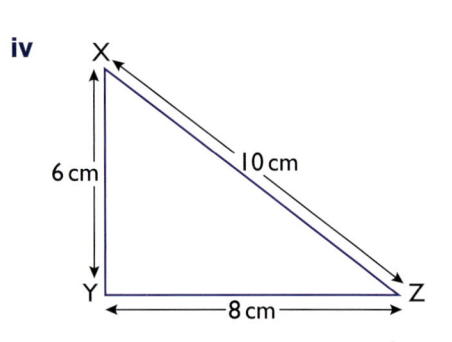

i Triangle XYZ with XY = 5 cm, XZ = 7 cm, YZ = 7 cm.

ii Triangle XYZ with XY = 6 cm, XZ = 7 cm, YZ = 9 cm.

iii Triangle XYZ with XY = 5 cm, XZ = 7 cm, YZ = 10 cm.

iv Triangle XYZ with XY = 6 cm, XZ = 10 cm, YZ = 8 cm.

5 a The diagram shows a triangle ABC. You are to find its area.

A line has been drawn through point A perpendicular to BC.

Copy and complete this working.
By measurement
BC = ☐ cm
AD = ☐ cm
So the area of triangle
ABC = $\frac{1}{2}$ × ☐ × ☐ cm^2
= ☐ cm^2 (to 1 decimal place)

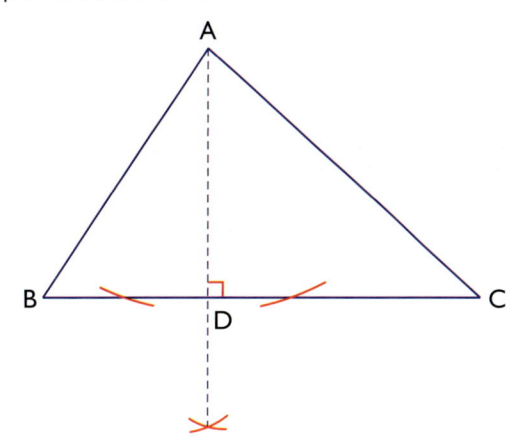

b Now draw the following triangles. Then use the method in part **a** to find their areas.

You should use only a ruler and a pair of compasses.
  i Triangles XYZ where XY = 8 cm, YZ = 10 cm and ZX = 7 cm
  ii Triangle LMN where LM = 5 cm, MN = 6 cm and NL = 8 cm
  iii Triangle PQR where PQ = 7 cm, QR = 10 cm and RP = 5 cm

Developing fluency

1 Draw a horizontal line AC 10 cm long. Mark the point T on the line 3 cm from A.
Construct a line perpendicular to AC that passes through T.
On one side of this line mark a point B such that BT = 4 cm.
On the other side mark a point D such that DT = 4 cm.
Join ABCD to make a quadrilateral.
Describe this quadrilateral.

2 a Draw a vertical line PR 8 cm long.
Construct the perpendicular bisector of PR. Mark the mid-point of the line PR as M.
Mark points Q and S on the perpendicular bisector of PR, on either side of the line, where QM = SM = 6 cm.
Join PQRS to make a quadrilateral.
Describe this quadrilateral.

b Repeat part **a** but this time let QM = SM = 4 cm.
What sort of quadrilateral do you have now?

3 a Use a ruler and a pair of compasses to construct a triangle LMN with LM = 8 cm, MN = 4 cm and NL = 6 cm.

b Construct the line through N perpendicular to LM.

c Work out the area of the triangle LMN.

Geometry and Measures Strand 4 Construction

4 a Construct the trapezium MNOP accurately.
Mark the point Q 2 cm from point M.

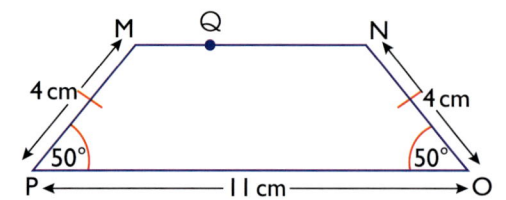

b Construct a line perpendicular to PO that passes through Q.

c Make suitable measurements and work out the area of the trapezium.

5 a Draw a circle of radius 10 cm.

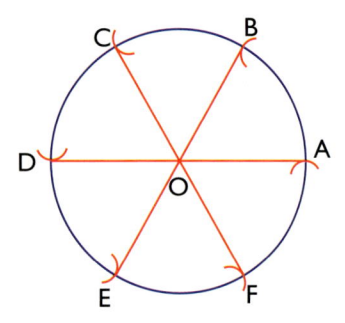

With your compasses still set at 10 cm, mark 6 points round its circumference, as shown. Call these points A, B, C, D, E and F and the centre of the circle O.
Join AD, BE and CF to make three diameters.
Now draw the bisectors of all the angles at the centre (∠AOB, ∠BOC, …). These give you three more diameters. Mark the points where they cross the circumference.
Now do the same again to get six more diameters. Mark the points where they cross the circumference.

b You now have 24 points on the circumference. Join them up to make a regular 24-sided polygon.

c By joining suitable points on the circumference you can construct other regular polygons. Which polygons can you make? Draw one example of each. (You may find it helpful to use different colours.)

d Now look at the angles at the centre.
List all the angles you can identify between 0° and 360°.

6 Draw a horizontal line of length 10 cm, allow space above and below your line.
You must now show all your construction arcs to answer these questions:

a Construct an angle of 60° at the right hand end.

b Bisect your 60° angle, mark each of the angles 30°.

7 Draw a vertical line 10 cm in the centre of your page.
You must now show all your construction arcs to answer these questions:

a Construct the perpendicular bisector of your 10 cm line.

b Bisect one of the 90° angles you have constructed.

Problem solving

1 Here is a line AB.

A•————•B

   a Using only a straight edge and a pair of compasses, draw
      i a triangle ABC where the angles at A and B are both 45°
      ii an equilateral triangle ABD.

   b Name the two possible shapes for the quadrilateral ACBD.

2 Wyn has a triangular garden. The lengths of the sides of his garden are 20 m, 16 m and 14 m. Draw a suitable scale diagram of the garden, using only a ruler and a pair of compasses. Construct a line through one vertex of the triangle perpendicular to the opposite side. Now make a suitable measurement and calculate the area of Wyn's garden.

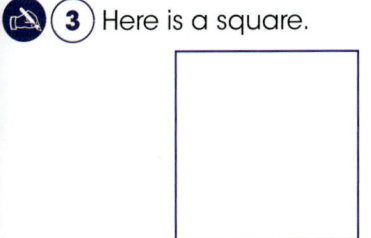

3 Here is a square.

Using only a straight edge and a pair of compasses, construct

   a a triangle that has the same area as the square

   b a rectangle that has the same area as the square, but half the height

   c a rhombus with the same area as the square.

4 Alys is designing a logo for her company. It is the shaded region in this sketch.

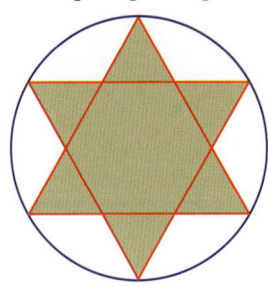

Diagram **not** accurately drawn.

The circle has radius 4 cm.
The logo must have rotational symmetry of the order 6.

   a Using only a ruler and a pair of compasses, construct an accurate drawing of the logo.

   b Measure the lengths of one side of the large equilateral triangles.

   c Without doing any further measurements, work out the area of the logo.

Geometry and Measures Strand 4 Construction

5 P and Q are two lighthouses 10 miles apart. P is due north of Q.
At 08:00 the *Whinlatter* is at point R, 14 km from P and 6 km from Q.

   a Show the information on a scale drawing.
   At 08:30 the *Whinlatter* is at point S, 8 km from P and 9 km from Q.

   b Add this to your scale drawing.

   c How far is it from R to S?

   d How fast is the *Whinlatter* sailing?

Reviewing skills

1 Use a ruler and a pair of compasses to draw triangle ABC accurately.

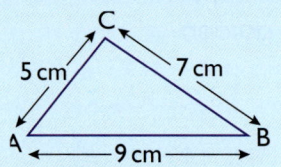

(Triangle with sides: AC = 5 cm, CB = 7 cm, AB = 9 cm)

   a Measure the angles of the triangle.
   b Construct a line through C perpendicular to AB.
   c Make a suitable measurement and use it to work out the area of the triangle.

2 a Use a ruler and a pair of compasses to construct triangle ABC.

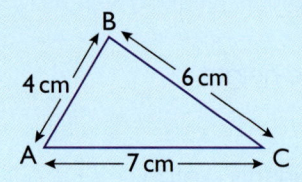

(Triangle with sides: AB = 4 cm, BC = 6 cm, AC = 7 cm)

   b Construct the perpendicular bisector of each of the three sides.
   c Mark the point M where the three perpendicular bisectors meet.
   d Draw a circle with centre M which passes through the points A, B and C.
   e Measure the circle's radius.

Unit 4 • Loci • Band g

Outside the Maths classroom

Cosmology
Are all orbits the same shape?

Toolbox

A **locus** is the path of all the points which obey a rule.
In two dimensions:

- The locus of all the points which are the **same distance from one point** is a circle.

- The locus of all the points which are the **same distance from two points** is the perpendicular bisector of the line which joins those two points.

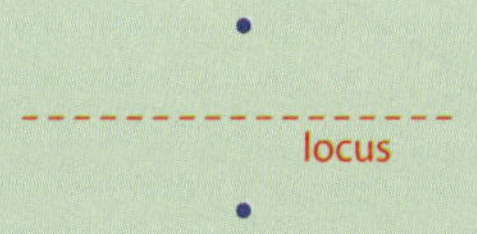

- The locus of all the points which are the **same distance from a line segment** is two parallel lines with semicircles joining the ends.

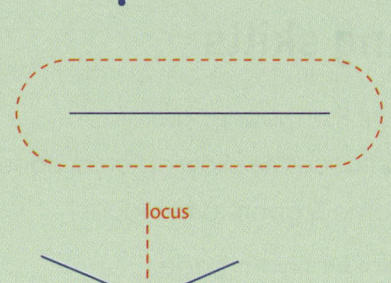

- The locus of all the points which are the **same distance from two lines that cross** is the angle bisector of the angles formed by the two lines.

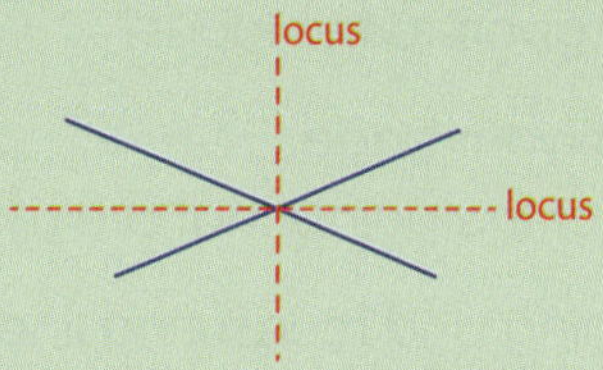

- The locus of all the points which are **the same distance from two lines that do not cross** is a line parallel to them, and midway between them.

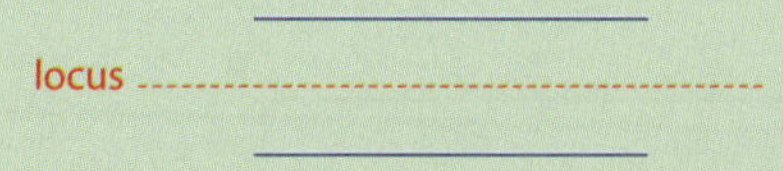

Note:
- Construct means do it accurately using instruments.
- Sketch means do it by eye illustrating the important features.
- Draw means somewhere between constructing and sketching. You should use your judgement to decide what is required.

Geometry and Measures Strand 4 Construction

Example – Loci equidistant from two points

A and B are the positions of two radio beacons.
An aeroplane flies so that it is always the same distance from each beacon.
Draw two crosses to represent the beacons.
Construct a line to represent the aeroplane's path.

A x

B x

Solution

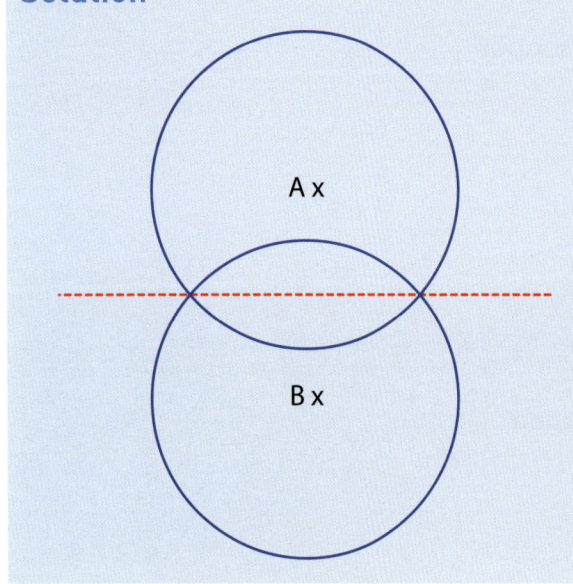

A x

B x

Practising skills

1. Mark a point P on your page.
   a. Make an accurate drawing of the locus of points that are 4 cm from the point P.
   b. What name is given to this locus?

2. Mark a point P on your page.
   Shade the locus of the points that are more than 4.5 cm from P but less than 6.5 cm from P.

3. Find, by constructing and measuring lines through P, the distance of point P from each of the sides of the rectangle ABCD.

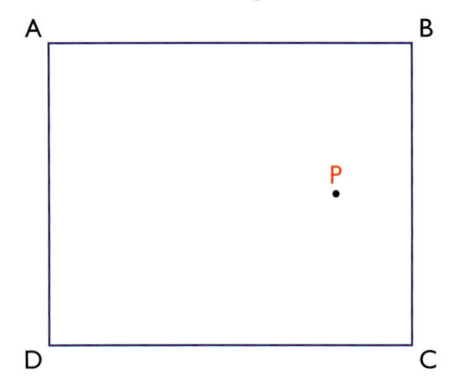

4 **a** Draw a straight line across your page.
  b Draw the locus of points on your page that are 2 cm from your line.

5 **a** Copy this diagram.

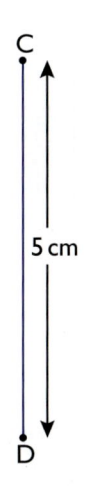

C
|
| 5 cm
|
D

  b Draw the locus of points that are the same distance from C as they are from D.

6 **a** Make a full size copy of this diagram.

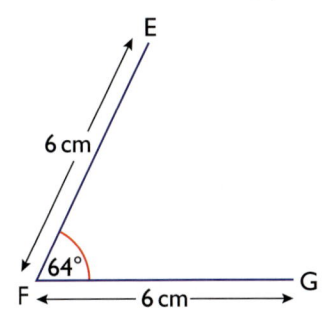

E, 6 cm, 64°, F, 6 cm, G

  b Make an accurate drawing of the locus of points that are the same distance from EF and FG.
  c What is the name given to this locus?

7 **a** Draw the square HIJK. Its sides are 5 cm long.

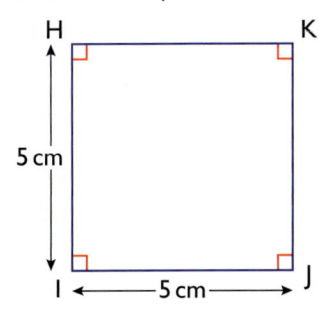

H, K, 5 cm, I, 5 cm, J

  b Draw the locus of points that are the same distance from HK and HI.

Geometry and Measures Strand 4 Construction

8 a Copy this diagram on to squared paper.

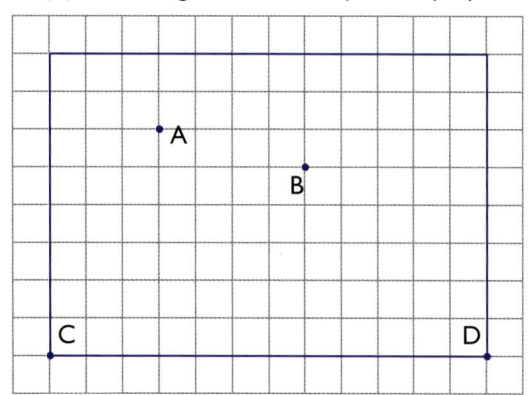

(Diagram: rectangle on squared paper with points A, B inside near the top-middle, and points C, D at the bottom-left and bottom-right corners of an inner rectangle.)

b Shade these regions.
  i Points that are at most 2 cm from A.
  ii Points that are at least $2\frac{1}{2}$ cm from point B.
  iii Points that are less than 1 cm from the line CD.

c Are there any points in all three regions?

Developing fluency

1 Hassan designs a logo.
He starts with an equilateral triangle with sides of length 6 cm.
He splits the triangle into 6 regions by drawing 3 lines. Each line is the locus of points inside the triangle that are the same distance from two of its sides.
Make an accurate full-size drawing of the logo.

2 PQRS is a square. Its sides are 6 cm long. T is the centre point.

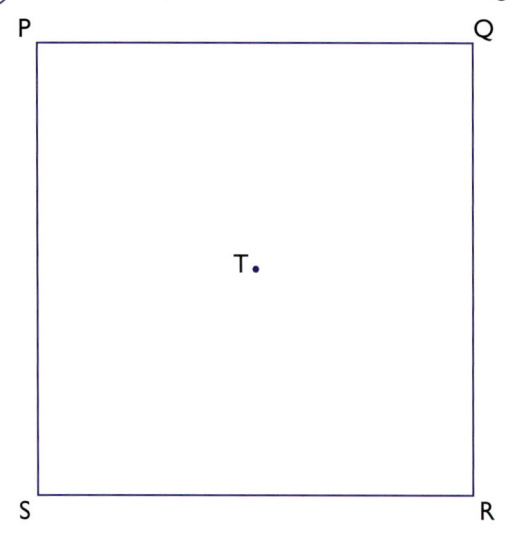

(Diagram: square PQRS with P top-left, Q top-right, R bottom-right, S bottom-left, and T marked at the centre.)

a Draw the square accurately.
b Shade the locus of points on the diagram that are
  • inside the square
  • and more than 3 cm from T
  • and closer to PQ than any of the other sides of the square
  • and closer to QR than PS.

3. This is a scale drawing of a mural called 'The hole in the wall'.
   The full size of the mural is 9 m by 6 m.

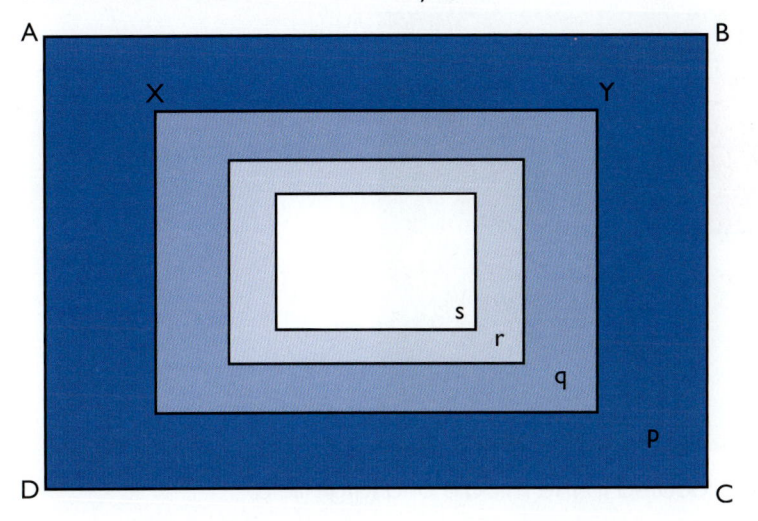

   a Describe the line XY as a locus, using ABCD as a reference.
   b A point is 3 metres from BC and 4 metres from AD. Which region is it in: p, q, r or s?
   c Describe the locus of points in the regions using ABCD as a reference.
      i s   ii r

4. a Construct triangle XYZ accurately.

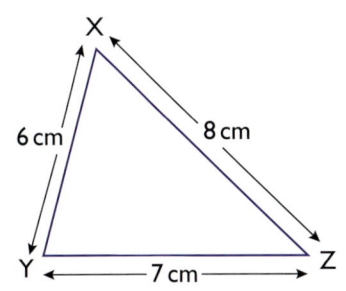

   (6 cm, 8 cm, 7 cm)

   b Draw the locus of points that are the same distance from X and Z.
   c Draw the locus of points that are the same distance from X and Y.
   d Mark the point Q that is the same distance from X, Y and Z. Measure QX.

Geometry and Measures Strand 4 Construction

5 The diagram shows 2 goats tied to a rectangular shed. One goat, Misty, is attached to point B by a rope that is 4 m long. The other goat, Billy, is attached to point D by a rope that is 8 m long.

The shed measures 8 m by 3 m and is located in the middle of a large field.

a Draw the diagram accurately, using a scale of 1 cm = 1 m.

b Using different colours, shade the areas where
  i Only Misty can graze
  ii Only Billy can graze
  iii Both goats can graze

6 a Draw a rectangle KLMN with side LM longer than side KL.

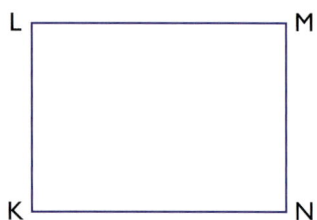

Now draw the locus of points in the rectangle that are the same distance from KL and KN.

b Draw also the locus of points that are the same distance from LM and LK.

c How many points are the same distance from the three lines LM, LK and KN?

d Explain why there are no points that are the same distance from all four edges of the rectangle.

e In a different rectangle PQRS there is a point O that is the same distance from all four edges. What can you say about the rectangle PQRS?

Unit 4 Loci Band g

7 Here is a part of a local chart for ships entering the port of Afonbedd.

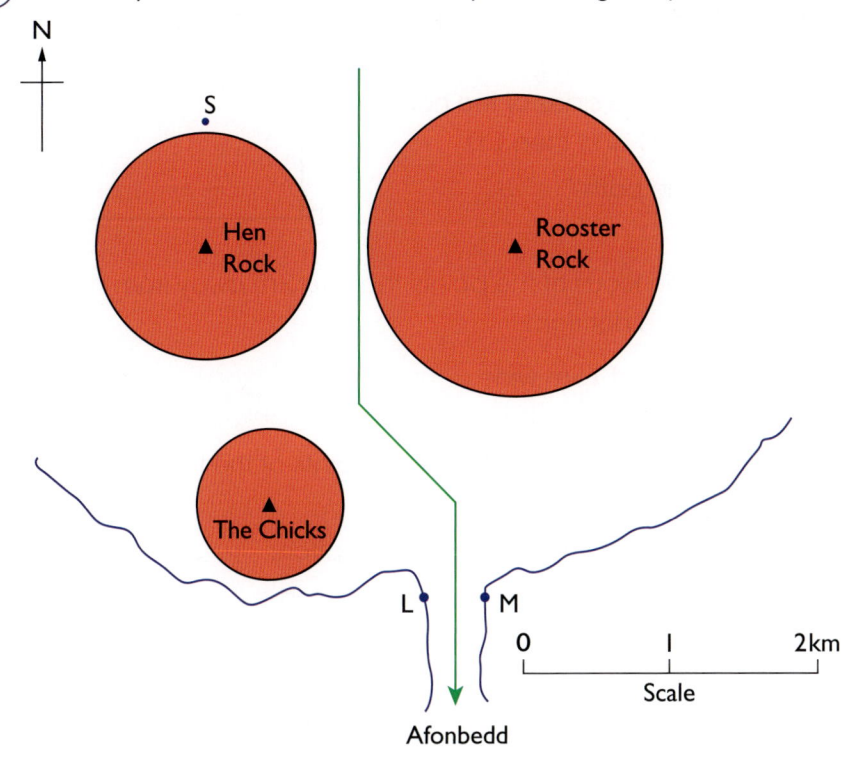

Ships follow the green route.
There are three dangerous areas round rocks, marked by the red circles.
The river entrance is marked by lights at L and M.

a Describe each of the three parts of the green route as a locus.

b Describe each of the red regions.

c A ship is at point S. It is going to Afonbedd.
Advise its captain what course to steer.

Problem solving

1 PQRS is a field in the shape of a rectangle.
PQ = 100 m and QR = 80 m.
There is a path crossing the field. All points on the path are the same distance from PS and PQ.
There is a different path crossing the field. All points on this path are the same distance from PS and QR.
These two paths cross at the point X.
Use a suitable drawing to find the distance of X from S.

2 A, B and C are three towns.
C is 20 miles due east of B.
A is 16 miles due north of B.
A mobile phone tower, T, is to be built such that it is the same distance from A and B, and it is 10 miles from C.

a Draw a scale diagram. Use it to locate the two possible positions of the tower.

b Find the shorter distance of the tower from A.

Geometry and Measures Strand 4 Construction

3) ABCD is the plan of a house.
AB = DC = 8m
BC = 6m
A path of width 2m is to be made round three sides of the house.
The path starts at A, goes along AB, then BC and then CD.

a Make an accurate scale drawing of the path.

b What is the total area of the path?

c Jake says, 'The outside of the path is the locus of the points that are 2m away from house.'
Give two reasons why Jake's statement is not right.

4) A pitch for five-a-side football is 32m long and 16m wide.

a Draw a diagram of the pitch, using a scale 1cm = 4m.
Lights are placed at the 4 corners of the pitch and at the mid-points of the two longer sides.
A light can light all points up to 10m away.

b Show that the 6 lights are not enough to light the whole football pitch.

c Show how some of the lights could be moved to light the whole pitch.

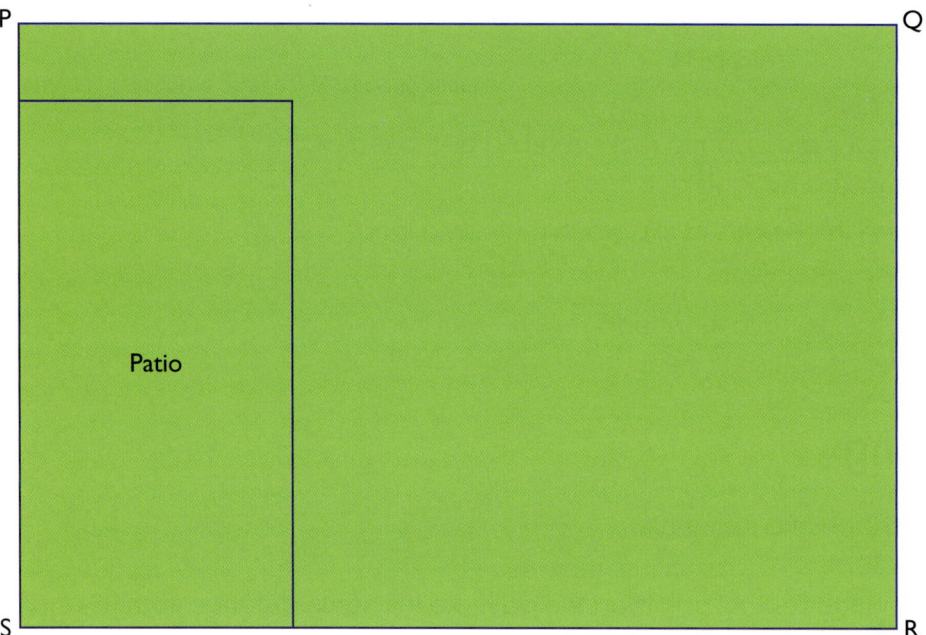

5) Here is a scale drawing of a rectangular garden PQRS.

Scale: 1cm represents 2m.
Siân wants to plant a tree in the garden at least 10m from the corner R, nearer to PQ than to PS and less than 6m from SR.
The tree cannot be planted on the patio.
On the diagram, shade the region where Siân can plant the tree.

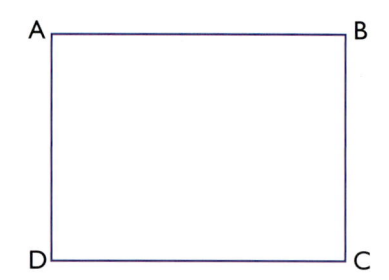

Unit 4 Loci Band g

6 PQRS is the plan of an enclosure at a zoo.
Its shape is an isosceles trapezium.

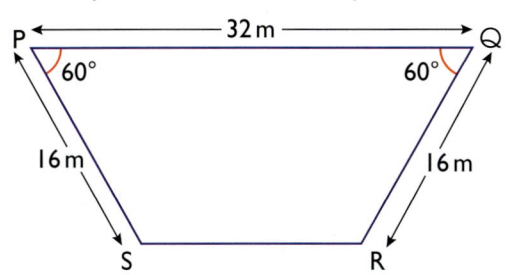

- P ← 32 m → Q
- 60°, 60°
- 16 m, 16 m
- S, R

a Make an accurate scale drawing of the enclosure.

The enclosure is divided up into four regions: p, q, r and s, by wire netting.

Region p is those points that are nearer to vertex P than to any other vertices, region q is those points that are nearer to vertex Q and so on.

b Draw lines on your diagram to show where the wire netting goes.

c Make suitable measurements and work out the total length of wire netting. Give your answer to the nearest metre.

d Work out the area of each region. Answer to the nearest square metre.

e Show that with another 32 m of wire netting the enclosure can be divided up into 6 regions of equal area.

Reviewing skills

1 Describe the loci represented by the red lines or curves in the following diagrams.

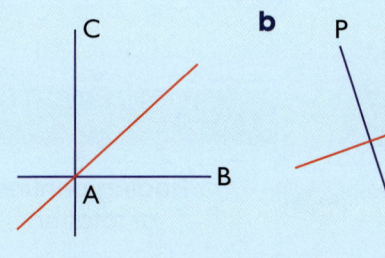

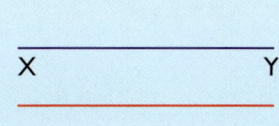

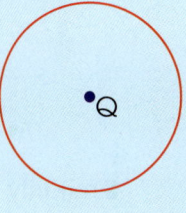

a (C, A, B axes with red diagonal line)

b (P, Q with red line)

c (X, Y with parallel red lines)

d (circle with centre Q in red)

2 Describe the regions shaded in these diagrams.

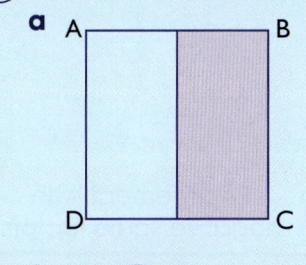

a (rectangle ABCD with shaded strip)

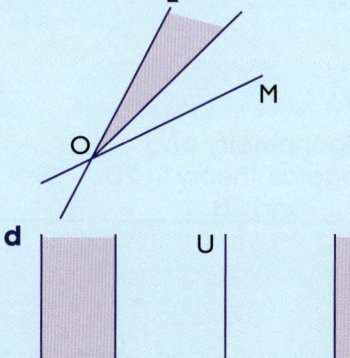

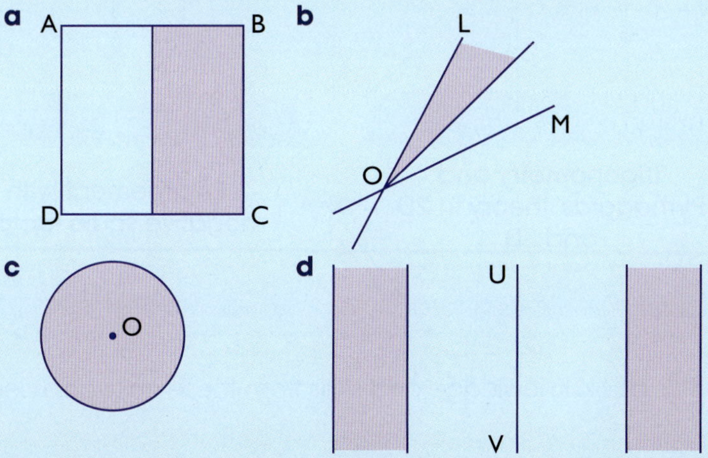

b (point O with rays to L, M; shaded wedge)

c (circle with centre O, shaded)

d (U, V with two shaded rectangular strips)

3 A watering pipe is laid in the shape of a circle of radius 40 m.
The region of the garden within 10 m of the pipe can be watered from the pipe.

a Draw a scale diagram to show this region.

b What is the area of the garden that can be watered from the pipe?

411

Geometry and Measures
Strand 5 Transformations

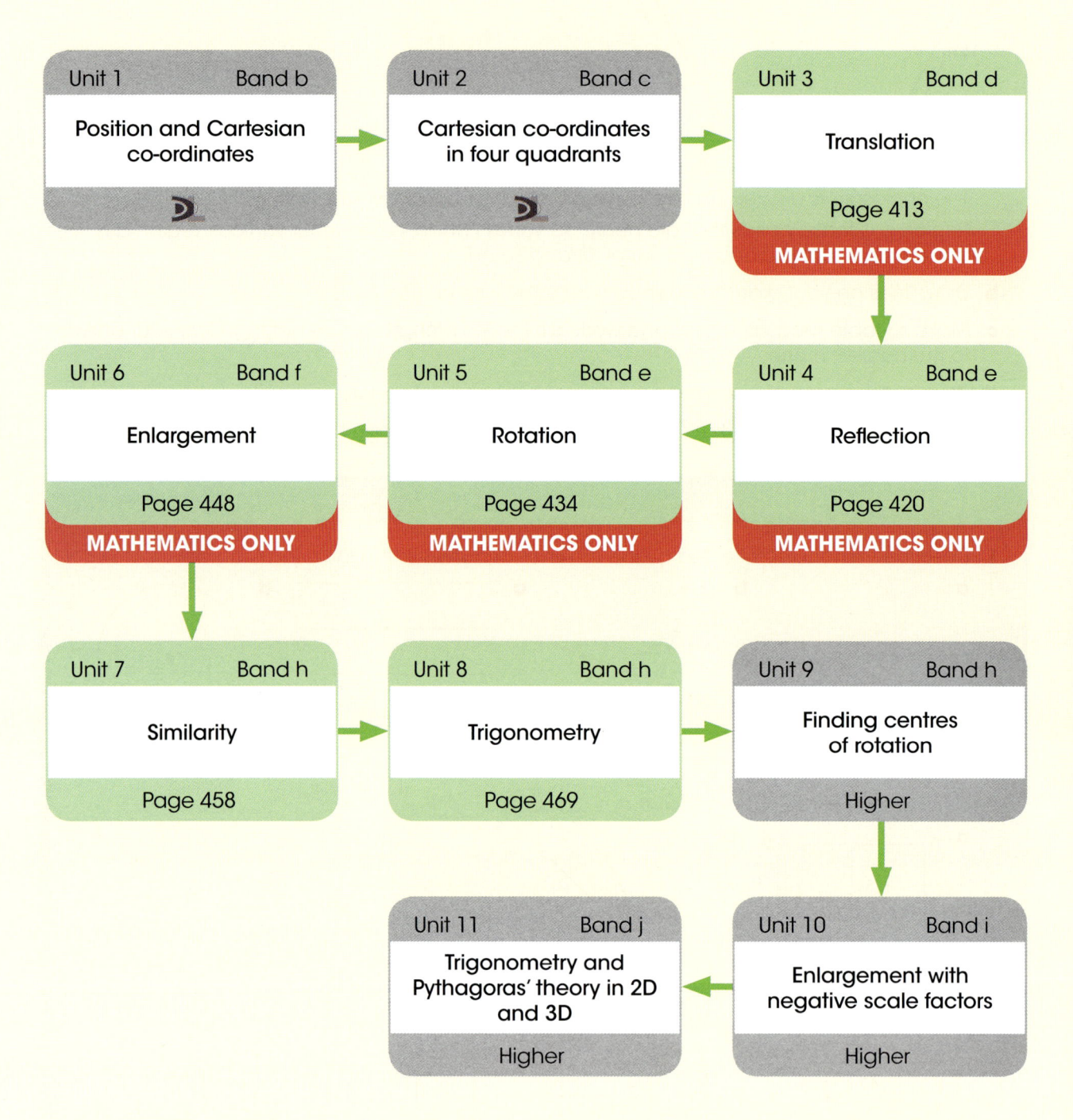

Unit 1 — Band b: Position and Cartesian co-ordinates

Unit 2 — Band c: Cartesian co-ordinates in four quadrants

Unit 3 — Band d: Translation — Page 413 — MATHEMATICS ONLY

Unit 4 — Band e: Reflection — Page 420 — MATHEMATICS ONLY

Unit 5 — Band e: Rotation — Page 434 — MATHEMATICS ONLY

Unit 6 — Band f: Enlargement — Page 448 — MATHEMATICS ONLY

Unit 7 — Band h: Similarity — Page 458

Unit 8 — Band h: Trigonometry — Page 469

Unit 9 — Band h: Finding centres of rotation — Higher

Unit 10 — Band i: Enlargement with negative scale factors — Higher

Unit 11 — Band j: Trigonometry and Pythagoras' theory in 2D and 3D — Higher

Units 1–2 are assumed knowledge for this book. Knowledge and skills from these units are used throughout the book.

Unit 3 • Translation • Band d

Outside the Maths classroom

Chess moves

All chess moves can be thought of as translations. What different moves can be made by a queen and a knight in chess?

Toolbox

A **transformation** moves an object according to a rule.
One transformation is a **translation**.
In the diagram object PQR is translated to the image P'Q'R'.
The object slides without turning.
The translation is described as 3 units right and 2 units up.

It can also be written as $\binom{3}{2}$ ← This way of writing it is called a **vector**.

The translation from A to B is sometimes written as $\overrightarrow{AB}$.
The image and the original object are **congruent**.
This means they are the same shape and the same size.

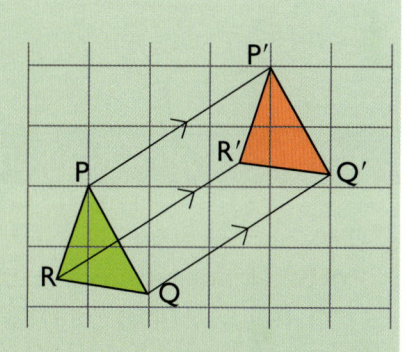

Example – Describing a translation

Describe the translation that maps
a A to C
b B to C
c C to A.

Solution

a The translation 8 units right and 1 down maps A to C.
b The translation 2 units right and 3 down maps B to C.
c The translation 8 units left and 1 up maps C to A.

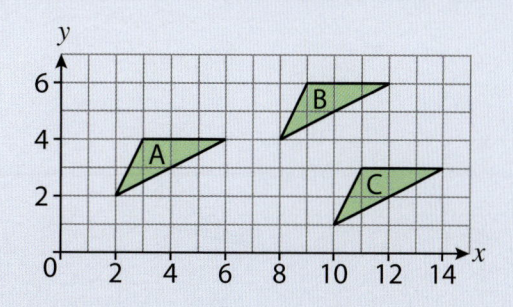

Geometry and Measures Strand 5 Transformations

Example – Translating an object

On a copy of this grid
a Translate A 5 units left and 2 up.
   Label this triangle B.
b Translate B 4 units right and 2 up.
   Label this triangle C.

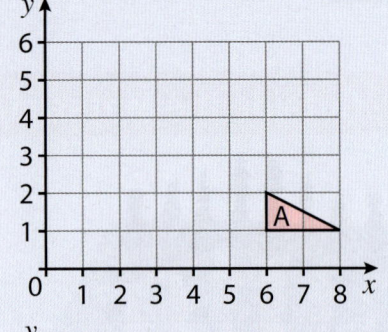

Solution

a Translating A 5 units left results in the blue triangle.
   Translating the blue triangle 2 units up results in image B.
b Translating B 4 units right results in the green triangle.
   Translating the green triangle 2 units up results in image C.

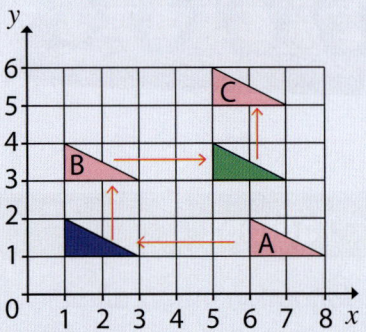

Example – Translating an object using a vector

a Draw and label an x axis from −5 to 7 and a y axis from 0 to 7.
   Plot and label these points.
      (1, 0), (3, 1), (4, 3), (5, 1)
   Join the points in order to form a quadrilateral.
   Label it A.
b Translate shape A by $\begin{pmatrix} 2 \\ 4 \end{pmatrix}$.
   Label the image B.
c Now transform shape B by $\begin{pmatrix} -7 \\ 0 \end{pmatrix}$.
   Label the image C.
d Describe the single transformation that maps A to C.

Solution

a–c

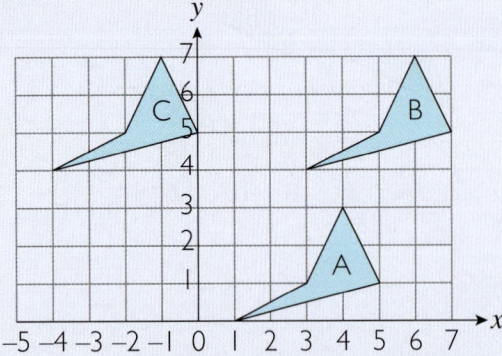

d The transformation A to C is a translation $\begin{pmatrix} -5 \\ 4 \end{pmatrix}$.

Practising skills

1 Copy this diagram.
  a Translate A, 4 to the left. Label the image B.
  b Translate A, 3 down. Label the image C.
  c Translate A, 2 to the right and 3 up. Label the image D.
  d Translate A, 2 to the left and 4 down. Label the image E.
  e Translate A, 2 up. Label the image F.

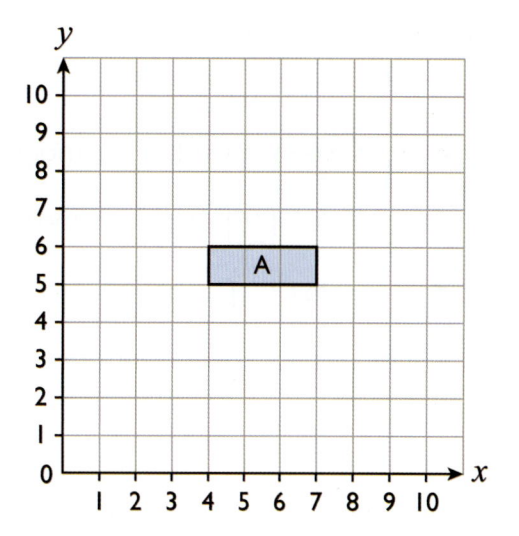

2 Write down in words the translation described by each column vector.
  a $\begin{pmatrix} 4 \\ 5 \end{pmatrix}$
  b $\begin{pmatrix} 6 \\ -1 \end{pmatrix}$
  c $\begin{pmatrix} -2 \\ 7 \end{pmatrix}$
  d $\begin{pmatrix} -6 \\ -3 \end{pmatrix}$
  e $\begin{pmatrix} 7 \\ 0 \end{pmatrix}$
  f $\begin{pmatrix} 0 \\ 7 \end{pmatrix}$
  g $\begin{pmatrix} -8 \\ 0 \end{pmatrix}$
  h $\begin{pmatrix} 0 \\ 5 \end{pmatrix}$

3 Write down a column vector for each of these translations.
  a 8 right and 2 down
  b 6 right and 1 up
  c 4 left and 3 up
  d 7 left and 4 down
  e 9 up
  f 6 right
  g 10 left
  h 12 down

Geometry and Measures Strand 5 Transformations

Developing fluency

1. Copy this diagram.
   a Translate T $\begin{pmatrix} 4 \\ 2 \end{pmatrix}$. Label the image V.
   b Translate T $\begin{pmatrix} 3 \\ -3 \end{pmatrix}$. Label the image W.
   c Translate T $\begin{pmatrix} -2 \\ -4 \end{pmatrix}$. Label the image X.
   d Translate T $\begin{pmatrix} -1 \\ 2 \end{pmatrix}$. Label the image Y.
   e Translate T $\begin{pmatrix} 3 \\ 0 \end{pmatrix}$. Label the image Z.

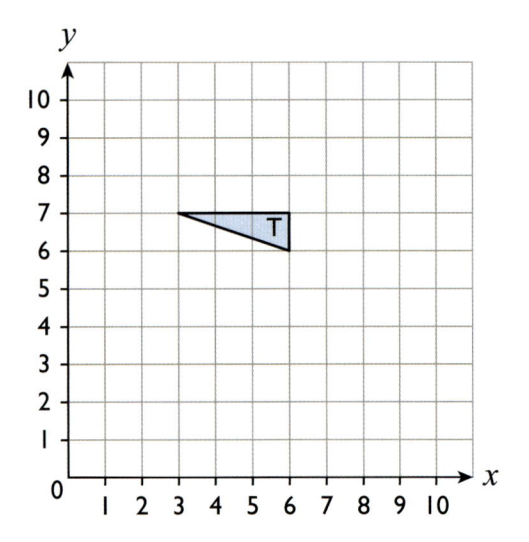

2. Look at this diagram.

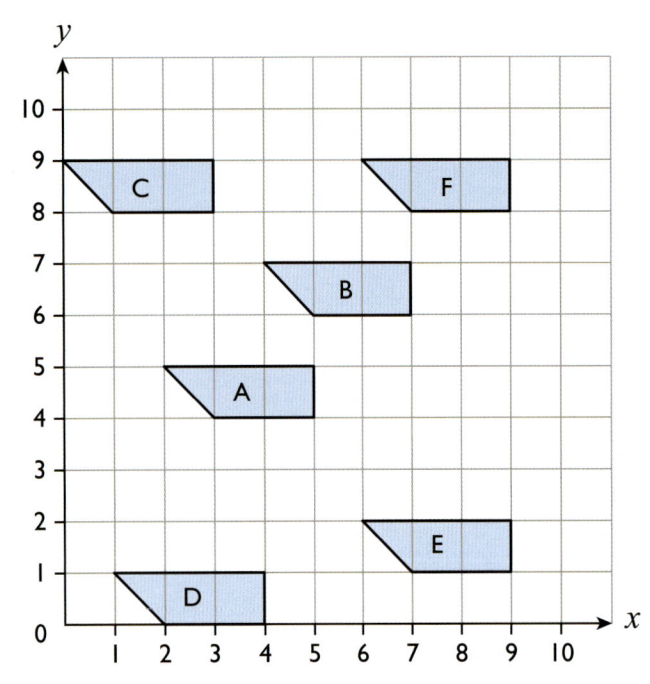

   a Describe fully the single transformation that maps
   - i   A to B
   - ii A to C
   - iii A to D
   - iv A to E
   - v   A to F
   - vi D to E
   - vii E to D
   - viii F to E
   - ix E to C
   - x   F to D
   - xi B to C
   - xii C to F.

   b Describe fully the transformations in part **a** using translation vectors.

Unit 3 Translation Band d

Intermediate tier only

3 Copy this diagram.
  a Translate M $\begin{pmatrix} 2 \\ 4 \end{pmatrix}$.
    Label the image N.
  b Translate M $\begin{pmatrix} -4 \\ 1 \end{pmatrix}$.
    Label the image O.
  c Translate M $\begin{pmatrix} -6 \\ -3 \end{pmatrix}$.
    Label the image P.
  d Translate M $\begin{pmatrix} 1 \\ -5 \end{pmatrix}$.
    Label the image Q.
  e Translate M $\begin{pmatrix} 0 \\ -2 \end{pmatrix}$.
    Label the image R.

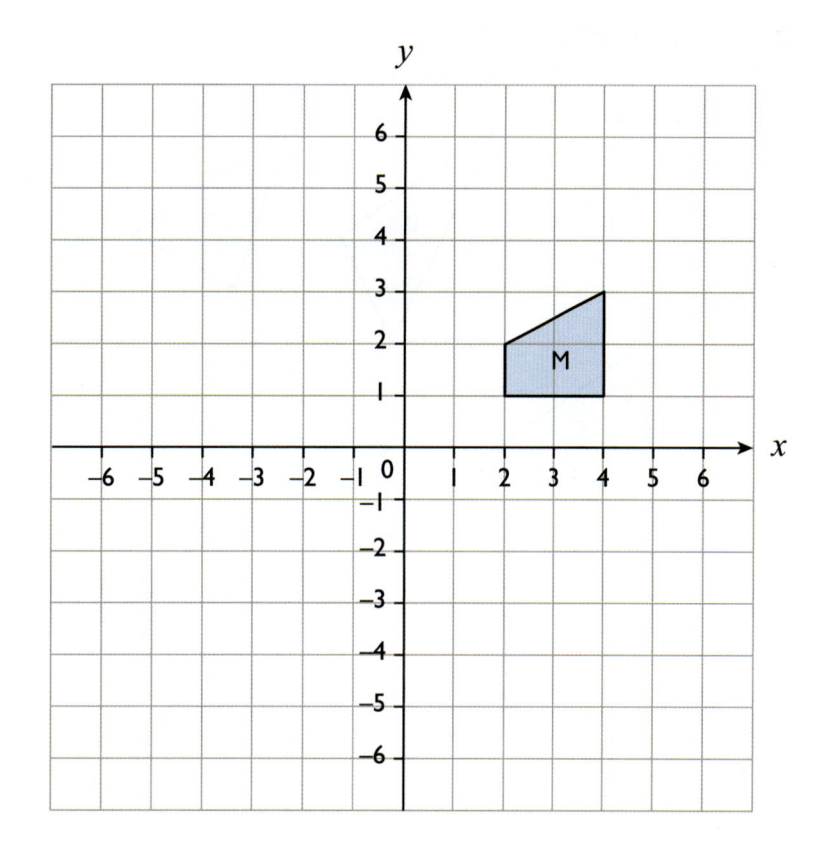

Problem solving

1 Look at this diagram.

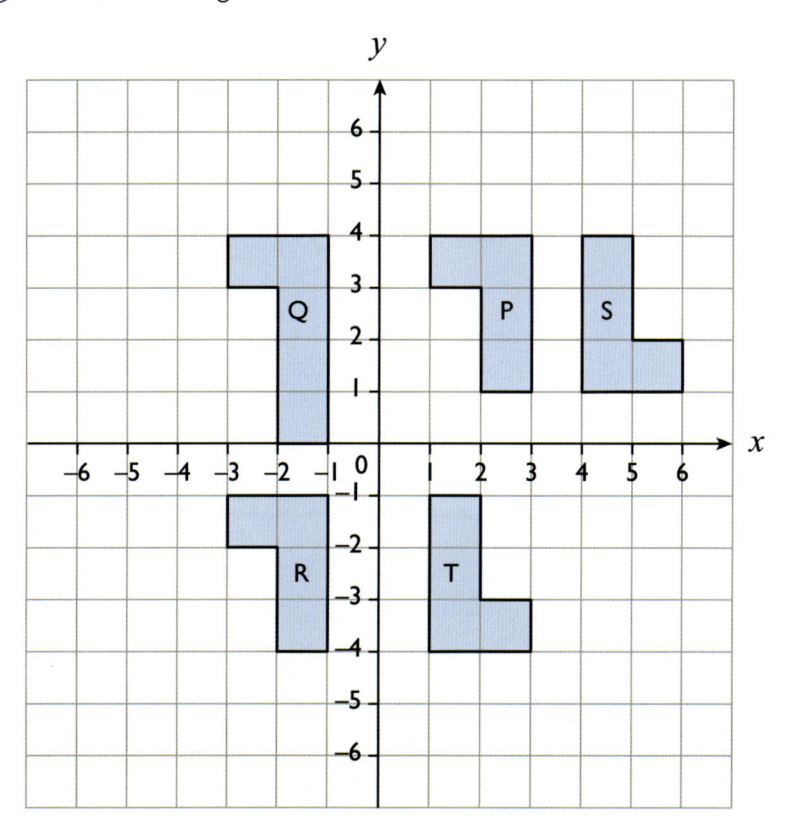

How many translations are there? Describe each fully.

Geometry and Measures Strand 5 Transformations

2 Look at this diagram.

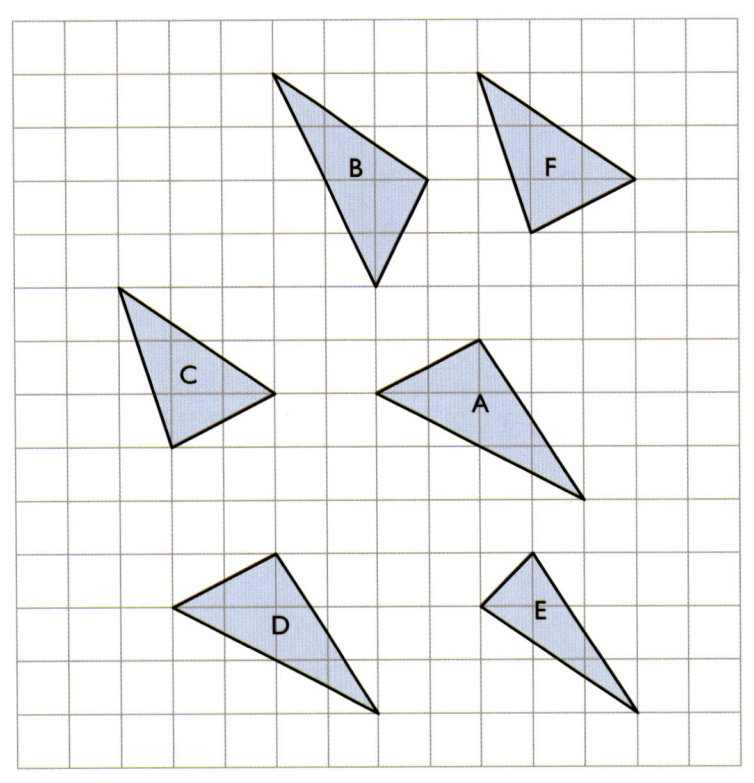

How many translations are there? Describe each fully.

Unit 3 Translation Band d

Reviewing skills

① Look at this diagram.

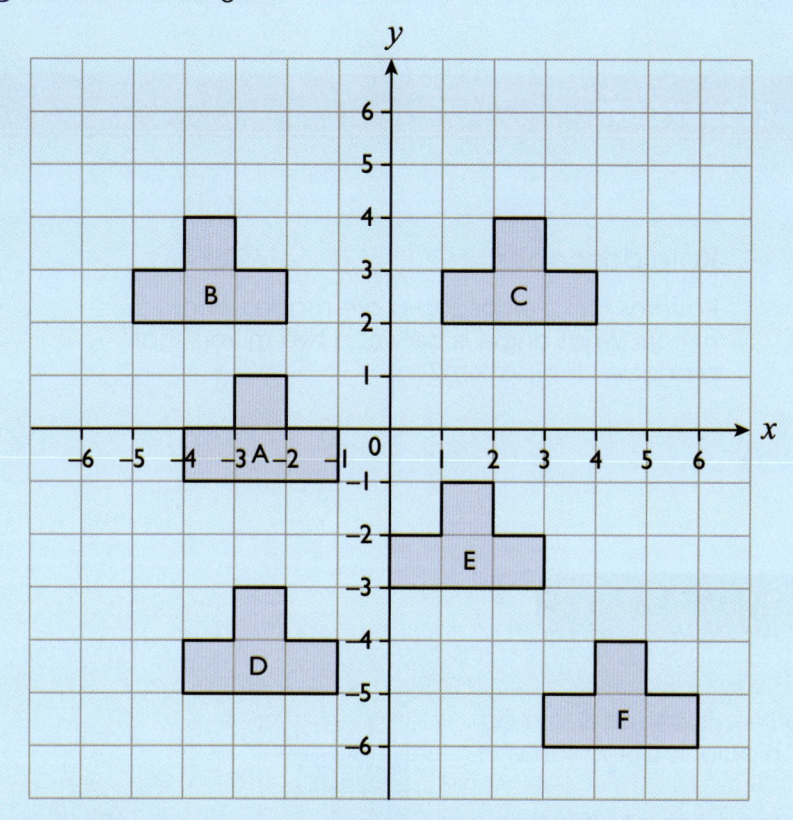

Describe fully the single transformation which maps

a A to B
b A to C
c A to D
d A to E
e A to F
f D to C
g B to E
h F to C
i E to C
j F to D
k C to B
l B to F.

Unit 4 • Reflection • Band e

Outside the Maths classroom

Kaleidoscopes

Patterns for kaleidoscopes are made using mirrors. What angle is between two mirrors that produced this pattern?

Toolbox

Reflection is a transformation.

When an **object** is reflected in a line, its **image** is formed on the other side of the line. Each point is at the same distance from the line.

The line is called the **mirror line** or the **line of reflection**.

The image and the original object are **congruent**.

They are the same shape and the same size.

The line of reflection does not have to be horizontal or vertical, it can be in any direction.

Common lines used for reflection are shown in the diagram below.

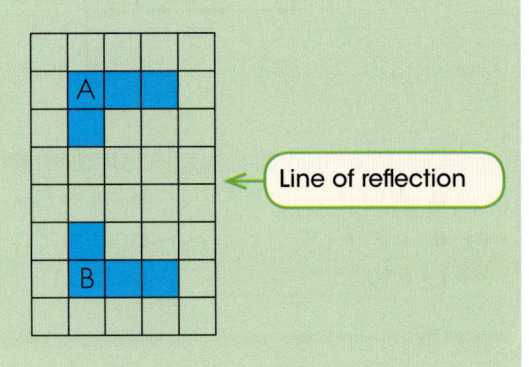

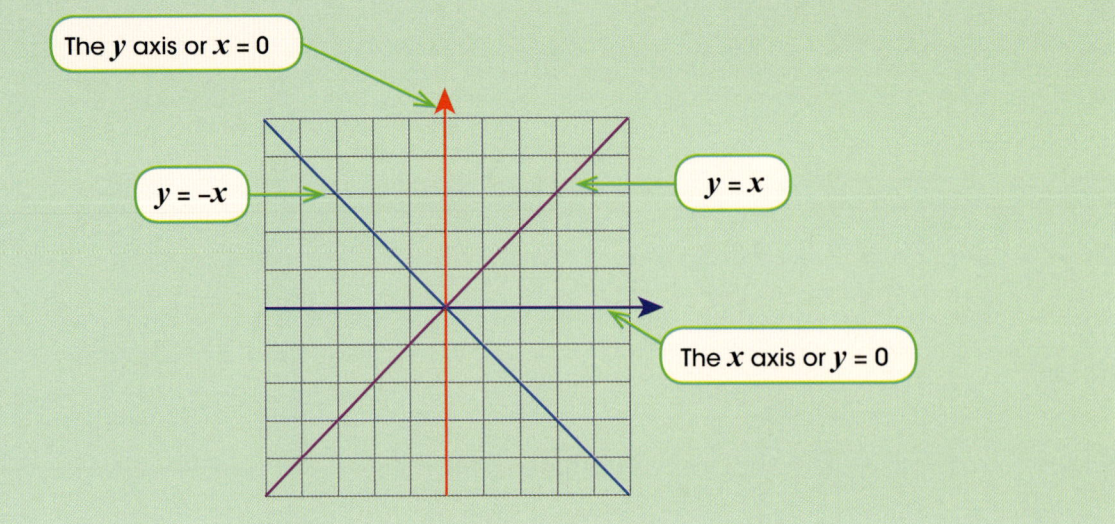

The y axis or $x = 0$

$y = -x$

$y = x$

The x axis or $y = 0$

Other commonly used lines of symmetry are
- vertical lines parallel to the y-axis e.g. $x = 3$, $x = -2$
- horizontal lines parallel to the x-axis e.g. $y = -3$, $y = 4$.

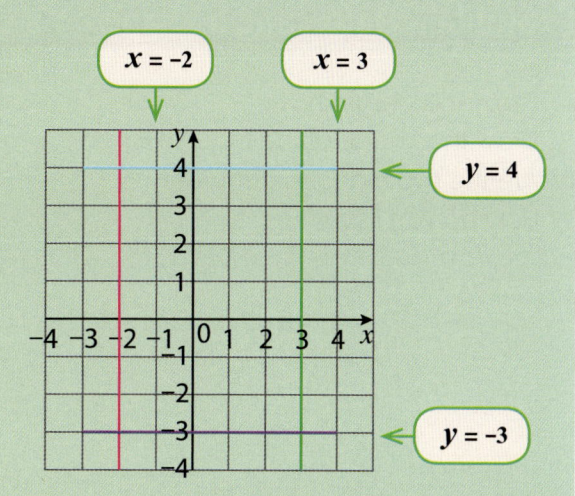

It is often obvious where the image should be, but sometimes you may need to do a drawing. To reflect a point P in a line l, take these steps.

- Draw a line through P at right angles to l. Call the point where they cross X.

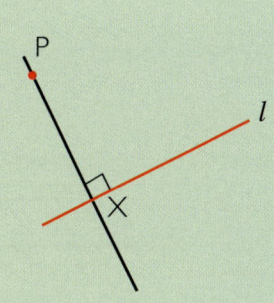

- Find P' where P'X = PX. P' is the image of P.

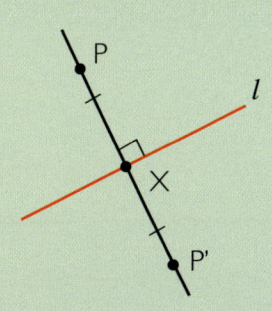

Geometry and Measures Strand 5 Transformations

Example – Reflecting a shape on a co-ordinate grid

a Copy this diagram.
   Draw the image of the triangle when it is reflected in the y-axis.

b Are the two triangles congruent?
   How do you know?

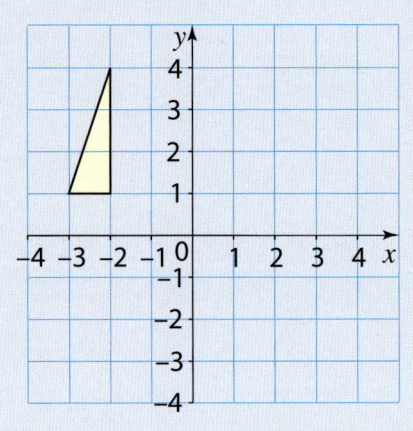

Solution

a

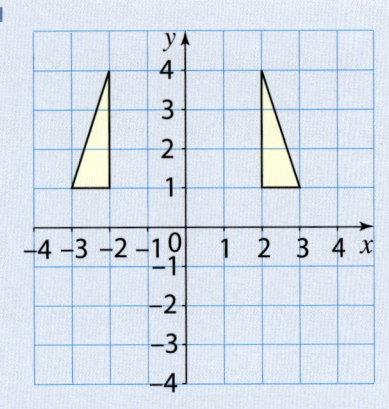

b When an object is reflected, all the lines and angles on the object and its image are the same size.
   So they are congruent.

Congruent shapes are the same size and shape.

Unit 4 Reflection Band e

Example – Reflecting a shape in a mirror line

Copy the diagram.
Draw the image of the shape after it is reflected.

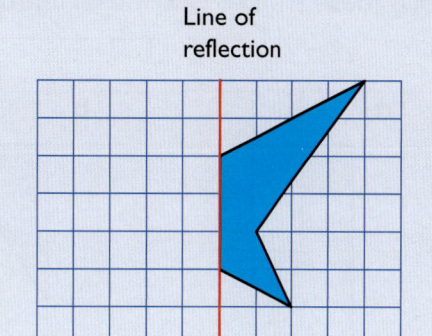

Solution

The points on the line of reflection stay in the same place.

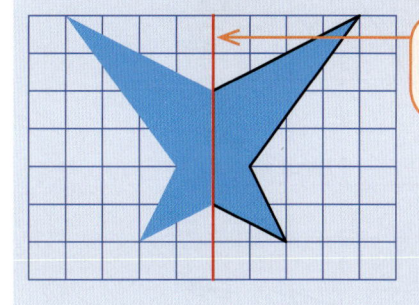

Example – Finding lines of reflection

For each of these diagrams show the line of reflection and give its equation.

a, **b**, 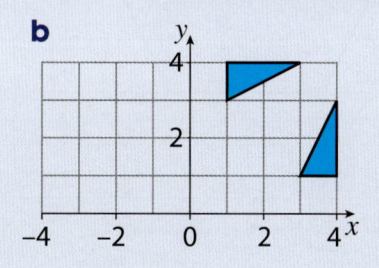 **c**

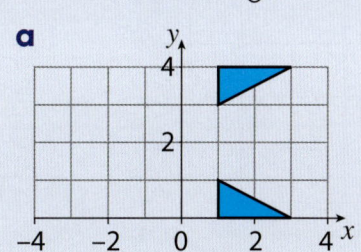

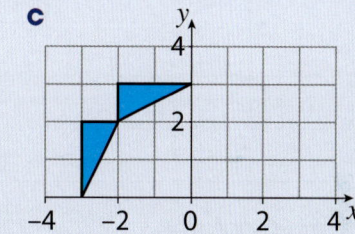

Solution

a The line of reflection is $y = 2$.

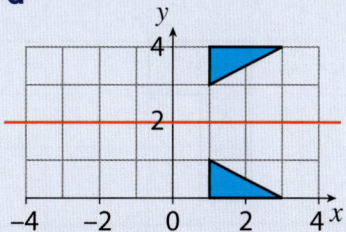

b The line of reflection is $y = x$.

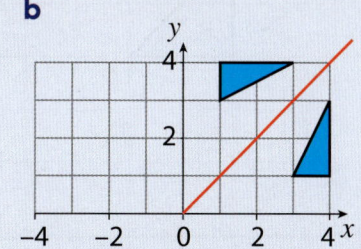

c The line of reflection is $y = -x$.

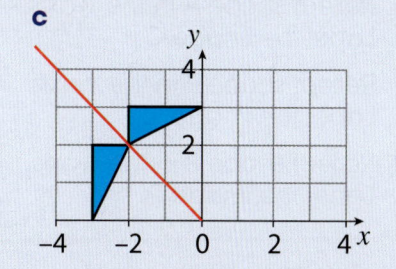

Geometry and Measures Strand 5 Transformations

Practising skills

1 Copy these shapes and reflect them in the mirror line.

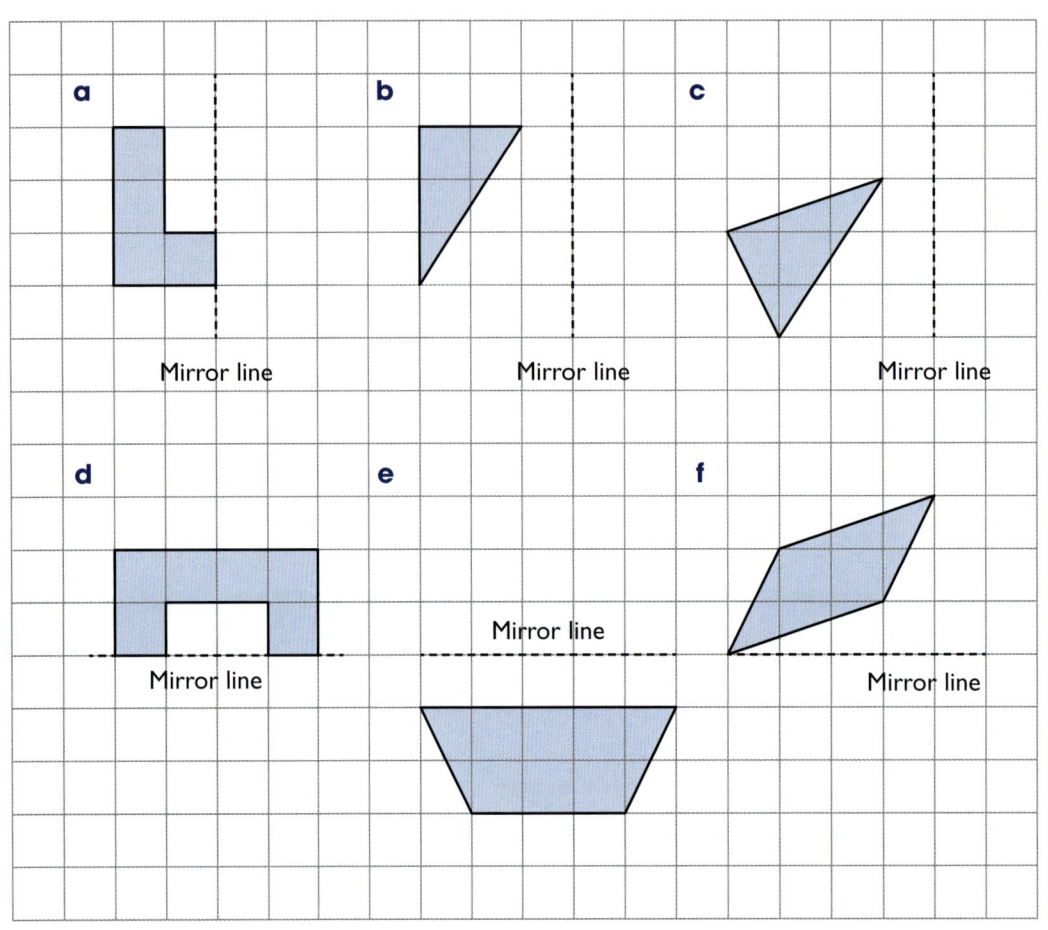

a   b   c
Mirror line   Mirror line   Mirror line

d   e   f
Mirror line   Mirror line   Mirror line

2 Copy this diagram.

- **a** Reflect shape A in the x-axis. Label the image B.
- **b** Reflect shape A in the y-axis. Label the image C.
- **c** Reflect shape P in the x-axis. Label the image Q.
- **d** Reflect shape P in the y-axis. Label the image R.

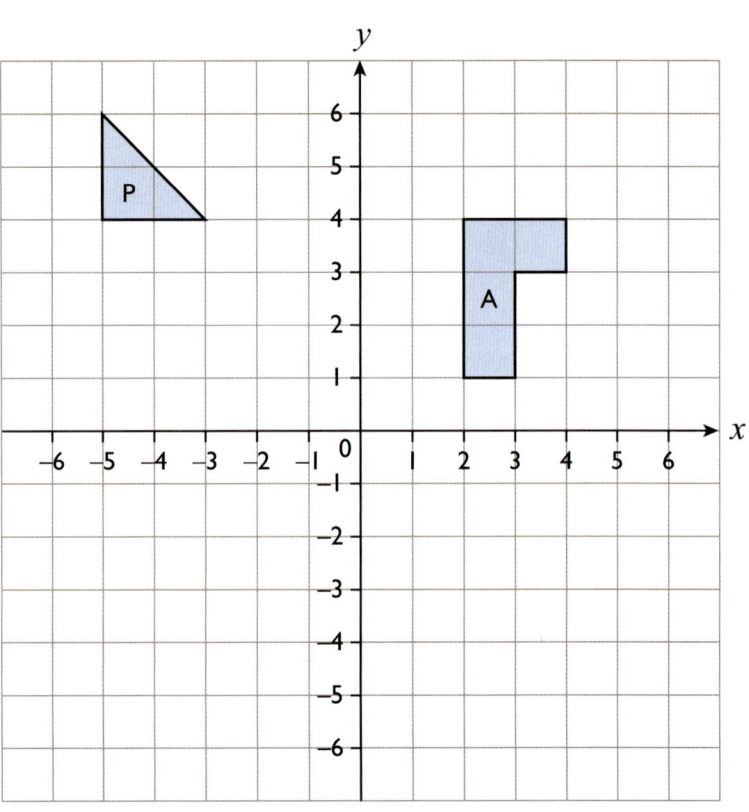

Unit 4 Reflection Band e

3 Write down the equation of the lines **a** to **f**.

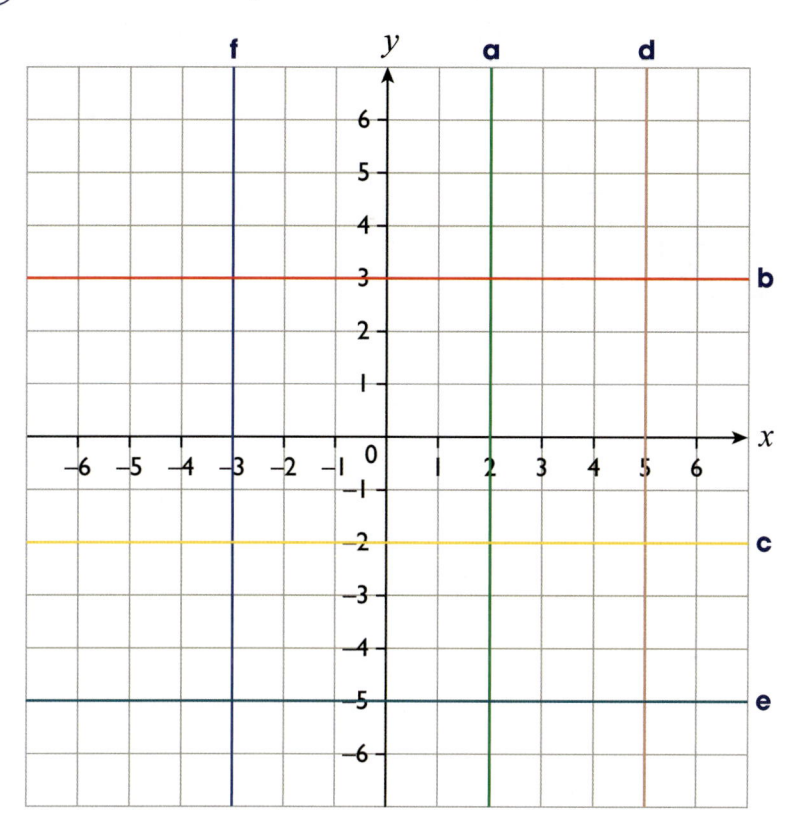

4 Copy this diagram.

a Draw and label the lines $x = 1$, $y = 3$ and $y = -1$.

b i Reflect shape T in the line $x = 1$. Label the image U.
  ii Reflect shape T in the line $y = 3$. Label the image V.
  iii Reflect shape T in the line $y = -1$. Label the image W.

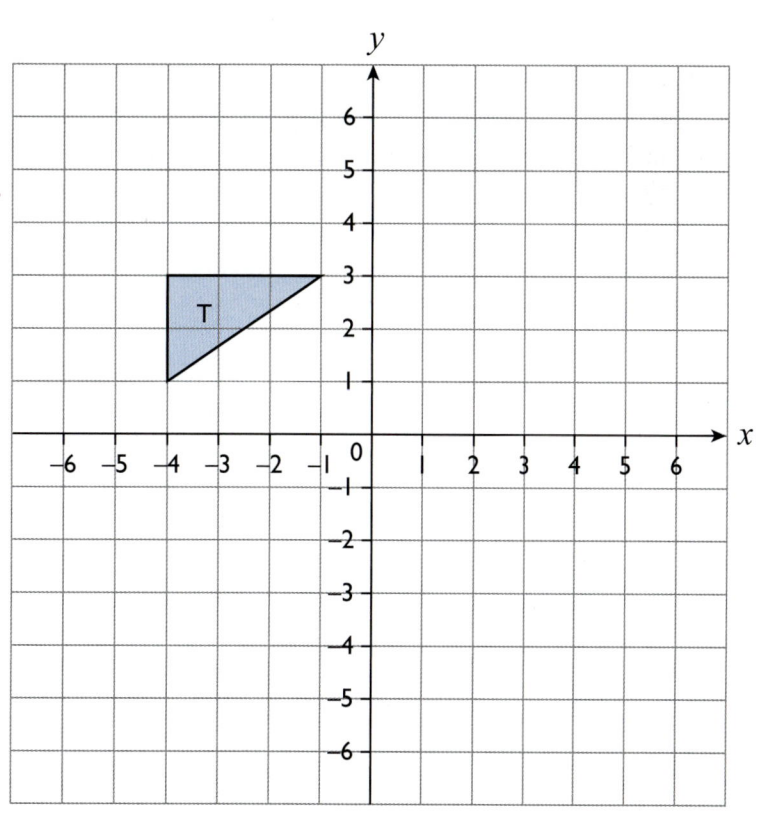

Geometry and Measures Strand 5 Transformations

5 Copy this diagram.

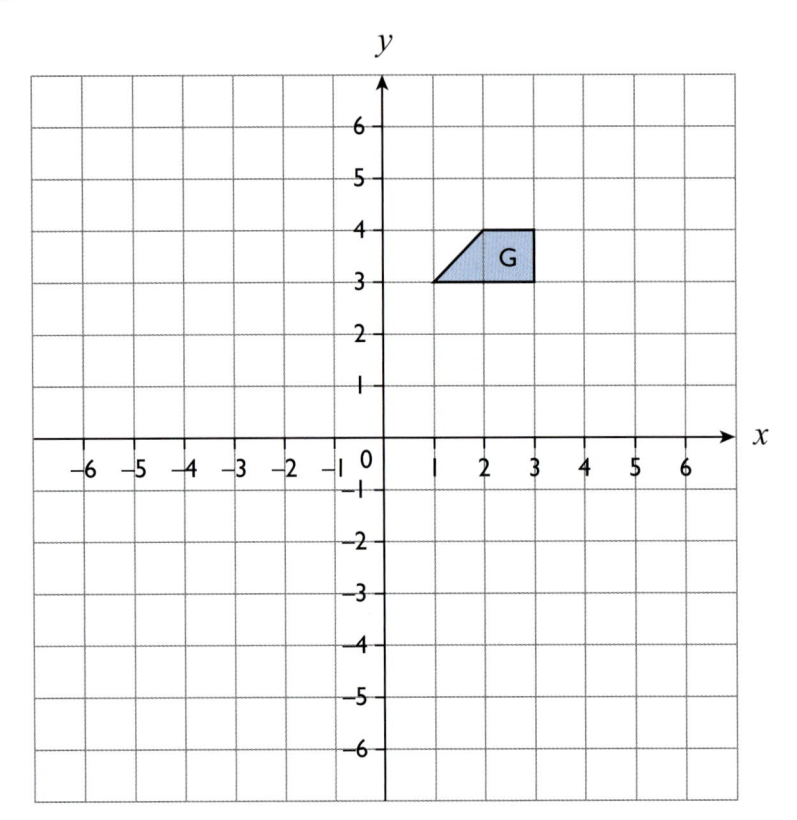

a Draw and label the lines $y = 1$, $y = 4$, $x = -1$ and $x = 3$.

b i Reflect shape G in the line $y = 1$. Label the image H.
  ii Reflect shape G in the line $y = 4$. Label the image I.
  iii Reflect shape G in the line $x = -1$. Label the image J.
  iv Reflect shape G in the line $x = 3$. Label the image K.

Unit 4 Reflection Band e

Developing fluency

1 Copy this diagram.

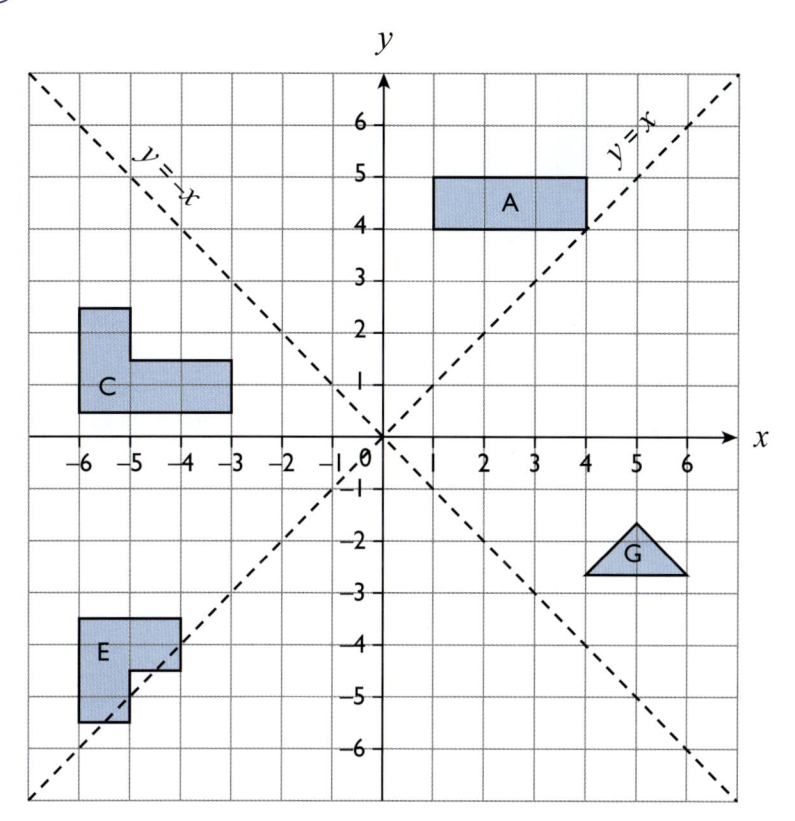

a Reflect shape A in the line $y = x$. Label the image B.
b Reflect shape C in the line $y = -x$. Label the image D.
c Reflect shape E in the line $y = x$. Label the image F.
d Reflect shape G in the line $y = -x$. Label the image H.

Geometry and Measures Strand 5 Transformations

2 Look at this diagram.

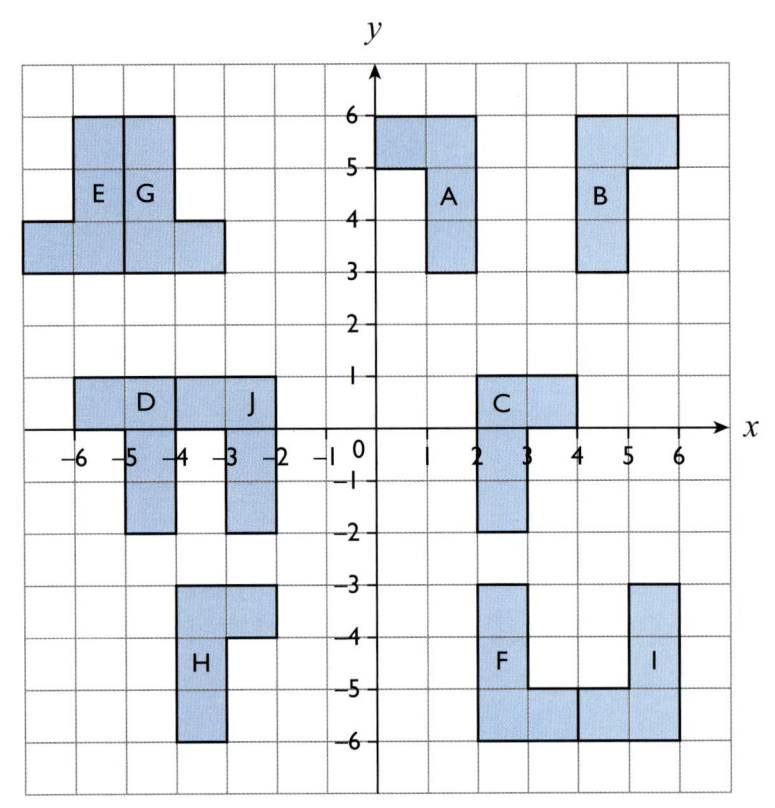

Describe fully the single transformation that maps

a   A to B
d   D to E
g   H to G

b   B to A
e   C to F
h   I to F

c   C to D
f   G to E
i   J to C.

3 Copy this diagram.

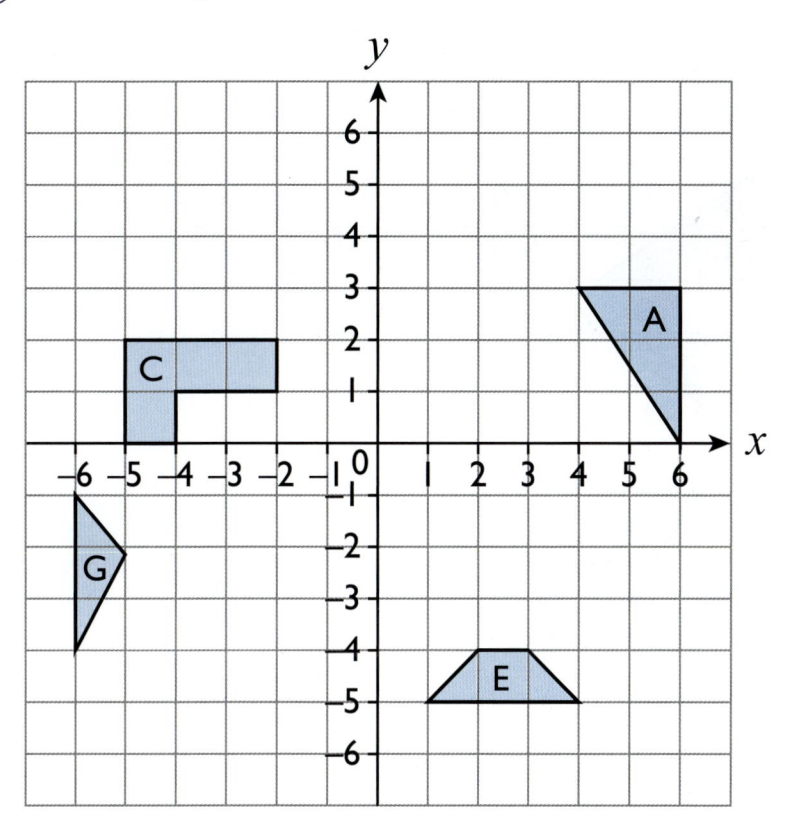

a Reflect shape A in the line $y = x$. Label the image B.
b Reflect shape C in the line $y = -x$. Label the image D.
c Reflect shape E in the line $y = -x$. Label the image F.
d Reflect shape G in the line $y = x$. Label the image H.

Geometry and Measures Strand 5 Transformations

4) Look at this diagram.

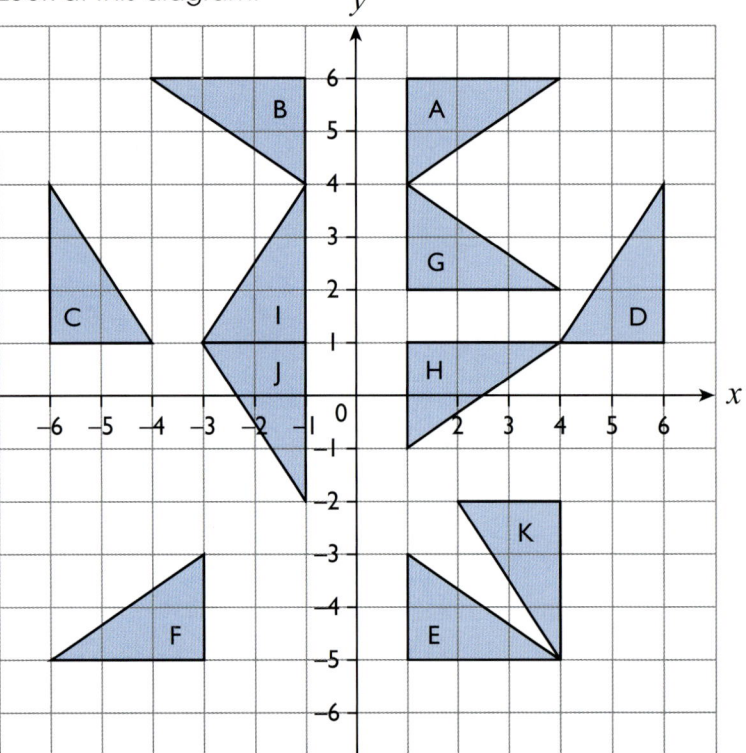

Describe fully the single transformation that maps

a A to B
b A to E
c E to F
d C to D
e A to D
f E to A
g B to C
h A to G
i H to E
j I to J
k C to I
l E to K.

5) The diagram shows a trapezium A drawn on a grid.

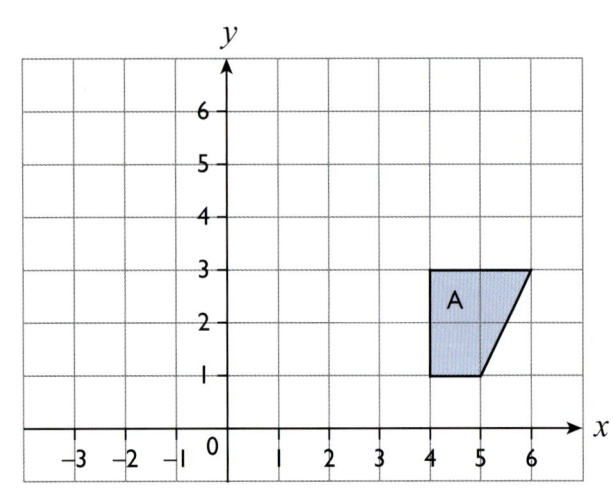

Reflect trapezium A in the line $y = x$. Label the image B.

Problem solving

1 a P and Q are points that are images of each other under a reflection.
P has co-ordinates (5, 8). Q has co-ordinates (5, 12).
Find an equation of the line of reflection.

b S and T are points that are images of each under a different reflection.
S has co-ordinates (4, 2). T has co-ordinates (−2, 4).
Find an equation of the line of reflection.

2 PQ is a line of length 6 units parallel to the x-axis.
PQ is reflected in the line $x = 5$ to give the line RS.
Find the length of the line RS

a when the line $x = 5$ does not cut the line PQ

b when the line $x = 5$ does cut the line PQ.
In each case give a reason for your answer.

3 P and Q are points that are images of each other under a reflection.
P has co-ordinates (4, b). Q has co-ordinates (4, 2b). The equation of the line of reflection is $y = 6$.
Find the value of b.

4 Two shapes, S and T have been drawn on a grid.

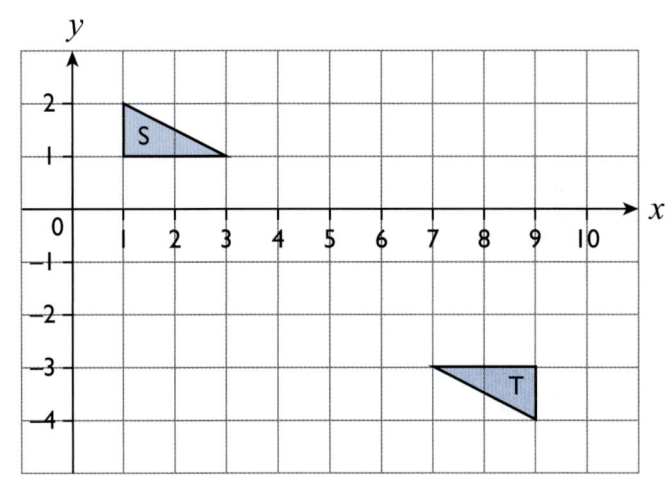

Shape S is mapped to shape T by a translation followed by a reflection.
Describe fully both the translation and the reflection.

Geometry and Measures Strand 5 Transformations

5 A shape has been drawn on a grid.

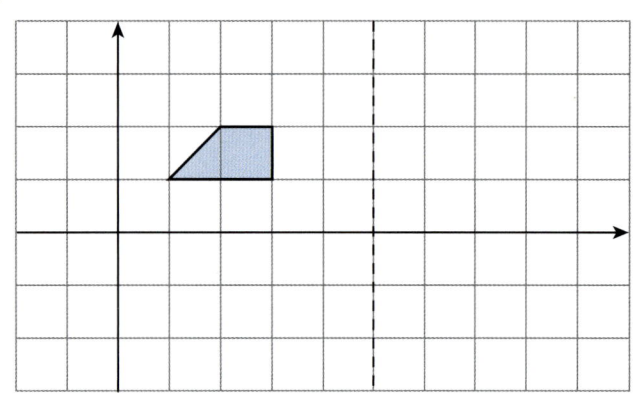

a Give an example to show that a translation followed by a reflection does not have the same effect as the same reflection followed by the same translation.

b Give an example to show that a translation followed by a reflection can have the same effect.

Reviewing skills

1 Copy this diagram.

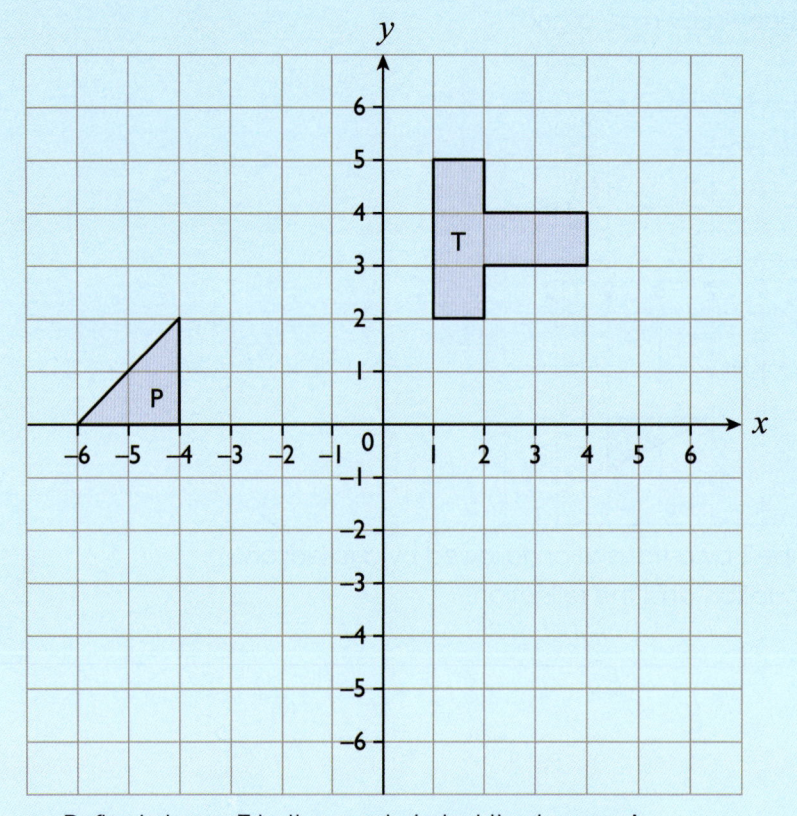

   a Reflect shape T in the x-axis. Label the image A.
   b Reflect shape T in the y-axis. Label the image B.
   c Reflect shape P in the x-axis. Label the image C.
   d Reflect shape P in the y-axis. Label the image D.

2 Copy this diagram.

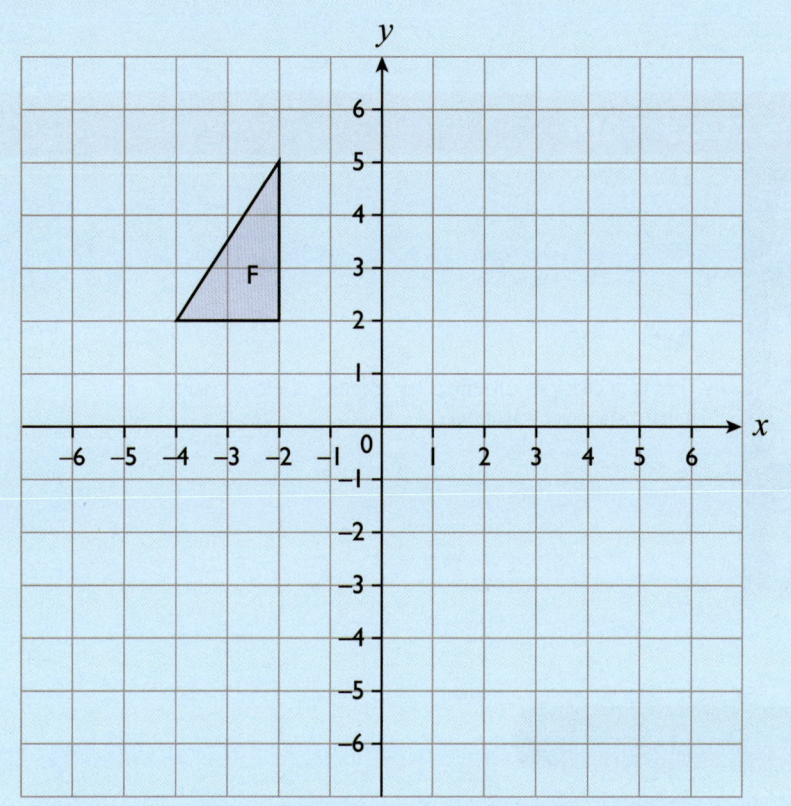

a Reflect shape F in the line $y = 2$. Label the image A.
b Reflect shape F in the line $x = -4$. Label the image B.
c Reflect shape F in the y-axis. Label the image C.
d Reflect shape F in the x-axis. Label the image D.
e Reflect shape F in the line $x = -1$. Label the image E.

Unit 5 • Rotation • Band e

Outside the Maths classroom

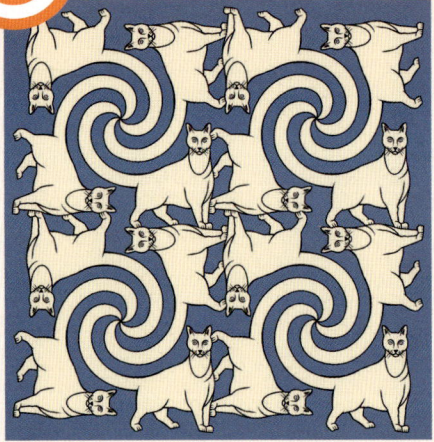

Art

This is a design created by rotations. How many rotations can you find?

Toolbox

Another transformation is a **rotation**.
Rotation is a movement made by **turning** an object.
The flag here has been rotated four times, each time by a quarter turn.
A full turn is 360°, so
- a quarter turn is 90° (a right angle)
- a half turn is 180°
- a three-quarters turn is 270°.

The flag has been rotated by holding the end of the stick still.
This is the **centre of rotation**.

In this diagram the red triangle is the image of the green triangle when it is rotated through 90° clockwise about the origin.

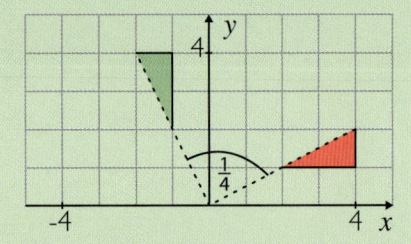

In this diagram the red flag is the image of the green one when it is rotated through 180° about the point (1, 0).
A rotation of 180° can be **clockwise** or **anticlockwise**.
Objects and their images as a result of a rotation are always **congruent**.

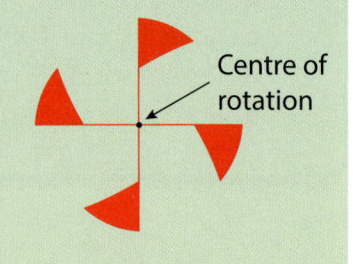

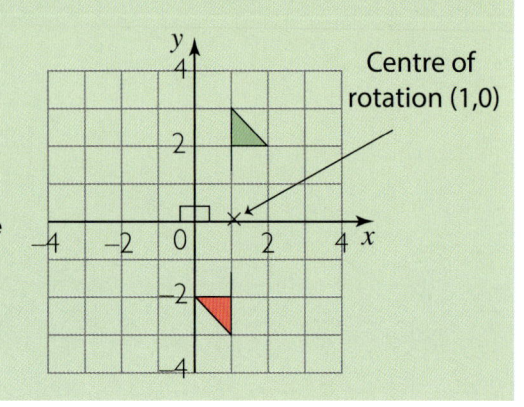

Unit 5 Rotation Band e

Example – Rotating a shape about the origin

a Rotate shape A by 90° in a clockwise direction, centre (0, 0). Label the resulting image B.
b Rotate shape A by 180°, centre the origin.
  Label the resulting image C.
  Why does the direction not matter for this rotation?

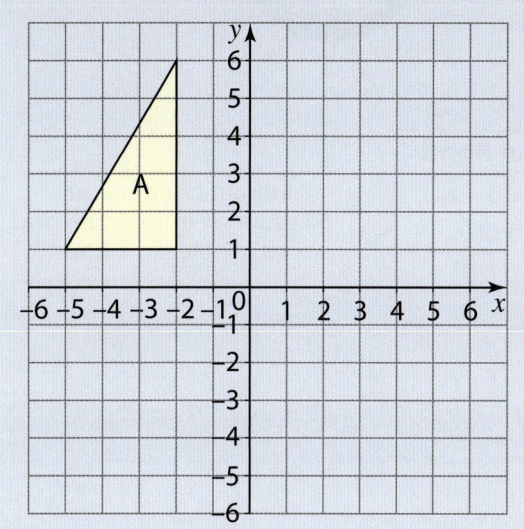

Solution

a, b

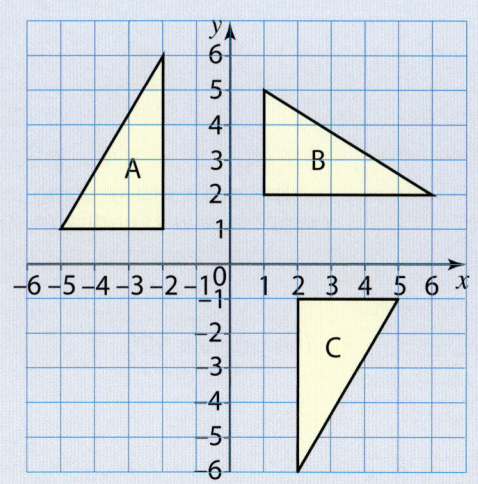

The direction does not matter because a turn of 180° is the same whichever direction you turn.

Geometry and Measures Strand 5 Transformations

Example – Describing a rotation

This clock has three hands.
What angles do the hands turn through in
a 1 minute
b 30 seconds
c 15 seconds?

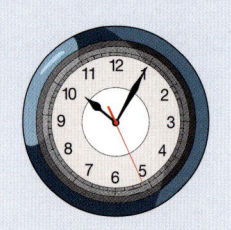

Solution

		Second hand	Minute hand	Hour hand
a	1 minute	360°	360° ÷ 60 = 6°	6° ÷ 60 = 0.1°
b	30 seconds	180°	3°	0.05°
c	15 seconds	90°	1.5°	0.025°

Remember there are 60 seconds in 1 minute and 60 minutes in 1 hour.

Example – Rotating a point

The point A is (2, 6).
It is rotated through 90° clockwise about the point (4, 2).
Find the co-ordinates of its image A'.

Solution

The centre of rotation is (4, 2).

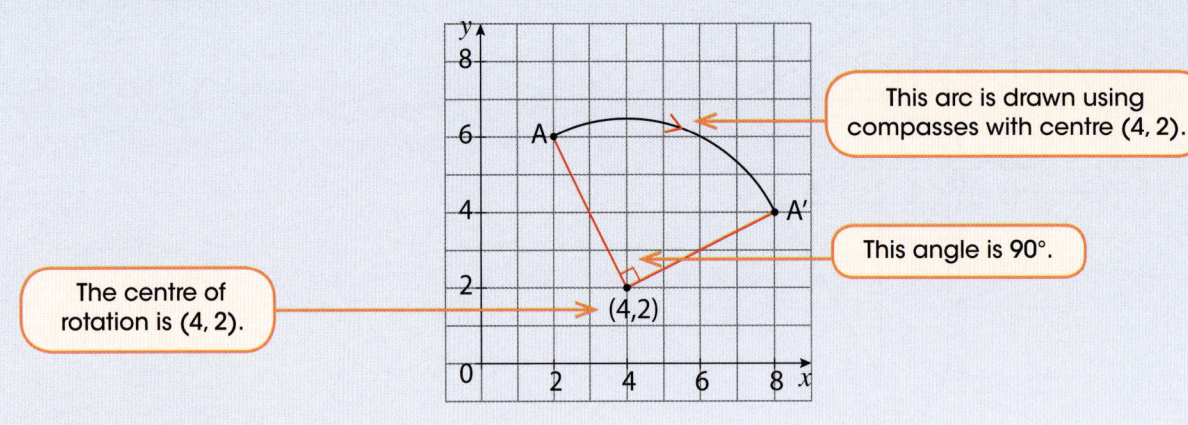

This arc is drawn using compasses with centre (4, 2).

This angle is 90°.

Its image A' is (8, 4).

Unit 5 Rotation Band e

Practising skills

1 Match the pairs.

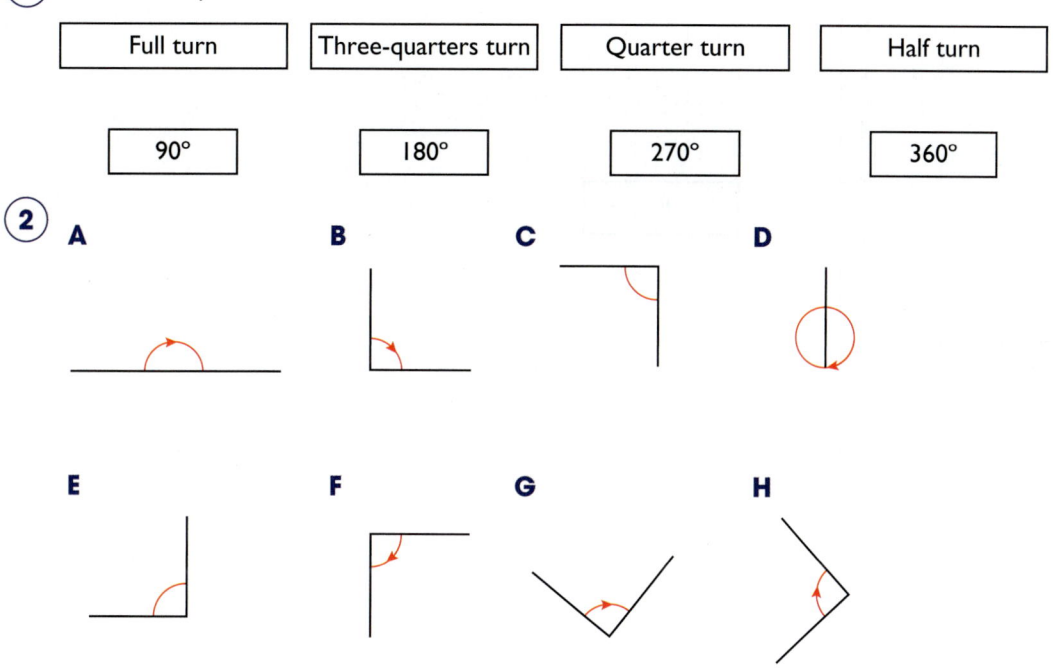

| Full turn | Three-quarters turn | Quarter turn | Half turn |

| 90° | 180° | 270° | 360° |

2 A B C D

E F G H

a Which of the above show a full turn?
b Which of the above show a 180° turn?
c Which of the above show a 90° clockwise turn?
d Which of the above show a 90° anticlockwise turn?

Geometry and Measures Strand 5 Transformations

3 Copy this diagram.

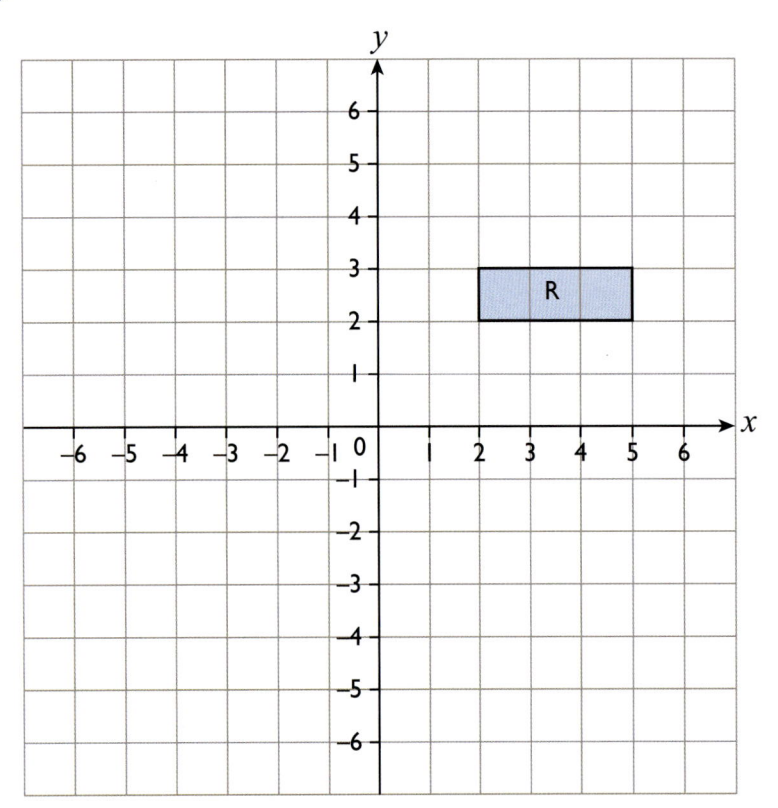

Use tracing paper to rotate the shape.

a Rotate shape R, 90° clockwise about the point (0, 0). Label the image A.

b Rotate shape R, 90° anticlockwise about the point (0, 0). Label the image B.

c Rotate shape R, 180° about the point (0, 0). Label the image C.

4 Copy this diagram.

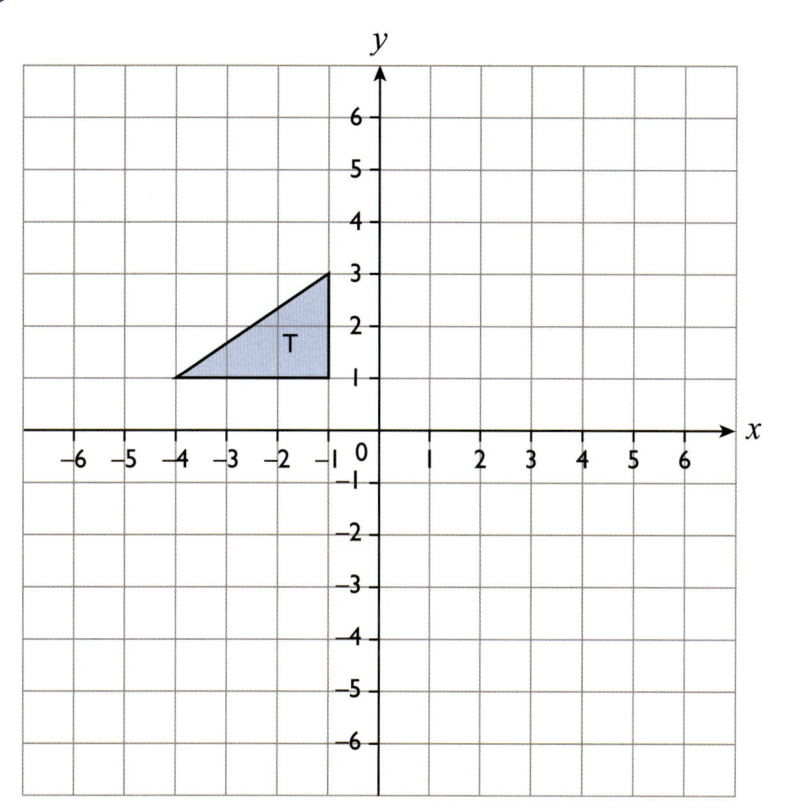

Use tracing paper to rotate the shape.

a Rotate shape T, 90° clockwise about the point (0, 0). Label the image A.

b Rotate shape T, 90° anticlockwise about the point (0, 0). Label the image B.

c Rotate shape T, 180° about the point (0, 0). Label the image C.

Geometry and Measures Strand 5 Transformations

5 Copy this diagram.

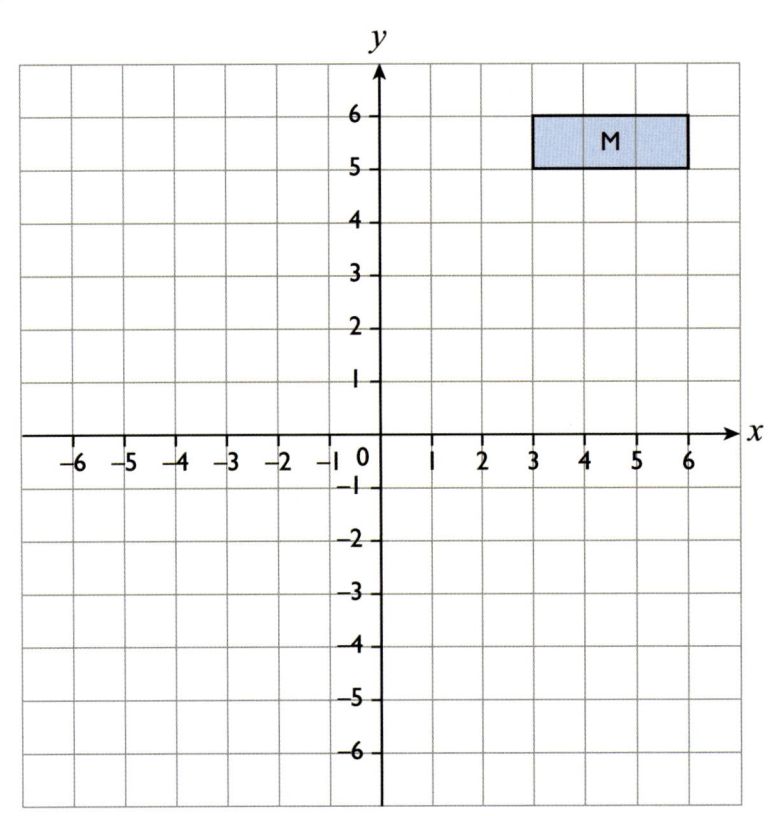

Use tracing paper to rotate the shape.

a Rotate shape M, 90° clockwise about (0, 0). Label the image A.
b Rotate shape M, 90° anticlockwise about (0, 0). Label the image B.
c Rotate shape M, 180° about (0, 0). Label the image C.
d Rotate shape M, 90° clockwise about (1, 2). Label the image D.
e Rotate shape M, 90° anticlockwise about (5, 3). Label the image E.
f Rotate shape M, 180° about (3, 4). Label the image F.

Unit 5 Rotation Band e

Developing fluency

1 Copy this diagram.

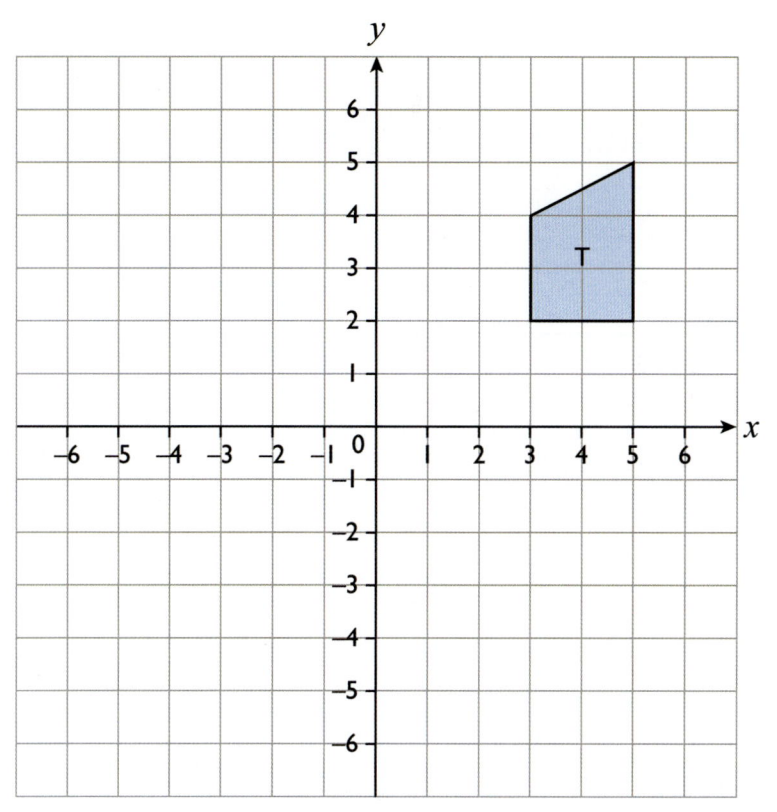

a Rotate shape T, 90° clockwise about (0, 0). Label the image A.
b Rotate shape T, 90° anticlockwise about (2, 3). Label the image B.
c Rotate shape T, 180° about (0, 0). Label the image C.
d Rotate shape T, 180° about (1, 2). Label the image D.
e Rotate shape T, 90° clockwise about (2, 2). Label the image E.

Geometry and Measures Strand 5 Transformations

2 Copy this diagram.

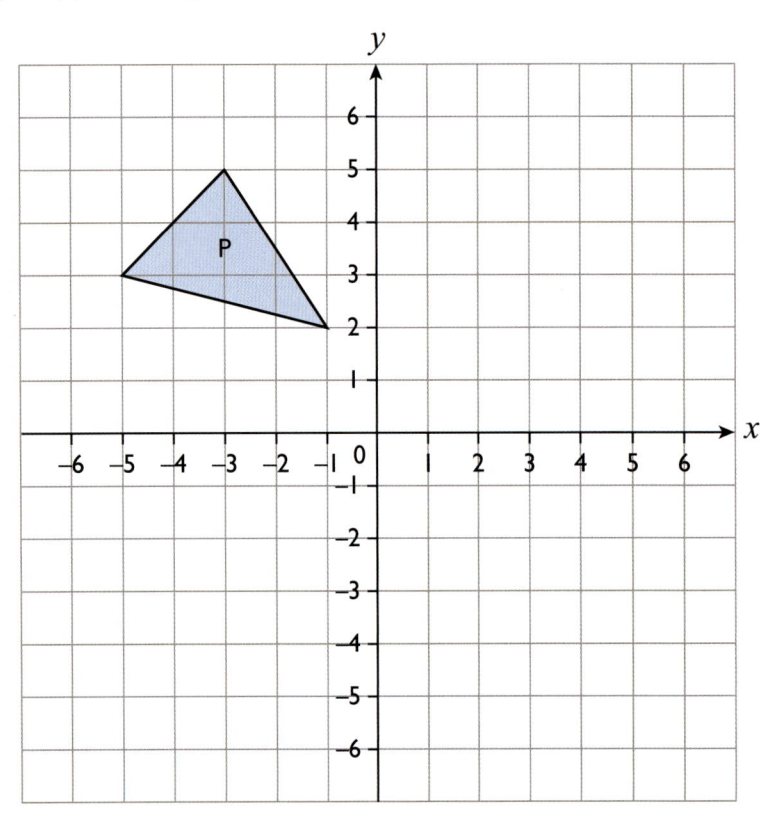

a Rotate shape P, 90° clockwise about (0, 1). Label the image A.
b Rotate shape P, 90° anticlockwise about (−2, 1). Label the image B.
c Rotate shape P, 180° about (0, 0). Label the image C.
d Rotate shape P, 90° anticlockwise about (0, 0). Label the image D.
e Rotate shape P, 180° about (0, 2). Label the image E.

3) Look at this diagram.

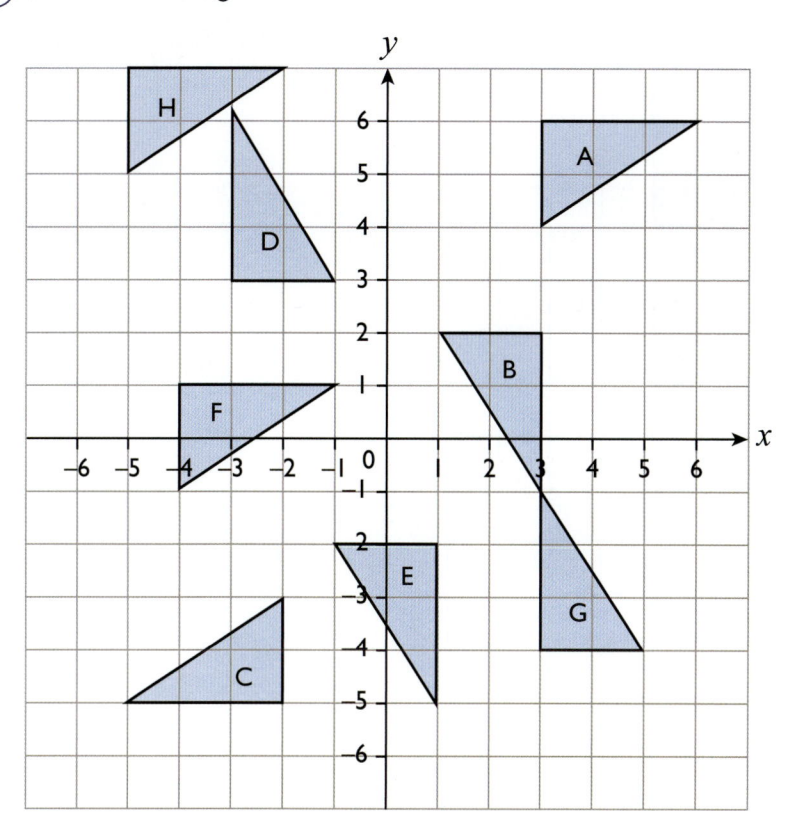

Describe fully the single transformation that maps

a A to B
b B to A
c A to C
d C to A
e B to D
f C to E
g D to F
h B to G
i H to D.

Geometry and Measures Strand 5 Transformations

4) Look at this diagram.

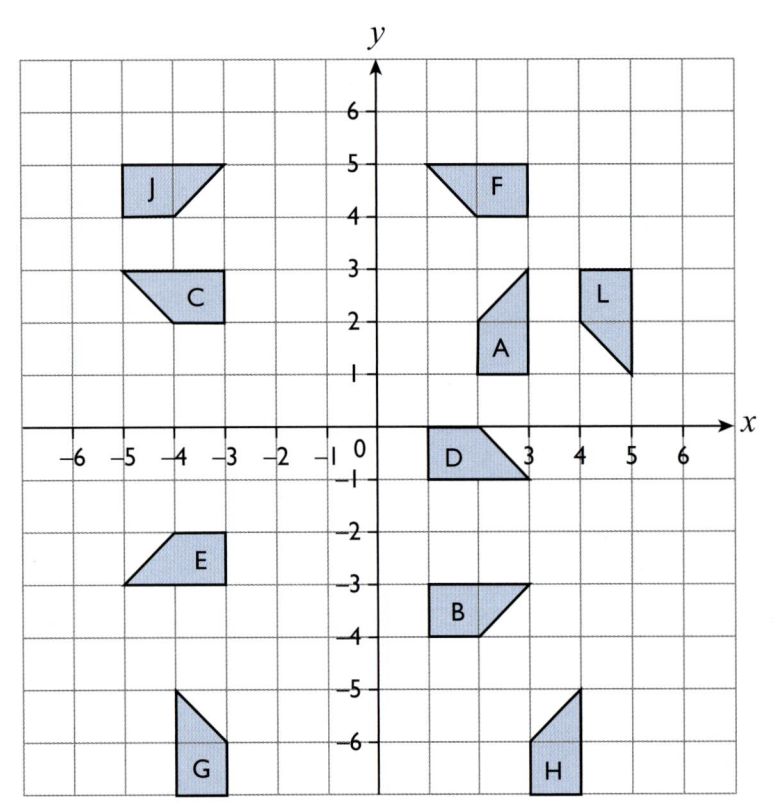

Describe fully the single transformation that maps

a B to D
b A to D
c C to F
d D to C
e E to C
f A to H
g G to H
h G to E
i E to G
j J to F
k B to J
l I to F.

Unit 5 Rotation Band e

Problem solving

1 Heddwen wants to make a wallpaper pattern. She practices first with a simple shape.

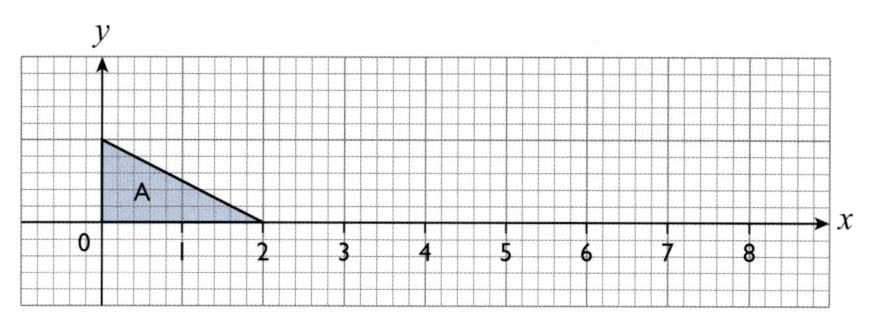

Her rules for transformation are:
- Rotate triangle A by 180° about the point (2, 0) to give triangle B.
- Rotate triangle B by 180° about the point (4, 0) to give triangle C.

a Describe the single transformation that maps triangle A to triangle C.

For a different design, Heddwen rotates the triangle A by 180° about the point (4, 0) to give triangle B, and then rotates triangle B by 180° about the point (8, 0) to give triangle C.

b Explain why the single transformation that maps A to C has to be a translation.

c Describe fully this translation.

2 Dewi wants to practice designing a wallpaper pattern.

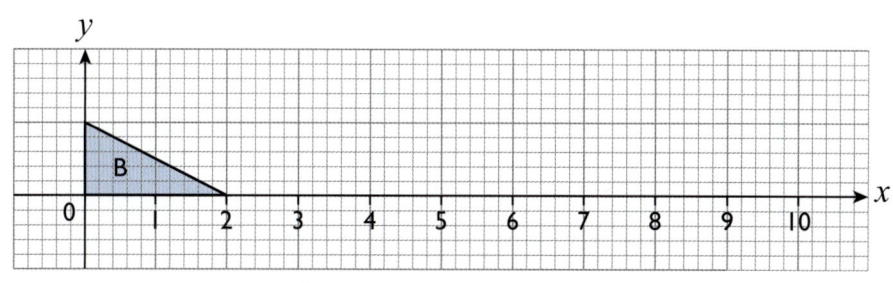

He rotates triangle B, 90° clockwise about (2, 0) to give triangle C.
He rotates triangle C, 90° anticlockwise about (4, 0) to give triangle D.

a Describe the single transformation that maps B to D.

b What type of single transformation is also equivalent to a rotation of 90° clockwise about a point followed by a rotation of 90° anticlockwise about a different point?

3 T is the translation with vector $\begin{pmatrix} 4 \\ 2 \end{pmatrix}$. R is the rotation of 90° anticlockwise about (0, 0).

Is it true that T followed by R will always have the same effect as R followed by T? You must give a reason for your answer.

Geometry and Measures Strand 5 Transformations

4 Here are the first two triangles in a sequence of triangles.

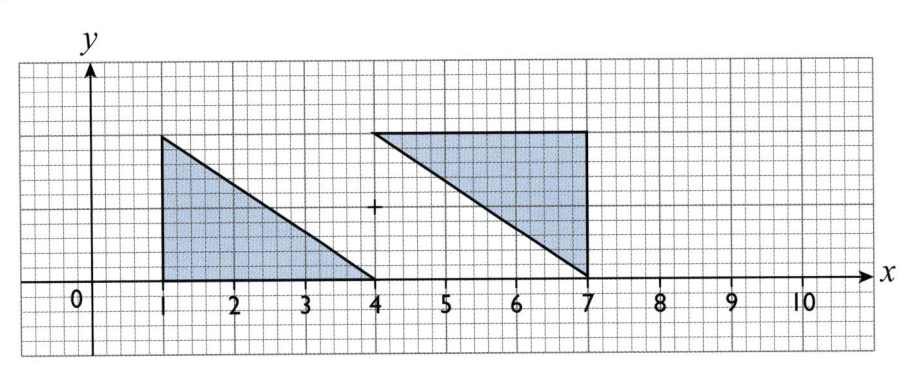

The rule for extending the sequence is:

rotate triangle T_n by 180° about the point $(4n, 1)$ to get triangle T_{n+1}.

a Draw triangle T_3.

b Describe fully the single transformation that maps T_1 onto T_{21}.

5 The diagram shows the start of a sequence of squares.

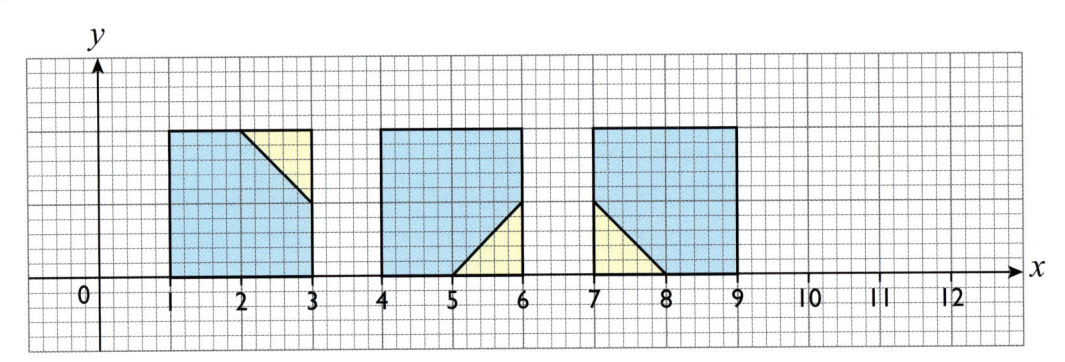

The rule for extending the sequence is:

rotate the square about its centre by 90° clockwise followed by a translation of 3 units to the right.

The sequence is continued for 25 squares.

What single transformation will map the first square to the last of the 25 squares?

6 The diagram shows a regular pentagon and a regular hexagon.

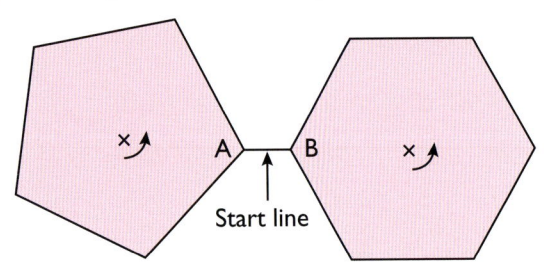

Corner A of the pentagon and corner B of the hexagon are also shown.

A and B are at opposite ends of a start line. Every second the pentagon rotates by 72° anticlockwise about its centre. Every second the hexagon rotates by 60° anticlockwise about its centre. The two polygons start at the same time.

After how many seconds will both A and B be at opposite ends of the start line?

Unit 5 Rotation Band e

7 The diagram shows a square and a regular hexagon.

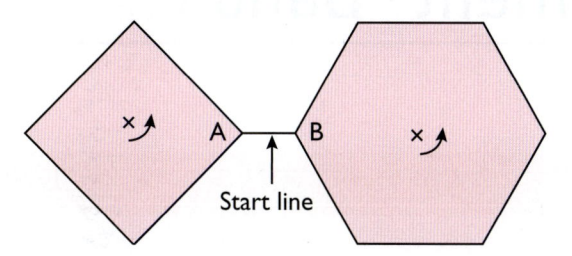

Corner A of the square and corner B of the hexagon are also shown.

A and B are at opposite ends of a start line. Every second the square rotates by 90° anticlockwise about its centre. Every second the hexagon rotates by 60° anticlockwise about its centre. The two polygons start at the same time.

After how many seconds will both A and B be at opposite ends of the start line?

Reviewing skills

1 Copy this diagram.

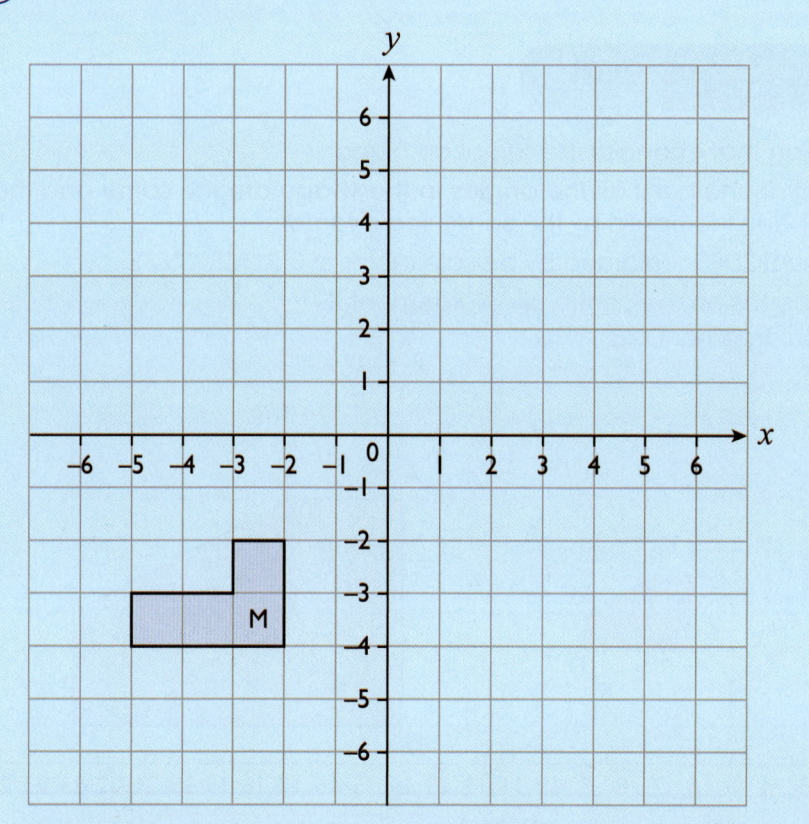

a Rotate shape M, 90° clockwise about (−1, −1). Label the image A.
b Rotate shape M, 90° anticlockwise about (−2, 1). Label the image B.
c Rotate shape M, 180° about (0, 0). Label the image C.
d Rotate shape M, 90° clockwise about (−1, 1). Label the image D.
e Rotate shape M, 180° about (0, −4). Label the image E.
f Describe fully the single transformation that maps A to D.
g Describe fully the single transformation that maps C to E.

Unit 6 • Enlargement • Band f

Outside the Maths classroom

TV screens

When you watch a film on TV, why do you sometimes get a thin rectangle of black along the top and bottom of the screen?

Toolbox

Enlargement is a transformation that changes the size of an object.

One shape is an enlargement of another if **all the angles in the shape are the same** and the **lengths of the sides** have all been increased by the **same scale factor**.

In this diagram the pentagon ABCDE is enlarged by a scale factor of 3 to A'B'C'D'E'.

The position of the image depends on the centre of enlargement X.

Because the scale factor of enlargement is 3

- side A'B' is three times as long as AB
- side E'D' is three times as long as ED, etc.
- the distance XB' is three times the distance XB
- the distance XD' is three times the distance XD, etc.

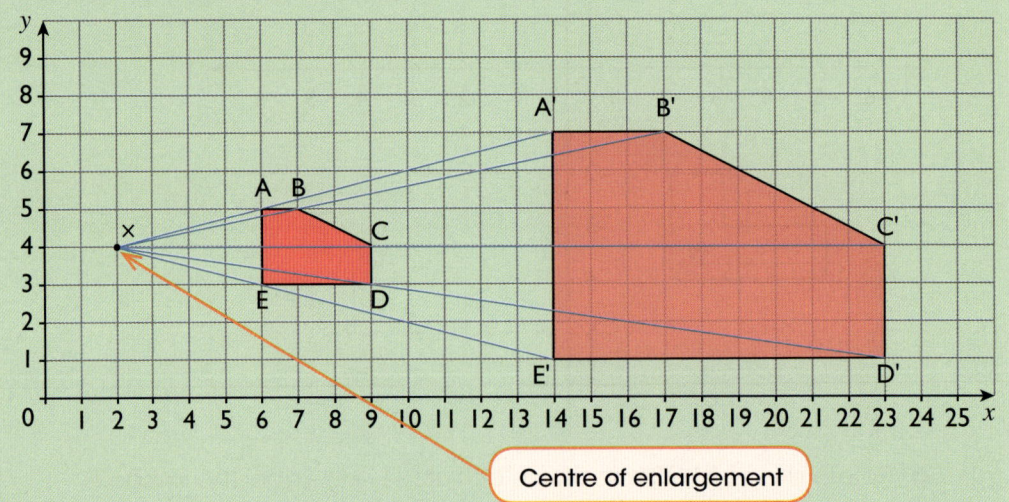

The term enlargement is also used in situations where the shape is made smaller.

In these cases the scale factor is a fraction, like $\frac{1}{2}$ or $\frac{1}{3}$.

In the diagram the scale factor for the enlargement of A'B'C'D'E' to ABCDE is $\frac{1}{3}$.

Unit 6 Enlargement Band f

Example – Finding the scale factor of an enlargement

The shape on the right shows an enlargement of a smaller rectangle from centre P, onto a larger rectangle.

a What is the scale factor of the enlargement?
b What happens if you change the centre of enlargement?

Solution

a The scale factor is 3 because all the sides of the second shape are three times as long as those of the first shape.
b The image would be in a different place.

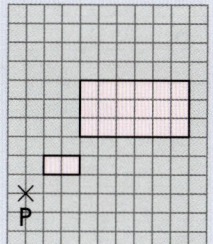

Example – Enlarging a shape

Plot the points A(2, 4), B(4, 4), C(4, 6) and D(2, 6).
Join the points to form a square.
Enlarge ABCD using (0, 5) as the centre of enlargement and a scale factor of 2. Label the image A'B'C'D'.

a What are the co-ordinates of the points A', B', C' and D'?
b What shape is A'B'C'D'?

Solution

a A'(4, 3), B'(8, 3), C'(8, 7), D'(4, 7)
b A square

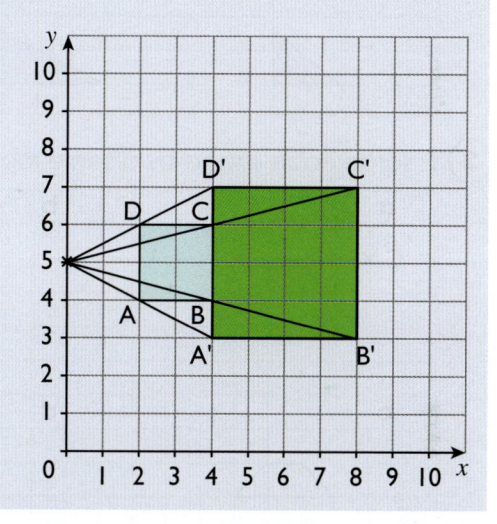

Example – Describing an enlargement

Emma draws the quadrilateral ABCD and then she transforms it as shown to A'B'C'D'.

a Describe fully the transformation from ABCD to A'B'C'D'.
b What can you say about the distance of the object and the image from the centre of enlargement?

Solution

a The enlargement scale factor is $\frac{1}{2}$.
The centre of enlargement is (0, −1).
b The image is half the distance that the object is from the centre.

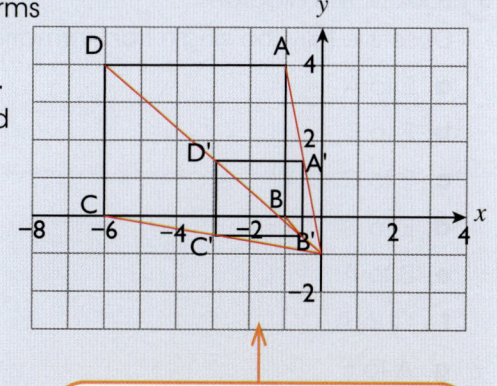

The lines joining the image and the object all meet at the centre of enlargement.

Geometry and Measures Strand 5 Transformations

Practising skills

1 Identify the pairs of triangles here. In each pair, one triangle is an enlargement of the other.

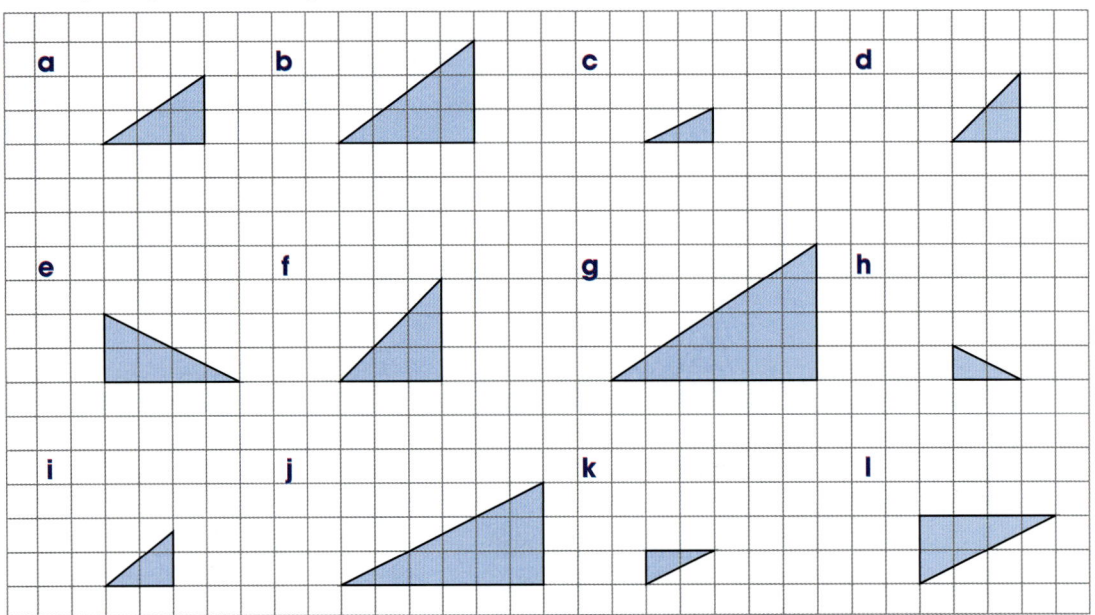

2 Enlarge each shape by a scale factor of 2, using C as the centre of enlargement.

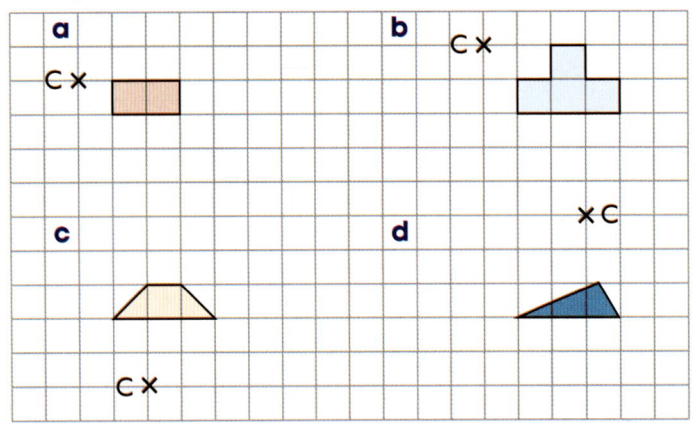

3 Look at this diagram.
Describe fully the single transformation that maps

- **a** E to A
- **b** E to B
- **c** E to C
- **d** E to D
- **e** B to A
- **f** C to A
- **g** A to E
- **h** B to E
- **i** D to E.

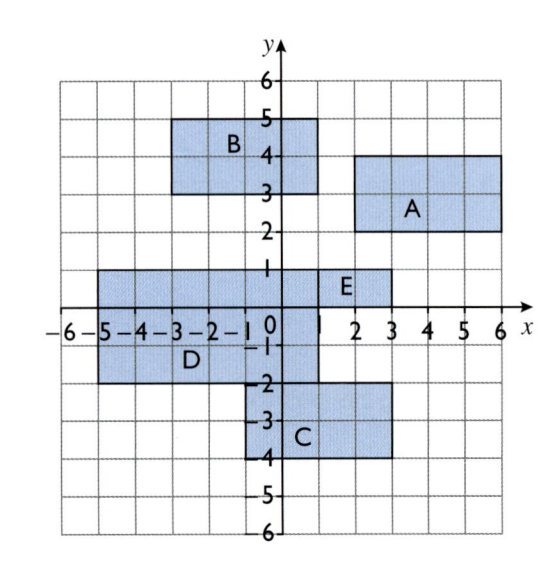

4 a An internet company have designed a new logo.

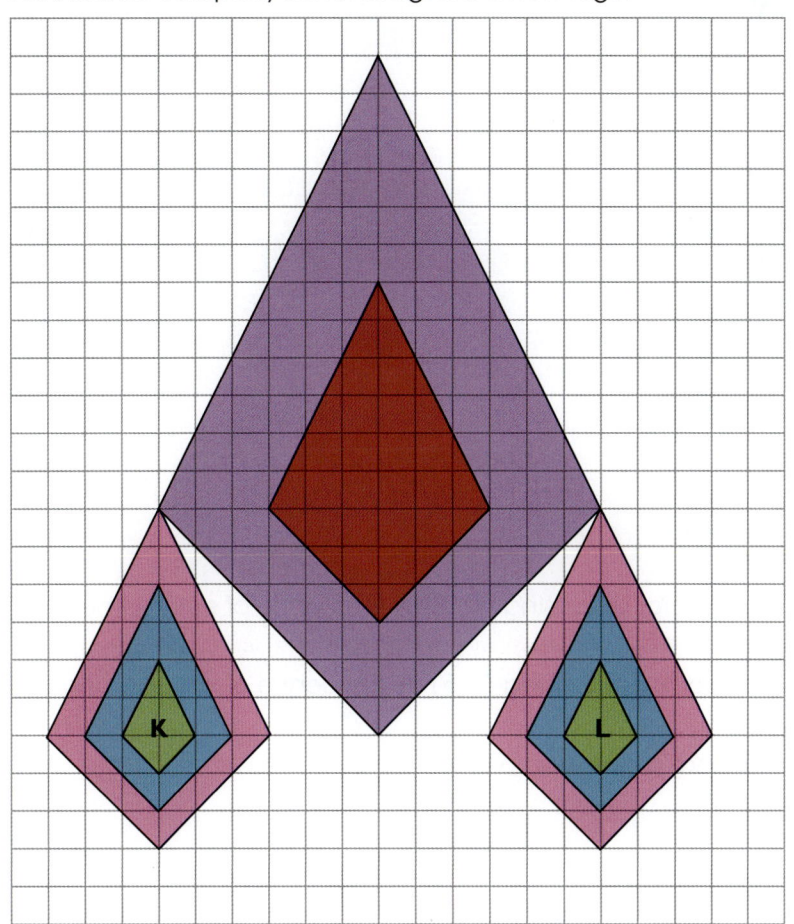

Describe the design fully.

b The green kite K is enlarged to be the same size as the
   i blue kite
   ii pink kite.
   Write down the scale factor of the enlargement for each.

c What transformation will map K to L?

d The blue kite is enlarged to give the purple kite.
   Describe the enlargement fully.

e The purple kite is enlarged to give the red kite.
   What is the scale factor of enlargement?

Geometry and Measures Strand 5 Transformations

Developing fluency

1. Copy this diagram.

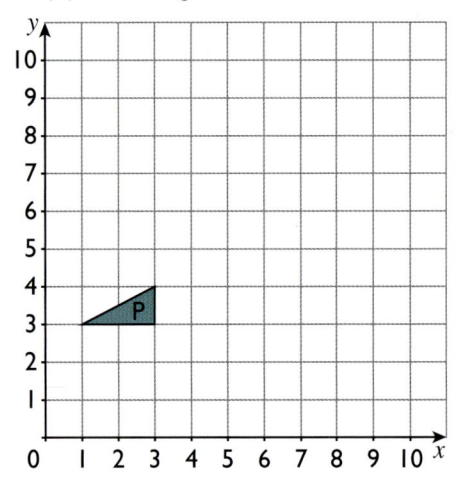

   a Enlarge triangle P by a scale factor of 2, using (0, 0) as the centre of enlargement. Label the image A.

   b Enlarge triangle P by a scale factor of 2, using (2, 5) as the centre of enlargement. Label the image B.

   c Describe the transformation that maps A onto B.

2. Copy this diagram.

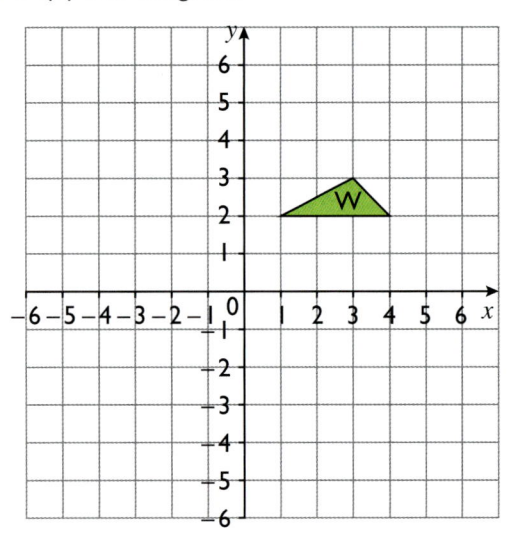

   a Enlarge shape W by a scale factor of 2, using (2, 1) as the centre of enlargement. Label the image A.

   b Enlarge shape W by a scale factor of 2, using (3, 6) as the centre of enlargement. Label the image B.

   c Describe the transformation that maps A onto B.

Unit 6 Enlargement Band f

3 Copy this diagram.

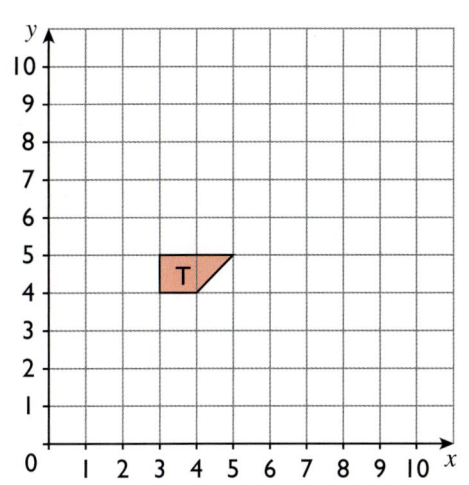

a Enlarge shape T by a scale factor of 2, using (1, 5) as the centre of enlargement. Label the image A.

b Enlarge shape T by a scale factor of 1.5, using (5, 9) as the centre of enlargement. Label the image B.

c Enlarge shape T by a scale factor of 3, using (2, 6) as the centre of enlargement. Label the image C.

d What do you notice about B and C?

4 In this diagram, triangles B and C are enlargements of triangle A.

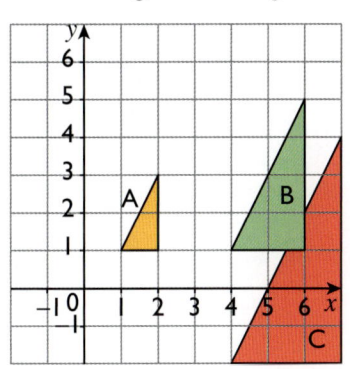

a Find the scale factor, f, and the centre of enlargement for A to B.

b Find the scale factor, g, and the centre of enlargement for B to C.

c The scale factor of the enlargement A to C is h. Use your answers for the scale factors f and g to predict the value of h.

Geometry and Measures Strand 5 Transformations

5 Look at this diagram.

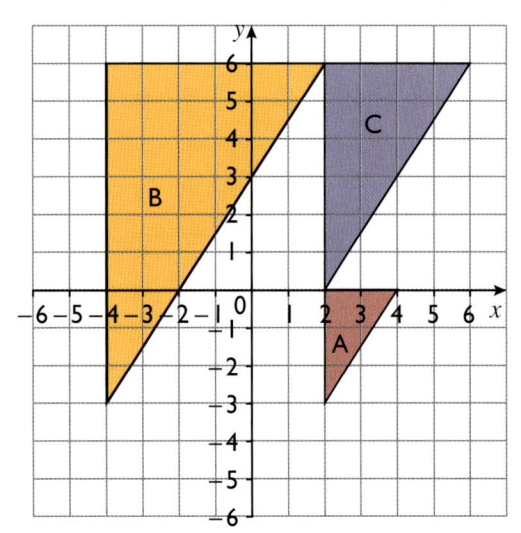

a Describe fully the single transformation that maps A to B.

b Describe fully the single transformation that maps B to A.

c Describe fully the single transformation that maps A to C.

d Describe fully the single transformation that maps C to A.

6 Copy this diagram.

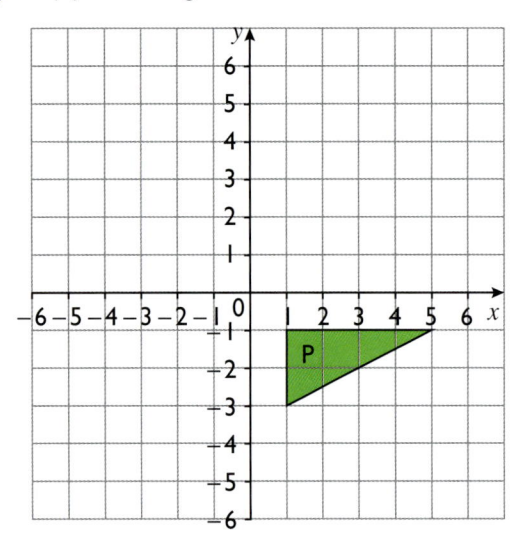

a Enlarge shape P by a scale factor of $\frac{1}{2}$, using (1, 5) as the centre of enlargement. Label the image A.

b Enlarge shape A by a scale factor of 2, using (6, 5) as the centre of enlargement. Label the image B.

c Describe the transformation that maps B to A.

Unit 6 Enlargement Band f

7 Alun makes this statement about enlargements.

'Start with a shape A, enlarge it with a scale factor k, centre O, to give shape B.
Enlarge shape B with a different scale factor m, centre O, to give shape C.
The single transformation that will map shape A to shape C is an enlargement with a scale factor $k + m$.'

a Give an example to show that Alun is wrong.

b What should Alun have said?

8 a Draw an equilateral triangle AXY.

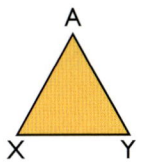

b On the same diagram, draw the enlargement of AXY, centre A, scale factor 2.
Label this triangle ABC.

c Still on the same diagram, draw the enlargement of ABC with scale factor $\frac{1}{2}$ and centres
   i B   **ii** C.

The new point on BC is Z.

d You have now drawn the net of a solid shape.
What shape is it?

e What happens if your original triangle is not equilateral?

Problem solving

1 Glenda has this picture of Tower Bridge.
She wants to enlarge the picture to fit exactly into the frame.
The dimensions of the picture and the frame are given.

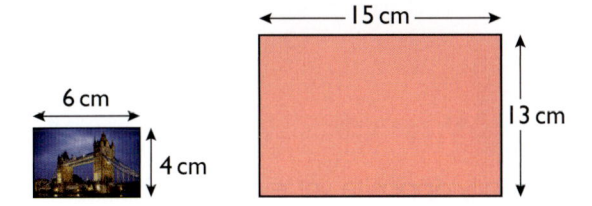

Will she be able to do this? Give a reason for your answer.

Geometry and Measures Strand 5 Transformations

2 Here is a scale drawing of a bedroom in a show home.

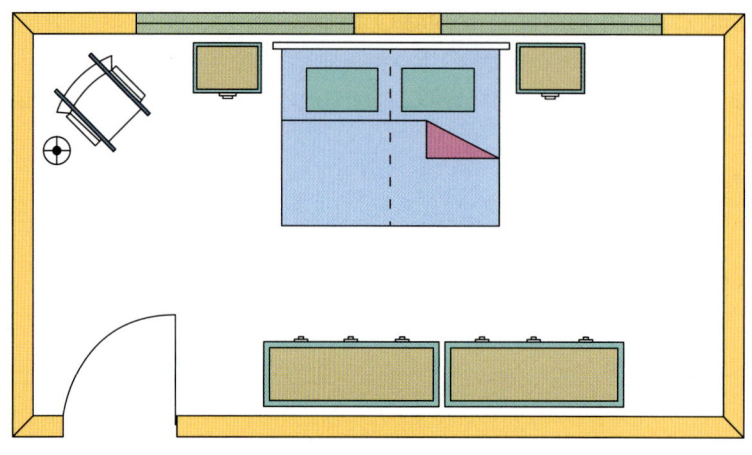

Bedroom

The bedroom has been drawn to a scale of 1 : 125.
Find the area of the bedroom floor.
Give your answer in m².

3 This is a diagram of a film projector from above.

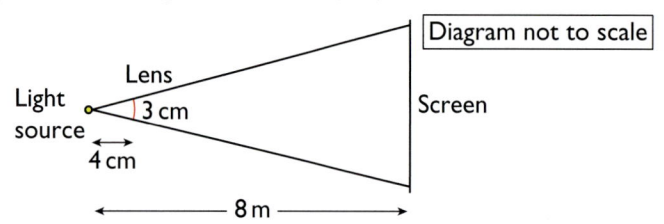

Diagram not to scale

Light source — Lens 3 cm — Screen
4 cm
8 m

Work out the width of the screen.

4 The vertices of the square S are (6, 4), (8, 4), (8, 6), and (6, 6).
S is enlarged by scale factor 2, centre (7, 5) to give shape T.
T is enlarged by scale factor 2, centre (7, 5) to give shape U.

a Draw S, T and U on graph paper.
The area of the region between S and T is A.
The area of the region between T and U is B.

b Work out the ratio A : B.

5 The point (3, 2) is a vertex of the square S. The diagonally opposite vertex is at (4, 3).
The square is enlarged by scale factor 3 to give the square T.
The point (3, 2) on S is mapped to the point (7, 4) on T.

a Find the centre of enlargement.

b Find the co-ordinates of the other vertices of T.

Unit 6 Enlargement Band f

6. The diagram shows a rectangle, R, a point A(1, 1) and a point Q(−1, −3).

   The point A is one vertex of a rectangle S which you can't see.

   The rectangle S is mapped onto R by an enlargement with centre Q.

   a Find the scale factor of the enlargement.

   b Find the co-ordinates of the other vertices of the rectangle S.

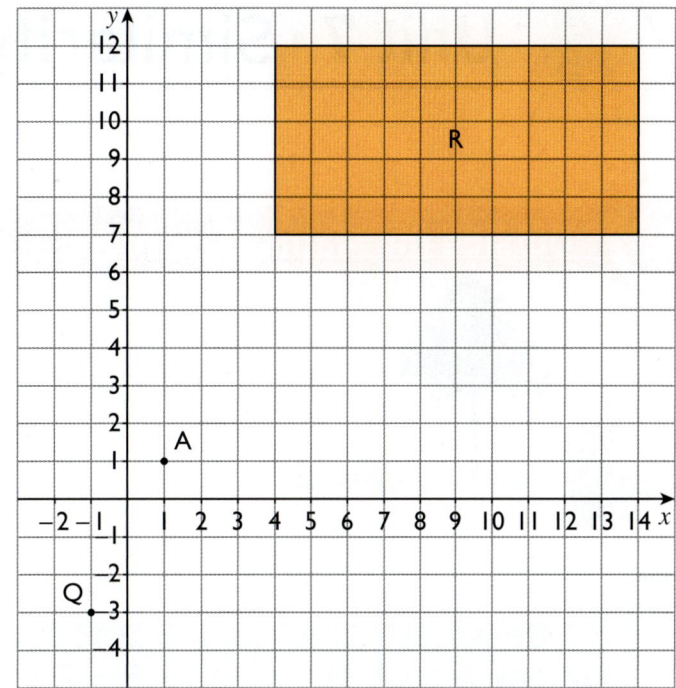

Reviewing skills

1. Enlarge each shape by a scale factor of 2, using C as the centre of enlargement.

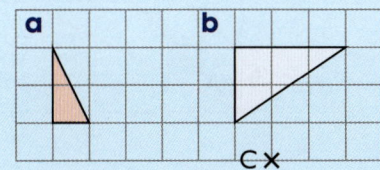

2. Copy this diagram.

   a Enlarge shape Q by a scale factor of 2, using (−4, 6) as the centre of enlargement. Label the image A.

   b Enlarge shape Q by a scale factor of 4, using (−5, 6) as the centre of enlargement. Label the image B.

   c Find the centre of enlargement and the scale factor of the enlargement that maps A to B.

   d Find the centre of enlargement and the scale factor of the enlargement that maps B to A.

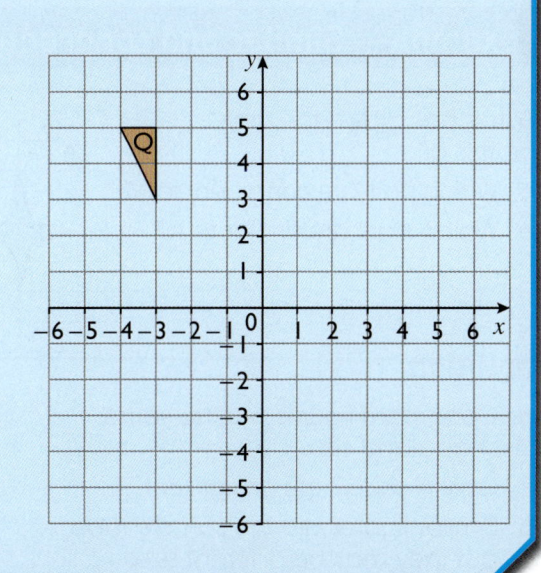

Unit 7 • Similarity • Band h

Outside the Maths classroom

Using shadows
What does the length of your shadow depend upon?

Toolbox

When you enlarge a figure with a scale factor of 3, all the lengths are made three times longer but the corresponding angles remain the same.

They are the same shape but different sizes.

The figures are **similar**.

The angles in the two figures are the same and the lengths of the sides are all in the same ratio.

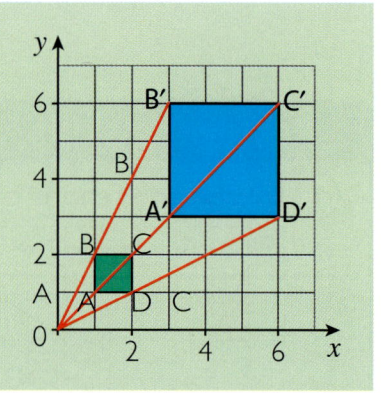

Example – Similar and congruent figures

Sarah has drawn the stars on this grid.

a Which stars are congruent to A?
b Which stars are similar to A?

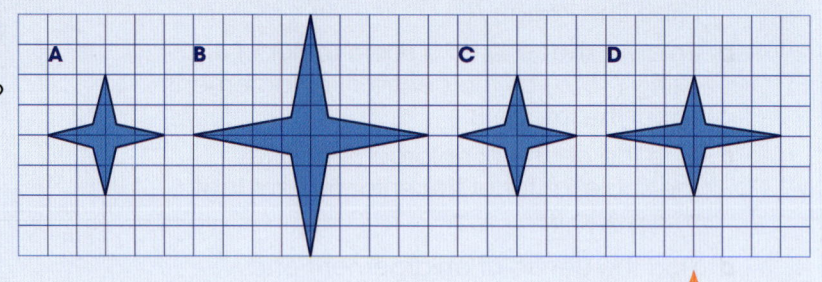

Solution

a Congruent figures are the same shape and size.

   Only A and C are congruent.

b Similar figures are the same shape but they may be different sizes.

   A, B and C are all similar.

Notice that D is a different shape.

Notice that congruent figures are always similar but similar figures need not be congruent.

Unit 7 Similarity Band h

Example – Using ratios of similar figures

These triangles are similar.

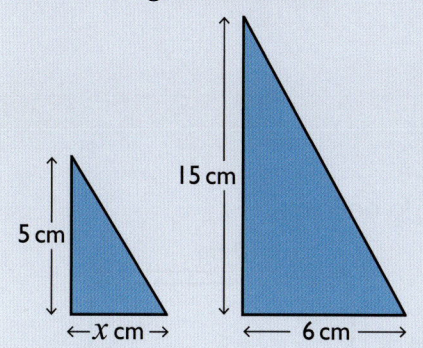

5 cm

15 cm

← x cm →

← 6 cm →

What is the value of x?

Solution

Method 1
The ratio of the vertical sides, small : large is $5:15 = 1:3$.
So the sides of the large triangle are three times as long as those of the small triangle.

For the bases
$3x = 6$
$x = 2$ ← The base of the small triangle is 2 cm long.

Method 2
In the large triangle the ratio of the sides,
base : height is $6:15 = 1:2.5$.
So the height of each triangle is 2.5 times the base.
For the small triangle
$2.5x = 5$
$x = 2$ ← The base of the small triangle is 2 cm long.

Geometry and Measures Strand 5 Transformations

Practising skills

1 P is a rectangle 3 cm by 1 cm.
Q is a rectangle 5 cm by 2 cm.

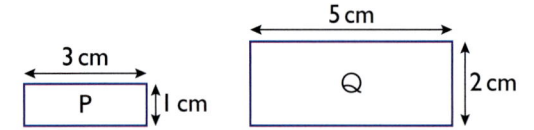

P: 3 cm by 1 cm
Q: 5 cm by 2 cm

Say whether the following rectangles are similar to P or to Q or to neither.

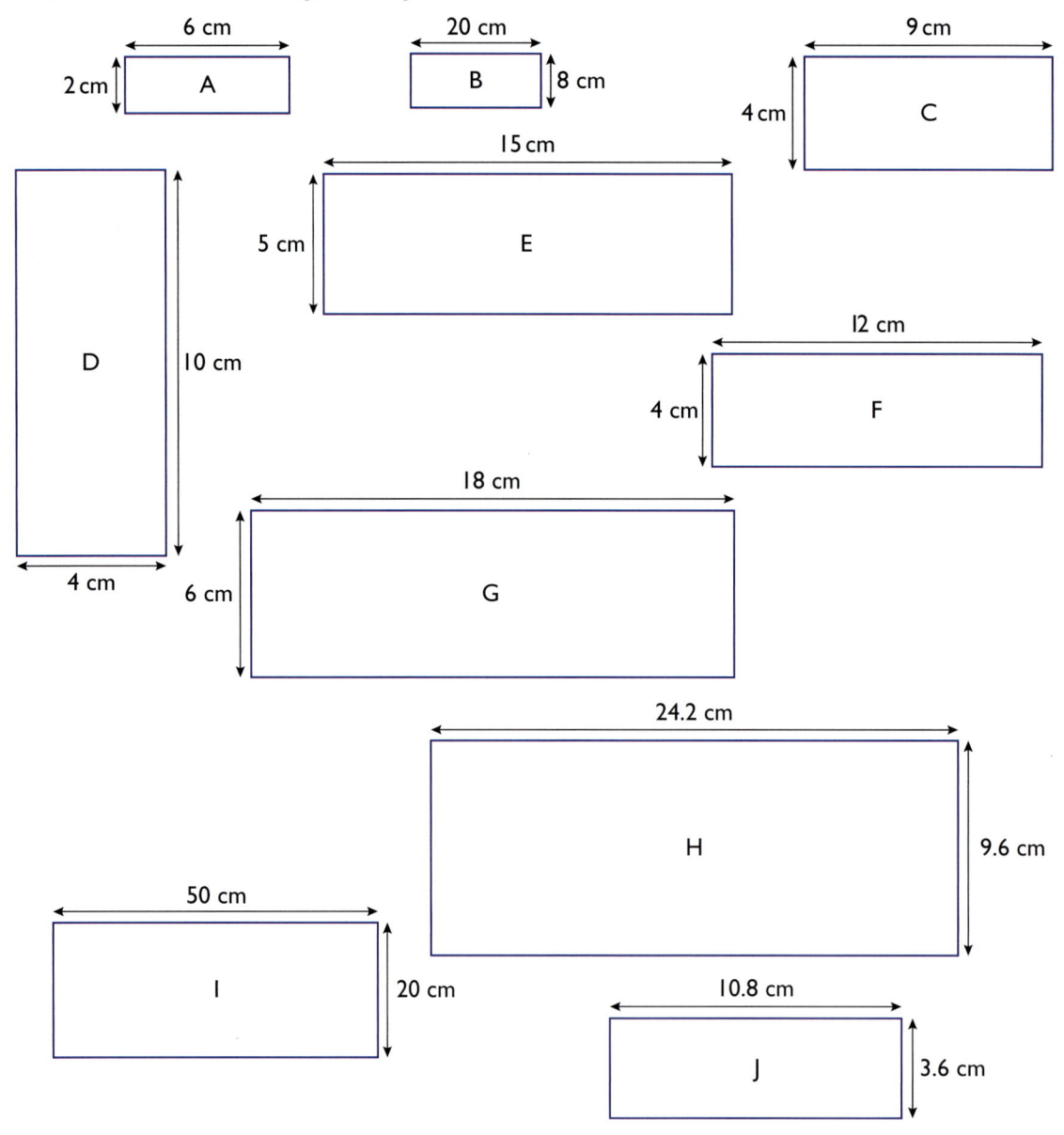

- A: 6 cm by 2 cm
- B: 20 cm by 8 cm
- C: 9 cm by 4 cm
- D: 4 cm by 10 cm
- E: 15 cm by 5 cm
- F: 12 cm by 4 cm
- G: 18 cm by 6 cm
- H: 24.2 cm by 9.6 cm
- I: 50 cm by 20 cm
- J: 10.8 cm by 3.6 cm

Unit 7 Similarity Band h

2 Triangle C is enlarged to give triangle D. The scale factor of the enlargement is 3.

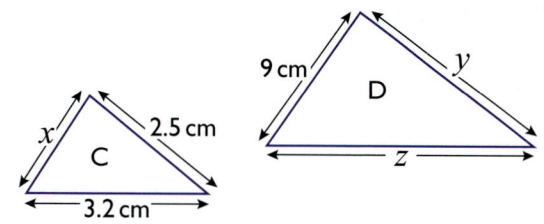

a Find the value of y.
b Find the value of z.
c Find the value of x.
d Are triangles C and D congruent or similar?

3 Triangle A is enlarged to give triangle B. The scale factor is 4.

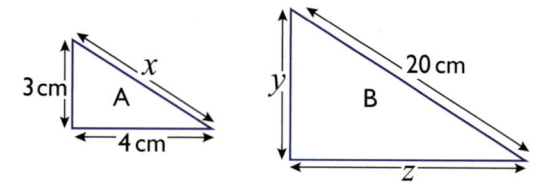

a Find the value of y.
b Find the value of z.
c Find the value of x.
d Are triangles A and B congruent or similar?
e What is special about both triangles?

4 Triangle E is enlarged to give triangle F.

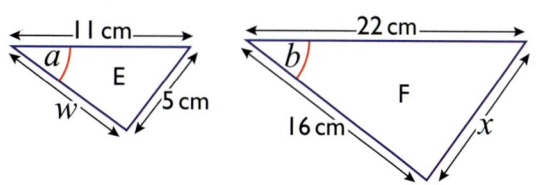

a What is the scale factor of enlargement?
b Find the value of x.
c Find the value of w.
d What do you know about the size of the angles labelled a and b?
e What is the relationship between triangles E and F?

Geometry and Measures Strand 5 Transformations

5 Shapes A and B are given below. In each case decide if shapes A and B are similar or not similar. You must explain your answer.

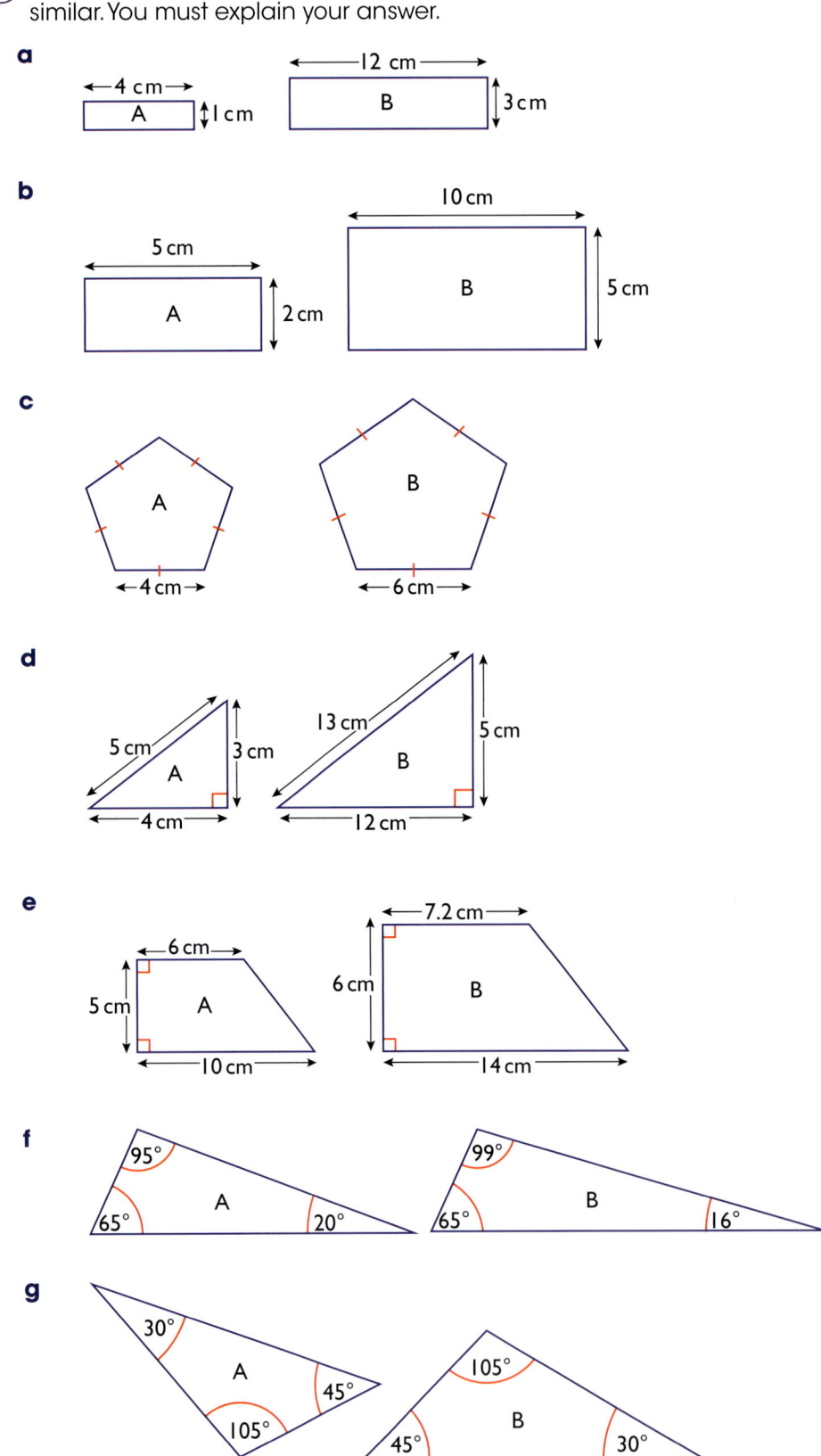

a Rectangle A: 4 cm × 1 cm; Rectangle B: 12 cm × 3 cm

b Rectangle A: 5 cm × 2 cm; Rectangle B: 10 cm × 5 cm

c Regular pentagon A with side 4 cm; Regular pentagon B with side 6 cm

d Right-angled triangle A: 5 cm, 3 cm, 4 cm; Right-angled triangle B: 13 cm, 5 cm, 12 cm

e Trapezium A: 5 cm, 6 cm, 10 cm; Trapezium B: 6 cm, 7.2 cm, 14 cm

f Triangle A: 95°, 65°, 20°; Triangle B: 99°, 65°, 16°

g Triangle A: 30°, 45°, 105°; Triangle B: 105°, 45°, 30°

462

6 For each pair of parallelograms, decide if P and Q are similar or not similar. You must explain your answer fully.

a
P: 4 cm, 6 cm, 52°
Q: 8 cm, 12 cm, 54°

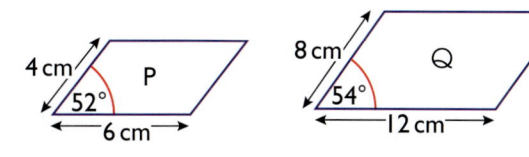

b
P: 4 cm, 9 cm, 55°
Q: 8 cm, 18 cm, 55°

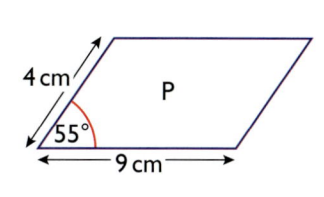

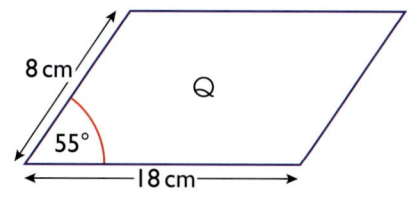

c
P: 4 cm, 9 cm, 50°
Q: 8 cm, 19 cm, 50°

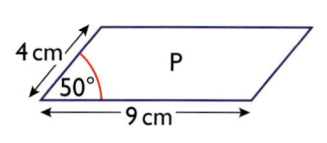

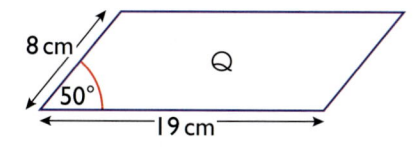

Developing fluency

1 A photograph is 6 inches by 4 inches. Which of these are similar to it?

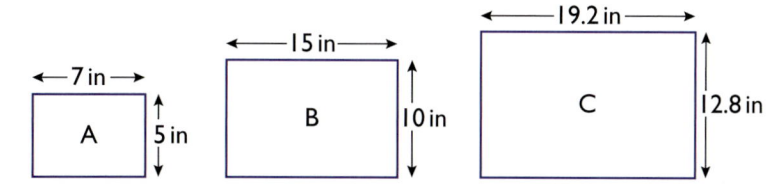

A: 7 in by 5 in
B: 15 in by 10 in
C: 19.2 in by 12.8 in

2 The diagram shows part of the landing stage for a ferry. The two triangles are similar.

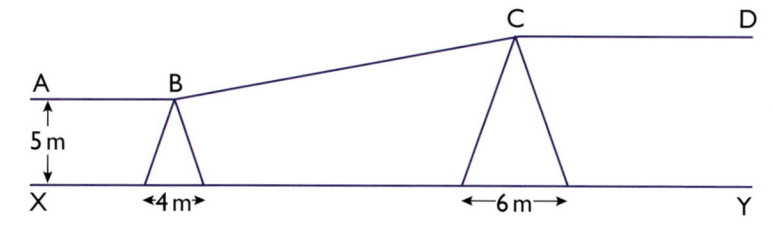

AB, CD and XY are horizontal.
AB is 5 m above the sea.
The bases of the triangles are 4 m and 6 m.
How much higher above sea level is CD than AB?

Geometry and Measures Strand 5 Transformations

3 The trapezia M and N are similar.

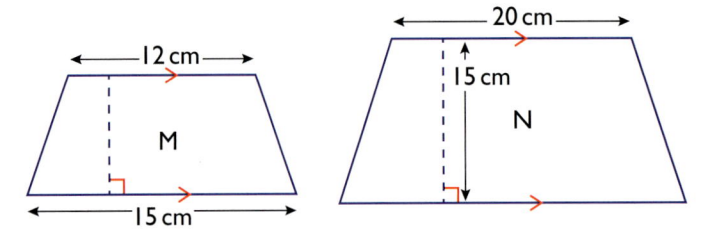

a Work out the area of trapezium M.

b Work out the area of trapezium N.

4 In the diagram, ABCDEF is a 6-pointed star with rotational symmetry of order 6.

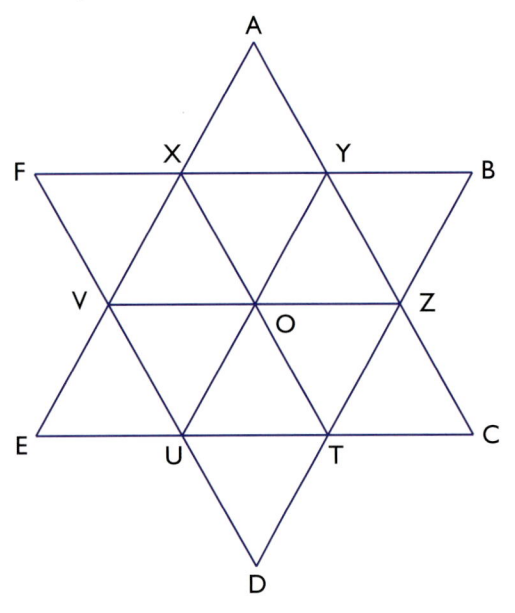

AXY is an equilateral triangle.

a How many triangles can you see that are congruent to AXY?

b Which triangles are similar to AXY but not congruent to it? Place them in groups that are congruent to each other.

c The perimeter of the star is 36 cm. What is its area?

5 Triangles A and B are similar.

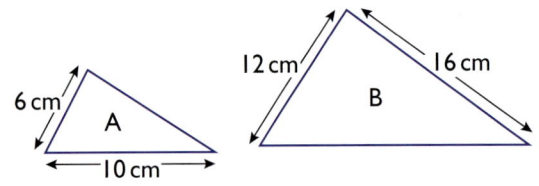

a Work out the perimeter of triangle A.

b Work out the perimeter of triangle B.

c Work out the areas of both triangles.

Unit 7 Similarity Band h

6 Shape P is reflected to give shape A.
Shape P is rotated to give shape B.
Shape P is translated to give shape C.
Shape P is enlarged to give shape D.

   a Which shapes are congruent?

   b Which shapes are similar?

Problem solving

1 The diagram shows a set of supports of two sizes made to support shelves.

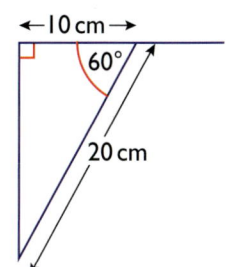

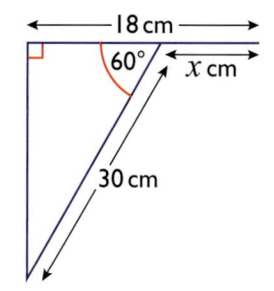

   a Explain how you know that the triangular parts of the supports are similar.

   b Find the value of x.

2 The diagram shows a step ladder on horizontal ground. DE is a horizontal bar inserted for stability.

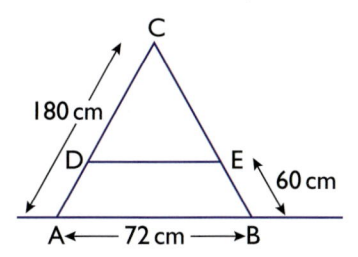

   What is the length of DE?

3 The diagram shows a support for a vertical wall. The ground is horizontal and the strut DE is perpendicular to AC.

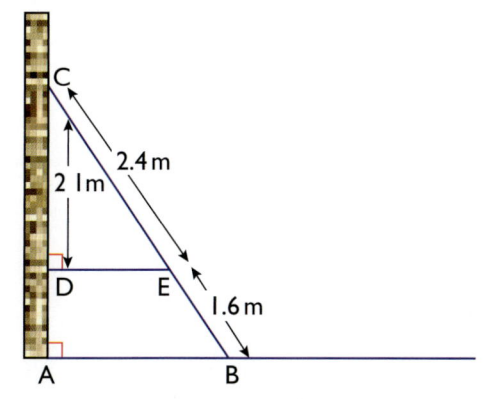

   a Show that triangles CDE and CAB are similar.

   b Work out the height of the point D above the floor AB.

Geometry and Measures Strand 5 Transformations

4 Here is a design for a fold-up seat.

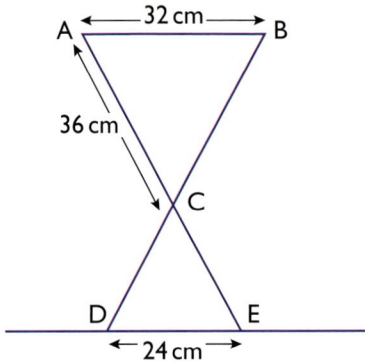

AB = 32 cm
AC = 36 cm
DE = 24 cm
The design has a vertical line of symmetry.
Work out the length of the leg AE.

5 In the diagram, the straight line DBA bisects ∠EAC.

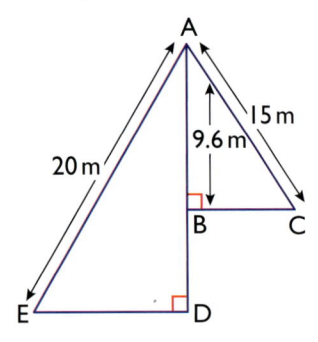

BC and DE are perpendicular to DBA.
AC = 15 m, AE = 20 m and AB = 9.6 m
Find the length of BD.

6 The diagram shows a framework used to support the top of a building. It is made of rods. The dimensions are marked on the diagram.

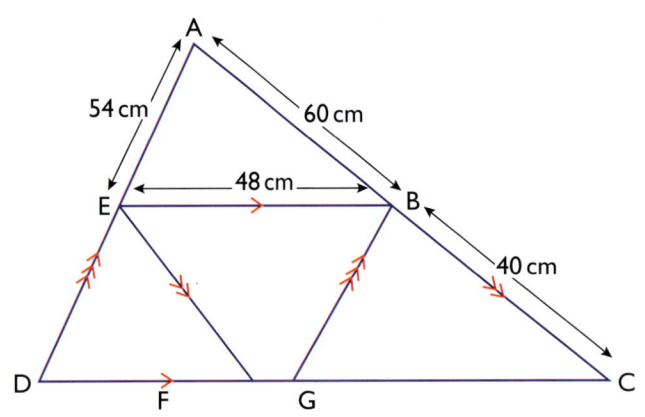

EB is parallel to DFGC, EF is parallel to BC and DE is parallel to GB.
Work out the total length of all the rods.

Unit 7 Similarity Band h

7 In the diagram, the lines AB and DE are parallel.
AC = 2CE

   a Copy and complete this proof that triangles ABC and DEC are similar.
      In triangles ABC and DEC
      ∠ACB = ∠☐ (vertically opposite)
      ∠ABC = ∠☐ (alternate)
      Therefore the triangles are similar (☐).

   b Write down the value of the ratio $\frac{AC}{EC}$.

   c What fraction of the way along AE is the point C?

8 ABC is a triangle.
X is the mid-point of AB.
Y is a point on AC such that XY is parallel to BC.

Prove that Y is the mid-point of AC and $XY = \frac{1}{2}BC$.

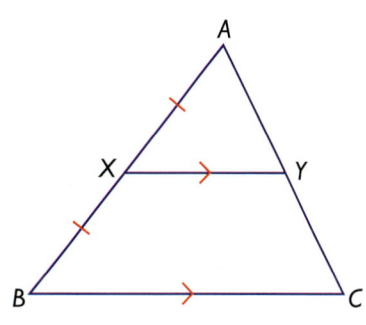

9 In the diagram,
L, M and N are the mid-points of the sides of triangle ABC
X, Y and Z are the mid-points of the sides of triangle LMN.

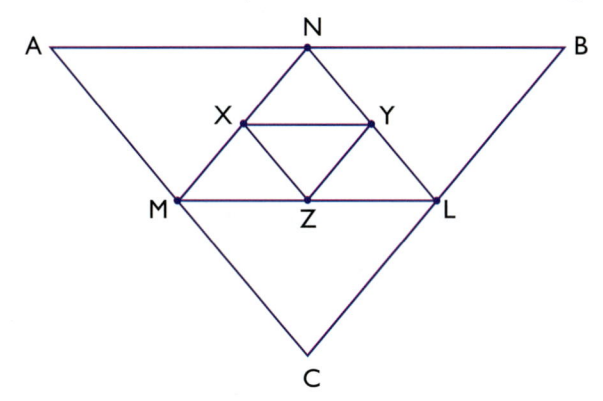

   a Prove that triangles ABC and ANM are similar.
   b What can you say about triangles ABC, LMN and XYZ?
   c Find the ratio of the sides of triangle XYZ to those of triangle ABC.

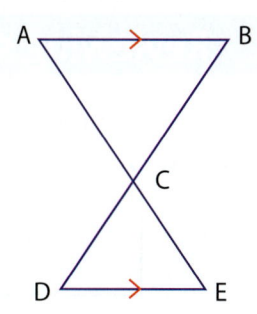

Geometry and Measures Strand 5 Transformations

Reviewing skills

1 Rectangles P and Q are similar. Find the value of x in each case.

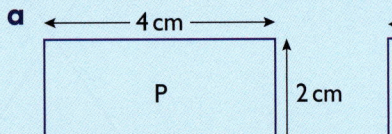

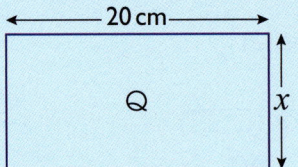

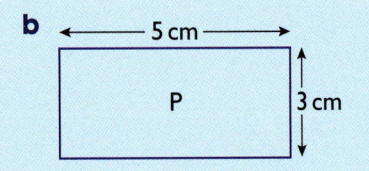

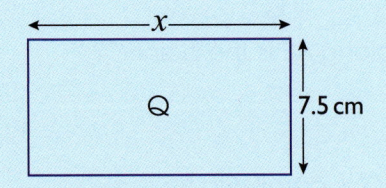

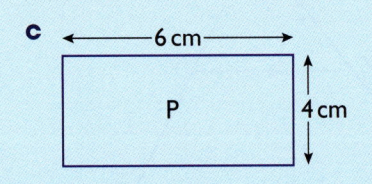

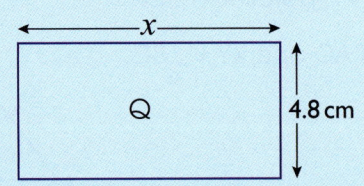

  a P: 4 cm × 2 cm; Q: 20 cm × x

  b P: 5 cm × 3 cm; Q: x × 7.5 cm

  c P: 6 cm × 4 cm; Q: x × 4.8 cm

2 a Prove triangles T and V are similar.

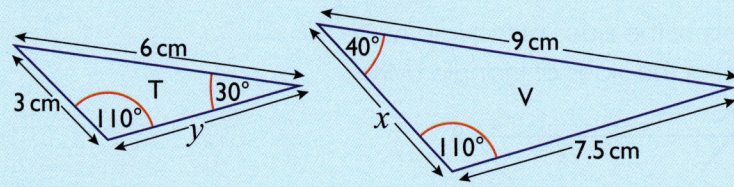

Triangle T: sides 6 cm and 3 cm, angles 30° and 110°, side y.
Triangle V: sides 9 cm and 7.5 cm, angles 40° and 110°, side x.

  b Find the value of x.
  c Find the value of y.

3 The diagram shows a flagpole PR standing on horizontal ground PST.

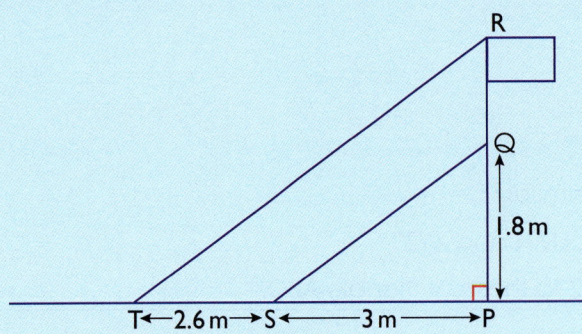

PQ is vertical rod, PQ = 1.8 m. TS = 2.6 m, SP = 3 m.

PQ is a vertical rod of length 1.8 m.
PS and PT are the shadows of the rod and the flagpole.
Work out the height of the flagpole.

Unit 8 • Trigonometry • Band h

Outside the Maths classroom

Size of the Earth
In about 240 BC, Eratosthenes estimated the size of the Earth. How did he do it?

Toolbox

Each side in a **right-angled triangle** has a name.
- The longest side is called the **hypotenuse (H)**.
- The side opposite the marked angle is called the **opposite (O)**.
- The remaining side, next to the marked angle, is called the **adjacent (A)**.
- The ratio of the lengths of the sides are given special names.

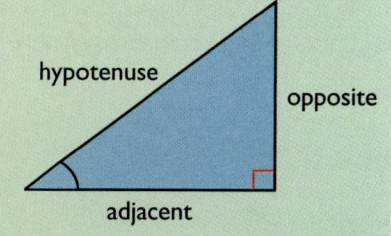

$$\text{cosine (cos) } \theta = \frac{\text{adjacent}}{\text{hypotenuse}}$$

$$\text{tangent (tan) } \theta = \frac{\text{opposite}}{\text{adjacent}}$$

$$\text{sine (sin) } \theta = \frac{\text{opposite}}{\text{hypotenuse}}$$

These ratios are constant for similar right-angled triangles. You can use this information to find angles and lengths in triangles.

For this triangle
$$\cos \theta = \frac{8}{17}$$
$$\sin \theta = \frac{15}{17}$$
$$\tan \theta = \frac{15}{8}$$

You will find keys for sin, cos and tan on your calculator.

Geometry and Measures Strand 5 Transformations

Example – Using trigonometry to find a length

John is a window cleaner. His ladder is 6 m long.
The angle between the ladder and ground is 70°.
Find the height that his ladder reaches up the wall.

Solution

$\sin \theta = \dfrac{\text{opposite}}{\text{hypotenuse}}$

$\sin 70° = \dfrac{y}{6}$

so $y = 6 \times \sin 70°$ ← Multiply by 6.

$\quad\; = 6 \times 0.94$ ← $\sin 70° = 0.94$ from a calculator.

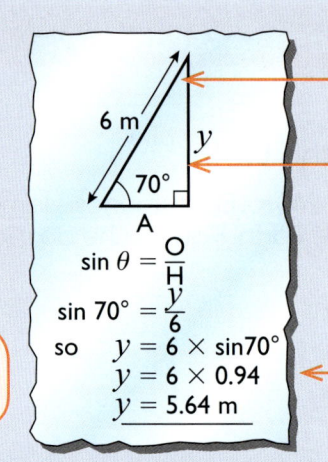

$\quad\; = 5.64\, m$

- The ladder is the hypotenuse. It is 6 m long.
- The height the ladder reaches up the wall is the opposite side to the angle of 70°.
- The distance from the bottom of the ladder to the wall is the adjacent side.

$\sin \theta = \dfrac{O}{H}$

$\sin 70° = \dfrac{y}{6}$

so $\quad y = 6 \times \sin 70°$
$\quad\quad y = 6 \times 0.94$
$\quad\quad y = 5.64\, m$

Example – Using trigonometry to find an angle

a Look at the diagram. Which ratio would you use to find the value of θ?
b Find the value of θ.

Solution

a Use $\cos \theta = \dfrac{\text{adjacent}}{\text{hypotenuse}}$

- The adjacent side is 6 cm.
- The hypotenuse is 11 cm.

b $\cos \theta = \dfrac{6}{11}$

$\theta = \cos^{-1}\left(\dfrac{6}{11}\right)$

$\theta = 56.9°$

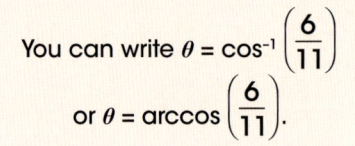

You can write $\theta = \cos^{-1}\left(\dfrac{6}{11}\right)$ or $\theta = \arccos\left(\dfrac{6}{11}\right)$.
Find this using your calculator.

Example – Angle of elevation and depression

The boat is 300 metres from the base of a cliff.
The height of the cliff is 180 metres.
Calculate the angle of elevation, correct to the nearest degree.

$\tan \theta =$
$\quad\quad = 0.6$
$\theta = \tan^{-1} 0.6$
$\quad\; = 30.96…°$

The angle of elevation is 31°.

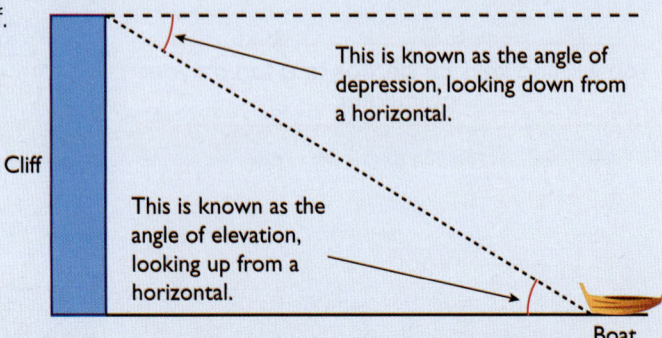

- This is known as the angle of depression, looking down from a horizontal.
- This is known as the angle of elevation, looking up from a horizontal.

Practising skills

1) Look at these triangles.

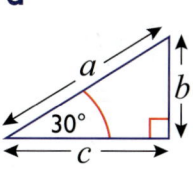

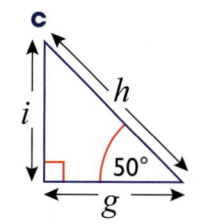

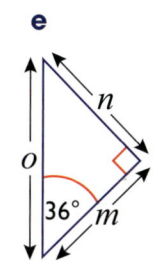

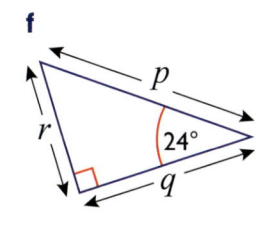

a — triangle with 30° angle, sides labelled a, b, c

b — triangle with 40° angle, sides labelled d, e, f

c — triangle with 50° angle, sides labelled h, i, g

d — triangle with 43° angle, sides labelled j, k, l

e — triangle with 36° angle, sides labelled n, o, m

f — triangle with 24° angle, sides labelled p, q, r

For each triangle, write down which side is

i the hypotenuse

ii opposite

iii adjacent.

2) Look at this triangle.

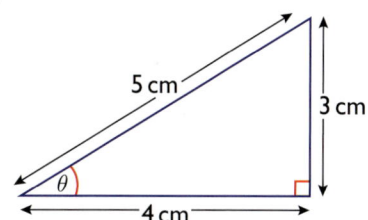

Triangle with sides 5 cm (hypotenuse), 3 cm, 4 cm and angle θ.

Which of these are true?

a $\sin \theta = \dfrac{3}{4}$ $\sin \theta = \dfrac{3}{5}$ $\sin \theta = \dfrac{5}{3}$

b $\cos \theta = \dfrac{3}{4}$ $\cos \theta = \dfrac{4}{5}$ $\cos \theta = \dfrac{4}{3}$

c $\tan \theta = \dfrac{3}{5}$ $\tan \theta = \dfrac{3}{4}$ $\tan \theta = \dfrac{4}{3}$

3) Look at this triangle.

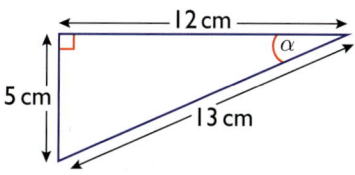

Triangle with sides 12 cm, 5 cm, 13 cm and angle α.

Which of these are true?

a $\tan \alpha = \dfrac{5}{12}$ $\sin \alpha = \dfrac{13}{12}$ $\cos \alpha = \dfrac{12}{5}$

b $\sin \alpha = \dfrac{5}{12}$ $\cos \alpha = \dfrac{5}{13}$ $\sin \alpha = \dfrac{12}{13}$

c $\cos \alpha = \dfrac{5}{12}$ $\tan \alpha = \dfrac{12}{5}$ $\tan \alpha = \dfrac{5}{13}$

Geometry and Measures Strand 5 Transformations

4 Look at these triangles. In each case you are going to find the value of x.

a 10 m, 30°, x m
b 7 m, 50°, x m
c 12 m, 48°, x m
d 15 m, 20°, x m
e 18 cm, 43°, x m

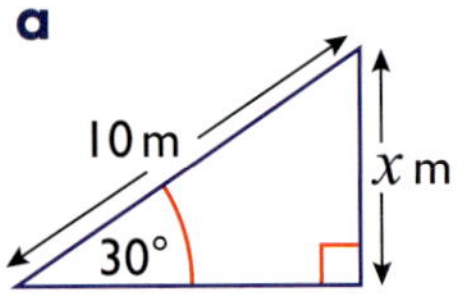

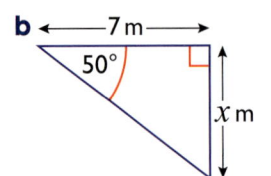

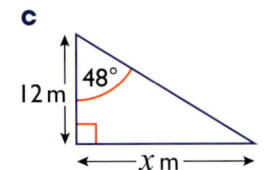

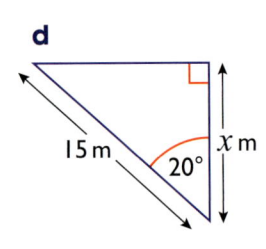

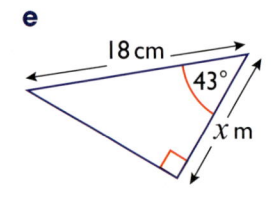

For each triangle
i sketch the triangle
ii label the sides H, O and A
iii decide whether to use sin, cos or tan
iv work out the value of x correct to 1 decimal place.

5 Use your calculator to find the value of θ to the nearest degree.

a $\sin \theta = 0.5$
b $\tan \theta = 1$
c $\cos \theta = 0.5$
d $\tan \theta = 0.839$
e $\sin \theta = 0.951$
f $\cos \theta = 0.139$
g $\sin \theta = \dfrac{4}{5}$
h $\cos \theta = \dfrac{2}{3}$
i $\tan \theta = \dfrac{9}{5}$

6 For each triangle
i sketch the triangle
ii label the sides H, O and A
iii decide whether to use sin, cos or tan
iv work out the value of θ correct to 1 decimal place.

a 8 cm, 4 cm, θ
b 4 cm, 3 cm, θ
c 10 cm, 7 cm, θ
d 9 m, 6 m, θ
e 7.2 m, 11.4 m, θ
f 13.2 m, 6.6 m, θ

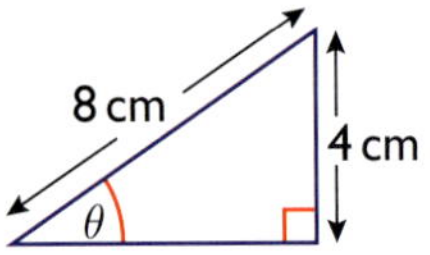

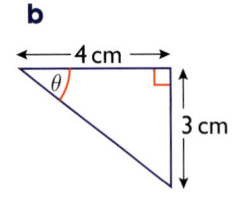

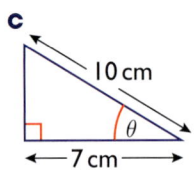

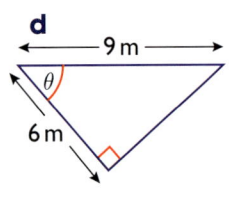

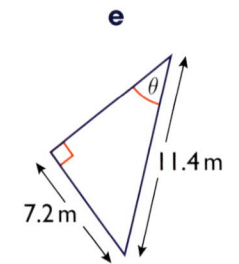

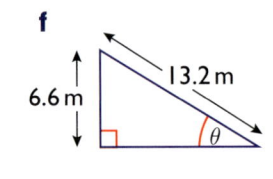

7) For each triangle
   i   sketch the triangle
   ii label the sides H, O and A
   iii decide whether to use sin, cos or tan
   iv work out the value of x correct to 1 decimal place.

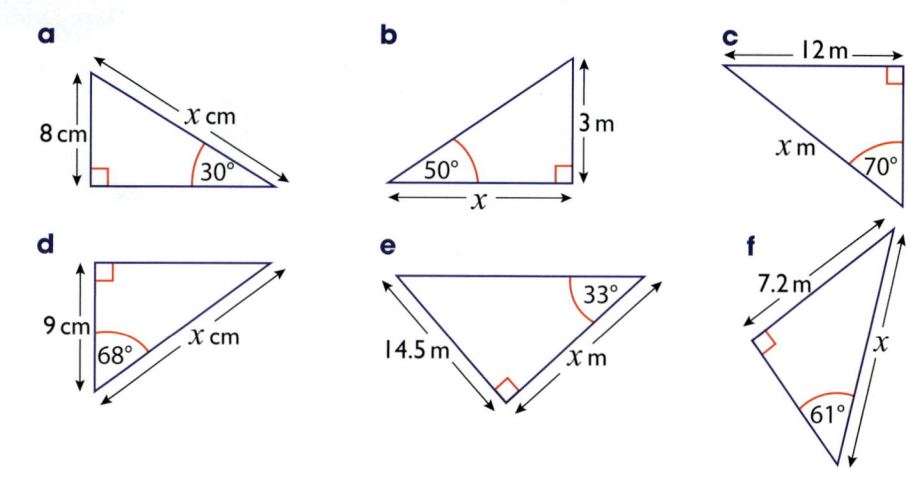

a 8 cm, x cm, 30°

b 3 m, 50°, x

c 12 m, x m, 70°

d 9 cm, 68°, x cm

e 14.5 m, 33°, x m

f 7.2 m, 61°, x

Developing fluency

1) **a** Work out the perpendicular height, h m, of this triangle.

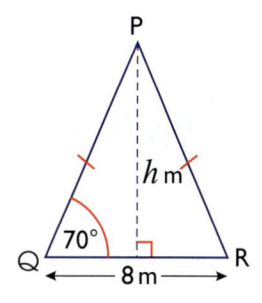

Triangle PQR with P at top, h m perpendicular height, angle 70° at Q, QR = 8 m.

   b Calculate the triangle's area.
   c Calculate the triangle's perimeter.

2) Work out the area and perimeter of this triangle.

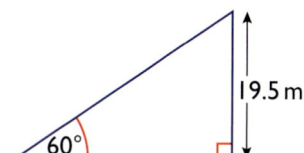

Right triangle with 60° angle and vertical side 19.5 m.

3) Joshua has made a 5-barred gate. The diagonal is 4 m long and makes an angle of 30° with the horizontal. What length of wood did he need?

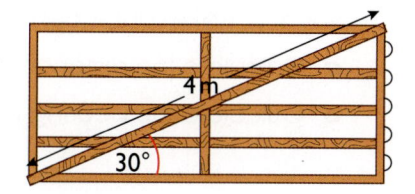

473

Geometry and Measures Strand 5 Transformations

4. Alys has lost her cat Truffles. After some searching she finds Truffles up a tree.
   When Alys is 30 m from the tree she sees Truffles at an angle of elevation of 25°.

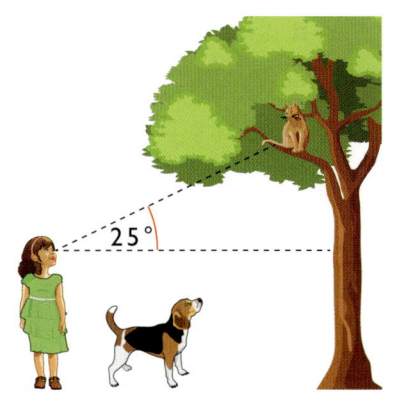

   a Alys's eye is 1.5 m above the ground.
      How high up the tree is Truffles?

   The dog barks and Truffles climbs a further 5 m up the tree.

   b Now what is the angle of elevation at which Alys sees Truffles?

5. A ship leaves Port Aura and sails for 5.8 miles on a bearing of 090° to a buoy. It then turns and sails on a bearing of 218° until it reaches Port Cambria which is due south of Port Aura.
   Calculate the distance between the Port Cambria and Port Aura.

6. Robin is standing on top of a vertical cliff looking at a small boat.

   He sees it at an angle of depression of 18°. The top of the cliff is 50 m above the sea and Robin's eye height is 1.5 m.

   a How far from the base of the cliff is the boat?

   The boat then sails directly out to sea.

   b How much further is it from the cliff when Robin sees it at an angle of depression of 10°?

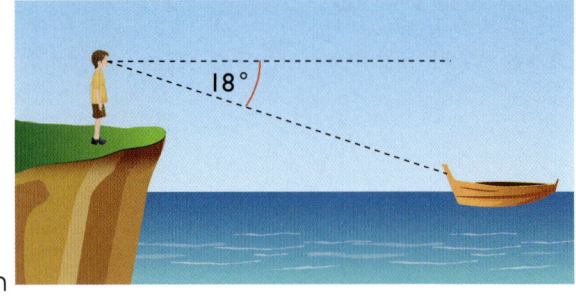

7. Look at triangle ABC.
   You are given the lengths of AB and AC.
   There are two different ways to find the length of BC.

   a i Use trigonometry to work out ∠ABC.
      ii Use trigonometry again to calculate the length of BC.

   b Without using any trigonometry, use Pythagoras' theorem to find the length of BC.

   c Do the two methods give the same answer?

8. A yacht is 2.4 km from a lighthouse. The bearing of the yacht from this lighthouse is 090°. The yacht is 1.5 km due north of a lightship.

   a Calculate the distance between the lightship and the lighthouse.

   b Calculate the bearing of the lighthouse from the lightship.

9 Point X is 1800 m due west of point Y.

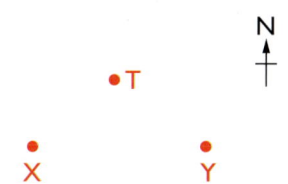

T is the base of a tower.
The bearing of T from X is 040° and the bearing of T from Y is 320°.
Floella walks from X to T and then from T to Y.
Work out how far she walks.

10 The diagram is the net of a square-based pyramid. The points V_1, V_2, V_3 and V_4 all come together at the vertex V when it is folded up.

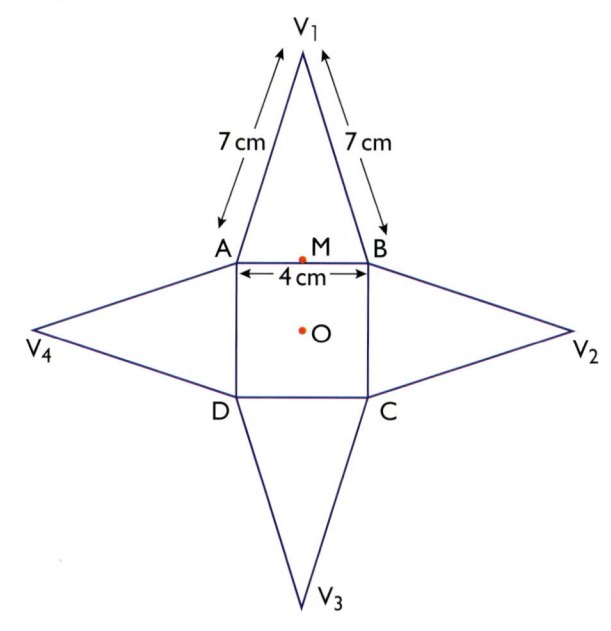

The four triangles in the net are all isosceles with sides 7 cm, 7 cm and 4 cm.
M is the mid-point of AB.
O is the middle of the base ABCD.

a Show that the length V_1M is $\sqrt{45}$ cm.

b Draw the triangle VMO when the net is folded up. Mark the right angle in your triangle.

c Work out the angle VMO to the nearest 0.1 degrees. This is the slant angle of the sloping faces of the pyramid.

d Calculate the height of the pyramid.

Geometry and Measures Strand 5 Transformations

Problem solving

1) The diagram shows a ramp for wheelchair access to a building.

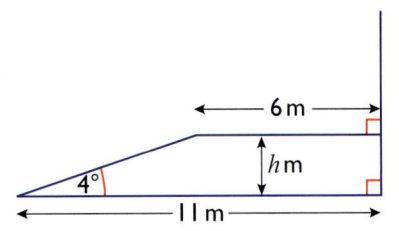

The slope of the ramp is 4°.
The top of the ramp is 6m from the building.
The bottom of the ramp is 11m from the building.
Find the value of h.

2) A ship leaves a port P and sails on a bearing of 040°.
There is a lighthouse L which is 36km from P on a bearing of 035°.
Work out the distance of the ship from L when it is at its closest.

3) The diagram shows the side view of a solar panel in a field.

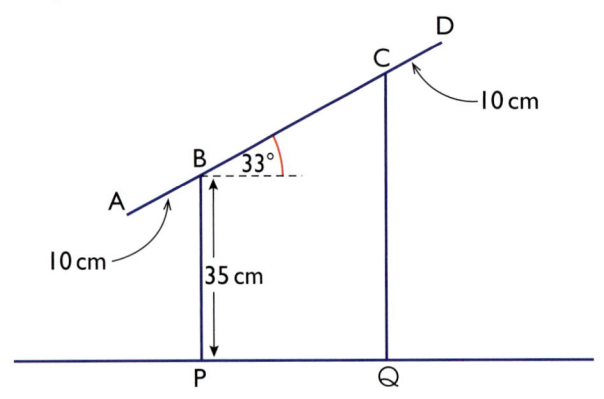

The straight line ABCD represents the panel edge.
PB and QC are vertical supports.
PQ is horizontal.
AB = CD = 10cm
AD = 102cm
PB = 35cm
To get the maximum efficiency the panel must be tilted at 33° to the horizontal.

  a Work out the distance PQ.
  b Work out the distance QC.

4) A supermarket has a moving walkway between the ground floor and the first floor.
The top of the walkway is 3.5m above the ground floor.
The walkway makes an angle of 10° with the horizontal.

  a Work out the horizontal distance covered by the walkway.
  b Find the length of the walkway.

5 The diagram shows a set of steps with a rail PQ.

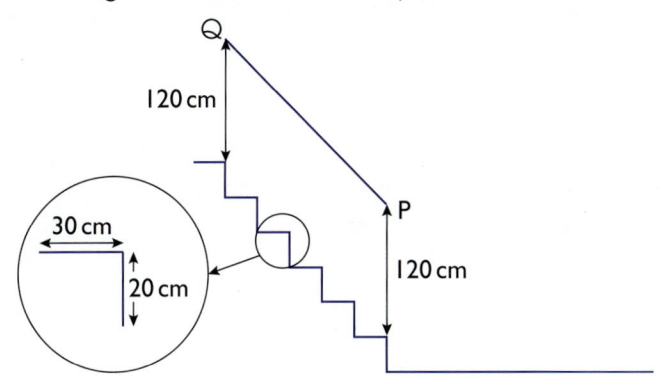

The height of each step is 20 cm.
The width of each step is 30 cm.
P is 120 cm above the first step.
Q is 120 cm above the last step.
There are 6 steps.

a Work out the angle that PQ makes with the horizontal.

b Explain why the angle you found in part **a** will always be the same no matter how many steps there are.

6 The diagram represents a framework that is going to support a vertical wall. It consists of 4 rods.

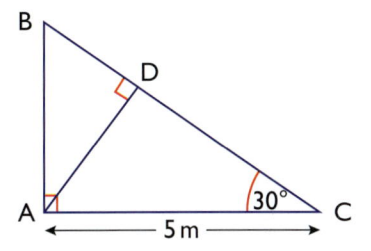

The dimensions are shown.
Work out the total length of the rods in the framework.

Reviewing skills

1 Look at these triangles. In each case you are going to find the length of the side marked x.

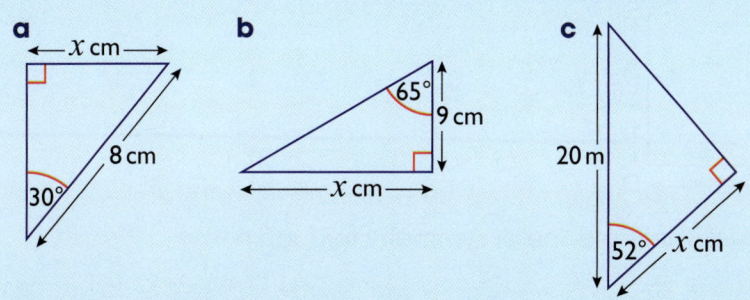

For each triangle, write down which side is
  i the hypotenuse   **ii** opposite   **iii** adjacent.

Then choose the best ratio to use to work out the value of x.

② For each triangle
  i sketch the triangle
  ii label the sides H, O and A
  iii decide whether to use sin, cos or tan
  iv work out the value of θ correct to 1 decimal place.

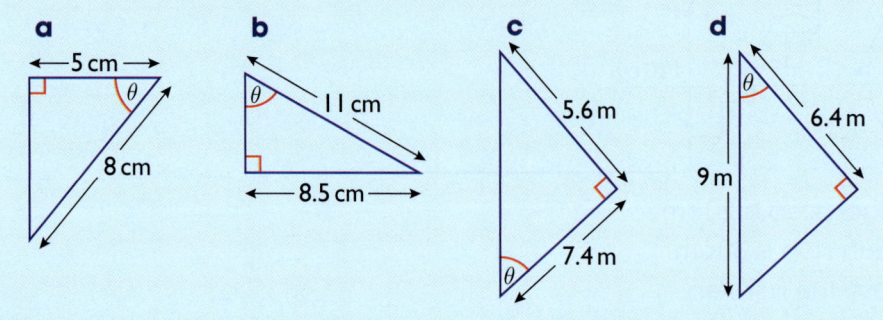

a 5 cm, 8 cm, θ

b 11 cm, 8.5 cm, θ

c 5.6 m, 7.4 m, θ

d 6.4 m, 9 m, θ

③ For each triangle, find the value of x correct to 1 decimal place.

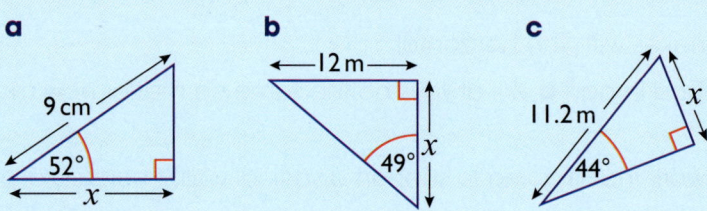

a 9 cm, 52°, x

b 12 m, 49°, x

c 11.2 m, 44°, x

④ For each triangle, find the value of x correct to 1 decimal place.

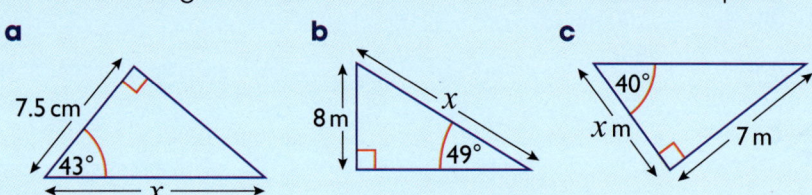

a 7.5 cm, 43°, x

b 8 m, 49°, x

c 40°, x m, 7 m

⑤ The diagram shows the end view of a house, ABCDE.

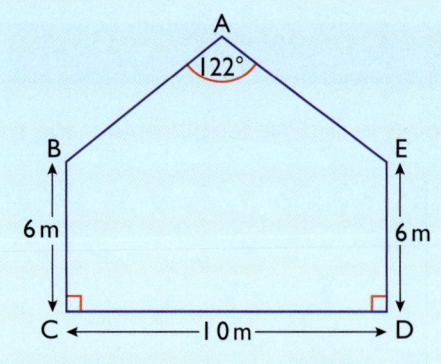

A 122°, B, E, 6 m, 6 m, C, 10 m, D

The dimensions are as shown. There is a line of symmetry through A. Find the height of point A.

Geometry and Measures
Strand 6 Three-dimensional shapes

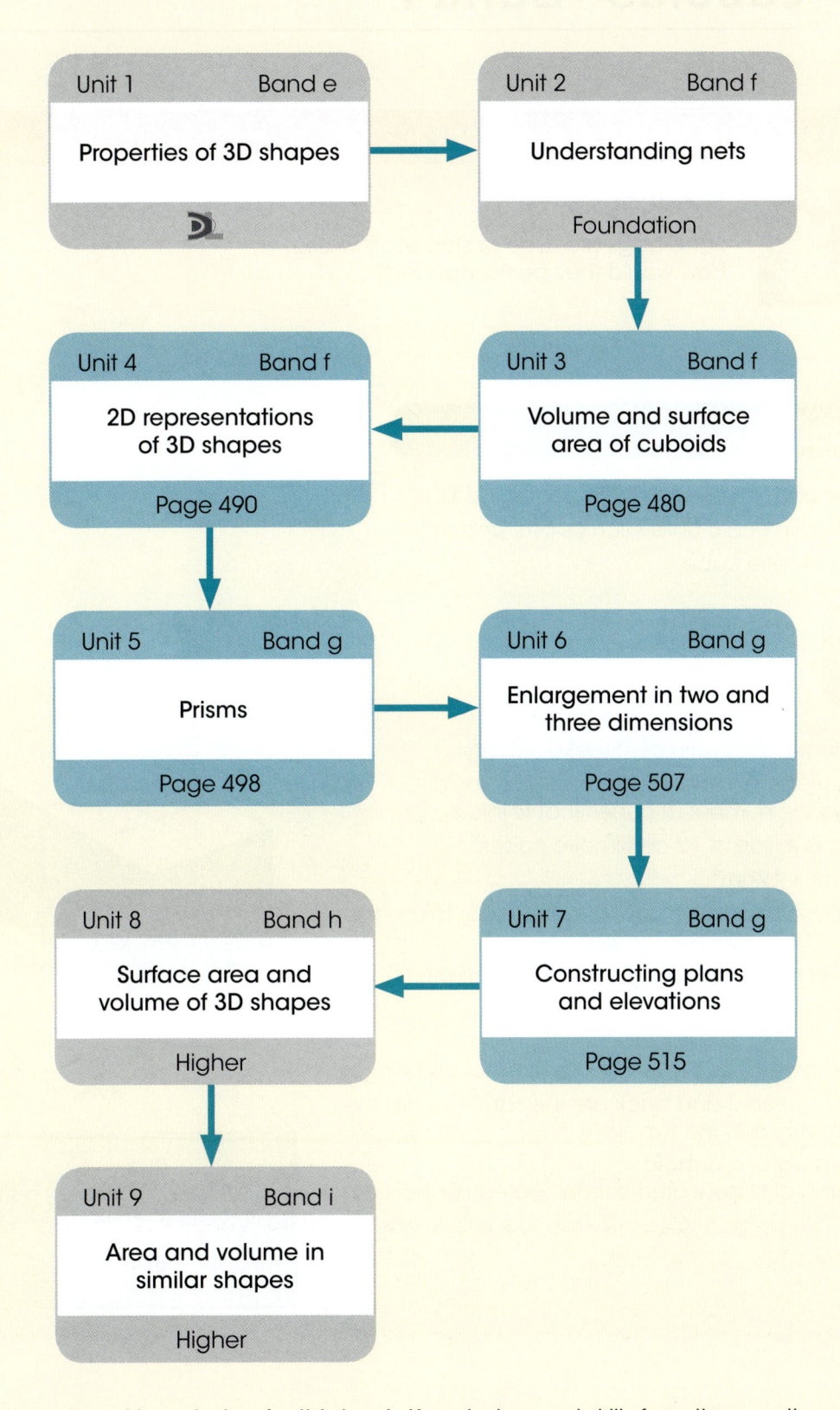

Unit 1 — Band e
Properties of 3D shapes

Unit 2 — Band f
Understanding nets
Foundation

Unit 3 — Band f
Volume and surface area of cuboids
Page 480

Unit 4 — Band f
2D representations of 3D shapes
Page 490

Unit 5 — Band g
Prisms
Page 498

Unit 6 — Band g
Enlargement in two and three dimensions
Page 507

Unit 7 — Band g
Constructing plans and elevations
Page 515

Unit 8 — Band h
Surface area and volume of 3D shapes
Higher

Unit 9 — Band i
Area and volume in similar shapes
Higher

Units 1–2 are assumed knowledge for this book. Knowledge and skills from these units are used throughout the book.

Unit 3 • Volume and surface area of cuboids • Band f

Outside the Maths classroom

Sandbags
Sand bags are used to stop flood water.
How would they be transported?

Toolbox

The **volume** of a solid shape is the space inside it.
It is measured in cubic units such as cm^3 and m^3.
This is a centimetre cube.

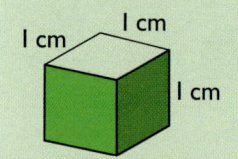

It has a volume of 1 cubic centimetre ($1\,cm^3$).
You can sometimes find the volume of a cuboid by counting the number of cubes that fit into it.
This cuboid is made of 12 centimetre cubes.
So its volume is $12\,cm^3$.
Another way to find the volume of a cuboid is to use the formula

volume of a cuboid = length × width × height.

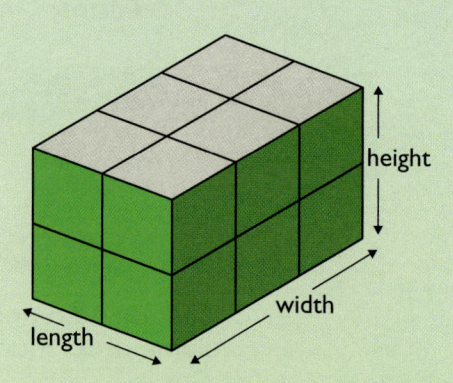

The surface area of a solid is the total area of all its faces.
In a cuboid, the front and back are the same; so are the top and bottom, and the two sides. So

surface area of a cuboid
= 2 × (area of base + area of front + area of one side)

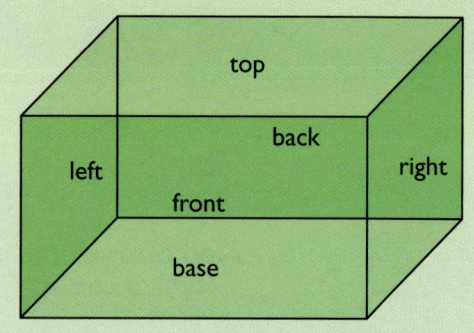

Unit 3 Volume and surface area of cuboids Band f

Example – Finding the volume and surface area of a cuboid

Find the volume and surface area of this cuboid.

Solution

Volume of a cuboid = length × width × height
$\qquad\qquad\qquad\quad$ = 4 × 6 × 2
$\qquad\qquad\qquad\quad$ = 48

The volume of the cuboid is 48 cm³.
The surface area of its faces is
$\qquad$Base: 4 × 6 = 24$\qquad$Top:$\quad$ 4 × 6 = 24
$\qquad$Front: 4 × 2 = 8$\qquad\;\;$Back: 4 × 2 = 8
$\qquad$Right: 6 × 2 = 12$\qquad\;$Left:$\quad$ 6 × 2 = 12

So the total surface area = 24 + 24 + 8 + 8 + 12 + 12
$\qquad\qquad\qquad\qquad\quad$ = 2 × (24 + 8 + 12)
$\qquad\qquad\qquad\qquad\quad$ = 2 × 44
$\qquad\qquad\qquad\qquad\quad$ = 88

The surface area of the cuboid is 88 cm².

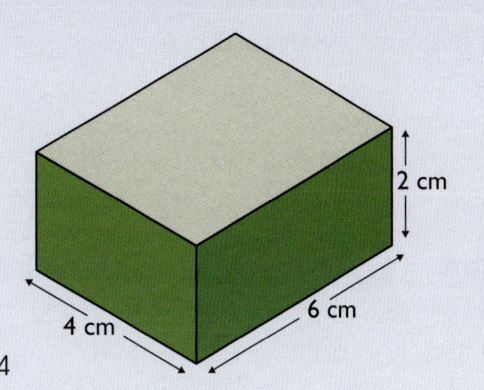

Example – Finding surface area from a net

Here is a net of a cuboid.
Find the surface area of the cuboid.

Each rectangle makes a face of the cuboid. The green rectangle is the bottom face.

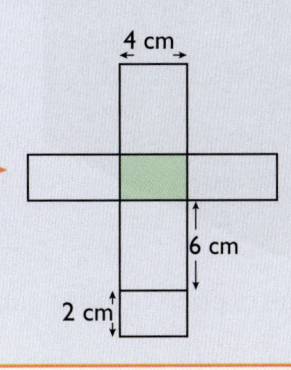

Work out the area of each face. Remember that the area of a rectangle is given by the formula area = length × width.

Solution

The surface area of the faces is
Base: 4 × 2 = 8$\qquad$Top:$\quad$ 4 × 2 = 8
Front: 4 × 6 = 24$\qquad$Back: 4 × 6 = 24
Right: 6 × 2 = 12$\qquad$Left:$\quad$ 6 × 2 = 12
Total surface area = 2 × (8 + 24 + 12)
$\qquad\qquad\qquad\quad$ = 88

The surface area of the cuboid is 88 cm².

Geometry and Measures Strand 6 Three-dimensional shapes

Example – Finding the surface area of an open box

Look at this open cardboard box.
It has no top.
Find its surface area.

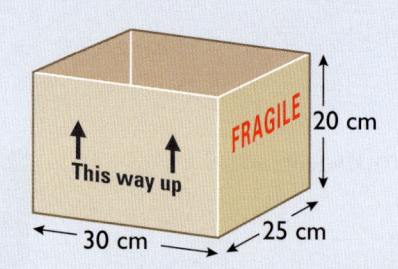

Solution

Area of bottom	$= 30 \times 25$	$= 750\,cm^2$
Area of front and back	$= 2 \times 30 \times 20$	$= 1200\,cm^2$ ← The front and back have the same area.
Area of both sides	$= 2 \times 25 \times 20$	$= 1000\,cm^2$ ← Both sides have the same area.
Total surface area	$= 750 + 1200 + 1000$	$= 2950\,cm^2$

Practising skills

1 Each cuboid is made up of $1\,cm^3$ cubes. Work out the volume of each cuboid.

a

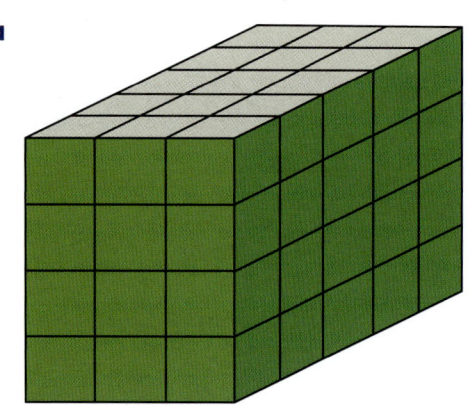

b

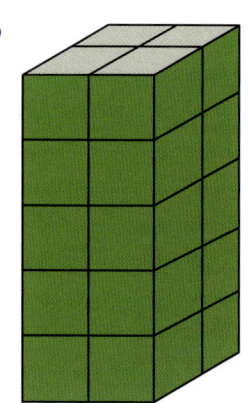

2 Work out the volume of each of these cuboids.

a 4 cm, 5 cm, 3 cm

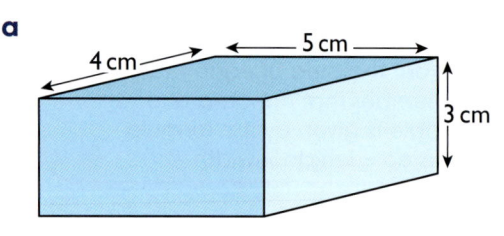

b 2 cm, 2 cm, 8 cm

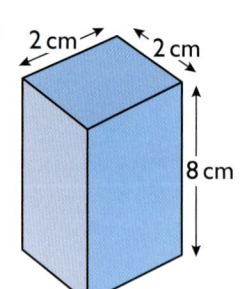

c 6 cm, 3 cm, 2 cm

482

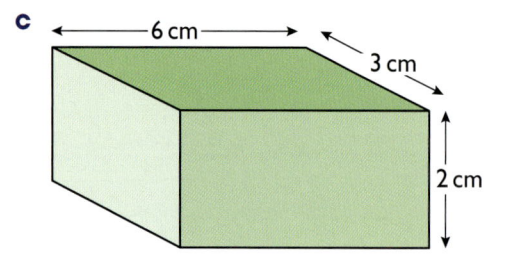

Unit 3 Volume and surface area of cuboids Band f

3) Work out the surface area of each of these cuboids.

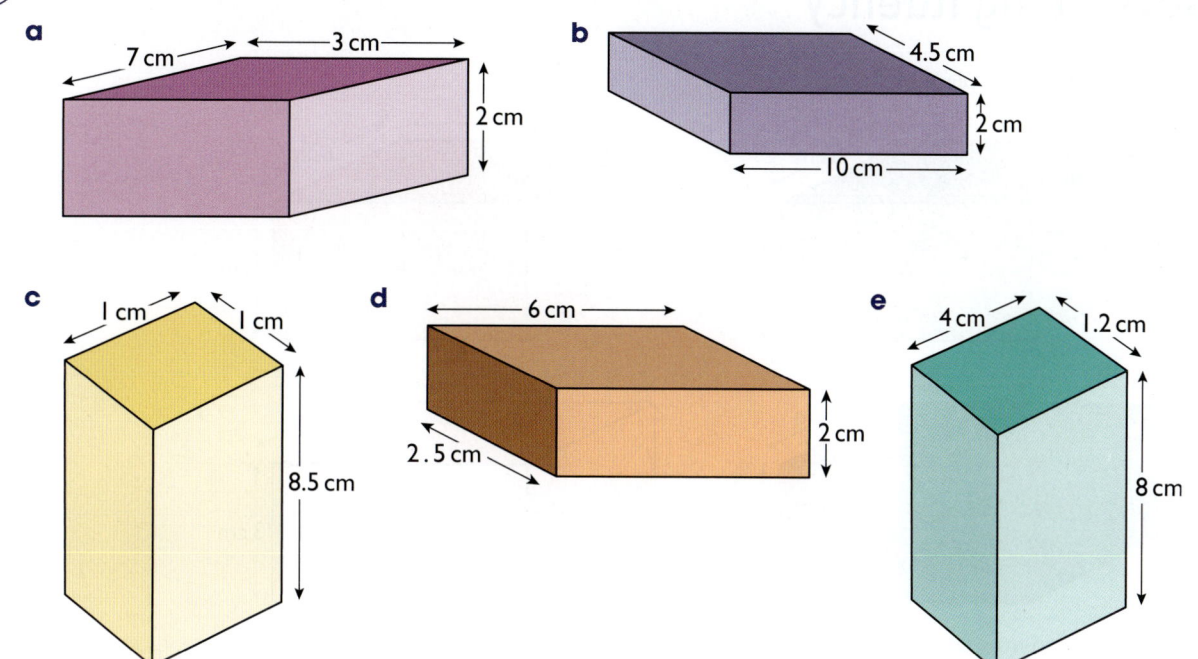

a) 7 cm, 3 cm, 2 cm

b) 4.5 cm, 10 cm, 2 cm

c) 1 cm, 1 cm, 8.5 cm

d) 6 cm, 2.5 cm, 2 cm

e) 4 cm, 1.2 cm, 8 cm

4) A cuboid has volume 72 cm³. Write down the dimensions of five different cuboids which have this volume. Only use whole numbers.

Length	Breadth	Height	Volume
			72 cm³
			72 cm³
			72 cm³
			72 cm³
			72 cm³

5) Copy and complete this table for cuboids.

	Length	Breadth	Height	Volume	Surface area
a	5 cm	3 cm	2 cm		
b	6 cm	2 cm	2 cm		
c	5 cm	4 cm		60 cm³	
d		5 cm	1 cm	35 cm³	
e	6 cm	4 cm		36 cm³	

483

Geometry and Measures Strand 6 Three-dimensional shapes

Developing fluency

1. Here are four cuboids.

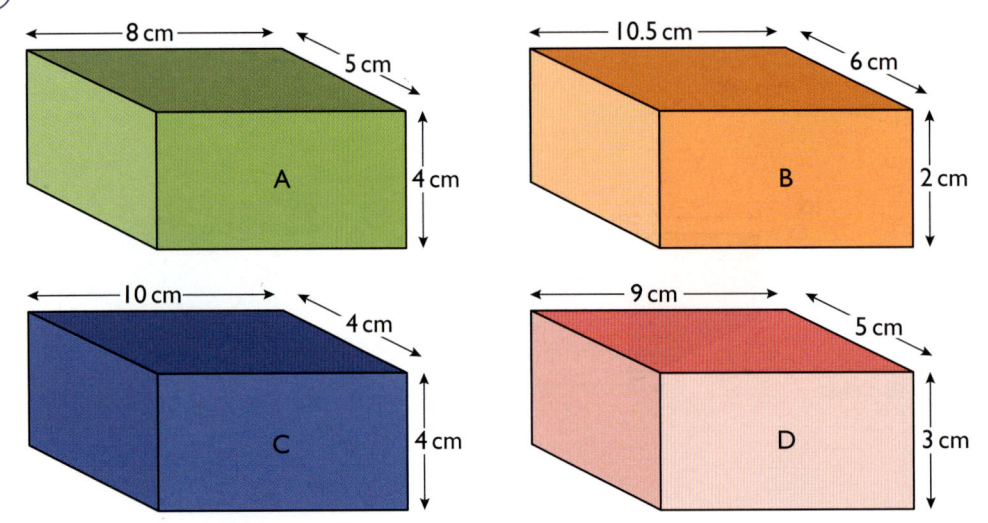

   A: 8 cm × 5 cm × 4 cm
   B: 10.5 cm × 6 cm × 2 cm
   C: 10 cm × 4 cm × 4 cm
   D: 9 cm × 5 cm × 3 cm

   a Which two cuboids have the same volume?
   b Which two cuboids have the same surface area?

2. Here are four cuboids.

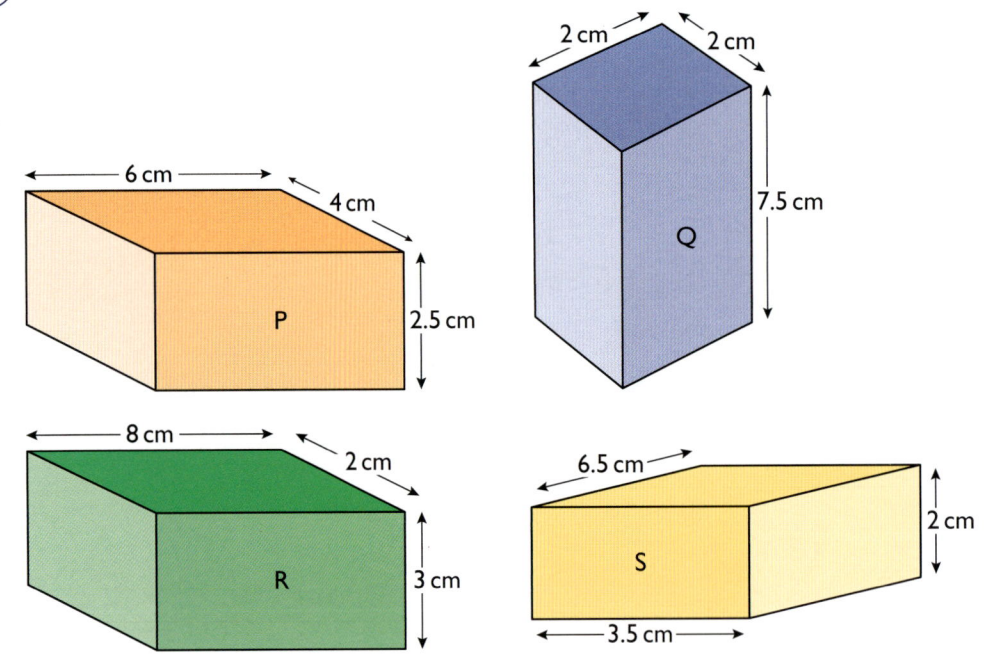

   P: 6 cm × 4 cm × 2.5 cm
   Q: 2 cm × 2 cm × 7.5 cm
   R: 8 cm × 2 cm × 3 cm
   S: 6.5 cm × 3.5 cm × 2 cm

   a Write the cuboids in order of the size of their surface areas starting with the smallest.
   b Name the cuboid with
      i the greatest volume
      ii the smallest volume.
   c Copy and complete these statements.
      The volume of ☐ is double the volume of ☐.
      The volume of ☐ is $\frac{4}{5}$ the volume of ☐.

Unit 3 Volume and surface area of cuboids Band f

3) All these statements are false. Explain why they are false.
   a A cube of side 1 cm has a volume of 1 cm².
   b A cube of side 2 cm has surface area 24 cm³.
   c A cube of side 4 cm has a volume of 12 cm³.
   d A cube of side 3 cm has surface area 45 cm³.
   e The volume of a cube of side 2 cm is twice the volume of a cube of side 1 cm.

4) A cube's total surface area is 294 cm².
   a What is the area of one square face?
   b What is the length of each edge?
   c What is the cube's volume?

5) Decide if these statements are true or false. If false, explain why.
   a The volume of a cuboid 2 m by 1 m by 20 cm is 40 cm³.
   b The volume of a cuboid 9 cm by 3 cm by 1 cm is the same as the volume of a cube of side 3 cm.
   c The surface area of a cuboid 6 cm by 4 cm by 2 cm is twice the surface area of a cuboid 3 cm by 2 cm by 1 cm.

6) A carton of juice measures 10 cm by 4 cm by 4 cm.
   A box measures 1 m by 40 cm by 20 cm.
   How many cartons of juice will fit into the box?

7) A solid wooden table top is in the shape of a cuboid and measures 2 m by 1 m by 4 cm.
   The top and the four sides are varnished but not the bottom.
   One tin of varnish covers 4 m².
   How many tins are needed to give the table two coats of varnish?

8) Two faces of Evi's jewellery box are squares with edges of s cm.

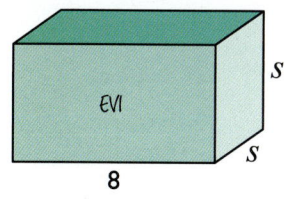

   The other faces are rectangles with edges of length 8 cm and s cm.
   The volume of the box is 72 cm³.
   a Work out the value of s.
   b Find the surface area of the box.

Geometry and Measures Strand 6 Three-dimensional shapes

9 The diagram shows the net of a solid shape.

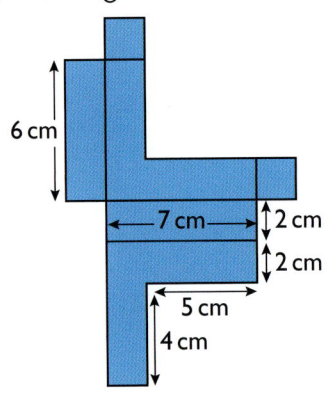

6 cm
7 cm
2 cm
2 cm
5 cm
4 cm

a Draw a sketch of the shape.
b Find the surface area of the shape.
c Find the volume of the shape.
d Write down
   i E, the number of edges
   ii V, the number of vertices
   iii F, the number of faces of the shape.
e Show that the shape obeys Euler's rule $V + F = E + 2$.

Problem solving

1 Here is a tank for storing water. The tank does not have a top.

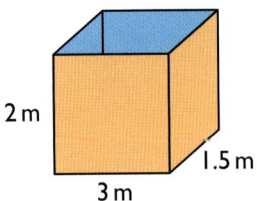

2 m
1.5 m
3 m

Liz is going to paint the five inside faces and the four outside faces.
One litre of paint covers $20 \, m^2$. Liz buys the paint in 2.5 litre tins.
Will one tin be enough?

2 Jo has a swimming pool.

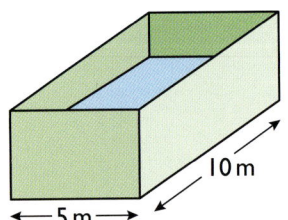

10 m
5 m

Jo wants to fill the pool to a depth of 180 cm.
The pump will pour water into the pool at a rate of 40 litres per minute.
Jo's friend says it will take more than a day to fill the pool from empty to a depth of 180 cm.
Show that Jo's friend is correct.

Unit 3 Volume and surface area of cuboids Band f

3 Iqbal is studying boxes for keeping shopping cool for a school science project.

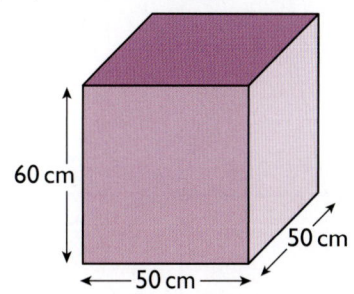

Iqbal measures the edges of the outside of a cool box.
The height is 60 cm.
The width is 50 cm.
The length is 50 cm.

a Use Iqbal's figures to estimate the capacity of the cool box.
Give your answer in litres.
($1 m^3$ = 1000 litres)

b State an assumption you have made and how it will affect your answer to part **a**.

c The sides, top and bottom of the cool box are all 2 cm thick.
What is the true value of its capacity?

4 The diagram shows a box on a table.
A and B are opposite faces.

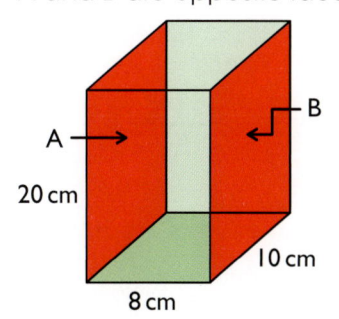

The box has length 10 cm, width 8 cm and height 20 cm.
Llew pours sand into the box until the level of the sand is 2 cm below the top.
Then he puts the lid on and turns the box over so that face A is on the table.
Work out how far the level of the sand is below face B.

5 The diagram shows a fish tank partly filled with water.

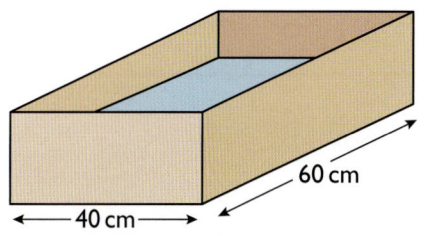

The tank is 40 cm wide and 60 cm long.
The water level is 28 cm from the bottom.
A stone is put in the tank and the water completely covers the stone.
The water level in the tank is now 30 cm from the bottom.
Work out the volume of the stone.

Geometry and Measures Strand 6 Three-dimensional shapes

6 This is the net for a scale model of a pyramid in Central America.

It has a flat top. The perimeter of the real pyramid is 180 m.

Make suitable measurements on the net to answer these questions.

  a What is the perimeter of the flat top of the pyramid?

  b What is the area of the flat top of the real pyramid?

  c How long are the slanting edges of the real pyramid?

  d Show that the total area of the four sloping faces is less than 7200 m².

7 Harri designs a net for a gift box on a centimetre grid.

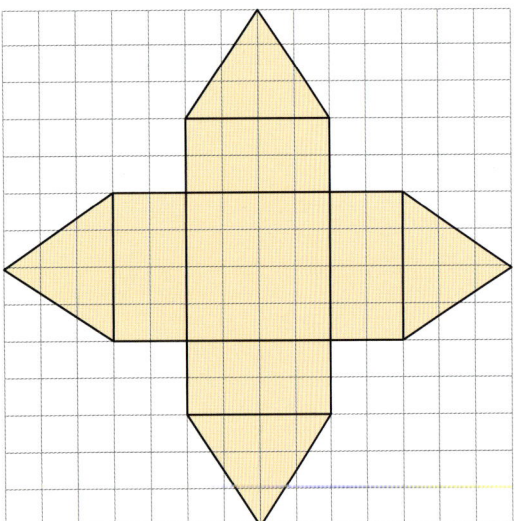

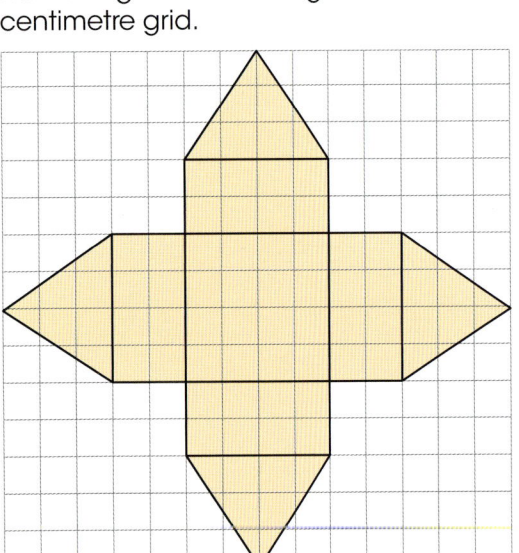

  a How many lines of symmetry does the net have?

  b What is the order of rotational symmetry of the net?

  c Harri cuts the net from a square piece of card measuring 14 cm by 14 cm.
   i What area of card does he waste?
   Harri folds the net to form the gift box.
   ii How many planes of symmetry does the gift box have?

  d The gift box has two parts.
   Write down the shape of
   i the lower part **ii** the top part of the gift box.

  e Find the volume of the lower part of the gift box.

  f Write down the number of
   i faces, F **ii** edges, E **iii** vertices, V of the gift box.

  g Euler's theorem states that $F + V - E = 2$.
   Show that Harri's gift box obeys Euler's theorem.

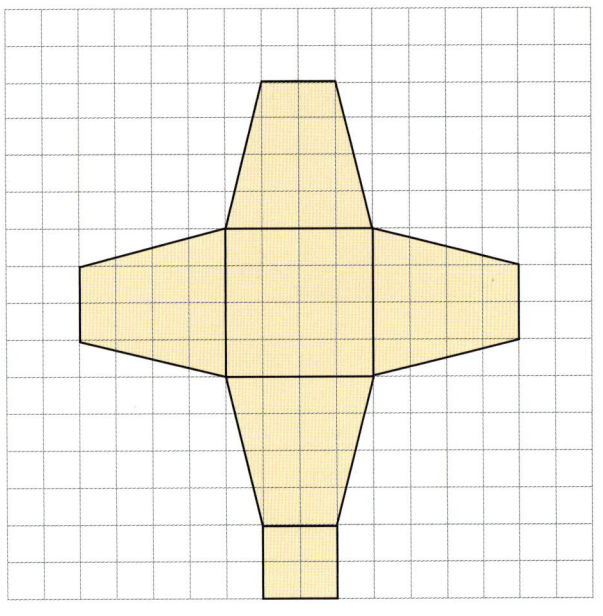

Reviewing skills

1 Work out the volume and surface area of each of these cuboids.

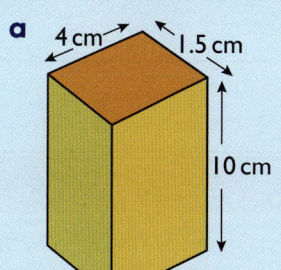

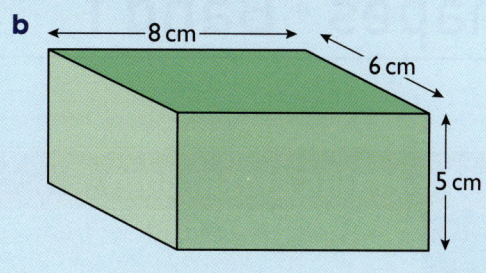

  a 4 cm, 1.5 cm, 10 cm

  b 8 cm, 6 cm, 5 cm

2 A company makes big sugar lumps. Their sides are 3 cm, 2 cm and $\frac{1}{2}$ cm.
The company wants to pack the lumps in a box.

  a Explain why a box 10 cm × 10 cm × 5 cm is not suitable.

  b The company decide the box should be 12 cm × 10 cm × 5 cm.
  How many sugar lumps does it hold?

Unit 4 • 2D representations of 3D shapes • Band f

Outside the Maths classroom

Architects
How does an architect represent all aspects of design in a drawing?

Toolbox

You can represent a three-dimensional (3D) object in two dimensions by drawing its plan and elevations separately.

- Plan view
- Side elevation
- Front elevation

You can also use isometric paper to draw a representation of a 3D object.

Unit 4 2D representations of 3D shapes Band f

Example – Drawing plans and elevations

Draw the plan, front elevation and side elevation of this solid.

Solution

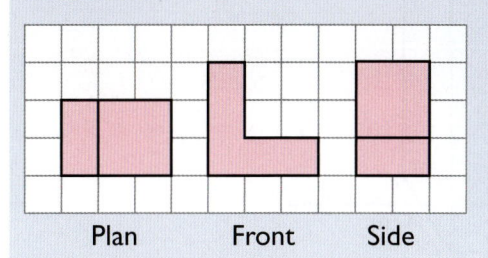

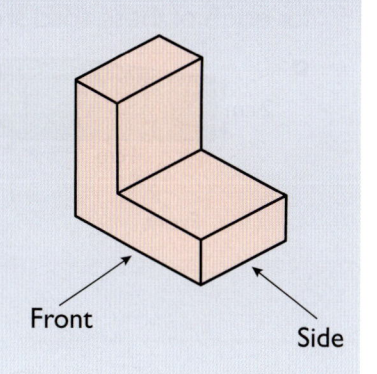

Plan   Front   Side

Practising skills

1 These shapes are made up from 1 cm cubes. Using squared paper, draw
  i the front elevation **ii** the side elevation **iii** the plan
of each shape.

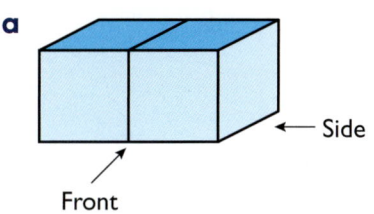

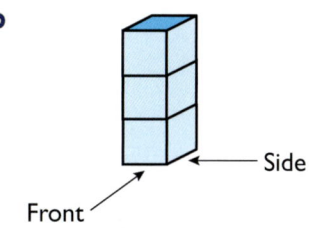

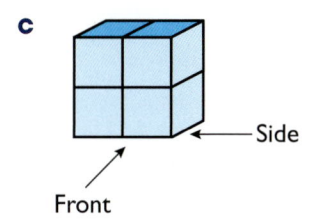

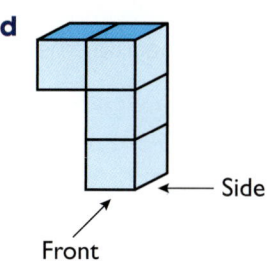

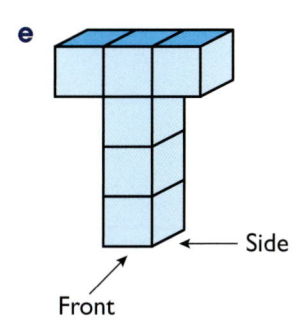

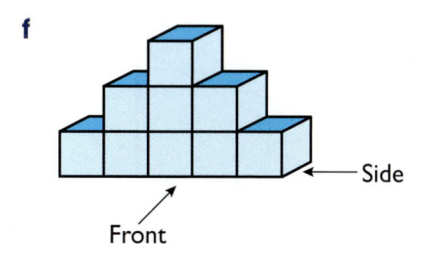

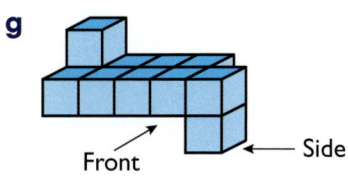

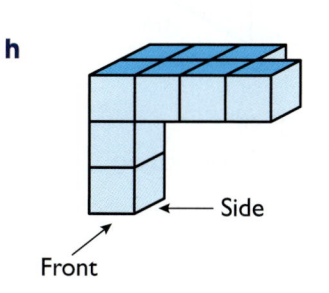

a

b

c

d

e

f

g

h

Geometry and Measures Strand 6 Three-dimensional shapes

2 Using squared paper, draw
  i the front elevation **ii** the side elevation **iii** the plan
  for each of these solid shapes

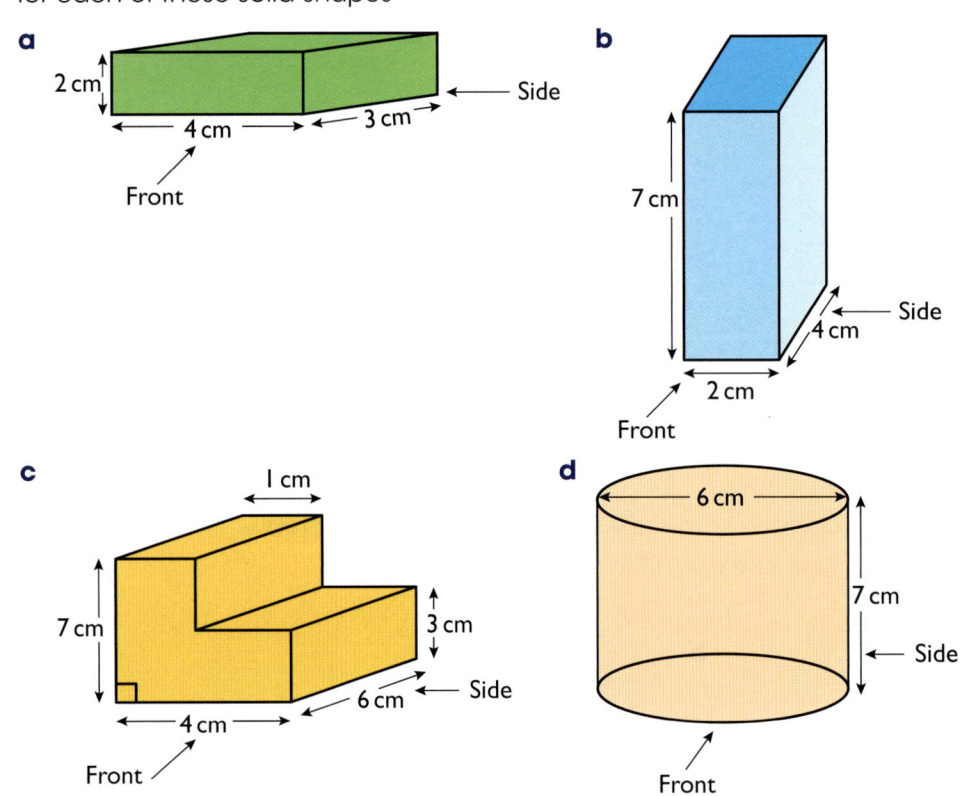

a 2 cm, 4 cm, 3 cm — Front, Side

b 7 cm, 2 cm, 4 cm — Front, Side

c 1 cm, 7 cm, 3 cm, 4 cm, 6 cm — Front, Side

d 6 cm, 7 cm — Front, Side

Developing fluency

1 This is a picture of a house. Some of the measurements are marked on it. Not all the windows are shown.

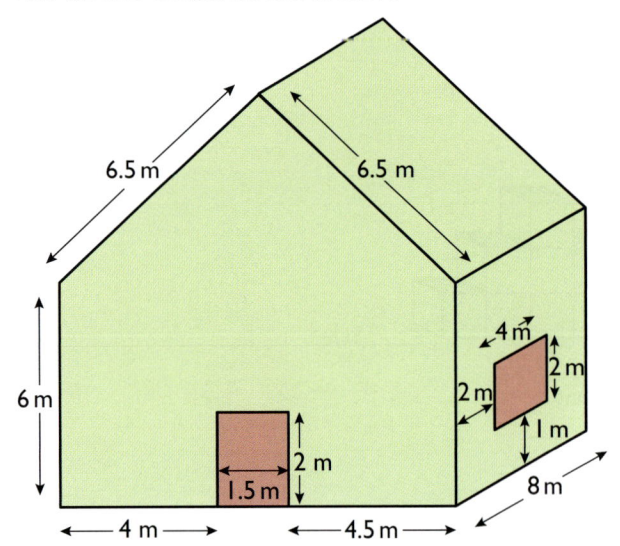

6.5 m, 6.5 m, 6 m, 4 m, 1.5 m, 2 m, 4 m, 2 m, 2 m, 1 m, 4.5 m, 8 m

a Make accurate scale drawings of
  i the front elevation **ii** the side elevation **iii** the plan.

b Use your drawings to find the height of the house.

c How many bedrooms do you think the house has?

Unit 4 2D representations of 3D shapes Band f

2) The front elevation, side elevation and plan are given for each solid. Draw a sketch of the solid.

	Front	Side	Plan
a	rectangle	rectangle	rectangle
b	triangle	rectangle	rectangle
c	square	square	circle
d	triangle	triangle	circle

3) Match together the 3D objects with their plans and elevations.
Some of the plans and elevations are used more than once.

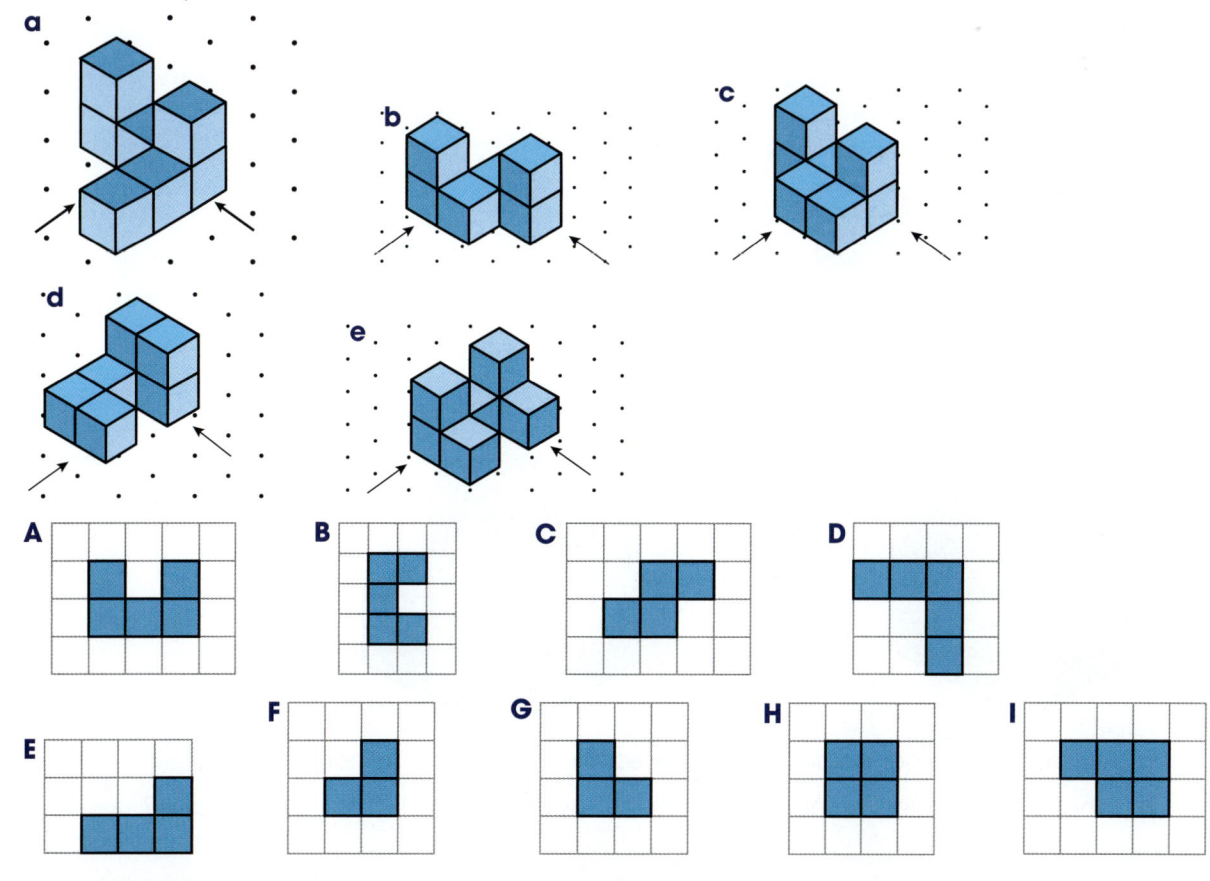

Geometry and Measures Strand 6 Three-dimensional shapes

4 Each diagram represents a plan view of a solid made from 1 centimetre cubes in stacks. The number in each square shows how many cubes are in each stack.
For each diagram
  i draw the solid on isometric paper
  ii draw the front and side elevations of the solid.

a
3	2
2	2
1	1

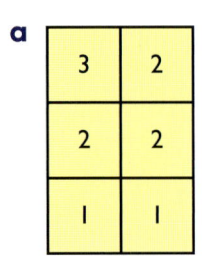

b
3	2	1
2	1	
1		

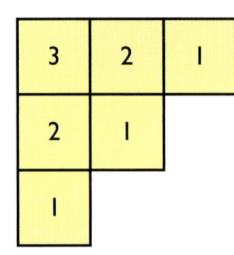

5 Here is the plan, front and side elevations of a child's toy.

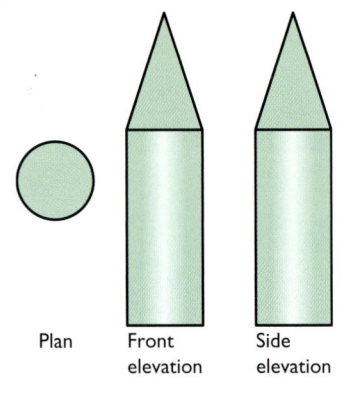

Plan   Front elevation   Side elevation

a What two 3D shapes is the toy made from?

b Sketch a net of the top and base of the toy.

Problem solving

1 Here are the three elevations for a 3D shape.

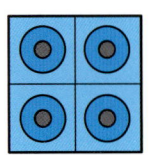

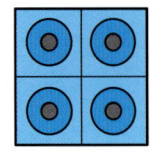

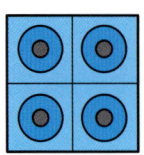

Front elevation   Side elevation   Plan view

The shape could look like this. 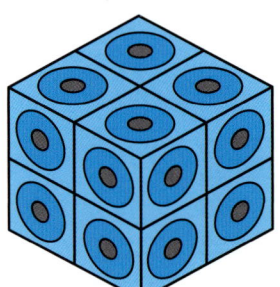   It could also look like this.

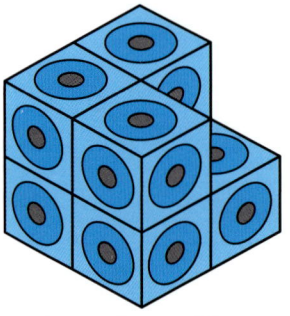

a Are there any other possibilities? Draw some on isometric paper.

b What is the smallest number of cubes that could be used to make the shape?

2 Ben made a shape, drew the three views and then destroyed the shape and made a different one. He did this five times.

Can you reconstruct each of the shapes, 1 to 5, that he made?

If you can, then draw it. If there is more than one possibility, draw them all.

If it is not possible to make it then explain why Ben must have made a mistake.

Shape 1

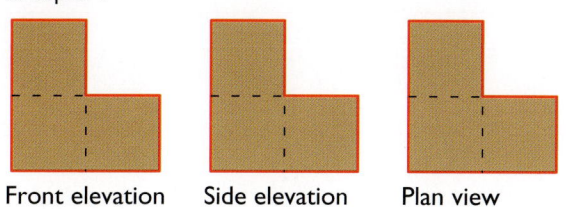

Front elevation   Side elevation   Plan view

Shape 2

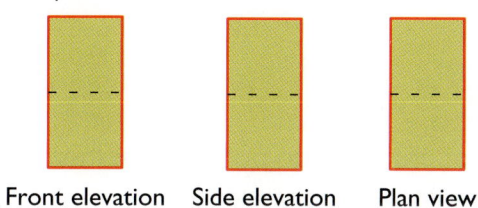

Front elevation   Side elevation   Plan view

Shape 3

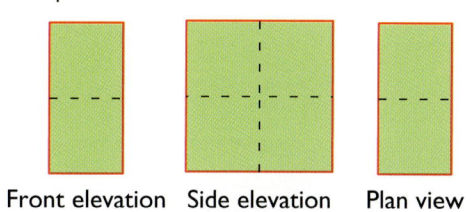

Front elevation   Side elevation   Plan view

Shape 4

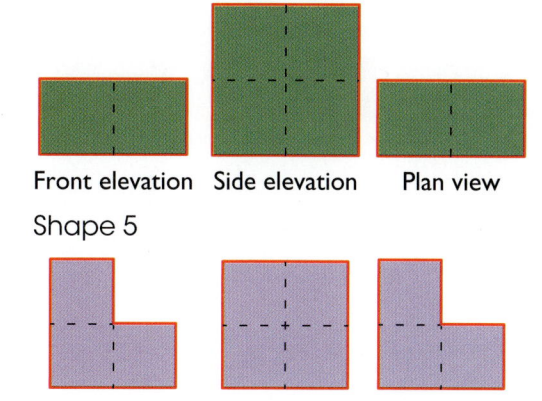

Front elevation   Side elevation   Plan view

Shape 5

Front elevation   Side elevation   Plan view

Geometry and Measures Strand 6 Three-dimensional shapes

3. The plan and elevations of a 3D shape are drawn on a 1 centimetre grid.

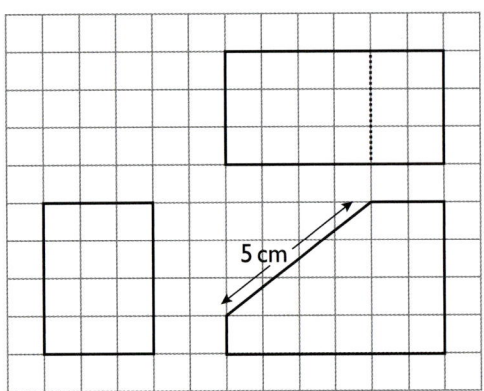

   a Draw the shape on isometric paper.
   b For the 3D shape, find
      i the surface area
      ii the volume.

4. A toy manufacturer produces large cardboard toys that children can put together themselves. Here is the plan and elevations for a small play house with a garage next to it.

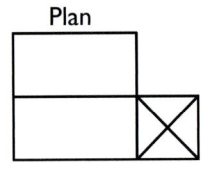

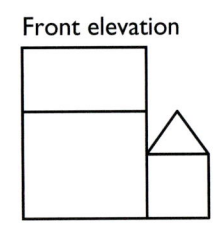

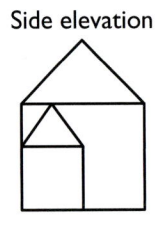

   Plan

   Front elevation   Side elevation

   a What shape is the roof of
      i the house
      ii the garage?
   b Make a 3D sketch of the house.
   c Sketch a net for the garage.

Unit 4 2D representations of 3D shapes Band f

Reviewing skills

1. The shapes are made up of 1 cm cubes.
   Using squared paper, for each shape draw
      i the front elevation   ii the side elevation   iii the plan.

   a

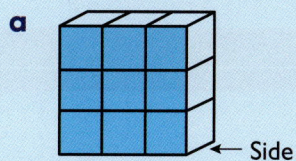

   b

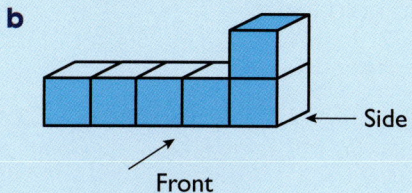

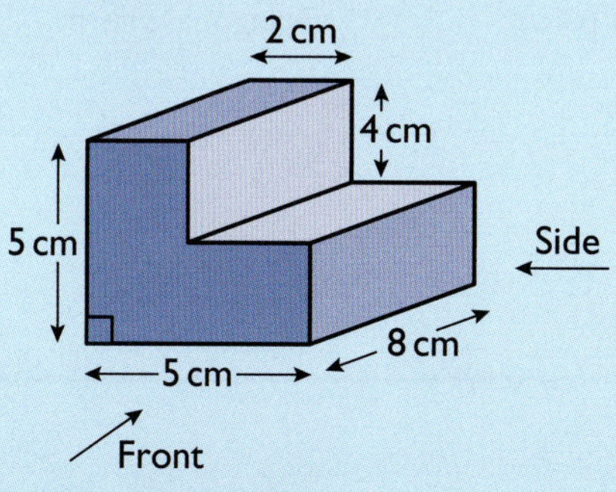

   c

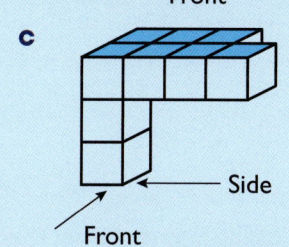

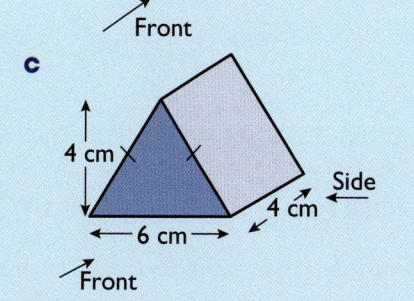

2. Using squared paper, for each solid draw
      i the front elevation   ii the side elevation   iii the plan.

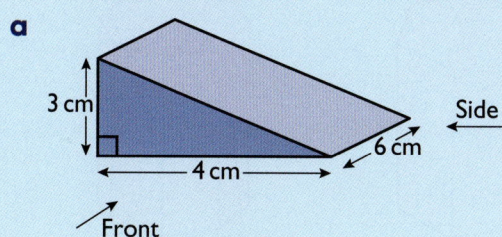

   a 3 cm, 4 cm, 6 cm

   b 2 cm, 4 cm, 5 cm, 5 cm, 8 cm

   c 4 cm, 6 cm, 4 cm

497

Unit 5 • Prisms • Band g

Outside the Maths classroom

Glass design

How would you design a glass to hold the entire contents of a 250 ml bottle?

Toolbox

A **prism** is a three-dimensional shape with the same cross-section all along its length.

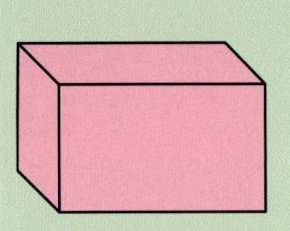

Cuboid 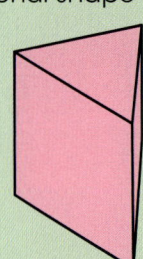   Triangular prism    Hexagonal prism 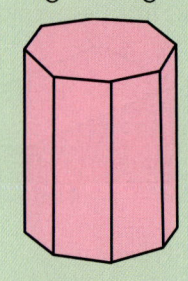   Octagonal prism

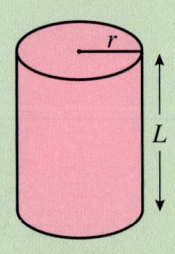

The cylinder is a prism with a circular base.
Its volume is $\pi r^2 L$.
Its surface area is $2\pi r L + \pi r^2 + \pi r^2 = 2\pi r L + 2\pi r^2$

Cylinder

To work out the **volume of a prism**, calculate the area of the cross-section and multiply by the height (or length).
The volume is measured in cubic units such as cubic centimetres (cm^3) or cubic metres (m^3).
The **surface area of a prism** is the total area of all the faces.

Example – Finding the volume of a prism

Work out the volume of this cylinder.

Solution

Area of circle = πr^2

$A = \pi \times 5^2$ ← The cross-section is a circle with a radius of 5 cm.

$ = 78.539...$

Volume of cylinder = area of cross-section × height

$ = 78.539... \times 10$ ← The height of the cylinder is 10 cm.

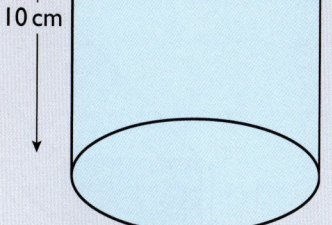

$ = 785.398...$

The volume of the cylinder is 785.4 cm³ (to 1 d.p.).

Example – Finding the surface area of a prism

Calculate the surface area of this prism.

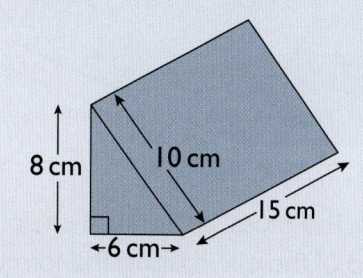

Solution

Work out the area of each face individually.

Area of one triangular face = $\frac{1}{2}$ × base × height

$ = \frac{1}{2} \times 6 \times 8$

$ = 24 \text{ cm}^2$

Area of other triangular face = 24 cm² ← The two triangular faces are identical.

Area of rectangular base: 6 × 15 = 90 cm²

Area of rectangular face: 8 × 15 = 120 cm² ← The rectangular faces all have a length of 15 cm.

Area of sloping rectangular face: 10 × 15 = 150 cm²

Total surface area = 24 + 24 + 90 + 120 + 150 ← Add the area of all the faces to find the total surface area.

$ = 408 \text{ cm}^2$

Geometry and Measures Strand 6 Three-dimensional shapes

Practising skills

1 Here are some prisms.
For each prism, work out
   i the area of the cross-section
   ii the volume.

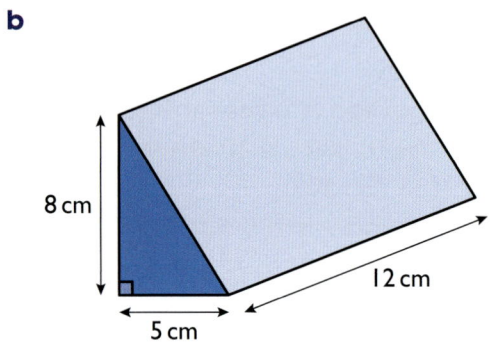

a 3 cm, 6 cm, 8 cm

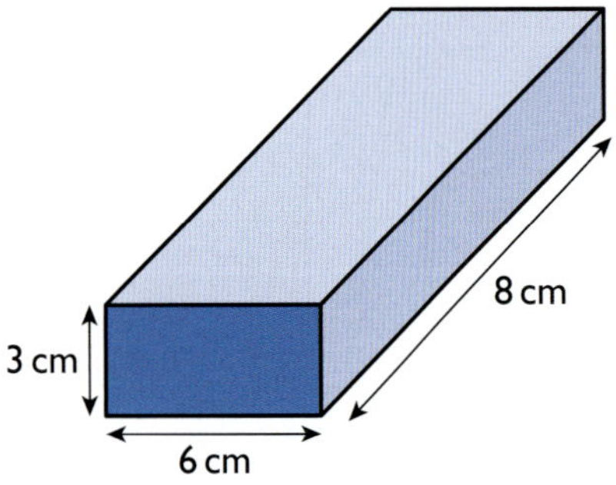

b 8 cm, 5 cm, 12 cm

c 2 cm (top), 4 cm (height), 6 cm (bottom), 11 cm (length)

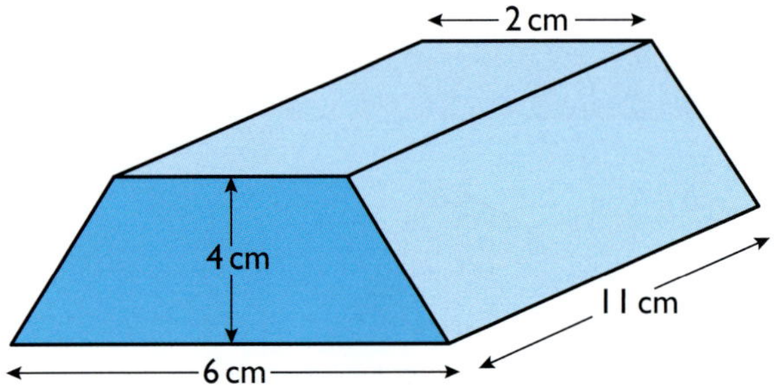

2 A cylinder is a prism. The cross-section is a circle. For each cylinder
   i work out the area of the circle using the formula Area = πr^2
   ii work out its volume.

a diameter 3 cm, length 10 cm

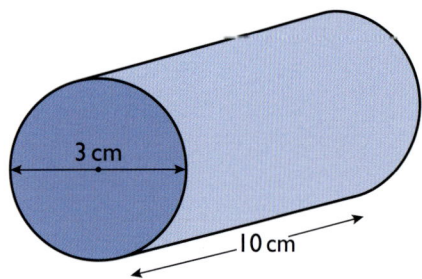

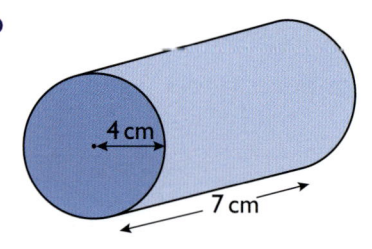

b radius 4 cm, length 7 cm

c diameter 10 cm, height 8 cm

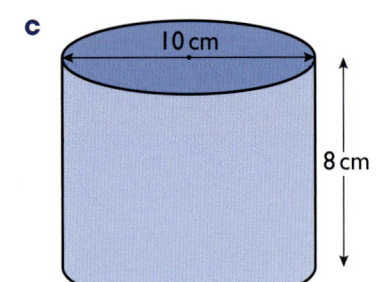

d diameter 14 cm, height 6 cm

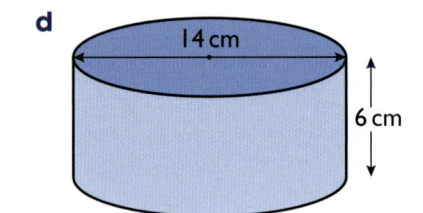

3) A prism has cross-sectional area 18 cm² and length 3 cm.
Work out its volume.

4) A prism has cross-sectional area 15 cm² and volume 120 cm³.
Work out its length.

5) The volume of this triangular prism is 280 cm³.

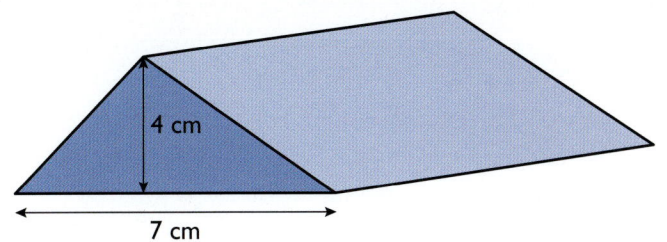

a Work out the area of the triangular face.
b Work out the length of the prism.

6) This diagram shows a triangular prism.

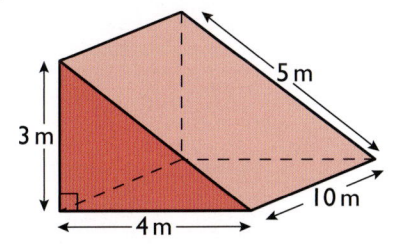

a i Find the areas of the three faces that are rectangles.
  ii What is the total area of their faces?
b i Find the perimeter of the triangular cross-section.
  ii Multiply the perimeter by the length of the prism.
c Comment on your answers to **a ii** and **b ii**.
d i Find the area of the triangular cross-section.
  ii What do you find when you multiply the area by the length of the prism?

7) Work out the volume of each of these prisms in cm³.

a

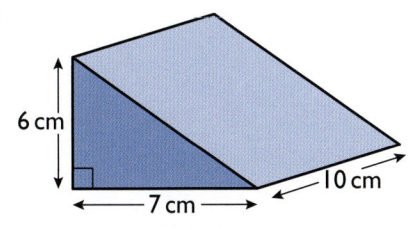

b

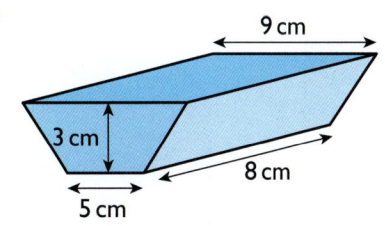

c

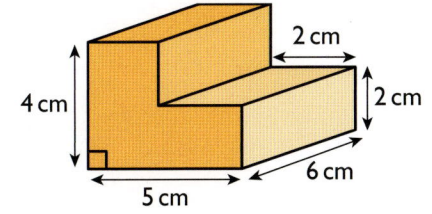

d

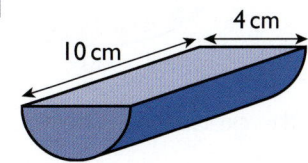

Geometry and Measures Strand 6 Three-dimensional shapes

Developing fluency

1. This is a sketch of a child's playhouse.

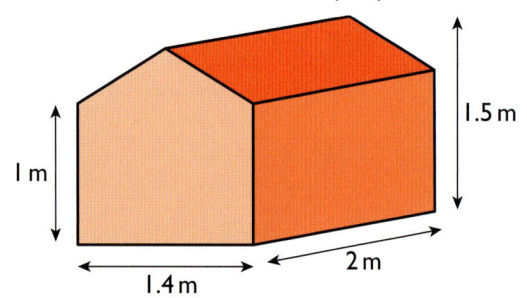

   Work out the volume of the playhouse.

2. This cylinder has a radius 10 cm and height 30 cm.

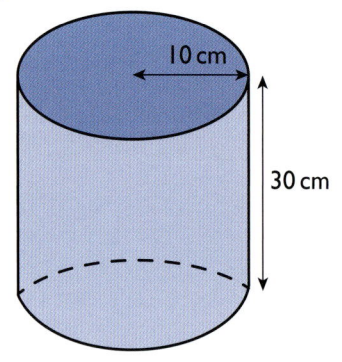

   a Find the circumference of the cross-section.
   b Find the surface area of the walls without the top and bottom.
   c Find the area of the top.
   d Find the total surface area: the walls, top and bottom all together.

3. A tin of beans has diameter 6.8 cm and height 10.2 cm.
   Work out its capacity (volume).

4. Susan has two cylindrical containers, P and Q.

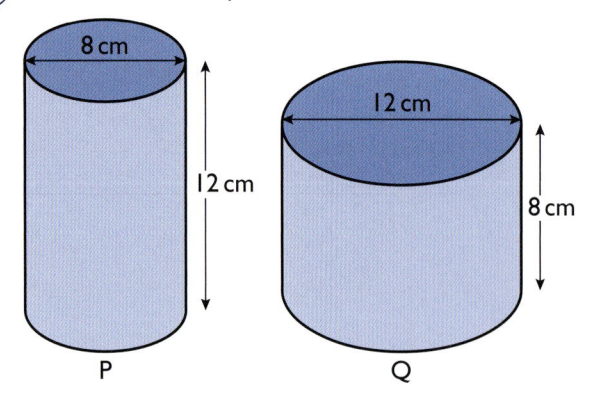

   a Which has the greater volume, P or Q?
   b What is the difference in volume between the two containers?

5 At the park, a cylinder is cut from a wooden cuboid to make a tunnel for children to crawl through.

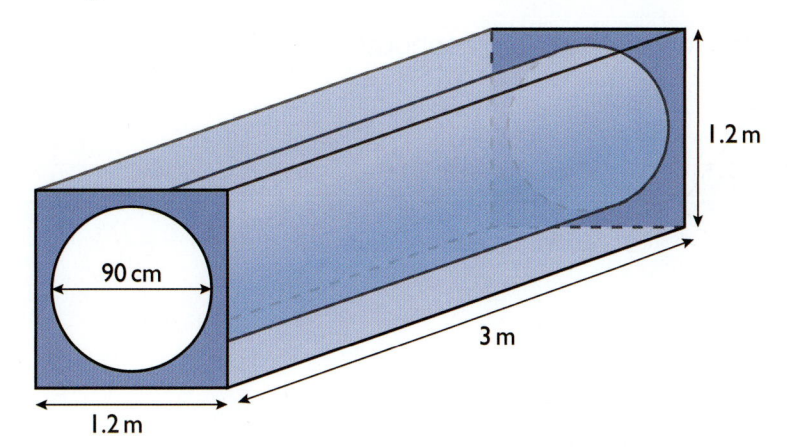

- 1.2 m
- 90 cm
- 3 m
- 1.2 m

a Work out the volume of wood remaining.

b Work out the surface area of the inside of the hole.

6 One summer's day two children, Zara and Anna, use their paddling pools. Zara's pool is in the shape of a cylinder and Anna's is in the shape of a cuboid. Zara fills her pool. Anna's pool is three-quarters full.

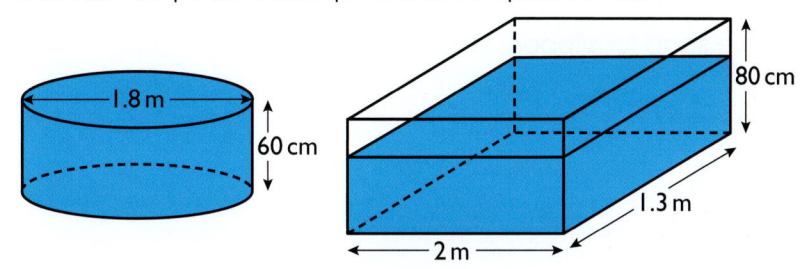

- 1.8 m
- 60 cm
- 80 cm
- 1.3 m
- 2 m

a Which pool contains more water?

b What is the difference in the volume of water in the two pools?

7 For each of these solids, say whether it is a prism. If it is a prism, write down the shape of its cross-section.

- **a** Cuboid
- **b** Wedge
- **c** Cylinder
- **d** Tetrahedron
- **e** Cone
- **f** Cube
- **g** Sphere

Geometry and Measures Strand 6 Three-dimensional shapes

Problem solving

1. The diagram shows a design for the roof space of a greenhouse.

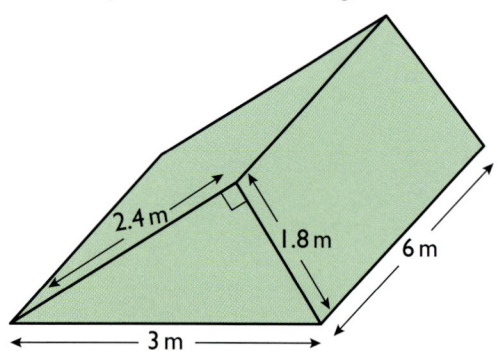

   The roof space is in the shape of a triangular prism of length 6 m.
   The cross-section of the roof space is a right-angled triangle.
   The sides of the triangle are 2.4 m, 1.8 m and 3 m.
   Find

   a the area of the glass used

   b the volume of the roof space.

2. A council wants to use bins to store sand for slippery roads.

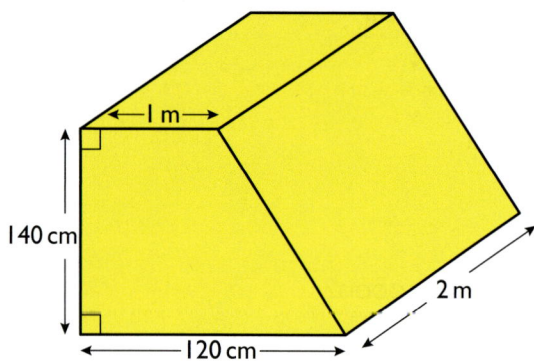

   The bins are in the shape of a prism.
   The cross-section of the prism is a trapezium; its dimensions are given on the diagram.
   The council wants to have enough bins to store 150 m³ of sand.
   Will 50 bins be enough to store this amount of sand?

3. A company digs a tunnel through a mountain.
   The tunnel is a cylinder with diameter of 8 metres.
   The length of the tunnel is 1 kilometre.

   a The material removed is taken away by lorries. Each lorry can carry 30 m³ of material. How many lorry trips are needed to take away all the material?

   b The walls inside the tunnel are covered in concrete.

   i What area of concrete is needed?

   ii The concrete is 10 cm thick. What volume of concrete is needed?

4 The diagram shows a prism-shaped cold frame.
Rectangle BCFE is open. All of the other surfaces are made of glass.
The dimensions of the cold frame are shown on the diagram.

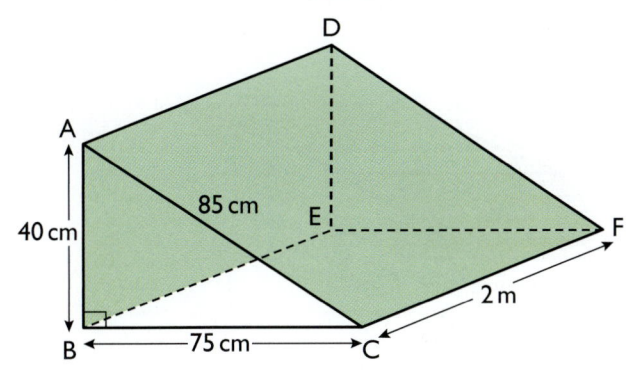

a Find the total area of glass.

b Find the volume of the cold frame.

5 Here is a container used to mix chemicals. It is a closed cylinder with the dimensions shown.

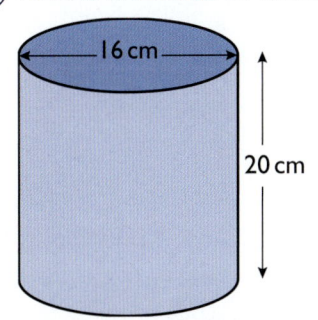

The inside surface of the cylinder has to be covered with a special chemical.

a Find the area of each end of the cylinder.

b Find the area of the inside wall of the cylinder.

It costs £1.20 to cover each square centimetre with the special chemical.

c Work out the total cost of covering the inside surface of the cylinder.

6 The diagram shows the cross-section of a water channel.
The cross-section is a trapezium.
The channel is 2 km long.

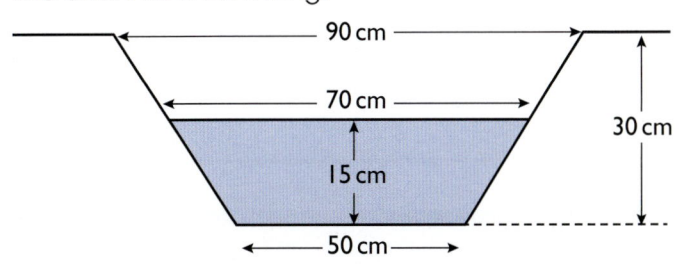

a One day the water is 15 cm deep, as shown in the diagram.
  i Find the cross-sectional area of the water.
  ii Find the volume of water in the channel.

b On another day, the channel is full. How much water does it contain?

Reviewing skills

1 Here are some prisms. For each prism, work out
  i the area of the cross-section
  ii the volume.

a (triangular prism: 7 cm height, 6 cm base, 10 cm length)

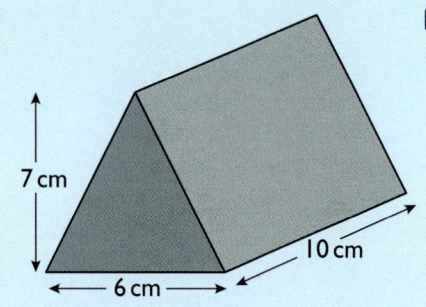

b (parallelogram prism: 4 cm, 7 cm, 9 cm)

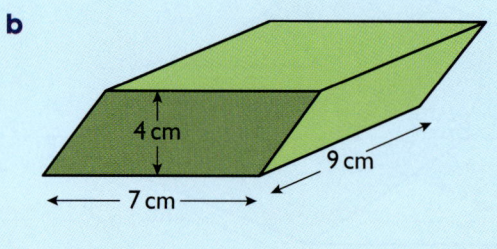

2 A prism has volume 5520 cm³ and length 1.2 m.
Work out its cross-sectional area.

3 A cylinder is a prism. The cross-section is a circle.
For each cylinder
  i work out the area of the circle using the formula Area = πr^2.
  ii work out its volume.

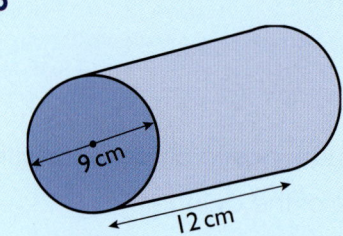

a (radius 6 cm, height 9 cm)

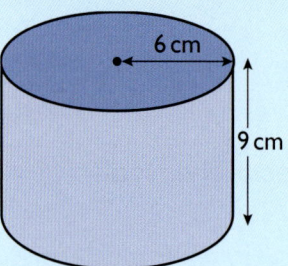

b (diameter 9 cm, length 12 cm)

c (radius 3 cm, length 8 cm)

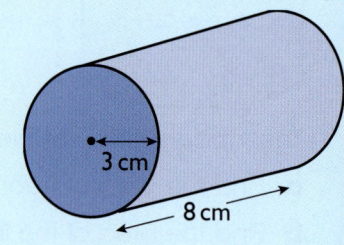

4 Work out the volume of this prism.

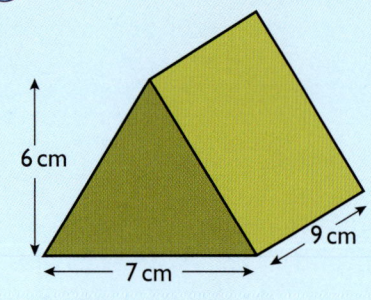

(triangular prism: 6 cm height, 7 cm base, 9 cm length)

Unit 6 • Enlargement in two and three dimensions • Band g

Outside the Maths classroom

Cost of enlargement
What will the actual cost of a print depend on?

Toolbox

When one shape is an **enlargement** of another, all the lengths are increased by the same scale factor.

The blue cuboid is an enlargement of the red cuboid because all dimensions of the blue cuboid are two times the dimensions of the red cuboid.

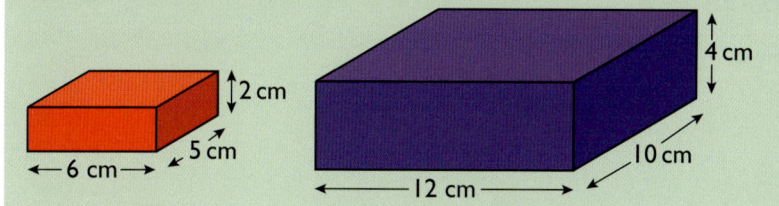

Length: 6 cm × 2 = 12 cm
Width: 5 cm × 2 = 10 cm
Height: 2 cm × 2 = 4 cm

The **surface area** is the area of all 6 surfaces.
Red surface area
$= 2 \times (6 \times 2 + 5 \times 2 + 6 \times 5) = 104 \, cm^2$
Blue surface area
$= 2 \times (12 \times 4 + 10 \times 4 + 12 \times 10) = 416 \, cm^2$
Red volume $= 6 \times 5 \times 2 = 60 \, cm^3$
Blue volume $= 12 \times 10 \times 4 = 480 \, cm^3$
The lengths, areas and volumes can be compared using ratios.
Lengths 6 : 12 or 1 : 2
Areas 104 : 416 or 1 : 4
Volumes 60 : 480 or 1 : 8

Higher tier only

Geometry and Measures Strand 6 Three-dimensional shapes

Example – Finding area

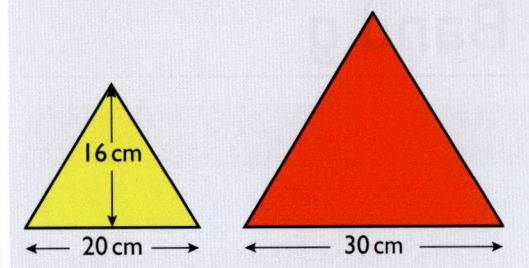

16 cm
← 20 cm →

← 30 cm →

The red triangle is an enlargement of the yellow triangle.
The yellow triangle has a base of 20 cm and a height of 16 cm.
The red triangle has a base of 30 cm.
a Calculate the height of the red triangle.
b Calculate the ratio of the areas of the triangles in its simplest form.

Solution

a First find the ratio of the lengths of the two triangles.
   Yellow : Red
   Base 20 : 30
        2 : 3
   or 1 : 1.5
   So the height of the red triangle is 1.5 × 16 = 24 cm   *this is the height of the yellow triangle*

b Area = $\frac{1}{2}bh$
   Yellow triangle area = $\frac{1}{2}$ × 20 × 16 = 160 cm²
   Red triangle area = $\frac{1}{2}$ × 30 × 24 = 360 cm²
   Ratio = 160 : 360   *divide by 40*
         = 4 : 9
         or 1 : 2.25

Example – Problem solving in 3-D

A cuboid has a square base of side 4 cm and a height of h cm.
Its volume is 192 cm³.
a Calculate the height of the cuboid.
b A new cuboid is an enlargement of the green one.
   Its base has side 12 cm.
   Find the ratio of their volumes.

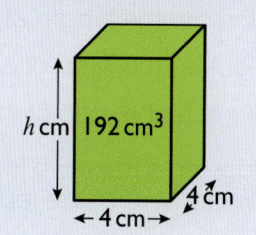

Solution

a Length × width × height = volume
   4 × 4 × h = 192
   $16h$ = 192
   h = 192 ÷ 16 = 12
The height is 12 cm.

b The ratio of the bases is 4 : 12   ← divide both sides by 3
                           = 1 : 3   ← in the simplest form
So the scale factor of enlargement is 3.
Therefore, the height of the new cuboid is 12 × 3 = 36 cm   ← multiplying the original height by the scale factor

So, the volume of the new cuboid = length × width × height
                                 = 12 × 12 × 36
                                 = 5184 cm³
Ratio of the volumes is 192 : 5184

= 48 : 1296   ← dividing by 4
= 12 : 324   ← dividing by 4
= 3 : 81   ← dividing by 4
= 1 : 27   ← dividing by 3

The ratio of the volumes is 1 : 27 in its simplest form.

Practising skills

1. Look at these two rectangles.

   a Write down the ratio of the lengths of the sides of A to the length of the sides of B, in its lowest terms.

   b i Calculate the perimeter of each rectangle.
     ii Find the ratio of the perimeter of A to the perimeter of B, in its lowest terms.

   c i Calculate the area of each rectangle.
     ii Find the ratio of the area of A to the area of B, in its lowest terms.

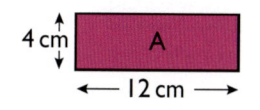

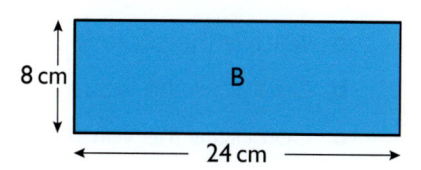

Rectangle A: 4 cm × 12 cm
Rectangle B: 8 cm × 24 cm

Geometry and Measures Strand 6 Three-dimensional shapes

2) The smaller of these two squares has side length of 15 cm.
The ratio of the sides of the two squares is 1 : 2.
   a Calculate the length of the side of the larger square.
   b Calculate the area of each square.
   c Calculate the ratio of the area of the squares, in its lowest terms.

3) The diagram shows two triangles. The blue triangle is an enlargement of the red triangle.
   a Calculate the ratio of their heights in its simplest form.
   b Calculate the ratio of their areas in its simplest form.

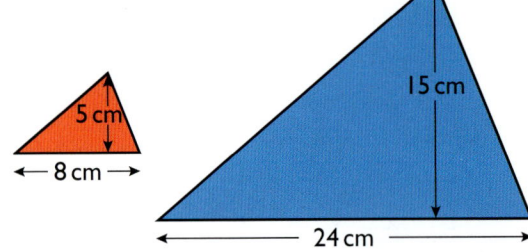

4) A box is in the shape of a cube with sides of 20 cm.
It is filled with small cubes with sides of 4 cm.
   a What is the volume of a small cube?
   b What is the volume of the box?
   c Write down the ratio of the lengths of a side of a small cube to the side of the box, in its lowest terms.
   d Write down the ratio of the volume of a small cube to the volume of the box, in its lowest terms.
   e How many small cubes fit in the box?

5) A cuboid is enlarged by a scale factor of 2.
   a Explain why the surface area is increased by a factor of 4.
   b By what factor is the volume increased?

Developing fluency

1) The green shape is an enlargement of the blue shape.

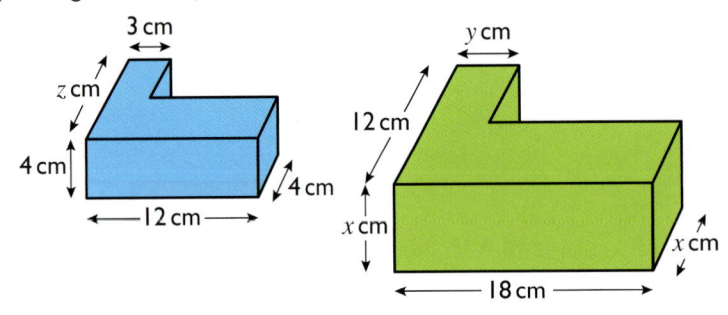

   a What is the scale factor?
   b Calculate the values of x, y and z.
   c Calculate the volume of each shape.
   d Calculate the ratio of the volumes in its simplest form.

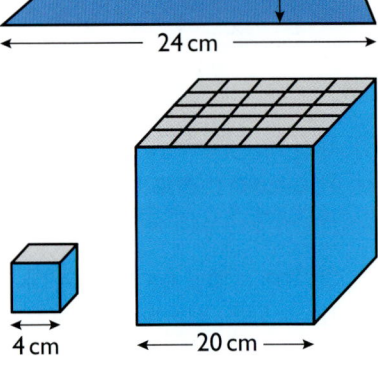

Unit 6 Enlargement in two and three dimensions Band g

2 Two squares have areas of 36 cm² and 100 cm².
  a Find the lengths of their sides.
  b Find the ratio of the lengths of their sides in its lowest terms.

3 A map is drawn to a scale of 1 : 500.
On the map, a rectangular building measures 4.8 cm × 3.2 cm.
Calculate
  a the dimensions of the actual building
  b the area of the building on the map
  c the actual floor area of the building
  d the ratio of the two areas in its simplest form.

4 This cuboid has a square base of side 6 cm. Its surface area is 162 cm².

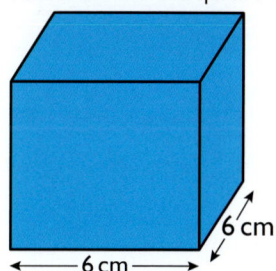

  a Calculate
    i the height of the cuboid   **ii** the volume of the cuboid.
  An enlargement of the cuboid is made with a scale factor of 3.
  b Calculate
    i the surface area   **ii** the volume
    of the enlargement.

5 Here are two cylinders.

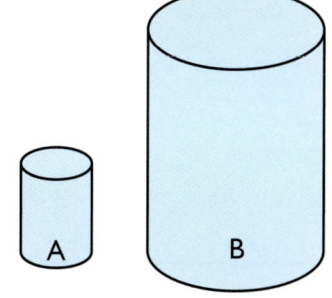

Cylinder A has radius 6 cm and height 15 cm.
Cylinder B is an enlargement of A.
The area of the circular top of B is 4 times the area of the top of A.
Find
  a the radius of cylinder B
  b the height of cylinder B
  c the scale factor of the enlargement
  d the ratio of the volumes of the two cylinders, in its simplest form.

511

Geometry and Measures Strand 6 Three-dimensional shapes

Problem solving

1) The diagram represents the two sails of a boat.

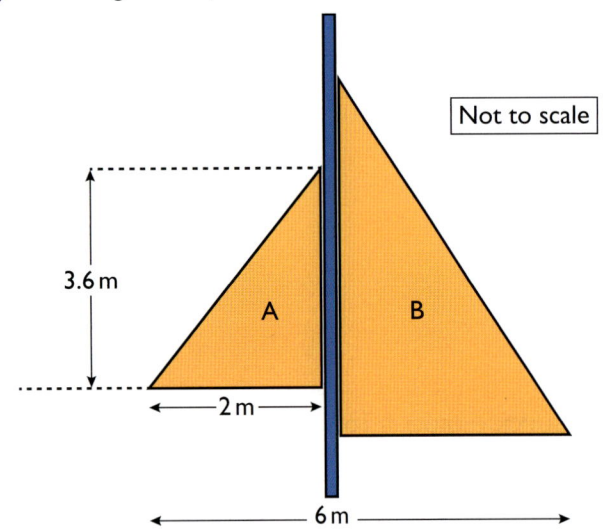

Not to scale

3.6 m

A B

2 m

6 m

The ratio height : base is the same for both sails.
Some of the dimensions are given on the diagram.
Work out the total area of the sails.

2) Iola owns a café.
He wants to put this banner across a space on his door after enlarging it.
The space is 1 m wide and 36 cm high.

Iola's Café 2 cm

5 cm

a What is the greatest size Iola's banner can be?
b What is the scale factor of the enlargement?
c What is the area of the banner?

3) A and B are two cubes. B is bigger than A.
The ratio of their sides is 2 : 5.
Block A has sides of length 40 cm.
a Work out the lengths of the sides of block B.
b Work out the surface area of each block.
c Show that the ratio of their surface areas is 1 : 6.25.

Unit 6 Enlargement in two and three dimensions Band g

4) Siân makes a model garage to the scale of 1 : 40. It has a flat roof.

The length of the real garage is 8 metres.

a Work out the length of the model garage. Give your answer in cm.

The width of the garage is $\frac{3}{4}$ of the length.

The height of the garage is $\frac{2}{5}$ of the width.

b Write down the width and height of the real garage.

c Find the volume of the real garage.

d Find the width, height and volume of the model garage.

e Show that the ratio of the volumes of the model and the real garage is $1 : 40^3$.

5) Olga makes wooden blocks for children's toys.

Here are two cubes.

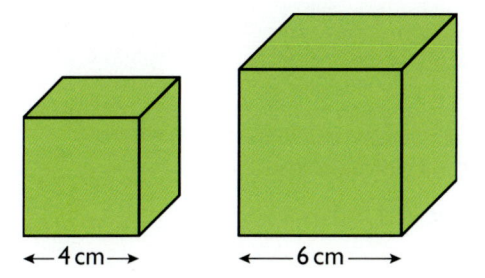

a Write down the ratio of the length of the sides.

b Emyr thinks that the ratio of the surface areas of the two cubes is the same as the ratio of the lengths of their sides.
Show that he is wrong.

c The blocks have the same density, so their masses are proportional to their volumes.
Show the ratio of their masses is $8 : 27$.

6) Here are two pictures.

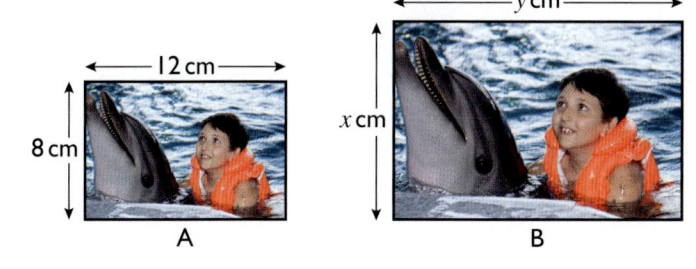

Picture B is a computer enlargement of picture A with scale factor 3.

a Work out the measurements of picture B.

b For the two pictures, find the ratios of
   i   the perimeters
   ii the areas.

Megan then stretches picture B by 8 cm in width and by 8 cm in height.

c Is the new picture an enlargement of picture A?
Give a reason for your answer.

513

Geometry and Measures Strand 6 Three-dimensional shapes

Reviewing skills

1 Look at the two cuboids.

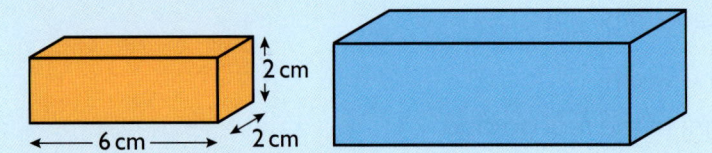

The edges of the larger one are $2\frac{1}{2}$ times the lengths of those in the smaller one.
The smaller cuboid has dimensions of 2 cm × 2 cm × 6 cm.

a Write down the dimensions of the larger cuboid.

Calculate

b the surface area of the smaller cuboid

c the surface area of the larger cuboid

d the volume of the smaller cuboid

e the volume of the larger cuboid

f the ratio of the surface areas of the two cuboids in its simplest form

g the ratio of the volumes of the two cuboids in its simplest form.

2 Dewi has to paint some cubes.
He knows that 1 litre of paint is enough to paint 200 cubes of edge 3 cm.
How many cubes of edge 4 cm can he paint with 1 litre of paint?

Unit 7 • Constructing plans and elevations • Band g

Outside the Maths classroom

Architecture
How do architects use constructions?

Toolbox

The most common types of 3-dimensional drawing are
- **a** **isometric** drawings
- **b** **plans and elevations**.

An **isometric drawing** is often made on a triangular grid.
Vertical edges are drawn vertically, but horizontal edges are not drawn horizontally.

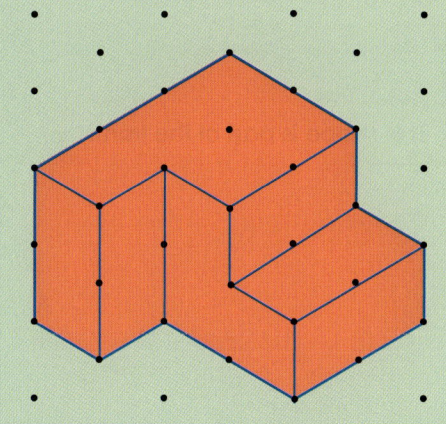

Plans and elevations show the view from above, the front and the side.

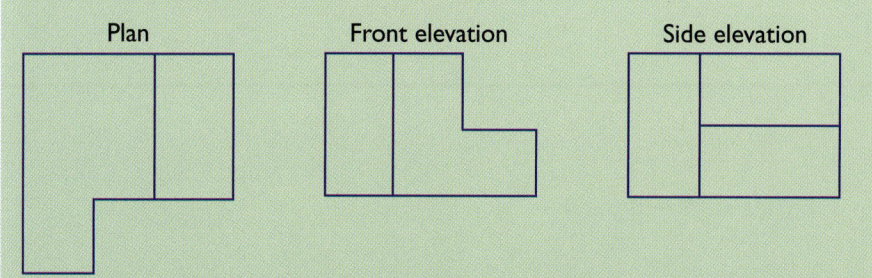

Plan   Front elevation   Side elevation

Geometry and Measures Strand 6 Three-dimensional shapes

Example – Isometric drawings

Here are the plan, front and side elevations of a shape.

Plan Front elevation Side elevation

Make an isometric drawing of the shape.

Solution

Plan

Front elevation

Side elevation

3-dimensional view

- A horizontal surface.
- A sloping top.
- And this is part of the side.
- This shape is part of the front.
- A sloping front.

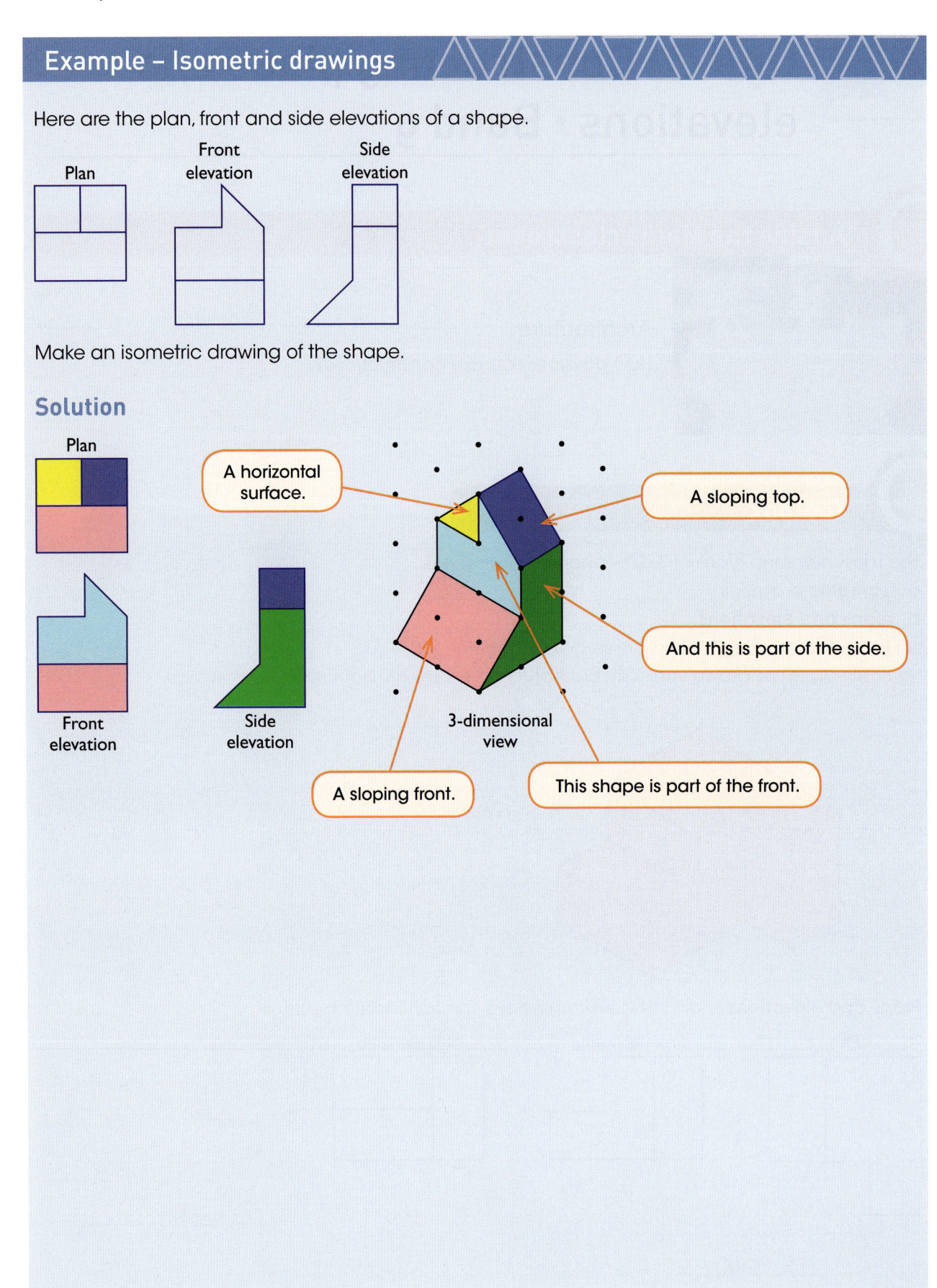

Practising skills

1. Match each shape at the top with the same shape at the bottom.

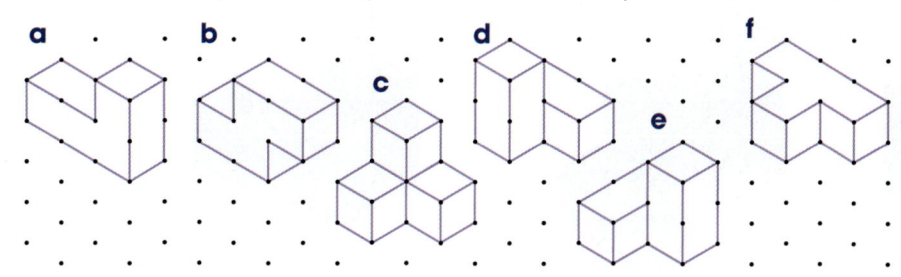

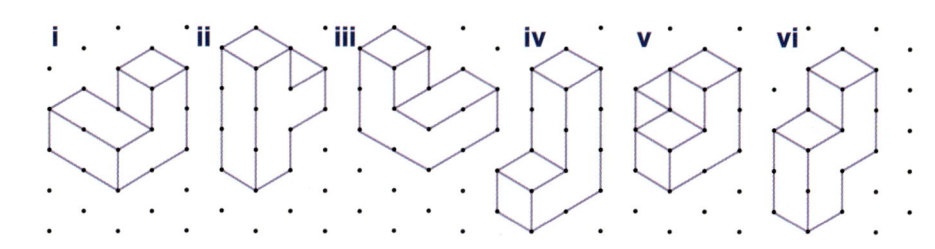

   a b c d e f

   i ii iii iv v vi

2. Copy these and add the missing lines to complete the drawings.

   a b c d

3. These shapes are made of cubes.
   Use isometric paper to draw the back view of each shape.

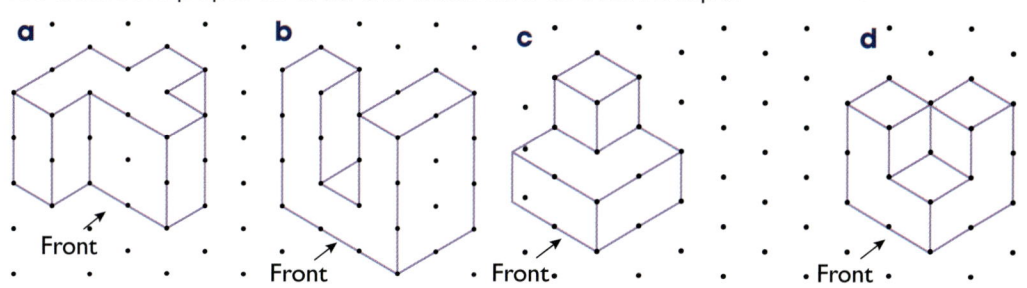

   a b c d

   Front Front Front Front

Geometry and Measures Strand 6 Three-dimensional shapes

4 Copy and complete the table by matching these isometric drawings to the views.

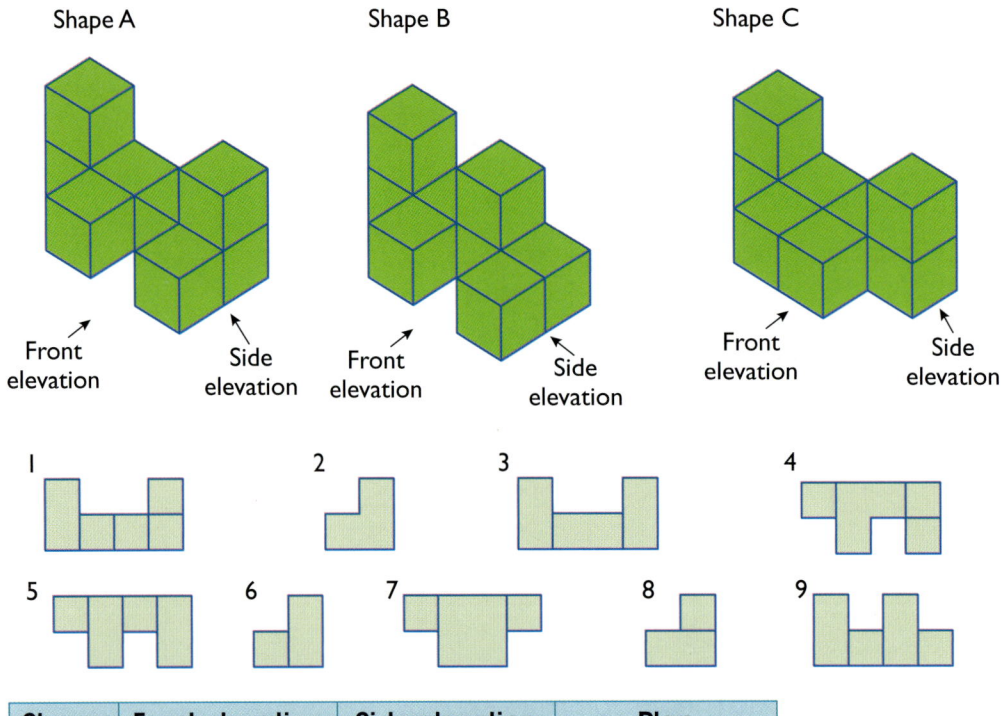

Shape A   Shape B   Shape C

Front elevation   Side elevation   Front elevation   Side elevation   Front elevation   Side elevation

1   2   3   4

5   6   7   8   9

Shape	Front elevation	Side elevation	Plan
A			
B			
C			

5 Sketch the plan, front elevation and side elevation of each of these shapes.

a   b

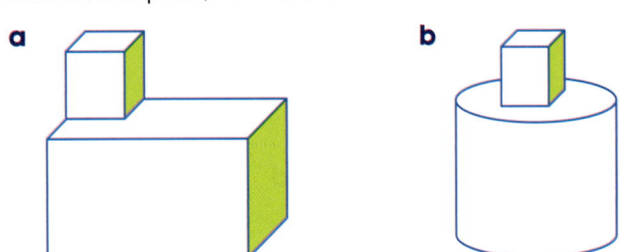

518

Developing fluency

1. Make isometric drawings of the shapes shown in these views.

   a. Plan / Front elevation / Side elevation

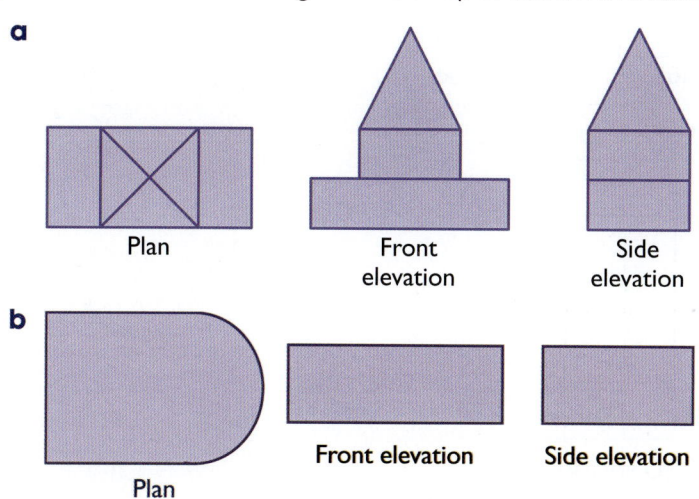

   b. Plan / Front elevation / Side elevation

2. Each of these shapes is made of 8 cubes.
   Draw the plan, front and side elevations of the shapes.

   a.

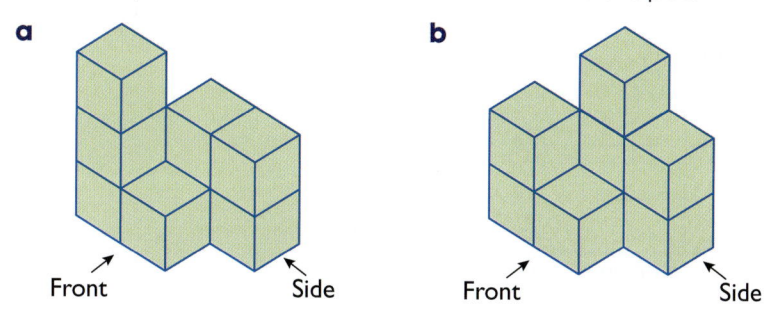

   b.

3. Draw plans, front and side elevations of these shapes.

   a.

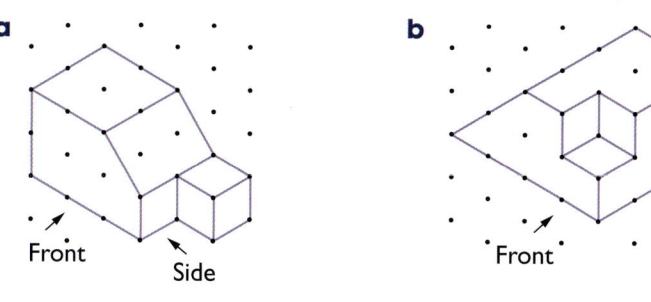

   b.

4. Draw the plan, front elevation and side elevation of this shape.

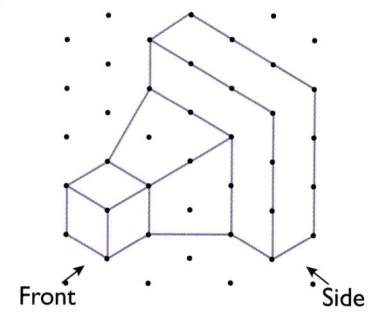

Geometry and Measures Strand 6 Three-dimensional shapes

5. Make an isometric drawing of this shape.

Plan   Front elevation   Side elevation

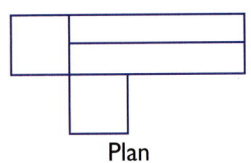

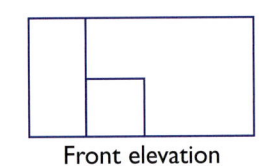

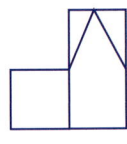

6. Here are the plan and elevations of a 3D shape.

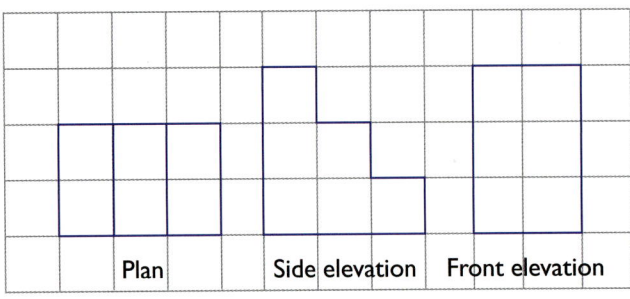

Plan   Side elevation   Front elevation

a Make an isometric drawing of this 3D shape.
   The solid is made from centimetre cubes.

b Find the
   i volume   ii surface area of the solid.

7. Here are the plan and elevations of a 3D shape.

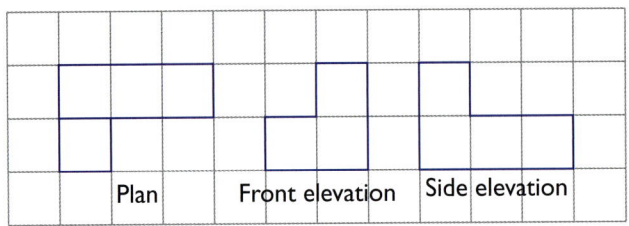

Plan   Front elevation   Side elevation

a Make an isometric drawing of this 3D shape.
   The solid is made from centimetre cubes.

b Add 1 more cube to your drawing, so that the drawing has plane symmetry.
   Find two different answers.

c Add 2 more cubes to your drawing from part a, so that the drawing has plane symmetry.
   How many different answers can you find?

Problem solving

1) Here is the plan view and elevations for a 3D shape.

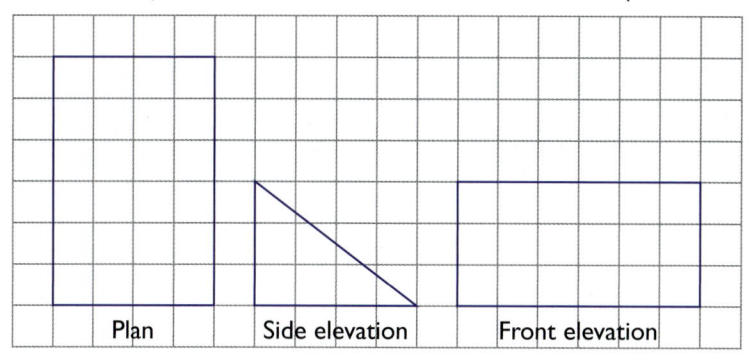

Plan Side elevation Front elevation

a Draw the 3D shape. What is the mathematical name for this shape?
b Find the volume of the 3D shape.
c Construct an accurate drawing of the net for the shape.
d Work out the surface area of the shape.

2) A child builds a shape out of multi-link cubes.
Here are the plan and elevations of the shape.

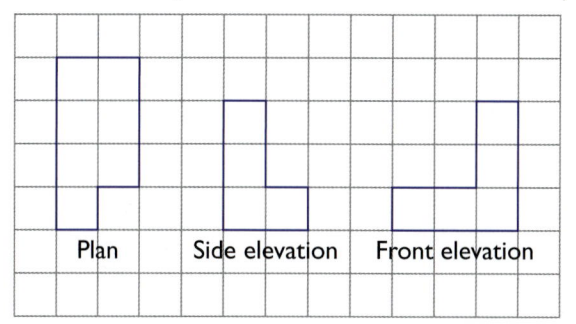

Plan Side elevation Front elevation

a Draw the 3D shape on isometric paper.
b Add one cube to your diagram so that the resulting shape has a plane of symmetry.

3) a Draw the plan, front and side elevations of this 3D shape.

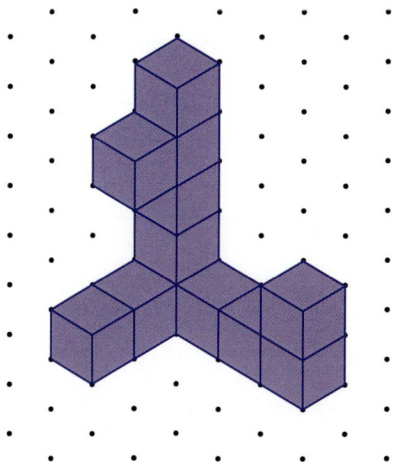

b Copy the 3D shape on isometric paper.
Add 3 cubes to your diagram so that the resulting shape has a plane of symmetry.

Geometry and Measures Strand 6 Three-dimensional shapes

Reviewing skills

1) This shape is made of cubes.
   Draw the shape viewed from the back.

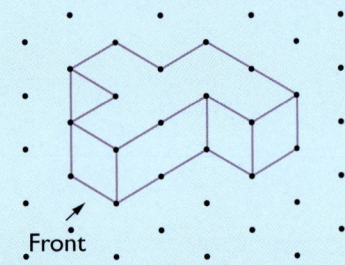

   Front

2) Make an isometric drawing of the shape shown in these views.

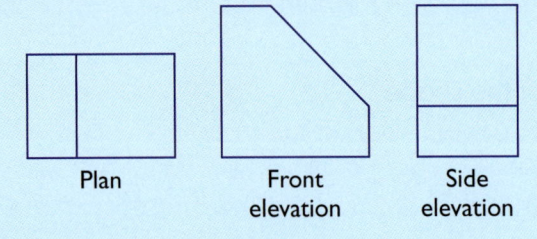

   Plan   Front   Side
           elevation elevation

3) This shape is made of 8 cubes.
   Draw the plan, front and side elevations of this shape.

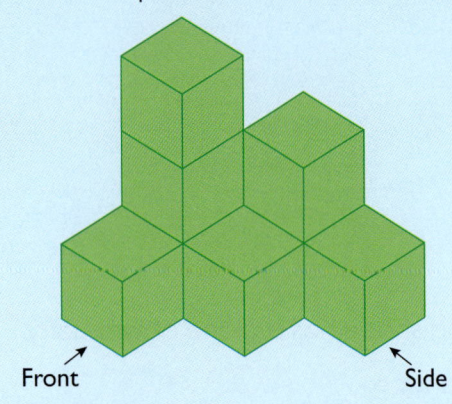

   Front   Side

Statistics and Probability
Strand 1 Statistical measures

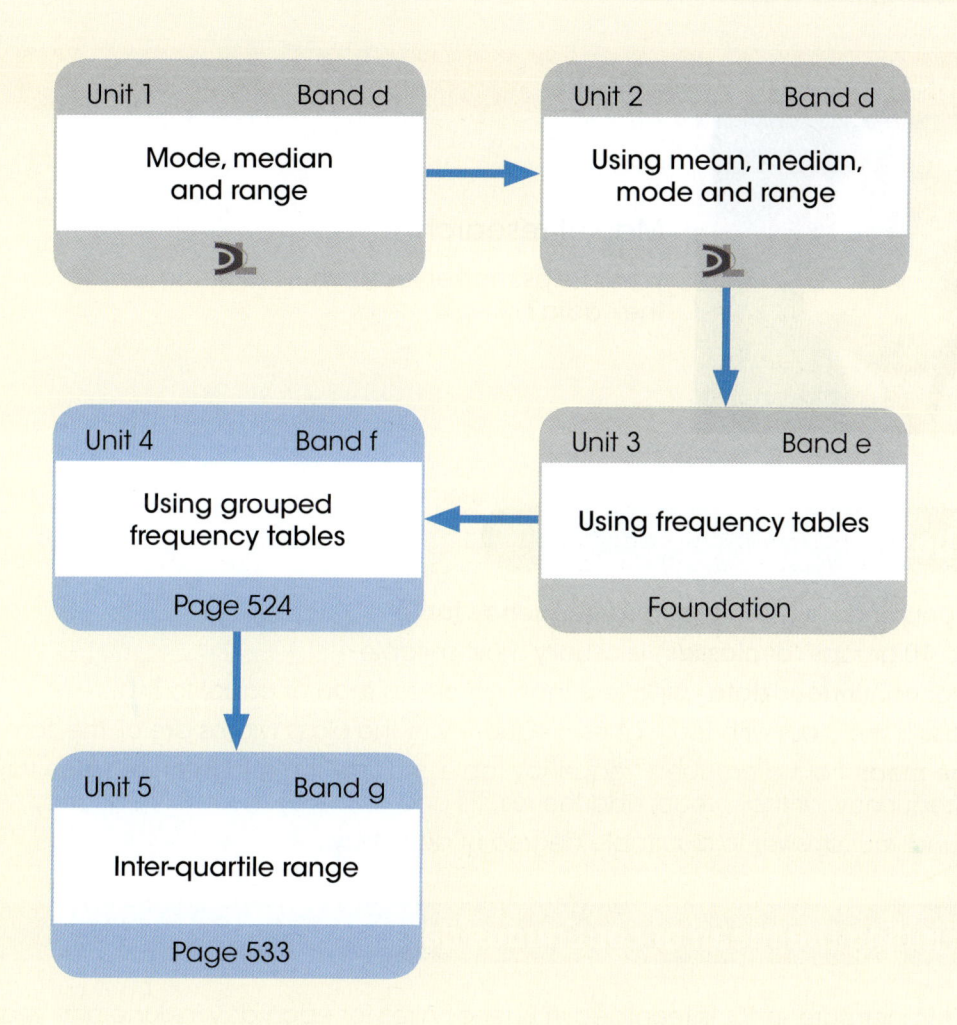

Unit 1 — Band d: Mode, median and range

Unit 2 — Band d: Using mean, median, mode and range

Unit 3 — Band e: Using frequency tables — Foundation

Unit 4 — Band f: Using grouped frequency tables — Page 524

Unit 5 — Band g: Inter-quartile range — Page 533

Units 1–3 are assumed knowledge for this book. Knowledge and skills from these units are used throughout the book.

Unit 4 • Using grouped frequency tables • Band f

Outside the Maths classroom

Market research
What helps market researchers make sense of their data?

Toolbox

For large amounts of data use a **grouped frequency table**.
Between 5 and 10 groups (or **classes**) is usually most suitable.
Show classes for **continuous data** using less than (<) or less than or equal to (≤).
The **modal class** is the class with the highest frequency (if the class widths are all the same).
To **estimate the mean** from a grouped frequency table, multiply the **mid-interval value** for each group by the frequency for that group, add the results and divide by the total frequency.
You should round your answer to a suitable degree of accuracy.

Example – Finding the mean of continuous data

The maximum temperature, in °C, is recorded in Buenos Aires for each day in June one year.

16.4	12.8	17.6	19.1	16.6	15.5
11.2	18.7	19.5	16.1	15.3	14.2
15.8	15.7	14.9	14.4	13.4	12.1
13.9	11.9	13.1	12.6	10.9	13.5
14.2	15.4	16.6	15.9	15.6	14.3

June

a Present these data in a grouped frequency table.
b Calculate an estimate for the mean temperature.

Temperature, T °C	Frequency, f	$m \times f$
$10 \leq T < 12$		
$12 \leq T < 14$		
$14 \leq T < 16$		
$16 \leq T < 18$		
$18 \leq T < 20$		

Solution

a

Temperature, T °C	Tally	Frequency
$10 \leq T < 12$	III	3
$12 \leq T < 14$	JHT II	7
$14 \leq T < 16$	JHT JHT II	12
$16 \leq T < 18$	JHT	5
$18 \leq T < 20$	III	3

b

Temperature, T °C	Midpoint, m	Frequency, f	$m \times f$
$10 \leq T < 12$	11	3	33
$12 \leq T < 14$	13	7	91
$14 \leq T < 16$	15	12	180
$16 \leq T < 18$	17	5	85
$18 \leq T < 20$	19	3	57
Totals		30	446

estimated mean = 446 ÷ 30 = 14.866 = 14.9 °C (1 d.p.)

Practising skills

1 The table shows the heights of 22 footballers about to play a match.

Height (cm), h	Frequency, f	Midpoint, m	$m \times f$
$150 \leq h < 156$	3		
$156 \leq h < 162$	6		
$162 \leq h < 168$	8		
$168 \leq h < 174$	3		
$174 \leq h < 180$	2		
Totals			

Copy and complete the table and use it to estimate the mean height of these footballers.

Statistics and Probability Strand 1 Statistical measures

2 Ruth's telephone bill shows the lengths, in minutes, of her last 20 calls.

47 min	30 min
19 min	44 min
32 min	18 min
41 min	12 min
57 min	24 min
28 min	36 min
9 min	42 min
17 min	16 min
46 min	32 min
33 min	29 min

a Copy and complete the frequency table.

Length of call (minutes), l	Frequency, f	Midpoint, m	$m \times f$
$0 \leqslant l < 10$			
$10 \leqslant l < 20$			
$20 \leqslant l < 30$			
$30 \leqslant l < 40$			
$40 \leqslant l < 50$			
$50 \leqslant l < 60$			
Totals			

b In which group does the median lie?

c Use the table to estimate the value of the mean.

3 A group of people do a puzzle as part of an aptitude test.
Here are the times (in seconds) that it takes them to solve the puzzle.

| 24 | 83 | 114 | 84 | 90 | 103 | 74 | 176 | 61 | 40 | 162 | 49 |
| 77 | 92 | 108 | 124 | 185 | 89 | 63 | 79 | 37 | 91 | 65 | 19 |

a i Find the times of the first and the last people to solve the puzzle.
  ii What is the range?

b Find the median for this data set.

c Copy and complete the frequency table.

Time (seconds), t	Frequency, f	Midpoint, m	$m \times f$
$0 \leqslant t < 40$			
$40 \leqslant t < 80$			
$80 \leqslant t < 120$			
$120 \leqslant t < 160$			
$160 \leqslant t < 200$			
Totals			

d In which group does the median lie?

e Use the table to estimate the value of the mean.

f The fastest 25% of the group are accepted and the slowest 25% are failed. The others have to do more tests.
What can you say about the marks of those who do more tests?

4 A speed camera recorded the speed of cars, v mph, on a road through a housing estate. Here are the results.

Speed (mph), v	Frequency, f	Midpoint, m	$m \times f$
$0 \leqslant v < 20$	13		
$20 \leqslant v < 30$	22		
$30 \leqslant v < 40$	4		
$40 \leqslant v < 60$	1		
Totals			

a Complete a copy of the table and use it to estimate the mean speed.
b What do you think the speed limit is?

Local residents say that any speed above 25 mph is unsafe.
c Estimate the percentage of cars that are travelling at 25 mph or faster.

5 A group of students record how many hours each week they spend on homework. Here are their results.

Hours, h	$0 \leqslant h < 8$	$8 \leqslant h < 12$	$12 \leqslant h < 16$	$16 \leqslant h < 20$
Frequency	18	14	9	4

a Estimate the mean number of hours a student spends doing homework.
b Most students do homework on six days. What is the average amount of homework they do each day?

Developing fluency

1 A sports centre records how many people use its facilities each day. Here are the results.

32　71　64　28　66　128　184　94　47　104
95　73　69　80　115　162　106　82　73　118

a Find the mean and the median for this data set.
b Copy and complete the frequency table.

Number of people, n	Frequency, f	Midpoint, m	$m \times f$
$0 \leqslant n < 50$			
$50 \leqslant n < 100$			
$100 \leqslant n < 150$			
$150 \leqslant n < 200$			
Totals			

c In which group does the median lie?
d Use the table to estimate the value of the mean.
e Compare your answers for parts **c** and **d** with those for part **a**.
f In what circumstances would you use an estimate of the mean and when would you need to calculate it exactly?

Statistics and Probability Strand 1 Statistical measures

2 A running club records the time members take to complete a cross-country race.

Time (minutes), t	Frequency, f	Midpoint, m	$m \times f$
$0 \leqslant t < 20$	1		
$20 \leqslant t < 30$	8		
$30 \leqslant t < 40$	14		
$40 \leqslant t < 50$	7		
Totals			

a Copy and complete the table and use it to estimate the mean time.

b What can you say about the range?

c Another club had a mean of 27.9 minutes and a range of 55 minutes. Compare the performance of the two clubs.

3 Harry travels to work by train.

He records the time, in minutes, that he waits for the train.

Waiting time (minutes), t	Frequency, f
$0 \leqslant t < 5$	6
$5 \leqslant t < 10$	5
$10 \leqslant t < 15$	11
$20 \leqslant t < 25$	9
$25 \leqslant t < 30$	4
Total	

a Complete a copy of the table, with any extra columns, and use it to estimate the mean waiting time.

b How many times does Harry have to wait at least 20 minutes?

c One day the waiting time was 72 minutes.

Can you explain what might have happened? Why did Harry exclude this time from his calculation?

4 The table shows the distance jumped by long jumpers at a school sports day.

Distance (metres), d	Frequency, f	Midpoint, m	$m \times f$
$0 \leqslant d < 2$	6		
$2 \leqslant d < 3$	12		
$3 \leqslant d < 4$	9		
$4 \leqslant d < 5$	8		
Total			

a Complete a copy of the table and use it to estimate the mean distance jumped.

b There were 14 jumpers and they had 3 jumps each. How many foul jumps were there?

c The qualification for the school team is a jump over 4.5 m.

What can you say about the number who qualified?

Unit 4 Using grouped frequency tables Band f

5 Alan plants two types of early potato, A and B. He weighs the potatoes, w grams, that each plant produces.
The results are summarised in this table.

	$700 \leq w < 750$	$750 \leq w < 800$	$800 \leq w < 850$	$850 \leq w < 900$	$900 \leq w < 950$	$950 \leq w < 1000$
A	5	8	4	2	5	0
B	2	4	5	7	3	3

Compare the yields of the two types of potatoes.

6 A small firm employs 25 people.

Salary, £s	Number of people
$0 \leq s < 10000$	6
$10000 \leq s < 20000$	11
$20000 \leq s < 30000$	5
$30000 \leq s < 40000$	2
$40000 \leq s < 50000$	1

The managing director is considering three schemes to increase the employees' pay.
Scheme 1: Give everyone a 5% increase on their current salary.
Scheme 2: Find 5% of the mean salary and increase all salaries by this amount.
Scheme 3: Find 5% of the median salary and increase all salaries by this amount.

a Copy and complete the table below to find out how much Sandra, Shameet and Comfort would earn under each scheme.

	Current salary	Scheme 1 increase	Scheme 2 increase	Scheme 3 increase
Sandra	£8000			
Shameet	£2200			
Comfort	£3600			

b Which member of staff would benefit most from each scheme?

c Which scheme do you think the managing director should use?
Give a reason for your answer.

Problem solving

1 An IT company give all applicants for a vacancy an aptitude test.
The applicants score s marks on the test.
The table shows the results.

Score, s	Frequency, f	Midpoint, m	$m \times f$
$0 \leq s < 10$	11		
$10 \leq s < 20$	6		
$20 \leq s < 30$	12		
$30 \leq s < 40$	10		
$40 \leq s < 50$	9		
Totals			

Statistics and Probability Strand 1 Statistical measures

    a Calculate an estimate of the mean mark.

    b The IT company interview all applicants who achieved 5 marks more than the mean. Estimate how many applicants were interviewed.

    c Explain why your answers are estimates.

2 The grouped frequency table gives information about the distance that 100 commuters travel to work.

Distance travelled, d km	Frequency, f	Midpoint, m	$m \times f$
$20 < d \leq 30$	6	25	
$30 < d \leq 40$			420
$40 < d \leq 50$	20	45	900
$50 < d \leq 60$			
$60 < d \leq 70$	11		715
Total	75	Total	

    a Copy and complete the table.

    b In which group does the median lie?

    c Estimate the mean distance travelled by the commuters.

    d A commuter expects that their journey will take $1\frac{1}{2}$ minutes for every kilometre commuted. Estimate the mean time spent commuting.

3 Chloe buys an IQ testing puzzle which she tests out on her friends.
She times how long each person takes to solve the puzzle.
The frequency table shows Chloe's results.

Time, t minutes	Frequency, f
$0 < t \leq 10$	5
$10 < t \leq 15$	6
$15 < t \leq 20$	8
$20 < t \leq 25$	18
$25 < t \leq 30$	13

    a What is the modal class?

    b Estimate the range of the data.

    c Estimate the mean time to solve the puzzle.

    d The puzzle carries this statement:
       'Are you a genius? You are if you can solve me in less than 10 minutes!'
       Comment on the statement.

4 A doctors' surgery surveys a group of adult male patients to find out their heights.
Here is a frequency table of the results.

Height in cm	Frequency
$150 < h \leq 160$	4
$160 < h \leq 170$	20
$170 < h \leq 180$	52
$180 < h \leq 190$	17
$190 < h \leq 200$	5
$200 < h \leq 210$	2

a How many people took part in the survey?

b In which class does the median lie?

c Dr Smith says the range of heights is 60 cm.
Is Dr Smith correct? Give a reason for your answer.

d Estimate the mean height of the patients.

Dr Smith decides a patient is classified as tall if he is 9.5 cm taller than the mean.

e Estimate the percentage of tall patients at the surgery.

5 The production team for a TV quiz show run a general knowledge test to identify suitable contestants.
The table below shows the number of correct answers from a group of hopeful contestants.

Number of correct answers, c	Frequency
$30 < c \leq 40$	41
$40 < c \leq 50$	16
$50 < c \leq 60$	10
$60 < c \leq 70$	7
$70 < c \leq 80$	8
$80 < c \leq 90$	10
$90 < c \leq 100$	8
Total	

a What is the modal group?

b In which group does the median fall?

c Estimate the mean number of correct answers.

The test has 100 questions.

A correct answer scores 2 points, an incorrect or missing answer scores −1 point.

d Estimate the mean score.

Contestants need a score of 125 or more to appear on the television show.

e Estimate the probability that a randomly chosen person will be selected for the show.

Statistics and Probability Strand 1 Statistical measures

6 A teacher wants to compare the performance of two different classes, X1 and Y1.
This table shows the results m% of a recent test.

Percentage	$0 < m \leq 20$	$20 < m \leq 40$	$40 < m \leq 60$	$60 < m \leq 80$	$80 < m \leq 100$
X1	2	5	11	9	3
Y1	6	4	3	9	8

Which class do you think is better? Explain your answer.

Reviewing skills

1 A group of people take an aptitude test for a flying school. Here are the results.

Score, s	Midpoint, m	Frequency, f	$m \times f$
$0 \leq s < 20$		6	
$20 \leq s < 40$		8	
$40 \leq s < 60$		15	
$60 \leq s < 80$		14	
$80 \leq s < 100$		5	
Totals			

a Complete a copy of the table and use it to estimate the mean score.
b The pass mark for the flying school is 75. Estimate how many people passed.
c The lowest $\frac{1}{3}$ of the group of people are told they cannot try again.

What can you say about the marks of this group?

Unit 5 • Inter-quartile range • Band g

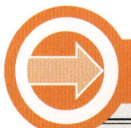

Outside the Maths classroom

THE NEWS
Too many toddlers underweight

Government targets
How does the goverment measure data on health?

Toolbox

The median and quartiles divide the data set into four equal groups.
The difference between the upper and lower quartile is called the **inter-quartile range**.
A **box and whisker diagram** shows the range of the data, the medians and the quartiles.
It is a useful diagram for comparing distributions.

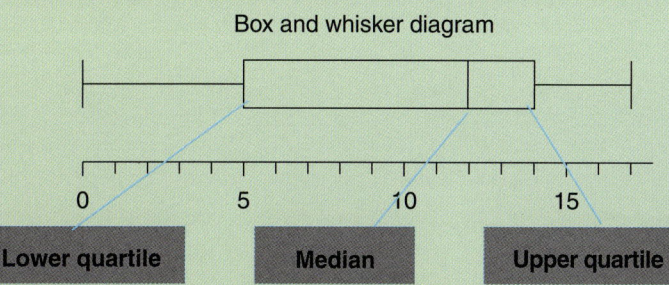

Box and whisker diagram

Lower quartile — Median — Upper quartile

You can use a **cumulative frequency graph** to find estimates for grouped data.

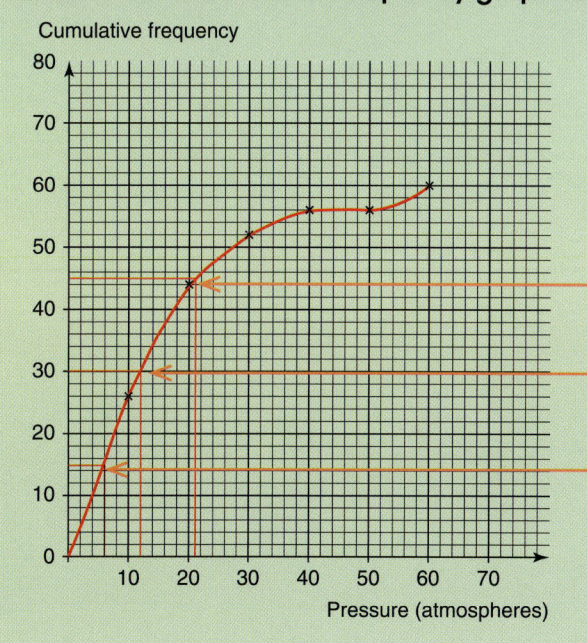

Upper quartile is 21 ($\frac{3}{4}$ of 60 = 45)

Median is 12 ($\frac{1}{2}$ of 60 = 30)

Lower quartile is 6 ($\frac{1}{4}$ of 60 = 15)

Pressure (atmospheres)

Statistics and Probability Strand 1 Statistical measures

Example – Drawing a box plot

Avonford High School holds a Sports Day every summer. This cumulative frequency graph shows the results from the Year 8 boys' shot putt.

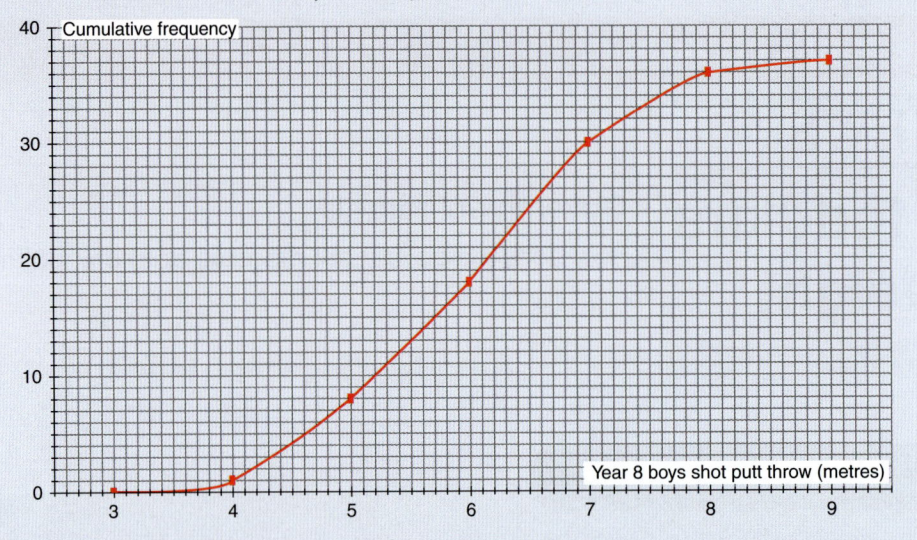

a Use the graph to find the median and quartiles for these results.
b Draw a box and whisker diagram and use it to find the inter-quartile range.

Unit 5 Inter-quartile range Band g

Example – Drawing a box plot

Solution

a The total frequency is 37 so the median is found by drawing a line from 18.5 on the cumulative frequency axis to the curve and down. It is 6.05 m.

The quartiles are found by dividing the cumulative frequency in half again, giving cumulative frequency values of 9.25 and 27.75.

The lower quartile is 5.15 m and the upper quartile is 6.75 m.

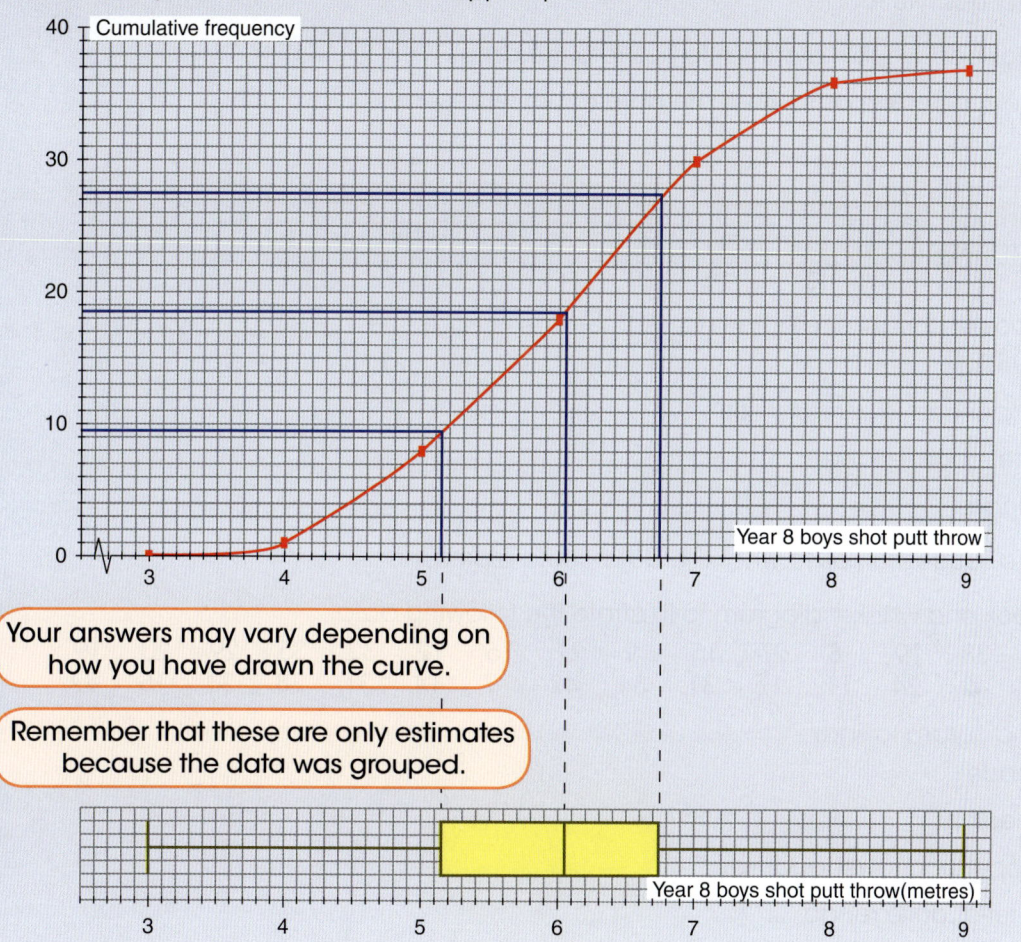

Your answers may vary depending on how you have drawn the curve.

Remember that these are only estimates because the data was grouped.

b The inter-quartile range is 6.75 − 5.15 = 1.6 m

Statistics and Probability Strand 1 Statistical measures

Practising skills

1 Look at this data set.

18 27 19 38 31 23 29 14 23 45 26 38 34 29 20

   a Find:
     i the median
     ii the upper and lower quartiles
     iii the inter-quartile range.

   b Draw a box and whisker diagram to illustrate the data.

   c Make one suggestion as to what the data could represent.

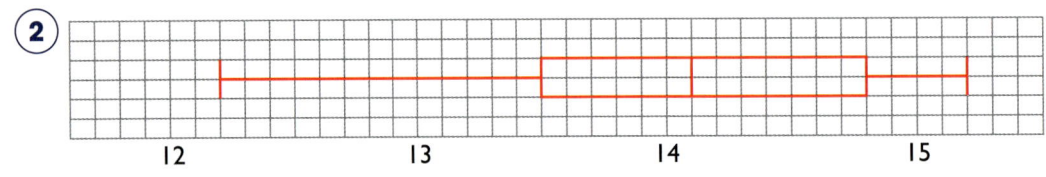

2

   a Use the box and whisker diagram to find:
     i the median
     ii the upper and lower quartiles
     iii the inter-quartile range
     iv the range.

   b Make one suggestion as to what the data could represent.

3 a Draw a box and whisker diagram to illustrate the following data.

24 16 38 19 8 27 15 9 27 16 12 32 35 29 20 19
7 12 42 24 11 17 31 34 42 7 14 31 38 23 15 42

   b Use your diagram to find:
     i the mode
     ii the median
     iii the upper and lower quartiles
     iv the inter-quartile range
     v the range.

Unit 5 Inter-quartile range Band g

4) The table shows the height of trees in a small plantation.

Height, h (feet)	$0 < h \leq 10$	$10 < h \leq 20$	$20 < h \leq 30$	$30 < h \leq 40$	$40 < h \leq 50$	$50 < h \leq 60$
Frequency	6	12	17	12	9	4

a Complete this cumulative frequency table.

Height, h (feet)	$h \leq 10$	$h \leq 20$	$h \leq 30$	$h \leq 40$	$h \leq 50$	$h \leq 60$
Frequency	6	18	35			

b Draw the cumulative frequency graph.

c Use the graph to estimate:
   i the median
   ii the inter-quartile range.

d The forester decides to cut down the smallest 20 trees to thin out the wood. Estimate the height of the smallest tree left standing.

5) The table shows the time, in minutes, to complete the journey to work for the employees of a company.

Time, t (min)	$0 < t \leq 10$	$10 < t \leq 20$	$20 < t \leq 30$	$30 < t \leq 40$	$40 < t \leq 50$	$50 < t \leq 60$
Frequency	3	8	15	6	7	3

a Draw the cumulative frequency graph.

b Use the graph to estimate:
   i the median
   ii the inter-quartile range.

c Five years ago the median was 22.3 minutes and the inter-quartile range was 23.4 minutes. How has the journey to work changed? Suggest a possible explanation.

d One day the median time was 24 minutes, the upper quartile was 50 minutes and the greatest value was 75 minutes. Suggest what might have happened.

Statistics and Probability Strand 1 Statistical measures

Developing fluency

1 The traffic police recorded the speeds of a number of cars on a motorway. The results are shown on this cumulative frequency graph.

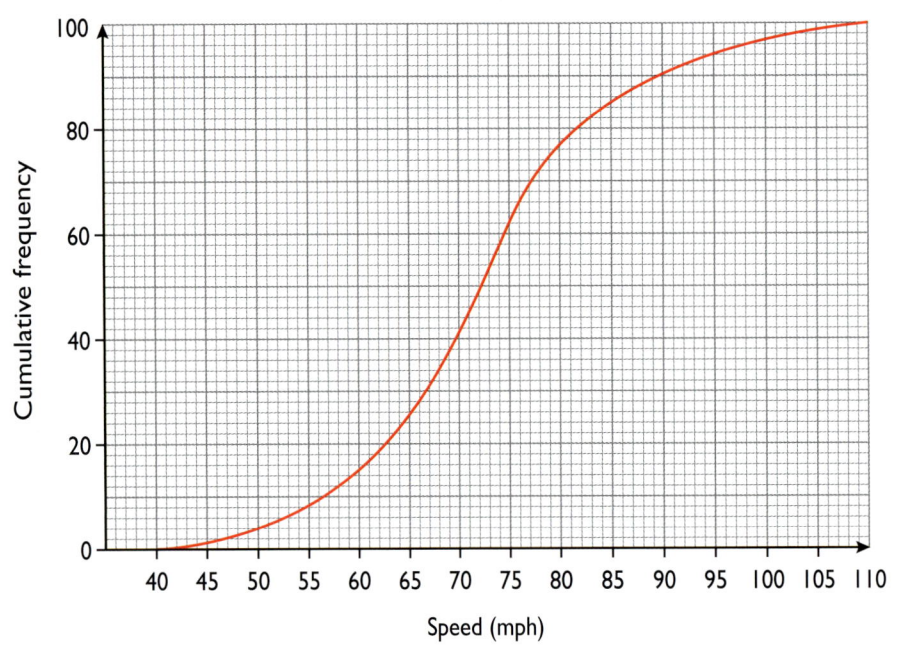

a How many cars did the police test?

b Estimate the median and quartiles of the speeds.

c Between what speeds were the middle half travelling?

d Estimate the percentage of the cars that were exceeding the speed limit of 70 mph.

e Cars travelling very fast or very slow are reckoned to be dangerous. Estimate how many of the cars were travelling at either 55 mph or less, or 90 mph or more.

2 Data were collected on the weekly rainfall, in millimetres, in two towns, over one year.

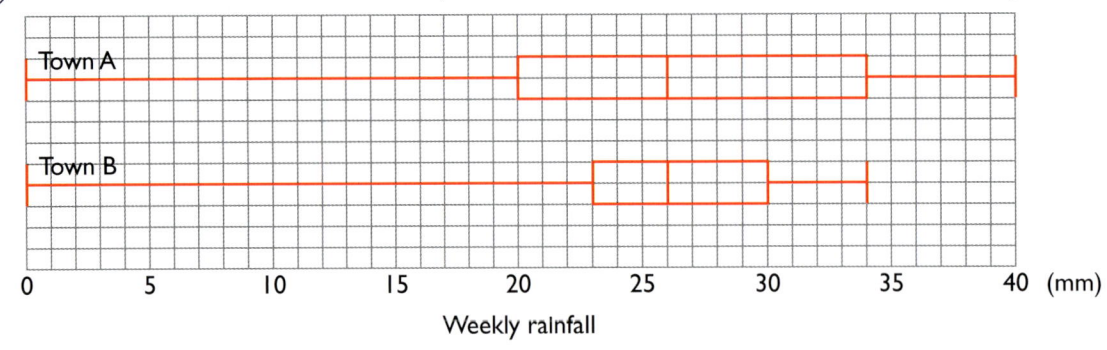

a Write down the median and the inter-quartile range for each town.

b Compare the weekly rainfall in both towns.

c If the data were collected over 10 years, would the box and whisker plots be exactly the same as those shown here? Explain your answer.

Unit 5 Inter-quartile range Band g

3 Here is a summary of the 100 m times, in seconds, for the members of an athletic club.

Time, t (s)	Frequency
$10.5 \leq t < 10.6$	1
$10.6 \leq t < 10.7$	3
$10.7 \leq t < 10.8$	8
$10.8 \leq t < 10.9$	14
$10.9 \leq t < 11.0$	17
$11.0 \leq t < 11.1$	7
$11.1 \leq t < 11.2$	4

a Make a cumulative frequency table.
b Draw the cumulative frequency graph.
c Use your graph to estimate the median and the inter-quartile range.
d Those taking less than 10.84 seconds can enter the county trials. How many members of the club qualified for the trials?

4 The table shows the weight by gender of all babies born in a hospital one month.

Weight, w (kg)	Frequency (boys)	Frequency (girls)
$2.6 \leq w < 2.8$	6	9
$2.8 \leq w < 3.0$	15	12
$3.0 \leq w < 3.2$	19	28
$3.2 \leq w < 3.4$	27	37
$3.4 \leq w < 3.6$	35	24
$3.6 \leq w < 3.8$	21	8
$3.8 \leq w < 4.0$	7	2

a Make a cumulative frequency table for each set of data.
   Draw the cumulative frequency curve for both sets on the same sheet of graph paper.
b Find the median and the inter-quartile range for each set of data and display them in a box and whisker plot.
c Compare the weights of the boy babies and the girl babies.
d A baby weighs 4.2 kg. Can you say whether it is a boy or a girl?

5 A large number of crews enter for a rowing event on a river. They row a certain distance, then they turn round and row back. The winner has the lowest total time for the two parts.
The table shows the times, in minutes, of boats on the first part.

Times, t (min)	$8 < t \leq 10$	$10 < t \leq 12$	$12 < t \leq 14$	$14 < t \leq 16$	$16 < t \leq 18$	$18 < t \leq 20$
Frequency	4	7	15	14	8	2

a Draw the cumulative frequency graph.
b Use your graph to estimate the median and the inter-quartile range for the first part.
c Twelve veteran crews entered the race and they were the twelve slowest over this part. Estimate the time for the fastest veteran crew.
d The second part has a median time of 10 minutes and an inter-quartile range of 3.5 minutes. Compare the two parts. Suggest a reason for the difference in the times.

Statistics and Probability Strand 1 Statistical measures

6 Say whether the following statements are true or false and justify your answers.
   a It is quite often the case that about half the data lie between the two quartiles.
   b The range is twice the inter-quartile range.
   c A box and whisker plot divides the data into four graphs with equal frequencies.
   d A cumulative frequency graph always goes from bottom left to top right and never has a negative gradient.
   e The median is midway between the lower quartile and the upper quartile.

7 At a county show there is a race for family pet dogs.
Some owners also take part. Their times are as follows

Time, t (s)	Frequency (dogs)	Frequency (owners)
$90 \leq t < 120$	1	0
$120 \leq t < 150$	5	0
$150 \leq t < 180$	27	2
$180 \leq t < 210$	12	5
$210 \leq t < 360$	3	9
$360 \leq t < 480$	0	14

   a What is the modal class for the dogs?
   b Copy the table and add columns for cumulative frequency.
   c Draw the two cumulative frequency curves on the same sheet of graph paper.
   d Estimate the median and the inter-quartile range for the dogs.
   e A rosette is awarded for the first five dogs and the first five owners.
      Estimate the greatest times of the rosette winners.
   f Compare the distributions of the dogs' and the owners' times.

Problem solving

1 A number of people took an aptitude test. Their scores are shown on the cumulative frequency graph.

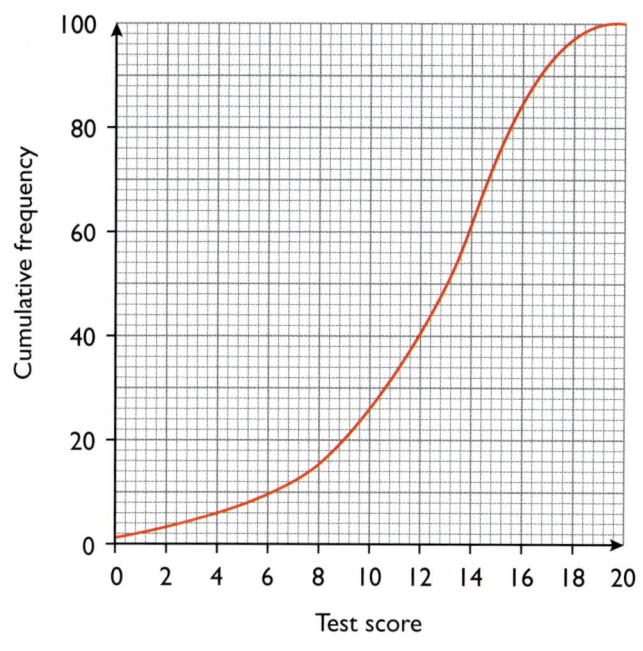

a How many people took the test?

b What can you say about the total mark for the test?

c James says 'My score of 15 puts me in the top 25% of the test.'
Is James right? Explain your answer.

2 Solomon has a moth trap. During one summer he captures 80 specimens of a particular type of moth. He records their wingspan and then lets them go free.
The results are shown in this cumulative frequency graph.

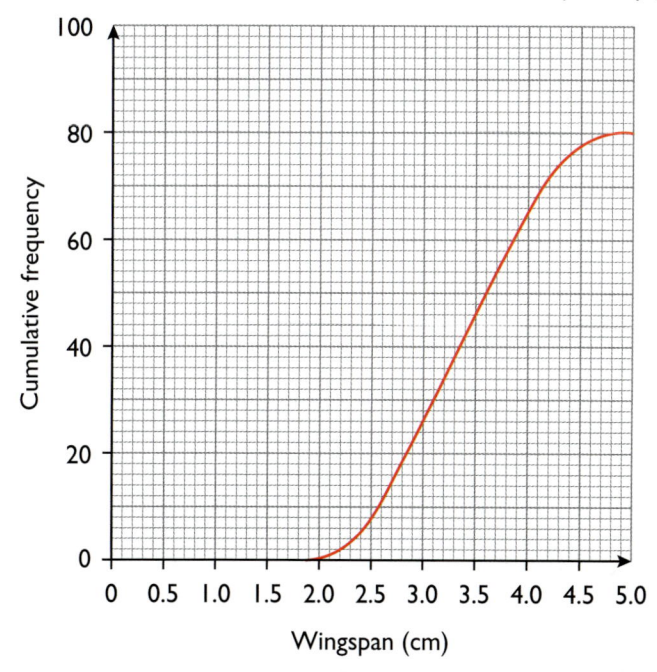

Statistics and Probability Strand 1 Statistical measures

a Use the graph to estimate the median wingspan.

b i Complete this table.

Wing span, w (cm)	$2.0 < w \leq 2.5$	$2.5 < w \leq 3.0$	$3.0 < w \leq 3.5$	$3.5 < w \leq 4.0$	$4.0 < w \leq 4.5$	$4.5 < w \leq 5.0$
Frequency	8	18				

ii Hence estimate the mean wingspan of the moths.

3) Some members of a hockey club took part in a 100 m trial. The cumulative frequency graphs show the times they took.

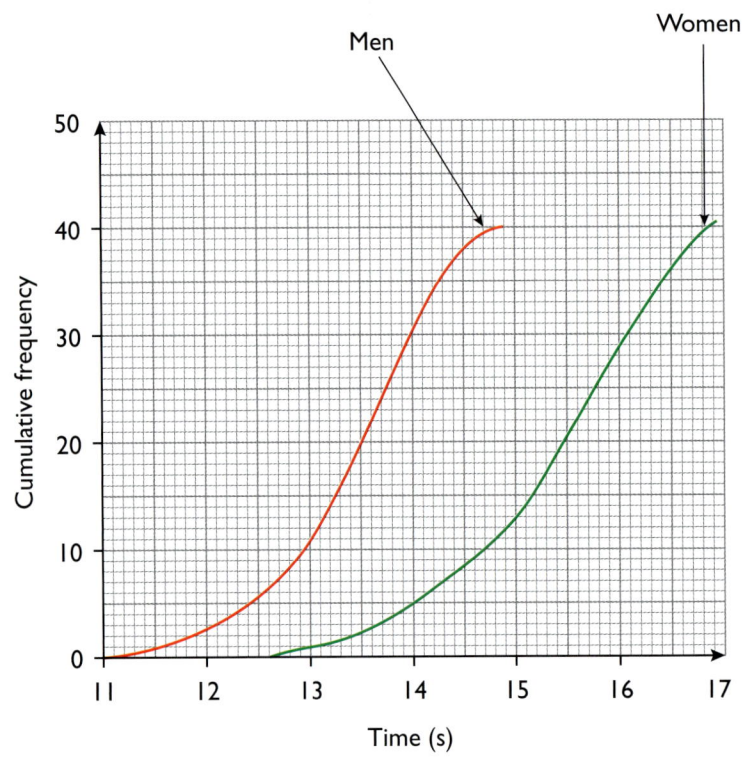

a How many people in total took part?

b Find the median, the upper quartile and the lower quartile for:
  i the men
  ii the women.

c Find the times of the fastest woman and the slowest man.

d How many men did the fastest woman beat?

e How many women beat the slowest man?

Unit 5 Inter-quartile range Band g

4) The box and whisker diagrams show the distribution of the weights of adult female and adult male elephants.

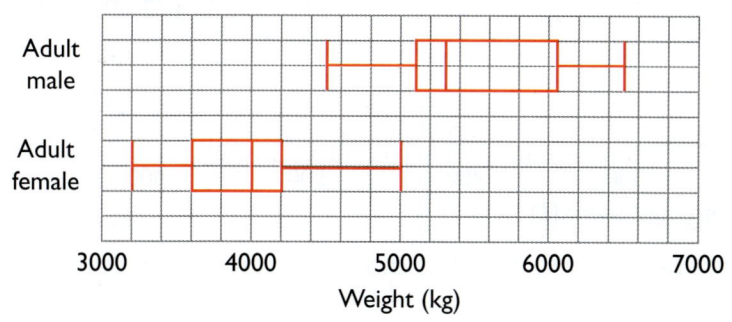

Compare the distribution of the weights of the adult male elephants with the distribution of the weights of the female elephants.

5) The box and whisker diagrams summarise the results of a medical study.
One group received a drug to aid recovery, the other group did not.

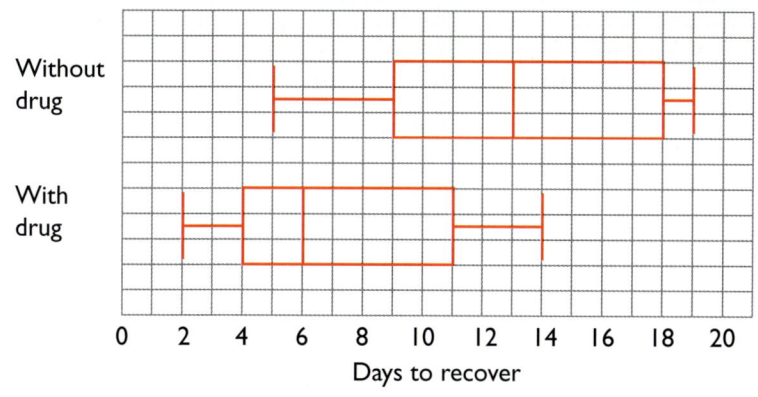

Compare and comment fully on the two distributions.

6) Maria carries out a survey to find out how much families spent on days out during the Easter holidays.
Here are her results.

Amount spent, A (£)	Frequency
$0 < A \leq 50$	3
$50 < A \leq 100$	6
$100 < A \leq 150$	12
$150 < A \leq 200$	17
$200 < A \leq 250$	28
$250 < A \leq 300$	16
$300 < A \leq 350$	11
$350 < A \leq 400$	7

a Draw a cumulative frequency graph for these data.

b Use your cumulative frequency graph to estimate:
  i the median
  ii the inter-quartile range.

c Maria surveys the same families to find out how much they spent on days out during the Christmas holidays.

543

Statistics and Probability Strand 1 Statistical measures

Here is a box and whisker diagram of her results.

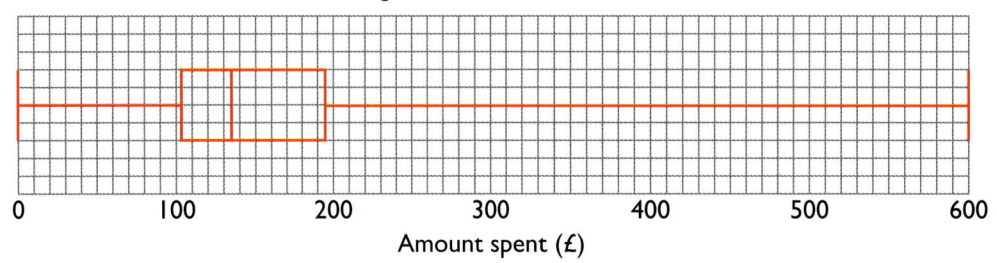

Amount spent (£)

Compare the amount of money spent during the Christmas holidays with the Easter holidays.

(7) The incomplete table of values and corresponding box plot show information about the length of time that a group of people took to solve a puzzle.

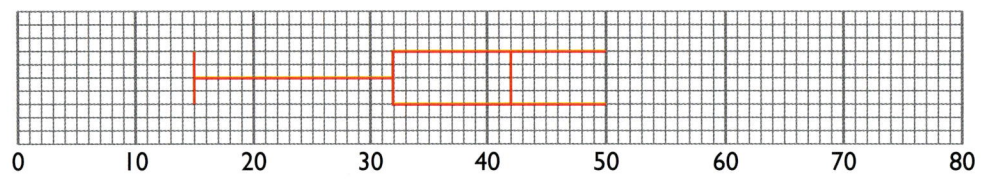

Slowest time	
Fastest time	
Range	63 minutes
Median	
Upper quartile	
Lower quartile	
Inter-quartile range	22 minutes

Copy and complete the table and the box plot.

Reviewing skills

1 A manager records the time at which employees arrive at work.

She records the number of minutes after 8.30 a.m. that each employee arrives. Here are her results.

Time after 8.30 a.m., t (min)	Number of employees
$0 \leq t < 5$	3
$5 \leq t < 10$	15
$10 \leq t < 15$	24
$15 \leq t < 20$	36
$20 \leq t < 25$	32
$25 \leq t < 30$	12
$30 \leq t < 35$	6
$35 \leq t < 40$	2

a Draw a cumulative frequency graph.

b Estimate the median arrival time.

c Estimate:

  i the lower quartile

  ii the inter-quartile range.

d Harry is the tenth person to arrive at work. Estimate his time of arrival.

e The manager marks an employee as late when they arrive after 9.02 a.m. Estimate the number of late employees.

Statistics and Probability
Strand 2 Statistical diagrams

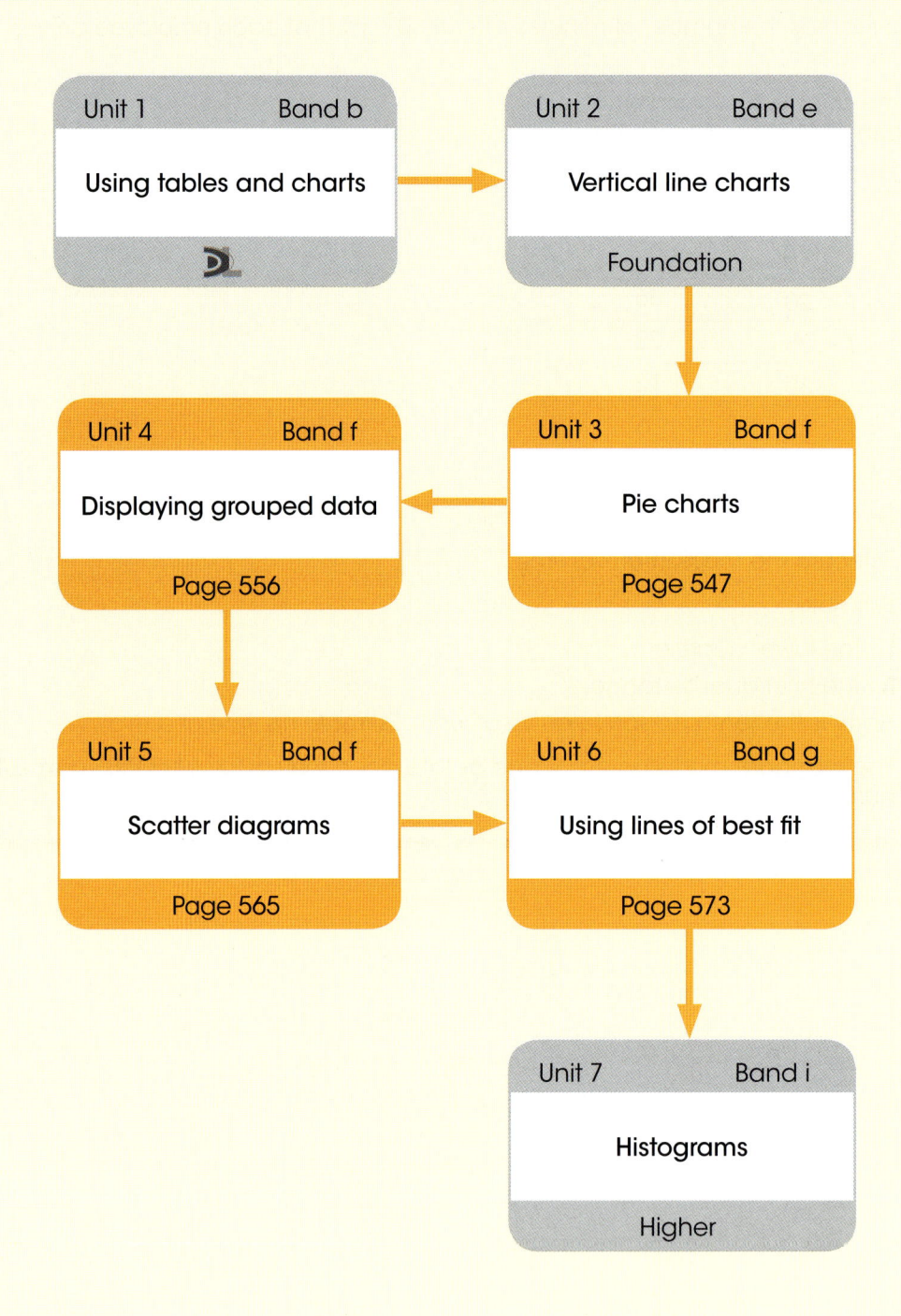

Unit 1	Band b
Using tables and charts	

Foundation

Unit 2	Band e
Vertical line charts	

Foundation

Unit 4	Band f
Displaying grouped data	

Page 556

Unit 3	Band f
Pie charts	

Page 547

Unit 5	Band f
Scatter diagrams	

Page 565

Unit 6	Band g
Using lines of best fit	

Page 573

Unit 7	Band i
Histograms	

Higher

Units 1–2 are assumed knowledge for this book. Knowledge and skills from these units are used throughout the book.

Unit 3 • Pie charts • Band f

Outside the Maths classroom

Budgeting

Why is a pie chart a good way to illustrate how you spend your money?

Toolbox

A pie chart shows the parts of a whole.

This pie chart shows that $\frac{1}{2}$ of the crisps sold were cheese and onion and $\frac{1}{4}$ were ready salted. The other two flavours are both the same size and take up $\frac{1}{4}$ of the pie chart in total. This means that they are each half of $\frac{1}{4}$, that is $\frac{1}{8}$.

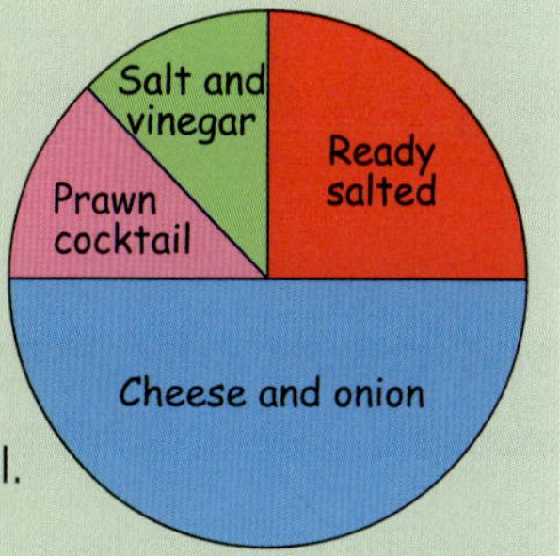

To find the size of each sector, find the angle that represents one individual. That is 360° divided by the total. Then multiply by the frequency for each category.

The data show which of four television channels thirty people were watching on Monday evening.

	BBC1	BBC2	ITV1	ITV3	Totals
Frequency	11	6	5	8	**30**
Pie chart angle	132°	72°	60°	96°	**360°**

360 ÷ 30 = 12° for one person, 12 × 11 = 132°

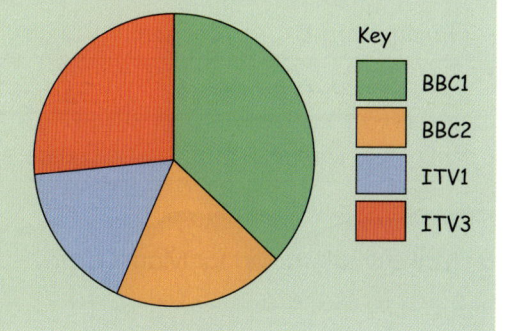

547

Example – Reading a pie chart

These pie charts show information about two football teams in the same season.

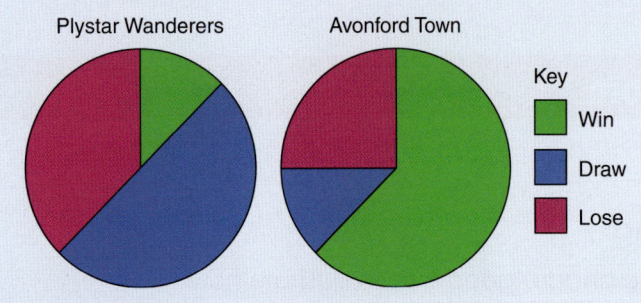

Plystar Wanderers   Avonford Town

Key
- Win
- Draw
- Lose

a Which team played better?
b What fraction of their matches did Plystar Wanderers draw?
c i What fraction of their matches did Avonford Town lose?
  ii Which angle is used to show this?
d Each team has played 32 matches. How many matches did Avonford Town lose?

Solution

a Avonford Town, as their pie chart shows a greater proportion of wins.
b $\frac{1}{2}$
c i $\frac{1}{4}$ ii $\frac{1}{4}$ of 360° = 90°
d $\frac{1}{4}$ of 32 = 8 matches

Example – Drawing a pie chart

Mark has made a list of the favourite type of music of his friends.

Dance	Pop	RnB	Dance	RnB	RnB	Dance	RnB
RnB	RnB	RnB	Garage	RnB	Pop	Dance	
Garage	RnB	Garage	Dance	RnB	Dance	RnB	
RnB	RnB	RnB	Garage	Pop	RnB	Pop	
RnB	Dance	RnB	Dance	Pop	RnB	Dance	

a Make a tally chart for Mark's data.

Mark draws this pie chart to show the data.

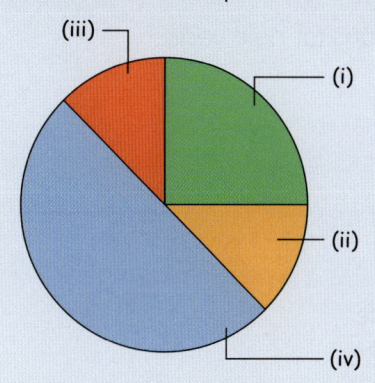

b What angle represents one person?
c Copy the pie chart and label each section with the correct type of music.
d What fraction chose Dance?
e What is the angle for Pop?
f What is the angle for RnB?

Solution

a

Favourite music	Tally	Frequency
Dance	卌 IIII	9
Pop	卌	5
RnB	卌 卌 卌 III	18
Garage	IIII	4
Total		**36**

b There are 36 people. The angle for each person is 360 ÷ 36 = 10
c i Green - Dance
  ii Orange - Pop
  iii Red - Garage
  iv Blue - RnB

d $\frac{9}{36} = \frac{1}{4}$
e 10° × 5 = 50°
f 10° × 18 = 180°

Statistics and Probability Strand 2 Statistical diagrams

Practising skills

1. Students in Abermawr School Year 13 were asked about their plans for next year. The pie chart shows their replies.

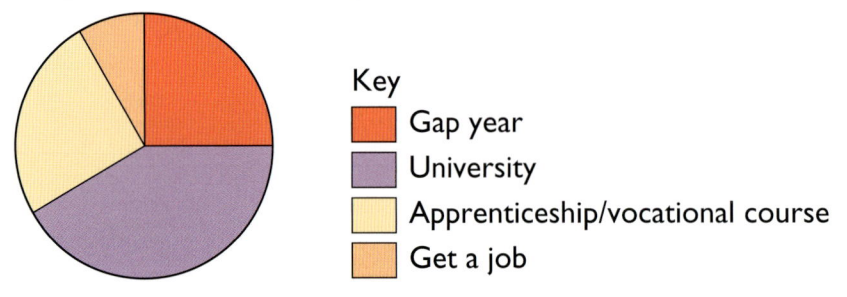

   Key
   - Gap year
   - University
   - Apprenticeship/vocational course
   - Get a job

   a Which option is the most popular choice?
   b What is the angle for gap year?
   c What fraction of the whole year choose gap year?
   d There are 168 students in Year 13.
      How many choose each of the four options?

2. A sample of people were asked which of the following best described their diet.

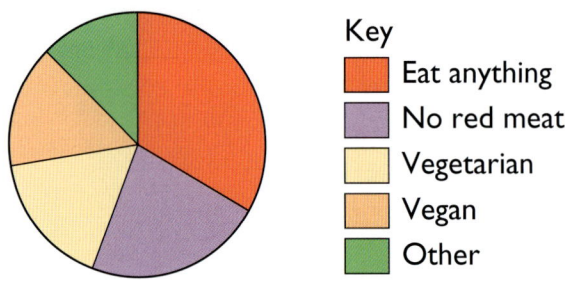

   Key
   - Eat anything
   - No red meat
   - Vegetarian
   - Vegan
   - Other

   a Which is the most popular option?
   b What is the angle for vegetarian?
   c What fraction chose the vegetarian option?
   d There were 120 people in the sample. How many chose each of the options?

3. A rail user group do a small survey of how people get to their local station. Here are their results.

Method	Walk	Bus	Taxi	Own car	Lift
Frequency	10	5	6	14	5

   They want to show the results on a pie chart.

   a How many degrees should they use for one person?
   b Draw the pie chart.
   c The rail user group are campaigning for more car parking space.
      1200 people use the station each day. How many of them do you expect to need a parking space?

Unit 3 Pie charts Band f

4 Jamini is a cat. Her owners watch how she spends her day.

Activity	Sleep	Prowling	Eating	Grooming
Time (hours)	16	5	1	2

They show this on a pie chart.

 a How many degrees do they use for one hour?

 b Draw the pie chart to show how Jamini spends her day.

 c Jamini's owners watch her some more. They decide that she spends $\frac{1}{2}$ an hour playing, $6\frac{1}{2}$ hours prowling and less time sleeping.
Describe the changes they must make to the pie chart.

5 The bar chart shows the types of drink that Sally sold in her café one day.

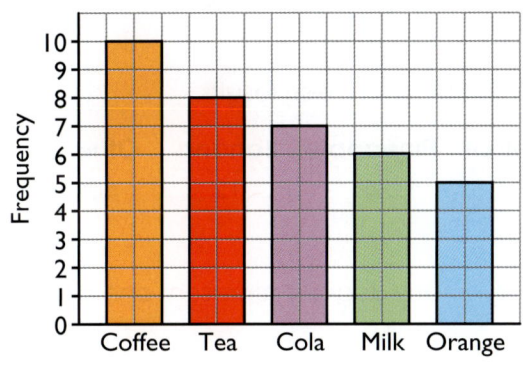

 a Draw a pie chart to show this information.

 b Which diagram do you find more helpful, the bar chart or the pie chart?

Developing fluency

1 This pie chart shows the favourite sports of 30 students.

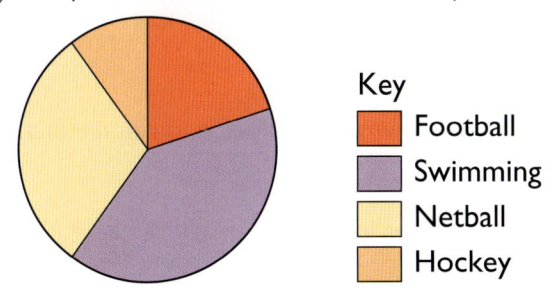

Key
- Football
- Swimming
- Netball
- Hockey

 a Which sport is the most popular choice?

 b What is the angle for the choice of football?

 c What fraction of the 30 students chose football?
What is this as a percentage?

There were actually 40 students in the group. Three said they didn't like any sports and the rest gave other sports (such as rugby).

 d What are the angles for a pie chart that shows the choices of all the students in the group?

Statistics and Probability Strand 2 Statistical diagrams

2 A travel operator carried out a survey of British people in a bar in a Spanish holiday resort. She asked them how they had travelled there.
Here are her results.

Method	Air	Drive	Coach	Live here	Other
Frequency	32	28	20	9	1

    a How many people were in the survey?
    b The travel operator draws a pie chart to show the information.
       How many degrees does she use for one person?
    c Draw the pie chart.
    d Draw a bar chart showing the same information.
    e Which do you personally find most helpful, the table, the pie chart or the bar chart? Explain why.

3 A fruit seller carries out a survey on people's favourite fruit, with these results.

Fruit	Apple	Orange	Peach	Grapefruit	Pineapple	Banana	Other
Frequency	11	8	9	6	4	12	40

    a How many people were in the survey?
    b The information is to be shown as a pie chart. How many degrees represent one person?
    c Draw the pie chart.
    d Comment critically on the data collection and the display of the results as a pie chart.

4 Emma works for an animal charity. It re-homes pets.
She keeps a record of the types of animals they re-home.
$\frac{3}{8}$ are dogs, $\frac{2}{9}$ are cats, $\frac{1}{4}$ are rabbits.
The rest (for example, snakes) come in the category of 'others'.
    a Work out the angles for a pie chart to show this information.
    b Draw the pie chart.

Emma's records covered 72 animals.
The next week she re-homes 12 cats, 4 rabbits and 2 snakes, which she adds to her record.
    c What should the angles in the pie chart be now?

5 Idris draws this diagram to show the different types of vehicles in a car park at 12 noon one day. He says it is a pie chart.

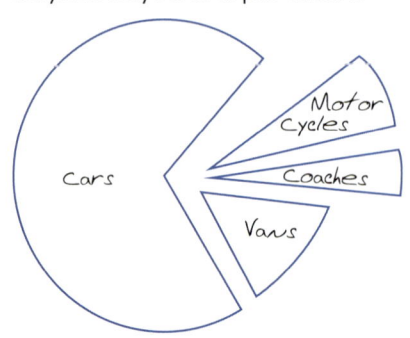

What things can you find that are wrong with it?

Problem solving

1) A cinema manager records the number of different types of tickets sold on Monday.

Tickets	Senior	Adult	Student	Child
Number sold	42	10	6	14

The manager draws a pie chart to represent these figures but it is wrong.
What mistakes has the manager made?

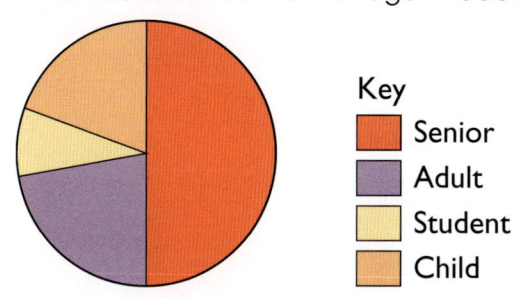

Key
- Senior
- Adult
- Student
- Child

2) In an election there were five candidates: Mrs Taylor, Mr Hussain, Ms Jones, Mr Williams and Ms Roberts. The table shows the number of votes each candidate received.

Candidate	Taylor	Hussain	Jones	Williams	Roberts
Number of votes	2567	1850	980	6751	2252

a Draw a pie chart to illustrate the data.

b Work out the percentage vote each candidate received. Give your answers to the nearest 1%.

c Mr Williams claims he got a majority of the vote.

How can you see that this is false from
   i the pie chart
   ii the percentages?

3) A careers adviser surveys a group of students to find out their career aims.

$\frac{7}{12}$ of the students plan to go to university.

$\frac{1}{4}$ of the students plan to start an apprenticeship.

The remainder plan to take a gap year.

a What fraction of students plan to take a gap year?

b Draw a pie chart to illustrate this data.

c 140 students plan to go to university.
   How many students were surveyed altogether?

Statistics and Probability Strand 2 Statistical diagrams

4 A clothes company collected data to find out why customers returned products to one of their stores last month. These are the results.

Reason	Frequency
Wrong size	27
Faulty	4
Wrong colour	16
Unwanted gift	5
Changed mind	8

a Draw and label a pie chart to represent this data.

b The clothes company has 15 000 returns annually.
Estimate how many items are returned because they are faulty.

5 The pie chart shows how Anwen spent her allowance last month.

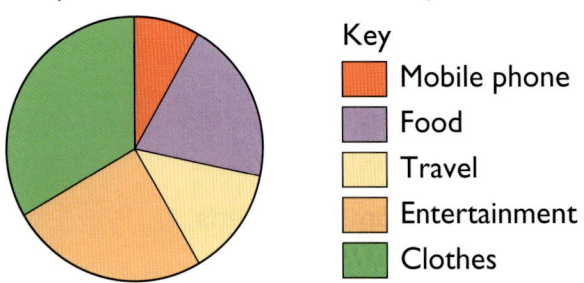

Key
- Mobile phone
- Food
- Travel
- Entertainment
- Clothes

Anwen spent £7.50 on her mobile phone.

Work out how much Anwen spent

a on entertainment

b altogether

c on travel.

6 Ted records the annual cost of running his car in a pie chart.

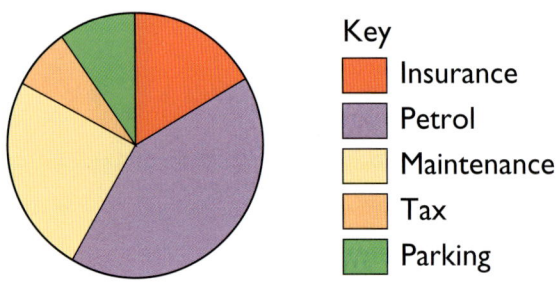

Key
- Insurance
- Petrol
- Maintenance
- Tax
- Parking

a What fraction of Ted's running costs are spent on petrol? Give your answer in its simplest form.

b Ted spent £160 on parking in this year.
Calculate the total annual running cost of the car.

Reviewing skills

1 There are 224 children at a primary school.

$\frac{1}{8}$ of the children go to art club.

$\frac{1}{4}$ of the children go to football club.

a What fraction of the children go to neither art club nor football club?

b What angle would this be represented by on a pie chart?

c Draw the pie chart.

d How many children do not go to either art club or football club?

Unit 4 • Displaying grouped data • Band f

Outside the Maths classroom

Investigating population trends

When a government looks at trends within a population the data it uses is usually grouped.

What are the advantages of grouping data for display?

Toolbox

How many pets have you got?

0	2	3	0	1
4	2	0	1	6
5	0	3	2	2
1	0	0	3	4
2	4	3	1	1

14 s	13.5 s	20 s	16.7 s	14.96 s
15 s	19 s	16.75 s	14.8 s	17.63 s
13.9 s	17.2 s	18 s	21 s	15.87 s
18.2 s	17.3 s	20 s	14.24 s	13.1 s
16 s	18.12 s	14 s	16.4 s	17 s

Coley times his classmates running 100 m.

Ava's data are **discrete**. Each value must be a whole number. You cannot own 4.2 pets!

Coley's data values are **continuous**. Any sensible value is possible. The time taken to complete 100 metres could be 14 seconds, 15.2 seconds or 13.98 seconds.

You can group both types of data in a frequency table.

A time of 14 seconds is included in the group $14 \leq t < 16$.

This frequency diagram shows the data in the table.

Time, t seconds	Frequency
$12 \leq t < 14$	3
$14 \leq t < 16$	7
$16 \leq t < 18$	8
$18 \leq t < 20$	4
$20 \leq t < 22$	3

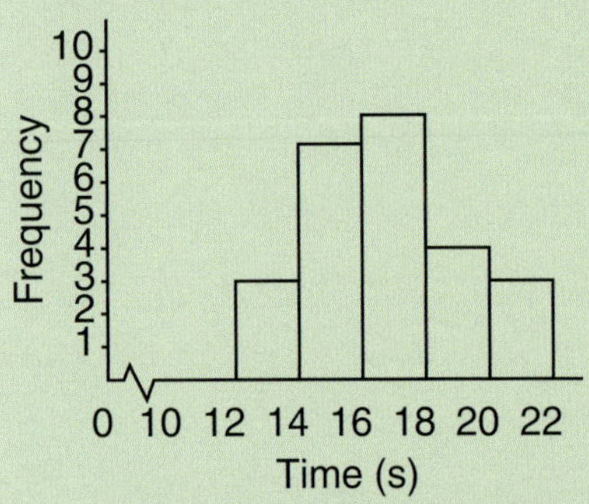

Use a jagged line to show the scale on an axis that does not start at zero. Sometimes just one axis has a broken scale, sometimes it is both. A broken scale can make it easier to plot a graph but it can also mislead you occasionally.

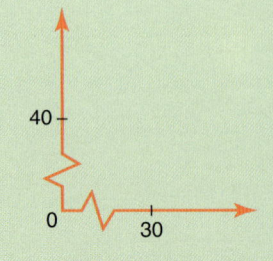

Unit 4 Displaying grouped data Band f

Example – Plotting a frequency diagram

Alex and Emily measured heights, h m, of girls in their athletics club.

1.45	1.57	1.60	1.48	1.60	1.77	1.56	1.55	1.66	1.66
1.70	1.62	1.60	1.42	1.52	1.55	1.59	1.72	1.52	1.62
1.80	1.52	1.75	1.55	1.70	1.63	1.44	1.73	1.50	1.54
1.36	1.62	1.54	1.64	1.55	1.82	1.47	1.68	1.55	1.70
1.60	1.75	1.63	1.75	1.44	1.60	1.60	1.42	1.58	1.80

a Display this information in a grouped frequency table.
b Use your grouped frequency table to plot a frequency diagram.
c Describe the distribution of the data.
d Draw a frequency polygon to display this information.

Solution

a

Height, h m	Frequency
$1.30 \leq h < 1.40$	1
$1.40 \leq h < 1.50$	7
$1.50 \leq h < 1.60$	15
$1.60 \leq h < 1.70$	15
$1.70 \leq h < 1.80$	9
$1.80 \leq h < 1.90$	3

b Frequency diagram showing the heights of girls in an athletics club.

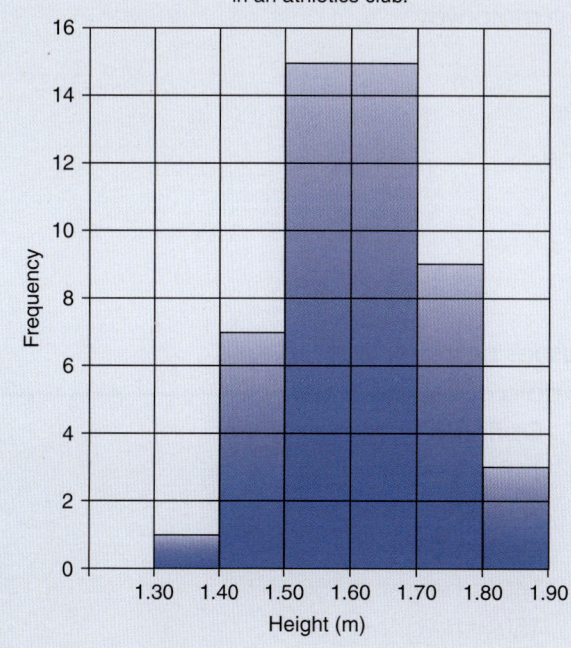

557

Statistics and Probability Strand 2 Statistical diagrams

c Most of the girls are between 1.5 and 1.7 m tall. A few are shorter than this and some are taller.

d Frequency polygon showing the heights of girls in an athletics club.

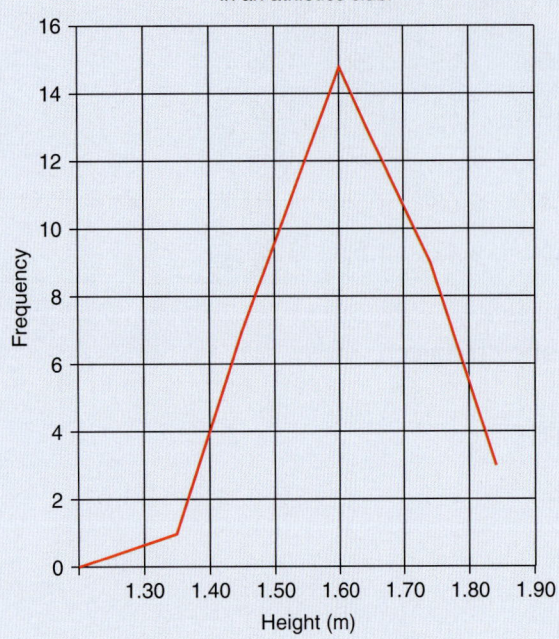

Practising skills

1) State whether each type of data is discrete or continuous.
  a i The number of cars passing a camera on a motorway.
   ii The speed of cars passing the camera on a motorway.
   iii The numbers of people in the cars.
   iv The numbers on the cars' registration plates.
  b i The number of passengers on an aeroplane.
   ii The masses of the passengers.
   iii The average age of the passengers.
   iv How long the aeroplane flight lasts.

2) Pam wants to investigate the heights, in cm, of rushes beside a river.
These are her ideas for the class intervals on her data collection sheet.

Option A
$140 \leqslant \text{height} \leqslant 150$
$150 \leqslant \text{height} \leqslant 160$

Option B
$140 < \text{height} < 150$
$150 < \text{height} < 160$

Option C
$140 - 150$
$150 - 160$

Option D
$140 \leqslant \text{height} < 150$
$150 < \text{height} \leqslant 160$

Criticise these suggestions and write a better one.

3 Trefor has recorded the masses of some people.
Here are the results, in kg.

a Copy and complete the tally chart.

Mass, w kg	Tally	Frequency
$40 \leqslant w < 50$		
$50 \leqslant w < 60$		
$60 \leqslant w < 70$		
$70 \leqslant w < 80$		
$80 \leqslant w < 90$		

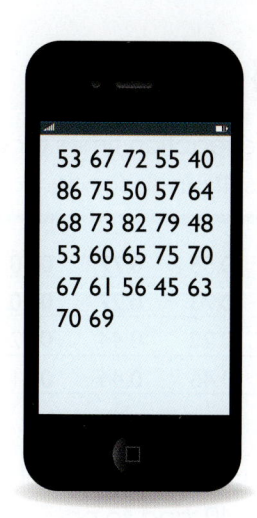

53 67 72 55 40
86 75 50 57 64
68 73 82 79 48
53 60 65 75 70
67 61 56 45 63
70 69

b Which class has the highest frequency?

c Draw a frequency diagram to show Trefor's data.

d Which shows the data most clearly, the tally chart, the frequency diagram or the original information?

e Draw a frequency polygon to display this information. You must draw new axes.

4 These are the numbers of people visiting a gym on each of 21 days.

23, 45, 31, 37, 63, 54, 36, 64, 60, 49, 50, 32, 45, 40, 38, 37,
41, 53, 71, 57, 62

a Copy and complete the tally chart.

Number attending, n	Tally	Frequency
$20 \leqslant n < 30$		
$30 \leqslant n < 40$		
$40 \leqslant n < 50$		
$50 \leqslant n < 60$		
$60 \leqslant n < 70$		
$70 \leqslant n < 80$		

b Which is the modal class?

c On how many days did fewer than 40 people attend?

d What can you say about the numbers of people who went to the gym over this period?

Statistics and Probability Strand 2 Statistical diagrams

Developing fluency

1 Mali records the reaction times for a group of people.
Here are her results, in seconds.

0.34	0.56	0.72	0.20	0.65	0.57	0.36	0.43
0.81	0.73	0.27	0.30	0.52	0.48	0.61	0.59
0.28	0.28	0.44	0.62	0.64	0.50	0.28	0.33
0.58	0.46	0.44	0.51	0.26	0.38		

   a Make a grouped frequency table using class intervals $0.20 \leqslant n < 0.30$, $0.30 \leqslant n < 0.40$, and so on.

   b Draw a frequency polygon to show the data.

   c What percentage of the group have a reaction time of less than 0.30 seconds?

   d Describe the shape of the distribution.

2 Henry plays a computer game and keeps a record of his scores.

   a Make a grouped frequency table using class intervals
$20 \leqslant n < 30$,
$30 \leqslant n < 40$, and so on.

   b Draw a frequency diagram to show the data.

   c What is the median? What is the easiest way to find it?

   d Describe the shape of the distribution. Is it easier to use the original data or the grouped data?

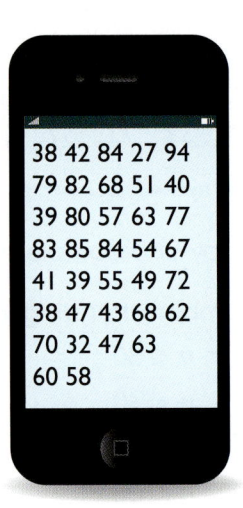

```
38 42 84 27 94
79 82 68 51 40
39 80 57 63 77
83 85 84 54 67
41 39 55 49 72
38 47 43 68 62
70 32 47 63
60 58
```

3 Here are the lengths of the tails of a group of rats, in mm.

156	184	157	173	165	180	191	186
169	170	173	153	147	168	154	166
182	145	153	160	152	185	159	166
155	176	158	153	147	172		

   a Make a grouped frequency table. Choose your own class intervals.

   b Draw a frequency polygon to show the data.

   c How many of the rats have tails longer than 169 mm?

   d Which of your groups is the modal group?

4) Tristan recorded the ages of people using the local swimming pool. His results are in this frequency diagram.

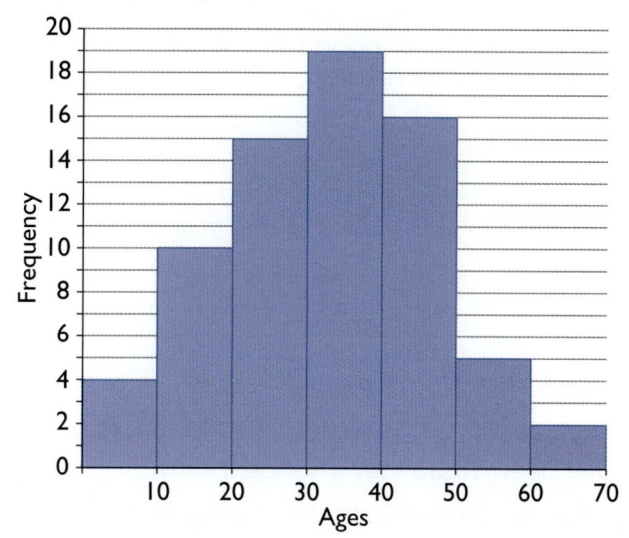

a How many people in the survey were aged 40 to 60?
b Make and complete a frequency table for the data.
c Explain why it is likely that this survey was taken in the evening.
d Sketch a frequency diagram to show what it might look like if the survey was taken in the day time.

5) The junior members of a cricket club record how long they can stay underwater, t seconds.

| Boys | 24 | 15 | 21 | 18 | 9 | 0 | 45 | 33 | 54 | 31 | 7 | 25 | 27 | 31 | 30 | 24 | 42 |
| Girls | 48 | 36 | 24 | 16 | 42 | 50 | 44 | 28 | 30 | 20 | 16 | 35 | 42 | 52 | 34 |

a Make grouped tally charts to show
  i the boys' data
  ii the girls' data.
Use the groups $0 \leqslant t < 10$, $10 \leqslant t < 20$, and so on.
b Find the medians for boys and for girls.
c Draw separate frequency diagrams for the boys and the girls.
d Who can stay underwater longer, boys or girls? Explain your answer.

6) Explain whether you think the following variables should be treated as discrete or continuous.
a The numbers of hairs on human heads.
b People's ages.
c The world's population.

Statistics and Probability Strand 2 Statistical diagrams

Problem solving

1 In an investigation, each of the 30 students in a biology class counts the number of poppies in a different patch of a meadow. All the patches have the same area.

Pat records their results as follows.

72	67	47	65	55	52
58	15	74	69	66	31
22	91	48	84	82	73
150	71	33	44	65	15
52	50	64	49	88	76

a One of the values is an outlier. Which one is it?

Give one reason why the students might exclude it and one reason why they might accept it.

Boris says the figure was his and it should have been 15. So they change it to 15.

b Make a grouped frequency table, using intervals of class width 10, starting at 0.

c Draw the frequency polygon.

d Find the mode and the median of the data. Which of them is more representative of the data? What about the modal class?

e The meadow is said to be "in good heart" where there are 60 or more poppies per patch. Estimate the percentage of the meadow that is "in good heart".

2 Zubert is a diver. He holds a competition to find out how far his friends can swim underwater without taking a breath.

He records the results in a frequency table.

Distance, metres		Frequency
At least	Less than	
0	10	2
10	20	11
20	30	4
30	40	2
40	50	1

a Display this information as a frequency diagram.

b Describe the distribution.

c Calculate the percentage of people in the modal group.

Zubert shows his friends some techniques and then tests them again.

This is the frequency diagram now.

d Describe the effect that Zubert's teaching has had.

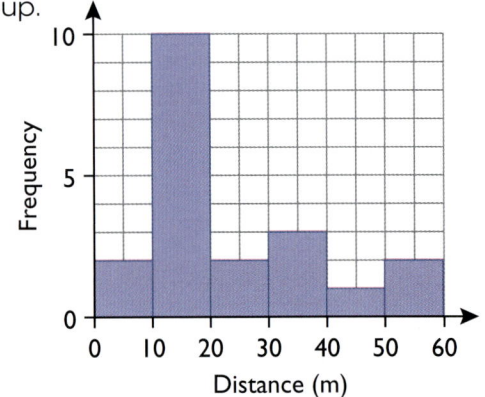

Unit 4 Displaying grouped data Band f

3 It can be very difficult to tell whether a newly hatched chicken is male or female.
Owen keeps a particular rare breed of chicken and he does an experiment to see if newly hatched cockerels are heavier than newly hatched hens. He weighs and marks newly hatched chickens and then records whether each one turns out to be a cockerel or a hen.
Owen's measurements are summarised in this table.

Mass, m g	Female	Male
$25 \leq m < 30$	1	0
$30 \leq m < 35$	6	0
$35 \leq m < 40$	18	2
$40 \leq m < 45$	23	10
$45 \leq m < 50$	7	27
$50 \leq m < 55$	3	26
$55 \leq m < 60$	2	13
$60 \leq m < 65$	0	2
Total	60	80

  a Draw frequency diagrams for females and males.
  b Say what your diagrams show you.
  Owen says, 'As a rule of thumb, any chick under 45 grams will turn into a hen and any chick over 45 g will turn into a cockerel.'
  c Estimate the percentages of
    i female chicks that Owen would judge to be male
    ii chicks overall that he would be right about.

4 Poppy asks her school friends to record how many minutes they spend playing computer games during one week in February.
Here are her results.

25	150	485	30	525	537	55	370	520	60
540	490	76	500	66	140	40	170	74	130
45	125	350	220	472	143	0	90	96	132
477	185	89	167	68	515	160	82	50	468

  a Display the data in a grouped frequency table.
  b Draw a frequency polygon to show this information.
  c Describe the distribution. What does it tell you about the way Poppy's friends spend their time?
  d Poppy plans to ask the same question in August. Predict the shape of the new diagram.

5 Prys and his sister Anna share a computer.
Prys and Anna each keep a record of the length of time, in minutes, that they use the computer each day for one month.

Prys
35 84 66 47 94 77 63 58 42
55 62 74 46 43 28 67 40 51
58 64 45 72 53 46 68 62 53
25 38 46 69

Anna
38 0 0 64 95 22 83 0 10
53 76 104 86 17 0 47 23 76
64 93 81 23 0 32 95 84 52
0 0 86 115

  a Compare the distributions of the length of time Prys and the length of time Anna use the computer this month.
  b Prys and Anna want their parents to buy them a second computer. They say, 'We often have to stay up late to do our work on the computer.' Comment on what they say.

563

Statistics and Probability Strand 2 Statistical diagrams

Reviewing skills

1 The frequency diagram shows the masses of cats taken into a vet's surgery one week.

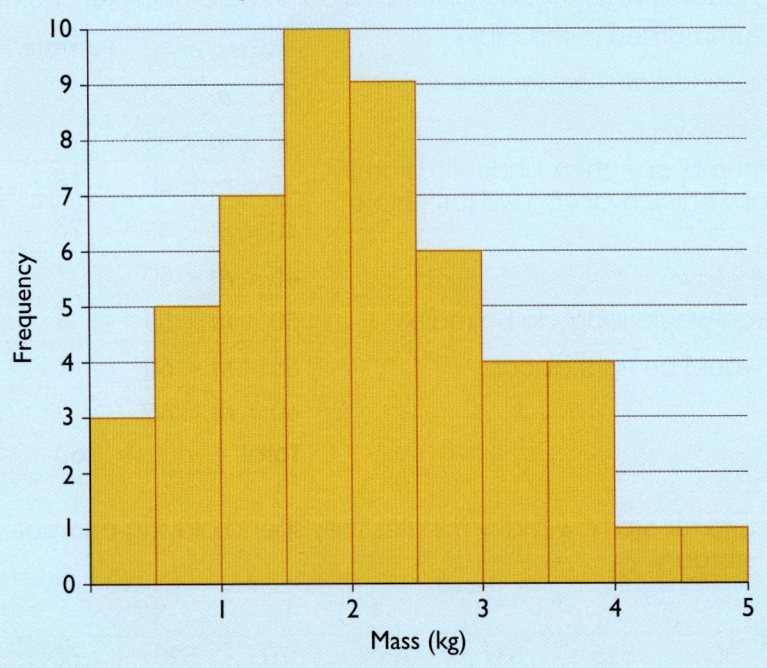

a Tabby weighs 832 g. Which group is she in?
b Which is the modal group?
c Make and complete a grouped frequency chart for these data.
d How many cats were taken in to see the vet that week?

Unit 5 • Scatter diagrams • Band f

Outside the Maths classroom

Looking for links

A statistician says, 'Correlation does not imply causation.'
What does this mean?

Toolbox

Scatter diagrams are used to investigate possible relationships between two variables affecting the same data (called bivariate data).

You do not join up the points on a scatter diagram.
If the variables increase together there is **positive correlation**.
If one variable decreases when the other increases there is **negative correlation**.
If there is **correlation** between the variables, you can draw a **line of best fit** through the points. This is a straight line that best represents the data.
The word 'correlation' describes the relationship between the values of the two variables.

Positive correlation   Negative correlation   No correlation

Example – Plotting a scatter diagram

Matthew and Aneesa are having an argument.

Matthew: *I think that people with long legs can jump further than people with short legs.*

Aneesa: *Rubbish! The length of a person's legs does not affect how far they can jump.*

565

Statistics and Probability Strand 2 Statistical diagrams

They decide to collect data from their friends to find out who is right.

	Alan	Barry	Claire	Dipak	Ernie	Flora	Gurance	Habib	Ivan
Inside leg measurement (cm)	60	70	50	65	65	70	55	75	60
Standing jump distance (cm)	85	90	65	90	80	100	80	95	70

a Draw a scatter diagram.
b i Describe the correlation in the scatter diagram for Matthew's and Aneesa's data.
   ii Does the scatter diagram support Matthew or Aneesa?
c i Draw a line of best fit.
   Jemima has an inside leg measurement of 70 cm.
   ii Use your graph to estimate what distance she is likely to jump.
d Have they got enough data to be certain about their findings?

Solution

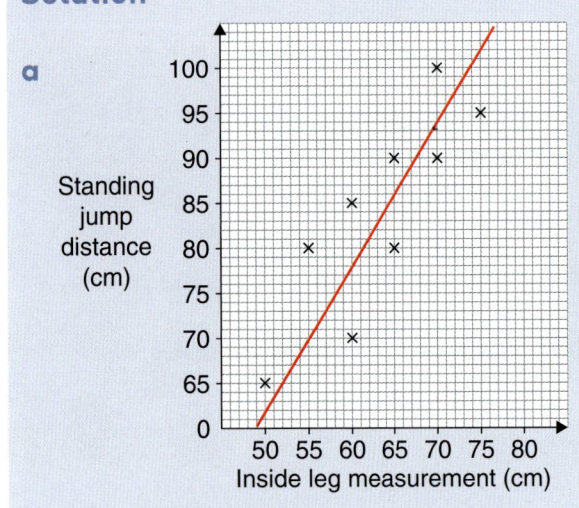

a

b i The graph shows positive correlation: as the inside leg measurement increases, so does the distance jumped.
   ii This supports Matthew's claim.
c i A line of best fit is drawn on the graph.
   The line of best fit leaves an even distribution of points on either side of the line.
   The line of best fit may go through some points or none at all.
   ii From the graph we can see that Jemima should jump about 93 cm.
d They do not have enough data to be certain. More points on the graph would help.

Practising skills

1) Give a description of the correlation shown in each of these scatter diagrams.

a   b   c   d

2. A number of people go on a hiking trip. The scatter graph shows the distances some of them walked in one day and the loads they carried.

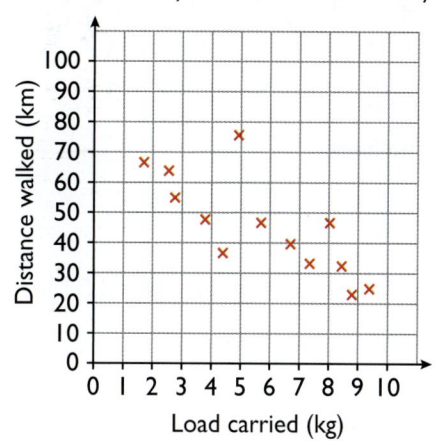

a Describe the correlation shown in the diagram.
b Copy the diagram and draw the line of best fit.
c Use the line of best fit to estimate the distance walked by someone with a 6 kg load.
d Use the line of best fit to estimate the load carried by someone who walked 70 km.

3. A car salesman draws three scatter graphs to show information about the cars on his forecourt.
The axes on the scatter graphs have no labels.

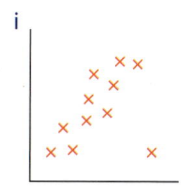

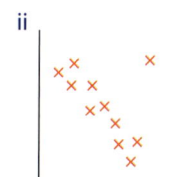

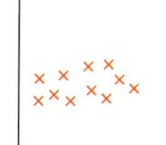

i   ii   iii

a How many cars does the salesman have on his forecourt?
b From the box below, choose an appropriate label for each axis.

> Age of car (years).
> Length of car (m).
> Petrol tank capacity (litres).
> Mileage (1000s of miles.)
> Mass of car (kg.)
> Value of car (£).

c Describe the correlation for each scatter graph.
d Two of the scatter graphs have an outlier. Give a possible explanation for the outlier in each case.

Statistics and Probability Strand 2 Statistical diagrams

4 The table shows the marks (out of 10) given by two judges at a local flower show.

Entrant	A	B	C	D	E	F	G	H	I	J	K	L
Judge 1	10	7	2	4	8	4	6	7	0	2	9	3
Judge 2	9	8	3	5	6	4	7	7	1	4	8	3

   a Draw a scatter diagram to show the marks of both judges.
   b Describe the correlation between the two judges.
   c Draw the line of best fit.
   d Use the scatter diagram to estimate Judge 2's score for an entrant awarded 5 by Judge 1.

5 This data shows the scores from two assessments taken by some school leavers who want a career in the media.

Assessment 1	Assessment 2
68	52
69	58
43	45
57	60
38	27
41	38
83	76
27	27

   a Plot the data and draw a line of best fit for the graph.
   b Fauzia scored 50% in the first assessment, but she missed the second assessment. Use your graph to predict what score she might have achieved.

Developing fluency

1 A group of language students took oral and written tests.

Oral (%)	16	30	65	32	62	55	45	74	63	33	67
Written (%)	27	32	62	47	73	57	43	82	76	32	51

   a Draw a scatter diagram to show the data.
   b Describe the correlation between the two tests.
   c How many got a higher mark in the oral test than the written test?
      How can you tell this easily from your graph?
   d Draw the line of best fit.
   e Use the line of best fit to estimate
      i   the oral mark for a pupil scoring 60 in the written test
      ii the written mark for a pupil who scores 40 in the oral test.

2 These data are from a football league. They show the numbers of goals some of the teams scored and the numbers of points they received.

Goals	79	36	63	50	54	81	31	58	46	68
Points	31	28	42	24	37	72	16	51	42	61

  a Draw a scatter diagram to show the data.
  b Describe the correlation between the goals scored and points received.
  c Draw the line of best fit.
  d Use the line of best fit to estimate the number of
     i points for a team scoring 60 goals
     ii goals for a team gaining 45 points.

3 Paula is looking at some crime statistics.

She records the numbers of police officers in a small sample of police forces and the numbers of reported crimes in one month, in their areas.

Number of police officers	58	38	16	72	34	57	78	12	33	42
Number of reported crimes	68	110	125	177	107	93	48	146	134	83

  a Draw a scatter diagram to show the data.
  b Which point represents a large police force operating in a high crime area?
  c Describe the correlation between the number of police officers and the number of reported crimes.
  d Draw the line of best fit.
  e Estimate the likely number of reported crimes if a police force employs 50 police officers.

4 A health visitor is investigating the relationship between a mother's height and the height of her daughter.

Height of mother (cm)	165	152	164	158	169	164	174	170	155	158	163	177	161	159	162
Height of daughter (cm)	167	154	161	159	173	160	177	169	161	160	164	175	162	162	164

  a Draw a scatter graph to illustrate the data.
  b Describe the correlation shown.
  c i Explain how you can use your scatter graph to find the median height of the group of mothers and find the median height of the group of daughters.
    ii Does the mother who is of median height have a daughter of median height?

Statistics and Probability Strand 2 Statistical diagrams

5 Here are some data about the members of a junior football team.

Name	Height (cm)	Goals this season
Nabil	138	16
Lee	150	11
Loamia	123	2
Younis	141	7
Lorraine	140	0
Chantel	152	3
Heidi	129	14
Sabrina	137	9
David	141	0
Rowena	138	17
Youssu	164	0
Patricia	149	2
Arwyn	128	15
Stuart	137	1
Nia	125	22

a Display this information on a scatter diagram.

b Which players are likely to be goal-keepers? Explain your reasoning.

The coach says, 'I always put the tall players in defence or in goal. Shorter players tend to be nippier and so are good in attack.'

c Is the scatter diagram consistent with the coach's policy? Explain your answer carefully.

Problem solving

1 An athletics coach thinks that athletes who are good at running are also good at high jump. The coach collects some data from his club.

Time to run 200 m (s)	25.3	27.4	26.4	27.5	29.0	30.2	27.3	26.6	30.1	32.0	28	28.3	29.4	27.0	31.3	31.7
High jump (m)	2.24	2.15	2.18	2.01	1.89	1.76	1.90	2.10	2.06	2.26	2	1.96	1.92	2.00	1.80	1.75

a Draw a scatter diagram to show the coach's data.

b Describe the correlation. Is the coach right?

c Find the median running time.

d Find the median height jumped. Is this the same person as in part **c**?

e The coach decides the top 25% of athletes in each sport should form an elite squad. How many athletes make it on to the squad?

Unit 5 Scatter diagrams Band f

2) Here is a scatter diagram it shows the mass and cost of 11 books in a shop.

Llinos says, 'You can see that heavier books cost more.'

Elfed says, 'There is no correlation between a book's mass and its cost.'

Assess the validity of the two statements. You must explain your reasoning.

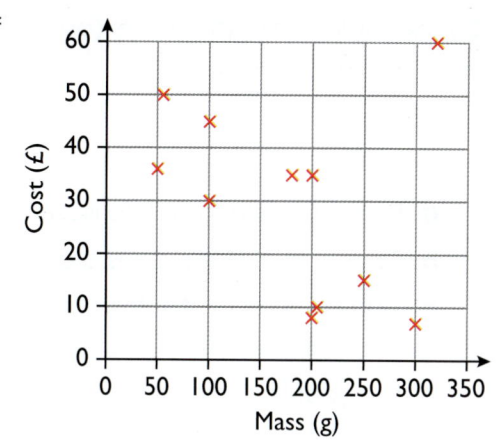

3) Mrs Jones collects information about how many hours students spent watching television in the week before a biology exam and their exam mark.

The scatter diagram shows the information.

Mrs Jones thinks that there is a connection between the number of hours spent watching television and the biology exam mark.

a Does the scatter diagram support this statement?
  Describe the correlation shown.

Mrs Jones collects some more data and finds that there is strong positive correlation between number of hours spent revising and the mark achieved in the test.

b i Sketch a scatter graph to illustrate this.
  ii Mrs Jones says, 'This shows you either watch television or you revise for biology, and you know which will definitely get you the better mark.'
     Is Mrs Jones right? Explain your reasoning.

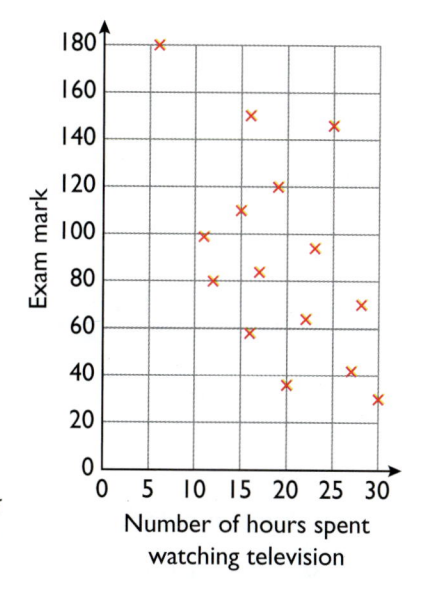

4) The table gives data for a number of diesel cars. For each car it shows the engine size and the distance it travels on 1 litre of diesel.

Engine size (litres)	3.0	.6	1.2	1.8	2.8	1.5	1.0	2.5
Distance (km)	6	15	13	10	7	11	12	9

a Draw a scatter diagram for the data.

b Comment on the correlation.

c Draw a line of best fit.

d Estimate the distance travelled for a car with an engine size of 1.4 litres.

5 The table shows the marks (out of 10) given by two judges for each of ten dancers in a competition.

| Judge 1 | 2 | 7 | 1 | 8 | 6 | 3 | 9 | 4 | 5 |
| Judge 2 | 3 | 8 | 2 | 10 | 8 | 3 | 7 | 6 | 5 |

a Draw a scatter graph to illustrate the data.

b Do you think the judges are consistent? Give a reason for your answer.

c Add a line of best fit to your scatter graph.
Judge 1 gives another competitor a mark of 3.

d Use your line of best fit to estimate the mark Judge 2 would give this competitor.
A twelfth competitor is judged.
Judge 1 gives him a mark of 7.
Judge 2 gives him a mark of 3.
The contestant objects and says, 'Judge 2 is being unfair as this makes this mark an outlier and is inconsistent with the other pairs of marks.'

e Comment on the validity of this argument.

Reviewing skills

1 Avonford Swimming Club keeps a record of the age of each swimmer and how many lengths they can swim in one go. This table shows the data for a few of the swimmers.

| Age | 16 | 38 | 53 | 36 | 63 | 46 | 22 | 55 | 58 |
| Number of lengths | 58 | 45 | 68 | 30 | 12 | 33 | 46 | 34 | 21 |

a Draw a scatter diagram to show the data.

b Describe the correlation between the age of the swimmer and the number of lengths they can swim.

c Draw the line of best fit.

d Use the scatter diagram to estimate
 i the number of lengths that a person aged 50 may swim
 ii the likely age of a person who can swim 40 lengths.

Unit 6 • Using lines of best fit • Band g

Outside the Maths classroom

Making predictions
How can statistics help us predict outcomes of future events?

Toolbox

Scatter graphs are used to show the relationship between **bivariate data** – this means the data contains pairs of values.

A **line of best fit** shows the overall trend of the data. It does not have to go through the origin.

An **outlier** is a pair of values that does not fit the overall trend.

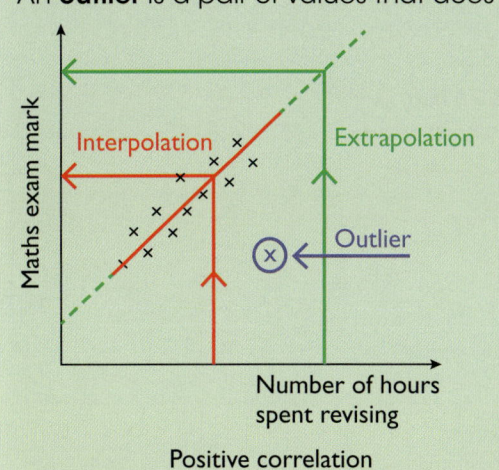

Positive correlation (Maths exam mark vs Number of hours spent revising): shows Interpolation, Extrapolation and an Outlier.

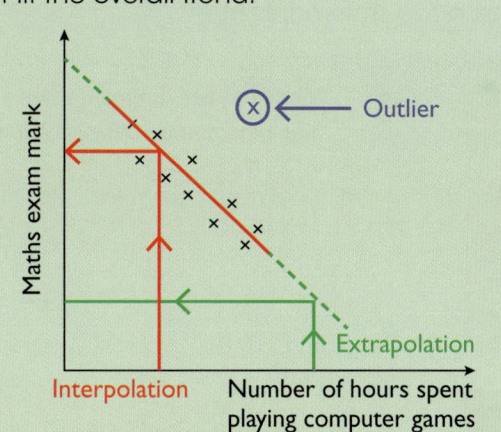

Negative correlation (Maths exam mark vs Number of hours spent playing computer games): shows Interpolation, Extrapolation and an Outlier.

Interpolation: this is where you use your line of best fit to estimate a value within the range of the data. Interpolation is reliable if there is a strong correlation.

Extrapolation: this is where you extend your line of best fit to estimate a value beyond the range of the data. Extrapolation is not very reliable because you cannot tell whether the trend will continue.

A strong correlation does not prove **causation**.

Spending more time revising will **cause** your maths mark to go up.

Computer games do not **cause** people to do badly in a maths test but they might cause them to revise less!

Statistics and Probability Strand 2 Statistical diagrams

Example – Extrapolation and causation

Country	Life Expectancy at birth	Birth rate per 1000
Australia	82.0	12.2
Barbados	75.0	12.0
Cambodia	63.8	24.4
Canada	81.7	10.3
Czech Republic	78.3	9.8
Guatemala	71.7	25.4
India	67.8	19.9
Italy	82.0	8.8
Libya	76.0	18.4
Samoa	73.2	21.3
Syria	68.4	22.8
Tajikistan	67.1	25.0
Uganda	54.5	44.2
Uruguay	76.8	13.2

a Draw a scatter diagram to show the figures for life expectancy and birth rate in different colours.

b Describe the correlation.

c Calculate the mean life expectancy and the mean birth rate per 1000.

d Draw a line of best fit through the mean point.

e Are either of these two statements true?

> The scatter diagram shows that a high life expectancy causes a low birth rate.

> You can see that a high birth rate causes low life expectancy.

f Someone looking at the line of best fit says, 'It shows that when the life expectancy in a country reaches 88, people will stop having children.' Comment on this statement.

Solution

a and d

[Scatter diagram: Birth rate per 100 (y-axis, 0 to 50) vs Life expectancy at birth (x-axis, 40 to 90), showing negative correlation with line of best fit drawn.]

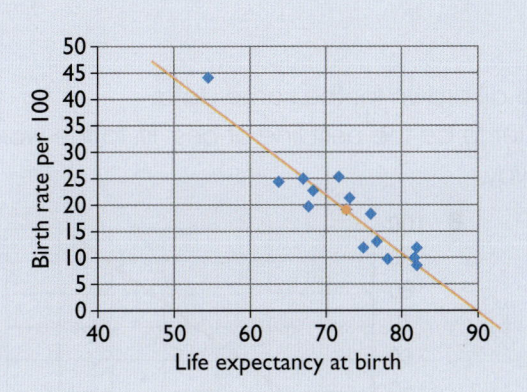

b The graph shows there is negative correlation between life expectancy and birth rate.

c Mean life expectancy = 72.74. Mean birth rate per 1000 = 19.12.

e A high life expectancy does not cause a low birth rate. Neither does a low birth rate cause a high life expectancy, although it could be true that more care can be given to older people if there are fewer babies to look after! It is more the case that both high life expectancy and low birth rate are the result of better access to medication and education.

> Notice that *Correlation does not imply Causation*. In this case a common underlying factor, economic development, seems to lie behind both the observed effects of low birth rate and high life expectancy.

f Common sense tells us this is definitely not true. We should not therefore **extrapolate** the line of best fit beyond the values given in the data. We can be fairly certain the relationship exists within the region of evidence but we cannot assume the relationship will exist outside of that region.

Practising skills

1 This table gives the power (in horsepower) and the fuel consumption (in miles per gallon) of a number of cars.

Power	Fuel consumption	Power	Fuel consumption
195	24.5	305	21.4
185	27.7	278	21.6
145	31.5	173	27.9
182	31.2	270	25.3
178	28.7	268	24.8
182	23.5	301	18.9
290	19.5	360	15.9
360	15.9	470	14.9
285	19.8	355	18.6
355	18.6	420	17
302	17.5	360	15.9
360	15.9	411	13.4
305	19.7	395	17.3
159	19.2	236	17

  a Find the smallest and greatest values of the power and of the fuel consumption.
  Use them to decide on suitable scales for a scatter diagram.

  b Draw the scatter diagram.

  c Draw a line of best fit through the mean points.

  d Use your line of best fit
  i To describe the relationship between power and fuel economy.
  ii To predict the power of a car that travels 15 miles on one gallon of petrol.
  iii To predict the fuel economy of a car that produces 450 horsepower.

  e Formula 1 racing cars produce around 800 horsepower. Can you use your graph to find their typical fuel consumption? Explain your answer.

Statistics and Probability Strand 2 Statistical diagrams

Developing fluency

1 Look at these four lines of best fit. They are all drawn for the same data.
Rank them in order from what you consider to be the best line of best fit, to the worst.
Explain why you've ordered them in this way.

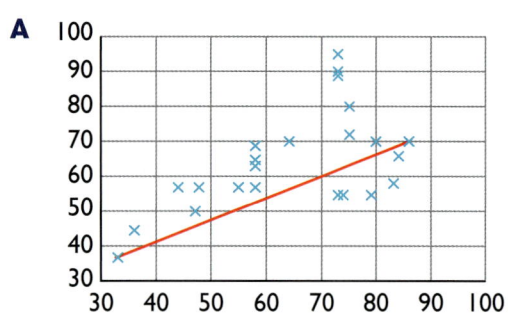

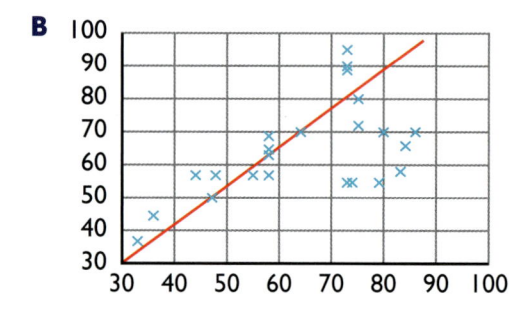

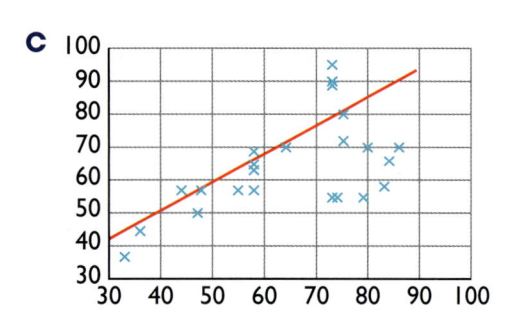

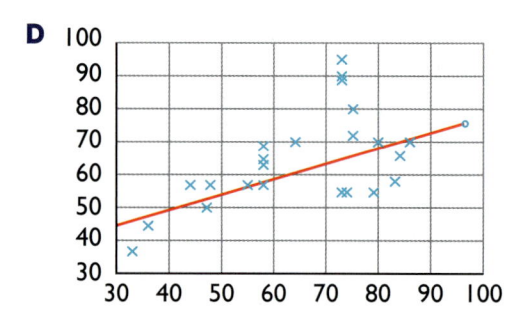

A

B

C

D

2 Here are the personal best performances of some athletes in a club.

Time to run 100m (s)	11.57	11.12	10.88	11.54	11.25	10.73	11.92	11.24
Time to run 1500m (s)	275	328	326	296	316	345	266	299
Distance jumped (m)	4.49	5.56	5.52	4.95	5.33	5.92	4.31	5.02

The data can be written as these pairs: 100m and 1500m; 100m and long jump; 1500m and high jump.

  a Investigate the correlations shown by the data.

  b What do these correlations tell you about who is good at these events?

  c How could you tell if the correlations hold for athletes in general?

  d Comment on these statements from the team coach.

   i 'One of these days we'll get a team member who can run the 100m in 10 seconds. He'll be able to do 7m in the long jump.'

   ii 'Being able to run the 100m in a low time makes you able to run the 1500m in a low time.'

3 This scatter diagram shows the science and maths marks of a class in two tests.

   a Describe the correlation between the two sets of marks.

   The science teacher says, 'This shows that doing well at science makes you good at maths.'

   The maths teacher says, 'This shows that doing well at maths makes you good at science.'

   b Which of them (if either) is right? Give your reasons.

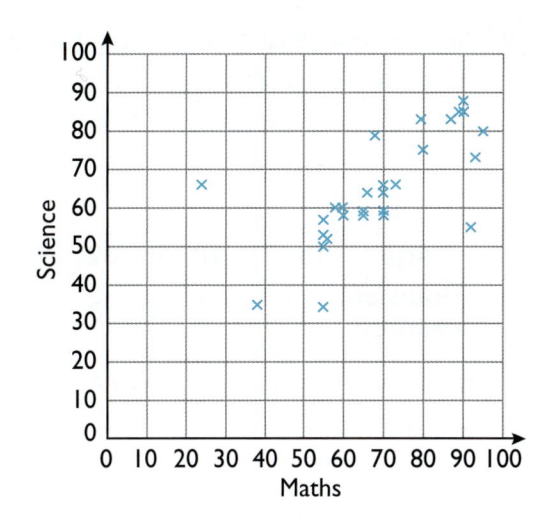

Problem solving

1 A life guard kept a daily record of the highest temperature and the number of people swimming in the sea at 3 p.m.
The results are shown below.

Temperature (°C)	32	30	31	34	27	26	25	24	25	23	22	23	24	22
Number of people swimming	203	180	188	144	171	164	155	140	145	135	120	132	129	110

   a Show these data on a scatter diagram.

   b Describe any correlation between the two variables.

   c There is an outlier in the data. State which it is and suggest a reason for it.

   d Calculate the mean temperature and mean number of people swimming.

   e Draw a line of best fit on your scatter graph through the mean values you have calculated.

One day the temperature is forecast to be around 15 °C.

   f Use your line of best fit to predict the number of swimmers.

   Comment on the reliability of your estimate, giving a reason for your answer.

An ice-cream vendor records number of people in the sea at 3 p.m. and number of ice-creams sold each day.
Here is the ice-cream vendor's graph.

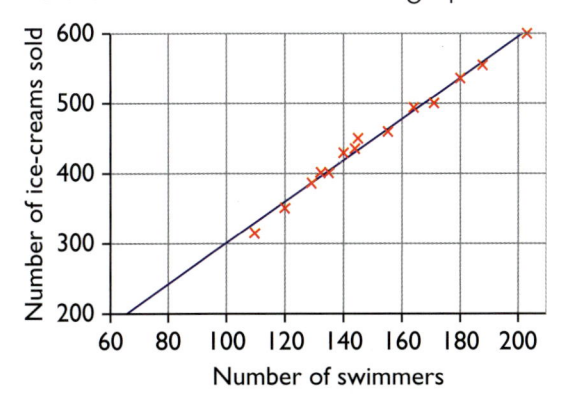

   g The ice-cream vendor says, 'My graph proves that swimming causes people to eat more ice-cream.'

   Explain why the vendor is not correct.

Statistics and Probability Strand 2 Statistical diagrams

2. Archie thinks that older people take less exercise.
   He carries out a survey.
   He chooses 20 adults of different ages.
   They each keep a record of how much exercise they take during one week.
   Here are his results.

Age	18	17	22	25	32	37	42	50	55	60	57	45	23	42	27	45	37	54	19	29
Hours of exercise	14	12	13	10	8	7	5	6	2	5	1	7	13	7	11	15	5	3	8	7

   a Draw a scatter diagram of Archie's results.
   b Is there any correlation between age and the amount of time spent exercising? What does this mean?
   c Identify any outliers.
   d Draw a line of best fit on your scatter diagram. Indicate the mean point plotted.
   e Archie takes 8 hours of exercise per week. Estimate his age.
     Comment on the reliability of your estimate, giving a reason for your answer.
   f Mary is 72 years old. Estimate how much exercise she takes.
     Comment on the reliability of your estimate, giving a reason for your answer.

3. The table gives some information about different types of aircraft.

Aircraft	A320	A318	B747	A350	B747	MD-11	A310	B737	AN225
Wingspan (m)	35.8	34.1	64.8	65	38	52	44	36	88
Maximum landing mass (tonnes)	66.0	57.5	251	205	88	185	124	66	640

   a Draw a scatter diagram to show the data.
   b Is there evidence from the scatter diagram to suggest there is a correlation between the wingspan of an aircraft and the maximum landing mass of the aircraft? You must explain your answer.
   c Draw a line of best fit.
   d Use your line of best fit to estimate the maximum landing mass of an aircraft with wingspan 58 m.
   e Peter has an aircraft with a wingspan of 12 metres. Would it be sensible for him to use the line of best fit to estimate the maximum landing mass of his aircraft? Explain your answer.

4) Megan is carrying out a science experiment.
She hangs a weight from a spring and measures the final length of the spring.
Megan repeats the experiment for different masses.
Here are Megan's results.

Mass (g)	50	100	150	200	250	300	350	400	450	500	550	600
Length of spring (cm)	6.5	8.3	10.1	12.2	14.3	20.1	18.3	20.3	22.6	24.1	26.5	28.7

a Draw a scatter diagram to show the data.

b Megan has made a mistake when she wrote down one of the results.
   The correct result should be 16.2 cm.
   Identify and correct the mistake.

c Draw a line of best fit through the mean mass and mean length of spring.

d Use your line of best fit to estimate the length of the spring when a mass of 180 g is hung from it.

e Comment on the reliability of using your line of best fit to estimate the length of the spring when a 1 kg mass is hung from it.

f Estimate the original length of the spring.

Reviewing skills

1) This table shows the height in metres above sea level and the temperature in Celsius, on one day at 8 different places in Europe.

Height (m)	1300	275	800	360	580	540	1300	690
Temperature (°C)	10	20	14	20	27	17	12	17

a Plot a scatter diagram and describe the correlation.
b Identify any outliers and suggest a reason for them.
c Use your diagram to estimate the temperature at a height of 400 m.
d Use your diagram to estimate the height of a place with a temperature of 25°C.
e Comment on the reliability of your answers in parts c and d.

Statistics and Probability
Strand 3 Collecting data

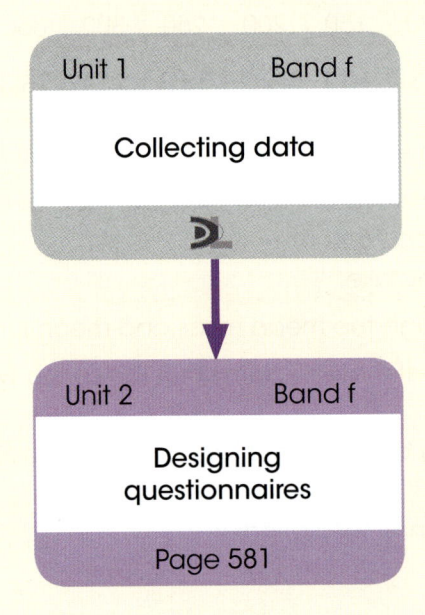

Unit 1 — Band f
Collecting data

Unit 2 — Band f
Designing questionnaires
Page 581

Unit 1 is assumed knowledge for this book. Knowledge and skills from this unit is used throughout the book.

Unit 2 • Designing questionnaires • Band f

Outside the Maths classroom

Environmental issues

What questions would you ask in a questionnaire about the environmental issues around wind forces?

Toolbox

Here are six key points when designing a questionnaire.

1. Are any of your questions **leading** towards a particular answer?
   For example, are you using overly positive language about one product or idea over another?

2. Are your questions **appropriate**?
   Some people may be offended or upset by direct questions about their age, weight or income, so it is much better to use response ranges for these questions.

3. Are your questions **open** or **closed**?
   Closed questions give a choice of responses and generate **quantitative** data, for example: would you rate the ice-cream as *outstanding, good, average, bad* or *terrible*?
   Open questions allow the person answering to express themselves freely and generate **qualitative** data, for example: what did you think of the ice-cream?

4. **Where, when and how** should you carry out your questionnaire?
   Different locations and times will mean that different groups of people are more or less likely to be walking past. Similarly, by carrying out your questionnaire by telephone or online, you might only reach one group of people.

5. Are your **categories suitable**?
   Make sure that your categories do not overlap.
   For example, in the question below, 25-year-olds could put themselves in two categories.

   How old are you?
   Under 20   20–25   25–30   30–35   35–40   Over 40

Statistics and Probability Strand 3 Collecting data

Make sure, too, that there are no gaps in your categories. Everyone must fit in exactly one category.

6 **Be specific** about a time scale.

If you are asking people how often they exercise or how much time they spend on social media, you need to state whether this is each day, each week or each month in order to ensure that each person answering the questionnaire is answering consistently.

Example – Designing questionnaires

A local primary school wants to change its menu so that more children eat school meals. Design a questionnaire that explores the type of food that the children enjoy, how much they would be willing to pay and whether they would change to school dinners if their favourite food was available.

Solution

For example:

1 Do you currently have school dinners:
- ☐ 5 days a week
- ☐ 2–4 days a week
- ☐ once a week
- ☐ less than once a week
- ☐ never

2 Is eating healthily important to you?
- ☐ Yes
- ☐ No

3 What are your three favourite meals?
1
2
3

4 How much would you pay for a school dinner?
- ☐ I would not have school dinner
- ☐ Up to £1
- ☐ £1–£1.50
- ☐ £1.51–£2
- ☐ Over £2

Practising skills

1 A medical centre is carrying out a survey to encourage patients to be more active.
A receptionist designs a survey. Here is a question from the survey.

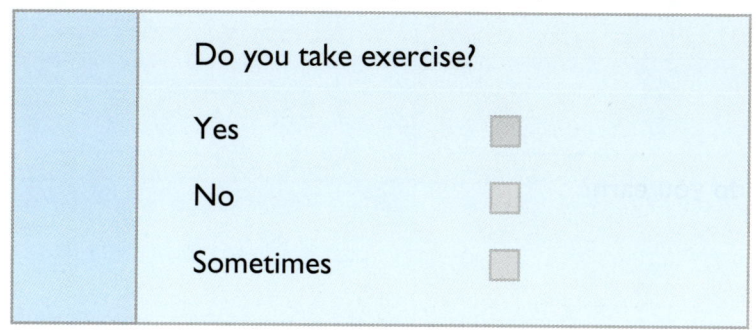

Do you take exercise?	
Yes	☐
No	☐
Sometimes	☐

    a Write down a criticism of the question.

    b Write down a criticism of the response options.

2 Gareth says that children who eat fish at least twice a week score the highest marks in mathematics tests.
How could Gareth test his hypothesis?

3 Mr. Harvey thinks that the girls in his class generally spend more time on their homework each week than the boys. He wants to find out if this is true.
Design a data collection sheet to help him.

4 Iona says that when a tap is fully opened the water does not flow at a constant rate.
How could Iona test her hypothesis?

5 A new coffee bar is to be opened in a factory. What is the population for a survey about the coffee bar facilities?

6 Lydia is conducting a survey about eating habits of teenagers. This is one of her questions.

Do you agree that burgers are bad for you?

Rewrite the question to remove bias.
Include response boxes for answers to the question.

Statistics and Probability Strand 3 Collecting data

7 A bank manager wants to find out how to attract more customers. He surveys some people. Here are the first two questions.

1.	How old are you?
	16–25 ☐
	26–35 ☐
	36–50 ☐
	51–70 ☐
2.	How much money do you earn?
	£0–£50 ☐
	£50–£100 ☐
	£100–£300 ☐
	£300–£500 ☐
	£500–£1000 ☐
	£1000–£5000 ☐

a Name one thing that is wrong with the responses for question 1.

b Name two different mistakes he has made with question 2.

Developing fluency

1 Write a question, with a selection of answer boxes, to find out how much people are prepared to pay for a sandwich.

2 Gill says that the mean price of a track of music is 69p. Dewi says she is incorrect.
How could Gill's hypothesis be checked?

3 Write a question, with a selection of answer boxes, to find out how many music DVDs people buy.

4 Sarah is conducting a survey to find out the views of local people about the town's library.
She asks people in the town centre at 11 a.m. on Monday morning. Here are the first two questions.

1.	How often do you use the library in a typical month?
	Never ☐
	On 1–2 occasions ☐
	On 2–5 occasions ☐
	More than 5 times ☐
2.	Do you agree that the library is well stocked?
	Yes ☐ No ☐

Make 3 criticisms of Sarah's survey.

584

5 Prisoners are often taught computer skills. The prison manager's hypothesis is:

'Prisoners taught computer skills are less likely to commit crimes after being released from prison.'

How could the prison manager test his hypothesis?

6 Mary is doing a survey on how people travel to the gym.
List two errors she could make when taking the sample.

7 Design a data collection sheet to record the heights and waist measurements of a group of people all aged over 20.

In your data collection sheet you should have sufficient options in boxes, with intervals that do not overlap.

8 Lily's hypothesis is that sugar dissolves in water more quickly if the water is hot.
How should Lily prove her hypothesis?

Problem solving

1 'The amount of sunshine impacts on the ripening of tomatoes on the vine.'
   a Is this likely to be true?
   b How could this hypothesis be tested?

2 'More pupils are absent during examination periods.'
   a Do you think this is a reasonable hypothesis?
   b How would you test this hypothesis?

3 'People taking vitamin C with zinc tablets have fewer colds.'
How could this hypothesis be tested?

4 Anna wants to use these questions in a survey about computer games.
Explain what is wrong with them and what Anna needs to do to improve them.

   a How old are you?
   10–15 years old
   16–20 years old
   21–30 years old

   b How many hours a week do you spend playing computer games?
   Less than 1 hour
   1–5 hours
   5–10 hours
   10–20 hours
   More than 20 hours

   c Why do you think computer games should be banned?
   Students play them instead of doing homework.
   They are too violent.
   Sitting for a long time at a computer is bad for your body.

5 Derek has gathered information from 100 women and 100 men on their height, mass and how many times they exercise each week.

Suggest some questions he could answer with these data.

Statistics and Probability Strand 3 Collecting data

6 Martin wanted to find out if people supported the local football team, Northfield City. He carried out a survey outside their football ground after a match. Here is his questionnaire.

1.	How old are you?
	Under 10 years old
	    10–18 ☐
	    18–25 ☐
	    25–40 ☐
	    Over 40 ☐

2.	How often do you attend football matches?
	    Once a week ☐
	    Once a month ☐
	    About 3 times a season ☐
	    More than 3 times a season ☐

3.	Do you support Northfield City?
	    Yes ☐
	    No ☐

a Explain why Martin's survey is biased and how that will affect the answer to question 3.

b Write down a criticism of each question in the questionnaire.

c Rewrite the questionnaire to improve it.

7 Malcolm wants to conduct a survey of the members of his cricket club to find out the types of sandwiches he should provide for the tea interval.
Should he sample the whole population or take a sample? Explain your answer.

8 A car manufacturer wishes to test how long their engines will run before breaking down. What type of experiment should they do?

9 Chris works for a consumer group. He is trying to find out if taxi fares are reasonable. He decides to ask 5 taxi companies how much they charge for each of 10 journeys.
Design an observation sheet for Chris to use to record the fare and distance of each journey.

Unit 2 Designing questionnaires Band f

Reviewing skills

1 Phil is interested in music. He thinks that younger people buy more music than older people. He also thinks that older people buy more CDs but younger people download more and buy more vinyl.

Design a data collection sheet he could use to find out if he is correct.

2 A survey is carried out to find out where people buy their groceries. These questions are asked of people as they leave a supermarket. A section of the questionnaire is shown below.

In questions 1 and 2 put a tick in a box
1. How old are you?   21 to 30 ☐   30 to 40 ☐   41+ ☐
2. Where do you buy your groceries?   Supermarket ☐   Local shop ☐

a Explain why this is a biased survey.

b State two criticisms of the design of question 1.

c What is wrong with question 2?

Statistics and Probability
Strand 4 Probability

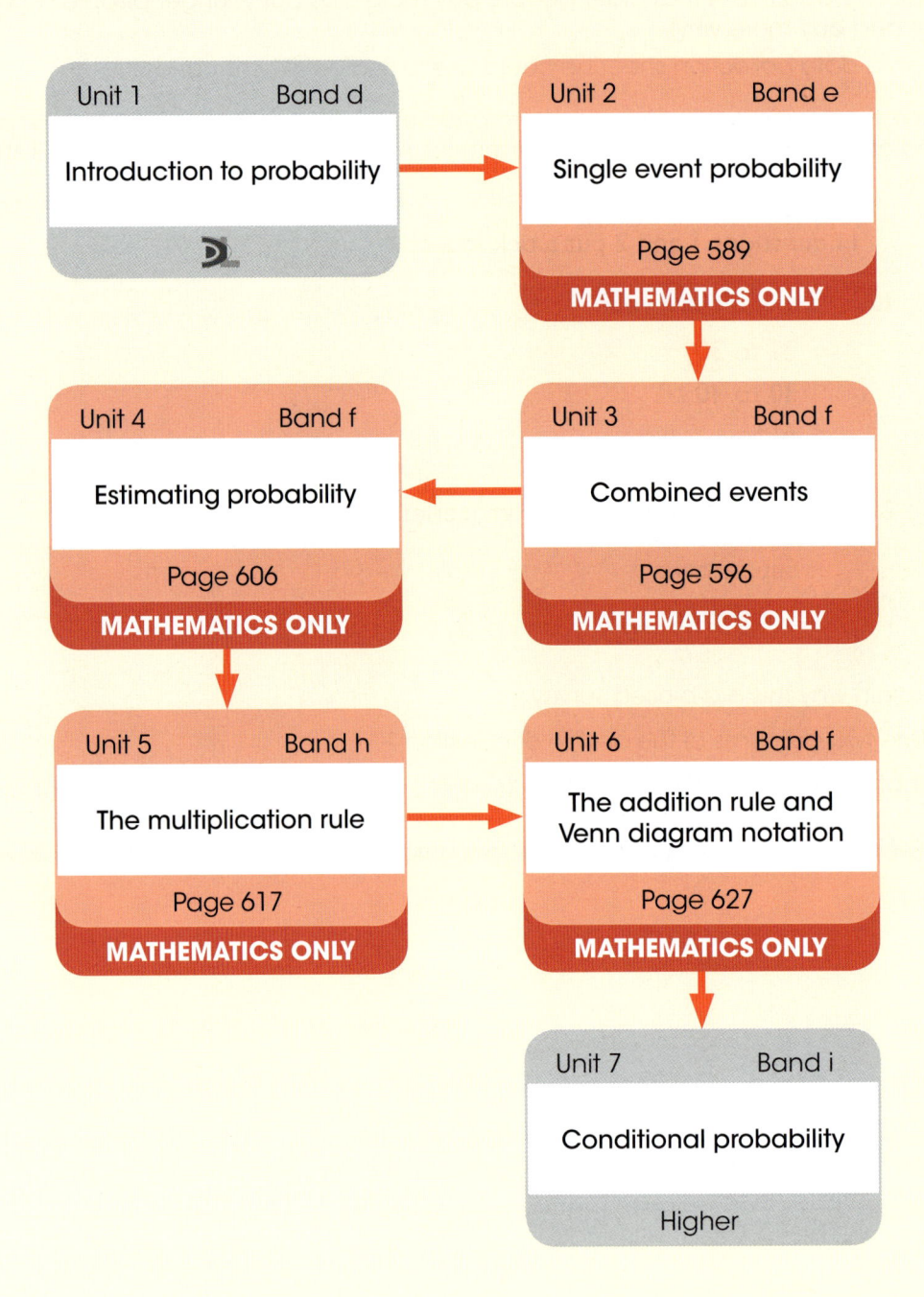

Unit 1 — Band d	Introduction to probability
Unit 2 — Band e	Single event probability — Page 589 — MATHEMATICS ONLY
Unit 3 — Band f	Combined events — Page 596 — MATHEMATICS ONLY
Unit 4 — Band f	Estimating probability — Page 606 — MATHEMATICS ONLY
Unit 5 — Band h	The multiplication rule — Page 617 — MATHEMATICS ONLY
Unit 6 — Band f	The addition rule and Venn diagram notation — Page 627 — MATHEMATICS ONLY
Unit 7 — Band i	Conditional probability — Higher

Unit 1 is assumed knowledge for this book. Knowledge and skills from this unit is used throughout the book.

Unit 2 • Single event probability • Band e

Outside the Maths classroom

Lotteries

Are the lottery numbers '1, 2, 3, 4, 5, 6' less likely to win than '5, 11, 18, 24, 31, 42'?

Toolbox

An **event** is something which may or may not occur. The result of an experiment or a situation involving uncertainty is called an **outcome**, like the score on a die.

The word **event** is also used to describe a combination of outcomes, like scores 5 or 6 on a die.

For any event with equally likely outcomes, the probability of an event happening can be found using the formula:

$$P(\text{event happening}) = \frac{\text{total number of successful outcomes}}{\text{total number of possible outcomes}}$$

Mutually exclusive events are events that cannot happen together. For example, you cannot roll a 2 and a 5 at the same time on one die!

The probabilities of all mutually-exclusive outcomes of an event add up to 1.

$P(\text{event not happening}) = 1 - P(\text{event happening})$

Example 1 – Equally likely outcomes

Kyle throws an ordinary die. He makes a list of all the possible outcomes.

| 1 | 2 | 3 | | | |

a Complete Kyle's list.
b Find the probability that Kyle gets
   i 6
   ii not a 6
   iii an even number
   iv 5 or more
   v less than 4
   vi a prime number.

Statistics and Probability Strand 4 Probability

Solution

a All possible outcomes: 1 2 3 4 5 6

b i P(6) $= \dfrac{1}{6}$ ← 1 possible throw out of 6 equally likely possibilities

 ii P(not a 6) $= 1 - P(6) = 1 - \dfrac{1}{6} = \dfrac{5}{6}$

 iii P(even) $= \dfrac{3}{6} = \dfrac{1}{2}$ ← 3 possible throws: 2, 4 and 6

 iv P(5 or more) $= \dfrac{2}{6} = \dfrac{1}{3}$ ← 2 possible throws: 5 and 6

 v P(less than 4) $= \dfrac{3}{6} = \dfrac{1}{2}$ ← 3 possible throws: 1, 2 and 3

 vi P(prime) $= \dfrac{3}{6} = \dfrac{1}{2}$ ← 3 possible throws: 2, 3 and 5

Example 2 – Explaining probabilities

A letter is picked at random, from the word PROBABILITY.
Find:

a P(letter B is chosen)
b P(a vowel is not chosen)
c P(letter C is chosen)

Solution

The letter is chosen at random. So all letters have equal chance of being chosen.

a There are 11 letters in PROBABILITY, 2 of which are B.

 P(letter B is chosen) $= \dfrac{\text{total number of letter Bs}}{\text{total number of letters}} = \dfrac{2}{11}$

b There are 4 vowels out of the 11 letters in the word PROBABILITY, and 7 letters that are not vowels.

 If the letter is chosen at random, all letters have equal chance of being chosen.

 P(vowel is chosen) $= \dfrac{\text{total number of vowels}}{\text{total number of letters}} = \dfrac{4}{11}$

 P(a vowel is not chosen) $= 1 - P(\text{vowel is chosen})$
 $= 1 - \dfrac{4}{11} = \dfrac{7}{11}$

 This is the same as $\dfrac{\text{total number of non-vowels}}{\text{total number of letters}}$.

c The letter C does not occur in PROBABILITY so it is impossible to choose it.
 The probability of picking a C is 0.

Practising skills

1 Here are 10 shapes.

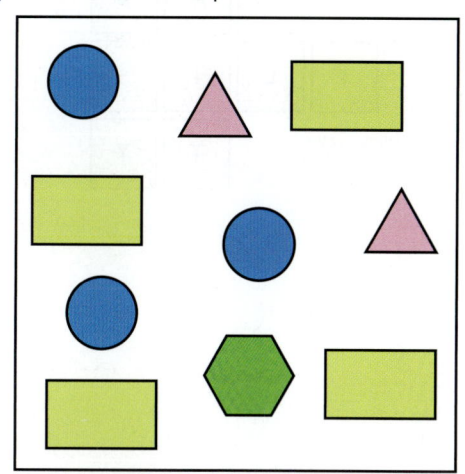

One is selected at random.
What is the probability that the shape selected is:

- **a** a rectangle
- **b** a circle
- **c** a hexagon
- **d** a shape with straight sides
- **e** a square?

2 Alwyn rolls a normal six-sided die.
What is the probability that he rolls:

- **a** a six
- **b** a three
- **c** an even number
- **d** a prime number
- **e** not a six?

3 Bronwen has a pack of 52 playing cards.

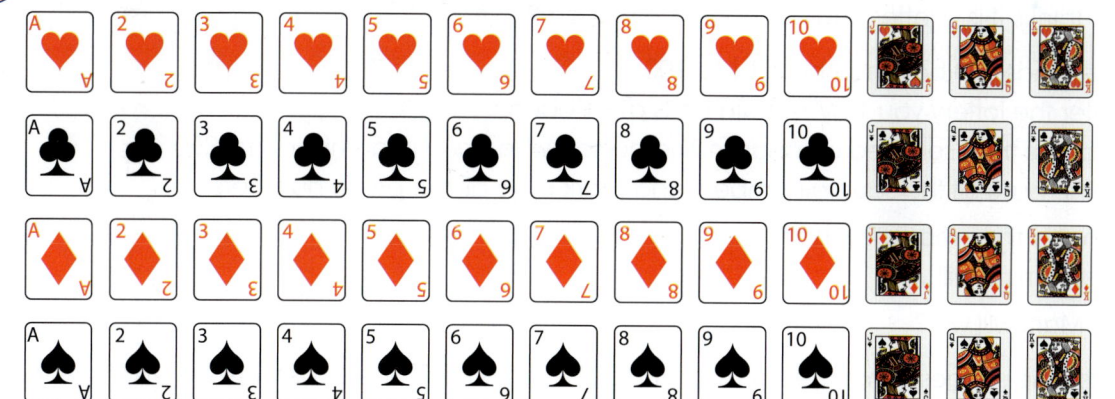

She picks one card at random.
What is the probability that the card she picks is:

- **a** **i** a Queen
  - **ii** a red Queen
  - **iii** the Queen of Hearts
  - **iv** not the Queen of Hearts?
- **b** **i** a five
  - **ii** a black five
  - **iii** the five of Clubs
  - **iv** not a five?

Statistics and Probability Strand 4 Probability

4 Here are some letter tiles.
Richard picks a tile at random.
What is the probability that he picks:

a the letter P
b the letter O
c the letter B
d the letter I
e the letter Z
f a blank tile?

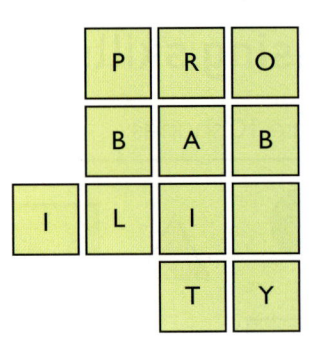

5 Bree has a spinner with 9 equal sides numbered 1 to 9.
What is the probability that:

a on the first spin the number is 1?
b on the second spin the number is 2?
c on the ninth spin the number is 9?
d on the tenth spin the number is 10?

Developing fluency

1 Here is Ahmed's password to his savings account: BADBOY6527.
Ahmed enters the first nine characters correctly but he has forgotten the last one.
He enters a character at random.
What is the probability that he is right if:

a he chooses from all the letters and numbers
b he remembers it is a number and chooses one of them
c he thinks it is a letter and chooses one of them?

2 A lottery has 100 balls numbered 1 to 100.
To enter the lottery you 'buy' certain balls at £1 each.
One ball is then selected at random. The person who has this number wins £50.
Jasmine buys all the square numbers and Mark buys all the prime numbers.

a What is the probability that:
   i   Jasmine will win
   ii Mark will win?

b Jasmine suggests that they form a syndicate. She says, 'If one of us wins, we will share the £50 equally, £25 each'.
Is this a fair arrangement?
Should Mark accept her offer?
Explain your answer.

Unit 2 Single event probability Band e

3 At a village fete there is a 'Lucky Dip' stall which has a barrel with packets in it.
At the start of the day there are 400 packets.
60 packets contain key rings.
20 packets contain chocolate coins.
16 packets contain £1 coins.
3 packets contain £5 notes.
1 packet contains a £20 note.
The remaining packets are empty.

  a How many empty packets are there?

  b On the first draw what is the probability that the packet contains:
   i nothing   ii a key ring   iii a chocolate coin
   iv a £5 note   v a £20 note?

  c Each draw costs £1.
   Jules says she is going to keep on buying tickets until she gets the £20 note.
   Do you think this is a good strategy?

4 A die with 6 faces is believed to be biased. It is rolled many times and the results are as follows.

Number	1	2	3	4	5	6
Frequency	70	38	45	30	52	15

  a How many times was the die thrown?

  b Estimate the probability of each of the outcomes 1, 2, 3, 4, 5 and 6.
   Show your answers in a table.

  c How can you check the figures in your table?

  d The die is rolled again.
   What is the probability that the number rolled is:
   i a 6
   ii a number less than 6
   iii a number greater than 6?

5 Caryl has a bag of counters which are either red, green or blue.
She chooses one at random.

  a The probability that Caryl gets a red counter is $\frac{5}{12}$ and for a green it is $\frac{1}{3}$.
   Find the probability that she gets a blue.

  b Caryl says, 'I think there are 18 counters in the bag.'
   Explain why she must be wrong.

  c What is the fewest possible number of counters in the bag?

6 Here is a spinner.
Hamid says, 'If I spin the spinner four times
I will get a 1, a 2, a 3 and a 4'.
Is Hamid right?
Explain your answer.

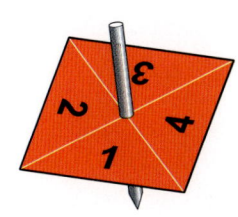

Statistics and Probability Strand 4 Probability

Problem solving

1. A bag contains red balls and blue balls.

   The probability of taking a red ball from the bag at random is $\frac{2}{3}$.
   There are 12 red balls in the bag.
   How many blue balls are in the bag?

2. The pie chart shows the sport last played by each member of a health club.
   The manager of the club displays this information using a pie chart.

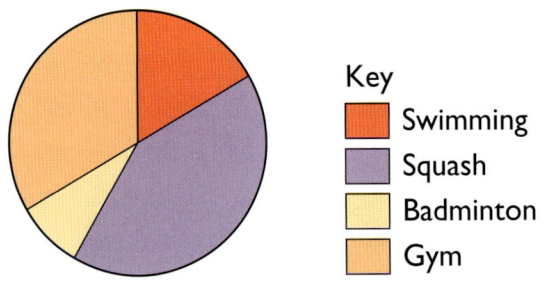

   Key
   - Swimming
   - Squash
   - Badminton
   - Gym

   Work out the probability that a randomly selected club member:

   a played badminton

   b went to the gym or played squash

   c went swimming

   d didn't go swimming.

3. Kyle and Isabelle are playing a game with a set of 21 cards, numbered 1 to 21.
   Kyle selects a card a random, it is the card with number 15.
   Isabelle shuffles the rest of the cards and picks one card at random.

   a What is the probability that the number on Isabelle's card is higher than 15?

   They put their cards back and play again.
   Kyle takes out a card at random.
   Isabelle shuffles the rest of the cards and picks one card at random.
   The probability that the number on this card is higher than the number on Kyle's card is 0.6.

   b What is the number on Kyle's card?

   c What is the probability that the number on Isabelle's card is lower than 15?

4. Ellie throws a biased die.
   The die is equally likely to score a 2 or 4.
   It is twice as likely to score a 1 as a 2.
   It is twice as likely to score a 6 as a 1.
   Find the probability that Ellie throws:

   a a 3

   b a 6

   c an even number.

5 Luc has a bag of toffees and pieces of fudge.
He takes a sweet at random from the bag.
The probability that the sweet is a toffee is $\frac{7}{12}$.

Luc eats four of the sweets and then chooses a sweet at random.
The next sweet is equally likely to be toffee or fudge.

a How many sweets were in the bag to start with?

b How many toffees were there?

c How many sweets of each type did Luc eat?
Find both possible answers.

6 A spinner has:
- eight equal sections and four different colours
- the probability of landing on red is greater than the probability of landing on green
- landing on yellow or blue has equal probability.

Draw the two possible designs.

Reviewing skills

1 Mal throws a die with 8 faces, numbered 1 to 8.
What is the probability that Mal rolls:

a i an 8

  ii a number between 1 and 8

  iii a number between 0 and 8

  iv zero?

b The die is described as 'fair'. What does this mean?

2 A cafe for long distance lorry drivers offers these breakfast dishes.
  Egg, sausage, beans and chips
  Egg, bacon, sausage, tomato and toast
  Bacon buttie
  Scrambled eggs on toast
  Sausage roll

a If a driver chooses his breakfast at random, what is the probability that his breakfast contains

  i egg

  ii sausage

  iii tomato?

b If his breakfast contains egg, what is the probability that it also contains bacon?

Unit 3 • Combined events • Band f

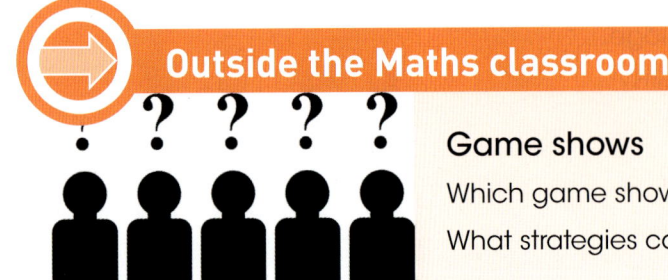

Outside the Maths classroom

Game shows

Which game shows involve probability?

What strategies can help you win?

Toolbox

You can use the formula that for any equally-likely event

$$P(\text{event}) = \frac{\text{total number of successful outcomes}}{\text{total number of possible outcomes}}$$

to find how likely a combination of events is.

To find the total number of combinations, list all of the outcomes if this is possible.

Be systematic and change one item at a time.

If it is not possible to list all the outcomes, you can use a **possibility space** diagram or a **Venn diagram**.

Example – Listing all possible outcomes

Sam is choosing her breakfast. She can choose one cereal and one drink.

Cereals: Wheatamix, Cornflakes or Sugarloops

Drinks: tea or coffee

a Draw a diagram to show all the possibilities for Sam's breakfast.
b Sam selects her cereal and drink at random. What is the probability that she has Sugarloops and coffee?
c How would the list change if Sam had three options for drinks, for example tea, coffee and orange juice?

Solution

a

Drink \ Cereal	Wheatamix	Cornflakes	Sugarloops
Tea	T&W	T&C	T&S
Coffee	C&W	C&C	C&S

b There are 6 possible outcomes and 1 successful outcome.

Probability = $\frac{1}{6}$

c There will be an extra row in the table in answer **a**.

Unit 3 Combined events Band f

Example – Probability space diagrams

Hannie throws two dice, one red and one green.
a Draw and complete a table to show all the possibilities for their total scores.
b What is the probability the total score is
   i   exactly 3
   ii 3 or less
   iii greater than 12
   iv a prime number?
c Would the answers be the same with two red dice?

Solution

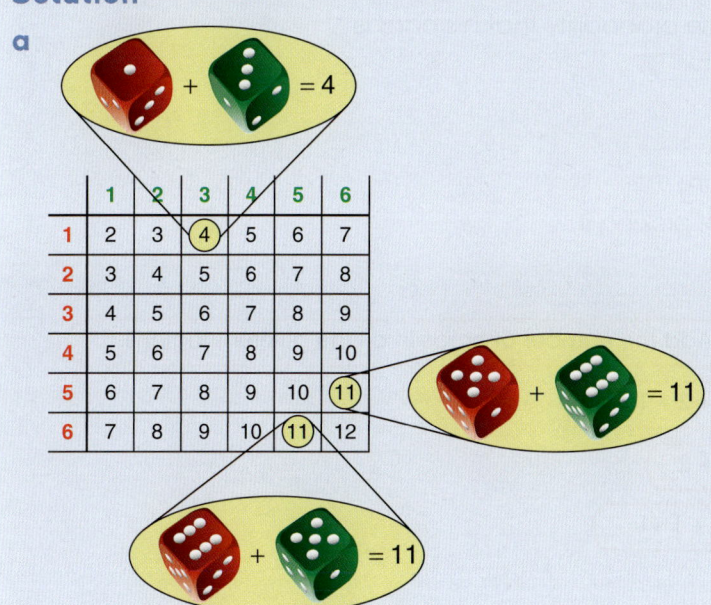

a

	1	2	3	4	5	6
1	2	3	4	5	6	7
2	3	4	5	6	7	8
3	4	5	6	7	8	9
4	5	6	7	8	9	10
5	6	7	8	9	10	11
6	7	8	9	10	11	12

b There are 36 possible outcomes.

i $\frac{2}{36} = \frac{1}{18}$ — There are 2 ways of getting 3, 1 + 2 and 2 + 1, so 2 favourable outcomes.

ii $\frac{3}{36} = \frac{1}{12}$ — There are 3 ways of getting 3 or less.

iii 0 — It is impossible to get more than 12.

iv $\frac{15}{36}$ — Prime numbers 2(1 way), 3(2 ways), 5(4 ways), 7(6 ways), 11(2 ways)

c The answers would be the same.
   The colour of the dice makes no difference. — Sometimes it is easier to see what is going on with different coloured dice.

Statistics and Probability Strand 4 Probability

Example – Venn diagrams

Owain has some cards with different shapes printed on them.
This Venn diagram describes the shapes printed on the cards.

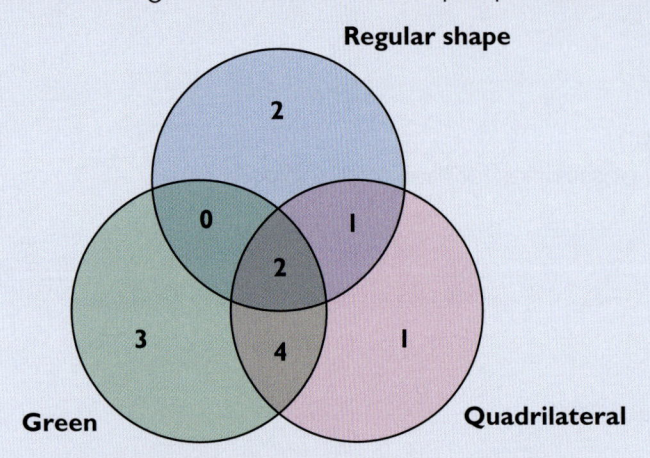

Regular shape: 2
Overlap Regular & Green: 0
Overlap Regular & Quadrilateral: 1
Central intersection: 2
Green: 3
Overlap Green & Quadrilateral: 4
Quadrilateral: 1

a How many cards are there in Owain's pack?
b Owain picks a card at random. What's the probability that his card is
   i a quadrilateral
   ii a green quadrilateral
   iii not green?
c Draw the shape in the central intersection.
   Write a sentence about the probability of picking it.

Solution

a There are 13 cards. ← Add the number of cards in all the different regions.

b i P(quadrilateral) = $\frac{8}{13}$ ← 4 + 2 + 1 + 1

  ii P(green quadrilateral) = $\frac{6}{13}$ ← 4 + 2

  iii P(not green) = $\frac{4}{13}$ ← 2 + 1 + 1

c

[green square]

← A regular quadrilateral is a square.
The intersection requires a green one.

The probability of picking a card with a green square at random is $\frac{2}{13}$.

Unit 3 Combined events Band f

Practising skills

1 Anwar is a keen cricketer. He is a bowler.
So far this season he has got 30 batsman from other teams out.
The table shows how they were out.

Bowled	Caught	LBW	Stumped
9	12	3	6

a One of the batsman Anwar got out is chosen at random.
What is the probability that he was:
   i bowled   **ii** LBW   **iii** caught   **iv** stumped?

b Add your answers to part **b** together.
What does your answer tell you?

c So far Anwar has played 10 matches.
He has 20 matches more to play.
How many more batsman can he expect to get out by being bowled?

2 A restaurant has 4 starters and 3 main course meals as shown on the menu card.

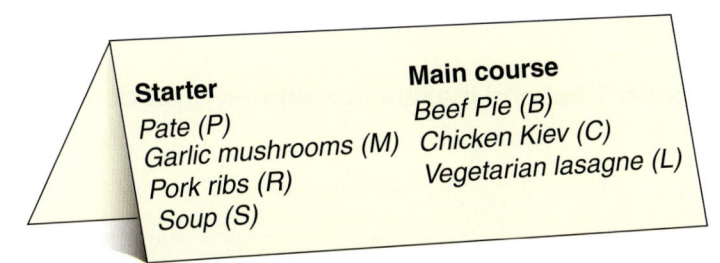

Starter
Pate (P)
Garlic mushrooms (M)
Pork ribs (R)
Soup (S)

Main course
Beef Pie (B)
Chicken Kiev (C)
Vegetarian lasagne (L)

a Make a list of the possible combinations of starter and main course.

b How many meals are there in your list?
How could you work it out quickly without listing them all?

c Rodric says, 'Get me anything'.
If the Starter and Main course are selected at random, what is the probability he gets soup and beef pie?

3 Two ordinary fair dice are rolled.
One die is red and the other is blue.
The numbers that come up are multiplied together.

a Copy and complete this table to show all the possible outcomes.

b What is the probability that the product is:
   i 8
   ii 25
   iii 7
   iv a number below 37?

c Do the colours of the dice make any difference?

d What types of numbers between 1 and 36 have a probability of $\frac{1}{36}$?

		\multicolumn{6}{c}{Red die}
×		1	2	3	4	5	6
Blue die	1						
	2						
	3						
	4						
	5						
	6						

599

Statistics and Probability Strand 4 Probability

4 Glynis has two spinners: the blue one has four equal edges numbered 1 to 4 and the green one has 6 equal edges numbered 1 to 6.
Glynis spins them and adds the two numbers together.

   a Make a table to show all the possible outcomes.

   b What is the probability that Glynis gets a score of:
      i 5   **ii** 12   **iii** 7?

   c Which other numbers between 1 and 20 have the same probability as:
      i 5   **ii** 12   **iii** 7?

5 Members of a sports club may play golf (G) or bowls (B).
Some play both and some play neither.
The numbers are shown on the Venn diagram.

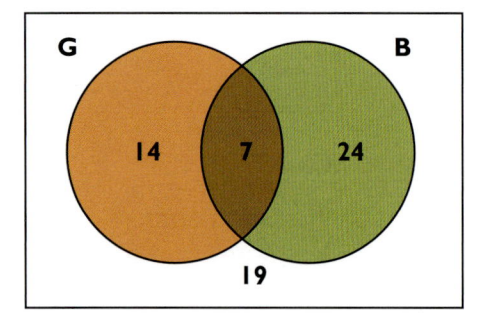

The club holds a raffle. Every member has a ticket and the winner is chosen at random.
Find the probability that the winner

   a plays golf

   b plays bowls

   c plays both golf and bowls

   d does not play golf

   e does not play bowls

   f does not play either bowls or golf?

Developing fluency

1 A mother cat has had a lot of kittens.
Her owner, Beca, classifies them as follows.

	Tabby	Ginger	Black & White	Tortoiseshell
Female	3	0	4	3
Male	3	4	3	0

   a Beca has a photo of each of the kittens.
     She selects a photo at random. What is the probability that the photo is of:
      i a female kitten   **ii** a tabby kitten   **iii** a female tabby?

   b Beca says, 'The kittens prove conclusively that all ginger cats are male and all tortoiseshell cats are female.'
     Comment on this statement.

Unit 3 Combined events Band f

2 Wyn is on holiday.
In his wardrobe he has four shirts and three pairs of shorts.

Shirts	Shorts
Green	Black
Red	Grey
Black	Cream
Cream	

  a Make a list of all the possible combinations to wear.

  b Wyn grabs one shirt and one pair of shorts in the darkness.
  What is the probability that he has:

  i a red shirt and grey shorts

  ii a shirt and shorts of the same colour?

3 Cari has two bags with coloured balls in each.
Bag 1 has 2 red and 3 blue balls.
Bag 2 has 4 red and 2 blue balls.

  a Copy and complete this table to show all possible outcomes when Cari selects a ball at random from each bag.

		\multicolumn{5}{c}{Bag 1}
		R	R	B	B	B
Bag 2	R					
	R					
	R					
	R					
	B		RB			
	B					

  b She selects a ball from each bag at random.
  What is the probability that they are:

  i one red and one blue

  ii two red

  iii two blue?

4 The Venn diagram shows the membership of a rugby club.
There are 30 members. Some of them are backs, others are forwards and there are some non-playing members.

  a Fill in the missing number on a copy of the Venn diagram.

  b A team of 15 players (8 forwards and 7 backs) is chosen for an away match.
  Another member of the club is chosen at random from the remaining players to be the travelling substitute.
  What is the probability that the substitute is

  i a forward

  ii a back?

  c A new player joins the club. He can play as a forward or as a back.
  Draw a new Venn diagram to illustrate the changed membership of the club.

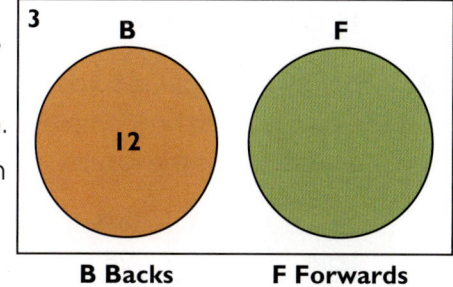

3, B (12), F

B Backs   F Forwards

601

Statistics and Probability Strand 4 Probability

5 Tiffany and Morgan are playing a game with a red spinner and a yellow spinner.
The red spinner is numbered 1 0 1 0 1.
The yellow spinner is numbered 0 1 0 1 0.
They are spun together.

   a Make a table showing the total of the numbers on the two spinners.

   b What is the probability that the total is:
      i 0   **ii** 1   **iii** 2?

   c Now make a table for the product of the numbers on the two spinners (when they are multiplied together).

   d What is the probability that the product is:
      i 0   **ii** 1   **iii** 2?

Problem solving

1 Rhys and Chloe are playing a game.
They each throw a die and the scores are multiplied together.

   a Complete the possibility space diagram.

	1	2	3	4	5	6
1						
2						
3				12		
4						24
5		10				
6						

   b Rhys wins if the product is odd. Is the game fair? Explain your answer fully.

   c Find the probability of getting a product of
      i 6
      ii a multiple of 6
      iii a factor of 60.

2 A factory manager records whether employees arrived late or on time one Friday.
She also records how employees got to work that day.
The table shows the results.

	Walk	Bus	Car	Cycle
Late	5	28	6	7
On time	95	85	142	32

   a An employee is selected at random. Find the probability that they
      i were on time
      ii walked and were late
      iii were late and came by bus.

   b The manager says that the results show that employees are not making enough effort to arrive at work on time. Comment on the manager's statement.

3 Baby Selwyn has lots of different bricks.

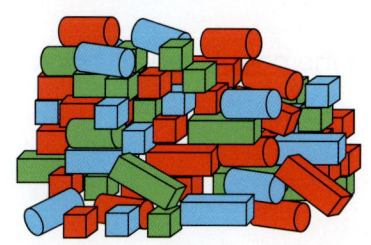

	Cube	Cuboid	Cylinder	Total
Red	14	40		71
Green	21		12	60
Blue		33		69
Total		100	42	

a Copy and complete the table.

b Find the probability that a randomly chosen brick is
  i a cuboid
  ii red
  iii a blue cube.

c Find the probability that a randomly chosen
  i cuboid is green
  ii green brick is a cuboid.

4 Isobel and Tomos are playing a game.
They each spin a spinner with sides numbered 1, 2 and 3.

a List all the possible outcomes of the two spinners.

b Isobel wins the game when one spinner shows an odd number and the other spinner shows an even number. Work out the probability that Isobel wins the game.

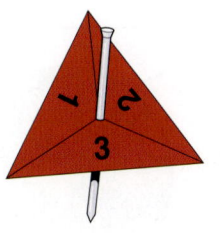

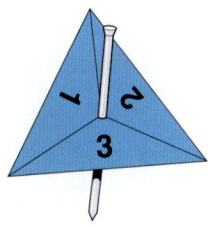

c How can they make the game fair?

Statistics and Probability Strand 4 Probability

5 A group of scientists find a remote population in the Amazon rainforest.
They estimate there are 1500 adults living in 30 villages.
The scientists spend time in one village and notice that many of the people are left-handed.
They record these data for the adults in that village.

	Women	Men
Right-handed	16	14
Left-handed	11	9

a An adult is chosen at random from the village. Find the probability that the person is
  i a woman
  ii left-handed
  iii a left-handed woman.

b One of the scientists says that the women in the village are more likely to be left-handed than the men.
Comment on this statement.

c The data from the village is used to estimate the number of left-handed adults in the complete remote population.
  i Calculate this estimate.
  ii Give a reason why this estimate may be very inaccurate.

6 A school has 200 Year 11 students. Of these, 136 study French, 96 study German and 8 students study neither French nor German.

a Copy and complete the Venn diagram.

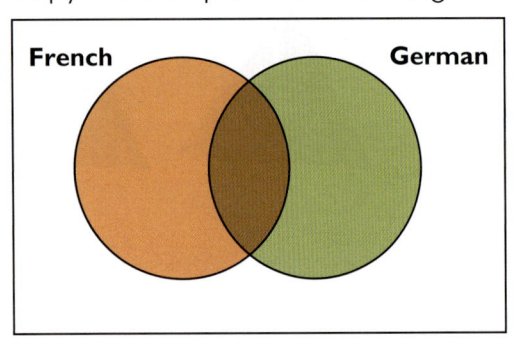

b Find the probability that a student selected at random studies
  i French
  ii French and German
  iii German but not French.

7 A café records what their customers order one morning.

The table shows the results.

	Coffee	Not coffee
Cake	82	35
No cake	90	43

a A customer is chosen at random.

Find the probability that they order:
  i   coffee and a cake
  ii neither coffee nor a cake
  iii coffee.

b The café is open 6 days a week and expects to have 400 customers a day.
  i   Estimate how many customers have a coffee in a week.

A 200 g bag of coffee beans makes 24 cups of coffee.
The café owner wants to order enough coffee to last for the next four weeks.
  ii How many kilograms of coffee should she order? Give your answer correct to the nearest kilogram.

Reviewing skills

1 Tudur and Bella are playing a game with a green die and a blue die.

The green die in numbered 1 3 3 4 6 6.

The blue die is numbered 2 3 4 4 5 5.

The dice are rolled and the scores that come up are added together.

a Make a table showing the possible outcomes.

b Find the probability of getting
  i   a 3 on both dice
  ii a total of 7
  iii a double
  iv a total of at least 6
  v   a number on the blue die that is 1 more than that on the green die.

Unit 4 • Estimating probability • Band f

Outside the Maths classroom

Insurance
What factors affect the cost of insurance?

Toolbox

A **population** is everything or everyone with some characteristic, for example
- All people over 100 years old
- All red squirrels
- All the students in a school
- All cars of a particular model.

A **sample** is a small set that is chosen from the population to provide information about it.

Samples are often used to **estimate** population probabilities.

To be useful a sample must be representative of the population. This is often achieved by choosing a **random** sample, but this is not always possible. The larger the sample, the more accurate it is likely to be.

Probability is estimated from what has been observed, using **relative frequency**.

Sometimes you need to carry out an experiment with **trials**.

Estimated probability (or relative frequency) = $\dfrac{\text{number of successful trials}}{\text{total number of trials}}$

You can estimate the number of times an outcome will occur using the formula

Expected number = P (a successful outcome) × number of trials

> In a random sample every item in the population has the same probability of being selected, so is equally likely.

Example – Using a sample

It is believed that a rare bird species has more males than females. After a long search, a team of scientists find a colony of these birds. 16 of them are male and 4 are female.

a Estimate the probability that a bird of this type is male.

b Comment on the sampling method.

Solution

a The total number of birds is 16 + 4 = 20.

The estimated probability that a bird in the population is male is $\frac{16}{20} = 0.8$.

b The sample is not random. It is just one group of the birds.

> This is an example of an opportunity sample.

The sample is small so the estimate is unlikely to be accurate. If the scientists can find more birds, and so have a larger sample, the estimate should be more reliable.

Example – Relative frequency

An insurance company investigates a number of speeding convictions in a country. It classifies them according to the age and gender of the offender and then summarises the data in this table.

		Age	
		Under 25	25 and over
Gender	Male	455	284
Gender	Female	120	141

a Calculate the probability that a speeding conviction belongs to
  i   a male person
  ii someone under 25.
b Do the data show that males drive faster than females?

Solution

Start by adding a Total row and column to the table

a

		Age		Total
		Under 25	25 and over	
Gender	Male	455	284	739
Gender	Female	120	141	261
Gender	Total	575	425	1000

i $P(\text{male}) = \frac{739}{1000}$ ← There are 739 convictions for males.
← There are 1000 convictions in total.

ii $P(\text{under 25}) = \frac{575}{1000}$ ← There are 575 convictions for under 25s.

b No. The data do not tell you how many male and how many female drivers there are.

It is possible that in that country there are only a few female drivers but they drive fast and get convictions.

It is also possible that there are about equal numbers of male and female drivers and the males do drive faster.

You do not have the information to draw a conclusion.

Statistics and Probability Strand 4 Probability

Example – Sampling systematically

Rowena plans a survey to find out if students enjoy the meals from the bistro each day.
Usually the bistro serves approximately 400 students per day. Far too many students for Rowena to cope with!

a Suggest a systematic method of sampling that Rowena could use to carry out her survey and have results based on approximately 80 students.

b How might Rowena improve the reliability of her results?

Solution

a $400 \div 80 = 5$, this means Rowena needs to sample $\frac{1}{5}$ of the 400 students.

She could do this by asking systematically every 5th student entering the bistro.

b Rowena might improve the reliability by asking more students.
Maybe she could cope with asking every 4th student entering the bistro.
This would mean asking $400 \div 4 = 100$ students.
This would mean her survey would be based on asking $\frac{100}{4} = \frac{1}{4}$ of the students about the bistro meals.

Practising skills

1 A shop sells newspapers.
Here are the results for a few days.

Newspaper	Daily Post	Gazette	The News	The Tribune
Frequency	186	84	216	105

a Estimate the probability that the next newspaper sold will be *The News*.

b The owners open a new shop in the same area. They expect to sell 1000 newspapers each day. How many of each one should they stock?

2 A computer repair company keeps a record of the faults in the computers it repairs.

Component	Motherboard	Power supply	Hard drive
Frequency	67	215	103

a Millie is called out to do a repair. Estimate the probability that she will find the fault is in the
   i motherboard   **ii** power supply   **iii** hard drive.

b The engineers say that it is more likely than not that the fault will be in the power supply. Are they correct?

c The computer company normally repair 5000 computers each year. Estimate how many of each component they will need.

Unit 4 Estimating probability Band f

3 Ben has a gold coin. It is going to be used for the toss in the World Cup Final.
Ben wants to be sure his coin is unbiased.
He throws his coin and records how many heads he gets.

Number of throws	20	50	100	400	1000	2000	5000
Number of heads	12	27	46	211	486	982	2516
Relative frequency	0.6						

a Copy and complete the relative frequency line of the table.

b Draw a graph to show the number of throws of relative frequency.

c Do you think his coin is unbiased? Give a reason for your conclusion.

4 During a local election a radio station conducts an exit poll. They ask people who they have voted for, as they came out of one polling station.
Here are the results.

Party	Blue Party	Red Party	Orange Party
Number of voters	84	72	33

a Work out the probability that one voter selected at random voted for
  i the Blue Party
  ii the Red Party
  iii the Orange Party.

b There are 20 000 voters in the community.
  i Estimate how many vote for the Orange Party.
  ii Comment on the reliability of your answer.

5 The police force in a large city select vehicles at random for road-worthiness checks.
The table shows the results of a traffic survey at a particular road junction.

Vehicle	Lorry	Van	Bus or coach	Car
Frequency	15 305	2411	1064	24 792

a Estimate the probability of each type of vehicle being selected on one occasion.

b In one week the police carry out checks on 190 vehicles at the same road junction.
Estimate how many of these vehicles are buses or coaches.

c On one occasion, across the whole city, the police select 2400 vehicles for checks.
Comment on the accuracy of using the data from the table to estimate the total number of lorries checked.
Give a reason for your answer.

Statistics and Probability Strand 4 Probability

6 Wyn has bought a die, he is not sure if the die is fair. He carries out an experiment and records the number of sixes he threw in every 10 throws of the die.

Number of throws	10	10	10	10	10	10	10	10	10	10
Number of sixes	4	5	1	2	3	4	3	4	3	3

Wyn creates a table to show the cumulative number of sixes thrown and to calculate the relative frequencies.

Total number of throws	10	20	30	40	50	60	70	80	90	100
Total number of sixes thrown	4	9	10	12						
Relative frequency of throwing a six	$\frac{4}{10}$	$\frac{9}{20}$								
	0.4	0.45								

a Complete Wyn's table.

b Draw a graph to illustrate the relative frequency of throwing a six on Wyn's die. Mark your axes like those below.

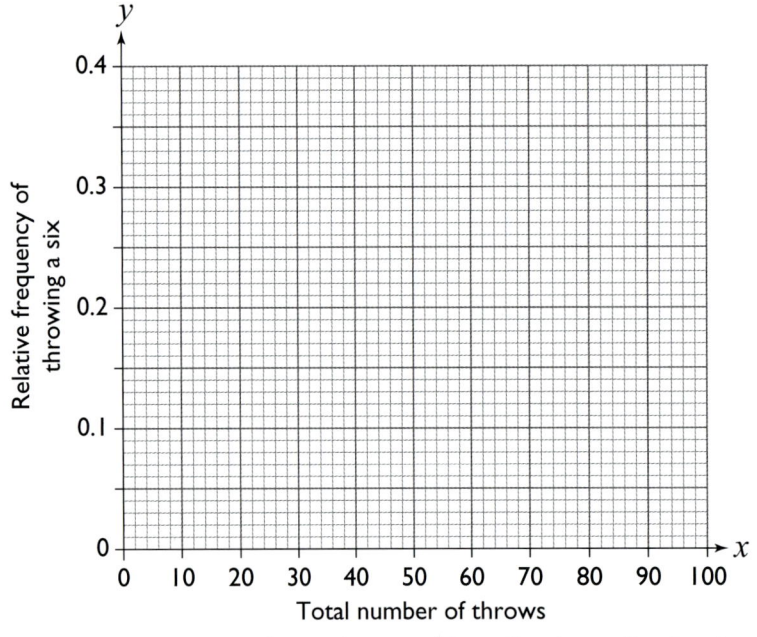

c Using your answers in parts **a** and **b**, write down the best estimate for the probability of **not** obtaining a six on Wyn's die. Give a reason for your answer.

d Wyn says that the die is not a fair die. Explain why Wyn's statement could be true.

Developing fluency

1 A bag contains some coloured balls. They are red, blue or green.
Eleanor takes a ball out at random, notes its colour and replaces it.
She does this 40 times.
Here are her results.

Colour	Red	Blue	Green
Frequency	12	18	10

a Estimate the probability that the next ball she draws is
   i red
   ii blue
   iii green.

b There are 12 balls in the bag.
Estimate how many there are of each colour.
What could Eleanor do to make her estimate more reliable?

2 A school conducts a small survey among its students to see if they like their uniform or if they want to change it.
Here are their results.

Decision	Frequency
Like it/Keep it	42
Change it	29
Don't know	16

a Use the data to estimate the probability that a student selected randomly will answer:
   i Keep it
   ii Change it
   iii Don't know.

b The governors say that if there are at least 400 students in the school who want to change the uniform then they will discuss it at their next meeting. There are 1240 students in the school. Are the governors likely to discuss school uniform at their next meeting?

3 The table lists the births in a maternity hospital in one week.

	Boys	Girls
Monday	5	3
Tuesday	2	4
Wednesday	6	3
Thursday	4	7
Friday	5	1

A baby is selected at random and called 'the baby of the week'.

a What is the probability that the baby of the week on this occasion is
   i male
   ii female?

b During one year, how many babies of the week would you expect to be male and how many female?

Statistics and Probability Strand 4 Probability

4) Kwame and Kofi are investigating a type of moth.
There are two varieties of this moth: light and dark.
They collect moths at different sites, A and B, and record which variety each moth it is that they collect.

Kwame (Site A)			
Light	Dark	Dark	Light
Dark	Light	Dark	Dark
Light	Dark	Dark	Dark
Light	Light	Dark	Dark
Dark	Dark	Dark	Dark

Kofi (Site B)			
Dark	Light	Light	Light
Light	Dark	Dark	Light
Light	Light	Light	Light
Dark	Light	Light	Dark
Light	Dark	Light	Light

a Estimate the probability that a moth is dark:
  i using all the data
  ii using only Kwame's data
  iii using only Kofi's data.

b Kwame says he thinks the moths are different at the two sites.
Explain why he says this.

c Kofi says, 'To be sure, we need to ...'
Complete Kofi's sentence.

5) Tim has a normal die.
Sara says that she normally throws a six every 3 throws.
Pete says he takes at least 20 throws to get a six.
Ian says that he never gets a six.

a Who is correct?

b Tim throws the dice 20 times and gets 5 sixes.
  i Is the die definitely biased?
  ii Alfie then throws the dice 100 times and gets 15 sixes. Is the die biased?

c How can they check that the die is unbiased?

6) Ceri has an unbiased coin. He says that if he throws the coin twice he should get one head.
Is he correct? Explain your answer.

7) Siân, Lowri and Gareth want to know the probability that a letter in written English is an E. (It can be upper case E or lower case e.) They each take a sentence as a sample to estimate this probability.

a In each case, use the sample sentence to estimate the probability that a letter in written English is an E.
  i Siân: *The quick brown fox jumps over the lazy dog.*
  ii Lowri: *To be or not to be, that is the question.*
  iii Gareth: *Never in the field of human conflict have so many owed so much to so few.*

b The probability of a letter being E is actually 0.12.
  i Which of the sentences gave the closest estimate?
  ii Explain why Siân's sentence cannot be regarded as random.

c Suggest how they can obtain a more accurate estimate.

d In a *Scrabble* set there are 100 tiles. Two of them are blank and the other 98 have letters on them. How many tiles would you expect to have the letter E in a set designed for players using English?
Find out how many Es there are in a standard *Scrabble* set.

Unit 4 Estimating probability Band f

8 Tom has been asked to carry out a survey to find out how many football supporters entering the ground at Gate A have ever been to a football match before.

It is likely that there will be 3000 supporters passing through Gate A before the match. He needs to sample approximately 20% of the supporters.

How can Tom carry out his survey by using a systematic sampling method?

9 Iona needs to record weather data throughout the year. She hasn't time to record all the data required every day.

Suggest a systematic method of sampling so that she will record data for at least 12 days every year.

Problem solving

1 Here is the result of a traffic survey a council did over one week on a busy road.
It shows the numbers of lorries, buses, motorbikes and cars that used the road.

	Lorries	Buses	Cars	Motorbikes
Frequency	16 000	10 000	240 000	9000

a Keith stands at the side of this road.
Estimate the probability that the next vehicle to go past Keith is
  i   a car
  ii a motorbike
  iii not a lorry.

b In one day, 15 000 vehicles go past a particular point.
Estimate the number of buses to pass that point.

2 A biased tetrahedral die has 4 sides numbered 1, 2, 3 and 4.
The die is thrown 20 times and the number it lands on is recorded.
1 3 4 2 4 4 3 2 2 1 1 2 2 4 3 2 1 1 1 2

a Copy and complete the relative frequency table.

Lands on	1	2	3	4
Relative frequency				0.2

These are the relative frequencies after the die is thrown 100 times.

Lands on	1	2	3	4
Relative frequency	0.3	0.4	0.15	0.15

b Which of the two relative frequencies for 'lands on 4' is the better estimate of the probability of the die landing on 4?
Give a reason for your answer.

The die continues to be thrown.

c Estimate the number of times it will land on '1' in 1000 throws.

Statistics and Probability Strand 4 Probability

3 A school is consulting students about changing the length of the school lunch time from 45 minutes to 30 minutes.

A sample of students gave the following opinions.

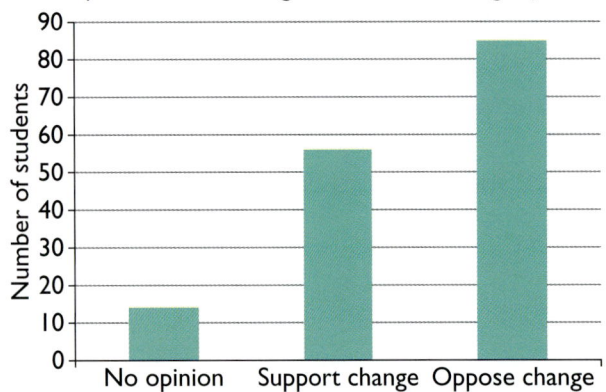

[Bar chart: No opinion ≈ 14, Support change ≈ 56, Oppose change ≈ 85; y-axis: Number of students, 0 to 90]

   a Estimate the probability that a randomly chosen student will support the change.

The school has 1200 students.

   b Use these sample results to estimate how many of the 1200 students are likely to oppose the change.

4 A four-sided spinner has the numbers 1, 3, 5 and 7 on it.
The table shows the probability that it will land on each number.

Number	1	3	5	7
Probability	0.15	0.4	0.25	0.2

Harry spins the spinner 150 times.

   a Work out how many times he expects to get
      i 3   **ii** 5.

   b How many times does he expect **not** to get 3?

   c What is the probability that he does not get 3?

5 At a charity fete there is a stall selling tickets.

The probability of winning £1 with one ticket is $\frac{1}{8}$.
Tickets cost 20p each.
The charity would like to make a profit of £120.
How many tickets do they need to sell?

6 A parsnip grower uses a machine to sort her parsnips. The parsnip grower carried out a survey to investigate the probability of oversized parsnips passing through her sorting machine. The relative frequency of oversized parsnips passing through the machine was calculated after a total of 100, 200, 300, 400, 500 and 600 parsnips. The results are plotted on the graph below.

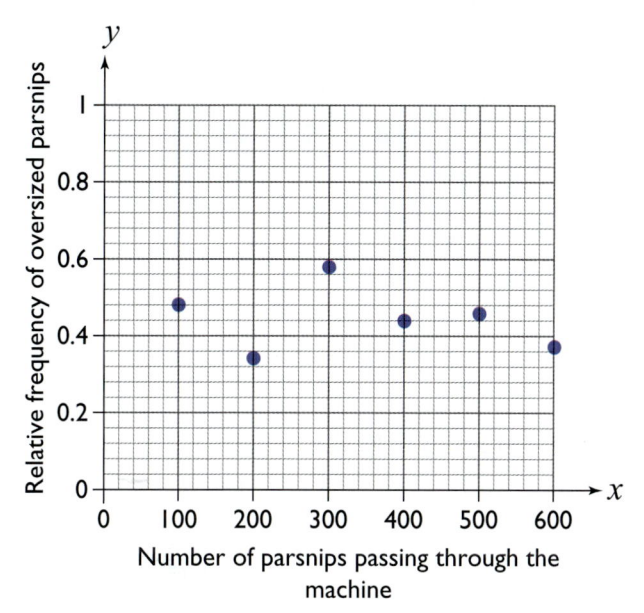

a Write down the best estimate for the probability that one of these parsnips, selected at random, will be oversized. You must give a reason for your answer.

A soup company offers to buy oversized parsnips at 8p each.

b How much would the parsnip grower receive if she decided to sell, to the soup company, all the oversized parsnips in the first 100 parsnips sorted by the machine?

The parsnip grower decides not to sell her parsnips to the soup company. She sells 900 parsnips to a small supermarket. The parsnip grower sells these parsnips for £3.50 per 100 parsnips. She has agreed with the manager of the supermarket that she will give a 3p refund per oversized parsnip discovered.

c What would your best estimate be for the amount you would expect the parsnip grower to make from this transaction?

Statistics and Probability Strand 4 Probability

7 Mr Thomas wants to find out how fit the students at his school are.

A bleep test involves running between two points that are 20m apart.

Each stage consists of several laps and a bleep signifies the start of the next stage. The bleeps get progressively closer together so the student has to run faster to complete the next level.

Mr Thomas asks a group of randomly chosen Year 9 students to perform a bleep test.

Here are the results.

Stage achieved	1	2	3	4	5	6	7	8	9	10
Girls	4	5	7	13	23	15	9	2	1	1
Boys	2	3	5	7	16	23	14	5	3	2

a Estimate the probability that a randomly chosen
   i boy achieves stage 10
   ii girl achieves stage 6 or better
   iii student achieves stage 4.

b Mr Thomas says a student is unfit if they achieve stage 3 or lower.
   There are 190 girls and 200 boys in Year 9.
   Estimate the number of
   i girls that are unfit
   ii boys that are unfit.

c There are 180 boys in Year 7, Mr Thomas says, 'I expect that about 36 Year 7 boys will achieve stage 5.'
   Is Mr Thomas's estimate too low, too high, or about right? Give a reason for your answer.

Reviewing skills

A doctors' surgery keeps a record of how early or late patients are seen.
The results are recorded in the table below.

At least $\frac{1}{4}$ hour early	4
Up to $\frac{1}{4}$ hour early	20
On time	8
Up to 5 minutes late	4
5 minutes to 10 minutes late	3
more than 10 minutes late	1

a Use the table to find the probability that a patient selected at random will be seen
   i up to 5 minutes late
   ii 5 minutes to 10 minutes late
   iii more than 10 minutes late.

b The next day the surgery sees 124 patients. Estimate how many of them will be seen more than 10 minutes late.

There is a larger doctors' surgery in the same town. In one day, the larger surgery sees 438 patients.

c Comment on the accuracy of using the data from the table to estimate the probability that a patient is seen late at the larger surgery.
   Give a reason for your answer.

Unit 5 • The multiplication rule • Band h

Outside the Maths classroom

Game shows
Why do so many game shows involve chance? How can contestants use the laws of probability to help them win?

Toolbox

Events are **independent** if the outcome of one does not affect the outcomes of the other.
For two independent events, A and B, then
P(A and B) = P(A) × P(B)

When a coin is flipped and a die is rolled then the score on the die does not change the likelihood of getting heads on the coin. So '*rolling a 6*' and '*heads*' are **independent**.

P('*6*' and '*heads*') = $\frac{1}{6} \times \frac{1}{2} = \frac{1}{12}$.

Events are **dependent** if the outcome of one event affects the outcomes of the other.
The events '*first marble is red*' and '*second marble is red*' without replacement are **dependent events**.
The first event has had an impact on the probability of the second event.

A **tree diagram** can be used to show all the possible outcomes of an event or sequence of events.

Statistics and Probability Strand 4 Probability

This tree diagram shows the possible outcomes of taking marbles from a bag containing 3 red marbles and 2 green marbles.

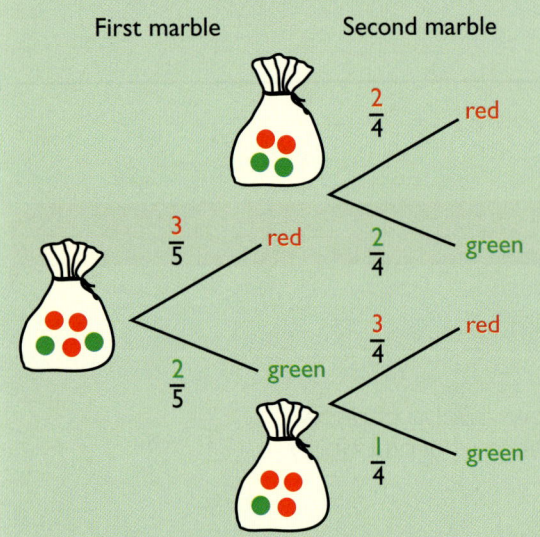

First marble   Second marble

- $\frac{3}{5}$ red
  - $\frac{2}{4}$ red
  - $\frac{2}{4}$ green
- $\frac{2}{5}$ green
  - $\frac{3}{4}$ red
  - $\frac{1}{4}$ green

You can multiply the probabilities as you move along the branches to find the probability of combined events.

P(red marble followed by a green marble) = $\frac{3}{5} \times \frac{2}{4} = \frac{6}{20}$

Example – Independent events

A coin is flipped and a die is rolled.
a   The coin is flipped 10 times and each time shows a tail.
    What is the probability that the 11th time it will also show a tail?
b   A die is rolled 100 times and a six has not yet been rolled.
    What is the probability that the next roll will give a six?
c   What is the probability of getting a 'tail' and a '6' together?

Solution

a   Each flip of a coin is an independent event. What has happened in previous flips does not affect it so the probability is $\frac{1}{2}$.

> Wrongly believing that a head is more likely to turn up as it is 'overdue' is known as the 'Gamblers fallacy'.

b   Each roll of a die is an independent event so the probability of scoring a six on each roll is exactly the same. The probability of scoring a six on the 100th roll is $\frac{1}{6}$.

c   The events are independent, so P(tail and 6) = P(tail) × P(6)

$$= \frac{1}{2} \times \frac{1}{6} \quad \left(\frac{1}{2} \times \frac{1}{6} = \frac{1 \times 1}{2 \times 6} = \frac{1}{12} \right)$$

$$= \frac{1}{12}$$

Unit 5 The multiplication rule Band h

Example – Without replacement

In an office there are 30 employees. Nine of them wear glasses.
Two employees are chosen at random from the group.
a What is the probability that the second employee chosen wears glasses?
b What is the probability that exactly one of the employees wears glasses?

Solution

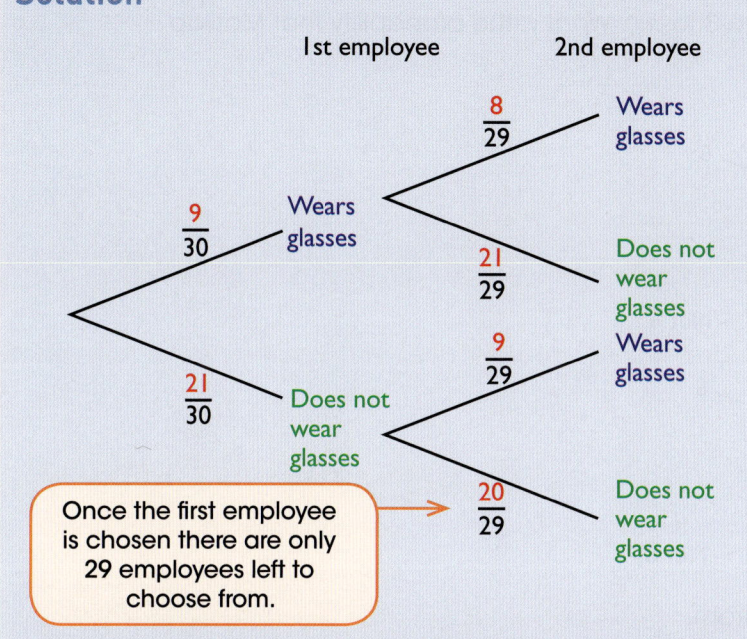

Tree diagram:

1st employee → Wears glasses ($\frac{9}{30}$) or Does not wear glasses ($\frac{21}{30}$)

2nd employee (from Wears glasses): Wears glasses ($\frac{8}{29}$), Does not wear glasses ($\frac{21}{29}$)

2nd employee (from Does not wear glasses): Wears glasses ($\frac{9}{29}$), Does not wear glasses ($\frac{20}{29}$)

Once the first employee is chosen there are only 29 employees left to choose from.

a The second employee wears glasses in two of the paths on the tree diagram.

$$P(\text{1st wears glasses and 2nd wears glasses}) = \frac{9}{30} \times \frac{8}{27} = \frac{72}{870}.$$

The probability that the second employee chosen wears glasses is found by adding these two probabilities together.

$$P(\text{1st does not wear glasses and 2nd wears glasses}) = \frac{21}{30} \times \frac{9}{29} = \frac{189}{870}.$$

So, $P(\text{2nd employee wears glasses}) = \frac{72}{870} + \frac{189}{870} = \frac{261}{870} = \frac{87}{290}$.

Simplify to $\frac{87}{290}$ by dividing the 'top' and 'bottom' by 3.

b There are two paths through the tree diagram that lead to exactly one employee wearing glasses.

$$P(\text{1st wears glasses and 2nd does not wear glasses}) = \frac{9}{30} \times \frac{21}{29} = \frac{189}{870}.$$

$$P(\text{1st does not wear glasses and 2nd does wear glasses}) = \frac{21}{30} \times \frac{9}{29} = \frac{189}{870}.$$

So, $P(\text{exactly one wears glasses}) = \frac{189}{870} + \frac{189}{870} = \frac{378}{870} = \frac{63}{145}$.

Statistics and Probability Strand 4 Probability

Practising skills

1 Matilda is playing *Snakes and ladders* with Gwyneth. They use one die.
   a Matilda rolls the die first. What is the probability that she rolls a 6?
   b Gwyneth rolls the die. What is the probability that she rolls a 6?
   c Matilda rolls the die again. What is the probability that she rolls a 6?
   d Gwyneth rolls the die again. What is the probability that she rolls a 6?
   e After a while Matilda needs to roll a 3 to win. What is the probability that Matilda rolls a 3 on her next turn?

2 Two dice are rolled.

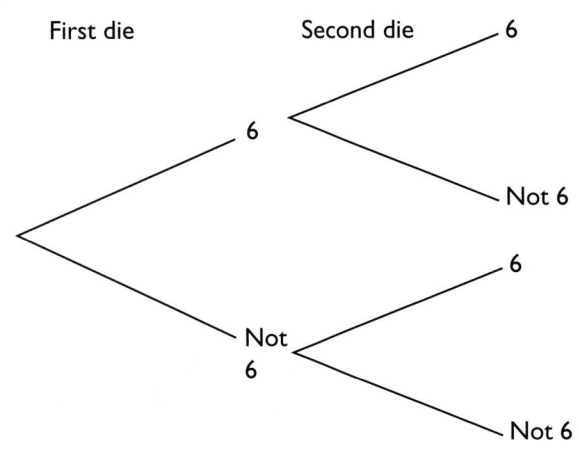

   a Copy and complete the tree diagram.
   Use this tree diagram to calculate the probability that
   b both dice show a 6
   c neither die shows a 6
   d at least one die shows a 6
   e exactly one die shows a 6.

3 Arlo and Bekah are playing cards. There are 52 cards in the pack; 4 of them are aces. They deal the cards and they are not replaced.
   a Bekah deals the first card. What is the probability that it is an ace?
   b Bekah's card is not an ace. Arlo gets the next card. What is the probability that it is an ace?
   c Arlo's card is not an ace. Bekah deals the next card. What is the probability that it is an ace?
   d Bekah's card **is** an ace. Arlo deals the next card. What is the probability that it is an ace?

Unit 5 The multiplication rule Band h

4 A coin is tossed and a die is rolled.

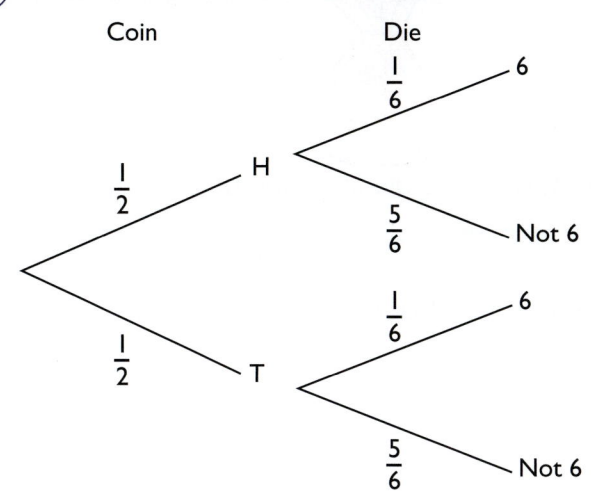

Coin — Die

H (1/2): 1/6 → 6, 5/6 → Not 6
T (1/2): 1/6 → 6, 5/6 → Not 6

Use this tree diagram to calculate the probability of scoring

a a head and a six

b a head and not a six

c a tail and a six

d a tail and not a six.

5 12 coloured counters are placed into a bag. Seven are red and five are blue.
A counter is drawn out of the bag. The counter is not replaced. A second counter is then drawn out of the bag.

a Copy and complete this tree diagram.

First counter   Second counter

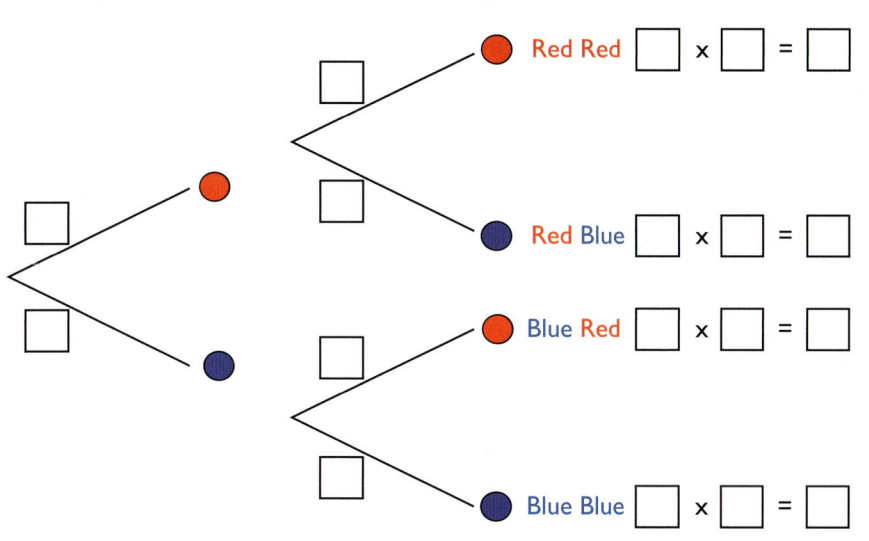

Red Red □ × □ = □

Red Blue □ × □ = □

Blue Red □ × □ = □

Blue Blue □ × □ = □

b Another time the first counter is replaced.
Draw the tree diagram for this situation.

Statistics and Probability Strand 4 Probability

6 Della has these coloured counters in a bag.

  a She takes out a counter without looking.
   What is the probability that it is red?

  b The first counter was red. Della does not put it back.
   How many red counters and how many yellow counters are left in the bag?

  c Della shakes the bag and takes out another counter.
   What is the probability that it is red?
   This counter too is red and again Della does not put it back.
   She takes out another counter from the bag.
   What is the probability that it is
     i red   **ii** yellow?

Developing fluency

1 A class of students has 16 girls and 13 boys.
 Two names are chosen at random from the register.

  a Draw a tree diagram to show the possible outcomes.

  b Use your tree diagram to find the probability that
     i both students are girls
     ii both students are boys
     iii at least one of the students is a boy
     iv exactly one of the students is a boy.

2 In each case, state whether P and Q are independent or dependent.

  a P: I toss a coin and record how it lands.
   Q: I roll a die and record its score.

  b P: It rains some time today.
   Q: It rains some time tomorrow.

  c P: A person lives to be 100 years old.
   Q: A person smokes.

  d P: A pet cat is ginger.
   Q: A pet cat wears a collar.

3) Lucie has two dice. One is blue and has eight sides numbered from 1 to 8. The other is red and is a normal, six-sided die.

   a Lucie rolls both dice.

   i What is the probability that she rolls a six on the blue die?

   ii What is the probability that she rolls a six on the red die?

   b Lucie rolls both dice again.

   i What is the probability that she rolls a six on the blue die?

   ii What is the probability that she rolls a six on the red die?

   c Lucie rolls both dice again. She rolls a six on the red die.
   What is the probability that she rolls a six on the blue die?

   d Are the outcomes on the two dice independent or dependent?

4) At the start of a game, a cricketer has a probability of 0.6 of holding a catch.
   If he holds the first catch he becomes more confident and the probability of holding the next catch goes up to 0.75.
   On the other hand, if he drops the first catch he becomes nervous and the probability of holding the next catch goes down to 0.5.
   In one match the cricketer receives two catches.

   a Draw a tree diagram to represent this situation.
   Fill in all the probabilities.

   b Use your tree diagram to find the probabilities that, out of the two catches, he holds

   i none   ii one   iii both.

5) The probability that Seb has toast for breakfast is 0.4.
   The probability that Seb has toast for lunch is 0.05.
   The events are independent.
   Select the right calculation for each of the following.

   a The probability that Seb doesn't have toast for lunch.

   b The probability that Seb doesn't have toast for breakfast.

   c The probability that Seb has toast for breakfast and lunch.

   d The probability that Seb has toast at least once a day.

$1 - 0.05$	0.95×0.4
$1 - 0.95 \times 0.6$	$1 - 0.4$
0.05×0.4	$1 - 0.05 \times 0.4$

Statistics and Probability Strand 4 Probability

Reasoning

6 James says that he tossed a coin 20 times and got tails every time.
Joe says that this is impossible and that James is not telling the truth.
Explain why Joe is wrong.

Problem solving

1 20 counters are placed into a bag. Seven are red and the rest are blue. A counter is drawn out of the bag and then replaced. A second counter is then drawn out of the bag.
Draw a tree diagram to show the possible outcomes and use it to calculate the probability of drawing out

   i two blue counters

   ii two red counters

   iii one of each colour

   iv at least one blue counter.

2 A box contains two white balls and one black ball.
A bag contains yellow and green balls in the ratio 2 : 3.
Mair takes a ball at random from the box.
She then takes a ball from the bag.
What is the probability that she will take

   a a white ball and a yellow ball

   b a black ball and a yellow ball

   c a black ball and a yellow or green ball?

3 A manager wants to select two people to look after a stand at a conference.
They are chosen from eight female staff, including Mrs Derwyn, and six male staff, including her husband Mr Derwyn.

   a His first plan is to select the two people at random from all 14 staff.
What is the probability that Mr and Mrs Derwyn are both chosen?

   b He then decides he should select one woman and one man.
What is the probability that Mr and Mrs Derwyn are both chosen now?

4 On the way to work, Millie has to pass through two sets of traffic lights.
The probability that the first set of lights is red is 0.8 and the probability that the second set of lights is red is 0.3.
Over a 25-day period Millie has to stop at both sets of lights 6 times on her way to work.

   a Millie thinks the lights work independently.
Do you agree? Given a reason for your answer.

   b If Millie is right, how often would you expect her to have to stop at just one set of lights?

Unit 5 The multiplication rule Band h

5 Naela takes the train to work. When it is raining the probability the train is late is 0.3. When it is not raining, the probability the train is late is 0.05.
In January, she worked on 22 days. It rained as she went to work on 8 of those days.

  a Find the probability that the train was late on a day in January.

  b The railway company advertised that fewer than 10% of their trains were late during January. Could this claim be true for Naela's train? Explain your answer.

6 Meilyr has a pack of 10 light bulbs of which 3 are faulty.
He takes 3 of the bulbs at random and fits them into 3 lamps.

  a Draw a tree diagram to represent this situation.

  b Use your tree diagram to find the probabilities that
     i none of the lamps works   **ii** 1 of the lamps works
     iii 2 of the lamps work   **iv** all 3 of the lamps work.

  c Add all 4 of yours answers to part **b** together. What does your answer tell you?

7 There are 6 blue socks and 4 red socks in a drawer.

Freddie takes out 2 socks at random.

  a Work out the probability that Freddie takes out 2 socks of the same colour.

  b What is the maximum number of socks he would need to take out at random to ensure he had a red pair?

8 Jamil has a bag containing 5 counters. 4 are blue and 1 is red.
Jamil wants the red counter. He takes them out one at a time until he comes to the red one. If he picks a blue counter, he does not replace it.

  a Copy and complete this tree diagram.

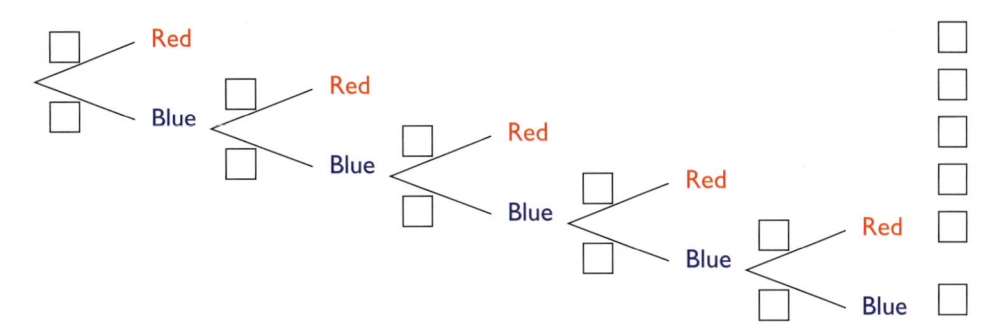

  b Jamil can take 1, 2, 3, 4 or 5 attempts to get the red counter. Before he starts, what is the probability that he will take each of these numbers of attempts?
  What does the total of these 5 probabilities tell you?

  Now investigate the situation if Jamil replaces any blue counters he takes out.

  c How does this affect the tree diagram?

  d What is the probability that he gets the red counter in his first 5 attempts?

Statistics and Probability Strand 4 Probability

Reviewing skills

Higher tier only

1. The probability that it will rain today is 0.2. If it rains today, the probability that it will rain tomorrow is 0.15. If it is fine today, the probability it is fine tomorrow is 0.9.
   a. Draw a tree diagram and calculate the missing probabilities.
   b. What is the probability that at least one of the two days will be fine?

2. 15 counters are placed in a bag. Five are red and the rest are green. Two counters are drawn from the bag in succession, without replacement. What is the probability of drawing out
   a. two red counters
   b. two green counters
   c. one of each colour
   d. at least one green counter?

Unit 6 • The addition rule and Venn diagram notation • Band f

Outside the Maths classroom

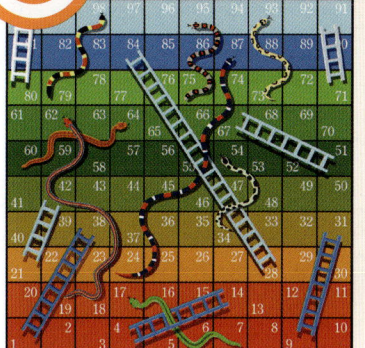

Games of chance
Which games involve probability? How can probability improve your strategy when you play a game of chance?

Toolbox

Mutually exclusive events

Two events or outcomes are **mutually exclusive** if they cannot both happen.

(When you toss a coin the outcomes '*heads*' and '*tails*' are mutually exclusive – you cannot get both heads and tails!)

When two events or outcomes are mutually exclusive then the probability that one or the other of them happens can be found by **adding** their individual probabilities.

The events must be mutually exclusive for the **Addition Rule** to work.

You can use **Venn diagrams** to show possible outcomes.

This Venn diagram shows 2 mutually exclusive events.

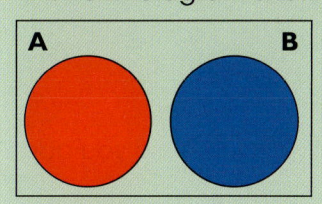

There is no intersection as A and B can never both happen!

$$P(A \text{ or } B) = P(A) + P(B)$$

For example, event A is '*throwing a die and getting an odd number*' and event B is '*throwing a die and getting 2*'.

Events that are not mutually exclusive

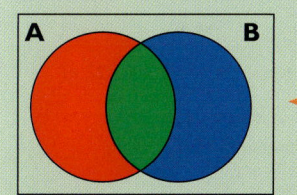

The intersection shows that A and B can happen at the same time:

$$P(A \text{ or } B) = P(A) + P(B) - P(A \text{ and } B)$$

For example, event A is '*someone owning a cat*' and event B is '*someone owning a dog*', the intersection is '*someone owning a cat and a dog*'.

Set notation: $\mathcal{E} = \{x : x \text{ is a factor of 24}\}$ means $\mathcal{E}$ is the set of all the numbers that are factors of 24, i.e. 1, 2, 3, 4, 6, 12, 24.

Statistics and Probability Strand 4 Probability

Venn diagram notation

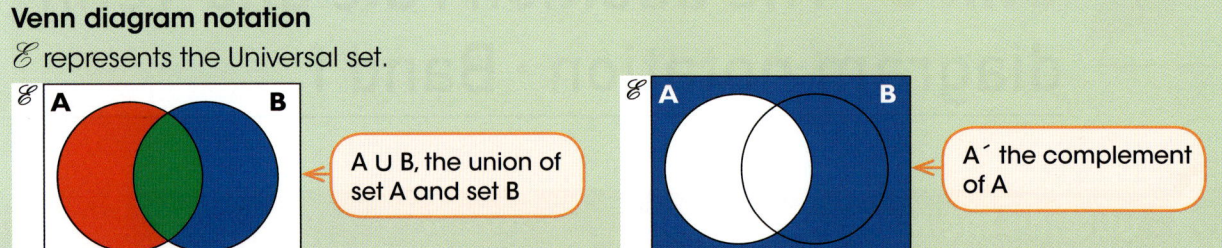

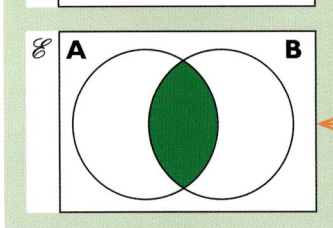

$\mathscr{E}$ represents the Universal set.

$A \cup B$, the union of set A and set B

A' the complement of A

$A \cap B$, the intersection of set A and set B

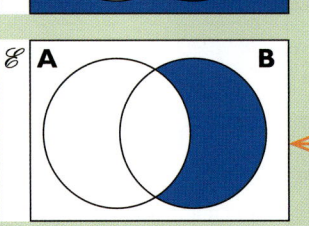

$A' \cap B$ the region where the complement of A intersects with B

Example – Mutually exclusive events

A bag contains 20 counters. Five of them are blue, two are green and the rest are other colours.
a Draw a Venn diagram showing this information.
b A counter is selected at random. What is the probability that it is
   i   blue
   ii green
   iii blue or green
   iv neither blue nor green?

Solution

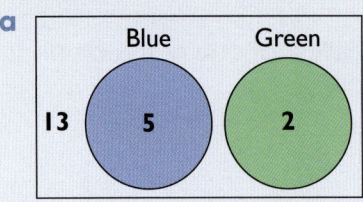

a

Blue   Green

13   5   2

b i $P(\text{blue}) = \dfrac{5}{20} = 0.25$

   ii $P(\text{green}) = \dfrac{2}{20} = 0.1$

   iii Choosing a blue counter and choosing a green counter are mutually exclusive, so you add their probabilities.
   $P(\text{blue or green}) = P(\text{blue}) + P(\text{green})$
   $= \dfrac{5}{20} + \dfrac{2}{20}$
   $= \dfrac{7}{20} = 0.35$

   iv Choosing a counter that is neither blue nor green is the opposite of choosing one that is either blue or green.
   So $P(\text{neither blue not green}) = 1 - 0.35 = 0.65$. ← The total probability is 1.
   Another way of doing this is to look at the Venn diagram.
   There are $20 - 5 - 2 = 13$ other colours.
   So the required probability is $\dfrac{13}{20} = 0.65$.

Unit 6 The addition rule and Venn diagram notation Band f

Example – Events that are not mutually exclusive

A fair die is rolled.
a Draw a Venn diagram to show the events A and B, where A = {*prime numbers on a die*} and B = {*even numbers on a die*}
b Use your Venn diagram to find
   i   P(score is prime)
   ii P(score is even)
   iii P(score is prime and even)
   iv P(score is prime or even).

Solution

a The prime numbers on a die are 2, 3 and 5. So A is {2, 3, 5}
   The even numbers on a die are 2, 4 and 6. So B is {2, 4, 6}

   1 is neither prime nor even so it goes outside of the circles.

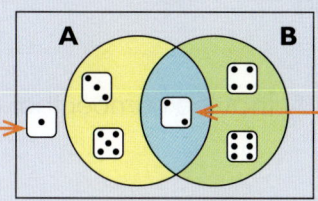

   2 is prime and even, and goes in the intersection.

b i   P(score is prime) = $\frac{3}{6} = \frac{1}{2}$ ← 3 out of the 6 possible scores are prime.

   ii P(score is even) = $\frac{3}{6} = \frac{1}{2}$ ← 3 out of the 6 possible scores are even.

   iii P(score is prime and even) = $\frac{1}{6}$ ← 2 is the only even prime.

   iv P(score is prime or even) = $\frac{3}{6} + \frac{3}{6} - \frac{1}{6} = \frac{5}{6}$ ← 2, 3, 4, 5 and 6 are prime or even.

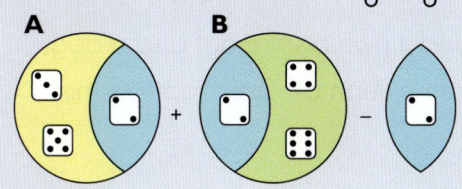

Practising skills

1) A bag contains 15 counters. Three are red, two are blue and the rest are yellow.
   A counter is chosen at random. Find the probability that the counter is

   a red
   b blue
   c red or blue.

629

Statistics and Probability Strand 4 Probability

2 A raffle has tickets numbered from 1 to 300. Osian has 5 tickets and Elen has 7 tickets. One ticket is drawn to find the winner of the star prize.
What is the probability that

   a Osian wins the star prize

   b Elen wins the star prize

   c Either Osian or Elen win the star prize?

3 Dewi is listening to his music on shuffle.
He has 600 songs. He has rated 57 of them as 5 star songs and 72 of them as 4 star songs.
What is the probability that the next song he plays is

   a a 5 star song

   b a 4 star song

   c either a four star or five star song

   d rated with 0, 1, 2 or 3 stars?

4 A die is rolled. What is the probability that the number that comes up is

   a 2 or less

   b 5 or more

   c either 2 or less, or five or more?

5 In a survey 50 students were asked whether they liked soccer or rugby.
   21 liked soccer.
   10 liked both.
   8 liked neither soccer nor rugby.

   a Draw a Venn diagram showing this information.

   b What is the probability that a student chosen at random from this group liked only rugby?

6 In a class of 30 students, 8 own a dog, 11 own a cat and 4 own both a cat and a dog.

   a Copy the Venn diagram. Add numbers to complete the Venn diagram to show this information.

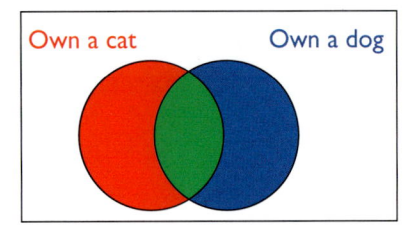

   b Find the probability that a randomly chosen student has

     i a dog

     ii a dog and a cat

     iii a dog or a cat or both

     iv no pets.

7 Emily has cards numbered from 1 to 15.
   a Write each number from 1 to 15 in the correct place in the Venn diagram.

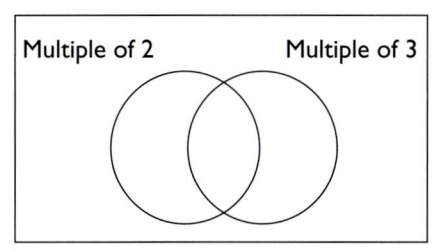

   b Find the probability that a card Emily selects at random is
      i   a multiple of 2
      ii   a multiple of 3
      iii a multiple of 2 and a multiple of 3
      iv   a multiple of 2 or a multiple of 3
      v   neither a multiple of 2 nor a multiple of 3.

Developing fluency

1 There are 52 cards in a pack. Each card is equally likely to be chosen.
   What is the probability that a card chosen at random is
   a a club
   b not a club
   c a spade, heart or diamond
   d a 2 or a 3
   e neither a 2 nor a 3?

2 The probability that there will be rain in London on a day in November is 60%.
   The probability that there will be sun in London on a day in November is 70%.
   Explain why the probability that there will be either rain or sun on a day in November in London is not 130%.

3 This two way table shows how many students in a class fit certain descriptions.

	Blonde hair	Brown hair	Black hair	Total
Wears glasses	3	4	0	
Does not wear glasses	9	10	3	

   a Copy the table and complete the cells in the Total column.
   b Use the table to find the probability that a student chosen at random has
      i   blonde hair
      ii   blonde hair or black hair
      iii blonde hair or wears glasses, but not both
      iv   black hair or wears glasses, but not both
      v   black hair and wears glasses.

Statistics and Probability Strand 4 Probability

4 Rosie always eats a bowl of cereal for breakfast.
The probability that Rosie eats cornflakes is $\frac{1}{4}$.
The probability that Rosie eats muesli is $\frac{5}{12}$.
Calculate the probability that
  a Rosie has cornflakes or muesli today
  b Rosie has neither cornflakes nor muesli today.

5 Ryan writes down each of the numbers from 1 to 20 on a separate card.
He then decides which cards belong in the following sets:
A = {$x:x$ is a factor of 18}
B = {$x:x$ is an odd number}
  a Draw a Venn diagram to show the two sets A and B.
  b Ryan shuffles his cards and selects a card a random.
  Find the probability that a number on a card selected at random is:
   i odd
   ii a factor of 18
   iii an odd number and a factor 18
   iv an odd number or a factor of 18
   v neither an odd number nor a factor of 18.

6 A vet is investigating the possible effects of inbreeding in a breed of pedigree dog.
Two possible effects are bad eyesight and weak hips.
The vet looks at a sample of 80 dogs and finds that 44 have neither condition, 24 have bad eyesight and 32 have weak hips.
  a Show this information in a Venn diagram.
  b Estimate the probability that a dog of this breed suffers from both defects.
  Say why your answer is an estimate and not necessarily accurate.
  c Find the probability that a dog of this breed suffers from at least one of the defects, by using
   i the formula P(A or B) = P(A) + P(B) − P(A and B)
   ii the numbers on the Venn diagram.

7 Make a copy of the Venn diagram to answer each part of this question.

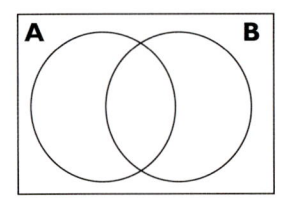

Shade the following regions:
  a A ∪ B´
  b (A ∪ B)´
  c (A ∩ B)´
  d A ∩ B´

Unit 6 The addition rule and Venn diagram notation Band f

Problem solving

1 100 patients take part in a trial of new medicines.
   36 patients receive medicine X only.
   25 patients receive medicine Y only.
   15 patients receive both medicine X and medicine Y.
The remaining patients receive a placebo.

   a Draw a Venn diagram showing this information.
   b What is the probability that a patient chosen at random receives a placebo?

2 100 people belong to a health spa club. It has a swimming pool and a gym.
   70 use the swimming pool only.
   10 use both the swimming pool and the gym.
   1 uses neither the swimming pool nor the gym.

   a Draw a Venn diagram showing this information.
Members are chosen at random to take part in a survey.
   b What is the probability that someone chosen for the survey uses the gym?
   c What is the probability that someone chosen for the survey uses one (but not both) of the club's facilities?

3 At a supermarket, 80% of customers bring their own carrier bags and 25% of customers have loyalty cards.
15% of customers have both their own bags and a loyalty card.

   a Draw a Venn diagram to show this information.
   b Find the probability that a randomly chosen customer has
       i a loyalty card but no carrier bag
       ii a carrier bag but no loyalty card
       iii a carrier bag or a loyalty card or both
       iv neither a carrier bag nor a loyalty card.

4 Ben always cycles, walks or drives to work.
On any day the probability that Ben cycles to work is $\frac{1}{3}$ and the probability that he drives is $\frac{1}{4}$.
Calculate the probability that

   a Ben walks to work
   b Ben either walks to work or he cycles.

5 There are 80 A-level students at a college. 40 of them do at least one science.
   28 students do physics.
   28 students do chemistry.
   3 students do physics and biology only.
   14 students do physics and chemistry only.
   1 student does chemistry and biology only.
   5 students do all three sciences.
One of the 80 students is chosen at random, to meet a visiting television science presenter.

633

Statistics and Probability Strand 4 Probability

a Identify the sets in this Venn diagram.

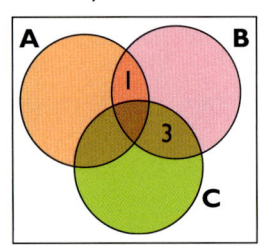

b Fill in all the missing numbers.
c Find the probability that the student chosen does 2 or 3 science subjects.
d Which is more likely: that the student chosen does some science or that the student does no science?

6) Make a copy of the Venn diagram to answer each part of this question.

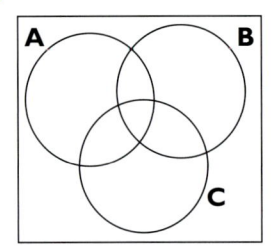

Shade the following regions:
a $A \cap B \cap C$
b $A \cup B \cup C$
c $A' \cap (B \cup C)$
d $A \cap (B \cup C)'$

Reviewing skills

1) a A die is rolled. What is the probability that the number that comes up is
   i even
   ii 3 or less
   iii either even, or is 3 or less.
   b Are the outcomes 'even' and '3 or less' mutually exclusive? Explain your answer.

2) In a group of 30 students
   8 study history only.
   5 study both history and geography.
   2 study neither history nor geography.
   a Draw a Venn diagram showing this information.
   b A student is chosen at random from this group. Find the probability that the student studies one out of history and geography but not both.